Fassett's Washington Pharmacy Law

2019 Edition

William E. Fassett, BSPharm, MBA, PhD, FAPhA
Shannon G. Panther, PharmD, BCACP

Fassett's Washington Pharmacy Law 2019
Published by Pharmacistlaw.com
Spokane, WA

Revision date: February 14, 2019

Cover Art: SEF Creations, Spokane, WA

Bill@pharmacistlaw.com

ISBN: 9781796856545

DEDICATION

This edition is dedicated to Jack E. Orr and Allen I. White, the two pharmacy deans at the University of Washington and Washington State University, respectively, who were prominent in ushering in the modern era of clinical pharmacy practice in the state of Washington through their advocacy of curricular change and their recruitment of new faculty into clinical positions. The curricular change championed by these men in the 1970s led in a large part to the major revision of Washington's Pharmacy Practice Act in 1978, which placed pharmacists in Washington in the forefront of expanded pharmacist's scope of practice. Dean White passed away in 2003 and Dean Orr in 2018.

CONTENTS

DISCLAIMER

This text is designed to provide accurate and authoritative commentary in regard to the subject matter covered. It is provided with the understanding that the author is not engaged in rendering legal or other professional services. If legal advice is required, the services of a licensed attorney should be sought.

The authors have academic training, pharmacy practice experience, and have undertaken scholarship in the matters herein discussed. They are licensed pharmacists in Washington, but are not attorneys, and neither represent that they are attorneys, nor intend to convey in any way that they are offering legal advice.

Care has been taken to assure the accuracy of the material as of the revision date shown on the copyright page. Users should verify with available official sources the current status of any law or regulation cited.

NATIONAL COMPETENCIES

A comment box at the beginning of each chapter indicates areas of competency specified in the following national standards documents:

MPJE - The 2016 Competency Statements for the Multistate Pharmacy Jurisprudence Exam (see Chapter 2) published by the National Association of Boards of Pharmacy, https://nabp.pharmacy/programs/mpje/

ACPE REQUIRED ELEMENTS – Appendix 1, Required Elements of the Didactic Doctor of Pharmacy Curriculum, Standards 2016, https://www.acpe-accredit.org/pdf/Standards2016FINAL.pdf

UDPATES

If needed, important updates to this text between annual editions will be provided at no charge in .pdf format at www.pharmacistlaw.com.

Photo Credit, Figure 4-1:
"Elixir Sulfanilamide" by Unknown - http://www.fda.gov/centennial/this_week/46_nov_12_nov_18.html. Licensed under Public Domain via Wikimedia Commons: http://commons.wikimedia.org/wiki/File:Elixir_Sulfanilamide.jpg#mediaviewer/File:Elixir_Sulfanilamide.jpg

1 - INTRODUCTION: THE LAW, COURTS, AND LAWS

LEGAL OBLIGATIONS AND CONSEQUENCES

To become a pharmacist is to voluntarily assume certain legal obligations; failing to fulfill these has consequences.

Follow the laws and regulations relating to the Practice of Pharmacy or be disciplined by the Pharmacy Commission: you may be fined, you may be put on probation, and/or your license may be suspended or revoked.

Violate certain criminal laws, such as the Controlled Substances Act, and you may be prosecuted in federal or state court: you may pay a fine and/or you may go to jail.

> COMPETENCY AREAS IN THIS CHAPTER
>
> 2016 MPJE COMPETENCY STATEMENTS – Area 3.1.1
>
> 2016 ACPE REQUIRED ELEMENTS – Pharmacy Law & Regulatory Affairs

Fail to perform according to legal and professional standards, and you may cause an injury to a patient, who can then sue you in state or federal civil court: you may be forced to pay damages

A PHARMACY LICENSE IS A REVOCABLE PRIVILEGE

Your license as a pharmacist, or the license of your pharmacy, gives you privileges that aren't available to most patients, and distinguishes you from other health professionals. It is issued by the state, and can be revoked by the state. Carrying out your professional duties, and being able to use your training to the fullest, requires an understanding of just how extensive these privileges are, and how to make the most of them. Once you've earned the license, however, you do have property and liberty interests that are protected by the Constitution, and your license may not be taken or restricted without due process of law (see 14th Amendment).

> PRIVILEGE – from the Latin for "private law;" a special right, advantage, or immunity granted or available only to a particular person or group of people.

PHARMACISTS ARE PRESUMED TO KNOW THE LAW

Ignorance of a law does not excuse a person from suffering the penalties for its violation. The law generally presumes that citizens – and especially licensees in certain professions – are able to learn the laws that apply to them. Boards of Pharmacy actually require pharmacists to pass an examination regarding pharmacy law to demonstrate that they understand it well enough to practice lawfully.

It is a requirement, however, that if an individual is to be held responsible for compliance with a law, the law itself must be clear and unambiguous, and not in conflict with other laws.

DIVISIONS OF THE LAW

Three important divisions of the world of law may affect the pharmacist, and determine the consequences of his or her actions.

ADMINISTRATIVE LAW

This is the law that is created and enforced by government agencies. It applies only to individuals or entities (such as licensees) under the *jurisdiction* of the particular agency.

THE POSSIBLE CONSEQUENCES OF DISCIPLINE are limited to placing restrictions on your license (probation, suspension, revocation), or, in some cases, to assessing fines or the costs associated with a hearing.

A decision by the agency that is adverse (has negative consequences) to a registrant or licensee can be made on the basis of evidence at a hearing by the agency. The licensee has an opportunity to appeal an agency decision in state or federal court.

PHARMACY COMMISSION JURISDICTION

The Pharmacy Commission can discipline pharmacists, interns, pharmacy technicians and assistants, wholesalers, and others who are required to be licensed by the Commission. It has no direct authority over patients, and cannot discipline physicians, nurses, or other health professionals, who are under the jurisdiction of other disciplinary boards (e.g., Nursing Quality Assurance Commission).

STANDARD OF EVIDENCE IN ADMINISTRATIVE HEARINGS

The current standard of evidence in Washington for decisions involving the license of pharmacists, physicians, and nurses, is a "clear, cogent, and convincing proof" standard,[1] which is more stringent than a preponderance of evidence standard, and less stringent than a requirement of proof beyond a reasonable doubt (see also chapter 7). In 2006, the Washington Supreme Court extended this standard to all licensees of the Department of Health in a case involving a nurse's aide.[2] In 2011, the Washington Supreme Court restricted the clear and convincing standard to learned professions, and retained a preponderance of evidence standard for licensees such as child day care providers, and overturned its 2006 ruling.[3] A plurality of justices continued to recognize the clear and convincing standard as it applies to physicians and other licensees who expend considerable time, expense, and education obtaining their licenses.

CIVIL LAW

Civil law applies to disputes between individuals, corporations, or other entities. The two types of disputes that pharmacists are most frequently involved in can primarily be classified into the following:

CONTRACTS, which are voluntary agreements between parties who are legally and actually capable of entering into those agreements. Warranties and guaranties are forms of contracts, as are employment agreements, leases, and sales of property.

TORTS, which are intentional acts committed by one individual that harm another. Common examples of torts include:

Assault and battery

Slander and libel

Negligence, which includes professional negligence (also called malpractice).

REMEDIES that can be ordered by the courts in civil suits include payment of damages, restraining orders (preventing one party from doing future acts), ordering disgorgement of funds obtained from the injured parties, and enforcement of contracts.

STANDARD OF EVIDENCE IN CIVIL LAWSUITS

Verdicts in civil cases can be by judges or by juries. The evidence used in the decision is presented at a trial. The verdict must be based on the preponderance of evidence (a majority of the evidence) favoring one party or the other.

CRIMINAL LAW

Criminal law covers acts of individuals "against the state," in which the lawsuit is filed by a state or federal prosecutor (prosecuting attorney, district attorney, attorney general, etc.).

Crimes are generally divided into misdemeanors and felonies. Both misdemeanors and felonies are further classified for purposes of sentencing. Certain felonies (such as premeditated murder) may be "capital crimes" in which the death penalty can be inflicted. Classifications of crime in Washington include the following.

MISDEMEANORS – minor violations punishable by up to 90 days in jail and/or fines of up to $1,000

GROSS MISDEMEANORS – minor violations punishable by up to 1 year in jail and/or fines of up to $5,000

FELONIES – CLASS A FELONIES include violent crimes such as murder, rape, kidnapping, or armed robbery, and may be punished by life imprisonment and/or a fine of up to $50,000. Washington State's death penalty law imposes capital punishment for aggravated murder, which is a class A felony.[4] First degree robbery is a class A felony, and requires commission of a robbery while armed with a deadly weapon, while displaying what appears to be a firearm or other deadly weapon, while inflicting bodily injury, or while committing a robbery within or against a financial institution.

CLASS B FELONIES include serious crimes including manslaughter, kidnapping, sexual crimes, drug crimes, theft, embezzlement, and white collar crimes. Class B felonies may be punished by up to 10 years in jail and/or a fine of up to $20,000. Second degree robbery, or robbery that doesn't qualify as first degree, is a class B felony.

CLASS C FELONIES include possession of stolen property, drug crimes, criminal trespass, theft, DUI, and felonious driving. These felonies are punishable by up to 5 years in prison and/or a fine of up to $10,000. DUI convictions may be made upon evidence of blood alcohol levels above 0.08%, of more than 5 ng/mL of Δ-9 THC, or of demonstrated physical impairment due to use *of prescribed or non-prescribed drugs.*

ROBBERY OF A PHARMACY. In Washington, conviction for committing first degree or second degree robbery against a pharmacy is accompanied by a mandatory sentencing enhancement of an additional 12 months of incarceration beyond standard sentencing ranges.[5]

PENALTIES for a criminal conviction can include fines, imprisonment, or loss of life. Disgorgement of funds obtained through criminal activities, and/or restitution of damages may be awarded to compensate victims of a crime.

STANDARD OF EVIDENCE IN CRIMINAL CASES. Trial by jury is guaranteed in criminal cases. Conviction of a crime requires the prosecutor to present evidence that proves every element of the offense *beyond a reasonable doubt.*

SELF-INCRIMINATION. Under the US and most state constitutions, no person may be compelled to testify against him or herself in a criminal matter. When an individual is in police custody, statements voluntarily made may be used against the individual, but police are required to warn individuals of their right to remain silent and avoid self-incrimination, in what is commonly called a *Miranda warning.*[6]

RELATIONSHIPS AMONG THE DIVISIONS OF LAW can be complex. It is important to understand that a given act, however, can give rise to actions in more than one arena.

ROBERT RAY COURTNEY's case is an example of this.[7] Courtney gained notoriety for operating a pharmacy in Kansas City in which he compounded chemotherapy drugs, and, for a number of years deliberately diluted these drugs to increase his profit margin. He entered a guilty plea in federal court to numerous counts of criminal acts. The Missouri Board of Pharmacy revoked his pharmacist's license and the license of his pharmacy. He also was the subject of a civil trial in Kansas City in which the jury awarded the plaintiffs $200 million in actual damages, and $2 billion in punitive damages, for the largest verdict ever assessed against a pharmacist ($2.2 billion).

THE NEW ENGLAND COMPOUNDING CENTER was the source of a nationwide outbreak of meningitis in 2012 due to fungus in the company's injectable methylprednisolone acetate suspension. The licenses of pharmacists Barry Cadden (NECC owner) and Glenn Adam Chin (NECC pharmacist supervisor) were revoked, the license of the pharmacy was also revoked, and injured parties have sued both NECC, its owners, and hundreds of clinics and physicians involved in the administration of the tainted drug. A $100-million dollar settlement was ultimately approved by the bankruptcy court handling NECC's dismantling,[8] and in December 2014, the United States Department of Justice announced the arrest of Cadden and Chin, plus 12 others on criminal charges. Cadden and Chin were charged with, among other crimes, 25 counts of 2nd degree homicide.[9]

THE O.J. SIMPSON case illustrates how the different levels of evidence required can lead to opposite outcomes. In his criminal trial, former NFL star running back and actor Orenthal James (O.J.) Simpson was acquitted of murder of Nicole Simpson (his ex-wife) and Ron Goldman, who was with her at the time of the murder.[10] However, a civil jury found him liable for $8.5 million in damages and $25 million in a punitive award to the estates of Simpson and Goldman.[11]

TABLE 1-1. OVERVIEW OF DIVISIONS OF LAW

	CIVIL LAW	CRIMINAL LAW	ADMINISTRATIVE LAW
EXAMPLE PARTIES	Miller v. Thomas	State v. Lewis	In re License of Johnson
APPLIES TO	Matters between private parties; torts, contracts	Violations of criminal statutes, enforced by state	Violations of administrative law and regulations by licensees
POSSIBLE CONSEQUENCES	Payment of damages, enforcement of contracts, disgorgement of funds, payment of court costs/attorney fees, disgorgement of funds, restraining orders or injunctions	Fines, disgorgement of funds, restitution, incarceration, capital punishment	Suspension or revocation of license, fines
EVIDENTIARY STANDARD	Preponderance of evidence	Beyond a reasonable doubt	Clear, cogent, and convincing or preponderance of evidence.

COURTS

HIERARCHY OF COURTS There is a hierarchy (ranking) of courts in which decisions are rendered and reviewed at the higher levels. Cases begin in lower courts, and decisions rendered there may be appealed to higher courts. Decisions within a court set precedents that bind the court in later decisions, and decisions of the higher level courts also set precedents which control later decisions in lower courts in the same jurisdiction.

JURISDICTION

The federal and state constitutions set forth how courts are established, and what kinds of cases each type of court can handle. The extent and scope of a court's powers are known as its jurisdiction.

ORIGINAL VERSUS DISCRETIONARY JURISDICTION. If a case may be begun or filed directly with a given court, it will be because that court has original jurisdiction over the matter (i.e., the case may originate in that court). On the other hand, a court may be able to choose to hear or not hear a particular case, in which its jurisdiction is discretionary.

SUBJECT MATTER JURISDICTION. Subject matter jurisdiction describes the types of cases a court may handle. For example, a bankruptcy court's subject matter jurisdiction is limited to bankruptcy cases, and the court may not hear other types of suits, such as negligence cases. Most trial courts in state systems have "general subject matter jurisdiction," and may hear any cases for which some other court does not have exclusive responsibility. At the federal district court level, courts have two types of subject-matter jurisdiction in non-criminal cases: (1)

where there is a question of federal law, or (2) where there is diversity of citizenship among the parties. Any judgment issued by a court in a case in which it did not have subject matter jurisdiction is null and void.

PERSONAL JURISDICTION. Sometimes also called "in personam" jurisdiction, defines which persons (or parties) are under the jurisdiction of a given court. Unless a given party is within the court's personal jurisdiction, no decision of the court may be binding on that person. A party not normally subject to a given court's jurisdiction may, however, consent to the case being tried in that court. A good example are provisions in contracts that agree to subject any disputes to a given jurisdiction (such as the home state of the corporate headquarters), and the parties to the contract agree in advance that *in personam* jurisdiction will not be challenged in the agreed-upon court.

IN REM JURISDICTION. Sometimes the court is asked to rule on the status of a *thing* rather than a person. In order to do so, the court must have jurisdiction over the property or item in question, subject to rules similar to determining *in personam* jurisdiction. The jurisdiction over a thing is called "in rem" (from the Latin *res*, or thing). A 1916 case testing the application of federal food and drug law is cited in Chapter 4 as *United States v. Forty Barrels and Twenty Kegs of Coca-Cola,* 241 U.S. 265. This case involved Coca-Cola seized by federal agents, and thus it was over the fate of the beverage, not any particular person, under the *in rem* jurisdiction of the United States Supreme Court.

TRIAL COURTS

At both the state and federal level, major civil lawsuits and prosecutions of felonies usually begin at courts of general jurisdiction, usually known as *trial courts*. Decisions of federal trial courts are often published, but state trial court decisions are not generally collected and published.

STATE TRIAL COURTS. In Washington, the trial courts are located in 30 judicial districts, and are called "superior courts." Most judicial districts consist of a single county, and there is a superior courthouse in every county, but some judicial districts are made up of more than one of the smaller counties (e.g., Garfield, Columbia, and Asotin counties comprise one judicial district), and judges in the district rotate among the counties as needed. A pharmacist living in Spokane who is to be tried under state law for diversion of a controlled substance would be tried in the "Superior Court of Washington for the County of Spokane."

FEDERAL TRIAL COURTS are called "district courts." Federal districts are established in every state and territory, and some states (like Washington) have more than one federal district. A pharmacist living in Spokane who is to be tried under federal law for violation of the Controlled Substances Act will be tried in the "United States District Court, Eastern District of Washington," which is located in Spokane (the district also has courtrooms in Yakima, Richland, and Walla Walla). Washington's other federal district, called the "Western District of Washington," has courtrooms in Seattle and Tacoma.

Each federal district houses the offices of a United States Attorney, who is appointed by the President. The US Attorney is assisted by career staff attorneys known as Assistant US Attorneys, or AUSAs. These attorneys are all part of the Department of Justice, which is headed by the U.S. Attorney General. The US Attorney is responsible for making prosecutorial decisions in all federal cases in the district, and his or her office also represents the US in lawsuits filed against it in the district.

Federal district courts have subject-matter jurisdiction when the plaintiff claims that the action arises out of a federal question, or under the Constitution, federal laws, or treaties. However, state courts may also hear claims based on federal law.

Subject-matter jurisdiction of federal district courts also extends to civil cases based on state law that are in (or removed to) the court based (1) on "complete diversity," in which no defendant is a citizen of the same state as any plaintiff; and (2) where the "amount in controversy" exceeds $75,000. Federal courts may dismiss cases where these conditions do not obtain, either as a result of a motion by one of the parties or on the court's own initiative (or *sua sponte*).

COURTS OF LIMITED JURISDICTION. A variety of special courts or lesser courts are also established at both the state and federal level.

STATE SPECIAL COURTS include District Courts, Municipal Courts established by cities, Family Courts (divorce), Juvenile Courts, and courts dealing with drug abuse or drunk driving. Nearly 7 out of 8 cases filed in Washington courts are filed in DISTRICT COURTS – almost 2 million cases per year. The majority of these cases involved traffic violations or prosecutions of misdemeanors. Cases that may be heard by Washington's district courts include:

Misdemeanors and gross misdemeanors involving traffic or non-traffic offenses.

Preliminary hearings in felony cases.

Civil cases where the claimed damages are not more than $75,000. (Claims under $5,000 are filed in the "small claims" department of the district court; parties may not bring attorneys to these hearings.)

Traffic and non-traffic *infractions*, which are civil proceedings in which a fine, but no jail may be imposed.

Motions for domestic violence or anti-harassment protection orders, or no-contact orders.

Changes of name petitions

Certain lien foreclosures.

Appeals of decisions of limited jurisdiction courts are made to the Superior Court.

FEDERAL SPECIAL COURTS include Bankruptcy Courts, International Trade Courts, Courts of Federal Claims, Veteran's Claims Courts, and the Military Court system.

APPEALS COURTS

Decisions at the trial court level may be appealed to the next higher court. In Washington, this court is called the COURT OF APPEALS, and it is divided into three divisions. Division I, headquartered in Seattle, receives appeals from lower courts in King, Snohomish, Skagit, Whatcom, San Juan, and Island counties. Division II, located in Tacoma, covers the remaining counties in Western Washington, including matters tried in Thurston County, the home of the state capital. Eastern Washington – consisting of the counties east of the Cascade Mountains – is covered by Division III, located in Spokane. Prior to 1969, Washington did not have a Court of Appeals, but only superior courts and the Supreme Court.

Federal appeals courts are called the CIRCUIT COURTS OF APPEALS, and cases from Washington are heard by the 9th Circuit Court of Appeals, with headquarters in San Francisco. Appellate court opinions at both the state and federal level are collected and published, and trial courts within the jurisdiction of a particular appellate court must follow the rules set down in those decisions.

SUPREME COURTS

The highest courts at both the state and federal level are supreme courts: the UNITED STATES SUPREME COURT and, in Washington, the WASHINGTON STATE SUPREME COURT. These courts resolve conflicts among lower courts, and resolve challenges to laws based on constitutional grounds.

RIGHT TO APPEAL. Criminal defendants and parties to civil cases generally have a right to appeal decisions to courts of appeal; appeals to supreme courts normally require permission of these courts, which have discretionary jurisdiction. The US Supreme Court has a special name for the document it issues when it accepts an appeal: a *writ of certiorari* (a "writ" means a written document; "certiorari" means a certification or formal statement to a lower court notifying it that an appeal has been granted).

Decisions of state supreme courts may be appealed to the US Supreme Court on constitutional grounds.

Decisions of a state supreme court are binding on all courts within the state. Decisions of the US Supreme Court are binding on all courts in the United States.

State appellate and supreme courts often rely upon or adopt, or "follow," the reasoning in decisions of other state courts of record making decisions in novel cases. According to a 2007 study, the Washington Supreme Court was the state supreme court whose decisions were the second most-followed decisions by other states between 1940 and 2005, with California being the first most-followed.[12] This indicates that Washington and California have long been regarded as bell-weather states in terms of modern jurisprudence.

LAWS, RULES, REGULATIONS, ACTS, STATUTES, CODES, AND THE COMMON LAW

"THE LAW" is a broad term that encompasses a set of societal expectations that can be enforced by government power. It is a form of social control that spells out requirements in the following ways: It may REQUIRE a person to act in a certain way – e.g., all pharmacies must maintain a record of each prescription dispensed; all persons operating a motor vehicle on the public highways of Washington must have a valid driver's license. It may PERMIT a person to undertake a specific action – e.g., pharmacists *may* enter into collaborative practice agreements with physicians; a person *may* designate another to act in his or her behalf to purchase property. Finally, the law may PROHIBIT a person from acting in a certain way – e.g., a pharmacist may not dispense a legend drug unless he or she has been presented a valid prescription; an individual may not park their automobile within five feet of a fire hydrant. In the *absence of a law* concerning a particular sphere of activity, individuals are presumed to have freedom of action.

> PRECEDENCE – the order in which rules from different sources of law must be followed.
>
> PRECEDENT(S) – prior court or administrative decisions regarding a legal subject that must be followed in subsequent cases involving similar circumstances.

HIERARCHY OF LAWS

Just as there is a hierarchy of courts, there is also a hierarchy of laws. Sources of law are ranked in the following order, from the highest level of precedence to the lowest.

CONSTITUTION. The highest law of the land is the US Constitution. Any law that is in conflict with the Constitution may be challenged, and can be declared unconstitutional by federal courts. Ultimately, the Supreme Court is the final arbiter of a law or treaty's conformance to constitutional law. Within a given state, on matters that are left to the States under the US Constitution, the state constitution is the supreme law. The state courts, and ultimately the state supreme court, decide whether a law is in conformance with the state constitution.

INTERNATIONAL TREATIES

Treaties approved by Congress with foreign powers, once established, create international law that has precedence over other state and federal laws.[13] Federal treaties with Native American tribes and nations are considered a form of international treaty, and the Native American treaty parties have many sovereign powers. States are allowed to create compacts with Native American nations and tribes, and may also have compacts as allowed by Congress with other countries. Perhaps the most significant treaty obligation of the United States affecting pharmacy law is the Single Convention on Narcotic Drugs[14] (see Chapter 5).

LEGISLATION

ACTS OF CONGRESS, which begin as BILLS in either chamber, create FEDERAL STATUTES.

ACTS OF THE LEGISLATURE, which begin as BILLS in the state legislature, create STATE STATUTES.

> BILLS – Proposals from legislators to be enacted
>
> ACTS – Bills that are approved by a legislature or Congress
>
> STATUTES – Laws resulting from acts of a legislative body that are signed into law by the President or Governor
>
> REGULATIONS – Rules promulgated by an administrative agency in accordance with the powers granted to the agency by Congress or the legislature in a statute

AMENDMENTS TO PRIOR LEGISLATION BY BILLS. When a congressperson or legislator proposes new legislation in the form of a bill, it almost always affects existing statutes. Congress differs from state legislatures in how a bill indicates which prior legislation is being amended by its proposed language. Congressional bills often amend earlier legislation by referring to the prior Act and its sections, as well as to the section of the US Code (see below) that is affected. For example, Congress passed The Secure and Responsible Drug Disposal Act of 2010, which was originally Senate Bill 3397 in the 111th Congress (S. 3397). Among its other provisions, section 3(a) of S. 3397 stated, "Section 302 of the Controlled Substances Act (21 U.S.C. 822) is amended by adding at the end the following: '(g)(1) An ultimate user who has lawfully obtained a controlled substance ...'" This Act became Public Law 111-273 (Pub. L. 111-273) when President Obama signed it on October 12, 2010, and it amended both Section 302 of the CSA as well as the corresponding Section 822 of title 21 of the United States Code.

State legislatures vary in how they cite legislation that is amended by newly-enacted statutes. Washington's legislature is required in each bill to state in the opening part of the bill the title of the act and the specific sections of the Revised Code of Washington that are amended. For example, Senate Bill 5516 (SB 5516) was passed by the Legislature on 2/28/10, and signed by Governor Gregoire on 3/10/10, becoming Chapter 9 of the Laws of 2010 (2010 c 9). The description read, "An Act Relating to drug overdose prevention; amending RCW 18.130.180; reenacting and amending RCW 9.94A.535; adding a new section to chapter 69.50 RCW; adding a new section to chapter 18.180 RCW; and creating a new section." (The news media may sometimes refer to pending legislation by a related, but unofficial name. SB 5516 was popularly known as the "9-1-1 Good

Samaritan Law," in part because it was similar to legislation by the same name previously enacted in New Mexico.)

When the Washington legislature amends prior law, the bill reprints the entire amended section, showing deletions with ~~strikethrough~~ text; additions are underlined. Washington bills are much easier to read and understand than federal bills.

FEDERAL "PUBLIC LAWS" AND "PRIVATE LAWS." Federal statutes result in two types of laws. The most common laws are "public laws," abbreviated "Pub. L." which affect all persons and entities in the US. Congress may also pass "private laws," abbreviated "Pvt. L." which resolve issues between a citizen or a small group of citizens and the government. Health care reform in 2010 was eventually passed as the Health Care and Education Reconciliation Act of 2010, which, when signed by the President, became Pub. L. 111-152.

Although hundreds of public laws may be enacted by a given Congress, private laws are rare. One private law was enacted by the 115th Congress: Pvt. L. 115-1, which authorized awarding of the Medal of Honor to John L. Canley for acts of valor during the Vietnam War. Many private laws resolve issues of citizenship for specific individuals; one such law was enacted in the 112th Congress (Pvt. L. 112-1, A bill for the relief of Sopuruchi Chukwueke).

FEDERAL PREEMPTION OF STATE LAWS

When Congress passes a federal statute in an area of its authority (for example, to regulate interstate commerce), federal law "preempts" state laws governing the same conduct, unless the federal statute allows for states to create their own laws. Preempted state laws may not be enforced. Three types of preemption exist.

EXPLICIT PREEMPTION. In this type of federal law preemption, the Congress includes specific language in the statute that preempts state law, which may include language that certain types of state law are allowed. For example, the Device Amendments to the FDCA (see Chapter 4) explicitly preempt state regulation of medical devices (21 U.S.C. § 360k(a)): "Except as provided in subsection (b) of this section, no State or political subdivision of a State may establish or continue in effect with respect to a device intended for human use any requirement which is different from, or in addition to, any requirement applicable under this chapter to the device, and which relates to the safety or effectiveness of the device or to any other matter included in a requirement applicable to the device under this chapter."

EXPLICIT – precisely and clearly expressed, as in a statute or contract, leaving nothing to infer.

IMPLICIT or IMPLIED – allowed, prohibited, or required as inherent in the nature of a statute or contract, or apparent from the actions of the parties.

An example of a federal statute that allows some state regulation is the Health Insurance Portability and Accountability Act (HIPAA) (Public Law 104-191, 104th Congress), which explicitly preempts state laws that are in conflict, but specifically allows the Secretary of the Department of Health and Human Services to permit state laws or regulations that are more stringent in protecting patient privacy (see section 1178 of the Act.)

CONFLICT PREEMPTION. If Congress is not explicit about a statute preempting any state regulation, then it may result that state and federal law will conflict. Either it will be impossible for a person to simultaneously comply with federal and state law, or it may be found that the state law interferes with the achievement of the goal or objective of federal law. The Hatch-Waxman amendments to the FDCA (see chapter 4) restrict generic manufacturers to labeling their products exactly in accordance with the label approved by the FDA for the originator's product, or with a class label approved by the FDA. State lawsuits alleging product liability typically argue that the labeling of the product should have been better at warning the plaintiff of the dangers of the drug. Because a generic manufacturer cannot simultaneously comply with the Hatch-Waxman requirements and with a stronger label under state product liability law, state product liability lawsuits based on label warnings have previously been held to be preempted (see below). Conflict preemption is a form of "implied" preemption.

FIELD PREEMPTION. The third type of preemption occurs when federal law has been held to "occupy the field" and it is apparent or implicit that Congress intended the law to preempt state law. Federal courts have repeatedly held that when Congress passed the Employee Retirement Income Security Act (ERISA), it intended to "occupy the field" of employment benefit law for plans subject to the Act. As discussed in Chapter 8, many attempts by pharmacy organizations to challenge the operations of 3rd party payment plans in state court have been affected by the federal preemption doctrine. As with conflict preemption, field preemption is a form of "implied" preemption.

US SUPREME COURT PREEMPTION CASES. Beginning in 2008, the US Supreme Court took up a series of federal preemption cases relating to the Food Drug and Cosmetic Act (FDCA).

MEDICAL DEVICES. In *Riegel v. Medtronic*,[15] the Court held that the regulatory scheme for Class III medical devices explicitly preempts any State requirement relating to a regulated device concerning the safety or effectiveness of the device. In *Warner-Lambert v. Kent*,[16] the Chief Justice recused himself from participating in the decision due to his ownership of stock in Warner-Lambert's parent company, and the remaining 8 justices split 4-4. The divided court resulted in affirming of the 2nd Circuit's ruling that the plaintiffs could continue their lawsuit involving Rezulin® under Michigan law, by asserting that W-L obtained approval of Rezulin by fraud.

BRAND-NAME PRESCRIPTION DRUGS. At the beginning of the 2008 Fall Term, the Court heard arguments in the case of *Wyeth v. Levine.*[17] The plaintiff was injured by Phenergan® injection administered by IV push, and sued Wyeth alleging that IV push administration should not have been recommended in the package insert. Wyeth asserted that "FDA's comprehensive safety and efficacy authority under the FDCA preempts state law claims that different labeling judgments were necessary to make drugs reasonably safe for use." In 2009, the Court ruled that under the facts of *Levine*, the FDCA does not preempt state laws related to product liability. It held that that *brand name drug* manufacturers could improve the labeling of their products without violating FDA rules.

GENERIC PRESCRIPTION DRUGS. Subsequent trial and appellate court decisions have held that the FDCA does not preempt product liability suits against manufacturers of *generic prescription drugs*.[18] The US Supreme Court, however, held in 2011 that the Hatch-Waxman Amendments to the FDCA, which establish labeling requirements for generic drugs, are more specific in requiring that all generic labeling must be identical to that of the brand name drug, thus it is impossible for generic manufacturers to simultaneously comply with state laws requiring them to improve or update their warnings and the requirements of federal law. Unlike brand name manufacturers, the Court held, generic manufacturers are not able to use the "Change Being Effected"(CBE) rule to modify their labeling. Thus, federal law was held to preempt state law suits against generic manufacturers arising from claims of defective labeling.[19]
Following this ruling, the FDA in 2013 proposed amendments to its rules that would allow generic manufacturers to use the CBE process to revise warnings on their labeling. The FDA would then review the CBE filing and determine whether to require adoption of the modified warning for the entire generic class.[20] The comment period on the proposed rule ended on January 13, 2014. If the rule were to be adopted, then generic manufacturers will be treated similarly to brand manufacturers under state product liability laws. In October 2014 the Generic Pharmaceutical Association (GPhA) threatened a lawsuit in the event that FDA finalizes the proposed rule.[21] The FDA continued proposed rule-making to allow generic manufacturers to update their labeling, but in December 2018, the Trump administration announced that the FDA had withdrawn the rule.[22]

REGULATIONS. Congress and legislatures may pass statutes that create administrative agencies, and extend limited rule-making power to those agencies. Such rules made by administrative agencies are called REGULATIONS or ADMINISTRATIVE RULES. As long as the regulations are *promulgated* (developed and announced) in accordance with the authority granted by the statute, they have the force of law.

The Washington Administrative Procedures Act (RCW 34.05) includes procedures that agencies must follow when promulgating regulations. In general, agencies publish notices when they propose to investigate a potential rule, when they begin the formal process of rule-making on the given topic, when a proposed rule has been developed, and when a final rule is adopted. These are filed with the Code Reviser, who publishes them in the *Washington State Register* (WSR) and the various notices are labeled CR-101 (Proposal Statement of Inquiry), CR-102 (Proposed Rule Making), CR-103 (Rule Making Order) and CR-105 (Notice of Expedited Rule Making). Public comments are received in response to CR-101 and CR-102 notices, and at rule-making hearings of state agencies.

LEGISLATIVE OVERSIGHT. In most states, the legislature maintains oversight over state agencies and persons affected by a proposed or enacted regulation may appeal to legislative oversight bodies to review the regulation to assure it is within the scope of the powers of the agency or that it was enacted following a statutorily-mandated process. In Washington, the review body is the Joint Administrative Rules Review Committee (JARRC). An example of how this process can alter agency actions arose in November 2005, when the Board of Pharmacy, acting in the place of the Department of Health, approved a regulation setting forth record keeping requirements for retail sales of methamphetamine precursor products (WAC 246-889-070 thru 110). The regulation was enacted without completion of a legislative rulemaking analysis or a small business economic impact statement, and the DOH indicated it was exempt from these requirements since "the rule does not cause any significant material changes to statute." The Washington Food Industry association appealed to JARRC, alleging that the rule did create a material change by enacting several provisions that were not set forth in the enabling statute (ESHB 2266; 2005 c 388). Following a JARRC hearing on December 8, 2005 the Board revised the rule on December 14.

COURT REVIEW. As with statutes, persons affected by a regulation who allege that it infringes a Constitutional right or violates a Constitutional limitation on government power may also seek a ruling by the courts as to the constitutionality of the regulation.

FEDERAL "NOTICE AND COMMENT" PROCESS. The federal rule-making process is known as a notice-and-comment process. The federal agency which proposes to change its rules must first publish a notice of the proposed rule-making in the Federal Register, and allow a period for public comment. The agency then may propose a rule in the Federal Register, and must discuss the comments it received and why or why not the agency agreed with the comments. The tentative rule is subject to further comment, after which the agency adopts a tentative final rule and announces its proposed effective date. Ultimately, the agency receives additional comment, after which it may publish a final rule, ending all public comment. However, at any time, citizens may petition the agency to modify its rules.

CONSTITUTIONALITY CHALLENGES. An individual affected by legislation or regulations who alleges that the legislation impairs a Constitutional right, or exceeds the powers granted to Congress or the Legislature, may seek a ruling in court as to the constitutionality of the legislation. For a good example of this, see the discussion of *Western States Medical Center v. Shalala*, 238 F.3d 1090 (9th Cir. 2001), in Chapter 4.

WASHINGTON AGENCIES OF INTEREST TO PHARMACISTS AND STUDENT PHARMACISTS. In Washington, the Pharmacy Practice Act (RCW 18.64), establishes the Washington State Pharmacy Quality Assurance Commission

(Pharmacy Commission), and gives it specific powers and duties (see RCW 18.64.001 to 18.64.009). The Pharmacy Commission is part of the Department of Health, which was established by RCW 43.70. The criteria for regulating health professions, which governs the purposes and scope of the Commission's rules, is specified in RCW 18.120, and its powers for disciplining pharmacists are described in the Uniform Disciplinary Act, RCW 18.130.

Washington's universities are also state agencies, established by statute under the authority of Article XIII of the State Constitution. The Regents of the universities have regulatory authority and do issue regulations that govern the universities.

SOVEREIGN IMMUNITY AND EMINENT DOMAIN

Throughout most of Western history, the King – also known as the Sovereign – had absolute power over his domain and subjects. Particularly in England, from which the US inherited most of its legal tradition, this meant that the Sovereign was considered unable to commit a legal wrong, and could take or give control of land as it pleases. In the early 13th century, arising from disagreements among Pope Innocent III, King John, and a lobby of powerful barons over the rights of the King, John agreed to the terms of the Magna Carta ("Great Charter"), which is the most conspicuous example of limitations on the power of the Sovereign. Among its enduring legacies is the right of *habeas corpus*, by which an accused is entitled to know the charges against him. Persistent to this day are notions that the Sovereign may not be sued against its will, and that the Sovereign may take property to meet its needs.

SOVEREIGN IMMUNITY IN THE US. In the US, the federal government and the states retain sovereign immunity, within Constitutional limits, and cannot be sued without their permission. Most states, including Washington, have by statute allowed the states to be sued for torts or certain breaches of contract. The federal government allows itself to be sued for torts, under the Federal Tort Claims Act, and has waived immunity for claims related to contracts to which the government is a party (under the Tucker Act). However, common law claims, such as unjust enrichment, or unfair practices, are not easy to bring in courts, but require legislative action to remedy (e.g., claims of Japanese Americans interned during World War II were only resolved by Congress, not the courts.)

EMINENT DOMAIN IN THE US. Eminent domain in the US is the right of the federal or state governments to seize an individual's property, or restrict his or her use of or rights in the property, without his or her consent. The legal process of taking the property is called condemnation. It is not uncommon for local independent retailers, such as community pharmacists, to find that their store is to be torn down to make way for highway construction. Protection against inappropriate use eminent domain is provided in the Fifth Amendment to the Constitution (the "Takings Clause"). It is allowed only for "public use," and the individual must be justly compensated for the property. That does not mean the compensation will be for its highest or best use, or what the owner would hope to receive. In the states, legislatures have extended the power of eminent domain to counties and municipal corporations. Recent Supreme Court decisions (particularly *Kelo v. City of New London*[23] in 2005) have extended the definition of what constitutes "public use" such that very little justification is actually needed to meet Constitutional limits. In *Kelo*, the Court approved of a New London, CT, condemnation of private property in order to transfer property from one private owner to another as part of an economic redevelopment plan. Under *Kelo,* a city might be able to close a group of small retail shops in order to build a shopping center which would be dominated by big box retailers. In response to the *Kelo* decision, President Bush issued Executive Order 13406[24] prohibiting federal agencies using eminent domain "for the purpose of advancing the economic interest of private parties to be given ownership or use of the property taken." A number of states have legislatively or by initiative reformed their eminent domain laws in response to the *Kelo* decision. The

Washington State Constitution has a fairly restrictive definition of eminent domain, which leaves determination of "public use" to the courts, [25] and the Supreme Court has interpreted public use narrowly. While the legislature has not made major changes to Washington's eminent domain statute since *Kelo*, a 2007 amendment required notification to owners by certified mail of the time and location where the public condemnation hearing involving their property will take place.[26] Pierce and Clallam counties have amended their charters to prohibit condemnation through eminent domain proceedings for the purpose of "economic development."

COMMON LAW

Common law is a body of law that is created by courts when decisions are made in specific cases in which there is no specific statute that applies. When the United States was established, at the moment that the Constitution was ratified, there were no specific federal laws in force. However, the country was not without federal law. Courts continued to render decisions based on the common law that was brought from England. (State laws and constitutions were in effect prior to ratification of the Constitution, and the Constitution appears to have given authority to treaties – such as the Peace Treaty of 1783 – that were enacted prior to its adoption.)

Common law does interpret existing constitutional law and statutes. For example, the "Miranda Warning" arose not from specific statutes, but from a history of cases dealing with claims that the police had coerced a defendant into an "involuntary confession." The Fifth Amendment to the Constitution states that no person "shall be compelled in any criminal case to be a witness against himself."

Congress and legislatures may enact specific legislation to supersede common law. For example, concern in the mid-1970s about the effects of court decisions concerning medical malpractice led the Washington legislature to enact "tort reform" law that put into statute specific rules for negligence suits relating to health care (see RCW 7.70). As regards the issues covered by these statutes, prior common law is no longer applicable in Washington.

CODES – COLLECTING AND ORGANIZING STATUTES AND REGULATIONS

Codes are a means to organize the many statutes and regulations into a meaningful and usable form. If not for *codification*, it would be almost impossible to track the currently applicable law. For example, the Pharmacy Practice Act we operate under today was first passed in 1935. When the Legislature passes a change to a current law, it does so by passing a new statute, but the new statute may be quite short, affecting only a portion of the original Act. The Washington Legislature refers to each law it enacts as a *session law*, and these acts are collected at the end of each session and numbered as "chapters" of that session's enactments. For example, the 1935 Pharmacy Practice Act was chapter 98 of the 1935 session laws, and is cited as "1935 c 98." Subsequent revisions to the Act occurred via session laws in 1963, 1971, 1979, 1981, 1984, and 2013. Imagine if you had to publish copies of all of these acts to track down the various changes! Instead, Washington has a legislative agency called the Office of the Code Reviser, and that agency maintains two major collections of code.

REVISED CODE OF WASHINGTON (RCW). The Revised Code of Washington (RCW) constitutes a current compilation of Washington statutes. The RCW is divided into 101 titles.[27] Each title covers a particular area of legislation. For example, Title 18 contains statutes relating to Businesses and Professions. The titles are subdivided into chapters, and Chapter 64 of Title 18 of the RCW is the section containing statutes relating to Pharmacists. The chapters are further divided into sections. The Definitions of terms used in the Pharmacy Practice Act are in Section 011 of Chapter 64 of Title 18 of the RCW. The citation of an RCW section is in the form RCW 18.64.011.

WASHINGTON ADMINISTRATIVE CODE (WAC). The Washington Administrative Code (WAC) is the current compilation of the various regulations promulgated by state agencies. Like the RCW, the WAC is divided into

Titles, Chapters, and Sections. WAC Titles are organized by agency. Each independent agency is assigned a title of the WAC. The Department of Health's regulations, which include those issued by all boards and commissions (such as Pharmacy) within the department, are placed in Title 246. Chapters are organized by subject matter. Most of the regulations of the Pharmacy Commission are contained within a consecutive series of chapters starting at Chapter 856 and ending with Chapter 907. The citation of a WAC section is in the form WAC 246-863-100. Note the use of dashes instead of periods as separators.

FEDERAL CODES. Federal law and regulation is organized into codes, also. Federal statutes are collected in the UNITED STATES CODE (USC), and federal regulations are collected in the CODE OF FEDERAL REGULATIONS (CFR). Both codes are divided into Titles and Parts. In general the Titles of the USC are unrelated to the Titles of the CFR, and the government publishes a "Parallel Table of Authorities and Rules" to assist in finding where federal statutes are implemented in agency regulations.[28] However, by fortunate coincidence, important federal drug laws – the FDCA and the CSA – are found in 21 USC and the related agency rules are in 21 CFR. Citation of these codes is in the form, 15 U.S.C. 2079(a) or 21 CFR 1700.1.

	WASHINGTON	UNITED STATES
STATUTES	Revised Code of Washington (RCW) "RCW 18.64.011"	United States Code (USC) "21 U.S.C. 2079(a)"
REGULATIONS	Washington Administrative Code (WAC) "WAC 246-863-100"	Code of Federal Regulations (CFR) "21 CFR 1700.1"

OTHER STATE CODES. Virtually all jurisdictions codify their statutes and regulations in some manner. Many states' systems parallel those of Washington, with statutes in one code series and regulations in another. Examples from nearby states include, for Oregon, Oregon Revised Statutes (ORS) and Oregon Administrative Rules (OAR); Idaho organizes its statutes as the Idaho Code (IC), and its regulations as the Idaho Administrative Code (IAC). California, on the other hand, has 29 "codes" that organize statutes. For example, pharmacy law is contained within the Business and Professions Code. California regulations are organized in a single code, called the California Code of Regulations (CCR). When preparing for practice in another jurisdiction, it is useful to start by learning how that state codifies its laws and regulations.

RESTATEMENTS OF COMMON LAW. Just as codes help organize statutes and regulations, common law is organized by "restatements," which, in the US, are developed by the American Law Institute.[29] Each deals with a general area of law, such as Contracts, Torts, Agency, Trusts, and Unfair Competition. There are currently upwards of 20 restatements, but the two of greatest importance to pharmacists are the Restatement of Torts and the Restatement of Contracts. The Restatement of Contracts is in its second edition, and a Third Restatement of Torts was completed in November 2012 with the publishing of volume 2 on Liability and Emotional Harm (volume 1, which covered most health care negligence, was issued in 2010).

LOCATING DECISIONS AND OPINIONS. To understand the application of common law, one may often wish to be able to find specifics of the common law or read the opinion in a key case. Court opinions in specific cases are often available on Internet search engines, and on the web site of the issuing court (at least for recent cases). The major source for court decisions, however, is a series of "reporters" published by Thompson-West Publishing, in which the important decisions in a given jurisdiction are collected and published.

FEDERAL COURT DECISIONS are published in three major categories of reporters. *US SUPREME COURT* decisions are published in the Supreme Court Reports (S.Ct.) and in the United States Reporter (U.S.) *FEDERAL APPELLATE*

COURT decisions are published in the Federal Reporter (F.) *FEDERAL DISTRICT COURT* decisions are published in the Federal Supplement (F.Supp.)

STATE SUPREME AND APPELLATE COURTS also publish their decisions, which are reprinted in individual state reporters, such as the Washington Reporter (Wn.), and are also printed in regional reporters, which assemble opinions from all the courts in geographic regions of the country. The seven regional reporters are Atlantic (A.), Northeastern (N.E.), Northwestern (N.W.), Pacific (P.), Southern (So.), Southeastern (S.E.), and Southwestern (S.W.).

Each volume of a reporter is bound into a fairly large book, and is numbered. When referring to a specific volume, the number is customarily placed ahead of the abbreviation for the reporter. So, the 100th volume of the United States Reports would be referred to as "100 U.S." Eventually, the numbers get too large to place on the spine of the book, so a new "series" of volumes is started, after volume 999 is published. The 100th volume of the second series of the United States Reports would be referred to as "100 U.S.2d." Some reporters (F., S.W.) are in their 3rd series, abbreviated "3d." The starting page number of a particular decision ("opinion") is placed after the volume number and abbreviation, so an opinion starting on page 409 of the 100th volume of the second series of the United States Reports would be cited as "100 U.S.2d. 409."

ELECTRONIC OPINION DATABASES. Two major services provide electronic access to court opinions (and also to many other legal resources): Westlaw and LexisNexis. Both services are available to the public on a per-use basis (via credit card payment), or may be available in university libraries. For example, LexisNexis Academic is available to faculty and students at UW and WSU. An opinion found on Westlaw will be cited in a manner similar to 2004 WL 68993 (Westlaw citation #68993 in 2004); Lexis citations will appear similar to 2008 U.S. Courts LEXIS 12345.

CITATION FORMAT. An opinion in a specific case is cited by the names of the parties, with the *plaintiff* listed first, then the *defendant*, thus: *McKee v. American Home Products.* If the opinion is reported in one of the published reporters, the reporter is cited, along with the date and jurisdiction. In some instances, multiple reporters will be cited for a given case. An important case forming Washington common law is the McKee case. The official case title was *Elaine McKee, Appellant, v. American Home Products Corporation et al., Respondents.* It may be cited as *McKee v. American Home Products,* 113 Wn.2d 701, 782 P.2d 1045 (1989). In the case of an appeal, the parties are often denoted the *appellant* and the *respondent* or *appellee.* The order in which they are listed may vary. In *McKee v. American Home Products*, McKee was the appellant and American Home Products the respondent. Citation formats for other countries as well as the US are summarized in an article on Wikipedia.[30]

STRUCTURE OF GOVERNMENT

EXECUTIVE BRANCH

The Executive Branch is established in federal and state constitutions to carry out and oversee the operations of government and implement the laws passed by the legislative branch. All the agencies of government are part of the executive branch. In both the federal and state system, the executive branch is divided into major departments, under which specific agencies are managed.

FEDERAL EXECUTIVE. The President (Donald J. Trump) is the chief executive officer of the US, and heads the executive branch. The President is supported by a Cabinet, consisting of the Vice President and the heads of the 15 major divisions of the executive branch, which are called Departments. Under Article II, Section 2 of the US

Constitution, the President "may require the Opinion, in writing, of the principal Officer in each of the executive Departments, upon any Subject relating to the Duties of their respective Offices."

CABINET – listed in order of succession to the Presidency:[31]

- Vice President – Mike Pence
- Secretary of State
- Secretary of the Treasury
- Secretary of Defense
- Attorney General (Department of Justice)
- Secretary of the Interior
- Secretary of Agriculture
- Secretary of Commerce
- Secretary of Labor
- Secretary of Health & Human Services
- Secretary of Housing & Urban Development
- Secretary of Transportation
- Secretary of Energy
- Secretary of Education
- Secretary of Veterans Affairs
- Secretary of Homeland Security
- Cabinet-rank Officials (not in line of succession)
    - White House Chief of Staff
    - Environmental Protection Agency Administrator
    - Office of Management & Budget Director
    - U.S. Trade Representative
    - U.S. Ambassador to the UN
    - Council of Economic Advisors Chairman
    - Small Business Administration Administrator

DEPARTMENT OF HEALTH & HUMAN SERVICES. Agencies within the DHHS are critical to pharmacy and medicine. The major agencies that administer programs or regulate in areas important to pharmacy are listed here.

AHRQ – Agency for Healthcare Research & Quality. This agency is responsible for studying health care delivery. Major research into the effectiveness of pharmacists' services is funded by this agency.

ATSDR – Agency for Toxic Substances and Disease Registry, which administers federal regulations related to hazardous waste and toxic substances.

CDC – Centers for Disease Control & Prevention. In addition to dealing with research into epidemic diseases, and monitoring for outbreaks, the CDC is the principal source of information on vaccines and on travel medicine recommendations.

CMS – Centers for Medicare & Medicaid Services. This agency administers Medicare and Medicaid, which together provide for over 40% of health care funding in the US. (See chapter 8)

FDA – Food & Drug Administration. Regulates food, drugs, cosmetics, and medical devices. (See Chapter 4)

HRSA – Health Resources & Services Administration. Charged with assessing and addressing health care manpower needs and providing programs to improve access to health care. Provides funds for education of health professionals, including administration of federal student loan repayment programs for pharmacists who work in underserved areas or certain government positions.

IHS – Indian Health Service. A major employer of pharmacists, supporter of research and education programs, and leader in many innovations in pharmacy practice.

NIH – National Institutes of Health. Major source of federal research funding related to health care.

OIG – Office of Inspector General. Oversees fraud control programs for the Department. (See Chapter 8)

SAMHSA – Substance Abuse & Mental Health Services Administration. Among its many duties, oversees the Office-based Narcotic Maintenance Program. Also a source of significant research and information on substances of abuse and mental health. (See Chapter 5)

DEPARTMENT OF JUSTICE – DRUG ENFORCEMENT ADMINISTRATION. The DOJ is the principal prosecution arm of the federal government, with US Attorneys in every state in the nation. Of particular importance to pharmacy, the Drug Enforcement Administration (DEA) is part of the DOJ (see Chapter 5.)

DEPARTMENT OF HOMELAND SECURITY. Created following the September 11, 2001 terrorist attacks, DHS has an overall mission of protecting the nation against threats, including environmental and human. The pharmacy profession and pharmaceutical industry are affected by several components of DHS, including FEMA (coordinating activities following natural disasters or emergencies), Customs and Border Protection (control against importation of banned drugs and illegal substances), Citizenship and Immigration Services (affecting pharmacists from other countries who wish to practice in the US, and those who would employ them), and the Office of Health Affairs, which deals with response to incidents having medical significance.

STATE OF WASHINGTON EXECUTIVE

The structure of Washington's government parallels that of the federal government. Both are divided into three branches: executive, legislative, and judicial. As with the federal system, there exists a balance of power among the three branches in Washington's government. The Governor (Jay Inslee) is the chief executive officer of the state, and all agencies (and all state employees) ultimately report to the governor, although there is not a direct chain of command for many state employees. The heads of the major departments do report directly to the governor, and they are appointed by the governor, but require the approval of the Senate.

THE DEPARTMENT OF HEALTH (DOH)[32] is one of the major departments of state government. It has several divisions, including the *DIVISION OF HEALTH SYSTEMS QUALITY ASSURANCE* (Kristin Peterson, Assistant Secretary). The *OFFICE OF HEALTH PROFESSIONS AND FACILITIES*[33] is the organization within HSQA that deals with the licensing of health professionals. The *OFFICE OF INVESTIGATIONS AND INSPECTIONS* in HSQA supervises a pool of investigators who inspect licensees' premises and investigate complaints. The HSQA office oversees all the various health care boards and commissions. Commissions, such as the Pharmacy Quality Assurance Commission, as well as the Medical Commission, and the Nursing Care Quality Assurance Commission, which regulate medicine and nursing, are currently semi-independent commissions within the DOH. Although the boards have certain independent powers, the executive director and staff of these boards are state employees that report through the chain of command to the Secretary of the Department of Health (currently John Wiesman). For the most part, the Department provides a general pool of investigators for the various boards and commissions who investigate complaints; the Pharmacy Commission has a specialized group of pharmacist investigators within the Departmental pool, but they report to the director of the Office of Investigation and Inspection. The Commission also has a team of inspectors, who are pharmacists, who now assist licensees in compliance using the revised inspection process (see Chapter 3). The inspectors report to the Assistant Executive Director.

The DEPARTMENT OF SOCIAL AND HEALTH SERVICES (DSHS)[34] manages a variety of state programs that provide services to the most vulnerable citizens of the state. The current Secretary is Cheryl Strange.

The HEALTH CARE AUTHORITY (HCA)[35] was reorganized in 2011 by the Legislature[36] to establish a single agency that coordinates all health care services purchased by the State. Medicaid was placed under the HCA and is generally no longer under the Secretary of Social and Health Services. Sue Birch is the Director of the HCA, and the Chief Medical Officer is Judy Zerzan. Health services purchased by the Department of Corrections, by the Department of Labor and Industries, public health programs, and the Department of Veterans Affairs remain with those agencies, although the HCA is charged with improving coordination and technology assessment. In 2017, the Legislature moved additional responsibilities, including behavioral health, to the HCA. The HCA now is responsible for the following programs, plus others:

Apple Health (Medicaid)
Behavioral health and recovery
Clinical collaboration & initiatives
Health Information Technology
Health Technology Assessment
Prescription Drug Program
Public Employees Benefits Board
School Employees Benefits Board
Uniform Medical Plan
Washington Health Program
Washington Wellness

The DEPARTMENT OF LABOR AND INDUSTRIES (L&I)[37] oversees workers' compensation programs and pays for medical services and medications provided to injured workers who are covered by the State fund, and sets rules for payment of claims by self-insured employers. L&I also enforces various worker-protection acts, including state laws setting minimum pay, overtime pay, and other rules governing working conditions. Joel Sacks is Director of Labor & Industries.

LEGISLATIVE BRANCH

WASHINGTON LEGISLATURE. The Legislature is bicameral (having two divisions, or "houses"), as is Congress (only Nebraska maintains a unicameral legislature). The state is divided into 49 legislative districts.[38] Two members of the HOUSE OF REPRESENTATIVES are elected from each district, and serve two-year terms; there are 98 state representatives. One senator is elected from each of the legislative districts, so the SENATE has 49 members, who are elected for four-year terms. The Legislature meets annually, starting on the second Monday in January. In odd-numbered years, when the biennial budget is determined, the Legislature meets for 105 days; in even-numbered years the session is scheduled for 60 days.

REDISTRICTING. State legislative and congressional district boundaries are subject to revision every 10 years following conduct of the U.S. Census. The Commission must be established in January

PQAC POWERS & DUTIES

RCW 18.64.005

- Regulate the practice of pharmacy and enforce the laws related to pharmacy and drugs.
- Prepare and supervise examinations for licensure (by agreement has delegated this to NABP).
- Establish qualifications for licensure of pharmacists or interns.
- Conduct hearings for revocation or suspension of licenses.
- Issue subpoenas and perform other judicial functions
- Assist law enforcement agencies in enforcing laws pertaining to drugs, controlled substances, and the practice of pharmacy
- Promulgate rules regulating pharmacy ... "for the protection and promotion of the public welfare and safety."
- Adopt rules regarding continuing education requirements for pharmacists and other licensees
- Be immune from suit based on official actions as commission members
- Suggest strategies for eliminating drug diversion, misuse, and abuse
- Conduct educational programs to reduce drug diversion, misuse and abuse by health care practitioners or facilities.
- Monitor trends of drug diversion, misuse and abuse
- Enter into written agreements with other state and federal agencies to promote coordination regarding controlled substances.

of each year ending in a "1" (e.g., 2021, 2031, etc.), and, as a result of voter approval of SJR 8210 in 2016, must approve a redistricting plan by November 15 of the same year. The legislature may revise the plan within the first 30 days of the next session a by a two-thirds vote of each house. If the Commission has not approved a plan by November 15, then the Supreme Court has until April 30 of the following year to devise a redistricting plan that complies with the Constitution.[39]

Washington was one of 8 states which gained a congressional seat as a result of the 2010 census; growing from 9 to 10 members of the House of Representatives. Between 2000 and 2010, the state population grew by 14% to 6.7 million persons.[40] Other states gaining one seat (unless otherwise indicated) include AZ, FL (+2), GA, NV, SC, TX (+4), and UT. States losing one or more seats were IN, LA, MA, MI, MO, NJ, NY (-2), OH (-2), and PA. The next census will be in 2020.

JUDICIAL BRANCH

The general structure of the courts[41] has been described above. Recall that in addition to state superior courts, there are a number of municipal (city) courts, district (county) courts, and special courts, such as juvenile courts.

> **PQAC MEMBERS & STAFF**
> (From PQAC website, January 2, 2019; appointments expire in January of the year shown)
>
> **10 PHARMACISTS**
> Tim Lynch, Chair (2022)
> Kat Wolf Khachatourian (2021)
> Steve Anderson (2022)
> Michael Sieg (2019)
> Elizabeth Jensen (2019)
> Matthew Ronayne (2019)
> Sepi Soleimanpour (2020)
> Teri Ferreira (2020)
> Kenneth Kenyon (2020)
> Vacant position
>
> **4 PUBLIC MEMBERS**
> Bonnie Bush (2022)
> Olgy Diaz (2021)
> Judy Guenther (2019)
> Jerrie Allard (2020)
>
> **1 TECHNICIAN MEMBER**
> Hoang-Uyen Thorstensen (2021)
>
> **EXECUTIVE DIRECTOR**
> Executive Director – Steven Saxe
> Deputy Exec. Dir. – Tracy West

THE PHARMACY QUALITY ASSURANCE COMMISSION (PQAC)

The Pharmacy Commission is a sub-agency of the Department of Health, and is part of the Executive Branch. Its powers and duties are set forth in the Pharmacy Practice Act, RCW 18.64 (see sidebar). Prior to 2013, the Commission was designated by the statute as the Board of Pharmacy, with 7 members.

NOTE ON REFERENCES TO THE PHARMACY COMMISSION OR BOARD OF PHARMACY: Throughout this textbook, historical actions taken prior to 2013 may be cited as decisions of the Board of Pharmacy. Also, note that while the statutes relating to the Commission were amended by the Legislature to refer to the Commission and not the Board, the Commission will need time to revise its regulations to reflect the change. This textbook will use the terms, "Pharmacy Quality Assurance Commission," "Pharmacy Commission," "Commission," or "PQAC" to refer to requirements in relevant WAC citations, even though the WACs themselves may still refer to the Board or Board of Pharmacy. Also note that Washington statutes and regulations refer to departments, boards and commissions without capitalization (e.g., "There shall be a state pharmacy quality assurance commission ..."); this text will fairly consistently capitalize Pharmacy Commission unless it is quoting directly from a statute or regulation.

COMMISSION MEMBERS. The Commission consists of 15 members, appointed by the governor, with the "advice and consent of the Senate." Ten members must be pharmacists, and must, at the time of their appointment, have been licensed to practice in Washington for at least five years, and they must remain licensed during their term on the Board. The statute (RCW 18.64.001) requires the governor to select members who are representative of all areas of practice and geographically representative of the state of Washington. Four "lay members," or "public members," are appointed by the governor, subject to Senate approval; these members must not be affiliated with pharmacy in any way. All pharmacist and public members of the commission must be US citizens and residents of the state. The final member must be a pharmacy technician licensed by the Commission. Commission members serve four year terms, and may be reappointed for a second term.

OVER-PRESCRIBING AND APPARENT LEGEND DRUG OVERUSE BY PRACTITIONERS

discovered by other state agencies, including DSHS and L&I, shall be reported to the Department of Health. Health maintenance organizations, health service contractors, and health care providers are also encourage to make such reports to the Department. The Commission is empowered to "Enter into written agreements with all other state and federal agencies with any responsibility for controlling drug misuse, diversion, or abuse and with health maintenance organizations, health care service contractors, and health care providers to assist and promote coordination of agencies responsible for ensuring compliance with controlled substances laws and to monitor observance of these laws and cooperation between these agencies." (RCW 18.64.005 (13))

LIMITS ON THE COMMISSION'S AUTHORITY

The Commission's authority (and the authority of the Department of Health) to regulate health professions or occupations is constrained by the provisions of RCW 18.120.010(2):

(2) It is the intent of this chapter that no regulation shall, after July 24, 1983, be imposed upon any health profession *except for the exclusive purpose of protecting the public interest*. [*Emphasis* added.] All bills introduced in the legislature to regulate a health profession for the first time should be reviewed according to the following criteria. A health profession should be regulated by the state only when:

> Unregulated practice can clearly harm or endanger the health, safety, or welfare of the public, and the potential for the harm is easily recognizable and not remote or dependent upon tenuous argument;
> The public needs and can reasonably be expected to benefit from an assurance of initial and continuing professional ability; and
> The public cannot be effectively protected by other means in a more cost-beneficial manner.

(3) After evaluating the criteria in subsection (2) of this section and considering governmental and societal costs and benefits, if the legislature finds that it is necessary to regulate a health profession not previously regulated by law, the least restrictive alternative method of regulation should be implemented, consistent with the public interest and this section:

> Where existing common law and statutory civil actions and criminal prohibitions are not sufficient to eradicate existing harm, the regulation should provide for stricter civil actions and criminal prosecutions;
> Where a service is being performed for individuals involving a hazard to the public health, safety, or welfare, the regulation should impose inspection requirements and enable an appropriate state agency to enforce violations by injunctive relief in court, including, but not limited to, regulation of the business activity providing the service rather than the employees of the business;
> Where the threat to the public health, safety, or economic well-being is relatively small as a result of the operation of the health profession, the regulation should implement a system of registration;
> Where the consumer may have a substantial basis for relying on the services of a practitioner, the regulation should implement a system of certification; or
> Where apparent that adequate regulation cannot be achieved by means other than licensing, the regulation should implement a system of licensing.

The 2016 Legislature also gave direction to the Commission in its interpretation of the licensing requirements of RCW 18.64, the pharmacy practice act. "This chapter must be interpreted in a manner that supports regulatory, inspection, and investigation standards that are reasonable and appropriate based on the level of risk and the type of services provided in a pharmacy, including pharmacy services provided in a hospital and pharmacy services provided in an individual practitioner office or multipractitioner clinic owned, operated, or under common control with a hospital regardless of the office or clinic's pharmacy address. The commission shall provide clear and specific information regarding the standards to which particular pharmacy services will be held, as appropriate, based on the type of pharmacy service provided at a particular location." (RCW 18.64.043 (b))

Sunset and Sunrise Reviews. Most states have processes in place to determine whether existing regulations, departments, agencies, or programs are meeting current needs; these include "sunset" and "sunrise" reviews. As required by statute, the Joint Legislative Audit & Review Committee of the Legislature periodically conducts "sunset reviews" to determine whether there is a continuing need for a program or an agency. Sunset reviews are usually triggered by legislative action which schedules a program or agency for termination. Continuation of the agency or program following a sunset review requires an Act of the Legislature. The Legislature may also direct the Department conduct a "sunrise" review to determine if new regulations should be promulgated regarding an occupation or profession. Sunrise reviews may be triggered by a request from the public (usually the occupation or profession), which is made to an appropriate Legislative Committee (either the Health Care and Wellness Committee of the House or the Senate Health Care Committee). The Department has an explanation of the process, which is overseen by the HSQA Division, on its website.[42] Members of the public or a profession may petition boards or commissions to amend existing regulations for currently regulated professions. An independent organization, the Council on Licensure, Enforcement & Regulation (CLEAR), tracks state-level sunset and sunrise reviews across the US on its website.[43]

INFLUENCING COMMISSION POLICY DECISIONS

It is important that pharmacy professionals and others who wish to influence the rule-making by the Commission always remember that the Commission's mandate is to regulate in the public interest. If arguments for or against particular policy changes are framed in those terms, then it is more likely that the Commission will be persuaded to accept those arguments. Engaging patients and other interested parties is also key to shaping regulatory policy.

REFERENCES

[1] *Bang Nguyen v. Dep't of Health*, 144 Wn.2d 516, 29 P.3d 689 (Wash. 2001).
[2] *Ongom v. Dep't of Health*, 159 Wn.2d 132; 148 P.3d 1029 (Wash. 2006); Cert. denied, 126 S.Ct. 2115 (2007).
[3] *Hardee v. Dep't of Social and Health Svcs*., 172 Wn.2d 1; 256 P.3d 339, (Wash. 2011)
[4] According to the Washington Department of Corrections, 78 persons have been put to death at the State Penitentiary in Walla Walla since 1904 – all were male (85% white, 9% black, 2% Asian, 2% Hispanic, and 1% Aleut). The most recent two executions were in 2010 and 2001. http://www.doc.wa.gov/offenderinfo/capitalpunishment/
[5] 2013 c 270 §1; RCW 9.94A.832; RCW 9.94A.533(14)
[6] *Miranda v. Arizona*, 384 U.S. 436 (1966)
[7] Draper R. The toxic pharmacist. *New York Times* 2003 Jun 8; http://www.nytimes.com/2003/06/08/magazine/the-toxic-pharmacist.html, accessed 12/23/14
[8] Yan H. Pharmacy owners agree to $100 million settlement after meningitis outbreak. CNN Health 2013 Dec 24; http://www.cnn.com/2013/12/24/health/meningitis-pharmacy-settlement/, accessed 12/23/14
[9] Bidgood J, Tavernise S. Pharmacy executives face murder charges in meningitis deaths. *New York Times* 2014 Dec 17; http://www.nytimes.com/2014/12/18/us/new-england-compounding-center-steroid-meningitis-arrests.html?_r=0, accessed 12/23/14
[10] Famous American Trials: The O.J. Simpson Trial 1995; School of Law, University of Missouri at Kansas City; http://law2.umkc.edu/faculty/projects/ftrials/Simpson/simpson.htm, accessed 12/20/2014
[11] Ayers Jr., BD. Jury decides Simpson must pay $25 million in punitive award. *New York Times* 1997 Feb 11; http://www.nytimes.com/1997/02/11/us/jury-decides-simpson-must-pay-25-million-in-punitive-award.html, accessed 12/23/14
[12] Jake Davis and Edward Jessen, "Followed Rates" and Leading State Cases, 1940-2005, *41 U.C. Davis L. Rev*. 683, 694 (2007)
[13] United States Constitution, Article VI.
[14] United Nations. Single Convention on Narcotic Drugs 1961 (amended by 1972 Protocol); https://www.unodc.org/pdf/convention_1961_en.pdf
[15] *Riegel v. Medtronic*. No. 06-179, U.S. Supr. Ct., 552 U.S. 312, 2008.
[16] *Warner-Lambert v. Kent*, No. 06-1498, U.S. Supr. Ct., 552 U.S. 440, 2008.

[17] *Wyeth v. Levine*, No. 06-1249, U.S. Supr. Ct., 129 S. Ct. 1187; 173 L.Ed. 2d 51, 2009
[18] See, e.g., *Mensing v. Wyeth et al.,* No. 08-3850, 4th Cir., November 27, 2009.
[19] *Pliva v. Mensing, Actavis Elizabeth v. Mensing, Actavis v. Demahy*, 131 S.Ct. 2567; 180 L.Ed.2d 580 (2011)
[20] USDHHS, FDA. 21 CFR Parts 314 and 601, Docket No. FDA-2013-N-0500. Supplemental applications proposing labeling changes for approved drugs and biological products. 78 Fed. Reg. 67985, 2013 Nov 13.
[21] Gaffney A. Generic drug industry threatens FDA with lawsuit over drug labeling proposal. Regulatory Affairs Professional Society *Regulatory Focus News,* 2014 Oct 7; http://www.raps.org/Regulatory-Focus/News/2014/10/07/20497/Generic-Drug-Industry-Threatens-FDA-With-Lawsuit-Over-Drug-Labeling-Proposal/, accessed 12/22/14
[22] USDHHS, FDA, 21 CFR Parts 314 and 601, Docket No. FDA-2013-N-0500, Withdrawal of proposed rule on supplemental applications proposing labeling changes for approved drugs and biological products. 83 Fed. Reg. 64299, 2018 Dec 14.
[23] *Kelo v. City of New London*, 545 U.S. 469 (2005)
[24] 71 Fed Reg 36973, 6/23/06.
[25] Wash. St. Const. Art. I § 16.
[26] HB 1458, 2007 c 68, 7/22/07.
[27] The titles are numbered from 1 to 91, but some titles have more than one part, such as the "education titles:" 28A (common schools), 28B (higher education), and 28C (vocational education).
[28] The Legal Information Institute republishes the PTOA on its website at https://www.law.cornell.edu/ptoa.
[29] www.ali.org
[30] http://en.wikipedia.org/wiki/Case_citation, accessed 1/3/13
[31] Note that the Speaker of the House (Nancy Pelosi as of January 3, 2019) and President pro tempore of the Senate (Charles Grassley as of January 3, 2019) follow the Vice-President in the line of succession, ahead of the Secretary of State.
[32] www.doh.wa.gov
[33] http://www.doh.wa.gov/AboutUs/ProgramsandServices/HealthSystemsQualityAssurance/HealthProfessionsandFacilities
[34] http://www.dshs.wa.gov/
[35] http://www.hca.wa.gov/
[36] 2011 1st sp.s, c 15; 2E2SHB 1738; RCW 41.05.021
[37] http://www.lni.wa.gov/
[38] https://app.leg.wa.gov/DistrictFinder/
[39] Wash. St. Const. Art. II § 43.
[40] http://2010.census.gov/2010census/data/
[41] http://www.courts.wa.gov/
[42] http://www.doh.wa.gov/AboutUs/ProgramsandServices/HealthSystemsQualityAssurance/SunriseReviews/HealthProfessionsCredentialing, accessed 12/23/14
[43] http://www.clearhq.org/

2 – BECOMING A PHARMACIST, INTERN, TECHNICIAN OR PHARMACY ASSISTANT

PHARMACISTS

WHAT IS A PHARMACIST?

Throughout most of the industrialized world, pharmacists are individuals who have been trained in an academic setting within a generally recognized curriculum related to drugs, their development and production, their storage and distribution, and their therapeutic uses. So, one answer to the question is a pharmacist is someone who has been trained as a pharmacist. From the perspective of the law, however, proper training is only one part of the equation. A pharmacist, by law, is a person licensed to practice pharmacy in a given jurisdiction. So, the answer to the question is entirely dependent upon the Legislature.

COMPETENCY AREAS IN THIS CHAPTER

2016 MPJE COMPETENCY STATEMENTS – Areas 1.1.2, 1.3.3, 2.1.1, 2.1.2, 2.1.4

2016 ACPE REQUIRED ELEMENTS – Pharmacy Law & Regulatory Affairs; History of Pharmacy; Public Health; Ethics

RCW 18.64.011 (10): "'Pharmacist' means a person duly licensed by the commission to engage in the practice of pharmacy."

CHANGE IN SCOPE OF PRACTICE SINCE THE 1960s

As seen below, a pharmacist in Washington is a person who can dispense, administer, monitor the use of, or, under protocol, prescribe medications. Prior to 1979, pharmacists in all states were only compounders and dispensers, and could not administer drugs, nor could they generally be involved in managing a patient's drug therapy, as we now understand the practice. Beginning in the 1960s, certain federal pharmacists, most notably in the US Public Health Service's Indian Health Service clinics, began to engage in expanded patient care roles, and by 1974 over 90% of IHS sites had one or more pharmacist-run disease management programs in place.[44] Washington was the first state in the US in 1979[45] to allow administration, monitoring, and/or prescribing of drugs as part of every pharmacist's scope of practice. Now, all states allow some form of administration of drugs – at least via provision of immunizations – and 48 states and the District of Columbia[46] allow by statute some form of collaborative practice for pharmacists, although several restrict it to institutional settings only, and/or require additional credentials beyond licensure.

FIGURE 1-1: STATES ALLOWING PHARMACIST COLLABORATIVE PRACTICE

The chart at right shows the number of states[47,48] – as reported in the literature in the years shown – which allowed some form of collaborative practice for pharmacists.[49,50,51,52,53,54] (See Chapter 8 for a discussion of how payers deal with pharmacists who are providers of care under collaborative drug therapy agreements.)

PRACTICE OF PHARMACY IN WASHINGTON.

> ### "PRACTICE OF PHARMACY" – WASHINGTON STATE – INCLUDES:
>
> - Interpreting prescription orders;
> - Compounding, dispensing, labeling, administering, and distribution of drugs and devices;
> - The monitoring of drug therapy and use;
> - The initiating or modifying of drug therapy in accordance with written guidelines or protocols previously established and approved for his or her practice by a practitioner authorized to prescribe drugs;
> - The participating in drug utilization reviews and drug product selection;
> - The proper and safe storing and distributing of drugs and devices and maintenance of proper records thereof;
> - The providing of information on legend drugs which may include, but is not limited to, the advising of therapeutic values, hazards, and the uses of drugs and devices.

The practice of pharmacy in Washington is defined in RCW 18.64.011 (11) – see text box at left. It is incumbent on every pharmacist to reliably know this definition, for it sets forth the boundaries of his or her scope of practice in the state of Washington. When this definition was adopted in, as suggested above, it added 3 key activities to the pharmacist's scope of practice: (1) administering of drugs and devices; (2) monitoring of drug therapy and use; and (3) initiating or modifying drug therapy under protocol or written guidelines approved by another authorized prescriber. These activities are discussed more fully elsewhere (particularly Chapter 4), but some important distinctions must be made.

First, nothing in the definition denotes "prescribing." This was done on purpose when the statute was written, to avoid alarming other professions concerning the implications to their practices. Instead, the phrase, "initiating or modifying" was used, but it implicitly gives the pharmacist authority to "prescribe" those drugs that are covered under the guideline or protocol.

Second, note that the initiating or modifying applies only to drug therapy, not to medical devices. Many medical devices require prescriptions, but the statute does not extend prescriptive authority for those devices to pharmacists. However, the definition of "administration" (see below) does include the use of devices to deliver therapy or to monitor therapy.

Finally, it must be recognized that nothing in the definition discusses "collaborative practice agreements," as they have become to be known in recent years. The statute implicitly allows written guidelines or protocols to be included in an agreement between one or more pharmacists and one or more authorized prescribers, but it does not require an "agreement," which implies a mutual relationship. The statute envisioned the use of protocols, which were emerging in hospitals at the time, and which could be approved by a Pharmacy & Therapeutics Committee, allowing pharmacists in the hospital who weren't even personally known to the committee members to initiate or modify therapy.

In late 2018, the Commission issued an "Interim Guidance on Collaborative Drug Therapy,"[55] which attempts to deal with the relationships among written guidelines, protocols, and what the Commission has defined as a collaborative drug therapy agreement, or CDTA. Under this interpretation, a CDTA is a subset of the universe of written guidelines or protocols, in which a particular protocol has been approved for a particular pharmacist's practice such that the pharmacist becomes the prescriber of the therapy authorized by the protocol. If the pharmacist is the prescriber, the guidance indicates he or she is operating under a CDTA. The guidance supposes that there could be protocols (perhaps refill authorizations based on non-discretionary guidelines) where the pharmacist could authorize the dispensing without being the prescriber, in which case the pharmacist is not operating under a CDTA. Chapter 4 discusses this guidance in further detail.

OTHER IMPORTANT DEFINITIONS. Several terms in the definition of the practice of pharmacy are key to an understanding other laws and rules. Among the more critical definitions a pharmacist needs to learn are the following (RCW 18.64.011 (15-18; 22-23):

"DELIVER" OR "DELIVERY" means the actual, constructive, or attempted transfer from one person to another of a drug or device, whether or not there is an agency relationship.

"DISPENSE" means the interpretation of a prescription or order for a drug, biological, or device and, pursuant to that prescription or order, the proper selection, measuring, compounding, labeling, or packaging necessary to prepare that prescription or order for delivery.

"DISTRIBUTE" means the delivery of a drug or device other than by administering or dispensing.

"COMPOUNDING" shall be the act of combining two or more ingredients in the preparation of a prescription.

"LABELING" shall mean the process of preparing and affixing a label to any drug or device container. The label must include all information required by current federal and state law and pharmacy rules.

"ADMINISTER" means the direct application of a drug or device, whether by injection, inhalation, ingestion, or any other means, to the body of a patient or research subject.

Note that "administer" includes drugs *and* devices. The authority of a pharmacist to perform finger-sticks for CLIA-waived screening and monitoring devices arises from the ability to "apply" the lancet to the patient's body. Similarly, pharmacists can likely insert continuous glucose monitoring devices as an act of "administering" the device to the patient. No pharmacist should administer devices for which he or she is not trained, and generally any truly invasive procedures, such as suturing or cutting the skin, are not part of administering devices, but the practice of medicine or surgery.

Also note that the authority to administer drugs is part and parcel of the definition of pharmacy practice, and does not require any other authorization. Thus, like a nurse, a pharmacist may administer any drug for which he or she has a valid order from a prescriber. In the case of vaccines, the pharmacist is usually the professional who also initiates the vaccine order, and to do so requires a written prescriptive authority protocol. Also note that a pharmacist does not have to be "certified" to administer drugs ordered by an authorized prescriber; most immunization protocols, however, require certification to be able to initiate the vaccine order.

The statute does not define "MONITORING OF DRUG THERAPY," so the Pharmacy Commission has done so by regulation (WAC 246-863-110):

> The term "monitoring of drug therapy" used in RCW 18.64.011(11) shall mean a review of the drug therapy regimen of patients by a pharmacist for the purpose of evaluating and rendering advice to the prescribing practitioner regarding adjustment of the regimen. Monitoring of drug therapy shall include, but not be limited to:
>
> (1) Collecting and reviewing patient drug use histories;
>
> (2) Measuring and reviewing routine patient vital signs including, but not limited to, pulse, temperature, blood pressure and respiration; and
>
> (3) Ordering and evaluating the results of laboratory tests relating to drug therapy including, but not limited to, blood chemistries and cell counts, drug levels in blood, urine, tissue or other body fluids, and culture and sensitivity tests when performed in accordance with policies and procedures or protocols applicable to the practice setting, which have been developed by the pharmacist and prescribing practitioners and which include appropriate mechanisms for reporting to the prescriber monitoring activities and results.

Ordering laboratory tests is within the scope of "monitoring of drug therapy," but the regulation requires that policies and procedures or protocols be developed and, by implication, maintained in the pharmacy, by the pharmacist and "prescribing practitioners." Such policies and procedures must include mechanisms for reporting to the patient's prescriber the results of the monitoring activities. However, unlike the protocols or guidelines that authorize the pharmacist to initiate or modify therapy, the laboratory test policies and procedures do not require the signature of an authorizing prescriber, nor must they be filed with the Commission.

Measuring vital signs is an activity that may be performed without guidelines or protocols.

Note that patient counseling is not part of dispensing, as defined in the statute, and that "administer" and "dispense" are quite different actions.

DO YOU NEED TO BE WORKING IN A PHARMACY TO BE PRACTICING PHARMACY? Because the practice of pharmacy includes both the physical processes of dispensing as well as many functions that involve interpreting information and providing advice about drug therapy, a person may be engaged in the practice of pharmacy without dispensing drugs. Pharmacists working in health systems or educational institutions, for example, are practicing pharmacy whenever they "advis[e] of ... hazards and the uses of drugs." Participating in a formulary committee, speaking to the public about drug use while holding oneself out to be a pharmacist, or consulting with other health care providers about drug use are all examples of practicing pharmacy without being involved in drug distribution. Even giving your neighbor advice about his or her drug therapy "over the fence" involves you in the practice of pharmacy if your neighbor has reason to know or believe that you're a pharmacist.

LICENSE REQUIRED FOR PRACTICE It is unlawful to practice pharmacy without a license, or to operate a pharmacy without placing a licensed pharmacist in charge. (RCW 18.64.020)

EMPLOYERS MUST VERIFY CREDENTIALS It is incumbent on employers to verify that each employee is currently licensed and free from restrictions on his or her practice. (RCW 18.130.180(10)) Pharmacies with DEA registration may not retain employees who have been previously convicted of a felony relating to controlled substances. (See Chapter 5) Pharmacies serving Medicare, Medicaid, or other federal beneficiaries may not employ persons who are excluded from participation in Medicare or Medicaid (See Chapter 8).

RETIRED OR INACTIVE PHARMACISTS Some persons trained as pharmacists are no longer in practice – such as a retired pharmacist or a person who has let his license lapse because he is engaged in a non-pharmacy business such as real estate. These individuals should refrain from giving advice about drugs to others, and should refer the person to a licensed pharmacist. Note that retired physicians and attorneys routinely adhere to this rule.

LICENSE MUST BE DISPLAYED A copy of the pharmacist's current license must be displayed openly in any licensed pharmacy location where the pharmacist is practicing. (RCW 18.64.140). Pharmacists who work in several locations should have a copy for each location. Because the "wallet card" bears the signature of the Secretary of Health, it is a valid copy of the pharmacist's license. The Commission has also indicated that a current printout from the Department's credential database is sufficient while waiting for a license copy to arrive following initial licensure or renewal.

This requirement does not apply to interns, technicians, or assistants. The Commission's inspection policy requires that licenses of all employees be readily available to the investigator, and most pharmacies display all employees' licenses in a central location.

PROTECTION FOR LICENSEE'S PERSONAL ADDRESS AND PHONE NUMBER

When communicating in writing to a person who has made a complaint concerning a health professional, the Department of Health is prohibited from disclosing the licensee's address and phone number. (RCW 18.130.085)

Information regarding a licensee's personal address and phone number, among other information, is protected from disclosure under Washington's Public Records Act (RCW 42.17; RCW 42.56 after 7/1/06).

A licensee who is the victim of domestic violence, sexual assault, or stalking may apply to the Secretary of State to participate in the Address Confidentiality Program. Washington Law (RCW 40.24.030, WAC 434.840) allows certain persons to participate in an Address Confidentiality Program[56] overseen by the Secretary of State. This program allows individuals who are victims of domestic violence, sexual assault, or stalking to obtain an alternate mailing address for all legal purposes, and thereby conceal from public disclosure their actual street address, school address, or work address. Mail is sent to the ACP address, and is then forwarded by the Secretary of State to the addressee.

LICENSES WILL DISPLAY ANY RESTRICTIONS Credentials issued by the Commission contain notations of any restrictions that have been placed on the license. For example, a pharmacist who is on probation will see "Active on Probation" printed on his or her license. Other restrictions are indicated by "Active with Restrictions."[57] It is improper for the licensee to alter or obscure these statements on the posted copy of his or her license.[58]

NOTIFICATION TO DEPARTMENT OF CHANGES The licensee must promptly notify the Department of any change in his or her name (WAC 246-12-300); or address (WAC 246-12-310)

Address changes may be mailed, faxed or e-mailed to the Department of Health. Mail should be sent to the HPQA Customer Service Office, P.O. Box 47865, Olympia, WA 98504-7865. Faxes may be made to 360-236-4818. The licensee must include complete identification and list the license number(s) affected by the change.

An Address Change form is also available on the Department's website at http://www.doh.wa.gov/LicensesPermitsandCertificates/ProfessionsNewReneworUpdate/ChangeyourContactorAddressInformation/HealthProfessions.aspx; this can be filled out online and submitted electronically.

LICENSE RENEWAL The license must be promptly renewed upon its expiration, which occurs annually on the licensee's birthday (WAC 246-907-030(1)). There is a penalty for late renewal, but, more important, the person whose license has not been renewed is not able to practice legally until the renewal and penalty fee are paid. A license that has expired for more than one year will require payment of a penalty fee plus completion of other requirements (WAC 246-863-090).

The Department of Health will send a renewal notice to the address on file with the Board, but this is considered only a "courtesy" reminder – the licensee is responsible for renewal even if this reminder is not received.

Pharmacists may renew their registrations using the on-line system provided their credential has not expired, and the registrant is not in inactive status. A $2.50 fee is charged for online renewals. (https://www.doh.wa.gov/LicensesPermitsandCertificates/ProfessionsNewReneworUpdate/LicenseRenewals)

CONTINUING PHARMACY EDUCATION

Pharmacists in virtually all states must complete continuing pharmacy education to be eligible to renew their licenses. Requirements differ among states, but most states specify a minimum for each renewal period, measured either in contact hours, or Continuing Education Units (CEUs). One contact hour equals 0.1 CEUs. The standards for continuing education for pharmacists are developed by the Accreditation Council for Pharmacy Education (ACPE), which accredits CPE providers. Each approved program is given an ACPE Program number which identifies the provider, date, and the CPE category covered by the program.[59]

Washington State requires 1.5 CEUs (15 contact hours) per year for pharmacist license renewal. (WAC 246-861-090) Qualifying programs include programs provided by approved program providers or programs approved for individual pharmacists by the Commission. Programs may be live, on-line, by correspondence, or in written format.

ACPE standards also describe 3 types of CPE activities. Knowledge-based activities are intended to transmit factual knowledge that is evidence-based, and requires a minimum of 15 minutes or 0.25 contact hours. Application-based activities are constructed to

ACPE DESIGNATIONS FOR CPE CATEGORIES

ACTIVITY TYPES:

Knowledge-based
Application-based
Practice-based (formerly named Certificate Programs)

FORMAT:

L – Live activities
H – Home study or other mediated activities
B – Both (for practice-based activities)

TOPIC:

01-P or 01-T Disease State Management/Drug Therapy
02-P or 02-T AIDS Therapy
03-P or 03-T Law (related to pharmacy practice)
04-P or 04-T General Pharmacy
05-P or 05-T Patient Safety
06-P or 06-T Immunizations
07-P or 07-T Compounding

AUDIENCE:

P – Pharmacists
T – Technicians

apply the information learned in the time allotted. Information presented must be evidence-based, and the minimum time required for credit is 60 minutes or 1 contact hour. Practice-based activities were formerly called Certificate Programs. Both didactic and practice experience components must be included and at least 15 contact hours must be involved in the program. To aid states in identifying specific topics that they may wish to require, ACPE has established 7 topic categories (see sidebar above). A given program will have an ACPE program number such as: 0197-0000-17-001-L05-P, using designations shown above.

Programs for Washington pharmacists must cover a topic from one of four areas: legal aspects of health care; properties and actions of drugs and dosage forms; etiology, characteristics, therapeutics, and prevention of the disease state; or specialized pharmacy practice (WAC 246-861-055). In practical terms, any ACPE-approved CPE in topic areas 01 through 07 (see side bar), other than "business management" programs, will qualify in Washington state. Presenters may claim credit for a program that they present, but only for the first time it is presented. (WAC 246-861-060)

The Commission does not currently specify a minimum number of hours in any category for pharmacists, other than when CE is part of a disciplinary order.

Approved providers may be either Commission-approved or can be accredited by the ACPE. All programs approved by ACPE qualify for Washington requirements, and do not require individual approval by the Commission. Non-accredited programs require approval by the Commission. Individuals may submit programs for approval using a form on the Commission's website.[60]

ATTENDANCE AT COMMISSION MEETINGS: The Commission awards 0.15 CEUs for attending a half-day session of the Commission, up to a total of 0.3 CEUs per license cycle. Attendees sign a form at the session to receive credit.[61]

PATIENT EDUCATION TRAINING INCENTIVE: A pharmacist may claim an incentive of 0.15 CEU for each hour of a qualified patient education training program (up to a maximum of 1.2 CEU) – see WAC 246-861-090 for details.

FIRST RENEWAL FOR NEWLY-LICENSED PHARMACISTS The Commission has established a policy that newly-graduated pharmacists do not need to submit CE for their first license renewal if the original license was issued within 12 months of graduation.[62]

CPE MONITOR ACPE and the National Association of Boards of Pharmacy (NABP) jointly manage the *CPE Monitor* program, which tracks all ACPE-accredited CE for pharmacists. Pharmacists must establish an e-Profile on the NABP website at no charge (https://nabp.pharmacy/cpe-monitor-service/) and must provide their NABP e-Profile ID number to program providers in order to receive credit.

MILITARY AND UNIFORMED SERVICE PERSONNEL (RCW 43.70.270; RCW 18.340; WAC 246-12)

PHARMACISTS IN UNIFORMED SERVICES. Pharmacists and other licensees of the Department of Health are entitled to have their licenses remain in force and not expired during any period of service in the armed forces, the U.S. Merchant Marine, and the U.S. Public Health Service Commissioned Officers Corps,[63] provided the license was in good standing at the time of entering the relevant federal service. This is called "military" status. (WAC 246-12-010(11)(e)) The statute requires that "Notwithstanding any provision of the law to the contrary, the license ... shall continue in full force and effect so long as such service continues, unless sooner suspended, canceled, or revoked for cause as provided by law." (RCW 43.70.270(1)) Within 6 months of retirement from federal service, the licensee may request renewal of the license and pay the current renewal fee. Continuing education requirements and license renewal fees are waived during this period. CE requirements will be waived until the first post-discharge renewal of the licensee's credential. Rules for military status are found in WAC 246-

12-500. Licensees on military status are expected to provide the Department with an official copy of his or service orders at the time of annual renewal to maintain his or her credential in military status. Complementary renewal notices will be sent to the licensee and the licensee "should return the courtesy maintenance notice to the department with an official copy of their service orders." (WAC 246-12-520(4))

INACTIVE MILITARY-RELATED SPOUSE LICENSE CATEGORY. Pharmacists or other licensees of the DOH who are spouses or domestic partners of federal personnel in the military or USPHS commissioned corps may request that their license to practice be placed in "Inactive Military Spouse" or "Inactive Military Registered Domestic Partner" status, if their spouse or partner is deployed outside the state of Washington. (WAC 246-12-010(11)(d)) "The Secretary shall return to active status the license of every such person who applies for renewal thereof within six months after the service member is honorably discharged from service, or sooner if requested by the licensee, upon payment of" the applicable renewal fee. Renewal requirements and CE obligations are treated the same for inactive military-related status as for military status.

EXPEDITED LICENSURE OF PHARMACISTS FROM OTHER STATES WHO ARE SPOUSES OF MILITARY PERSONNEL TRANSFERRED TO WASHINGTON STATE. Pharmacists or other DOH licensees who are spouses of active duty military, merchant marine, or USPHS commissioned corps personnel are entitled to expedited registration in the state of Washington if they hold an unrestricted license in another state when the requirements for licensure in the other state are substantially equivalent to Washington, and they are following their spouse/domestic partner to Washington upon his or her transfer by the federal government.

The Pharmacy Commission is required to establish procedures for promptly granting a temporary permit to allow the applicant time to complete any specific additional requirements that differ in Washington from the state of their current license. (RCW 18.340.020) This has more applicability for pharmacy assistants and technicians than for pharmacists.

Rules implementing the "inactive military-related" and "military" license status categories were adopted by the are found in WAC 246-12-010, 090, 100, and 110, and in WAC 246-12-500 through 560.

TEMPORARY PERMITS (WAC 246-863-035). In November 2010, the Commission revised the terms for the issuance of temporary permits to practice pharmacy in Washington. Temporary permits are only available to applicants seeking license via license transfer (reciprocity) and who hold an unrestricted license in another state that participates in the license transfer process. The rule provides for a temporary permit when the applicant meets all other qualifications for licensure except for completion of a fingerprint-based national background check. The applicant must have completed the MPJE for Washington and all other requirements to receive a license in Washington. Temporary permit holders may not serve as a pharmacy's responsible pharmacist manager. The permit expires after 180 days, when a permanent license is issued, or a decision on the applicant's permanent license is reached, whichever is sooner. An applicant for a temporary permit must submit the required fingerprint card, a written request for a temporary permit, and must pay the permit fee of $100.

INACTIVE LICENSES (WAC 246-863-070; WAC 246-12-090)). A pharmacist may apply for an inactive license, which does not allow the pharmacist to practice, but maintains a credential with the Pharmacy Commission. The annual license fee is the same for an inactive license as for an active license. The inactive license may be reactivated without payment of a penalty fee.

RETIRED PHARMACIST LICENSES (WAC 246-863-080). A pharmacist who has been licensed in WA for 25 consecutive years or more may maintain a retired pharmacist credential upon application to the Department. This credential does not allow the pharmacist to practice, but the annual fee is currently only $25, and allows the pharmacist to continue to receive mailings from the Commission. This license may be reactivated without payment of a penalty fee.

REACTIVATION of inactive, expired, or retired licenses (WAC 246-12) require similar procedures, based on length of time that the license has been inactive and whether the pharmacist has been in active practice elsewhere.

For reactivations within less than 3 years, the pharmacist must pay a reactivation fee and provide evidence of having met the CE requirements. After more than 3 years: (1) if the pharmacist has been active in another state, provide evidence of active status and retake the MJPE for Washington; (2) if the pharmacist has not been active in another state, but applies for reactivation within 5 years, must take and pass the MPJE for Washington, and serve 300 hours of internship or pass a practical exam specified by the Commission in specific cases.

After more than 5 years without being active in another state, must take the MPJE for Washington and complete 300 hours of internship.

A fee of $265 is required for a reissued license.

ALLOWING UNLICENSED PRACTICE

Allowing another person to practice pharmacy without a license is a basis for discipline (RCW 18.130.180 (10)). The Pharmacy Commission has specifically identified a list of PROFESSIONAL RESPONSIBILITIES THAT THE PHARMACIST MAY NOT DELEGATE TO PHARMACY **a**ncillary personnel (see side bar). Allowing technicians or assistants to perform any of these functions may constitute allowing the unlicensed practice of pharmacy.

SUPERVISION OF INTERNS REQUIRED

As discussed under Internship, below, a pharmacy intern may perform any function that is part of the practice of pharmacy when under supervision of a licensed pharmacist.

OTHER PROFESSIONS SHARE AUTHORITY

Remember that other health professionals, including nurses and physicians, are allowed by their own licenses to perform

PROFESSIONAL RESPONSIBILITIES THAT MAY NOT BE DELEGATED TO TECHNICIANS OR ASSISTANTS

(WAC 246-863-095)

- RECEIPT OF A VERBAL PRESCRIPTION other than a refill authorization;
- CONSULTATION WITH THE PATIENT regarding the prescription and/or regarding any information in the patient medication record; (Note, however, that the Commission has previously approved a technician utilization plan at some hospitals which allows specially trained technicians to interview patients to obtain medication histories for medication reconciliation purposes – see discussion in text.)
- CONSULTATION WITH THE PRESCRIBER regarding the patient and the patient's prescription (see also WAC 246-901-010(1) for a definition of "consultation");
- EXTEMPORANEOUS COMPOUNDING of the prescription (except for bulk compounding from a formula by a technician or preparation of IV admixtures by a technician in accordance with WAC 246-871);
- INTERPRETATION OF THE DATA in a patient medication record system;
- ULTIMATE RESPONSIBILITY for the correctness of a dispensed prescription (see also WAC 246-901-010(10) for a definition of "verification");
- PROVIDING PATIENT INFORMATION as required by WAC 246-869-120;
- SIGNING OF DOCUMENTS or registry books that require a pharmacist's signature;
- PROFESSIONAL COMMUNICATIONS with physicians, dentists, nurses and other health care practitioners;
- DECISION TO NOT DISPENSE lawfully-prescribed drugs or devices or to not distribute drugs and devices approved by the U.S. Food and Drug Administration for restricted distribution by pharmacies.

many of the same functions as can pharmacists. For example, nurses may administer drugs, and may consult with patients about their drug therapy. To do so is part of the practice of nursing, not the practice of pharmacy.

PENALTIES What can happen when a person performs functions for which they are not licensed? A 2003 case in Washington[64] resulted in criminal charges being filed against a Registered Counselor who administered flu vaccines in his clinics. A *Seattle Post-Intelligencer* report[65] indicated that Bellevue's Shahid Shiekh was being charged with nine felony counts, and that the counselor may have administered outdated vaccine. The report noted that physicians, pharmacists, and nurses are licensed to give flu shots, but not counselors.

QUALIFICATIONS FOR LICENSURE AS A PHARMACIST

Washington's statutory requirements for licensure as a pharmacist are specified in RCW 18.64.080. In Washington, as well as in the US generally, pharmacists must provide evidence of having the following qualifications to be licensed: (1) Must be an adult – age 18 or over; (2) Must be of "good moral and professional character," which includes freedom from impairment by reason of mental or physical illness, or abuse of alcohol or other chemical substances; (3) Must have achieved an earned accredited degree in Pharmacy (Bachelors or Doctorate in Pharmacy – PharmD only in US for graduates after 2010); (4) Must have completed a period of practical experience, which may include advanced pharmacy practice experiences as part of the PharmD program and/or internship (see below); and (5) successful completion of license examinations in fitness for practice and pharmacy law – the NAPLEX in all states and the MPJE (in Washington and most states) or another jurisprudence exam in the remaining states, except Idaho, which requires only that the applicant attest they have read and understand the pharmacy laws of the state.[66]

FOREIGN PHARMACY GRADUATES. Graduates of non-US-accredited programs are considered foreign pharmacy graduates.[67] Prior to taking the NAPLEX, foreign graduates must first qualify for and complete the Foreign Pharmacy Graduate Equivalency Exam (FPGEE) offered by the NABP.[68] CANADIAN PHARMACY GRADUATES are considered foreign graduates. For many years the Washington Board of Pharmacy allowed pharmacists who graduated after 1994 from Canadian pharmacy programs to take the NAPLEX without completing the FPGEE, under Board Policy Statement No. 30. At its April 7, 2011 meeting the Board discontinued this policy, and now requires Canadian graduates to follow the same procedures as all other foreign pharmacy graduates.[69]

HIV/AIDS EDUCATION. RCW 70.24.280 requires all licensees of the Pharmacy Commission to have completed four or seven hours of HIV/AIDS prevention and information education. Such training shall include: etiology and epidemiology; testing and counseling; infection control guidelines; clinical manifestations and treatment; legal and ethical issues to include confidentiality; and psychosocial issues to include special population considerations. (WAC 246-12-270). Pharmacists must have seven hours of HIV/AIDS education as a requirement for licensure (WAC 246-863-120). The Commission recognizes that graduates of pharmacy programs accredited by the ACPE have met the minimum requirements for HIV/AIDS education.[70]

SUICIDE AWARENESS AND PREVENTION TRAINING.

The 2016 Legislature amended RCW 43.70.442 to include pharmacists among health professional who must complete a one-time training in suicide assessment, treatment, and management. Pharmacists and individuals with active or retired pharmacist credentials will need to complete this training prior to their first full continuing education reporting period following January 1, 2017, or during the first full CE reporting period following licensure. Where the disciplinary authority determines that the professional role includes only screening and referral, it may set a 3 hour CE requirement; otherwise the requirement is 6 hours. The Pharmacy Commission established a 3-hour requirement in WAC 246-861-105. The pharmacist training must include "content related to the assessment of issues related to imminent harm via lethal means." After July 1, 2017, the training program must be on a list of approved programs established by the Department. The statute allows a disciplinary authority to exempt individual licensees from the training requirement "if the professional has only brief or limited patient contact." (RCW 43.70.442(4)(b))

REFUSAL TO ISSUE LICENSES The Commission may refuse to license an otherwise qualified pharmacist who has (1) engaged in fraud, misrepresentation, or deceit in procuring a license; or (2) has violated laws relating to drugs, controlled substances, cosmetics, or nonprescription drugs, or the rules of the Pharmacy Commission, or has been convicted of a felony. (RCW 18.64.165).

LICENSE FEES Significant changes were made to the fee structure for pharmacy registrant licenses starting on January 1, 2019. The original fee for a pharmacist's license in Washington is $200.00, and the fee for renewal is $265.00 (WAC 246-907-030(4)(b)). Licenses expire on the registrant's birthday. A late payment penalty fee is $135. Note, however, that during the period between the expiration of the annual license period, and the payment of the fee to the Department, the pharmacist is not eligible to practice. Pharmacists may renew their registrations using the on-line system provided their credential has not expired, and the registrant is not in inactive status. A $2.50 fee is charged for online renewals.
(https://www.doh.wa.gov/LicensesPermitsandCertificates/ProfessionsNewReneworUpdate/LicenseRenewals)

DISCIPLINE Pharmacists in Washington are subject to the Uniform Disciplinary Act for health professionals. (RCW 18.130 – See Chapter 7 on Avoiding Discipline and Liability.)

PHARMACISTS IN FEDERAL FACILITIES Pharmacists who practice in federal facilities (Veterans' Affairs, Public Health Service, Indian Health Service, federal prisons, or the military), including federal civilian employees, in Washington do not need to be licensed in Washington, unless they also practice outside of these facilities. To be a federal pharmacist, however, you must maintain a license in at least one US state or territory. Under federal policy, federal pharmacists and federal pharmacies must adhere to the standards of care in the state in which they are located. See also the discussion above concerning the Active Military Credential available to pharmacists in Washington who are on active duty.

INTERNS

WHAT IS AN INTERN?

In Washington, an intern is a person registered by the Commission pursuant to its rules to "engage in the practice of pharmacy, and the selling of items restricted to sale under the supervision of a licensed pharmacist, only while the intern under the direct and personal supervision of a certified preceptor or a licensed pharmacist designated by the preceptor to supervise that intern during the preceptor's absence from the site." (See WAC 246-858-040(2))

ALLOWED ACTIVITIES

Because interns are allowed to practice pharmacy, they may perform any act that their supervising pharmacist allows within the scope of practice of a pharmacist (other than supervising technicians or checking IV admixtures prepared by technicians). Not all states' laws are interpreted to allow interns to do certain acts.

One such act is the transfer of refill information to another pharmacy concerning controlled substances prescriptions. Interns may do this in Washington. Interns in Washington may also sell Schedule V controlled substances and sign the record book, and Washington interns may take oral prescriptions over the phone.

It is not necessary for the supervising pharmacist to perform a final check on every prescription an intern dispenses, although the pharmacist is liable for any errors made by an intern under his or her supervision.

ELIGIBILITY "Any person enrolled as a student of pharmacy in an accredited college may file with the department an application for registration as a pharmacy intern ... but in no instance shall the certificate be valid if the individual is no longer making timely progress toward graduation, provided, however, the commission may issue an intern certificate to a person to complete an internship for initial licensure or the reinstatement of a previously licensed pharmacist." (RCW 18.64.080(3))

The Commission website notes that the Commission will grant an internship certificate "to a person to complete an internship to be eligible for initial licensure and up to 18 months after graduation." A certificate may also be issued to foreign-trained pharmacists to complete internship requirements in Washington, as a condition of a disciplinary order, or to foreign-trained pharmacists seeking to complete APPE requirements as part of a non-traditional PharmD program.

"STUDENT OF PHARMACY" The Commission defines "student of pharmacy" as a person enrolled in an accredited college or school of pharmacy or any graduate of an accredited college or school of pharmacy. (WAC 246-858-020(1)). The Commission's definition may seem to include students in a college of pharmacy who are not actually studying pharmacy, such as PhD students enrolled in a graduate program. However, the underlying statute is clear that the intern must be a "student of pharmacy."

In February 2018, the Commission adopted Procedure #54 on Pharmacy Intern Registration[71] which defines "Enrolled" as: "1) The student that has accepted an offer of admission in writing; and 2) The student has made the appropriate deposit to the school or college of pharmacy, securing his or her admission." An intern's credential may become "inoperable" when he or she is not actively making satisfactory progress or participating in a pharmacy program. The Commission may revoke an internship credential when the student is dismissed from the program due to unprofessional conduct. The Commission may choose to notify the student that his or her credential is inoperable when the student is temporarily withdrawn from the program without unprofessional conduct (e.g., family reasons, financial reasons, etc.).

WHEN MAY A PHARMACY STUDENT APPLY FOR INTERNSHIP? Students may apply for internship upon acceptance into the PharmD program, and upon completion of enrollment into the University. They may work as interns as soon as certified by the Commission, but the hours spent in internship activities will not count until the student has completed the first term (semester or quarter) of the PharmD program. The Commission requires that proof of enrollment for individual intern applicants must be provided directly by the school or college of pharmacy to the Commission.

CONTINUING PROGRESS To remain registered as an intern, the student must make continuing satisfactory progress in completing the pharmacy course. (WAC 246-858-020(2)(c))

Release of educational records by colleges of pharmacy is governed by the requirements of the Family Educational Rights and Privacy Act (FERPA), also known as the Buckley Amendment. In general, colleges will not provide information about educational decisions (such as decertification from the PharmD program) to others without the written permission or request of the student. Currently, the Commission does not make routine requests to colleges for information on student progress. However, a student who has been decertified or placed on probation and required to retake one or more pharmacy courses before proceeding in the curriculum, is not entitled to retain an internship certificate and will be practicing pharmacy without a license during the period of decertification or probation. The student is obligated to report to the Commission, and failure to so report, if discovered at a later date, could result in the Commission's refusal to issue a license, or in other discipline.

The Commission requires a certification by the intern at the time of credential renewal that he or she is currently enrolled as a student of pharmacy in an accredited college, or otherwise authorized by the Commission for registration.[72]

INTERN APPLICATION FORM The Commission requires completion of an application form,[73] which includes questions about prior registration, fitness for practice, use of controlled substances, or prior convictions or lawsuits, and requires granting of permission to the Commission to obtain health and other personal information. The applicant agrees to notify the Commission regarding any convictions (including for driving under the influence) or changes in mental or physical conditions that might impair his or her ability to practice. The applicant certifies that he or she has read RCW 18.130.170 and 18.130.080 of the Uniform Disciplinary Act. Any evasions or misleading answers on this application can result in refusal by the Commission to grant a license to practice pharmacy.

SUPERVISION BY A PRECEPTOR Interns must generally be supervised by a licensed pharmacist who is certified by the Commission as a preceptor. The Commission envisions that an intern works at a particular site, and the intern is required to notify the Commission prior to starting internship at that site. The notification form is available on the Commission's website.[74] However, interns may change sites without Commission permission, as long as they notify the Commission of the new site prior to earning internship hours. The Commission will notify the intern if the site and preceptor are approved. (WAC 246-858-040(1)). The intern is responsible for submitting training reports to the Commission. These must be submitted within 30 days after the intern has left the site with no intention of obtaining future experience at that site. (WAC 246-858-050). Thus, interns working over the summer at a pharmacy, and intending to work as interns at the same pharmacy the following summer, do not need to file a report at the end of each summer. The final reports of all intern experience – by both the intern and any preceptors – must be on file with the Commission 30 days prior to taking the NAPLEX or MPJE. (WAC 246-858-070(4)) The Commission reiterated the importance of the preceptor-intern relationship in its January, 2013 newsletter.[75]

WHEN THE PRECEPTOR IS ABSENT The Commission allows interns to continue to work at a site if their preceptor is not present for periods of time (for example, during lunch), provided the preceptor has designated another pharmacist at the site to supervise the intern. If that pharmacist is not a preceptor, the time spent working at the site that is not under a preceptor's supervision does not count towards the time required for internship.

QUALIFICATIONS FOR PRECEPTORS Pharmacists who wish to be preceptors must be actively practicing in a Class A pharmacy in Washington, and must complete a Commission-approved training program every five years. A pharmacist must have been licensed and actively practicing pharmacy for 12 months prior to becoming a preceptor. (WAC 246-858-060(1,2)) These requirements would seem to eliminate the possibility of externship or clerkship training in non-traditional settings, such as physician's offices, nursing homes, or other patient care settings that are not pharmacies. However, the Commission can approve special internship programs, and by practice has accepted those programs that are conducted under the auspices of the UW or WSU. This policy would also be implied by the Commission rule that gives credit for experiential classes as part of accredited pharmacy programs.

The Commission provides preceptors with an Experiential Training Manual[76] that may be downloaded from its website. Successfully completing an examination over the material in the manual satisfies the continuing education requirement for becoming a preceptor. The examination answer sheet is combined with the Preceptor Application Form. At its September 30, 2016 meeting, the Commission discussed a need to revise the 15-year old preceptor training process and manual. The matter was referred to the Commission's counsel to "review the proposal and compare the rules along with the requirements for interns."[77]

ONE PRECEPTOR – ONE INTERN ENGAGED IN DISPENSING Washington regulations specify that "The pharmacist preceptor may supervise more than one intern during a given time period; however, two interns may not dispense concurrently under the direct supervision of the same preceptor. (WAC 246-858-070(5))" If there is more than one pharmacist at the site, but only one preceptor, it is implied by the regulation that more than one intern may "dispense" at the site at the same time, but only one can count hours, and the other(s) must be supervised by a designated pharmacist. Ideally, all pharmacists working at a site that hires interns should become preceptors as soon as they are eligible.

Fassett's Comment: This rule is obviously out of date, and reflects a focus on the distributive aspects of practice, rather than the clinical aspects. If strictly interpreted, it allows one intern to be "dispensing," another to be "compounding," and another to be "delivering" drugs to patients along with patient counseling, and so on. At the time the rule was written, the Commission probably intended "dispensing" to encompass all the steps involved in providing medications to patients. Preceptors, who are ultimately responsible for the quality of patient care, must not oversee more interns than can be safely supervised.

"DIRECT SUPERVISION" does not absolutely preclude the intern from working in areas of a pharmacy or institution without a pharmacist immediately at his or her side, nor does it preclude the supervising pharmacist from being absent for short periods of time while the intern is working. However, the supervising pharmacist must use judgment and be sure that the intern is operating under sufficient supervision for his or her ability level to assure patient safety.

An intern in the 4th professional year, for example, may reasonably be allowed to take telephoned prescriptions, and reduce them to writing, while the pharmacist is at the other end of the prescription department counseling patients. That same latitude might not be appropriate for an intern in the 1st professional year.

On the other hand, the Commission has taken disciplinary action against both the intern and the pharmacist when the pharmacist allowed the intern to open the pharmacy prior to the arrival of the pharmacist and the pharmacist was a half hour late in arriving at the pharmacy.

REQUIRED INTERNSHIP HOURS The basic requirement for internship in Washington is 1,500 hours, which may be satisfied as follows (WAC 246-858-020):

Up to 1,200 hours is granted for completion of clinical courses as part of the PharmD program. Both UW and WSU have a clerkship requirement of a minimum of 36 weeks of clinical rotations in patient care settings during the 4th professional year that provides 1,440 hours of patient care experience, well over the 1,200 hour maximum.

The remaining 300 hours for graduates of Washington programs can be earned after completing the first semester of the 1st professional year.

Some states require more than 1,500 hours of internship credit, so the Commission will allow students to document excess hours so as to be able to report the hours to other states in which they may wish to be licensed.

Graduates from other states that do not certify internship hours may submit a letter from their institution attesting that their program met the requirements for internship in Washington.[78,79]

LICENSE FEE - INTERN The annual intern registration fee is $45.00 (WAC 246-907-030(14)). The registration expires on the intern's birthday. (WAC 246-907-030(1)).

RENEWALS – INTERN PERMIT The Commission in recent years has had to deal with several cases of interns who continued to renew after no longer being in a pharmacy program, or otherwise eligible. As a result, the Department of Health began in August 2012 to require a "Pharmacist Intern Renewal Attestation" to be filed with the intern's renewal request, in which the intern declares under penalty of perjury that he or she remains eligible for an internship.

CURRENT NAME AND ADDRESS - INTERNS As do other licensees, interns must promptly notify the DOH of any change in name or address. (See above)

DISCIPLINE – INTERNS Pharmacy interns are subject to discipline for the same reasons and under the same procedures as are pharmacists.

PHARMACY ANCILLARY PERSONNEL

Licensed health care practitioners in the US are now allowed in most jurisdictions to enlist the aid of ancillary personnel in providing care to their patients. In general, there are at least two levels of ancillary providers associated with each profession – an intermediate-level provider with certain technical or advanced care skills whose functions are performed under the supervision of the practitioner, and a lower level provider whose functions are limited to those that call for little or no discretion. For example, physicians are assisted by physician assistants who have prescriptive authority and may perform certain invasive procedures, and by medical assistants with quite circumscribed activities. Similarly, dentists are joined in patient care by dental hygienists, and also by registered dental assistants, dental anesthesia assistants, or expanded function dental auxiliaries. Registered nurses may supervise practical nurses or nursing assistants ("nursing technicians" is a designation used for nursing students who are working in hospitals, clinics, or nursing homes under the supervision of a nurse). For pharmacists, the two levels of ancillary providers are pharmacy technicians and pharmacy assistants, in most states.

PHARMACY ANCILLARY PERSONNEL TYPES IN WASHINGTON

TECHNICIANS – may perform **functions related to the practice of pharmacy** that are (1) Delegated to them by a pharmacist and (2) Non-discretionary

PHARMACY ASSISTANTS – employees of the pharmacy who perform **clerical and related functions** under the supervision of a licensed pharmacist. Typical duties include: *typing* of labels, filing, re-filing, bookkeeping, pricing, stocking, delivery, non-professional phone inquiries, and documentation of third party reimbursements

STATUTORY AUTHORITY FOR ANCILLARY PERSONNEL

The authority for the use of pharmacy assistants in Washington's pharmacies was granted by the Legislature in RCW 18.64A. The statute defines two types of ancillary personnel that may be utilized in the practice of pharmacy: technicians and assistants. This statute has several significant elements.

DEFINITIONS RELATED TO ANCILLARY PERSONNEL It is important to note here that pharmacists are defined, but interns are not, and are not mentioned in the statute. The Board has in the past interpreted this to mean that the duties of pharmacists relative to supervision of ancillary personnel are not included in the definition of the practice of pharmacy in RCW 18.64.011. Under this interpretation, interns may not supervise ancillary pharmacy personnel or fulfill any other duties required of licensed pharmacists that are specified in RCW 18.64A.

Fassett's Comment: My interpretation of this rule is that interns may not specifically supervise technicians who are preparing IV admixtures, including performing the final check on an IV admixture. Some Commission staff members have made comments that seem to allow for this. However, given that interns are often novices themselves in the IV preparation area, and given the consequences to patients of an improperly prepared IV, and given further the difficulty of discovering many problems with IVs at the bedside, I do not believe that interns should be allowed to perform the final check on technician-prepared IVs in most cases. The Board indicated in 2008 that it would review this issue, but has not done so at present. (See discussion of "specialized functions" for technicians, below.)

TRAINING PROGRAMS ARE REQUIRED FOR TECHNICIANS, as specified in Commission Rules. According to the statute, a licensed pharmacist must supervise the training of technicians. The training shall consist of instruction and/or practical training, and the Commission may include requirements for completion of specific examinations. (RCW 18.64A.020)

TECHNICIAN CERTIFICATION New applicants for licensure as a pharmacy technician after January 1, 2009 must provide proof to the Commission that they have passed a "Commission-approved national standardized pharmacy technician certification examination." (WAC 246-901-060(2)) The Commission has approved two national exams: the PTCE from the Pharmacy Technicians Certification Board,[80] and the ExCPT from the National Healthcareer Association.[81]) Completion of either examination and fulfillment of annual continuing education requirements allows the technician to use the designation CPhT. Maintaining CPhT status is not a requirement for technician licensure in Washington, but the Commission may, and does, require continuing education for technicians.

STATUTORY LIMITS ON PHARMACIST-TECHNICIAN RATIO The statute established a ratio of 1 pharmacist to 1 technician in retail pharmacies, and a 1:3 pharmacist-to-technician ration in institutional pharmacies. This statutory ratio has been overridden by subsequent rules, because the statute gives the Commission the right to establish other ratios for pharmacies that have filed a utilization plan. (RCW 18.64A.040) *In practice, the ratios established in regulation, i.e., 3 technicians to 1 pharmacist in sites with approved utilization plans, is the ratio that actually applies.* The statute also gives the Commission authority to authorize pilot projects designed to investigate different ratios or use of technicians.

The statute specifies the various institutional pharmacies covered by the higher ratio by referring to specific chapters of the RCW. The specific institutional types (and the chapters referred to in RCW 18.64A) are: Hospitals (RCW 70.41); Mental Health Institutions (RCW 71.12); Residential Habitation Centers (RCW 71A.20); Nursing Homes (RCW 74.42).

PHARMACIST-TECHNICIAN RATIOS IN CLOSED-DOOR LTC PHARMACIES. In 2016,[82] the Legislature amended RCW 18.64 to require the Commission to "adopt reasonable, task-based standards regarding the ratio of pharmacists to pharmacy technicians in a closed door long-term care pharmacy." Specifically, such regulations should not consider a technician to be practicing as a technician while performing administrative tasks such as medical records maintenance, billing, prepackaging unit dose drugs, inventory control, delivery, or processing returned drugs. (RCW 18.64.580)

While the Commission is developing proposed new rules governing technician ratios in different settings, it has adopted a procedure for individual settings to propose technician ratios that exceed 3:1, by submitting a Request for Consideration Form and a revised pharmacy services plan. The policy is available at https://www.doh.wa.gov/Portals/1/Documents/2300/2018/PhamPharmTechRatio.pdf. As noted below, the Commission has also issued a guidance document on the use of technicians for administrative roles in a closed-door pharmacy; such technicians are not counted in the ratio.

DISCIPLINE – TECHNICIANS AND ASSISTANTS Pharmacy technicians may have their registration revoked for violation of the Uniform Disciplinary Act (RCW 18.130), and for other reasons, specified in RCW 18.64A.060, that are similar to those for which pharmacists may be disciplined. Discipline of technicians is subject to the requirements and procedures of RCW 18.130, the Uniform Disciplinary Act. (RCW 18.64A.055)

CURRENT INFORMATION ON FILE – ANCILLARY PERSONNEL As for all licensees, ancillary personnel must maintain current address information with the Commission of Pharmacy (see above).

PHARMACY MUST HAVE PRIOR APPROVAL TO USE ANCILLARY PERSONNEL No pharmacy may use ancillary personnel unless it has applied to the Commission and received approval. (RCW 18.64A.060) The Commission also may assess a fee for the use of ancillary personnel, and the current original fee is $100, with an annual renewal fee of $100. (WAC 246-907-030(4)) In March 2016, the Commission adopted a revised procedure for intake and approval of ancillary personnel utilization plans (AUPs). New pharmacy permit applications with AUPs must be submitted 60 days prior to a regularly scheduled Commission business session. Separate specialized function requests must also be submitted. The Commission reviews existing AUPs on a schedule to be determined, and the Commission staff notifies pharmacies when they should submit their existing AUPs for review and approval. A pharmacy may continue to operate under an AUP that is set for review until the Commission has notified them otherwise. Pharmacies with approval for specialized functions will need to submit their specialized functions requests for review along with their AUP.[83]

COMMISSION RULES FOR ANCILLARY PERSONNEL

The Pharmacy Commission's regulations relating to pharmacy assistants are found in WAC 246-901. The Commission's rule sets forth three key definitions that clarify the ability of pharmacists to delegate duties to ancillary personnel (see text box next page). The Commission demands a specific level of patient profile review when the pharmacist is assisted by ancillary personnel that is often overlooked in daily practice.

ACTIVITIES RESTRICTED TO TECHNICIANS, INTERNS, OR PHARMACISTS Only technicians, interns and pharmacists may (1) enter a new medication order into the pharmacy computer system; (2) retrieve the drug product to fill a prescription (WAC 246-901-020(4)); or participate in stocking of drugs in an automated drug distribution device (WAC 246-862-030(4)). (Note, however, that the Nursing Quality Assurance Commission has stated that stocking of these devices is within the scope of practice of a registered nurse.)

TECHNICIAN TRAINING (WAC 246-901-030) Technicians may receive training either in a formal academic training program approved by the Commission or from on-the-job training programs approved by the Commission. Prior to entering a technician training program the trainee must have a high school diploma or G.E.D. Applicants for registration must submit to the Commission proof of completion of an approved training program and "proof of passing a commission-approved national standardized pharmacy technician certification examination." (WAC 246-901-060)

The principal national certification program is the Pharmacy Technician Certification Board (PTCB), which issues a CPhT credential. Individuals must recertify every 2 years to maintain the CPhT credential. By 2020, the applicants for initial certification will need to have completed an ASHP/ACPE accredited training program.

The Commission currently approves the training programs of the following pharmacy chains: Fred Meyer, Rite Aid, Safeway, Sav-On (Albertsons), Walgreens, and Walmart.

KEY DEFINITIONS RELATED TO ANCILLARY PERSONNEL ADOPTED BY COMMISSION RULE

(WAC 246-901)

"'CONSULTATION' is defined to mean:
"A communication or deliberation between a pharmacist and a patient, a patient's agent, or a patient's health care provider in which the pharmacist uses professional judgment to provide advice about drug therapy.
"A method by which the pharmacist meets patient information requirements as set forth in WAC 246-869-220." (WAC 246-901-010(1))

"'VERIFICATION' means the pharmacist *has reviewed a patient drug order initiated by an authorized prescriber, has examined the patient's drug profile, and has approved the drug order after taking into account pertinent drug and disease information to insure the correctness of a drug order for a specific patient*. The verification process must generate an audit trail that identifies the pharmacist. The pharmacist who performs the verification of a drug order is responsible for all reports generated by the approval of that order. The unit-dose medication's fill and check reports are an example." (WAC 246-901-010(10))

"'IMMEDIATE SUPERVISION' means visual and/or physical proximity to a licensed pharmacist to ensure patient safety." (WAC 246-901-010 (11))
The Commission has allowed a pharmacist to supervise a technician at a remote location under certain circumstances, for example, preparing IV admixtures while under two-way video contact, with the admixture room closed to other personnel, if the pharmacist assured that all IV admixtures were verified before distribution to patient care areas.

Technicians must complete 4 hours of HIV/AIDS prevention and information education. (WAC 246-901-120). The Department of Health maintains a list of training sites on its web page.[84] The Commission has found that for graduates of technician training programs approved by the Commission, where "the program materials on file with the Commission office document four hours of AIDS education, the applicant is deemed to meet the AIDS education requirement for initial certification."[85]

Out-of-state applicants must meet the same requirements as in-state applicants, and the Board must approve any out-of-state training programs. Out-of-state technicians must also provide proof of 8 hours of study of Washington pharmacy law under the direction of a pharmacist.

Foreign-trained pharmacists or physicians may apply to become technicians subject to the additional requirements in WAC 246-901-030(5).

SPECIALIZED FUNCTION TRAINING
Additional, specialized training programs are required for technicians who wish to perform either of the following "specialized functions:"
Unit-dose medication checking. Such training must include proficiency testing demonstrating 99% accuracy in checking unit-dose medications.
Intravenous admixture preparation. Such training must include proficiency testing demonstrating 100% accuracy in preparing a representative sample of IV admixtures using aseptic technique.

SPECIALIZED FUNCTIONS The Commission may approve utilization plans which allow technicians to perform specialized functions. (WAC 246-901-035, 246-901-100). Three functions have been approved in regulation by the Commission, and others have been approved on a plan-by-plan basis.

PARENTERAL ADMIXTURES may be prepared by technicians who have met the special training requirements. A "licensed pharmacist" must check each parenteral product prepared by a technician (WAC 246-901-035(2)). (See discussion concerning statutory authority and implications for interns in section 3.a. above.)

REQUIRED ELEMENTS FOR PHARMACY ANCILLARY PERSONNEL UTILIZATION PLANS

The pharmacy's utilization plan must contain the following elements. (WAC 246-901-100)

- It must describe the manner in which ancillary personnel will be utilized.
- A job description for each category of job.
- Task analysis for each job category defining duties and conditions under which they may be performed.
- The number of positions to be used in each category
- If technicians will be used for **specialized functions**, the plan must indicate: (1) criteria for selecting which technicians will perform the specialized functions; (2) a description of how training will be performed for these technicians, and how the assessment will be made to prove proficiency as required in the rules (99% for unit-dose, 100% for IV admixtures; (3) a copy of the pharmacy's quality assurance plan that relates to these specialized technicians
- The plan need only list the job title or function for each pharmacy assistant position.

TECH-CHECK-TECH PROGRAMS. Technicians may check other technicians or interns who have filled unit-dose medication cassettes in institutional settings. This is often called a "tech-check-tech" program. (Note that the language of the rule does not specify that interns may check the work of technicians.) No more than a 48-hour supply may be placed in a cassette that is part of a tech-check-tech procedure. Another "licensed health professional" must again check the medication prior to administration to a patient. (WAC 246-901-035(2))

STOCKING OF AUTOMATED DRUG DISTRIBUTION DEVICES by technicians has been allowed by Commission rule (WAC 246-872-030(4)). This is treated as a specialized function for which the technician must be specially trained. Note: On January 5, 2017, the Commission adopted a new rule (WAC 246-874, Pharmacy Technology) that repealed the older rules on automated devices; it retained the role and for technicians in replenishing medications in ADDDs, and allows a technician with specialized function qualifications to perform a double check of medications in the ADDD. (WAC 246-874-040)

TELEPHARMACY programs approved by the Commission almost always involve technicians at the remote dispensing site who are supervised by a pharmacist using telecommunications technology.

MEDICATION RECONCILIATION ACTIVITIES The Commission can approve specialized functions without requiring a pilot program or demonstration project (see below). At its January 22, 2009 meeting, the then Board of Pharmacy approved a plan by a hospital to train pharmacy technicians for the special function of interviewing patients, under pharmacist supervision, to obtain a medication list for purposes of medication reconciliation. Under this plan, specially trained pharmacy technicians will be used in the following process: (a) Patient is admitted through the emergency department; (b) ED-based pharmacy technician obtains complete medication list; (c) ED-based pharmacist reviews and verifies the list; (d) physician reviews and reconciles pharmacist-verified medication list.[86]

ADMINISTRATIVE ACTIVITIES IN CLOSED DOOR LTC PHARMACIES. In response to RCW 18.64.580, and pending adoption of permanent rules, the Commission has adopted a guidance document on the use of pharmacy technicians in administrative roles, such as reconciling of insurance claims, shipping, or ordering. The policy applies only for closed-door pharmacies serving LTC facilities. Technicians operating in administrative roles are not counted in the pharmacist-to-technician ratio. A revised auxiliary utilization plan must be submitted to the Commission, and technicians operating in an administrative role must be identified as such on their name tag.[87]

FEES – PHARMACY TECHNICIANS. Technicians pay a $70 application fee and a $70 annual renewal fee. The penalty fee for late renewal of a technician's certificate is also $70 (WAC 246-907-030(13)). Technicians may renew their registrations using the on-line system provided their credential has not expired, and the registrant is not in inactive status. A $2.50 fee is charged for online renewals. (https://www.doh.wa.gov/LicensesPermitsandCertificates/ProfessionsNewReneworUpdate/LicenseRenewals)

Continuing Education - Technicians The Commission has established requirements of 10 hours of CE (0.1 CEU) per year for technicians for "every renewal cycle following their first certification renewal." 1 hour must be in pharmacy law, and the remaining 9 hours must be in pharmacy technician-related education. (WAC 246-901-061). The requirements are compatible with the annual CE requirements needed to maintain the CPhT certification, but maintaining the certification *per se* is not a requirement for registration in Washington. Starting in 2016, CPhT recertification through the PTCB requires 20 hours of CE every 2 years, of which 2 hours must be in pharmacy law and 1 hour in patient safety.

ACPE and the NABP jointly operate the *CPE Monitor* program, which tracks all ACPE-accredited CE for pharmacists and technicians. Technicians must establish an e-Profile on the NABP website; there is no charge (www.nabp.net/technicians). However, currently, the *CPE Monitor* does not report technician CE directly to PTCB for recertification, but does report to pharmacy boards.

The rule does allow for non-ACPE approved programs submitted for approval to the Board, when submitted by a pharmacist under WAC 246-861-050, if the course work directly relates to the scope of practice of a technician.

Pharmacy Assistants may be utilized to perform "Any duties not otherwise reserved to pharmacists or technicians;" prepackaging and labeling of drugs for subsequent use in prescription dispensing operations; counting, pouring, and labeling for individual prescriptions. Note, however, that they may not retrieve the drug from the shelf to be used for the particular prescription, though they may replace the container on the shelf after the prescription is verified. (See WAC 246-901-020(4)) The Commission received a request to allow a modification of this rule when bar code scanning was used, but declined to do so in December 2005.

No limit on number of pharmacy assistants There is no maximum ratio of pharmacy assistants to pharmacists, provided the pharmacy has Commission approval for use of ancillary personnel, and the number of positions is specified in the utilization plan.

There are no restrictions on age or educational preparation for pharmacy assistants. Note, however, that other state laws (i.e., RCW 26.28) establish rules regarding the age of majority for minors in Washington, and generally prohibit employment of minors below the age of 14. (See Chapter 3)

Registration, Fees, and Renewal – pharmacy assistants Pharmacy assistants must submit an application for registration prior to working as an assistant, must notify the Commission of any change in their mailing address within 30 days, and must renew their registration every year, on their birthday. The 2016 Legislature amended RCW 18.64A to place pharmacy assistants under the Uniform Disciplinary Act and to require a fee for registration or renewal of registration. The Commission has established a $35 fee for initial registration or renewal. (WAC 246-907-030(4)(e)) Pharmacy managers and assistants should note that placement of assistants under the UDA means some new responsibilities and expectations are now in place for assistants, such as reporters of evidence of abuse of vulnerable adults (see below), and mandatory reporting of suspected impaired professionals.

Job shadowing by students. The Commission has determined that students should be encouraged to explore pharmacy as a career, and thus allows for job shadowing by students who are (1) affiliated with an organized educational program; (2) do not perform any functions reserved for licensed, certified, or registered pharmacy personnel; and (3) are limited to not more than 3 days of time in the pharmacy. The Commission recommends that the job shadowing students sign a confidentiality statement. Job shadowing that goes beyond these limits require the student to become registered as a pharmacy assistant.[88]

ID BADGES REQUIRED FOR TECHNICIANS AND ASSISTANTS

All pharmacy ancillary personnel who are in the pharmacy and who interact with patients or the general public must wear ID badges clearly indicating that they are Pharmacy Assistants or Pharmacy Technicians. (WAC 246-901-090)

TECHNICIAN RATIOS ALLOWED BY COMMISSION RULE

The Commission utilized the authority granted in statute to modify the pharmacist-to-technician ratios specified in the statute. (WAC 246-901-130)

1:3 Pharmacist-to-Technician Ratio for All Licensed Pharmacies.

Under the Commission's rule, all pharmacies with a utilization plan properly on file may have a 1:3 technician ratio, not just institutional pharmacies. The Commission has yet to promulgate rules in response to the direction given it by the 2016 Legislature regarding closed-door LTC pharmacies (see RCW 18.64.580), but, as noted above, the Commission has adopted a procedure for individual settings to propose technician ratios that exceed 3:1, by submitting a Request for Consideration Form and a revised pharmacy services plan. The policy is available at https://www.doh.wa.gov/Portals/1/Documents/2300/2018/PhamPharmTechRatio.pdf

Which pharmacists may be included in the ratio?

Pharmacists who are *actively practicing* pharmacy at the site are included in the ratio, but not, for example, the pharmacy CEO in the business office. For inpatient settings, pharmacists *actively practicing* outside the central pharmacy may be included if: (1) the pharmacy is not open to the public; (2) enough pharmacists are available in the central pharmacy to safely oversee the technicians' work; (3) any dispensed medications are checked by a licensed health care professional (e.g., nurse) immediately prior to administration to the patient; and (4) no orders are dispensed from the pharmacy unless they are checked by a pharmacist or intern, or dispensed subject to a tech-check-tech program.

Higher ratios of technicians to pharmacists may be approved for specific pharmacies with a well-developed plan meeting the specifications of WAC 246-901-140. The Commission may give conditional approval to pilot or demonstration projects.

MILITARY PERSONNEL AND SPOUSES SEEKING TECHNICIAN LICENSES

The Commission provides information on its website concerning how military spouses (or domestic partners) may apply to have their applications as pharmacy technicians processed more rapidly, and how former military personnel may apply to have their military training and experienced evaluated for registration as pharmacy technicians.

ACCREDITED PHARMACY PROGRAMS

Commission policy recognizes as accredited those colleges and schools of pharmacy that are accredited by the Accreditation Council for Pharmaceutical Education.[89]

LICENSING EXAMS FOR PHARMACISTS

The Commission has established a policy of using examinations provided by the National Association of Boards of Pharmacy Foundation, specifically the North American Pharmacy Licensure Examination (NAPLEX) and the Multi-state Pharmacy Jurisprudence Exam (MPJE). (As noted above, the Commission has approved 2 national certification exams for technicians.)

NAPLEX/MPJE REGISTRATION BULLETIN

The 51-page .pdf file containing the NAPLEX/MPJE Candidate Registration Bulletin is available from NABP's website.[90] This describes the procedures for registering for both the NAPLEX, NAPLEX Score Transfer, and the MPJE in those states that use the MPJE. Registration is online for all states. NOTE: NABP urges candidates to download the bulletin only from the NABP official site, since NABP is aware of out-of-date or fake bulletins available elsewhere on the Internet.

NAPLEX is a computer-adaptive examination that is now accepted for licensure in all 50 states. Students may take the NAPLEX at any Pearson VUE[91] Testing Center site and may transfer scores to other states for an additional fee of $75 per state. The basic fee for the NAPLEX is $575, which includes a $100 application fee and a $475 exam fee. Pearson VUE has locations in Spokane Valley, Seattle, Renton, Yakima, Boise, Helena, Salem, Beaverton and Portland. The NAPLEX is scheduled for 6 hours and has 250 test items. The NAPLEX is based on a blueprint, or set of competencies, which was revised in 2016 and became effective in November 2016. The competencies are contained in the Candidate Registration Bulletin.

NAPLEX Score Transfers to Multiple States Exam takers identify a "primary state" at the time of registration to take the NAPLEX. NAPLEX does not offer an examination window (test date) unless the student has been recognized as eligible by the primary state. However, student pharmacists may specify score transfer to states other than the primary state without having currently met all requirements to take the exam in those states. The exam take specifies jurisdictions to receive the transferred score at the time of the exam, or he or she may submit original or additional requests for score transfers for up to 90 days following the exam.

All 50 states, DC, Guam, Puerto Rico, and the Virgin Islands accept score transfers.

California accepts score transfers from applicants completing the NAPLEX after January 1, 2004. California has placed an updated bulletin[92] on its website concerning the NAPLEX and the California Pharmacy Jurisprudence Exam (CPJE). California allows NAPLEX score transfers.

Applicants who select Colorado or Utah as their primary state must submit a NAPLEX/MPJE Eligibility Request form to NABP, which has agreed to confirm eligibility to test for those states.

TIME LIMITS TO COMPLETE LICENSURE AFTER SCORE TRANSFER Many states limit how long a student has to complete licensure application following a score transfer – typically one to three years. Washington requires that applications for licensure must be completed within one year of the time of score transfer (WAC 246-863-020(5)). Failure to complete licensure within the time limit will require the applicant to re-start the application process and either use license transfer (see below) or retake the NAPLEX.

On-Line NAPLEX Score Reports NAPLEX scores are reported online only by states that participate in the online score reporting service. Washington, Montana, and California do not participate. Idaho, Alaska, Oregon and Wyoming do participate. If a student intends to become licensed in a state that does not participate, as well as in a state that does participate, he or she will only be able to see his or her score online if a participating state is listed as the primary state.

Pre-NAPLEX Trial Exam Students may take a Pre-NAPLEX trial exam for $65 per attempt to help prepare for the NAPLEX. The test is on-line, and students are allowed 140 minutes to answer 100 questions. The test may be taken twice. (See NABP web page.[93])

MPJE is a computer-adaptive examination administered at the same Pearson VUE testing sites as is the NAPLEX. All states require some form of law examination, and a handful of jurisdictions do not use MPJE, but write their own jurisprudence exam. You must take the MPJE once for each state in which you wish to register, since the exam is adapted to the rules of each state. The fee for each MPJE exam is $210. The MJPE is scheduled for 2 hours, with no breaks during testing. The exam consists of 120 questions, of which 100 are used to determine the candidate's score; the remaining items are being tested for future use.

The MPJE, like NAPLEX, is based on a blueprint. The blueprint was revised in 2016 and became effective for exams taken on or after April 1, 2016. The new MPJE competency statements are available in the Candidate Registration Bulletin.

48 jurisdictions use the MPJE. Jurisdictions that do NOT use the MPJE are Arkansas, California, Idaho, Puerto Rico, and the Virgin Islands.[94]

MPJE scores are reported online only for participating states. Washington, Montana, and California do not participate. Alaska, Oregon and Wyoming do participate.

California has used the NAPLEX since January 1, 2004, and developed its own California Pharmacy Jurisprudence Exam, which is administered at Psychological Services, Inc. (PSI) Testing Centers in California. PSI locations offering the CPJE are located only in California. The fee for the CPJE is $30.50. It is a 2-hour computerized exam.

DISABILITY ACCOMMODATIONS for NAPLEX and MPJE may be requested by contacting NABP as set forth in the Registration Bulletin. However, any accommodation granted must be approved by the applicant's Board of Pharmacy prior to testing. An applicant seeking disability accommodations should also check with any states to which a score might be transferred to assure the score will be accepted.

SECURITY PROVISIONS for NAPLEX and MPJE are set forth in the Candidates Guide, and are strictly adhered to. Among the specifications are

- Digital photographs taken at the testing site
- Palm vein scan taken at the testing site
- Candidates must present a digital signature at the time of testing
- Prohibited items must not be taken into testing center – even inadvertently – and if discovered, will disqualify the examination:
    - Pagers, cell phones, PDAs, digital watches, recording or photographic devices, including glasses with cameras
    - Bags, cases, purses, backpacks or other containers
    - Wallets, contents of pockets, facial tissue, food or beverages must be left outside the testing room
    - The NAPLEX provides an on-screen calculator, or a calculator may be borrowed from the testing center. Calculators are not allowed for the MPJE.

MISSING AN EXAMINATION APPOINTMENT Applicants who miss a scheduled testing appointment without previously following the cancellation procedure forfeit their testing fees. Applicants may reschedule an exam by contacting Pearson VUE at least 2 business days prior to the appointment and paying a $50 rescheduling fee.

RETAKING EXAMINATIONS Pharmacist applicants in Washington may take the NAPLEX up to 3 times within a 3-year period, after which the Commission will specify additional required training before allowing further attempts (RCW 18.54.080). According to Commission Policy #40, the applicant must submit an updated application and pay the applicable fee, and submit a study plan for approval by the Commission. An additional

750 hours of internship must be completed before the applicant will be allowed to take the NAPLEX.[95] The Commission will require additional law instruction for any applicant who has taken and failed the MPJE 3 times (WAC 246-863-020).

NAPLEX requires a 45-day wait between administrations. MPJE requires a 30-day wait between administrations for a given jurisdiction.

LICENSE TRANSFER ("RECIPROCITY")

Pharmacists who are already licensed by examination in another state may become licensed in Washington by transferring their licenses through the License Transfer services of the National Association of Boards of Pharmacy (web site[96]). In Washington regulations, this process is also called "reciprocity." (WAC 246-863-030) The NABP now uses an electronic license transfer process that takes less time than formerly. However, the transfer fees involved make license transfer somewhat more expensive than retaking the NAPLEX. In addition to the fees charged by NABP, Washington assesses a $465.00 fee for license transfer.

ORIGINAL LICENSE BY EXAMINATION REQUIRED IN MANY STATES

Many states require that a pharmacist using license transfer must maintain an original license by examination in another state.[97] In 2016, NABP reported that the following states required maintenance of an original license by examination include: AL, AZ, AR, CT, DC, GA, IA, LA, NV, NH, NJ, NM, NY, NC, ND, OK, SC. The NABP no longer compiles this listing, but advises applicants to check with the pharmacy board of the intended state.

As of 2016, states that do not require maintenance of an original license by examination, but require that "the license transfer applicant must have a license in good standing from a member board and transferred their license through the NABP Clearinghouse after," included: AK, CA, CO, DE, FL, HI, ID, IL, IN, KS, KY, MA, MD, ME, MI, MN, MO, MS, MT, NE, OH, OR, PA, PR, RI, SD, TN, TX, UT,VT, VA, WA, WI, WV, WY.

"ORIGINAL LICENSE" EXAMPLE

A 2017 PharmD graduate takes the NAPLEX, naming Idaho as the primary state, and **transfers scores** to Washington and Oregon, becoming licensed in all 3 states. All 3 licenses are "original licenses by examination."

2 years later, the pharmacist uses **license transfer** to become licensed in California and Montana. Those licenses are "transferred licenses," not "original licenses by examination."

If the pharmacist later wishes to use **license transfer** to become licensed in Arizona, Nevada, or New Mexico, he or she will not be able to register in these states using his or her California or Montana license; the pharmacist will have had to keep at least one license fully active in Washington, Idaho, or Oregon.

California allows license transfer only for pharmacists who took and passed the NAPLEX after January 1, 2004.The majority of states, including WA, have conditions on license transfer from California – the most common restriction being that the license must have first been obtained after January 1, 2004.

The following states have previously had special conditions regarding license transfers from Florida: AZ, CO, DE, ME, PA.

The reciprocity applicant must take the MPJE for Washington within 2 years of completing the transfer application process. If the reciprocity applicant has been out of active practice for between 3 and 5 years, the Board may require additional practical exams or 300 hours of internship prior to licensing. If the reciprocity applicant has been out of active practice for over 5 years, the applicant must retake the NAPLEX and serve a 300 hour internship prior to licensure.

WAC 246-863-035 allows for temporary permits to practice pharmacy while a transfer applicant is awaiting a return on the fingerprint-based national background check, provided all other application steps (including passage of the MPJE) are complete.

FEDERAL INSTALLATIONS

Pharmacists practicing in federal installations, such as the Indian Health Service, the armed forces, or the Veterans Administration, must be licensed in one of the 50 states or territories, but do not need to be licensed in the particular state in which they are stationed. However, pharmacists practicing in federal installations may not practice outside of those facilities unless they are also licensed by that state. See the discussion above concerning Active Military and Inactive Military Spouse license status categories in Washington.

POST GRADUATE TRAINING

Post graduate training for pharmacists includes residencies, fellowships, and graduate degree programs.

RESIDENCIES are post-graduate training opportunities for pharmacists that are one or more years in duration. A comprehensive description of pharmacy residencies is available on the ASHP website.[98] To participate in a residency, you must be licensed in the state in which the residency is located, unless it is in a federal installation. Washington allows recent graduates who are participating in residency programs to register as interns.[99]

General institutional residencies, managed care, and community practice residencies provide a broad range of experiences, and are usually required if one wishes to complete a specialty residency or a fellowship.

Specialty residencies (e.g., infectious disease, pediatrics) focus on a specialty area and often require applicants to have completed a general residency.

The ASHP Residency webpage contains information on the standards for accredited residencies, as well as information on how to apply for a residency that participates in the national matching program. After 2007, accredited residencies are described by the same terms used for post-graduate training of physicians:

PGY1, or Post Graduate Year 1, residencies are those that provide broad training, but may have a focus in special populations. Most current general and community residencies, and some specialty residencies such as geriatrics or pediatrics, will meet the requirements for PGY1 residencies.

PGY2, or Post Graduate Year 2, residencies, will be advanced residencies that require PGY1 training and will be focused in a specialty area.

Accreditation of residencies is undertaken primarily by ASHP, but guidelines for non-institutional residencies are developed jointly by ASHP and other organizations: for community PGY1 residencies, ASHP and APHA, and for managed care PGY1 residencies, ASHP and AMCP. Other organizations cooperate with ASHP in preparing guidelines for accreditation of PGY2 residencies include ASCP (geriatrics), SIDP (infectious disease), and ACCP (pharmacotherapy), among others.

FELLOWSHIPS are one or two years in duration and focus on development of both advanced skills and the ability to research in a specific area.

QUALIFICATION "BY EDUCATION, TRAINING OR EXPERIENCE"

Certain practice roles require training or experience beyond the entry-level pharmacy degree. Included among these in Washington are directors of hospital pharmacies (WAC 246-873-040(1)), and pharmacists in charge of home IV compounding (WAC 246-871-040(1)). Residencies or fellowships can provide this training or experience.

Nuclear pharmacists must complete either six months of on-the-job training under the supervision of a qualified nuclear pharmacist, or must have completed a nuclear pharmacy training program in an accredited college of pharmacy. (WAC 246-903-030(3))

CONSCIENTIOUS OBJECTION

Pharmacists, technicians, and other licensees of the state are required to follow the laws and regulations established for practice, which generally includes an obligation to provide services to patients or potential clients on a non-discriminatory basis and to provide all lawful or required services needed by these patients or clients. There is a formal recognition in society, however, that certain dictates of a person's conscience can overrule these obligations. A pharmacist or technician who refuses to complete an otherwise required action by appealing to matters of conscience, is said to have justified the refusal as a matter of conscientious objection. Certain categories have become more prominent in recent years.

REFUSING TO PARTICIPATE IN ABORTIONS As a matter of Washington state law, no individual may be compelled to participate in an abortion. One does not have to be a "conscientious objector" to opt out of such participation in Washington.

Under Washington's Reproductive Privacy Act[100] (Initiative 120 -1991), "No person or private medical facility may be required by law or contract in any circumstances to participate in the performance of an abortion if such person or private medical facility objects to so doing. No person may be discriminated against in employment or professional privileges because of the person's participation or refusal to participate in the termination of a pregnancy." (RCW 9.02.150)

Federal law similarly protects the right of individuals to refuse to participate in termination of PREGNANCIES BY ANY HEALTH CARE ENTITY THAT RECEIVES FEDERAL FUNDS. THE CHURCH AMENDMENTS (42 U.S.C. § 300A-7) PROHIBITS DISCRIMINATION AGAINST PERSONS OR ENTITIES WHO PARTICIPATE IN HEALTH SERVICE PROGRAMS funded by DHHS and who choose to participate in or refuse to participate in sterilization or abortion because of religious or moral belief.

REFUSING TO PARTICIPATE IN AID-IN-DYING. Oregon and Washington Death with Dignity laws specify that participating in providing aid-in-dying is limited to willing health care providers, and prohibit discrimination against persons who participate in or refuse to participate in aid-in-dying. Washington's law permits hospitals and clinics to prohibit participation in aid-in-dying on their premises, but this applies only to the acts of physicians as specified in the law. Pharmacies are not permitted to prohibit their employee pharmacists from filling prescriptions issued under the law.

REFUSING TO PARTICIPATE IN OTHER HEALTH CARE SERVICES. The Church Amendments further specify that "No individual shall be required to perform or assist in the performance of any part of a health service program or research activity funded … under a program administered by the Secretary of Health and Human Services *if his performance or assistance in performance of such part of such program or activity would be contrary to his religious beliefs or moral convictions."* (42 U.S.C. § 300a-7(d))

The Illinois Supreme Court allowed a lawsuit to go forward in December 2008 that challenges the Illinois regulation requiring that pharmacies promptly fill prescriptions for contraceptives, including emergency contraception. The plaintiffs cited contrary Illinois statutes, including the Illinois Health Care Right of Conscience Act and the Illinois Religious Freedom Restoration Act.[101]

As noted in Chapter 3, a similar challenge to Washington's "prompt fill" regulation has been rejected, and the Washington rule upheld by the 9th Circuit. The U.S. Supreme Court declined to hear an appeal.[102]

PHARMACY ORGANIZATIONS' POLICIES

State and national pharmacy organizations have adopted policy statements that endorse the exercise of conscience by pharmacists, but they believe that pharmacists must balance their moral stance with the right of patients to receive lawful therapies.

WASHINGTON STATE PHARMACY ASSOCIATION POSITION STATEMENTS

The WSPA has adopted two statements regarding the responsibility of pharmacists to assure that patients have access to the lawful care they need.

DUTY TO FACILITATE CARE

"... the WSPA supports the following statements as meeting the 'duty to facilitate' and the appropriate components of a standardized referral process:

Pharmacies have a duty to facilitate the delivery of lawfully prescribed and medically appropriate drugs or devices and those approved for restricted distribution by pharmacies, or to facilitate the delivery of therapeutically equivalent drugs or devices to patients in a timely manner, except under the following circumstances:

Prescriptions containing obvious or known errors, inadequacies in the instructions, known contraindications, or incompatible prescriptions;

Potentially fraudulent prescriptions; and

National or state emergencies or guidelines affecting availability, usage, or supplies of drugs or devices.

A pharmacy fulfills the duty to facilitate the delivery of lawfully prescribed medically appropriate drugs or devices if, when presented with a lawful, medically appropriate prescription, or request for distribution, a pharmacy:

Dispenses the lawfully prescribed and medically appropriate drug or device or a therapeutically equivalent alternative drug or device;

Facilitates the patient's access to the lawfully prescribed and medically appropriate drug or device by referring the patient to a healthcare provider who will provide the care. To complete the referral, the referring pharmacy shall contact the provider of the patient's choice to confirm that the drug or device is available, and transfer the prescription to the new provider; or

If the patient or the patient's caregiver prefers to self-refer, returns the patient's unfilled prescription."[103]

ACCESS TO CARE

WSPA **believes** a pharmacist's professional responsibility is to provide optimum patient care.

WSPA **opposes** any pharmacist obstructing a patient's access to care.

WSPA **supports** patient access to timely care in the event a pharmacist is unable to dispense a lawful prescription.[104]

As the former executive director of the WSPA has put it, the association believes that pharmacists may *stand aside* from participation in activities they object to, but cannot *stand in the way* of patient care. The majority of WSPA members support a patient's right to receive lawful medications, and Washington pharmacists are nationally recognized for their participation in the prescribing of emergency contraception.[105]

MORAL OBLIGATIONS OF THE CONSCIENTIOUS OBJECTOR

A pharmacist or technician who intends to refuse to participate in otherwise lawful activities has two important moral obligations, authenticity and publicity.

AUTHENTICITY

The objection must be based on sincerely held, carefully considered, moral or religious convictions. It cannot be due to mere squeamishness concerning the activity.

The objection must be based on evidence that the activity actually offends the moral principle invoked by the objector. For example, if a pharmacist's objection to emergency contraception is based on a moral or religious opposition to terminating a pregnancy, current pharmacological evidence does not support the conclusion that Plan B does, in fact, result in pregnancy terminations.[106]

The objection must be applied consistently. A pharmacist who objects to dispensing ECP should object to doing so regardless of which patient is seeking the drug. Conscientious objection cannot be a cover for discrimination or bias.

PUBLICITY

Pharmacists enter into relationships with patients that entail expectations on the patients' part that the pharmacist will provide care upon request. A pharmacist who provides services to women of childbearing age must be public and candid with these clients about whether he or she will dispense emergency contraception, so that the patients can decide whether to enter into a professional relationship with that pharmacist. Likewise, a pharmacist who practices hospice care in Washington or Oregon should be open about whether he or she will participate in aid-in-dying.

Employers have a right to know whether an employee will fill all lawful prescriptions. As with other antidiscrimination laws, employers are required to make reasonable accommodations for religious practices, but they are entitled to know in advance of the need for such accommodations. (See also Chapter 7).

MANDATORY REPORTING OF ABUSE OR OTHER NOTIFIABLE PUBLIC HEALTH CONDITIONS

Social service agencies and public health departments rely on health care providers to serve as sentinels who alert these agencies to abuse of vulnerable individuals or certain public health concerns.

ABUSE REPORTING Pharmacists are among the professionals who are required by Washington law to report suspected abuse of children or vulnerable adults.

CHILDREN RCW 26.44.030 reads, in part: "(1)(a) When any ... pharmacist ... has reasonable cause to believe that a child has suffered abuse or neglect, he or she shall report such incident, or cause a report to be made, to the proper law enforcement agency or to the department [of social and health services] as provided in RCW 26.44.040."

VULNERABLE ADULTS RCW 74.34.035 describes reports that must be made to the Department of Social and Health Services when health providers are aware of abuse of vulnerable adults. Pharmacists, pharmacy technicians, and pharmacy assistants are among the "mandated reporters" by virtue of being subject to the Uniform Disciplinary Act. "Abuse" includes "willful action or inaction that inflicts injury, unreasonable confinement, intimidation, or punishment on a vulnerable adult." It "includes sexual abuse, mental abuse, physical abuse, and exploitation of a vulnerable adult." Specific definitions of these types of abuse are found in RCW 74.34.020 (2)(a) through (d).

A registrant's obligation to report abuse arises under the law only as it relates to their professional duties. A 2018 decision by the Washington State Supreme Court held that a teacher's obligation to report possible child abuse did not require her to report the spanking of her own children when it occurred at home and was administered by another family member: "A teacher's failure to comply with the mandatory reporting duty must have some connection to his or her professional identity."[107]

NOTIFIABLE CONDITIONS As a public health measure, health facilities, laboratories, and health care providers are required to notify their local health officer or the State Department of Health when they encounter certain reportable conditions. Pharmacists are among the health care providers subject to this law. Most of the conditions are communicable diseases, and the pharmacist is unlikely to be the health care provider who identifies the disease and manages the patient care for those conditions. However, some notifiable conditions will confront pharmacists who are acting as immunizers, or are engaging in collaborative practice agreements that make them primary care providers for certain patients.

A "HEALTH CARE PROVIDER" under the rule is any person "having direct or supervisory responsibility for the delivery of health care" who is licensed under Title 18 RCW (this includes pharmacists) or military personnel providing health care in Washington.

A "PRINCIPAL HEALTH CARE PROVIDER" is the attending health care provider who is primarily responsible for diagnosis or treatment for a patient, or "in the absence of such, the health care provider initiating diagnostic testing or treatment for the patient."

THE RESPONSIBILITY FOR NOTIFYING THE HEALTH DEPARTMENT OR LOCAL HEALTH OFFICER rests with the principal health care provider, but other health care providers in attendance are responsible for reporting unless a report has already been made.

NOTIFIABLE CONDITIONS WHICH HEALTH CARE PROVIDERS must report are listed in Table HC-1 of WAC 246-101-101. Table 2-1 contains a highly selective list of conditions that are more likely to be identified by pharmacists who could find themselves in the position of the principal health care provider, followed by the required time frame and whether the local or state health department should be notified:

TABLE 2-1. SELECTED LIST OF NOTIFIABLE CONDITIONS

CONDITION	REQUIRED TIME FRAME	LOCAL OR STATE
Animal bites	Immediately	Local
Asthma, occupational	Monthly	State
Diseases of suspected bioterrorism	Immediately	Local
Domoic acid poisoning ("red tide")	Immediately	Local
Emerging conditions with outbreak potential	Immediately	Local
Influenza, novel or unsubtypable strain	Immediately	Local
Influenza-associated death (lab confirmed)	3 business days	Local
Outbreaks of suspected foodborne origin	Immediately	Local
Outbreaks of suspected waterborne origin	Immediately	Local
Pesticide poisoning (hospitalized, fatal, or cluster)	Immediately	State
Pesticide poisoning (other)	3 business days	State
Serious adverse reactions to immunizations	3 business days	Local

Pharmacists who enter into collaborative practice agreements to manage or screen for communicable diseases should review the list of notifiable conditions and include in the collaborative practice agreement an understanding of how the pharmacist and authorizing prescriber will assure appropriate reporting. Even when the pharmacist is not the principal health care provider, there is no prohibition of reporting by other health care providers for any notifiable condition.

CRIMINAL BACKGROUND CHECKS AND OTHER REQUIREMENTS

CRIMINAL BACKGROUND CHECKS

Individuals who might have unsupervised access to children, developmentally disabled persons, or vulnerable adults may not be hired by agencies or firms providing services to these individuals if they have a relevant criminal background. The Washington State Patrol is authorized to perform background checks on prospective employees or licensees at the request of employers or state agencies (RCW 43.43.832). Health care facilities that have received criminal background checks on prospective employees are permitted to share this information with other facilities under certain circumstances. The statute also authorizes the WSP to provide background checks at the request of any law enforcement agency. The Pharmacy Quality Assurance Commission seeks criminal background checks from the State Patrol on applicants for credentials issued by the Commission.

Because the WSP background check is limited to records in Washington State, employers (and colleges of pharmacy) are likely to require prospective employees (or students) to permit a national background check performed by an outside firm. In certain cases, state agencies are empowered to seek an FBI background check for prospective state employees.

The Department of Health now requires federal fingerprint-based background checks for out-of-state applicants (including interns). These applicants must arrange to have their fingerprints taken, pay the cost for that if any, and also pay a fee of approximately $32 for the background check. The background check typically adds 5 to 10 working days to the approval process.[108]

SEXUAL CONTACT WITH CLIENTS OR PATIENTS IS PROHIBITED (See also Chapter 7)

Pharmacists and other health providers are prohibited from engaging in or attempting to engage in sexual misconduct with a current patient, client, or "key party," inside or outside the health care setting. (WAC 246-860-100). This applies to other licensees of the Department of Health, including pharmacy ancillary personnel. The rules also prohibit offering professional services in exchange for sexual favors, and/or using health care information to attempt to engage in sexual misconduct or to "meet the provider's sexual needs." A health care provider is prohibited from attempting to engage in sexual conduct during a 2-year period after the provider-patient relationship ends. The Commission revised the rule in 2016 to include "sexual contact with any person involving force, intimidation, or lack of consent; or conviction of a sex offense as defined in RCW 9.94A.030," in the definition of sexual misconduct.[109]

MANDATORY REPORTING OF UNPROFESSIONAL CONDUCT OR IMPAIRMENT

(See also Chapter 7)

Reporting Unprofessional Conduct of Other Licensees

The Uniform Disciplinary Act (RCW 18.130.170) requires that all persons licensed by the Department of Health in Washington (including pharmacists and ancillary personnel) report to the appropriate disciplinary authority (e.g., the Pharmacy Commission) when

- They are aware that another licensee has been subject to a conviction, determination, or finding that he or she has committed an act which constitutes unprofessional conduct;
- They are aware that another licensee may not be able to practice his or her profession with reasonable skill and safety to consumers as a result of a mental or physical condition (this information may generally be reported to an impaired practitioner or substance abuse monitoring program instead of the disciplinary authority)

Self-Reporting Unprofessional Conduct

The statute also requires licensees to report to the Commission when *they themselves* have been

- Subject to any conviction, determination, or finding that he or she has committed unprofessional conduct or is unable to practice with reasonable skill or safety, or
- Disqualified from participating in the federal Medicare or Medicaid programs. (See also Chapter 8.)

Specific rules on how to make these reports to the Department of Health are contained in WAC 246-16-200 through 265. (See also Chapter 7.)

Employer Reporting of Unprofessional Conduct

Washington law sets forth mandatory reporting requirements for employers.[110] The statute clearly requires all employers to report termination or restriction of health care providers' privileges when due to unprofessional conduct or impairment. The current regulation specifies that "Every license holder, corporation, organization, health care facility, and state and local government agency that employs a license holder shall report to the department of health when the employed license holder's services have been terminated or restricted based on a final determination or finding that the license holder:

- Has committed an act or acts that may constitute unprofessional conduct; or

- May not be able to practice his or her profession with reasonable skill and safety due to a mental or physical condition." (WAC 246-16-270(1))

Reports must be submitted no later than 20 days after a final determination or finding is made. A "'Determination or finding' means a final decision by an entity required to report ... even if no adverse action or sanction has been imposed or if the license holder is appealing the decision." (WAC 246-16-210(3)) Note, however, that the requirement for employers is triggered only by termination or restriction, both of which are generally considered to be adverse employment actions.

SOCIAL SECURITY NUMBERS. All applicants for a license or credential must supply the agency with a Social Security number, as required in RCW 23.23.150. This statute implements a federal requirement to aid enforcement of child support decrees.

Some individuals who may need a credential from the Commission, such as foreign pharmacy students who wish to participate in an exchange program, cannot currently obtain a social security number. These individuals may certify to the Commission their inability to obtain a social security number, using a form provided by the Commission, and the Department of Health will issue the credential.

NATIONAL PROVIDER IDENTIFIERS. Requirements of the Health Information Portability and Accountability Act (HIPAA) require that all health care providers, including pharmacists, who are covered entities under the Act obtain a National Provider Identifier (NPI). See Chapter 7 for details.

REFERENCES

[44] Giberson S, Yoder S, Lee MP. *Improving Patient and Health System Outcomes through Advanced Pharmacy Practice. A Report to the U.S. Surgeon General.* U.S. Public Health Service; 2011 Dec: 18. http://www.usphs.gov/corpslinks/pharmacy/documents/2011AdvancedPharmacyPracticeReporttotheUSSG.pdf
[45] Wash. Sess. L. 1979 c 90 § 5
[46] CDC. Advancing team-based care through collaborative practice agreements: a resource and implementation guide for adding pharmacists to the care team. Atlanta, GA: Centers for Disease Control and Prevention, US Department of Health and Human Services; 2017; https://www.cdc.gov/dhdsp/pubs/docs/CPA-Team-Based-Care.pdf
[47] The 2013 figures (47 states) include pending rules in the District of Columbia; rules were now finalized in Missouri, but still pending in Oklahoma, and Kansas allowed collaborative practice by 2013. Only Alabama, Delaware, Illinois, South Carolina and the territories of Guam and Puerto Rico do not allow some form of prescriptive authority for pharmacists. NABP Survey of Pharmacy Law 2013.
[48] The 2011 figures (45 states) recognized pending legislation or rules in Missouri, New York, and Oklahoma; Maine only allows CPAs regarding oral contraceptives. As of 2012 New York's rules were in effect for teaching hospitals only, and rules remained pending in Missouri and Oklahoma; collaborative practice was not allowed in Alabama, Delaware, the District of Columbia, Illinois, Kansas, South Carolina, Guam, or Puerto Rico; NABP Survey of Pharmacy Law 2012.
[49] Shefcheck SL, Thomas J III. The outlook for pharmacist initiation and modification of drug therapy. JAPhA 1996; NS36:597-604
[50] Ferro LA, Marcrom RE, Garrelts L et al. Collaborative practice management agreements between pharmacists and physicians. JAPhA 1998; 38:655-65
[51] Mitrany D, Elder R. Collaborative pharmacy practice: an idea whose time has come. JMCP 1999 Nov-Dec; 5(6): 487-491
[52] Punekar Y, Lin S, Thomas J. Progress of pharmacist collaborative practice: status of state laws and regulations and perceived impact of collaborative practice. JAPhA 2003 Jul-Aug; 43(4):503-510

[53] Ukens C. Most states now allow collaborative practice. Drug Topics 2006 Jul 24; http://drugtopics.modernmedicine.com/drugtopics/Community+Pharmacy/Most-states-now-allow-collaborative-practice/ArticleStandard/Article/detail/359816
[54] Thompson CA. Collaborative practice comes to New York, expands in Indiana. ASHP Pharmacy News 2011 Jul 15; http://www.ashp.org/menu/News/PharmacyNews/NewsArticle.aspx?id=3568
[55] WSDOH, PQAC. Interim Guidance on Collaborative Drug Therapy. DOH 690-327, 2018 Dec; https://www.doh.wa.gov/Portals/1/Documents/Pubs/690327.pdf
[56] http://www.secstate.wa.gov/acp/
[57] Article No. 987, Washington Board of Pharmacy Newsletter 2009 Jan; 30(3):1.
[58] RCW 9A.60.020 – Forgery.
[59] Accreditation Council for Pharmacy Education, Definition of Continuing Education for the Profession of Pharmacy, https://www.acpe-accredit.org/pdf/DefinitionofCE.pdf
[60]See "other forms," at http://www.doh.wa.gov/LicensesPermitsandCertificates/ProfessionsNewReneworUpdate/Pharmacist/ApplicationsandForms
[61] WSDOH, PQAC. Procedure No. 35, 2014 Dec 11; https://www.doh.wa.gov/Portals/1/Documents/2300/2017/PQAC-35-CEAttendCommMtg.pdf
[62] WSDOH, PQAC. Policy No. 38, 2014 Dec 11; https://www.doh.wa.gov/Portals/1/Documents/2300/2017/PQAC-38-CE-ReqNewGrads.pdf
[63] 2012 c 45 § 2(1)
[64] http://www.doh.wa.gov/Publicat/2003_News/03-205.htm
[65] Johnson T. Flu-shot 'doctor' in serious trouble. Seattle P-I . 2003 Dec 30; http://seattlepi.nwsource.com/local/154737_flu31.html
[66] https://bop.idaho.gov/forms/2018-03-27_MPJE-Attestations.pdf
[67] ACPE currently accredits one international PharmD program – Lebanese American University School of Pharmacy in Byblos, Lebanon.
[68] http://www.nabp.net/programs/examination/fpgee
[69] Minutes, Washington State Board of Pharmacy, April 7, 2011
[70] WSDOH, PQAC. Policy/Procedure No. 47, 2016 Aug 18; https://www.doh.wa.gov/Portals/1/Documents/2300/2017/PQAC-47-HIV-AIDSEdInitialCred.pdf
[71] PQAC Procedure #54, effective February 2, 2018; https://www.doh.wa.gov/Portals/1/Documents/2300/2018/PQAC-54-PharmInternReg.pdf
[72] Article No. 1157 – Pharmacy Intern Registration. Washington State Board of Pharmacy News 2013 Oct; 35(2):5.
[73] http://www.doh.wa.gov/Portals/1/Documents/Pubs/690110.pdf
[74] Internship Site and Preceptor Notification, WSDOH, WSPQAC.; http://www.doh.wa.gov/Portals/1/Documents/Pubs/690033.pdf
[75] Article No. 1129, Preceptor-Intern Relationship. Washington Board of Pharmacy News 2013 Jan; 34(3): 4.
[76] O'Sullivan T, Bray B, Morrison RD, Woodard L., Fuller T. Experiential Training Manual for use by pharmacy preceptors, interns, and technicians. 3rd Ed., 2001; WSPQAC; http://www.doh.wa.gov/Portals/1/Documents/2300/etmanual.pdf
[77] Minutes, Pharmacy Commission meeting, September 30, 2016.
[78] Minutes, Board of Pharmacy Meeting, September 17, 2009.
[79] This interim policy was permanently adopted in 2012; Minutes, Board of Pharmacy Meeting, June 7, 2012.
[80] https://www.ptcb.org
[81] http://www.nhanow.com/pharmacy-technician.aspx
[82] 2016 c 148 §5
[83] Article No. 1228 – Application for Utilization of Ancillary Personnel – Pharmacy Technicians and Assistants, Washington State Pharmacy Quality Assurance Commission News, 2016 Apr; 37(4):4.
[84] http://www.doh.wa.gov/cfh/hiv/prevention/training/default.htm
[85] WSDOH, PQAC. Policy/procedure No. 47, 2016 Aug 18; https://www.doh.wa.gov/Portals/1/Documents/2300/2017/PQAC-47-HIV-AIDSEdInitialCred.pdf
[86] Minutes, Washington State Board of Pharmacy, 2009 Jan 22.
[87] WSDOH, PQAC. Guidance Document No. 50, 2017 Mar 30; https://www.doh.wa.gov/Portals/1/Documents/2300/2017/PQAC-50-ClosedDoorLT-Pharm.pdf
[88] WSDOH, PQAC. Policy/procedure No. 34, 2014 Dec 11; https://www.doh.wa.gov/Portals/1/Documents/2300/2017/PQAC-34-JobShadowing.pdf

[89] https://www.acpe-accredit.org/pharmd-program-accreditation/
[90] https://nabp.pharmacy/wp-content/uploads/2018/11/NAPLEX-MPJE-Bulletin-November-2018.pdf
[91] http://www.pearsonvue.com/nabp/
[92] http://www.pharmacy.ca.gov/forms/exam_info_update.pdf
[93] https://nabp.pharmacy/programs/pre-naplex/
[94] https://nabp.pharmacy/help/which-states-require-the-mpje/
[95] WSDOH, PQAC. Policy/Procedure No. 40, Qualifications for re-exam – NAPLEX. 2014 Dec 11; https://www.doh.wa.gov/Portals/1/Documents/2300/2017/PQAC-40QualsRe-examNAPLEX.pdf
[96] https://nabp.pharmacy/programs/licensure-transfer/
[97] https://nabp.pharmacy/wp-content/uploads/2016/11/State-Requirements-and-Conditions_11112016.pdf
[98] http://www.ashp.org/menu/Residency/Residents
[99] Washington Board of Pharmacy Procedure #36, approved October 30, 2008.
[100] RCW 9.02
[101] Morr-Fitz Inc. v Blagojevich, No. 104692, Ill. Supr. Ct., December 18, 2008.
[102] Stormans et al. v Wiesman et al, 794 F.3d 1064, 9th Cir., 2015; 136 S.Ct. 2433 (2016)
[103]http://www.wsparx.org/associations/7310/files/Pharmacist%20Duty%20to%20Facilitate.pdf
[104]http://www.wsparx.org/associations/7310/files/WSPA%20Position%20Statement%20on%20Access%20to%20Care.pdf
[105]http://www.wsparx.org/associations/7310/files/Facts%20For%20Pharmacist%20Access%20to%20Care.pdf
[106] Cantor J, Baum K. The limits of conscientious objection – May pharmacists refuse to fill prescriptions for emergency contraception? N Engl J Med 2004; 351(19):2008-12.
[107] State of Washington v. James-Buhl, No. 94409-1, S.Ct. Wash., 190 Wn.2d 470, April 19, 2018.
[108] http://www.doh.wa.gov/LicensesPermitsandCertificates/ProfessionsNewReneworUpdate/FingerprintBackgroundCheck
[109] WSR 17-01-143, eff. 2017 Jan 20.
[110] 2008 c 134.

3 – ESTABLISHING, OPERATING, OR CLOSING A LICENSED OR REGISTERED PRACTICE SITE OR BUSINESS

GENERAL CONSIDERATIONS FOR ESTABLISHING A BUSINESS IN WASHINGTON

RESOURCES for businesses are available on the Access Washington web site at the following URL: http://access.wa.gov/business/index.aspx

FORM OF BUSINESS – The Secretary of State of Washington has provided the following definitions of forms of business available in Washington on its website.[111]

A **Sole Proprietorship** is one individual or married couple in business alone. Sole proprietorships are the most common form of business structure. This type of business is simple to form and operate, and may enjoy greater flexibility of management and fewer legal controls. However, the business owner is personally liable for all debts incurred by the business.

A **General Partnership** is composed of two or more persons (usually not a married couple) who agree to contribute money, labor, and/or skill to a business. Each partner shares the profits, losses, and management of the business, and each partner is personally and equally liable for debts of the partnership. Formal terms of the partnership are usually contained in a written partnership agreement.

COMPETENCY AREAS IN THIS CHAPTER

2016 MPJE COMPETENCY STATEMENTS – Areas 1.1.1, 1.2.1, 1.4.3, 1.4.4, 1.4.10-13, 1.7.1, 1.7.2, 2.2.1, 2.2.2, 2.2.3, 2.2.4, 2.3.1, 2.3.2, 3.1.1

2016 ACPE REQUIRED ELEMENTS – Pharmacy Law & Regulatory Affairs; Practice Management

A **Limited Partnership*** is composed of one or more general partners and one or more limited partners. The general partners manage the business and share full in its profits and losses. Limited partners share in the profits of the business, but their losses are limited to the extent of their investment. Limited partners are usually not involved in the day-to-day operations of the business.

A **Limited Liability Partnership*** is similar to a General Partnership except that normally a partner does not have personal liability for the negligence of another partner. This business structure is used most commonly by professionals such as accountants and lawyers.

A **Corporation*** is a more complex business structure. As a chartered legal entity, a corporation has certain rights, privileges, and liabilities beyond those of an individual. Doing business as a corporation may yield tax or financial benefits, but these can be offset by other considerations, such as increased licensing fees or decreased personal control. Corporations may be formed for profit or nonprofit purposes.

The **Limited Liability Company (LLC)*** and the Limited Liability Partnership (LLP)* are the newest forms of business structure in Washington. An LLC or LLP is formed by one or more individuals or entities through a special written agreement. The agreement details the organization of the LLC or LLP, including: provisions for management, assignability of interests, and distribution of profits or losses. Limited liability companies and limited liability partnerships are permitted to engage in any lawful, for profit business or activity other than banking or insurance.

*Registers with the Secretary of State

NONPROFIT ORGANIZATIONS may take the form of nonprofit corporations or nonprofit professional services corporations. The latter are formed when licensed health professionals (or other professionals) join to provide professional services as a nonprofit group (e.g., charitable clinic).

MASTER LICENSE APPLICATION. The state uses a Master License Application to apply for tax registration, Labor & Industries registration, corporation registration, and trade name registration.

LABOR AND INDUSTRIES REGISTRATION. Businesses that have employees are required to register with the Department of Labor and Industries, whether they are for profit or nonprofit organizations.

REGISTRATION WITH DEPARTMENT OF HEALTH. PHARMACIES, HOSPITALS, NURSING HOMES, SHOPKEEPERS, AND OTHERS registered by the Department of Health must also apply to the DOH and/or the appropriate board or commission.

REGISTRATION WITH DEA. PHARMACIES AND HOSPITALS will also need to apply to the Drug Enforcement Administration and register as dispensers. A WA Pharmacy Commission controlled substances registration number will be required by DEA.

ADVANCE INSPECTION REQUIRED. The Department of Health and/or the Pharmacy Commission requires advanced notice and conducts an inspection of health care facilities prior to licensure.

CERTIFICATE OF NEED. Certain types of health care facilities (but not community pharmacies) must obtain a Certificate of Need prior to opening.

PHARMACY COMMISSION AND DEA APPLICATIONS

THE PHARMACY COMMISSION has traditionally used a single application form (690-152)[112] for all pharmacy types, with supplemental forms required for differential hours[113] or utilization of ancillary personnel.[114] In September 2016, in response to direction from the Legislature, the Commission created a separate application form for hospital pharmacies (690-302),[115] with a supplemental addendum for hospital pharmacy associated clinics (see below).

Applications must be submitted 30 days prior to a regularly scheduled Pharmacy Commission meeting. (WAC 246-869-030 (1))

Any change of ownership or location must be communicated to the Commission immediately (RCW 18.64.043(2)). This includes relocating the pharmacy within the same building or facility.

THE DRUG ENFORCEMENT ADMINISTRATION now utilizes an online application[116] procedure to submit DEA Form 224 – Application for Retail Pharmacy, Hospital/Clinic, Practitioner, Teaching Institution, or Mid-Level Practitioner. The DEA requires that a state license have been granted prior to obtaining a DEA registration.

Individual pharmacists with prescriptive authority for controlled substances will need to register using DEA Form 224.

TYPES OF FIRMS LICENSED BY THE PHARMACY COMMISSION

The Pharmacy Commission has recently summarized the kinds of licensed firms in Washington State. 2,026 firms were licensed as of January 2011, of which 71% were pharmacies.[117]

- Pharmacies: Community (1,223); Hospital (114); LTC (50); Parenteral (19); Jail (8); Nuclear (7); Mail order (4); Other (10)
- Non-pharmacies: Drug/controlled substances researcher (241); Drug wholesaler (121); Other controlled substance (35); Health care entities (60); Animal control/humane society (46); Drug manufacturer – in state (25); Dog handlers (24); Emergency response warehouse (16); Itinerant vendor (11); Fish and wildlife (6); Precursor chemicals (3); Poison distributors (3).

COMMISSION INTERPRETATION OF RCW 18.64 MUST BE REASONABLE AND APPROPRIATE TO TYPE OF PHARMACY PRACTICE

The 2016 Legislature gave direction to the Commission in its interpretation of the licensing requirements of RCW 18.64, the pharmacy practice act. "This chapter must be interpreted in a manner that supports regulatory, inspection, and investigation standards that are reasonable and appropriate based on the level of risk and the type of services provided in a pharmacy, including pharmacy services provided in a hospital and pharmacy services provided in an individual practitioner office or multipractitioner clinic owned, operated, or under common control with a hospital regardless of the office or clinic's pharmacy address. The commission shall provide clear and specific information regarding the standards to which particular pharmacy services will be held, as appropriate, based on the type of pharmacy service provided at a particular location." (RCW 18.64.043 (b))

GENERAL REQUIREMENTS FOR LICENSED PHARMACIES

EVERY OPERATOR OF A PHARMACY MUST BE A PHARMACIST OR PLACE A PHARMACIST IN CHARGE OF THE PHARMACY. (RCW 18.64.020)

EACH OWNER OF A PHARMACY MUST PAY AN ANNUAL LICENSE, FILE A STATEMENT OF OWNERSHIP AND LOCATION, AND PROMPTLY NOTIFY THE DEPARTMENT OF ANY CHANGE IN OWNERSHIP OR LOCATION. The pharmacy location license must be posted in the pharmacy. (RCW 18.64.043(2))

RECORDS OF ALL PRESCRIPTIONS AND DISPENSING OF PRESCRIPTION DRUGS SHALL BE KEPT FOR A MINIMUM OF 2 YEARS. (RCW 18.64.245) However, see Chapter 8 for the longer record requirement for Medicaid prescriptions and documentation, which is 6 years.

CONTROLLED SUBSTANCES RECORDS MUST BE MAINTAINED FOR 2 YEARS. (See also Chapter 5)

ACCESS TO PHARMACIES RESTRICTED. Several regulations of the Commission restrict access to pharmacies by non-pharmacy personnel.

Lay persons may not converse with pharmacist while compounding. WAC 246-869-140 prohibits lay persons from conversing with a pharmacist while he or she is engaged in the act of "compounding a prescription"

Lay persons may not enter pharmacy. WAC 246-869-140 also protects the "prescription department of every licensed pharmacy in the state of Washington from trespass by the lay public."

Pharmacies must be secured. WAC 246-869-160(7) requires that "the prescription department shall be situated so that the public shall not have free access to the area where legend drugs, controlled substances, poisons, or other restricted items are stored, compounded, or dispensed."

WAC 246-869-020 requires pharmacies with differential hours from the rest of the store to provide adequate security to assure that in the absence of a pharmacist only those individuals designated by the pharmacist, such as janitors or persons doing inventory, can have access.

May high school students "shadow" a pharmacist? As noted in Chapter 2, the Commission allows students to undertake job shadowing for limited periods of time – up to 3 days, provided they are involved in an organized educational program and do not perform any functions reserved to registrants of the Commission. The pharmacy is encouraged to obtain a confidentiality agreement from the student.[118]

Qualifications of Employees Must be Verified. Employers must verify qualifications and license status of employees when hired and periodically thereafter. Employers who hire pharmacists, technicians, or other personnel for whom a license or registration is required must assure these qualifications are met at the time the person is hired, and must re-verify employees' credentials on an ongoing basis as is reasonable – at least annually is recommended by most consultants. Otherwise, the employer will be guilty of aiding or abetting unlicensed practice (RCW 18.130.180(10)).

No DEA registrant may employ any person who has been previously convicted of a felony involving controlled substances in any position which would give that person access to controlled substances. (21 CFR § 1301.76) The DEA does provide for an application for a waiver of this prohibition in individual circumstances (see Section V of the Pharmacist's Manual). (See also Chapter 5)

No pharmacy that provides services to recipients of federal assistance programs (Medicare, Medicaid, TriCare, etc.) may employ or retain a person who has been excluded from participation in federal programs. Lists of excluded individuals are maintained by states as well as by the federal government. The federal list is available at a website maintained by the Office of the Inspector General of HHS, as well as a searchable site where individual names may be entered.[119] An additional list of excluded persons is maintained by the General Services Administration in its System for Award Management (SAM) web portal.[120] (See also Chapter 8)

The National Practitioner Healthcare Integrity & Protection Data Bank ("The Data Bank") is maintained by the Department of Health and Human Services – it lists individual practitioners who have been disciplined, excluded, or otherwise had a final action taken against their license. It is available for search by hospitals and other qualified entities.[121]

The Department of Health maintains a "Provider Credential Search" page that allows individuals to determine if a given provider or practitioner is currently licensed, and whether there is any restriction or other discipline related to the license.[122]

In the event that a pharmacist or technician has recently submitted a renewal application (or has just been notified of his or her initial licensure) and has not yet received a printed license certificate, a printout from the credential search database at the DOH may be used as evidence of current licensure or registration.

COMMUNITY PHARMACIES (AMBULATORY CARE PHARMACIES) – WAC 246-869

RESPONSIBLE PHARMACIST MANAGER. It is unlawful to operate a pharmacy without placing a pharmacist in charge (RCW 18.64.020). The Commission requires each non-licensed proprietor of a pharmacy to appoint a responsible pharmacist manager (RPM) and to notify the Commission of the name of the RPM, and when employment of that RPM has terminated (WAC 246-869-070). Similarly, each person appointed as an RPM must notify the Commission of his or her appointment, and when that appointment is terminated (WAC 246-863-060). The RPM is responsible for compliance with all laws and regulations governing the practice of pharmacy at the pharmacy.

OVERALL AUTHORITY OF RPM. Every portion of the establishment coming under the jurisdiction of the pharmacy laws shall be under the full and complete control of such responsible manager. (WAC 246-869-070)

The Commission has interpreted this rule to hold the RPM of a pharmacy responsible for problems with the labeling of OTC drugs stocked elsewhere in the pharmacy.

AUTHORITY FOR ANCILLARY PERSONNEL. The responsible pharmacist manager shall retain all professional and personal responsibility for any assisted tasks performed by personnel under his or her responsibility, as shall the pharmacy employing such personnel. The responsible pharmacist manager shall determine the extent to which personnel may be utilized to assist the pharmacist and shall assure that the pharmacist is fulfilling his or her supervisory and professional responsibilities. (WAC 246-863-095).

A PHARMACIST MAY BE RPM FOR MORE THAN ONE LOCATION. The Commission has indicated that one pharmacist may accept appointment as the RPM for more than one pharmacy location.[123]

LIMITS ON COMMISSION'S LATITUDE IN DISCIPLINING PHARMACIES LEADS TO DISCIPLINE OF RPM. When the current version of the Uniform Disciplinary Act was enacted, it was made applicable only to individual registrants, such as pharmacists, physicians, nurses, etc., and does not apply to firms. The UDA gives the Commission latitude to fashion discipline for pharmacists that may range from a notice of correction up to license revocation (see Chapter 7), and may include fines. However, the principal power the Commission has over a pharmacy license is to suspend or revoke the license, which might be considered a "nuclear option," and one that is therefore difficult to enforce. Therefore, the Commission will assess fines or lesser penalties on the RPM when the pharmacy operations under the RPM's supervision violate laws or regulations. In the event that the pharmacy has terminated the appointment of a pharmacist as the RPM, but fails to notify the Commission, it will treat the pharmacist as responsible for the pharmacy's operations if the pharmacist has also failed to inform the Commission that he or she is no longer the RPM.

ABSENCE OF A PHARMACIST. The Commission has approved a policy/procedure on temporary absence of a pharmacist in a community pharmacy/retail practice setting. The policy defines "immediate and direct access" as meaning "that the pharmacist is on the premises and maintains contact with the pharmacy." The policy states that "the pharmacist must be accessible to the patient or patients' representative when a prescription requires counseling or counseling is requested. Under the guidelines, "No new prescription or medication that requires counseling shall be delivered without immediate and direct access to a pharmacist, excluding prescriptions delivered outside the pharmacy premises. If a pharmacist is readily available but not within direct and immediate access, the pharmacy may continue with dispensing, non-discretionary functions and delivery of prescriptions that do not require counseling."[124] This policy must be read in the context of the Commission's guidance on patient counseling[125] – see Chapter 6.

DIFFERENTIAL HOURS.

Community pharmacies in chain stores or other settings may operate with different hours than the main establishment, subject to the following requirements. (WAC 246-869-020)

- The pharmacy must be separately secured from the rest of the establishment.
- All equipment, records, drugs, devices, poisons or other products that are restricted to sale by a pharmacist must be kept in the pharmacy area.
- If written prescriptions are to be dropped off during non-pharmacy hours, there must be a secure "drop box" or "mail slot" that allows the prescription to be put into the secured pharmacy area.
- No prescriptions can be dispensed or released unless the pharmacist is present.
- No restricted products can be sold unless the pharmacist is present.
- The pharmacy must have a distinct telephone number that is not answered by the main establishment when the pharmacy is closed. However, if all phone calls are recorded for playback to the pharmacist, the phone may be answered elsewhere in the establishment when the pharmacy is closed.
- Oral prescriptions may be taken on a recording device when the pharmacist is not present, but the device must announce the hours of the pharmacy.
- Pharmacy operating hours must be permanently displayed on or adjacent to the entrance to the pharmacy. If the pharmacy is in a larger establishment, the hours must be posted at the pharmacy and on or adjacent to the entrance to the larger establishment.
- If the larger establishment advertises the presence of the pharmacy, or refers to products that may only be sold in a pharmacy, the advertisement must list the operating hours of the pharmacy.
- A 30-day notice is required before adopting differential hours to allow for a Commission inspection.

COMPLIANCE WITH BUILDING AND FIRE CODES.

New pharmacies located in new or remodeled buildings must provide evidence of being built or remodeled in accordance with local building and fire codes. (WAC 246-868-040)

PHYSICAL STANDARDS FOR COMMUNITY PHARMACIES.

ADEQUATE STOCK.

(WAC 246-869-150) "The pharmacy must maintain at all times a representative assortment of drugs in order to meet the pharmaceutical needs of its patients." Although the Commission does not specify any particular products, it conditions a pharmacy's obligation to deliver all legally-prescribed drugs to patients in a timely manner in part on the need to maintain adequate stock (see discussion above; also see Poison Control, below).

- No outdated drugs may be in the regular stock.
- Stock must be free from contamination, deterioration, and adulteration.
- Stock must be properly labeled.
- Devices not approved as fit for an ultimate consumer by the FDA may not be stocked.
- The regulation incorporates USP standards for storage of drugs in a pharmacy, and requires that storage conditions meet USP standards.

ADEQUATE FACILITIES (WAC 246-869-160) The Commission requires pharmacies to meet the following minimum standards for drug storage and dispensing:

- Lighting must be adequate, with 30 to 50 foot-candles of illumination in the dispensing area
- Adequate ventilation with constant air flow
- A minimum of three linear feet of bench space (18 inch minimum depth) for each pharmacist or intern who will be working at a given time.
- Prescription counter must be maintained in a clean and uncluttered state.
- There must be a sink with hot and cold running water.
- A refrigerator with a thermometer in the compounding area that must be maintained between 2 °C and 8 °C (36 °F and 46 °F) as required by USP standards. The Commission investigators usually require that food not be kept in this refrigerator.
- The pharmacy must be situated so that public does not have free access.

SANITARY CONDITIONS. (WAC 246-869-170)

- The walls, and ceiling of the pharmacy must be in good repair, with no peeling or cracked paint, etc.
- Adequate trash receptacles must be provided (see later chapters on the demands of HIPAA for disposal of material containing protected health information, and of the Department of Ecology for separation of forms of hazardous waste).
- A restroom, if provided, must have hot and cold water, soap and towels, and the toilet kept clean and sanitary.
- All equipment must be clean and in good repair.
- Professional personnel and staff working at the pharmacy shall keep themselves and their apparel neat and clean.

ADEQUATE EQUIPMENT. (WAC 246-869-180) Washington differs from many states in avoiding lists of required equipment, but only requires that the pharmacy have the equipment needed to compound the type of prescriptions dispensed therein. However, the rule does require equipment and supplies necessary to "compound, dispense, label, administer, and distribute drugs." Such equipment as the pharmacy possesses must be properly maintained.

Specific reference books are not required. The rule only requires that up-to-date references must be available as needed for pharmacists to furnish patients and practitioners with information concerning drugs.

The pharmacy must have in place one up-to-date copy of Washington statutes and rules governing the practice of pharmacy, the sale and dispensing of drugs, poisons, controlled substances and medicines. Electronic or on-line versions are acceptable. (WAC 246-869-180(2))

PROMPT DISPENSING OF ALL LAWFUL PRESCRIPTIONS

In response to controversy concerning the refusal by some pharmacists to dispense certain drugs (e.g., emergency contraception) as a matter of moral objection, the Commission adopted new requirements for pharmacies. In general, it requires all licensed pharmacies to deliver all lawfully-prescribed drugs to patients in a timely manner, while permitting pharmacies to attempt to accommodate the religious or moral beliefs of individual employee pharmacists. A pharmacy may not choose to omit particular products from its stock based on factors such as the religious objection of the pharmacy owner. This rule became effective on July 26, 2007 (WAC 246-869-010).

Pharmacies have a duty to deliver lawfully prescribed drugs or devices to patients and to distribute drugs and devices approved by the U.S. Food and Drug Administration for restricted distribution by pharmacies (e.g., Plan B®); or provide a therapeutically equivalent drug or device in a timely manner; consistent with reasonable expectations for filling the prescription. (WAC 246-869-010(1))

Note the use of the term "deliver," as opposed to "dispense." Pharmacies do not "dispense" drugs, because to "dispense" is part of the practice of pharmacy, which only pharmacists can do. Firms, however, are licensed to distribute or deliver drugs.

EXCEPTIONS TO THE "TIMELY MANNER RULE" include the following:

- Prescriptions containing an obvious or known error, inadequacies in the instructions, known contraindications, or prescriptions requiring action in accordance with WAC 246-875-040 (the Drug Use Review regulation);
- National or state emergencies or guidelines affecting availability or supplies of drugs or devices (e.g., flu vaccine restrictions when the supply is short);
- Lack of specialized equipment or expertise needed to safely produce, store, or dispense drugs or devices, such as certain drug compounding or storage for nuclear medicine;
- Potentially fraudulent prescriptions (i.e., taking time to verify a prescription); or
- Unavailability of drug or device despite good faith compliance with WAC 246-869-150 (the minimum stock requirement – see below).
- Failure of the patient to pay the pharmacy's usual and customary or contracted charge.

ACTIONS NEEDED IF THE DRUG IS NOT AVAILABLE in a timely manner, which will provide the patient with a "timely alternative for appropriate therapy which, consistent with customary pharmacy practice, may include obtaining the drug or device. These alternatives include but are not limited to:"

- Contacting prescriber to address and resolve concerns with the prescription, or to obtain authorization for a therapeutically equivalent alternative;
- Return the prescription to the patient if requested;
- Transmit the information to another pharmacy of the patient's choice if requested.
- Note: this rule prohibits the pharmacy from transferring the prescription to another pharmacy unless the patient requests.

ENGAGING IN OR PERMITTING THE FOLLOWING ACTIONS WILL SUBJECT THE PHARMACY TO DISCIPLINE: Destroy an unfilled lawful prescription; Refuse to return unfilled lawful prescriptions; Violate a patient's privacy; Discriminate against patients or their agent in a manner prohibited by state or federal law; (WAC 246-863-095 (4)(d)) or Intimidate or harass a patient.

LEGAL CHALLENGES TO PROMPT DISPENSING RULE

PROHIBITION OF THE "TRANSFER OPTION" ENJOINED BY THE US DISTRICT COURT

In 2007, a group of plaintiffs, including pharmacists who object to dispensing Plan B® for religious reasons, sued the Department of Health and the then Board of Pharmacy in the Federal District Court for the Western District of Washington, on the basis that the rule constitutes an infringement of free exercise of religion, in conflict with the First Amendment to the US Constitution.[126] The district court issued a preliminary injunction against enforcement of the rule against a pharmacy that immediately refers a patient to a nearby source of Plan B. Following an appeal to the 9th Circuit, which invalidated the injunction, and additional Board of Pharmacy actions that ultimately did not alter the rule, a bench trial was held and the judge found the rule unconstitutional as applied to the plaintiffs. The case was originally *Stormans, Inc. et al. v. Selecky et al.,* but by the time it reached the US Supreme Court, it was known as *Stormans, Inc. et al. v. Wiesman et al.*

The State appealed to the 9th Circuit, and in 2015 the 9th Circuit again overturned the district court's ruling.[127]

Plaintiffs appealed to the U.S. Supreme Court, which denied certiorari.[128] The rule remains enforceable, as a result. Note: a more complete history of these proceedings was presented in the 2015 edition of this text.[129]

POISON CONTROL. (WAC 246-869-200)

Pharmacies must have the telephone number of the nearest poison control center readily available. The Washington Poison Center web page: http://www.wapc.org/

THE NATIONAL POISON CENTER NUMBER: 1-800-222-1222

The NATIONAL POISON CENTER NUMBER IS 1-800-222-1222.[130]

In Washington, this is the only number to call for immediate poison information, and it automatically connects with the Washington Poison Center.

TDD services for deaf persons are available at the following number: 1-800-572-0638

Ipecac Syrup Required

As of January 2019, the Commission's regulation still requires that "Each pharmacy shall maintain at least one ounce bottle of Ipecac syrup in stock at all times."(Technically, the pharmacy must maintain 2, so that one can be sold!)

However, no formulation of syrup of ipecac is currently marketed or available in the United States.

Studies have shown that ipecac causes vomiting but makes no difference in poisoning outcomes, and has contributed to morbidity in numerous instances. The national poison control center organization recommends not to keep or use ipecac.

In June 2017, the Washington Poison Center posted a notice on the lack of availability of ipecac syrup and recognized that national authorities no longer recommend use of syrup of ipecac for childhood poisoning. While its notice recommends that requirements for stocking ipecac syrup should be eliminated, but, paradoxically, encourages persons who have ipecac syrup to retain it, noting that it may keep its potency for up to 20 years.[131]

Ipecac for Licensed Childcare Providers

Washington's Department of Early Learning regulates licensed childcare providers. Among its regulations for first aid supplies is the requirement for "at least one unexpired bottle of Syrup of Ipecac that must be given only at the direction of a poison control center." (WAC 170-295-5010(3)(k)) In response to the shortage of ipecac syrup, the Department issued an advisory in 2008 suggesting that, according to the Washington Poison Center, syrup of ipecac is effective for up to 30 years after its expiration date, and noting ways for a child care center to gain an exception if it is impossible to obtain syrup of ipecac. Pharmacists can assist childcare providers in documenting the non-availability of ipecac syrup. Selling an outdated bottle of ipecac syrup, regardless of the opinion of the Washington Poison Center, violates the Food, Drug and Cosmetic Act (see Chapter 4).

In February 2011 the DEL issued another guidance stating that "We have learned from the Washington Poison Center that ... Syrup of Ipecac has been found online and in some stores carrying pharmaceutical products." It urged care providers to continue to keep expired bottles.[132]

PHARMACY COMMISSION INSPECTIONS OF PHARMACIES.

(WAC 246-869-190). The Commission significantly revised its inspection rules effective March 2018, which replace the older system of awarding ratings of "A," "Conditional," or "Unsatisfactory."

SELF-INSPECTIONS REQUIRED

The responsible manager or a designee is required to complete an annual self-inspection using a self-inspection worksheet supplied by the commission. The annual inspection must be completed within the month of March each year. Completed work sheets must be signed by the responsible manager and must be maintained for 2 years in the pharmacy's records.

When a change in the responsible manager occurs, the new responsible manager must complete an additional self-inspection, and retain the record of the inspection for 2 years. This self-inspection must be completed, signed, and dated by the new responsible manager within 30 days of his or her appointment.

PHARMACY COMMISSION-CONDUCTED INSPECTIONS

Commission Investigators inspect pharmacies on a routine basis, and when a complaint has been filed with the Commission. Inspections will end with an "exit meeting" with the responsible manager or designee(s) to address "unresolved deficiencies" identified during the inspection.

- A written inspection report will be provided to the pharmacy within 14 calendar days of the exit meeting.
- The inspection report may include unresolved deficiencies, describing them in detail with a reference to applicable laws.

PHARMACY PLANS OF CORRECTION

A pharmacy must submit a plan of correction addressing each unresolved deficiency identified in the inspection report.

- A plan of correction is "a proposal devised by the applicant or pharmacy that includes specific corrective actions that must be taken to correct identified unresolved deficiencies with time frames to correct them."
- The Commission will set a time frame in which it will notify the pharmacy whether or not a submitted plan of correction adequately addresses the unresolved deficiencies.
- Implementation of an approved plan must be completed within the time frame established in the plan; the Commission may require a follow-up report from the pharmacy, or may schedule a re-inspection.

DISCIPLINARY ACTIONS

WAC 246-869-040 now specifies that new pharmacies will not be licensed unless they have completed an inspection without deficiencies, or with an approved plan of correction.

Pharmacies whose inspection reveals "deficiencies that represent an imminent or immediate risk or threat to public health, safety, and welfare may be subject to summary suspension of the pharmacy license" at the Commission's discretion. (WAC 246-869-190 (c))

Disciplinary actions against pharmacy licenses proceed under the Administrative Procedures Act, rather than the Uniform Disciplinary Act, and require a quorum of the Commission to open an investigation.[133]

NO REQUIREMENT TO POST INSPECTION CERTIFICATE

The current rule no longer requires a pharmacy to post a "certificate of inspection" in public view. However, as noted above, the pharmacy location license must be posted in the pharmacy (RCW 18.64.043 (3)).

FDA INSPECTIONS OF PHARMACIES.

The FDCA (21 U.S.C. § 374(a)) allows FDA personnel to "… enter, at reasonable times, any … establishment in which food, drugs, devices, or cosmetics are manufactured, processed, packed, or held, for introduction into interstate commerce or after such introduction, … and to inspect, at reasonable times and within reasonable limits and in a reasonable manner, such … establishment … and all pertinent equipment, finished and unfinished materials, containers, and labeling therein."

The Act also allows that "in the case of any … establishment … in which prescription drugs, nonprescription drugs intended for human use … are manufactured, processed, packed, or held, the inspection shall extend to all things therein (including records, files, papers, processes, controls, and facilities) …" (21 U.S.C. § 374(a)(1)). However, pharmacies are exempt from this additional level of inspection, which is called the "records provision," when they operate "in conformance with local laws regarding the practice of pharmacy and medicine and which are regularly engaged in dispensing prescription drugs or devices … and which do not … manufacture, prepare, propagate, compound, or process drugs or devices for sale other than in the regular course of their business of dispensing or selling drugs or devices at retail …" (21 U.S.C. § 374(a)(2))

Under the terms of the Drug Quality and Security Act[134], the FDA may inspect "Outsourcing Facilities" in the same manner as other FDA-registered establishments. Outsourcing facilities are facilities that compound sterile products or other drugs outside of the normal pharmacist-physician-patient relationship, but are overseen by a licensed pharmacist. (See Chapter 4)

OTHER AGENCY INSPECTIONS AND AUDITS. Pharmacies are also subject to other inspections by government agencies, including local agencies such as the fire department, sanitation department, etc.

THE US DEPARTMENT OF HEALTH AND HUMAN SERVICES is now required to conduct periodic audits of entities covered under HIPAA (see Chapter 6) to assess compliance with rules governing the security and privacy of patients' protected health information.

PHARMACIES ARE SUBJECT TO AUDITS BY THIRD PARTY PAYERS**,** including the Washington Department of Health and Human Services (for Medicaid), the Department of Labor and Industries, and Medicare Part D plans. (See Chapter 8)

PHARMACY SITE ACCREDITATION. Pharmacies may voluntarily choose to become accredited by one of several organizations, in which case they are subject to self-study requirements and peer-review, including on-site reviews. In some cases, accreditation is necessary to be eligible for payment for certain services. As discussed below, hospitals and their pharmacies are accredited by the Joint Commission or ACHC. Example organizations for non-institutional pharmacies include:

Center for Pharmacy Practice Accreditation (CPPA)[135] – community and ambulatory pharmacies; specialty pharmacies; telehealth pharmacy practice

URAC[136] – community pharmacies; drug therapy management programs; mail service pharmacies; pharmacy core programs

Community Health Accreditation Partner (CHAP)[137] – home medical equipment providers; ambulatory or LTC pharmacies; infusion therapy providers

Accreditation Commission for Health Care (ACHC)[138] – specialty and infusion pharmacy; compounding pharmacy (see PCAB below); community pharmacy; LTC pharmacy; durable medical equipment providers (eligibility for federal DMEPOS contracts)

DONATIONS OF PRESCRIPTION DRUGS AND SUPPLIES FOR FREE REDISTRIBUTION (RCW 69.70) – THE "CANCER CAN'T CHARITABLE PHARMACY ACT"

Pharmacies in Washington may receive donated drugs from any practitioner, pharmacist, medical facility, drug manufacturer, or wholesaler to be redistributed to uninsured or needy individuals without fee or compensation. Drugs may also be donated by the patient or the patient's agent under certain circumstances. A pharmacy electing to participate in the program may also transfer donated drugs to another pharmacy, pharmacist, or prescribing practitioner for use pursuant to the program. Priority for distribution of the drug is to uninsured individuals, or, if no uninsured individuals have been identified, another person expressing a need may receive the drug. "Uninsured" means that the individual does not have private or public health insurance; or the insurance does not cover the particular drug.

Donated drugs must meet the following criteria:

- In the original sealed and tamper evident packaging, or, opened, if the package contains intact single unit doses;
- Bears an expiration date more than 6 months from the time donated;
- The drug or supplies are inspected by a pharmacist before dispensing and determined not to be misbranded or adulterated;
- The drug meets other safety standards established by the department; and
- If the drug is donated by a patient or representative, the package bears a time temperature indicator that allows the pharmacist to determine it was properly stored, and is accompanied by a donor form adopted by the department that releases the drug for distribution and certifies that the drug has not been opened, used, adulterated, or misbranded. A "time temperature indicator" is a device or smart label that shows the accumulated time-temperature history of the product throughout the entire supply chain.
- Knowledge of recalls, must be communicated between pharmacies distributing or collecting the drugs and the recipient must comply with the recall notice.

Donated drugs may only be distributed pursuant to a prescription. Drugs for programs requiring registration (e.g., REMS programs) may only be dispensed to patients who are properly registered and eligible.

No dispensing fee or other charge may be made for distributing the drugs. Certain types of immunity from suit is provided to manufacturers who donate the drug or to other donors. Pharmacies have immunity as well if they comply with Commission rules , maintain records of donated and dispensed drugs, and identify themselves to the public as participating in the program.

"Nothing in this chapter restricts the use of samples by a practitioner during the course of the practitioner's duties at a medical facility or pharmacy."

The statute was first passed in 2013, and changes became effective on January 1, 2017, and the Commission has announced it will develop rules.

NON-RESIDENT PHARMACIES (NRP). Pharmacies in other states that deliver medications to patients in Washington must register with the Commission as Non-Resident Pharmacies. The statutory authority of the Commission to conduct these registrations is contained in RCW 18.64.350 through RCW 18.64.480.

NRPS MUST BE LICENSED AND REGULATED by the Board of Pharmacy or its equivalent in their home state or *province of Canada**.

REQUIREMENTS FOR NRPS INCLUDE THE FOLLOWING:

- A TOLL FREE NUMBER must be provided during operating hours so that Washington residents may communicate with the out-of-state pharmacy. This number must be printed on the prescription label. (Note: in-state pharmacies are not required to place their phone number on the prescription label, though almost all do.)
- NRPs must MAINTAIN PATIENT PROFILES in compliance with Washington regulations,
- NRPs must PROVIDE INFORMATION TO PATIENTS as required by Washington law.

NRPS MUST DESIGNATE AN AGENT IN WASHINGTON for service of process (the receipt of legal claims, subpoenas, etc.), and must SUBMIT INFORMATION WHEN REQUESTED CONCERNING CONTROLLED SUBSTANCES SHIPPED TO A WASHINGTON RESIDENT; or submit to an on-site inspection of the pharmacy's records.

DISCIPLINE OR FINES. The Department may discipline or fine a NRP if the home state Board of Pharmacy or *provincial authority** fails to initiate an investigation on a matter referred to that state *or province** by Washington within 45 days. Note that the Commission does not have authority to issue fines to in-state pharmacies.[139]

CANADIAN NRPS INCLUDED IN STATUTE BUT CANNOT BE LICENSED DUE TO FEDERAL LAW. The 2005 Legislature passed legislation to deal with importation of drugs from outside the US, an enacted a scheme to license Canadian pharmacies. RCW 18.64.350(3) was amended to read, "... all out-of-state pharmacies, <u>including those located in Canada</u>, that provide services to Washington residents shall be licensed by the department of health ..." However, because the federal Food, Drug and Cosmetic Act (see Chapter 4) preempts state law, a waiver would need to be issued by the FDA to allow this to take place. The Washington request was denied by the FDA on March 17, 2006 (see section on wholesalers, below). (See also chapter 4) Thus, any sections of the rules listed above or below that related to Canada are inoperative and are marked by an *asterisk (*)*.

GENERAL ISSUES RELATING TO NON-AMBULATORY CARE PHARMACIES

Pharmacies operated by entities other than retail businesses are typically regulated under a somewhat different set of assumptions than community or ambulatory care pharmacies. Not the least important reason for this is that the patient being seen in these non-ambulatory care settings is in a different position regarding responsibility for his or her care than the normal ambulatory patient. In addition, the role of the pharmacist has traditionally been integrated into the care setting along with other care providers in a different manner than for community-based pharmacy practitioners.

MULTIPLE REGULATORS. Several agencies in addition to the Pharmacy Commission regulate non-ambulatory care pharmacies, which are located in institutional settings. Examples are:

THE JOINT COMMISSION[140] (formerly known as JCAHO or "jayco"). Although The Joint Commission does accredit ambulatory care organizations, such accreditation is not currently applied to community pharmacies; however, pharmacies in certain kinds of ambulatory clinics may be involved in a Joint Commission accreditation. Other accreditation organizations are also active in the non-ambulatory space, including the Accreditation Commission on Health Care (ACHC)[141] and URAC[142].

THE BOARD OF HEALTH

MEDICAID (HEALTH CARE AUTHORITY IN WA)

MEDICARE

TYPES OF FACILITIES. The state defines a wide variety of health care and medical facilities, not all of which have pharmacies, but most of which store, use, or administer drugs and devices.

HEALTH CARE FACILITIES defined in RCW 70.38.025(6) include: hospices, hospice care centers, hospitals, psychiatric hospitals, nursing homes, kidney disease treatment centers, ambulatory surgical facilities, and home health agencies.

RCW 70.40.020 further defines the following:

"HOSPITAL" includes public health centers and general, tuberculosis, mental, chronic disease, and other types of hospitals, and related facilities, such as laboratories, outpatient departments, nurses' home and training facilities, and central service facilities operated in connection with hospitals;

"PUBLIC HEALTH CENTER" means a publicly owned facility for the provision of public health services, including related facilities such as laboratories, clinics, and administrative offices operated in connection with public health centers;

"MEDICAL FACILITIES" means diagnostic or diagnostic and treatment centers, rehabilitation facilities and nursing homes as those terms are defined in [Title VI of the Federal Public Health Service Act].

"REHABILITATION FACILITIES." The federal definition of "rehabilitation facilities" is found in 42 CFR 124.2: "a facility which is operated for the primary purpose of assisting in the rehabilitation of disabled persons through an integrated program of medical evaluation and services, and psychological, social, or vocational evaluation and services ... and either the facility is operated in connection with a hospital, or all medical and related health services are prescribed by, or are under the general direction of persons licensed to practice medicine or surgery in the State."

"RESIDENTIAL TREATMENT FACILITIES" in Washington are "licensed, community-based facilities that provide 24-hour inpatient care for people with mental health and/or chemical dependency disorders in a residential treatment setting." RFTs are licensed under RCW 71.12, along with other establishments for treatment of mental illness. Regulations governing RTFs, including medication management, are found in WAC 246-337. In 2016, the Pharmacy Commission issued Policy Procedure No. 46, in which it found that RTFs are eligible to use automated drug dispensing devices (ADDS) if they are "rehabilitation facilities" associated with a hospital or supervised by a physician, or if they obtain a health care entity license.[143]

HEALTH CARE ENTITIES (HCEs) are organizations that "provide health care services in a setting that is not otherwise licensed by the state to acquire or possess legend drugs." They are defined in the Legend Drug Act (RCW 18.64.011(15)) HCEs include outpatient surgery centers, residential treatment facilities, or freestanding cardiac care center. Individual practitioner or multipractitioner clinics are not required to be licensed as HCEs, but may elect to do so. HCEs also do not include a practitioner clinic identified as associated with a hospital that acquires or possesses legend drugs under the hospital's pharmacy license; such a clinic is known as a hospital pharmacy associated clinic (HPAC).

IN-HOME SERVICES AGENCIES are licensed and regulated by the Department of Health under RCW 70.127, these entities include home health agencies and hospice agencies. The department's rules governing use of legend drugs or controlled substances "shall reference and be consistent with pharmacy quality assurance commission rules." (RCW 70.127.130)

REGULATORY SCHEME The regulatory scheme for institutional pharmacies differs in important ways from that applied to community pharmacies.

It is more likely to be POLICY DRIVEN. Institutional pharmacies establish policy and procedure manuals that govern their activities. Increasingly, however, the Commission is trying to use a policy-based approach more often in community pharmacies as well, such as the Ancillary Personnel Utilization Plan requirement.

The scheme relies on INSTITUTIONAL CHECKS AND BALANCES, counting on nurses and physicians, for example, to be active participants with the pharmacist in assuring the quality of the drug use process, and in setting policy regarding drug use in the institution.

The institution often follows A MEDICAL STAFF MODEL, in which the physicians who have admitting privileges in the institution participate in governing health care services. Hospitals have a physician who is Chief of Staff. Nursing homes have a physician who is Medical Director.

AN INSTITUTIONAL COMMITTEE IS RESPONSIBLE FOR SETTING DRUG USE POLICY. In hospitals, this is usually called the Pharmacy & Therapeutics Committee; in nursing homes it is the Pharmaceutical Services Committee. The pharmacist is often the secretary of this committee.

There are key differences in labeling requirements, distribution systems, and methods for accounting for and disposing of controlled substances.

HOSPITALS. (WAC 246-873)

DIRECTOR OF PHARMACY. Each hospital pharmacy must have a Director of Pharmacy, who is "qualified by education, training, and experience." The hospital must define this position and its responsibilities in hospital policy. The rules allow small hospitals to contract with a part-time pharmacist to serve as director. (WAC 246-863-040) The Commission may be moving away from using the term "director of pharmacy" in future rule revisions; its recent rewrite of WAC 246-873-060 referred instead to "responsible manager."

There must be sufficient supportive personnel to assist the director.

The director, or his or her pharmacist designee, must manage all the activities of the hospital pharmacy. Each decentralized unit of a hospital pharmacy must have a pharmacist supervisor.

PHARMACY SERVICES MUST BE PROVIDED ON A 24-HOUR BASIS. This requires either full-time pharmacy staffing or the availability of on-call pharmacists in accordance with a policy to provide for services.

If, under the policy, a pharmacist is not present after hours, a nurse may enter the pharmacy to obtain a needed drug. The nurse entitled to enter the pharmacy must be designated by the pharmacy and the hospital, and only one such nurse may be designated for a given shift. (WAC 246-873-050)

- Written policy and procedures must be in place to guide the designated nurse.
- The stock container from which the nurse drew the drug must be left along with the drug order for inspection by the pharmacist.
- Only enough drug to sustain the patient until the pharmacy opens may be removed by the nurse.

Note that this rule is different from the rule related to emergency outpatient medications distributed by emergency departments.

IMPORTANT DEFINITIONS RELATED TO HOSPITAL PHARMACY (WAC 246-863-010).

The Commission has defined several terms in ways that are consistent with hospital practice and need. Among those that are important for pharmacists to learn are the following:

"AUTHENTICATED" OR "AUTHENTICATION" means authorization of a written entry in a record by means of a signature which shall include, minimally, first initial, last name, and title.

"DRUG ADMINISTRATION" means an act in which a single dose of a prescribed drug or biological is given to a patient by an authorized person in accordance with all laws and regulations governing such acts. The complete act of administration entails removing an individual dose from a previously dispensed, properly labeled container (including a unit dose container) reviewing it with a verified transcription, a direct copy, or the original medical practitioner's orders, giving the individual dose to the proper patient, and properly recording the time and dose given.

"PROTOCOL" means a written set of guidelines

"SELF-ADMINISTRATION OF DRUGS" means that a patient administers or takes his/her own drugs from properly labeled containers: Provided, that the facility maintains the responsibility for seeing that the drugs are used correctly and that the patient is responding appropriately.

EMERGENCY OUTPATIENT MEDICATIONS.

The 2015 Legislature made several changes related to pharmacy services in hospital emergency rooms and clinics, including a new section, RCW 70.41.480, concerning emergency outpatient medications. Under the revised statute, hospitals may allow a practitioner to prescribe prepackaged emergency medications to patients being discharged from hospital emergency departments. A practitioner or registered nurse may distribute such drugs to the patient pursuant to the prescription or order:

- During times when community or outpatient hospital pharmacy services are not available within 15 miles by road, or
- When, in the judgment of the practitioner and consistent with hospital policies and procedures, the patient has no reasonable ability to reach the local community or outpatient pharmacy.

The hospital may allow this in its policy and procedures only when the director of pharmacy in collaboration with the medical staff develops the following policies and procedures:

- A list preapproved by the director of the types of emergency medications to be prepackaged;
- All medications must be prepared by a pharmacist or under the supervision of a pharmacist;
- Specific criteria under which emergency medications may be prescribed and dispensed;
- Practitioners and dispensing nurses must be trained on the types of medications available and the circumstances under which they may be distributed to a patient;

- Prescriptions for the emergency medications must be maintained in writing or electronically within the patient's records;
- No more than 48-hours' supply of medications may be distributed, unless community or hospital outpatient pharmacy services will not be available within 48 hours, in which case up to a 96-hour supply may be allowed;
- Assure that prepackaged medications are stored securely near the emergency department such that entry to the pharmacy is not required;
- Distribution of emergency medications to the patient may only occur after the practitioner has counseled the patient on the medication.

OPIOID REVERSAL DRUGS. As discussed further in Chapter 4, RCW 69.41 allows improved access to naloxone and other drugs to reverse opioid overdose. RCW 69.41.095 allows practitioners to directly provide patients with reversal medications. In light of the legislative imperative, the Commission has interpreted the statute to allow emergency department practitioners, or their agents by protocol, to distribute opioid reversal agents to emergency department patients at discharge, notwithstanding the provisions of RCW 70.41.480 or WAC 246-873-060.[144] "The Commission's policy is that current state law authorizes a hospital emergency department, pursuant to a practitioner's prescription, standing order, or protocol, to dispense, distribute, or deliver opioid overdose medication to people at risk or to first responders, family members, or other persons or entities in a position to assist such at-risk people."

The Pharmacy Commission revised WAC 246-873-060, effective January 19, 2017:

> **WAC 246-873-060 Provision of emergency department discharge medications when pharmacy services are unavailable.** The responsible manager, as defined in WAC 246-869-070, of a hospital or free standing emergency department may, in collaboration with the appropriate medical staff committee of the hospital, develop policies and procedures in compliance with RCW 70.41.480 which must be implemented to provide discharge medications to patients released from hospital emergency departments during hours when community or outpatient hospital pharmacy services are not available. The delivery of a single dose for immediate administration to the patient is not subject to this regulation. Such policies shall allow the practitioner or registered nurse to distribute medications, pursuant to the policies and procedures, as specified in RCW 70.41.480 and the following:
>
> (1) An order of a practitioner authorized to prescribe a drug is presented. Oral or electronically transmitted orders must be verified by the practitioner in writing within seventy-two hours.
>
> (2) A department credentialed pharmacy technician or a licensed pharmacist shall prepackage the medication. Medication prepackaged by a department credentialed pharmacy technician must be checked by a licensed pharmacist. The prepackaged medication must contain any supplemental material provided and an affixed label that contains:
>
> (a) Name, address, and telephone number of the hospital.
>
> (b) The name of the drug (as required by chapter 246-899 WAC), strength and number of units.
>
> (c) Cautionary information as required for patient safety and information on use is provided.
>
> (d) An expiration date after which the patient should not use the medication.
>
> (e) Directions for use.
>
> (3) No more than a forty-eight hour supply is provided to the patient except when the pharmacist has informed appropriate hospital personnel that normal services will not be available within forty-eight hours. A final quantity of medication supply shall not exceed ninety-six hours.
>
> (4) The practitioner or registered nurse will ensure the container is labeled before presenting to the patient and shows the following:
>
> (a) Name of the patient;

(b) Complete directions for use, which should include at a minimum the number of units distributed, frequency, and route of administration;

(c) Date of distribution;

(d) Identifying number (i.e., RX number or similar indicator)

(e) Name of prescribing practitioner;

(f) Initials of the practitioner or registered nurse who distributed the medication.

(5) A registered nurse or practitioner will distribute prepackaged emergency medications to patients only after a practitioner has counseled the patient on the medication.

(6) The original hard copy or electronically transmitted order by the practitioner is retained for verification by the pharmacist after completion by the practitioner or registered nurse and shall contain:

(a) Name and address of patient if not already listed in the medical records;

(b) Date of issuance;

(c) Units issued;

(d) Initials of the practitioner or registered nurse.

(7) The medications distributed as discharge medications must be stored in compliance with the laws concerning security and access. They must be stored in or near the emergency department in such a manner as to preclude the necessity for entry into the pharmacy when pharmacy services are not available.[145]

HOSPITAL PHARMACY GENERAL STANDARDS for physical requirements, access, drug storage, and flammable storage are specified in WAC 246-873-070. They include:

- Adequate space and related facilities:
- Appropriate transportation and communications facilities for drug distribution throughout the hospital.
- Space and equipment for secure, environmentally controlled storage of drugs and pharmaceutical supplies.
- Space for management and clinical functions.
- Space and equipment for the preparation of parenteral admixtures, radiopharmaceuticals, and other sterile compounding and packaging.
- Controls to prevent unauthorized access to pharmacy department areas.
- Drugs shall be stored under proper conditions of sanitation, temperature, light, moisture, ventilation, segregation, and security. The Commission, in coordination with other DOH divisions, has amplified these regulations with a position statement on "Medication Security in Hospitals."[146]
- Adherence to proper storage policies and practices is a joint responsibility of the Director of Pharmacy and the Director of Nursing.
- Locked storage units or locked medication carts must be provided on each nursing unit.
- Policies and procedures for storage and disposal of flammable materials must be in place and in accordance with applicable local and state fire regulations.

SECURITY CONCERNS. In the wake of national concerns about controlled substance abuse, the DEA and the Commission have begun to hold pharmacy managers and pharmacists responsible for failure to take necessary steps to prevent diversion and theft. In 2016, responding to the theft of several hundred thousand tablets of narcotics by an employee of a hospital, the Commission entered an order censuring the hospital pharmacy director for failing to institute "a higher level of vigilance toward storage of controlled substances than was in place," and which the Commission found was required by the complexity and high volume of prescriptions in the outpatient pharmacy. The pharmacist paid a $1,000 fine and was required to prepare and deliver a presentation on the nature of the diversion and the remedial measures that have been put in place. The Commission recognized that the director had no direct involvement in the diversion, and cited several mitigating factors in reaching its decision to restrict the order to a censure, but still held that as the responsible pharmacy manager, the ultimate responsibility rested on the pharmacist's shoulders. See Chapter 5 for a more complete discussion of the steps expected of pharmacy managers to protect against diversion.

RECOMMENDED AND REQUIRED ACTIVITIES. The regulations set forth required activities, and recommended activities of the hospital pharmacy relating to drug distribution and control. (WAC 246-873-080)

MUSTS – REQUIRED ACTIVITIES

The pharmacy department of the hospital, under the direction of the director of pharmacy, must assure or provide:

- Control of all drugs throughout the hospital
- Monthly inspections of all areas where drugs are stored or used
- Monitoring of drug therapy (see again the definition in WAC 246-863-110, discussed in Chapter 2).
- Provision of drug information to patients, physicians, and others
- Surveillance and reporting of adverse drug reactions and drug defects.

SHOULDS – RECOMMENDED ACTIVITIES

The following activities are recommended by the regulation, but not required, to be performed by the hospital's pharmacy department:

- Obtaining and recording drug use histories and participation in discharge planning
- Preparation of all sterile products, except in emergencies
- Distribution and control of radiopharmaceuticals
- Administration of drugs
- Prescribing

UPDATED POLICY AND PROCEDURES MANUAL. The director must develop (in collaboration with the medical staff, nursing service, and the hospital) policy and procedures for the pharmacy, and must annually update these policies and procedures. As noted in the section on Commission inspections of hospitals (below), failure to maintain updated manuals is one of the most common faults found in hospital pharmacy inspections.

LABELING REQUIREMENTS differ for inpatient and outpatient drugs (see also Chapter 4).

INPATIENT MEDICATIONS must show the

- drug name,
- strength,
- expiration dates as appropriate, and
- additional cautionary labeling

OUTPATIENT MEDICATIONS must be labeled in accordance with outpatient pharmacy requirements specified in RCW 18.64.246.

PARENTERAL MEDICATIONS must be labeled with

- name and location of the patient,
- name and amounts of drugs added,
- appropriate dating, and

- Initials of the personnel who prepared and checked the solution

PHARMACIST REVIEW OF ORDERS. Except in emergencies, no medication may be distributed unless the pharmacist has reviewed the original order or a direct copy of the order. (WAC 246-873-080 (6))

REMOTE ORDER ENTRY

Many hospitals, particularly in rural settings, are utilizing telepharmacy services to provide pharmacist entry of orders during evening and weekend hours. Remote order entry involves a pharmacist at a remote site reviewing and entering orders that allow administration of drugs at the hospital, often using automated dispensing devices. The Commission reviews proposals for remote order entry on a case-by-case basis, and typically require follow-up reports following implementation of the proposal. Details of these reviews may be found in published minutes of the Commission. For example, the March 2014 minutes reflect Commission review of a follow-up report on remote order entry services provided by Providence Centralia Hospital to Olympic Memorial Hospital (Sequim, WA); a proposal by Providence Centralia Hospital to provide similar services to Providence St. Mary Medical Center (Walla Walla, WA); and a proposal from Forks Community Hospital to use the telepharmacy services provided by Medication Review, Inc., of Spokane, WA.[147]

ORDERS VERSUS PRESCRIPTIONS

A PRESCRIPTION is a written or verbal instruction from an authorized prescriber for an individual patient to permit dispensing of a drug or device. If verbal, it is reduced to writing by the pharmacist or other dispenser.

An ORDER is a verbal or written communication by an authorized prescriber, recorded in a medical record, which authorizes treatment, procedures, tests, or other facets of a patient's care in a clinic, hospital, or other patient care setting.

ADMINISTRATION OF DRUGS. (WAC 246-873-090)

Drugs may only be administered subject to an order from a licensed practitioner who has been granted clinical privileges in the hospital.

This is a characteristic of institutional practice; before a practitioner can admit patients or issue orders, that person must be admitted to the medical staff with privileges to issue orders. This is typically the responsibility of the medical staff credentials committee.

Pharmacists in hospitals with prescriptive authority must also be granted clinical privileges before their orders may be implemented.

VERBAL ORDERS. Verbal orders for drugs shall only be issued in emergency or unusual circumstances and shall be accepted only by a licensed nurse, pharmacist, or physician, and shall be immediately recorded and signed by the person receiving the order. Such orders shall be authenticated by the prescribing practitioner within 48 hours.

In 2014, the Nursing Quality Assurance Commission issued an advisory opinion that reiterated that nurses may carry out medical regimens on the basis of verbal orders, and reiterated the requirement in WAC 246-873-090 that the verbal order must be authenticated by the prescriber within 48 hours.[148]

MEDICATIONS BROUGHT IN TO HOSPITAL BY OR FOR PATIENTS

Written procedures and policies must be developed for dealing with drugs brought into the hospital by or for patients. Although many hospitals do not allow patients' drugs from home to be used in their care while in the institution, certain drugs obtainable only through specialty pharmacies are often needed in the hospital.

- Such drugs may only be administered if properly ordered. Prior to use, a pharmacist must examine the drugs to identify them and assure they meet quality standards of the hospital pharmacy.
- Such drugs, if stored in the hospital and not used during the patient stay, must be packaged and sealed and returned to the patient at discharge or given to the patient's family upon discharge.
- The hospital may develop policies to not return such drugs if it would be dangerous to the patient.
- Policies must be developed for destruction of non-used, non-returned patient medication.

SELF-ADMINISTRATION OF MEDICATIONS (SAM) may only be done in accordance with approved protocols and a formal policy and a program of self-care or rehabilitation. The policy developed by the Director of Pharmacy must be approved by the administration and by medical and nursing staff units. Note: SAM protocols are not the same as protocols for using Patient Controlled Analgesia (PCA).

RECORDS OF DRUGS ADMINISTERED TO PATIENTS

All medications administered to inpatients shall be recorded in the patient's medical record. (WAC 246-873-080 (9))

A PERPETUAL INVENTORY OF SCHEDULE II drugs must be maintained, with policies established regarding the control, storage, and distribution of other controlled substances. Specific requirements are discussed later in Chapter 5.

MECHANICAL DEVICES. The WAC formerly contained two regulations that deal with the use of automated drug dispensing devices in hospitals: MECHANICAL DEVICES IN HOSPITALS (WAC 246-869-120), adopted in 1992, and AUTOMATED DRUG DISTRIBUTION DEVICES (WAC 246-872), adopted in 2006. In January 2017, the Commission repealed WAC 246-859-120 and WAC 246-872, replacing them with a new chapter on Pharmacy Technology, WAC 246-874 (see below.)

HANDLING OF RECALLS, REPORTING OF ADRS, AND REPORTING OF ERRORS, shall be according to a policy established by the Director of Pharmacy.

All adverse drug reactions shall be appropriately recorded in the patient's record and reported to the prescribing practitioner and to the pharmacy. (WAC 246-873-080 (10))

All drug errors shall upon discovery be recorded in an incident report and reported to the prescribing practitioner and to the pharmacy. (WAC 246-873-080 (11))

OTHER PROGRAMS AND RESPONSIBILITIES

The pharmacy is responsible several additional activities within the hospital, including:

- use of investigational drugs;
- participation in appropriate hospital committees; and
- establishing a quality assurance program

The Commission also states that the pharmacy department *should* develop clinical programs including the following

- maintenance of drug histories and participating in discharge planning,
- drug information service,
- prescribing, and/or

- administering of drugs

COMMISSION INSPECTION OF HOSPITAL PHARMACIES

The Commission has previously published the "Top Hospital Inspection Violations" on its web site.[149] Among the issues the Commission has highlighted for hospital pharmacies are the following:

- Policies and procedures: (1) are they in writing; (2) are they updated/reviewed annually; (3) is there documentation of the annual review; and (4) do they reflect current practice?
- Patient medication records: (1) do they maintain allergies, idiosyncrasies and chronic conditions in the patient record that may affect drug utilization; and (2) do pharmacists use that information to conduct prospective DUR?
- Ancillary personnel: does the pharmacy have a Commission approved utilization plan that reflects current practice procedures?
- Completed prescription labels: do the labels of containers dispensed by the pharmacy comply with all requirements?
- DEA Order Forms: (1) are DEA forms 222 filled out completely, including date(s) and quantity of drug(s) received; and (2) is a proper power-of-attorney designation available in the records when applicable?
- Necessary equipment: is equipment appropriate and in good repair, and are appropriate references available to the pharmacist, including the law book?

The Commission has more recently emphasized that it has now developed a list of functions that must be completed by a pharmacist in ALL hospital pharmacies, and that compliance with this list will be a feature of hospital pharmacy inspections:[150]

- Pharmacists monitoring of drug therapy. This would include daily visits by the pharmacist (to a hospital without full-time pharmacy services) unless there were no new patients or orders. Policies and procedures must be developed to include a description of the pharmacist's duties and a copy of the ongoing arrangement between the facility and the pharmacist.
- Monthly inspections of all units where medications are dispensed, administered, or stored. (This may be delegated to a staff pharmacist or pharmacy technician.[151])
- Report quality assurance and continuing quality improvements, ADRs, and incident reports.
- Monitor ordering, stocking, and security of all legend drugs.
- Verify emergency access to the pharmacy.
- Document and review emergency room dispensing.
- Review sterile IV admixture programs.

DOCUMENTATION REQUESTED AT TIME OF INSPECTION

In April 2014, the Commission announced that inspections of hospitals will now be conducted by 2 investigators, and will be unannounced. The Commission indicated that investigators can be expected to ask to see a number of documents during the inspection from the following list:[152]

- Policies and procedure manual, including policies and procedures for nursing unit inspections, controlled substance distribution records, controlled substance losses, emergency outpatient medications, emergency access to the pharmacy, quality assurance programs, IV preparation, and drug recalls
- 2 randomly selected surgery patient medical records
- 2 randomly selected general inpatient medical records
- Copies of the most recent Joint Commission and DOH survey reports
- Quality assurance summary reports for the past year
- Pharmacy & Therapeutics Committee meeting minutes

- Nursing inspection reports for the past 12 months
- Copies of any prescriptive authority protocols and resulting QA reports
- Pharmacy assistant/technician utilization plans
- Technician training records and IV recertification training records (including end product testing, glove fingertip sampling, etc.)
- DEA biennial inventory and schedule II perpetual inventory logs
- Controlled substances loss reports for the past 24 months
- Copies of controlled substances orders
- Controlled substances power-of-attorney forms
- Sterility and environmental testing reports of ISO classified space
- Investigational drug use protocols
- Refrigerator and freezer temperature logs
- Drug references
- A list of all pharmacy employees and verification of licenses/credentials

HOSPITAL PHARMACY ASSOCIATED CLINICS. The 2015 Legislature modified RCW 18.64 to allow hospitals to include associated individual or multipractitioner clinics on their pharmacy license,[153] but by the time of the 2016 legislative session, the Commission had failed to implement the change. The 2016 Legislature then reiterated the directive to the Commission to implement the statute and set a timeline for the Commission to promulgate the necessary regulations.[154]

RCW 18.64.043(2)(a) now specifies that hospitals licensed under RCW 70.41, and notwithstanding the definition of "hospital" in RCW 70.41.020, the license location may include

- Any individual practitioner's office or multipractitioner clinic
- Owned, operated, or under common control with a hospital and
- Identified by the hospital on the pharmacy application or renewal

The hospital must describe the type of services relevant to the practice of pharmacy provided at each such office or clinic as requested by the Commission.

The Commission promulgated WAC 246-873A as an emergency rule in August, 2016,[155] and re-promulgated the chapter, again as an emergency rule, in November, 2016,[156] in December 2017,[157] in April 2018,[158] and in July 2018.[159] The most recent re-enaction of the emergency rule was on November 29, 2018.[160]

DEFINITIONS (WAC 246-873A-010): Some definitions are repeated from other rules. Those specific to HPACs include the following:
(1) "Clinic" means a facility that is established primarily to furnish outpatient health care services by an individual or a group of practitioners. ...
(4) "Hospital pharmacy associated clinic" or "HPAC" means an individual practitioner's office or multipractitioner clinic owned, operated, or under common control of a parent hospital or health system, where the physical address of the office or clinic is identified on a hospital pharmacy license.
(5) "Parent hospital pharmacy" means a hospital licensed under 70.41 RCW, adding hospital pharmacy associated clinics to their hospital pharmacy license in accordance with chapter 18.64 RCW and this chapter. ...
(10) "Transfer" means to move drugs from the parent hospital pharmacy to the hospital pharmacy associated clinic.

LICENSING (WAC 246-873A-020): Parent hospitals applying for a new license or change of ownership may submit an addendum to add HPACs. Currently licensed hospitals may submit an addendum at any time to add HPACs.

Unlike the requirements for new pharmacy applications, there is no minimum time limit prior to a Commission meeting for adding HPACs. However, added HPACs must be inspected prior to approval. A hospital removing an HPAC must notify the Commission 15 days prior to the removal. When adding HPACs, the parent hospital must classify the clinic as either a Category 1 HPAC (does not perform sterile or non-sterile compounding), or Category 2 HPAC (does perform sterile or nonsterile compounding). The HPAC must obtain a DEA location registration if it intends to possess controlled substances.

The responsible manager must comply with WAC 246-873-080 requirements for establishing policies and specifications for drug procurement, distribution, and accountability, controlled substance accountability, and drug recalls in subchapters (3), (4), (7) and (8). Physical requirements must conform to applicable sections of WAC 246-873-070, in accordance with HPAC category type.

Transfer and control of drugs to the HPAC may be general drug transfer under the hospital's authority to engage in intracompany sales, or may transfer patient-specific drugs pursuant to a valid prescription or order recorded in the medical record. Nothing in the regulation prohibits practitioners from storing or dispensing drug samples according to law.

Labels dispensed to patients of the HPAC must comply with RCW 69.41.050 (see Chapter 4). Parenteral and irrigation solutions in Category 2 HPACs must include a label with at least: the patient name; name and amount of drugs added; a suitable beyond-use date; and initials of personnel who prepared and checked the solution.

Drugs may only be administered by Washington state credentialed personnel with their scope of practice, and only upon the valid order of a practitioner who is licensed to prescribe and has been granted clinical privileges.

HPACs will be inspected in conjunction with inspections of the associated hospital pharmacy. A representative sample of Category 1 HPACs will be selected by the investigator, and all Category 2 HPACs will be inspected.

LONG-TERM CARE FACILITIES (EXTENDED-CARE FACILITIES)

In 2012, there were about 58,500 regulated providers of long-term care in the United States, according to the CDC. This figure included 4,800 adult day care centers, 12,200 home health agencies, 3,700 hospices, 15,700 nursing homes, and 22,200 assisted living centers and residential communities. 8 million persons were provided long-term care services in 2012. In 2012, approximately 2.6% of persons aged 65 or over resided in nursing homes, approximately 1.5% were in residential care communities, and 0.4% utilized adult day care centers. 9.4% of seniors used the services of home health care agencies, and about 2.8% of persons 65 and over were served by hospices in 2012.[161] The oldest members of the Baby Boom generation turned 65 in 2011, and approximately 10,000 Boomers will turn 65 every day until 2029. Because the Boomers account for 26% of the population, by 2029 approximately 1 in 5 persons in the US will be 65 or older. Pharmacists graduating this year can expect that care for seniors will be a major feature of their career. Providing pharmacy services to this population will depend on where and in what setting the individual resides, and upon their ability to care for themselves.

TYPES OF SENIOR HOUSING

Seniors currently typically progress over time through three major types of senior housing:

INDEPENDENT LIVING, leading to ASSISTED LIVING, leading to NURSING CARE. For individuals who develop Alzheimer's disease or other forms of dementia, their nursing care may be rendered in a facility designed specifically to provide ALZHEIMER'S CARE.

CONTINUOUS CARE RETIREMENT COMMUNITIES (CCRCs), are integrated communities in which seniors may reside that allow them to move among these types of facilities easily while living in the same general location.

CONSIDERATIONS IN LIVING/CARE RESOURCES

A series of considerations that will affect the choice of residential type include the following:

- What is the patient's overall health?
- Activities of daily living (ADL) – what is the resident's need for assistance in performing daily tasks? For example, a person may be quite independent but unable to prepare his or her own meals due to cognitive issues.
- Desire for community activities (golf, social events, outings)
- Community services – how easily can the resident access shopping, entertainment, post-office, travel, etc.?
- Health services – what mix of health care services must be provided?
- Environment (degree of personal freedom) – does the resident require a lot of guidance and monitoring daily, or can he or she function with considerable personal freedom?

LEVELS OF CARE

The resident's specific health care conditions may require different levels of care, which may vary over time. For example, following an acute injury, the resident may require more assistance than when that injury has healed. The levels of care needed are also associated with levels of reimbursement available to provide the level of care.

BASIC CARE

Provides daily assistance with personal care, some level of supervision, and provision for safety needs at a level that may be provided by an aide or family caregiver.

SKILLED CARE

Involves care services provided by licensed providers with significant training. It may include supervised drug therapy or provision of specific treatment modalities. Skilled care is provided by nurses, respiratory therapists, physical therapists, and similar others.

SUB-ACUTE CARE

Is a form of skilled care that delivers comprehensive in-patient care for a patient who is recovering from an illness; it includes daily review and assessment of the patient's progress. This care may be provided following a hospitalization prior to release to independent or assisted living, or transfer to nursing care.

LONG-TERM CARE FACILITY NOMENCLATURE

Facilities serving individuals requiring long-term care may be generally described as either Long-Term Care Facilities (LTCFs) or Extended Care Facilities (ECFs).

INDEPENDENT LIVING IS PROVIDED BY

- Congregate care facilities
- Retirement communities
- Senior apartments

These types of facilities provide meals and activities, and the residents are responsible for managing their own medications. Some pharmacies provide special services to these communities, such as bingo cards (blister packs) or similar dosage organizers, but they follow all community pharmacy rules for dispensing drugs.

ASSISTED LIVING IS PROVIDED IN

- Adult family homes
- Board and care facilities
- Residential care facilities
- Adult living facilities
- Adult foster care
- Adult habitation centers (a legal term in WA)

Nurses may provide medication assistance to these residents, or they may assume responsibility for their own medications. Medication organization packaging that helps assure the resident takes the correct medication at the right time and dose is widely provided to residents by pharmacies – again under the rules governing ambulatory dispensing.

SPECIALIZED PACKAGING FOR ASSISTED LIVING

Washington pharmacy rules allow for "Med-pack" containers, which it defines as follows: "'Med-pack' containers are prepared under immediate supervision of a pharmacist for a specific patient comprising a series of containers and containing one or more prescribed solid oral dosage forms including multifill blister packs" (WAC 246-869-235(4))

The Commission allows pharmacies to provide "customized patient medication packages" by use of med-pack containers. (WAC 246-869-255) The following requirements apply to this packaging:

- Original bulk bottle must stay in pharmacy
- No more than a 31-day supply may be supplied per container
- Patient or agent requests non-child resistant container

The label must contain the following items that are also required on regular ambulatory prescriptions:

- Pharmacy name and address
- Patient's name
- Drug name, strength, and quantity
- Directions
- Serial prescription number, date
- Prescriber's name, pharmacist's initials

NURSING CARE IS PROVIDED in SNF's – skilled nursing facilities. Washington Pharmacy Commission rules refer to these facilities as extended-care facilities

PRACTICE OF PHARMACY – LONG-TERM CARE SETTINGS: 2016 LEGISLATION

Among many mandates from the Legislature to the Commission in 2016 was SSB 6203,[162] which established revised standards for pharmacy services in LTCFs. The legislation included:

AMENDMENTS TO RCW 18.64.011 – definitions were added for the following terms:
"Chart order" – a lawful order for a drug or device entered on the chart or medical record of an inpatient or resident of an institutional facility by a practitioner or his or her designated agent.
"Closed door long-term care pharmacy" – a pharmacy that provides pharmaceutical care to a defined and exclusive group of patients who have access to the services of the pharmacy because they are treated by or have an affiliation with a long-term care facility or hospice program, and that is not a retailer of goods to the general public.

"Hospice program" – a hospice program certified or paid by Medicare under Title XVIII of the federal social security act, or a hospice program licensed under chapter 70.127 RCW.
"Institutional facility" – any organization whose primary purpose is to provide a physical environment for patients to obtain health care services including, but not limited to, services in a hospital, long-term care facility, hospice program, mental health facility, drug abuse treatment center, residential habilitation center, or a local, state, or federal correction facility.
"Long-term care facility" – a nursing home licensed under RCW 18.51, assisted living facility licensed under RCW 18.20, or an adult family home licensed under RCW 70.128.
"Shared pharmacy services" – a system that allows a participating pharmacist or pharmacy pursuant to a request from another participating pharmacist or pharmacy to process or fill a prescription or drug order, which may include but is not necessarily limited to preparing, packaging, labeling, date entry, compounding for specific patients, dispensing, performing drug utilization review, conducting claims adjudication, obtaining refill authorizations, reviewing therapeutic interventions, or reviewing chart orders.

NEW SECTION CLARIFYING CHART ORDERS

A new section was added to RCW 69.41.550. A "chart order" must be considered a valid prescription if it contains

- The full name of the patient
- The date of issuance
- The name, strength, and dosage form of the drug prescribed
- Directions for use, and
- An authorized signature

Written orders must contain the prescribing practitioner's signature, *or the signature of the practitioner's authorized agent,* including the name of the prescribing practitioner. Electronic or digital orders must contain either the electronic signature of the prescriber, *or the digital signature of the prescriber's authorized agent,* including the name of the prescriber. The Commission has determined that chart orders may only be used for legend drugs – not controlled substances. See below.[163]

A licensed nurse, pharmacist, or physician practicing in a long-term care facility or hospice program may act as the prescriber's agent – without a specific agency relationship – for the purposes of this chapter, to

- document a chart order in the patient's medical record on behalf of the prescriber pending the prescriber's signature, or
- communicate a prescription to a pharmacy telephonically, via facsimile, or electronically (fax of a controlled substances prescription signed by the prescriber would conform to the Commission's guidance)
- the communication to a dispenser by the prescriber's agent has the same force and effect as if communicated directly by the authorized practitioner.

RCW 69.41.055 was amended to provide that the electronic or digital of the agent constitutes a valid electronic communication of prescription information.

EMERGENCY KITS AND SUPPLEMENTAL DOSE KITS

Limited quantities of drugs may be supplied by a pharmacist or pharmacy to a nursing home or hospice program without a prescription for emergency administration. Note, these are specific to nursing homes (E-kits and SD-kits) or hospice programs (E-kits), and are not available for other long-term care settings (e.g., assisted living).

- Drugs provided in emergency kits must be limited to those typically required to meet immediate needs

- Supplemental dose kits may be provided to nursing homes that are using unit dose drug distribution.
- Emergency kits and supplemental dose kits must be stored in a locked room, container, or device to prevent unauthorized access and proper storage environment.
- Administration of drugs from emergency kits or supplemental dose kits must be pursuant to a valid prescription or chart order
- The types and quantities of drugs in emergency kits and supplemental dose kits must be determined by a pharmacy services committee of the nursing home or hospice program. The pharmacy services committee must consist of a pharmacist, a physician or ARNP, and appropriate clinical or administrative personnel as set forth in rules adopted by the Commission.
- An RN or LPN "operating under appropriate direction and supervision by a pharmacist" may restock an emergency kit or supplemental dose kit.

PHARMACY SERVICES

- Valid chart orders as defined in the statute are sufficient to allow a pharmacy to resupply a legend drug to a patient at a nursing home or hospice program as long as the order is signed by the prescriber, is not time limited, and has not been discontinued.
- Shared pharmacy services are allowed to ensure timely availability of drugs to patients in the facility or program.

  First-dose dispensing. The LTC pharmacy may arrange for a local pharmacy to dispense and deliver a first dose or partial fill of a new chart order. It is not necessary for the LTC pharmacy to "fully transfer" the prescription to the supplying pharmacy, as would otherwise be required for prescription transfers. The supplying pharmacy must retain a copy of the order, and must notifying the LTC pharmacy of the quantity and service provided.

  Approval of the facility or program is required to outsource shared pharmacy services

- Drug repackaging and re-dispensing may be performed by a pharmacy for unused drugs returned by a LTC or hospice program in "per-use, blister packaging, whether in unit dose or modified unit dose form, except as prohibited by federal law."

  The Commission is directed to adopt rules for the "safe and efficient repackaging, reuse, and disposal of unused drugs returned to a pharmacy" from an LTC or hospice program, taking into consideration the "acceptance and dispensing requirements of RCW 69.70.050 (1), (2), and (5)" (the statute dealing with donations of drugs and supplies – see above).

In September 2016, the Commission issued a preproposal statement of inquiry (CR-101) indicating potential rule making regarding long-term care pharmacies to comply with the revised Chapter 69.70 RCW.[164] In October 2018, the Commission withdrew the CR-101 and indicated that revisions would be part of the ongoing rules rewrite.[165] Until the revised rules are in place, the existing rules discussed below must be interpreted in light of the changes to the underlying statute, and areas of potential interpretation are indicated below by an asterisk (*).

Commission Policy on Chart Orders. While awaiting revision of its rules for LTC facilities, the Commission has issued a guidance document that indicates the Commission does not believe that the agent's signature can validly communicate a chart order for controlled substances.[166] This is discussed in more detail in Chapter 5.

EXTENDED-CARE FACILITIES (WAC 246-865) (See also WAC 388-97-1300)

MUST PROVIDE DRUGS TO RESIDENTS

ECFs must ensure the provision of TIMELY DELIVERY OF DRUGS and biologicals to provide care for patients (WAC 246-865-060). The facility may OPERATE ITS OWN LICENSED PHARMACY; or may have WRITTEN AGREEMENT(S) WITH ONE OR MORE LICENSED PHARMACIES to provide pharmaceutical consultant services. WAC 388-97-1300 provides that a PATIENT HAS A RIGHT TO CHOICE OF PHARMACY, provided that the pharmacy timely delivers drugs in packaging appropriate to the facility's distribution system. *Shared pharmacy services provisions may affect this section.

NO MEDICATIONS MAY BE ADMINISTERED UNLESS ORDERED BY A PHYSICIAN. As in hospitals, orders are typically entered into the patient's chart by the prescriber or by a licensed nurse receiving the order from the prescriber. The rule is silent on how the nurse then communicates these orders to the pharmacy. The exact method of transmission of new and continuing orders to the pharmacy must be detailed in the facility's policy and procedures as approved by the pharmaceutical services committee. In crafting these policies, attention must be paid to state as well as DEA rules regarding prescriptions for controlled substances. *Pharmacists practicing at the facility are allowed to be the prescriber's agent under the 2016 law.

In April 2011, the Board issued a clarification by e-mail to licensees concerning nursing home transmission of orders to pharmacies, which stated, in part:

The Board's extended care facility rule, chapter 246-865 WAC does not address the method of relaying new or refill drug orders to the pharmacy when received by the licensed nurse in writing or verbally from the prescriber as authorized in WAC 246-865-060(7)(e). WAC 246-865-060 (1)(b) requires all nursing homes without a licensed pharmacy or employing a director of pharmaceutical services to have a written agreement with one or more licensed pharmacists who provide pharmaceutical consultant services. The entire spectrum of pharmaceutical services for the nursing homes are the responsibility of the staff pharmacist or consultant pharmacist – including the process, policies and procedures for conveying prescription orders.[167]

PHARMACEUTICAL SERVICES COMMITTEE

ECFs must establish a Pharmaceutical Services Committee, which performs a function for the nursing home similar to the P&T Committees in hospitals. This committee sets policies for use of drugs in the facility.

MEMBERSHIP - THE COMMITTEE MUST CONSIST OF

- At least one staff or consultant pharmacist
- A physician – generally the "medical director"
- Director of nursing or his or her designee
- The facility administrator or his or her designee

RESPONSIBILITIES

The committee must develop written policies and procedures to assure:

- Safe and effective drug therapy
- Distribution of drugs
- Control of drugs
- Use of drugs
- P&P are current and followed in practice
- Procedures must be established for recording and reporting of medication errors and adverse drug reactions

WRITTEN REFERENCE MATERIALS regarding drugs must be available to staff regarding

- Use of medications
- Adverse reactions
- Toxicology
- Poison control center information

STAFF PHARMACIST OR CONSULTANT PHARMACIST shall be responsible for

- Provision of pharmaceutical services evaluations and recommendations to the administrative staff
- On-site reviews to ensure that drug handling and utilization are carried out in conformance with recognized standards of practice
- Regularly reviewing each resident's therapy to screen for potential or existing drug therapy problems, and documenting recommendations
- Provision of drug information to nursing home staff and physicians as needed
- Planning and participating in the nursing home staff development program ("in-service training")
- Consultation with other departments (nursing, housekeeping, etc.)

DRUG STORAGE AND SECURITY MUST INCLUDE:

- Proper sanitation, humidity, temperature, etc.
- Locked cabinets, rooms, or carts, accessible only to personnel licensed to administer or dispense drugs.
- Schedule III drugs must be stored separately from other legend drugs, but may be stored with Schedule II drugs.
- External use drugs stored separately from internal use drugs
- Keys to drug storage areas must be carried by on duty personnel who are licensed to administer drugs
- May use supplemental dose kit or emergency drug kit

LABELING OF MEDICATIONS (WAC 246-865-060(4))

The pharmacy serving a nursing home has a choice between 2 systems for packaging and labeling medications provided to patients. The facility will not intermix these systems.

"TRADITIONAL SYSTEM" – NOT UNIT DOSE

Packaging may be traditional prescription vials without child-resistant caps. These vials are labeled as if they were outpatient prescriptions, except:

- Directions for use need not be on label
- Controlled substances classification must be on label
- If compounded drug with controlled substances, the concentration/quantity of controlled substances must be shown.

Packaging may also be blister packs (bingo cards) or other modified unit dose packages; these must adhere to these labeling rules.

UNIT DOSE

Require individual storage compartment for each patient clearly labeled with patient name; individual doses do not include patient name, and each individual package must contain name of drug, strength, lot number, controlled substance schedule, and expiration date

NON-PRESCRIPTION DRUGS
May be treated as prescription drugs and labeled accordingly, or may simply retain the manufacturer's label with a note on the label of the date received by the facility and the patient's name.

The facility may also purchase certain bulk OTC drugs (e.g., acetaminophen), which do not require the patient's name, but must maintain the manufacturer's original label.

NO LABEL CHANGES ON A PATIENT'S MEDICATION (Rx or OTC) may be made by the facility; must be made by pharmacist.

DRUG CONTROL AND ACCOUNTABILITY (WAC 246-865-060(5))

Written procedures must be followed for control and accountability of all drugs in the facility.

No drugs may be returned to the pharmacy except if in qualifying unit dose packaging. *Qualifying packaging will include single-dose blisters in modified unit dose.

No drugs released to resident on discharge unless ordered by prescriber. A receipt as specified in the regulation must be entered into the health care record.

Discontinued drugs (including CSA III, IV, and V) must be destroyed by a licensed nurse employee in the presence of a witness within 90 days, with accurate records maintained. Sealed unit dose packages may be returned to pharmacy for credit.

Discontinued schedule II drugs be destroyed within 30 days by one of the following methods:

- By two of the following individuals: licensed pharmacist, director of nursing or RN designee, registered nurse employee of the facility;
- Destroyed at the nursing home by a Pharmacy Commission investigator if so requested.
- By another system if unit dose drugs are involved and specified conditions are met. (See WAC 246-865-060 (6)(g))

In September, 2014 the DEA finalized its rule on disposal of drugs by nursing homes and consumers, and now allows pharmacies to provide disposal services to nursing homes (see Chapter 5). The Commission will need to consider the impact of this change in its rules for nursing homes. The Commission has been approving individual drug disposal plans, and presumably could do so for pharmacies serving nursing homes. *The Commission is directed in the 2016 amendments to redevelop rules in this area.

EMERGENCY KITS (WAC 246-865-030)

Each ECF may establish an emergency kit, regardless of the type of distribution system that is used in the facility. The contents of the kit may be used for emergencies in which drug therapy must be started immediately. The kit is not used to provide "starter doses" of routine drugs for newly admitted patients. The specific contents of the kit is determined by pharmaceutical services committee, which is responsible for ensuring proper storage, security, and accountability, and the kit is obtained from the in-house pharmacy or the consulting pharmacy. The emergency kit is considered a physical extension of the supplying pharmacy and remains owned by the supplying pharmacy (WAC 246-865-020) When items are used from the kit, the ECF notifies the pharmacy, which replaces the items and charges the facility for the cost of the item used. (Note that providing the items at no charge would constitute a kick-back; see Chapter 8.) The Commission's rules specify the following requirements for emergency kits:

- Copy of contents on outside of kit

- Record keeping by nursing home and the supplying pharmacy
- Must be locked or stored in a locked area
- Accessible only to licensed nurses. *Licensed nurses will be able to restock these kits in accordance with policy and procedure and appropriate pharmacist supervision.

SUPPLEMENTAL DOSE KIT FOR UNIT-DOSE SYSTEMS. (WAC 246-865-040)

If the ECF uses a unit-dose distribution system (not modified unit dose), then the pharmaceutical services committee may establish the contents of a supplemental dose kit which may be used to provide starter doses for newly admitted residents, or to provide supplemental doses when the dose is changed. As with an emergency kit, the supplemental dose kit is considered a physical extension of the supplying pharmacy; when starter doses are removed for a given resident, the pharmacy will deduct the starter dose from the initial supply provided for the resident receiving the medication and replace the starter dose in the kit on the next delivery to the facility. The Commission's requirements for supplemental dose include the following:

- Used only in nursing homes using unit-dose drug dispensing systems.
- May be used for non-emergency supplemental doses.
- Pharmaceutical services committee determines the contents.
- Remains the property of the supplying pharmacy
- Pharmacy and PSC responsible for proper storage, security and accountability. *Licensed nurses at the facility may be allowed to restock these kits.

CONTINUITY OF DRUG THERAPY ("PASS MEDS") (WAC 246-865-070)

When a resident takes a short-term leave, it is necessary to send a supply of medications with the resident. This policy permits nurses at the facility to prepare up to a 72-hour supply of medications to send with the resident. This procedure is not available for planned leaves that allow time for a pharmacist to prepare therapy. In the case of blister packs or bingo cards, as long as the labels include complete directions for use, the entire card may be sent with the resident with no alterations. Otherwise, protocols must be established by the pharmaceutical services committee for the nurses to follow.

FEDERAL REGULATIONS OF LTCFS

The federal government regulates long-term care institutions to the extent that they provide services to Medicare or Medicaid patients. Significant involvement of pharmacists in the care of federally-funded patients in nursing homes was required by certain provisions of the Omnibus Budget Reconciliation Act of 1987 (OBRA-87).[168] Key elements include:

Development of a COMPREHENSIVE CARE PLAN for each resident, which may include appropriate self-medication. (42 CFR 483.10(n))

Each resident's drug therapy must be FREE FROM UNNECESSARY DRUGS: this requirement is designed to reduce excessive doses or duplicative therapy; excessive duration of therapy; inadequate monitoring; inadequate indications for use of drugs; and use of drugs in presence of adverse consequences that suggest the dose should be reduced or the drug discontinued. (42 CFR 483.25(l)(1))

Special attention is given to LIMIT THE USE OF PSYCHOTROPIC AGENTS IN RESIDENTS, and to require specific documented reasons for using psychotropic agents. Comprehensive reviews and continual efforts must be made to reduce the use of psychotropic agents in each patient receiving them. (42 CFR 483.25(l)(2)) These comprehensive reviews by a patient care team, including the pharmacist, are typically conducted every 90 days.

PHARMACEUTICAL SERVICES must be provided or arranged for by the facility. (42 CFR 483.60)

THE FACILITY MUST EMPLOY OR OBTAIN THE SERVICES OF A CONSULTANT PHARMACIST. (42 CFR 483.60(b))

EACH RESIDENT'S DRUG REGIMEN MUST BE REVIEWED EVERY 30 DAYS BY A PHARMACIST. (42 CFR 483.60(d))

PHARMACIES IN CORRECTIONAL FACILITIES

PRISONERS' RIGHTS TO HEALTH CARE

Prisoners have a constitutional right to health care equivalent to non-jailed populations.[169] This right arises under the 8th Amendment, which prohibits cruel and unusual punishment. The courts have ruled that "Deliberate indifference to serious medical needs" contravenes the 8th Amendment.

Prisoners have 3 basic rights related to medical care:[170]

- Access to care. All correctional facilities must provide for emergency care, "sick call," and access to specialists and inpatient hospital treatment, when warranted by the inmate's condition.
- Ordered care. When a health care professional has ordered care for a prisoner, jail authorities must provide that care and not interfere with it. The care must be provided in a timely manner.
- Professional judgment. The professional judgment of health care providers treating prisoners is given significant deference by the courts. However, prisoners have a right to demand that decisions are based on sound medical judgment.

CORRECTIONAL FACILITY TYPES.

PRISONS – facilities that house convicted felons, whose sentences generally exceed 1 year, and which may be operated by the federal government or states

JAILS – facilities that house individuals awaiting trial or those convicted of misdemeanors with sentences less than one year. Most commonly operated at the county level. There are upwards of 1,600 jails nationwide.

FEDERAL DETENTION CENTERS house individuals awaiting federal trial

Cities have small facilities, often called "LOCK-UPS" which may hold persons for up to 72 business hours or 5 days while awaiting appearance before a judge

HALF-WAY HOUSES AND RESIDENTIAL RE-ENTRY CENTERS house individuals who have been released on parole for a period of time determined by the parole board

JUVENILE DETENTION CENTERS house minors who have been sentenced to incarceration

KEY MEDICAL CARE ISSUES IN INMATE POPULATIONS

MAJOR DISEASE STATES - Mental health issues afflict a large portion of jail inmates, and a large proportion of prison inmates are infected with Hepatitis C. Further, the jail population of long-term inmates is aging and thus have chronic conditions associated with this aging, such as hypertension, diabetes, hyperlipidemia, and cardiovascular disease.

SELF-ADMINISTRATION NOT ALLOWED. Inmates (other than in re-entry centers) are not allowed to self-administer care, but may only receive medications by order of the medical staff.

MEDICAID AND MEDICARE do not currently cover otherwise eligible individuals who are in jail. This places a significant health care cost burden on states and counties who operate jails and prisons. For example, in 2014, Spokane County expended $4.3 million on medical care for inmates at the Jail and the Geiger Confinement Facility. This was the 3rd largest item in the expenditure budget for detention services, after the cost of confinement itself in the Jail ($10.7 million) and at Geiger ($5 million).[171]

JAIL PHARMACY SERVICES

Most jails do not have full-time pharmacies. Many jails contract with local pharmacies and drugs are often supplied in modified unit dose as they would be for assisted living centers. A growing number of jails contract with national firms that specialize in correctional health.

Most prisons and many larger county jails have full-time pharmacists. Health services – including pharmacy services – in federal prisons are provided by pharmacists in the U.S. Public Health Service.

WASHINGTON REQUIREMENTS FOR MEDICATION USE IN JAILS. The Washington Pharmacy Commission currently applies community-pharmacy rules to its inspection of pharmacies in jails. When the Board attempted to promulgate rules governing medication use in jails without pharmacies, the Department of Corrections and jail administrators objected. The Legislature addressed medication management in correctional facilities with revised legislation (SSB 5252) in July, 2009.[172]

The legislation excluded from Pharmacy Commission regulation any jail that does not operate, in whole, or in part, a pharmacy, but does allow the Commission to regulate a pharmacist who has entered into an agreement with a jail for provision of pharmaceutical services. (RCW 18.64.510)

New definitions were established related to medication administration in jails by jail staff who are not physicians, nurses, pharmacists or other practitioners: (RCW 70.48.020):

- NONPRACTITIONER JAIL PERSONNEL (NJP) – appropriately trained jail staff who may manage, deliver, or administer medications
- MEDICATION ASSISTANCE – assistance rendered by NJPs to an inmate to facilitate the individual's self-administration of medications
- ADMINISTRATION (WITHIN A JAIL) – direct application of a drug by ingestion or inhalation, to the body of an inmate by a practitioner or NJPs.

The statute allows jails to provide for delivery and administration of medications and medication assistance for inmates in their custody by NJPs, subject to the following actions by the jail administrator (JA) or chief law enforcement executive (CLEE): (RCW 70.48.490):

- JA, CLEE, or designee shall enter into an agreement between the jail and a licensed pharmacist, pharmacy or other facility to ensure access to pharmaceutical services on a 24-hour basis, including consulting and dispensing services.
- JA or CLEE shall develop policies addressing the designation and training of NJPs, and other specific issues addressed in statute. Training of NJPs in proper medication procedures must be performed by a designated physician, RN, or ARNP.
- JA or CLEE shall consult with one or more licensed pharmacists and one or more licensed physicians or nurses in the course of developing the policies.

PROVISION OF MEDICATIONS BY A PRACTITIONER OR NJP to an inmate requires a prescription or order (in the case of OTC drugs) for the drug to be administered; if the inmate is a minor, parental or guardian permission to administer medications must be obtained.

NJPs may assist in preparation of legend drugs or controlled substances for self-administration. Medication assistance does not include assistance with intravenous or injectable drugs.

NJPs may not be inmates.

REMOTE DISPENSING, CENTRAL FILL, AND AUTOMATED DRUG DISTRIBUTION

Community pharmacies as well as hospital pharmacies are increasingly becoming involved in automated dispensing at sites remote from the pharmacy. In ambulatory settings, these systems include methods for counseling patients using video technology. In hospital and nursing home settings, the systems may involve shared patient record systems between the local and remote site. Some community pharmacies have utilized telepharmacy technology to provide service to remote areas. Another consulting pharmacy in Spokane provides review and approves release of drugs from Pyxis dispensing systems in several rural hospitals in Eastern Washington. These systems are being used in hospice facilities, nursing homes, and hospitals. As noted above, these rules may apply equally well to non-remote devices used within a hospital.

The Commission adopted new rules in January 2017 governing automated drug dispensing devices. The new chapter, 246-874 WAC, is entitled "Pharmacy and Technology," and over time the Commission will add additional sections governing other forms of technology. The section on automated drug dispensing devices is designated as "Part 1" in the regulation, and it is likely that qualifying devices will become known as "Part 1 Devices."

"AUTOMATED DRUG DISPENSING DEVICES" (ADDD) includes, but is not limited to "a mechanical system controlled remotely by a pharmacist that performs operations or activities, related to the storage, counting, and dispensing of drugs to a credentialed health care professional consistent with [his or her] scope of practice." ADDD does NOT include:

- Technology that solely counts or stores (e.g., counting machines in the pharmacy)
- Kiosks
- Robots
- Emergency kits
- Supplemental dose kits
- Automation for compounding, administration, or packaging

PART 1 – WAC 246-874-020 THROUGH WAC 246-874-070 applies to ADDDs managed by the following:

- Licensed pharmacies
- Health care entities
- Assisted living facilities
- Nursing homes
- Health maintenance organizations
- Public health centers
- Other entities authorized by the Commission that choose to use them

NOTICE TO COMMISSION REQUIRED. Use of a Part 1 ADDD does not require Commission approval, but pharmacies (resident or non-resident) must provide written notice to the Commission of the physical address of the facilities where ADDDs they manage are located. (WAC 246-874-020(2)) Facilities using ADDDs under previous approval by the Commission will have 1 year from the effective date of the regulation to comply with part 1.

RESPONSIBLE MANAGER. Each pharmacy and facility using an ADDD shall designate a responsible manager who must be a pharmacist licensed in Washington state. (WAC 246-874-025) The responsible manager is responsible for oversight of the ADDDs, and to assure that drugs are procured, stored, delivered, and dispensed in compliance with all applicable state and federal statutes and regulations.

The responsible manager may designate a "Washington state credentialed health care professional acting within their scope of practice as a designee to perform tasks in part 1." The responsible manager retains personal and professional responsibility for assisted tasks. (WAC 246-874-030(6)) As noted the Nursing Care Quality Assurance Commission staff has determined that stocking automated drug dispensing devices is within the scope of practice of a registered nurse.[173]

POLICIES AND PROCEDURES, ANNUAL REVIEW. (WAC 246-874-030 (1,2))

- Written policies and procedures must be in place prior to use of an ADDD
- Responsible manager shall review policies and procedures at least annually and make necessary revisions
- Annual review must be documented (may do so electronically) and made available to Commission or its designee upon request
- Current copies of all policies and procedures must be maintained at the facility or pharmacy and be available on request

POLICIES AND PROCEDURE REQUIRED CONTENT. (WAC 246-874-030 (3)) The policies must include at least the following:

- All sections of part 1;
- User privileges based on user type
- Criteria for selection of medications subject to override
- Override list approved by the pharmacy or facility's pharmacy services committee
- Diversion prevention procedures
- Record retention and retrieval requirements that adhere to state and federal laws; retention must be for a minimum of 2 years

TRANSACTION INFORMATION. (WAC 246-874-030 (4)) An ADDD must collect and retain the following minimum transaction information:

- Identity of individuals accessing the system
- Identity of all personnel loading the ADDD
- Movement of drugs into and out of the system to provide security, accountability, and accuracy
- Transaction information must be made readily available to the Commission on request

INVENTORY CONTROL. (WAC 246-874-030 (5))

- Drugs must be placed into the ADDD by authorized personnel in the manufacturer's original sealed unit dose or unit-of-use packaging, in repackaged unit-dose containers, or in other suitable containers
- Patient owned medications that have been properly identified and approved in accordance with facility's policies, may be stored in accordance with policies defining safe and secure handling of medications

SECURITY AND SAFETY (WAC 246-874-040 (1,2,7,8)) requirements shall be assured by the responsible manager to include:

- Secure access to ADDD by users requires biometrics or other secure technology;
- Removal of system access for prior employees or persons whose privileges have changed must be implemented immediately or upon notification;
- Removal of profiles for discharged patients shall occur as soon as possible and no later than 12 hours after notification
- Responsible manager or designee shall assign, discontinue, or change access priveleges.
- Access to ADDD is limited to Washington state credentialed health care professionals acting within their scope of practice
- Replenishment of stock is reserved to (1) a pharmacist, intern, or technician under supervision of a pharmacist; or (2) a state licensed RN or LPN using an electronic verification system that ensures exact placement of secured compartments into the ADD;
- Pharmacists must provide independent double check manually or using an electronic verification system or other approved technology. A technician with specialized function approval may perform the manual double check for the pharmacist.
- Methods must be in place to address security breaches, including tracking of ADDD malfunctions and downtime procedures in the event of disaster or power outages
- ADDDs in assisted living facilities must be located in a secure area which, along with the ADDD, is locked when the ADDD is not in use.

PROSPECTIVE DRUG UTILIZATION REVIEW (WAC 246-874-040 (3,4,5)) by a pharmacist is required for each medication order, with the following exceptions:

- The drug is a subsequent dose from a previously reviewed order;
- The prescriber is in the immediate vicinity and controls the drug dispensing process;
- Access is being provided on override and the quantity dispensed is limited to the immediate need of the patient; or
- When 24-hour pharmacy services are not available, in which a retrospective drug use review shall be performed within 6 hours of the pharmacy being opened
- A retrospective review is not required for a drug dispensed on override as a one-time dose, or if the order was for a discharged patient
- All orders added to a patient's profile outside of the facility's normal discharge transfer process shall be reviewed and reconciled by the pharmacist no later than the next business day.

RETURN OF MEDICATIONS OR DEVICES TO THE ADDD. (WAC 246-874-040 (6)) Medications or devices may be returned to the ADDD in accordance with policies and procedures that provide at least the following:

- Items (other than controlled substances) stored in unsecured patient-specific bins, matrices, or open pockets (e.g., home meds, multiple-use patient-specific bottles) may be returned if adequate controls are in place.

- Medications stored in patient-specific containers may not be returned to general stock for reuse

Accountability. (WAC 246-874-050)

- The **facility** shall have a mechanism for securing and accounting for wasted, discarded, expired, or unused medication and its removal from the ADDD in accordance with state and federal laws
- The **responsible manager** shall implement procedures and maintain records regarding use and accountable of drugs, including controlled substances.
- Controlled substances shall be perpetually inventoried with a "blind count," or a physical inventory made by a pharmacist or other credentialed professional without access to the quantities shown in the electronic or other inventory records. A blind count is not needed when the drug is dispensed in dose specific amounts to a credentialed health care professional.
- An inventory count of controlled substances must be performed each time a controlled substance is replenished.
- Controlled substances must be stored in individually secured pockets or compartments, and not in "matrix" drawers or open pocket drawers.
- Facilities using a closed canister system must be able to verify the accuracy of controlled substances counts by perpetual inventories that are regularly reviewed and reconciled by pharmacy staff.
- The responsible manager shall assure that the facility maintains an ongoing medication discrepancy resolution and monitoring process; a discrepancy report is generated for each transaction where the count does not reflect inventory; and discrepancies are reviewed by the responsible manager or designee within 7 days.
- A wastage record is maintained for all controlled substances and wastage is witnessed by a credentialed professional and both individuals sign the wastage record. The rule has specific requirements for the content of the wastage record and a minimum retention for 2 years.

QUALITY ASSURANCE PROGRAM. (WAC 246-874-060) Each pharmacy and facility shall establish a quality assurance program in accordance with the rule, and which includes annual audits of compliance by the responsible manager.

NURSING STUDENT ACCESS. (WAC 246-874-070) The rule provides for access to ADDDs by students in Washington state accredited nursing programs in facilities that are providing a clinical experience for the students.

REMOTE MEDICATION ORDER PROCESSING (RMOP) is a related activity to remote dispensing, but can also include such activities as pharmacist authorization of refills under protocol. As in other areas, the Pharmacy Commission has issued guidelines concerning remote processing of medication orders[174] to interpret its other regulations. These guidelines allow pharmacies that are not owned by a common entity to enter into agreements for remote processing of orders.

MEDICATION ORDER PROCESSING involves the following without dispensing the medication:

- Receiving, interpreting, or clarifying orders
- Data entry and transferring of medication order information
- Performing drug regimen review
- Interpreting clinical data
- Performing therapeutic interventions
- Providing drug information concerning medication orders or drugs

OUTSOURCING RMOP. A Washington pharmacy may outsource medication order processing to another pharmacy if the pharmacies have the same owner, or have entered into a written contract or agreement outlining responsibilities and accountability. Commission approval must be sought.

- All pharmacists involved in RMOP must be trained on each pharmacies policies and procedures.
- The pharmacies must share common electronic files or have secure access to the pharmacy information system by the remote pharmacy.
- A pharmacy using RMOP services must maintain records of all orders entered from a remote location and must be able to audit activities of remote pharmacies.
- Pharmacies and pharmacists providing RMOP services to Washington pharmacies must be licensed in Washington. Out-of-state RMOP pharmacies must be licensed in Washington as non-resident pharmacies.

POLICIES AND PROCEDURES REQUIRED. Pharmacies involved in RMOP must develop and maintain current policies and procedures relating to their operations:

- Outline the responsibilities of each of the pharmacies
- List the name, address, telephone number and all license/registration numbers of the pharmacies involved
- Include policies and procedures for
  - Protecting the confidentiality and integrity of patient information
  - Maintaining records of the names, initials, or ID codes for each pharmacist involved
  - Complying with federal and state laws
- A continuous quality improvement program designed to objectively and systematically monitor the quality and appropriateness of patient care, pursue opportunities to improve care, and resolve identified problems
- Annual review of the policies and documentation thereof

CENTRALIZED FILLING AND FULFILLMENT. It is common now for mail order pharmacies, some hospitals, many chains, and HMOs to use centralized facilities to process prescriptions, particularly refills. Some hospital systems also use centralized sterile product processing. A simple diagram of the process would be:

As it has for RMOP, the Washington Pharmacy Commission has published a guideline entitled "Requirements for Central Filling of Prescriptions by Washington Pharmacies and Central Prescription Filling Service Providers."[175] These are similar in many ways to the requirements for RMOP, which is understandable since RMOP is a typical element of central filling processes.

A pharmacy desiring to provide central filling services must provide the Commission with its policies and procedures for approval.

A Washington licensed dispensing pharmacy may outsource prescription filling to another pharmacy under the same ownership, or based on a written contract or agreement outlining responsibilities and accountability of each pharmacy. Unless there is common ownership, the CENTRAL FILL PHARMACY SHALL DELIVER PRESCRIPTIONS TO THE DISPENSING PHARMACY FOR DELIVERY TO PATIENTS.

CONTROLLED SUBSTANCE central filling must be in compliance with DEA regulations.[176]

The pharmacies must share COMMON ELECTRONIC FILES OR APPROPRIATE TECHNOLOGY to allow secure access to information needed to dispense and process the prescription.

The licensed dispensing pharmacy must maintain records of all prescriptions processed by their pharmacy and the central fill pharmacy. The pharmacist at the dispensing pharmacy must comply with the minimum required information for the patient medication record (WAC 246-875-020) prior to sending the prescription order to the central fill pharmacy. The information system must provide for the ability to audit the activities of the central fill pharmacists.

PQAC PROPOSED RULES RELATED TO COMPOUNDING AND STERILE PRODUCTS

On October 1, 2014 the Pharmacy Commission published a set of DRAFT COMPOUNDING PRACTICE RULES which would revise its current regulations in light of major changes in federal law (see Chapter 4). It would modify regulations now contained in WAC 246-878 – Good Compounding Practices, WAC 246-903 – Nuclear Pharmacies and Pharmacists, and WAC 246-871 – Pharmaceutical-Parenteral Products for Nonhospitalized Patients. The Commission in October 2018 withdrew its CR-101 filing; indicating that revisions to compounding rules would be part of the ongoing rules rewrite project.

A pharmacy that uses central filling must, PRIOR TO OUTSOURCING THE PRESCRIPTION, INFORM THE PATIENT THAT PRESCRIPTION FILLING MAY BE OUTSOURCED TO ANOTHER PHARMACY. The patient shall be given the option of not having the prescription outsourced.

The PRESCRIPTION LABEL OF THE CENTRALLY FILLED PRESCRIPTION must show the name and address of both the dispensing pharmacy and the central fill pharmacy, except when there is common ownership of the pharmacies.

The dispensing pharmacy must designate staff members who are responsible for signing for the receipt of prescriptions delivered from the central fill pharmacy. The receipt shall be maintained as part of the prescription records.

All pharmacies providing central prescription filling services to Washington pharmacies MUST BE LICENSED IN WASHINGTON, either as resident or non-resident pharmacies.

The dispensing and central fill pharmacies shall maintain a policy and procedure manual. The requirements for this manual are identical to those for RMOP (see above).

PARENTERAL PRODUCTS FOR NON-HOSPITALIZED PATIENTS (HOME IV THERAPY) – WAC 246-871

Home IV Therapy, now more commonly called Home Infusion Therapy, is an important facet of pharmaceutical services that allows patients requiring a wide variety of infusion products to live at home or otherwise go about their lives without the restrictions associated with clinic or hospital-based infusion. The major association for pharmacies providing home infusion therapy is the National Home Infusion Association (NHIA), which has significant resources on its website.[177] NHIA defines a home infusion therapy pharmacy as a "pharmacy-based, decentralized patient care organization with expertise in USP 797-compliant sterile drug compounding that provides care to patients with acute or chronic conditions generally pertaining to parenteral administration of drugs, biologics and nutritional formulae administered through catheters and/or needles in home and alternate sites. Extensive professional pharmacy services, supplies and equipment are provided to optimize efficacy and compliance."

WASHINGTON REGULATION OF HOME INFUSION PHARMACIES

Pharmacies that prepare and dispense home IV therapy are regulated similarly to other non-ambulatory care pharmacies, in particular the Commission requires that their operations are subject to a developed POLICY AND PROCEDURE MANUAL (WAC 246-871-020) that is REVISED ANNUALLY. The manual must cover the following topics:

- Clinical services
- Parenteral product handling, preparation, dating, storage, and disposal
- Major and minor spills of antineoplastic agents, if applicable
- Disposal of unused supplies and medications
- Drug destruction and returns
- Drug dispensing
- Drug labeling and relabeling
- Duties and qualifications for professional and nonprofessional staff
- Equipment
- Handling of infectious waste pertaining to drug administration
- Infusion devices and drug delivery systems
- Dispensing of investigational medications
- Training and orientation of professional and nonprofessional staff
- Quality assurance
- Recall procedures
- Infection control
- Suspected contamination of parenteral products
- Orientation of employees to sterile technique
- Sanitation
- Security
- Transportation
- Absence of a pharmacist

PHYSICAL REQUIREMENTS

A home infusion pharmacy must meet the following minimum physical requirements:

- Adequate space, light, and restricted entry.
- Capable of containing laminar flow hood
- Class 100 environmental conditions. A Class 100 environment restricts particulate matter to no more than 3,500 particles greater than or equal to 0.1 micrometers (μm) per cubic foot. The federal standard that defined a Class 100 environment was cancelled in 2001, but it is still widely used. The current standard definition for clean rooms is the ISO 14644-1 standard, normally indicated as ISO 1 through ISO 9; ISO 5 is the current standard that is equivalent to the old Class 100 designation. (The Commission's proposed revisions use the ISO 5 standard.)

  - Annual certification of Class 100 environment by independent contractor
  - Incorporates Federal Standard 209B or National Sanitation Foundation standard 49
  - Reports maintained for 2 years
- Pre-filters are cleaned regularly and replacement date documented
- Sink with hot and cold running water
- Disposal containers for sharps, etc.
- Refrigerator/freezer with thermometer
- Temperature controlled delivery container (if appropriate)
- Infusion devices, if appropriate
- Reference library related to parenteral products (e.g., Trissel)

PHARMACIST IN CHARGE MUST HAVE BEEN TRAINED in specialized functions related to parenteral products, including aseptic technique and quality assurance. (The Commission's proposed rules will require all pharmacists or technicians involved in sterile compounding to obtain a "sterile compounding endorsement," to their licenses.)

"MAY USE A LEVEL-A PHARMACY ASSISTANT." This rule has not been updated since the revision of the Ancillary Personnel statute and rules. This would correspond to a technician. The technician must have been trained in specialized functions similar to those required for hospital IV admixture technicians. (Proposed rules would create a "sterile compounding endorsement" for technicians' licenses.)

DRUG DISTRIBUTION AND CONTROL. (WAC 246-871-050)

PRESCRIPTIONS REQUIRED. Pharmacist or intern must receive written or verbal order for any parenteral products dispensed. May be filed within the pharmacy by patient-assigned consecutive numbers. A new order is required every 12 months or upon any prescription change. The elements of the prescription are the same as required for ambulatory care prescriptions.

PATIENT PROFILES ARE REQUIRED. Minimum elements required in the patient profile include several items not mandated for community pharmacies. Items required are

- Patient full name
- Age or date of birth
- Weight, if applicable
- Sex, if applicable
- Parenteral products dispensed
- Date dispensed
- Drug content and quantity
- Patient directions
- Prescription number
- ID of dispensing pharmacist and ID of technician, if applicable
- Other drugs the patient is receiving
- Known drug sensitivities and allergies to drugs and foods
- Primary diagnosis, chronic conditions
- The completed prescription record must record the name of manufacturer and lot numbers of components. If lot numbers not recorded, a policy must be established for return of recalled products.

LABELING. Required labeling is discussed in chapter 4, and Table 4-8c.

DELIVERY TO PATIENTS. TIMELY DELIVERY of parenteral products to the patient's home must be assured. ENVIRONMENTAL CONTROLS DURING DELIVERY must be maintained, and must adhere to USP standards for temperature control. PROPER STORAGE FACILITIES must be maintained in patient's home

The chain of custody for CONTROLLED SUBSTANCES is documented, and a receipt received.

Must assure that PATIENT DISPOSAL OF INFECTIOUS WASTES does not pose a health hazard.

Must provide nurse (or other licensee) administering or starting therapy with authorized EMERGENCY KIT.

ANTINEOPLASTIC MEDICATIONS. Protections are required for personnel involved in compounding antineoplastic drugs. (WAC 246-871-060)

- Compounding must take place in a VERTICAL LAMINAR FLOW hood
- PROTECTIVE APPAREL is required
- Safety containment techniques must be used
- DISPOSAL OF WASTE must conform to state, local, and federal requirements (i.e., OSHA and WISHA rules)
- Written procedures for handling major and minor SPILLS, and provision of spill kits, must be provided
- Prepared doses must be dispensed and shipped in a manner to minimize risk of container rupture
- Documentation must be maintained of employee training related to antineoplastic medications

CLINICAL SERVICES REQUIRED (WAC 246-871-070) – the pharmacy must provide the following patient clinical services:

- Patient records must identify authorizing practitioner who is primary provider for the patient.
- Medication use review
- Patient monitoring requires access to clinical and laboratory data concerning each patient
- Must document ongoing drug therapy monitoring
    - Avoiding therapeutic duplication
    - Validating appropriateness of therapy
    - Clinical laboratory or clinical monitoring
- Patient training must be documented to show that patient or caregiver is capable of handling home parenteral therapy
    - Pharmacist responsible for training related to compounding, labeling, storage, stability, or incompatibility
    - Must see that patient's competence is reassessed regularly
- Must verify that administration of a product the patient has not received before will be handled by a person trained in management of anaphylaxis.

QUALITY ASSURANCE (WAC 246-871-080) – a quality assurance program must meet the following requirements:

- Documented QA program reviewed annually
- Must include methods to document
    - Medication errors
    - ADRs
    - Patient satisfaction

  - Product sterility and stability
    - Documentation that the end product has been tested on a sampling basis for microbial contamination – at least quarterly.
    - Nonsterile compounding rules require adhering to end product testing approaches identified in Remington. (This would now be superseded by the requirements for USP <797>)
    - Written justification for choosing expiration dates.

USP <797> STANDARDS. Although the regulation does not incorporate USP standards for compounding of sterile products, legislation enacted in 2013 amended RCW 64.270 to read "Any medicinal products that are compounded for patient administration or distributed to a licensed practitioner for patient use or administration shall, at a minimum, meet the standards of the official United States pharmacopeia as it applies to nonsterile and sterile administered products."[178] (See chapter 4)

The Commission has placed a "Sterile Compounding [USP <797>] Self-Assessment Compliance Checklist" on its website.[179]

NUCLEAR PHARMACIES – WAC 246-903

The practice of nuclear pharmacy primarily involves the preparation, calibration and delivery of radioactive diagnostic and therapeutic drug products to be administered to patients. Nuclear Pharmacy was the first practice area recognized as a specialty area by the Board of Pharmaceutical Specialties. As with other pharmacies, nuclear pharmacies are regulated by state pharmacy boards, but also must comply with regulations of state and federal nuclear regulatory commissions.

WASHINGTON REQUIREMENTS FOR A NUCLEAR PHARMACY LICENSE

Permit to operate issued only to QUALIFIED NUCLEAR PHARMACIST. (WAC 246-903-020) All personnel must be under supervision of a nuclear pharmacist.

The nuclear pharmacy must be segregated from other pharmacy facilities.

May waive requirements for permits for handling non-nuclear products if nuclear pharmacy deals exclusively with nuclear pharmaceuticals

NUCLEAR PHARMACIST is a licensed pharmacist who has submitted evidence to Commission that he or she meets requirements of WAC 246-903-030

- Meets standards of the state radiation control agency
- Licensed to practice pharmacy in WA
- Submits to Commission
  - Certification of at least 6 months on the job training in a licensed nuclear pharmacy under supervision of a licensed nuclear pharmacist, or
  - Has completed a nuclear pharmacy training program in an accredited college of pharmacy
  - Commission may grant partial credit to non-college of pharmacy programs
- Has received a letter from the Commission that the person is recognized as a nuclear pharmacist

MINIMUM EQUIPMENT

Must submit detailed equipment list to Commission and radiation control agency prior to approval of license application. May waive requirements for equipment related to compounding of non-radiopharmaceuticals if nuclear pharmacy deals exclusively with radiopharmaceuticals.

LABELING REQUIREMENTS.

The IMMEDIATE OUTER CONTAINER shall be labeled with:

- The standard radiation symbol
- The words, "Caution-Radioactive Material"
- The name of the radiopharmaceutical
- The amount of radioactive material contained, in millicuries or microcuries
- If a liquid, the voume in mL
- The requested calibration time for the amount of radioactivity contained
- Expiration data, if applicable
- Specific concentration of radioactivity

The IMMEDIATE CONTAINER shall be labeled with

- The standard radiation symbol
- The words, "Caution-Radioactive Material"
- The name of the nuclear pharmacy
- The prescription number
- The name of the radiopharmaceutical
- The date
- The amount of radioactive material contained in millicuries or microcuries

CLOSING OF A PHARMACY (WAC 246-869-250)

THE COMMISSION MUST BE NOTIFIED PRIOR TO THE CLOSING OF ANY LICENSED PHARMACY, REGARDLESS OF SETTING.

15 Days Prior to Closing

A notice shall be provided to the Commission indicating:

- The intended date of closing
- The names and addresses of persons who shall have custody of the pharmacy's records of: prescriptions, bulk compounding, repackaging, and controlled substances.
- The names and addresses of any persons who will acquire any of the legend drugs from the pharmacy, if known at the time.
- The 15-day pre-closing notice to the Commission is a requirement as well for Hospital Pharmacy Associated Clinics (WAC 246-873A-095). Similar elements must be reported.

Within 15 Days After Closing

The Commission must be provided with the following documents:

- The pharmacy license
- A written statement containing the following:

- Confirmation that legend drugs were transferred to persons authorized to receive them (along with names and addresses of the transferees), or destroyed
- For any transferred controlled substances, a list of drugs, quantities, date transferred, and names and addresses of transferees
- Confirmation that the DEA registration and all unused DEA order forms were returned to the DEA
- Confirmation that pharmacy labels and blank prescriptions were destroyed
- Confirmation that all signs and symbols indicating the presence of the pharmacy have been removed.
- Similar reporting requirements must be met within 15 days of closing for Hospital Pharmacy Associated Clinics (see WAC 246-873A-095)

In 2015, the Commission disciplined a pharmacist who closed a pharmacy and failed to comply with these regulations. The pharmacist was placed on probation for 2 years, required to complete 4 hours of CE on law and ethics, prohibited from supervising or serving as a preceptor for interns, and fined $5,000.[180]

NOTIFICATION OF PATIENTS. In some circumstances, owners have closed a pharmacy, with advanced notice to the Commission, but with no notice to staff or patients until the actual date of closing. The Commission has developed Policy No. 39, on "Closing a Pharmacy – Patient Notification."[181]

The Commission expressed a policy that "adequate patient notification of a pharmacy's closing is an important public health and patient access issues *[sic]*. In addition to applicable state and federal laws and rules, the Commission urges all pharmacies to notify patients, fifteen days in advance, of the closing or the execution of the sale of a pharmacy."

- The notification should be by direct mail or by public notice in a local newspaper, and by posting a closing notice sign conspicuously in a public area of the pharmacy.
- The notice should include
  - The intended last date the pharmacy will be open for business;
  - The name and address of the pharmacy to which prescription records will be transferred after closing; and
  - Instructions on how patients can arrange for transfer of their prescription records to a pharmacy of their choice and the last day a transfer may be initiated.

EMPLOYEE NOTIFICATION. Under certain conditions, a federal law requires prior notice to employees when a plant or facility is closed. The Worker Adjustment and Retraining Notification (WARN) Act [182] of 1989 requires 60-day prior notice to employees (or their union) if the company employs 100 or more workers, and either a plant closing or mass layoff is anticipated.

PLANT CLOSING. The notification is required if an employment site will be shut down and the shutdown will result in an employment loss of 50 or more employees during any 30-day period.

MASS LAYOFF. Notice must be given when a mass layoff, not resulting from a plant closure, will result in an employment loss for more than 500 employees in a 30-day period or for 50-499 employees if they make up more than 1/3 of the company's active workforce.

SALE OF A BUSINESS. A sale that triggers a covered plant closing or layoff must provide the 60-day notice to affected individuals.

LOSS OF EMPLOYMENT means an employment termination or a layoff exceeding 6 months or a reduction of employee's hours of work more than 50% in each month of any 6-day period.

EXEMPTIONS INCLUDE (1) closing of a temporary facility; (2) completion of a project.

EXCEPTIONS TO THE 60-DAY NOTICE include a faltering company, unforeseeable business circumstances, or natural disasters.

ENFORCEMENT OF THIS LAW is via lawsuits filed in federal district court by affected employees or bargaining groups.

SHOPKEEPERS AND ITINERANT VENDORS

GROCERY STORES, CONVENIENCE STORES, AND OTHER RETAILERS WHO WISH TO BE ALLOWED TO SELL OTC DRUGS must register through the Master License System as Shopkeepers (RCW 18.64.044), if they are not already licensed as a pharmacy. Door-to-door salespersons who wish to sell OTC drugs must register with the Commission as Itinerant Vendors (RCW 18.64.047). The law specifies the following restrictions on these registrants

They MAY NOT SELL LEGEND DRUGS OR OTC CONTROLLED SUBSTANCES.

OTC DRUGS may only be sold in the MANUFACTURER'S ORIGINAL PACKAGE.

METHAMPHETAMINE PRECURSORS. Products containing any detectable amount of EPHEDRINE, PSEUDOEPHEDRINE, OR PHENYLPROPANOLAMINE (EPP) may only be purchased from a wholesaler or manufacturer licensed by the Commission.

If a shopkeeper or itinerant vendor has been found to have sold EPP in a "suspicious transaction" (RCW 69.43.035), then it will be subject to limits on sales of EPP, as follows:

- March through October – sales of EPP must be not greater than 10% of total prior monthly sales; or
- November through February – sales of EPP must be not greater than 20% of total prior monthly sales.

PROPER STORAGE AND LABELING. Shopkeepers and Itinerant Vendors must meet the storage, stability, labeling, and other requirements for drugs, and are subject to the misbranding or adulteration provisions of the FDCA and the state Legend Drug Law.

WHOLESALERS AND MANUFACTURERS

Individuals or firms that distribute drugs at wholesale (wholesalers) or manufacture and distribute drugs (manufacturers) must be licensed by the Commission (RCW 18.64.046, RCW 18.64.044).

Federal law requires wholesalers who are not **authorized distributors of record (ADR)** for a particular manufacturer or drug – including pharmacies who transfer drugs at wholesale other than emergency accommodation sales or intracompany transfers – to provide a pedigree statement for each drug transfer. The Drug Supply Chain Security Act requires manufacturers and wholesalers to develop an interoperable system of exchanging "track and trace" information over a period of time starting in 2015, and will phase out the specifics of the earlier legislation (see Chapter 4).

WHAT IS A MANUFACTURER?

The Pharmacy Practice Act (RCW 18.64.011 (21), (22)) defines manufacture and manufacturer as follows:

> (21) "Manufacture" means the production, preparation, propagation, compounding, or processing of a drug or other substance or device or the packaging or repackaging of such substance or device, or the labeling or relabeling of the commercial container of such substance or device, but does not include the activities of a practitioner who, as an incident to his or her administration or dispensing such substance or device in the course of his or her professional practice, personally prepares, compounds, packages, or labels such substance or device. "Manufacture" includes the distribution of a licensed pharmacy compounded drug product to other state licensed persons or commercial entities for subsequent resale or distribution, unless a specific product item has approval of the commission. The term does not include:
>
> (a) The activities of a licensed pharmacy that compounds a product on or in anticipation of an order of a licensed practitioner for use in the course of their professional practice to administer to patients, either personally or under their direct supervision;
>
> (b) The practice of a licensed pharmacy when repackaging commercially available medication in small, reasonable quantities for a practitioner legally authorized to prescribe the medication for office use only;
>
> (c) The distribution of a drug product that has been compounded by a licensed pharmacy to other appropriately licensed entities under common ownership or control of the facility in which the compounding takes place; or
>
> (d) The delivery of finished and appropriately labeled compounded products dispensed pursuant to a valid prescription to alternate delivery locations, other than the patient's residence, when requested by the patient, or the prescriber to administer to the patient, or to another licensed pharmacy to dispense to the patient.
>
> (22) "Manufacturer" means a person, corporation, or other entity engaged in the manufacture of drugs or devices.

The Commission has set forth Good Manufacturing Practices for Finished Pharmaceuticals in Chapter 246-895 WAC. In its license application for Manufacturer, it recognizes 3 types: controlled substances manufacturer, non-controlled substance manufacturer, or repackager; a firm may register in more than one category.

OUTSOURCING FACILITIES The Commission has not yet modified its rules or achieved modifications of statute to specifically recognize outsourcing facilities that are federally registered under §503B of the FDCA (see Chapter 4). Currently, federally-registered outsourcing facilities located in Washington are required to obtain a manufacturer's license; outsourcing facilities located outside of Washington are required to obtain a non-resident wholesaler's license.[183]

THE COMMISSION'S REGULATIONS GOVERNING WHOLESALERS are found in WAC 246-879.

WHOLESALER TYPES:

"FULL-LINE" – licensed to wholesale legend, OTC, and controlled substances (if registered) to other licensed or authorized purchasers

"OTC-ONLY" – licensed only for OTC wholesaling; may wholesale EPP within restrictions

"CONTROLLED SUBSTANCES" wholesaler

"EXPORT WHOLESALER" – licensed to sell legend or OTC drugs to foreign countries

The Pharmacy Commission addressed the issue of exportation of controlled substances at its January 2014 meeting and determined that the exportation of diazepam by an otherwise licensed Export Wholesaler was outside the scope of the commission.[184]

PHARMACIES DO NOT NEED TO REGISTER AS WHOLESALERS in order to engage in "the sale, purchase, or trade of a drug or an offer to sell, purchase, or trade a drug for emergency medical reasons." (WAC 246-879-010 (10)(e))

Intracompany sales or transfers may be made by pharmacies without registering as a wholesaler. (WAC 246-879-010 (10)(d)) The Legislature has made it clear that hospital pharmacies may also engage in intracompany sales, or transfers between any division, subsidiary, parent company, or related company under common ownership and control of the corporate entity. (RCW 70.41.490)

"EMERGENCY MEDICAL REASONS" includes transfers of prescription drugs by retail pharmacy to another retail pharmacy or practitioner to alleviate a temporary shortage, except that the gross dollar value of such transfers shall not exceed 5% of the total prescription drug sale revenue of either the transferor or transferee pharmacy practitioner during any twelve consecutive month period. The Commission has indicated that it may challenge distributions to prescribers by pharmacies on a routine basis when the prescriber could otherwise obtain the product from a wholesaler. Given that a 5% limitation applies to the receiving practitioner, it is unlikely that a pharmacy can legally be the regular source of drugs for a physician unless it is also a wholesaler.

In permitting hospital pharmacies to transfer drugs for emergency reasons, the Legislature also specified that the 5% limit applies to the "total prescription drug sale revenue of either the transferor or transferee pharmacy during any twelve month consecutive period." (RCW 70.41.490)

WHOLESALING ALSO DOES NOT INCLUDE the following:

- Sales or trades that constitute dispensing pursuant to a prescription
- The lawful distribution of samples by manufacturers' representatives or their distributors' representatives
- Sale, purchase, or trade of blood or blood components (regulated separately)

METHAMPHETAMINE PRECURSORS. Wholesalers who distribute precursor drug products (EPP) are subject to the following restrictions:

- March through October – EPP sales may not exceed 5% of the prior month's total sales of all products
- November through February – EPP sales may not exceed 10% of the prior month's total sales of all products

The Commission may exempt a wholesaler from the above limits if its sales of EPP are intracompany sales and there is no history of suspicious transactions in precursor drugs.

Sales of EPP may be only made to licensed pharmacies, a shopkeeper or itinerant vendor, a practitioner authorized to prescribe or use the particular drug, or a traditional Chinese herbal practitioner. (See also Chapter 5)

CANADIAN WHOLESALERS. The 2005 Legislature required the Commission (then Board) to submit by September 1, 2005, a request to the FDA for a waiver to permit the licensing in Washington of "Canadian, United Kingdom, Irish, and other nondomestic prescription drug wholesalers ..." (RCW 18.64.490) The FDA denied the waiver request on March 17, 2006. References to Canadian wholesalers in Commission regulations are without force.

REFERENCES

[111] http://www.secstate.wa.gov/corps/registration_structures.aspx
[112] http://www.doh.wa.gov/Portals/1/Documents/Pubs/690152.pdf
[113] http://www.doh.wa.gov/Portals/1/Documents/Pubs/690152.pdf
[114] http://www.doh.wa.gov/Portals/1/Documents/Pubs/690056.pdf
[115] http://www.doh.wa.gov/Portals/1/Documents/Pubs/690300.pdf
[116] https://www.deadiversion.usdoj.gov/webforms/jsp/regapps/common/newAppLogin.jsp
[117] Article No. 1060, Washington State Board of Pharmacy Newsletter 2011 Jan; 32(3):5.
[118] WSDOH, PQAC. Policy/procedure No. 34, 2014 Dec 11;
https://www.doh.wa.gov/Portals/1/Documents/2300/2017/PQAC-34-JobShadowing.pdf
[119] https://oig.hhs.gov/exclusions/index.asp
[120] https://www.sam.gov/portal/public/SAM/
[121] http://www.npdb-hipdb.hrsa.gov/
[122] https://fortress.wa.gov/doh/providercredentialsearch/
[123] Article No. 979, Washington State Board of Pharmacy Newsletter 2008 Oct;30(2):1.
[124] WSDOH, PQAC. Procedure No. 49, 2017 Feb 17; https://www.doh.wa.gov/Portals/1/Documents/2300/2017/PQAC49.pdf
[125] WSDOH, PQAC. Procedure No. 52, 2017 Mar 30; https://www.doh.wa.gov/Portals/1/Documents/2300/2017/PQAC-52%20PatientCounseling.pdf
[126] http://www.usconstitution.net/xconst_Am1.html
[127] Stormans, Inc. et al. v. Wiesman et al., 9th Cir., 794 F.3d 1064 (2015)
[128] Stormans, Inc. et al. v. Wiesman et al., 136 S.Ct.2433 (2016)
[129] Fassett WE. Washington Pharmacy Law: A User's Guide 2015. Spokane, WA: pharmacistlaw.com; 2015: 64-64.
[130] This is funded by the federal government. Reauthorization for 2015 through 2019 was enacted in the Poison Center Network Act of 2013, Pub. L. 113-77.
[131] Syrup of Ipecac, Lack of Availability. Washington Poison Center, 2017 Jun. 5;
https://www.wapc.org/resources/trainingandeducationalmaterials/syrup-of-ipecac-lack-of-availability-2/
[132] https://del.wa.gov/sites/default/files/imported/publications/licensing/docs/SyrupOfIpecacLetter.pdf
[133] Article No. 1273, Washington State Pharmacy Quality Assurance Commission Newsletter, 2018 Jan; 39(3):1,4.
[134] Pub. L. 113-54
[135] https://www.pharmacypracticeaccredit.org
[136] www.urac.org
[137] www.chapinc.org
[138] www.achc.org
[139] The Commission has an established policy/procedure for handling potential enforcement actions against non-resident pharmacies. See Minutes, PQAC, 2016 Sep 30: 2; http://www.doh.wa.gov/Portals/1/Documents/Mtgs/2016/20160930-MN-PH.pdf
[140] http://www.jointcommission.org
[141] www.achc.org
[142] www.urac.org
[143] WSDOH, PQAC. Policy/Procedure No. 46, Residential treatment facilities use of automated drug distribution devices. 2016 May 26; http://www.doh.wa.gov/Portals/1/Documents/2300/2016/GuidanceRTFAutoDrugDistDevices.pdf
[144] WSDOH, PQAC. Policy Statement No. 59, 2018 Apr 27;
https://www.doh.wa.gov/Portals/1/Documents/2300/2018/NaloxoneDist-ED.pdf
[145] WSR 17-01-108, 2016 Dec 29
[146]http://www.doh.wa.gov/Portals/1/Documents/2300/MedicationSecurityHospital_Position_Statement.pdf

[147] Minutes, Washington Pharmacy Quality Assurance Commission, 2014 Mar 6; http://www.doh.wa.gov/Portals/1/Documents/Mtgs/2014/20140306-MN-PH.pdf, accessed 1/14/15
[148] WSDOH, NQAC. Advisory Opinion NCAO 6.0, Standing orders and verbal orders, 2014 Sep 12; http://www.doh.wa.gov/Portals/1/Documents/6000/StandingAndVerbalOrders.pdf
[149]http://www.doh.wa.gov/hsqa/Professions/Pharmacy/Documents/Hospital_Pharmacy_violation.pdf (as of January 2015, this link is not active)
[150] Article No. 1019, Washington State Board of Pharmacy Newsletter, 2010 Jan; 31(3):4.
[151] Article No. 1046, Washington State Board of Pharmacy Newsletter, 2010 Jul; 32(1):5.
[152] Article No. 1165. Hospital inspections. Washington Pharmacy Quality Assurance Commission News, 2014 Apr;35(4):1.
[153] 2015 c 234 §4
[154] 2016 c 118
[155] WSR 16-18-074
[156] WSR 17-01-144
[157] WSR 18-01-003
[158] WSR 18-08-070
[159] WSR 18-16-097
[160] WSR 18-24-055; http://lawfilesext.leg.wa.gov/law/wsr/2018/24/18-24-055.htm
[161] Harris-Kojetin L, Sengupta M, Park-Lee E, Valverde R. Long-term care services in the United States: 2013 overview. National health care statistics reports; no 1. Hyattsville, MD: National Center for Health Statistics. 2013.
[162] 2016 c 148
[163] WSDOH, PQAC. Guidance Document No. 51 – Chart orders and the use of practitioner authorized agent signatures in long-term care settings. March 30, 2017.
[164] WSR 16-19-077
[165] WSR 18-21-145
[166] WSDOH, PQAC. Guidance document No. 51, 2017 Mar 30; ttps://www.doh.wa.gov/Portals/1/Documents/2300/2017/PQAC-51-ElectSigDelegatAuthority.pdf
[167] Beebe DE. Announcement sent to WSBOP-NEWSLETTER@LISTSERV.WA.GOV: Clarification of April 2011 Pharmacy Newsletter Article No. 1064. 2011 Apr 11.
[168] Pub. L. 100-203.
[169] Estelle v. Gamble, 429 U.S. 97 (1976).
[170] Rold WJ. Thirty years after Estelle v. Gamble: a legal retrospective. J Correctional Health Care. 2008 Jan;14(1):11-20.
[171] Spokane County 2014 Annual Budget, p. 64; http://www.spokanecounty.org/data/budgetandfinance/pdf/countybudget/Main%20Document%202014.pdf, accessed 1/14/15
[172] 2009 c 411
[173] Minutes, WA Board of Pharmacy, October 25, 2007 (http://www.doh.wa.gov/hsqa/Professions/Pharmacy/Documents/Documents/20071025.pdf)
[174]http://www.doh.wa.gov/Portals/1/Documents/2300/Remote_Order_Processing_Guidelines.pdf
[175]http://www.doh.wa.gov/Portals/1/Documents/Pubs/690274.pdf
[176] 68 Fed. Reg. 37405-37411, 2003 Jun 24
[177] www.nhia.org
[178] 2013 c 146; RCW 18.64.270
[179] WSDOH, PQAC. Sterile compounding [USP <797>] self-assessment checklist, 2016 Apr; http://www.doh.wa.gov/Portals/1/Documents/Pubs/690296.pdf
[180] WSDOH, PQAC, Case No. 2015-251, June 23, 2015
[181] WSDOH, PQAC, Policy/procedure No. 39, 2014 Dec 11; https://www.doh.wa.gov/Portals/1/Documents/2300/2017/PQAC-39-ClosingPharm-PatientNot.pdf
[182] Worker Adjustment and Retraining Notification Act (WARN), Pub. L. 100-379; 29 USC §§ 2101 et seq.
[183] Personal communication, A. Pauley, Pharmacist Consultant, PQAC, 2017 Jan 25.
[184] Christopher Barry, personal communication, 1/30/2014. (This is not reflected in the minutes of the meeting because the Commission, by deeming it beyond its scope, took no action.)

4 – PROVIDING DRUGS AND MEDICAL DEVICES TO PATIENTS

REGULATION OF FOOD, COSMETICS, DRUGS, AND DEVICES

The Food and Drug Administration[185] is responsible for regulating foods, drugs, cosmetics, and medical devices in the United States, under authority of the Food, Drug and Cosmetic Act[186] (FDCA – 21 USC Chapter 9).

The FDA web site provides several articles on the History of the FDA[187] and the food and drug laws.

THE PURE FOOD AND DRUG ACT, also known as the Wiley Law, was passed in 1906, as the first comprehensive federal statute to assure purity and truthful labeling for foods and drugs.

The Act required accurate labeling, and attempted to assure that food and drugs were "pure," i.e., contained only what should be in wholesome food or the drug as labeled.

Two ways in which drugs or food could violate the act:

ADULTERATION, which is the presence of any added injurious substance, food which is deteriorated, contains toxic substances, drugs which differ from compendia standards, or food or drugs which are stored in unsanitary places or at improper temperatures. After 1962, includes failure to be produced in accordance with GMPs (see below).

COMPETENCY AREAS IN THIS CHAPTER

2016 MPJE COMPETENCY STATEMENTS – Areas 1.1.1, 1.2.1, 1.2.2, 1.3.1, 1.3.2, 1.3.3, 1.3.4, 1.3.6, 1.4.1, 1.4.2, 1.4.3, 1.4.5, 1.4.6, 1.4.7, 1.4.8, 1.4.9, 1.4.11, 1.4.15, 1.6.1, 1.6.2, 1.6.3, 1.8.1, 1.8.2, 1.8.3, 1.8.4, 2.3.3, 3.1.1

2016 ACPE REQUIRED ELEMENTS – Pharmacy Law & Regulatory Affairs; Medication Dispensing, Distribution and Administration

MISBRANDING consisted in 1906 of false and fraudulent statements on the *label*. Currently, misbranding includes any false or misleading statements in the *labeling,* which includes both the label as well as any additional statements about the product made by its manufacturer.[188]

FOOD, DRUG AND COSMETIC ACT (FDCA). Growing problems with modern chemicals, and limits on the applicability of the Wiley Law, led to the passage in 1938 of the FDCA, that has been amended several times since then. A major impetus to the passage of the FDCA was an influential book by Ruth DeForest Lamb, "American Chamber of Horrors."[189] A precipitating event was the marketing by the S.E. Massengill Company of

"Sulfanilamide Elixir,[190] which contained diethylene glycol as the solvent – 107 deaths occurred before the FDA could get the product removed from the market. The FDCA is often referred to as "the 1938 law."

NEW DRUGS. All drugs marketed after 1938 are "new drugs." The FDCA required that manufacturers of "new drugs" PROVIDE PROOF OF SAFETY BEFORE MARKETING DRUGS. The law specified that "'new drug' means ... any drug ... the composition of which is not generally recognized, among experts qualified by scientific training and experience to evaluate the safety and effectiveness of drugs, as safe for the use under the conditions prescribed, recommended, or suggested in the labeling thereof ..." Drugs "generally recognized as safe" (GRAS) were not "new drugs." Other products required proof of safety prior to marketing.

FIGURE 4- 1. ELIXIR SULFANILAMIDE

The law also requires that manufacturers OBTAIN PRE-MARKETING APPROVAL of "new drugs" by the FDA. Approval was to be sought by filing of a NEW DRUG APPLICATION (NDA) with the FDA.

HOMEOPATHIC DRUGS. The FDCA's definition of a "drug" includes items listed as official in the Homoeopathic Pharmacopoeia[191] of the United States (HPUS). Homeopathy emerged as a medical theory suggesting that drugs producing symptoms similar to those of the underlying disease would act a curatives for that condition ("like cures like"). For example, capsicum (derived from cayenne pepper) is thought to stimulate blood flow and sweating and is an anodyne for stinging pain, since capsicum itself produces such pain. The chief proponent of homeopathy was Samuel Hahnemann (c. 1796) and the principles he elucidated include the notion that the more dilute the drug, the more powerful it is. The most potent homeopathic remedies are prepared by a series of 100-fold dilutions; expressed as factors of C (e.g., 6C has a concentration of $1{:}\,10^{6}$). Hahnemann is said to have advocated 30C dilutions, or a dilution by a factor of 10^{60}. Above about 13C, the concentration of the drug falls below $1\ x\ 10^{-26}$, which is less dilute than the reciprocal of Avogadro's number; thus there would not likely be a single molecule of the drug left in the resulting solution. Homeopathic practitioners often assert that the compounding process modifies the water to give it the "memory" of the drug substance.

OTC versions of homeopathic remedies are labeled in concentrations expressing factors of "X", or 10-fold dilutions. The original version Zicam Cold Remedy nasal spray was labeled with 2X zinc acetate and 1X zinc gluconate; or 1:100 zinc acetate and 1:10 zinc gluconate (current versions of the nasal swabs are labeled with active ingredients that include "Galphimia glauca 4x; Luffa operculata 4x, and Sabadilla 4x").

Prescription versions of homeopathic remedies are dispensed by licensed practitioners, including naturopaths. OTC versions are treated by FDA as if they were herbal remedies and generally only acted on if, like the original Zicam – which allegedly caused anosmia – adverse effects emerge.[192] However, the Federal Trade Commission is now evaluating marketing claims for OTC homeopathic products with greater scrutiny (see below).

OLD DRUGS. Drugs marketed prior to 1938 are not covered by the FDCA, unless changes are made in their formulation or labeling. Examples of these "old drugs" include some dosage forms of phenobarbital and various narcotic drugs. The FDA believes that few, if any of the pre-1938 drugs now marketed are in their original formulation or labeling, and thus require submission of a NDA to allow them to be marketed legally.

IDENTICAL, RELATED, OR SIMILAR DRUGS. After 1938 and before the subsequent passage of the Kefauver-Harris amendments in 1962, whenever FDA approved a New Drug, all existing (pre-1938) drugs that were "identical, related, or similar" (IRS) to the new drug were also considered approved, and were marketed without ever completing a specific NDA for the product.

GENERALLY RECOGNIZED AS SAFE. Also between 1938 and 1962, many manufacturers introduced drug products into the market based on their own conclusion that the drugs were "generally recognized as safe" (GRAS) OR based on opinions from the FDA that the drugs were not new drugs. The FDA formally revoked all these "opinions" in 1968 (21 CFR 310.100).

PRESCRIPTION ONLY DRUGS. Prior to 1951, pharmacists could dispense most drugs – except narcotics – without a prescription. As a matter of professional ethics and courtesy, however, most pharmacists required prescriptions for many drugs, although refill procedures were somewhat lax. After 1951, however, the DURHAM-HUMPHREY[193] AMENDMENTS created a new class of drugs that could not be dispensed without a prescription. These have become called "LEGEND DRUGS," because they were required to bear a "legend" on their label: "Caution: Federal Law prohibits dispensing without prescription."

All existing drugs could be sold over the counter (OTC), without prescription.

New drugs that could not bear adequate labeling for safe use by the consumer would now be able to be marketed if information was provided to the physician, and these required a prescription.

The law allowed for oral prescriptions, and for refills.

KEFAUVER-HARRIS AMENDMENTS – EFFECTIVENESS REQUIRED. In 1962, additional amendments, the KEFAUVER-HARRIS AMENDMENTS,[194] were passed, triggered by problems with thalidomide,[195] a drug which had not actually been marketed in the US, but which caused birth defects (phocomelia) in many babies born in Europe and Canada. However, the stage was set for the legislation

FEDERAL FOOD, DRUG, AND COSMETIC ACT AND ITS MAJOR AMENDMENTS

FDCA – 1938 (Replaced Pure Food and Drug Act, established proof of safety prior to marketing)

DURHAM-HUMPHREY AMENDMENTS – 1951 (Rx Only)

KEFAUVER-HARRIS AMENDMENTS – 1962 (Effective as well as Safe)

MEDICAL DEVICE AMENDMENTS – 1976 (Established safety and effectiveness requirements for medical devices)

ORPHAN DRUG ACT – 1983 (Economic amendment to bring low-demand drugs to market)

WAXMAN-HATCH AMENDMENTS – 1984 (Economic amendment to allow marketing of generics, extend patent life)

PRESCRIPTION DRUG MARKETING ACT – 1987 (Economic amendment – restrict reimportation of drugs from outside of US, restrict distribution of samples, regulate wholesalers)

FDAMA – 1997 (Regulatory reform of FDA, create safe harbor for pharmacy compounding in §503A, create user fees)

FDAAA – 2007 (Reauthorize user fees, give more power to FDA regarding drug safety issues, establish REMS)

FDASIA – 2012 (Reauthorize and expand user fees, reform rules regarding pediatric drugs, deal with drug shortages)

DRUG QUALITY & SECURITY ACT - 2013 (Reinstate §503A, establish outsourcing facilities, establish 10-year timeline for track-and-trace drug supply chain security)

21ST CENTURY CURES ACT – 2016 (Multiple revisions of requirements for drug development and approval)

FDA REAUTHORIZATION ACT – 2017 (Revise and extend various user-fee programs, among other purposes)

by a series of hearings led by Senator Kefauver's Senate Committee on Antitrust and Monopoly starting in 1959, which were initially focused on drug pricing and monopoly issues. The 1962 amendments required:

- Proof of efficacy (effectiveness) as well as safety prior to marketing.
- Established regulations called Good Manufacturing Practices (GMPs) requiring significant monitoring of manufacturers' facilities and processes
- Moved control of advertising for Rx drugs from the Federal Trade Commission to the FDA
- Improved procedures and requirements for obtaining informed consent during clinical trials of new drugs.

GENERALLY RECOGNIZED AS SAFE AND EFFECTIVE (GRASE). The GRASE status is conferred on existing products, especially for OTC use, that meet the 1962 standards.

DRUG EFFICACY REVIEW. The 1962 amendments mandated the FDA to review the *efficacy* of drugs which were previously approved only on the basis of *safety*. The result of this review left three categories of drugs on the market.

APPROVED DRUG PRODUCTS. All *prescription* drugs marketed between 1938 and 1962 *for which an NDA was approved on the basis of safety only* were reviewed in a long-lasting effort by FDA known as the Drug Efficacy Study Implementation (DESI).

60 panels of experts reviewed submissions of evidence from the manufacturers, and classified each proposed indication for a product as "ineffective," "ineffective as a fixed combination," "possibly effective," "probably effective," or "effective." Only those products which were found to have at least one "effective" indication could continue to be marketed.

Drugs with no "effective" indications were given a Notice of an Opportunity for Hearing (NOOH), and an opportunity to submit data to substantiate the effectiveness of their claims. Drugs without an effective indication are called "Less-than-effective" products (LTE).

Of 3,400 products reviewed, over 1,000 were removed from the market by this process.[196]

NONPRESCRIPTION (OVER-THE-COUNTER OR OTC) DRUGS were separated from the DESI process in 1972 and potential OTC *ingredients* were subject to a review by groups of experts formed into OTC Review Panels. These expert panels developed monographs for therapeutic classes of drugs (e.g., antacids, cold remedies). Products comprised of ingredients listed in these monographs, and formulated in conformance with the monographs, may be used in formulating OTC products without submission of an NDA.[197]

DRUGS FOR WHICH AN NDA WAS NEVER APPROVED.
At least 6 categories of drugs might still be found on the US market that have never been subject to an approved NDA:

- *DRUGS STILL PART OF THE DESI PROCESS*. Believe it or not, over 50 years after the passage of the Kefauver-Harris amendments, some drugs are being marketed "subject to the ongoing [DESI] review" as of 2014, including Donnatal® (belladonna and phenobarbital) and Librax® (chlordiazepoxide and clidinium bromide).[198]
- *DRUGS "IRS" TO A WITHDRAWN DESI DRUG.* Drug products which were not included in the DESI program, but which are identical, related, or similar (IRS) to a DESI product which was withdrawn.
- *DRUGS "IRS" TO AN EFFECTIVE DESI DRUG WITH NO NDA.* Drug products which are IRS to a DESI product which was found effective, but for which an NDA has never been filed or approved.

- *"PRESCRIPTION DRUG WRAP UP" DRUGS.* These drugs include those that were not approved prior to 1962 and are not IRS to DESI drugs, plus the majority of pre-1938 drugs that the FDA believes are no longer covered by the "grandfather clauses" of the 1938 and 1962 acts.
- *DRUGS FIRST MARKETED AFTER 1962 OR CHANGED AFTER 1962 WITHOUT AN NDA.*
- *OTC PRODUCTS THAT DO NOT COMPLY WITH THE OTC MONOGRAPHS AND DO NOT HAVE INDIVIDUAL APPROVED NDAS.*

UNAPPROVED DRUGS TODAY. The FDA issued a Compliance Policy Guide on Marketing Unapproved Drugs (CPG Section 440-100) in June 2006 that allowed the agency to take a closer look at pre-1938 drugs and possibly remove them from the market, or require manufacturers to bring market only dosage forms that have met FDCA requirements. The guide was updated and revised in 2011.[199]

REMOVING UNAPPROVED DRUGS from the market is a renewed initiative of the FDA, and pharmacists will be facing more issues surrounding an estimated 2% of all marketed drugs which can still be found on pharmacy shelves.

ENFORCEMENT PRIORITIES. Because of limited enforcement resources, the FDA has set a priority for dealing with unapproved drugs, with highest priority assigned to:

- Drugs with potential safety risks
- Drugs that lack evidence of effectiveness
- Health fraud drugs
- Drugs that present direct challenges to the new drug approval and OTC monograph systems
- Unapproved drugs that specifically violate other provisions of the FDCA
- Drugs that are reformulated to evade FDA enforcement actions

Enforcement actions listed on the FDA website in early 2015 have removed the following products from the market that were being marketed without an approved NDA: balanced salt solution (ophthalmic); carbinoxamine products; various codeine oral dosage forms; colchicine products; quinine sulfate products; trimethobenzamide suppositories; and other unapproved drugs.[200]

The FDA has also pursued lawsuits under the Federal False Claims Act (see Chapter 8) against several manufacturers, obtaining settlements in excess of $450 million in 2010 and 2011, with additional claims pending.

WHEN AN NDA IS APPROVED FOR A FORMERLY UNAPPROVED DRUG. The FDA, on a case-by-case basis, will take more aggressive action when an approved NDA is granted for one product in a class, when other manufacturers continue to market unapproved versions of the drug.

However, FDA noted in 2011 that it will "balance the need to provide incentives for voluntary compliance against the implications of enforcement actions on the marketplace and on consumers who are accustomed to using the marketed products." This appears to be in response to the experience with its approval in February 2011 of Makena® (hydroxyprogesterone caproate injection) for use in threatened preterm births. The manufacturer (KV Pharmaceutical) released the product at $1,500 per dose, or approximately 100 times the cost of the drug when it was being compounded by pharmacies. By March 2011, the FDA publicly announced it would exercise discretion and not take action against pharmacies compounding hydroxyprogesterone caproate injection in full compliance with state laws. The manufacturer reduced its price to $690 per dose.[201,202] In June, 2012, the FDA issued a statement that it would apply its normal enforcement policies to pharmacies compounding hydroxyprogesterone caproate.

FEDERAL FUNDS CAN'T BE USED FOR LTE DRUGS. Federal regulation relating to the Medicaid program prohibits use of federal funds to pay for drugs which have been rated LTE. If states wish to pay for any of these drugs, they must do so with state funds only. Similarly, LTE drugs have been excluded from Medicare Part D coverage.

"ECONOMIC" AMENDMENTS. Other amendments since 1976 have largely dealt with economic issues, including marketing, patent rights, and promotion of generic drugs. These include:

ORPHAN DRUG ACT OF 1983, extending patent protection and giving tax relief to companies that develop needed drugs without significant market potential.

WAXMAN-HATCH AMENDMENT OF 1984, which streamlined processes for approval of generic drugs, and gave extended terms of patents for certain drugs.

PRESCRIPTION DRUG MARKETING ACT OF 1987, which controls distribution of legend drug samples, reselling of drugs by hospitals, and requires state licensing of drug wholesalers. (Many of the provisions of the PDMA have been replaced by the Drug Supply Chain Security Act (see below).)

FDAMA. The Food and Drug Administration Modernization Act of 1997 created significant changes in the FDCA, predominantly affecting manufacturers.

- Required studies of drugs in pediatric patients
- Set forth FDA authority to regulate compounding of solutions used in PET scans
- Created a system of fast-track approvals of critical drugs
- Established user fees for processing of NDAs
- Simplified labeling, allows "Rx only" instead of the former legend
- Allowed for manufacturers to disseminate information on "off-label" uses – this provision is now "sunsetted"

A major section dealt with pharmacy compounding, but the section's ban on advertising was challenged as an unconstitutional violation of the First Amendment. The section was invalidated by the 9th Circuit in *Western States Medical Center v. Shalala,* 238 F.3d 1090 (2001), and upheld as to certain parts by the Supreme Court in *Thompson v. Western States Medical Center,* 238 F.3d 1090 (2002).[203] The 5th Circuit ruled that the compounding provisions of FDAMA, absent the ban on advertising, remain in force.[204] The 2013 enactment of the Drug Quality and Safety Act reenacted this section. (See section on Compounding).

FDAAA. The Food and Drug Administration Amendments Act of 2007[205] was passed primarily to reauthorize the use of user fees to support FDA NDA review activities, and to allow user fees related to review and approval of medical devices. However, several additional reforms were included in the Act. Among the most important for pharmacists are:

FDA AUTHORITY TO REQUIRE NEW SAFETY LABELING IN PRESCRIPTION DRUG LABELING. The FDA can force the manufacturer to include specific "new safety information" in the prescription drug labeling, rather than "negotiate" the language to be used.

FDA AUTHORITY TO REQUIRE POST-MARKETING CLINICAL TRIALS FOR APPROVED DRUGS. The FDA can now insist that a manufacturer conduct additional trials on marketed drugs:

- To assess a known serious risk related to the use of the drug involved.
- To assess signals of serious risk related to the use of the drug.
- To identify an unexpected serious risk when available data indicates the potential for a serious risk

REMS. The FDA may require manufacturers to develop Risk Evaluation and Mitigation Strategies (REMS) as a condition of approval of a new drug, or as a post-approval requirement pursuant to new safety information. A REMS may apply to a single drug product or to an entire class (e.g., NSAIDs or long-acting opioids). A list of drugs with approved REMS is on the FDA website.[206]

ELEMENTS OF A REMS PLAN MAY INCLUDE ANY OR ALL OF THE FOLLOWING:

- Assessments at 18 months, 3 years, and 7 years
- Medication Guide or PPI development
- Communication plan to health professionals
- Access plans to insure safe use for drugs with high risk, which may include one or more of the following strategies:
- Limit prescribing to providers with special training
- Limit dispensing to certified providers
- Limit administration to patients in certain settings
- Limit distribution to patients with documentation of safe-use conditions, such as laboratory tests
- Require monitoring for each patient receiving the drug
- Require each patient to be enrolled in a registry

Examples of current control programs that could be considered REMS with access plans include the controlled distribution and blood monitoring system for Clozaril®, and the iPledge[207] program for Accutane® prescribing and dispensing. In 2009 the FDA published a proposed REMS for long-acting opioids, including fentanyl, methadone, and long-acting forms of oxycodone and morphine. A REMS was approved in July 2012 and significantly revised in September 2013 (See also Chapter 5).

REMS ARE ENFORCEABLE against both manufacturers and practitioners

- The drug sponsor (manufacturer) may not introduce a product into interstate commerce if in violations of the provisions of a REMS for the drug
- A dispenser who distributes the drug in violation of the REMS has created a misbranded product
- FDA can impose civil penalties against manufacturers or providers who violate FDAAA; and criminal penalties may be imposed on manufacturers
- Some courts have held that failure to distribute a required Medication Guide could constitute evidence of negligence on the part of the pharmacist.[208]

THE NATIONAL INSTITUTES OF HEALTH WILL EXPAND ITS "CLINICAL TRIALS DATABASE," and manufacturers will be required to provide information on all of their sponsored clinical trials. This information will be accessible online to the general public.

THE FDA MAY REQUIRE PRE-BROADCAST REVIEW OF TELEVISION ADVERTISING FOR PRESCRIPTION DRUGS. Manufacturers may submit direct-to-consumer advertising for prior review by FDA. The FDA may review DTC ads to assure that the "major statement" concerning the drug's name, conditions of use, side effects and contraindications is presented in a "clear, conspicuous, and neutral manner."

PHARMACISTS MUST DISTRIBUTE TO PATIENTS A "SIDE EFFECTS STATEMENT." (See section on prescription labeling, below.)

FDASIA. The Food and Drug Administration Safety and Innovation Act of 2012[209] is the most recent attempt by Congress to enhance the authority of the FDA to deal with emerging issues and technologies. It consists of 11 major sections (titles):

- Reauthorization and expansion of user fees charged by FDA to review applications for new drugs and medical devices (Titles I through IV). These provisions increase fee levels for prescription drug and medical device user fees, and add new user fees for generic drug applications and biosimilar drugs applications.
- Makes permanent the provisions of the Best Pharmaceuticals for Children Act and the Pediatric Research Equity Act previously enacted or reenacted as part of FDAMA and FDAAA (Title V).
- Revision of regulatory requirements for medical devices (Title VI).
- Enhancing FDA's authority to inspect producers and distributors of drugs throughout the drug supply chain (Title VII).
- Incentives to encourage development of products for antibiotic-resistant infections (Title VIII).
- Expanding the range of products that qualify for accelerated approval, including a category of "breakthrough therapies. (Title IX).
- Addressing the problem of drug shortages (Title X).
- Reauthorization of certain portions of FDAAA, and enacting miscellaneous provisions related to medical gases, prescription drug abuse, controlled substances, nanotechnology, and controlled substances, among others.

FDASIA provisions are discussed where appropriate in other sections of this text.

FDARA. The FDA Reauthorization Act of 2017,[210] in a manner similar to the FDAAA, primarily reauthorizes the user-fees previously enacted by the Prescription Drug User Fee amendments (PDUFA), the Medical Device User Fee Amendments (MDUFA), the Generic Drug User Fee Amendments (GDUFA), and the Biosimilar User Fee Act (BsUFA). Changes are made to the inspection process used by FDA for medical devices, and the statute makes changes to the process by which generic drug developers can gain exclusivity.

BIOLOGICS PRICE COMPETITION AND INNOVATION ACT OF 2009

The BPCIA is for biological products the counterpart to the Hatch-Waxman amendments, and creates a pathway for follow-on biological products that are highly similar to a reference product to be marketed without completing a full NDA or BLA. Until March 2020, it is possible for a biologic product to be approved under an NDA, and an approved NDA is deemed equivalent to a "license" issued under a BLA. Follow-on biologics that are highly similar are approved based on a "351K" application to be declared "interchangeable," which is a biologic product's alternative to being a generic equivalent. The BPCIA gives the reference product 12 years of "data exclusivity" following its initial approval, which means that a 351K application for an interchangeable product cannot be approved during that time. After March 23, 2020, biologic products can no longer be approved based on an NDA, but only on the basis of a BLA. See further discussion of biologic drug products below.

DRUG QUALITY & SECURITY ACT OF 2013. In November 2013, largely in response to the New England Compounding Center meningitis epidemic,[211] Congress passed the Drug Quality & Security Act.[212] The first part of the Act dealt with pharmaceutical compounding, and the second part established a 10-year timeline for electronic track and trace of drug products. See following sections on Compounding and on the Drug Supply Chain.

21ST CENTURY CURES ACT OF 2016. Unusual for the 114th Congress, drug industry lobbyists generated widespread bipartisan support for H.R. 34, "An Act to accelerate the discovery, development, and delivery of 21st century cures, and for other purposes," otherwise known as the 21st Century Cures Act.[213] It featured $6.3 billion of new funding, much going to support research supported by the National Institutes of Health (NIH). About $1 billion of the funding went to state grants to fight the opioid epidemic as envisioned by the Comprehensive Addiction and Recovery Act (CARA), passed earlier in 2016 (see Chapter 5). Its major impact on the FDCA is to revise requirements for drug approval, ostensibly to expedite drug approvals. A major revision is to allow the use of "data summaries," or "real world evidence," such as observational studies, insurance claims data, and anecdotal information including patient input, to substitute in some cases for controlled clinical studies. (See below) The Act strengthens regulations requiring that insurers cover mental health treatments on a par with coverage for other medical conditions (see Chapter 8), and provides for some changes to HIPAA rules for "compassionate communication" (see Chapter 6) and directs DHHS to revise part 2 of 42 CFR governing disclosures for persons in substance abuse treatment programs (see Chapter 5).

PUBLIC HEALTH SERVICE ACT.[214] The PHSA was enacted in 1944 and has been amended frequently since then. It is a wide-ranging set of federal laws that have a significant impact on health professionals, including pharmacists. Federal law governing health maintenance organizations, accountable care organizations, research ethics, healthcare quality research, health information technology, and health professions education are all subsumed within the PHSA. The so-called "340B" drug pricing program is described in section 340b of the PHSA. The Act also provides for regulation of biological products by the FDA (see below).

RX-TO-OTC SWITCHES. Most modern new drugs begin their marketed lives as legend drugs. However, after some time on the market, their general safety and usefulness for the lay public may become better known, and manufacturers may seek to have them moved to OTC status. This process is known as an Rx to OTC switch.

One way by which Rx-OTC switches are initiated is by "Citizens Petitions" to the FDA (which may be submitted by the manufacturer). The conversion of Plan B® from Rx only to OTC for women 15 and over was initiated by a citizen's petition (and a federal lawsuit).

DRUGS THAT ARE BOTH RX AND OTC. A few drugs have for many years been available without prescription, but restricted to sale in a pharmacy. Until very recently, these consisted almost exclusively of OTC products in Controlled Substance Schedule V (see Chapter 5), for which the purchaser had to sign a log book that was also signed by a pharmacist. Methamphetamine precursor products containing PSEUDOEPHEDRINE have now been restricted to sale and recording in a log book, but are not specifically restricted to sale by pharmacists (see below and Chapter 5).

PLAN B® (and its generics) require a prescription for persons under age 17, but may be sold without a prescription to persons 17 and older. (Note that Plan B One-Step® is OTC and after March 2014 there are generic versions available, such as Next Choice One-Dose, Take Action, and My Way, and all are labeled for use by women of child-bearing age.)

DEXTROMETHORPHAN-containing products may not be sold OTC in Washington to persons under 18 years of age, and retailers must verify the age of the purchaser, unless the purchaser's outward appearance would reasonably indicate they are 25 or older. (RCW 69.75)

FDA SOLICITS COMMENTS ON A CLASS OF "BEHIND THE COUNTER" (BTC) DRUGS. In October of 2007, the FDA issued a notice of public meeting[215] to receive input on a proposed class of BTC drugs. BTC drugs would be available without prescription, but only from pharmacists who provide an appropriate level of patient assessment and counseling prior to delivery of the drug to the patient. The most frequently mentioned potential class of drugs for BTC status is the statin group of HMG Co-A reductase inhibitors. In general, organized medicine (e.g., the American College of Physicians[216]) has opposed the concept, asserting, among other things, that pharmacists lack the training and time to properly supervise the distribution of BTC medications. The American Medical Association testimony at the November hearing also questioned whether FDA had statutory authority to approve such a class. Pharmacy groups generally supported the concept, with recommendations that would make the distribution of BTC drugs subject to rigorous processes designed to promote patient care. The National Association of Boards of Pharmacy (NABP) has advocated a BTC class of drugs since 1993. Representatives of non-pharmacy retailers (e.g., the Food Marketing Institute) and OTC drug manufacturers were not supportive. Consumer representatives were generally supportive. The comment period was subsequently extended to December 17, 2007.[217] A 2011 commentary by Pray and Pray noted that there are already several drugs or devices that are available without prescription but only from pharmacies, including older forms of beef and pork insulin, OTC Schedule V cough syrups (see chapter 5), and syringes, as well as more recent additions of pseudoephedrine, and emergency contraceptives.[218] Naloxone and epinephrine injectors are being handled in the states in ways to make them more accessible (see below). As noted in Chapter 5, the FDA is actively promoting the development of an OTC version of naloxone.

FDA HOLDS HEARING ON "CONDITIONS OF SAFE USE TO EXPAND ACCESS TO NONPRESCRIPTION DRUGS" IN 2012.**[219]** A revised paradigm for "BTC" drugs was announced by FDA in late February 2012. Under this new approach, FDA was considering ways to make the distinction between prescription and nonprescription drugs less rigid, so that certain drugs could be made available to patients under "conditions of safe use." These conditions would require a pharmacist's intervention or use of "innovative technologies." Possible approaches would include

- Including under certain conditions of safe use:
- Requiring pharmacist intervention to ensure appropriate nonprescription use
- Use of innovative technologies approved or cleared by FDA for use in the pharmacy or other setting
- Requiring an initial prescription for some drugs, but allowing refills as a nonprescription product under conditions for safe use
- Some drugs which would otherwise require a prescription could be approved for nonprescription use with some type of pharmacist intervention as a condition of safe use
- Making the same drug product simultaneously available as both a prescription and nonprescription drug product with conditions of safe use
- The FDA has not updated its website covering this issue since April 2012, and the site is currently "archived."

The growing expansion of pharmacists' scope of practice and eligibility for payment as providers and prescribers of drugs may well obviate the need for a BTC class of drugs.

FEDERAL OTC DRUGS REQUIRING PRESCRIPTIONS IN WASHINGTON. Washington statue (RCW 69.41.075) gives the Pharmacy Commission to require prescriptions for some drugs that are otherwise OTC under federal law.

EPHEDRINE. The Commission has classified federal OTC ephedrine-containing products as prescription-only in Washington (WAC 246-883-030). The rule exempts certain OTC combination bronchodilator products containing 25 mg or less of ephedrine (e.g., Tedral, Bronitin). Subsequently, the FDA has proposed to reclassify ephedrine combinations as not GRASE for OTC use.[220] The FDA continues to allow marketing of single-ingredient bronchodilator products containing ephedrine, but these products will remain prescription-only in Washington.

REGULATION OF BIOLOGIC DRUGS AND THERAPEUTIC BIOLOGICAL PRODUCTS. CBER AND CDER are two FDA Centers that review and approve applications for new drugs or devices.

CBER (the Center for Biologics Evaluation and Research) regulates:

- Allergenics – allergen patch tests and allergenic extracts
- Blood and blood products – blood, blood components, blood bank devices, and blood donor screening tests
- Tissue and tissue products – bone, skin, corneas, ligaments, tendons, stem cells, sperm, and heart valves
- Vaccines and tuberculin tests
- Xenotransplantation – transplantation of non-human cells, tissues, or organs into a human

CDER (the Center for Drug Evaluation and Research), in addition to regulating small-molecule therapeutic drugs, tests, and devices, deals with therapeutic biologic applications for the following types of products:

- Monoclonal antibodies for in-vivo use
- Cytokines, growth factors, enzymes, immunomodulators and thrombolytics
- Proteins intended for therapeutic use that are extracted from animals or microorganisms, including recombinant versions (except clotting factors)
- Other non-vaccine therapeutic immunotherapies

BIOLOGIC LICENSE APPLICATION (BLA). Whereas most drugs are regulated under the FDCA, biologics are subject to the Public Health Service Act. The Act requires a firm who manufactures a biologic for interstate sale to hold a license for the product. These manufacturers submit a Biologics License Application (BLA) to FDA in lieu of an NDA. Biologic products evaluated by CDER are subject to the provisions of PDUFA – and sponsors must pay the applicable user fee.

BIOSIMILAR AND INTERCHANGEABLE BIOLOGICAL PRODUCTS are the "generic equivalents" of biological products. These are also known as "follow-on" biologics. Until 2010, there was no statutory route to allowing licensing of drugs that were similar or interchangeable with existing biologic drugs, except for the follow-on manufacturer to submit a BLA. In March 2010, President Obama signed the Biologics Price Competition and Innovation Act (BPCI Act)[221], which amended the Public Health Services Act to provide a pathway for approval of follow-on biological in a manner not unlike the Waxman-Hatch amendments did for generic drugs. However, the BPCIA allows for greater variation in certain areas between the biosimilar and the reference product.

Applications to market a biosimilar are becoming called "351(k)" applications, because they are allowed under §351(k) of the PHS Act. Such an application must demonstrate that (1) the proposed biologic product is "highly similar to the reference product notwithstanding minor differences in clinically inactive components" and (2) there are "no clinically meaningful differences between the biological product and the reference product in terms of safety, purity, and potency."

Biosimilar labeling. In January 2017, the FDA issued a guidance on nonproprietary labeling for biosimilar drugs.[222] See below.

The 2015 Legislature amended Washington law to allow for interchange of biosimilar drugs that are on a listing provided by the FDA.[223]

STATE REGULATION OF FOOD, DRUGS AND COSMETICS. States generally have adopted a regulatory scheme that parallels the federal approach. Washington statutes implementing this scheme include the following acts.

INTRASTATE COMMERCE IN FOOD, DRUGS AND COSMETICS (formerly the Uniform Food, Drug and Cosmetic Act – RCW 69.04). This is the "FDCA" for Washington, which defines, as does the federal law, misbranding and adulteration, and requires that drugs regulated under the federal law must conform to that law.

Administration of the law is vested in the Director of the Washington State Department of Agriculture. The Director is Derek Sandison. Enforcement and administration of all provisions of the statute that pertain to drugs and cosmetics, however, are placed with the Pharmacy Commission. (RCW 69.04.730) Persons wishing to manufacture drugs in the state file applications with the Pharmacy Commission

CAUSTIC POISON ACT OF 1929 (RCW 69.36). This statute regulates the labeling of specific caustic products sold for household use at retail.

"Dangerous caustic or corrosive substances" subject to the Act include:

- HCl – in concentrations ≥ 10%[224]
- H_2SO_4 – in concentrations ≥ 10%
- HNO_3 – in concentrations ≥ 5%
- Phenol – in concentrations ≥ 5%
- Oxalic acid – in concentrations ≥ 10%
- Acetic acid – in concentrations ≥ 20%[225]
- Hypochlorous acid (HClO) – in any preparation yielding ≥ 10% chlorine
- KOH – in preparations yielding ≥ 10% KOH
- NaOH – in concentrations ≥ 10%
- $AgNO_3$ – in concentrations ≥ 5%
- Ammonia water – in preparations yielding ≥ 5% NH_3

Misbranding of covered caustic poisons is defined as a retail parcel, package, or container of the covered substances that does not contain the following:

- Name of substance
- Name and address of manufacturer, packager, seller, or distributor
- The word "POISON" in contrasting color and letters of at least 24 point size
- Directions for treatment in case of injury
- Labeling requirements do not apply to products
    - sold to pharmacists for dispensing, compounding, or preparing prescriptions,
    - for use by or under the direction of a physician, dentist, or veterinarian
    - for use by a chemist in the practice or teaching of his profession
    - for any industrial or professional use
    - for use in any of the arts or sciences

Community pharmacies (particularly in rural areas) are often sought as a source for these chemicals. The key element here is that retail packages of these products must be labeled according to the Act.

POISON SALES AND MANUFACTURING (RCW 69.38). This act requires that pharmacies or other retailers of specified poisons must maintain a poison register in which sales of specified poisons are recorded. Covered poisons include:

- Arsenic and its preparations
- Cyanide, hydrocyanic acid, and preparations

- Strychnine
- Other substances designated by the Pharmacy Commission – none are currently designated

Excluded products include those regulated under the Caustic Poisons Act of 1929 (RCW 69.04), the Legend Drug Law (RCW 69.41), the Controlled Substances Act (RCW 69.50), the Pesticide Control Act (RCW 15.58), the Pesticide Application Act (RCW 17.21), and the Drug Samples statute (RCW 69.45).

No sales can be made of covered products unless the seller is satisfied as to the identity of the purchaser and that the sale is for a lawful purpose. The register must contain the date and time of sale, the full name and home address of the purchaser, the kind and quantity of poison sold, and the purpose for which the poison is being purchased. The name and address of the purchaser must be verified by examination of photo ID. Pharmacies may dispense poisons on prescription without obtaining a poison distributors license.[226]

POISONS AND DANGEROUS DRUGS (RCW 69.40). This statute prohibits placing poisons in edible products, such as crackers, biscuit, bread or other edible product (e.g., hamburger). It also prohibits distributing milk containing formaldehyde.

POISON INFORMATION CENTERS (RCW 18.76). This statute established a statewide poison information center program.

LEGEND DRUG ACT (RCW 69.41). This is the principal law governing the sale, prescribing, dispensing, and use of legend drugs. Its elements are discussed throughout this textbook where applicable.

CONTROLLED SUBSTANCES. The laws relating to controlled substances are discussed in Chapter 5:

- UNIFORM CONTROLLED SUBSTANCES ACT (RCW 69.50). This is the state parallel to the federal CSA.
- PRECURSOR SUBSTANCES (RCW 69.43). This supplements the Controlled Substances Act by regulating the sale and distribution of chemicals which are used in the production of controlled substances.
- CONTROLLED SUBSTANCES THERAPEUTIC RESEARCH ACT (RCW 69.51)
- MEDICAL MARIJUANA (RCW 69.51A)
- IMITATION CONTROLLED SUBSTANCES (RCW 69.52)
- USE OF BUILDINGS FOR UNLAWFUL DRUGS (RCW 69.53)
- DEATH WITH DIGNITY ACT (RCW 70.245)
- 9-1-1 GOOD SAMARITAN ACT (RCW 69.50.315; RCW 18.130)
- INITIATIVE 502 – MARIJUANA[227] This initiative was passed to "stop treating adult marijuana use as a crime," and authorizes the state liquor control board to regulate and tax marijuana for persons 21 and older, and sets a threshold for DUI related to marijuana. It made a number of amendments to the Controlled Substances Act (RCW 69.50)

OVER-THE-COUNTER MEDICATIONS (RCW 69.60). This statute, now superseded by federal regulations, required that OTC solid dosage forms be imprinted with an identification symbol or code. Because federal requirements (21 CFR 206.01-10) exempted certain products that were subject to the Washington Act, the Pharmacy Commission established by regulation that OTC drugs not covered by federal rules could not be marketed in Washington in the absence of a complying imprint or Board exemption. (WAC 246-885-030)

DRUG DEVELOPMENT IN THE US. The development of new drugs in the United States follows a multistage process.

PRECLINICAL TESTING, *in vitro* and in animals. Preclinical testing begins when the sponsor (manufacturer) files with the FDA of a NOTICE OF INVESTIGATIONAL NEW DRUG (IND). This allows the drug to shipped in interstate commerce for purposes of testing

CLINICAL TESTING.
Before a drug may be marketed for human use, the sponsor must conduct 3 phases of testing in humans.

PHASE I – a small number of healthy volunteers to determine pharmacodynamic and pharmacokinetic properties

PHASE II – a limited number of patients who have the target disease, to determine efficacy and dose-response.

PHASE III – large-scale clinical trials in patients with the disease. At least two clinical trials must be conducted that are double-blinded and placebo-controlled.

Under the 21st Century Cures Act the FDA will have from 2 to 5 years after January 2017 to make changes to the drug approval process that allow for use of "real world evidence," "novel clinical trial designs," and "patient experience data" in making approval decisions.[228]

FILING OF A NEW DRUG APPLICATION (NDA). This filing describes the drug, the results of preclinical and clinical trials, sets forth the proposed labeling, a Risk Management Plan, and describes manufacturing and testing processes. If the NDA is approved, the drug may be marketed. A single NDA may refer to more than one product marketed by the NDA holder as a brand-name drug and one or more "approved generics."

POST-MARKETING SURVEILLANCE (ALSO CALLED PHASE IV). Once a product is released for marketing, the manufacturer must maintain records and file annual reports which include summaries of adverse reactions and problems discovered after marketing. Significant problems must be reported promptly, which may lead to revisions in the labeling. Additional clinical trials may be required by FDA for assessment of safety issues, and manufacturers may utilize additional clinical trials to establish new indications, or new routes or forms of administration, for currently marketed products.

SUPPLEMENTAL NDAS are filed when the manufacturer seeks additional indications or changes in the labeling or production of the drug. These are often preceded by Phase IV trials.

CHANGE BEING EFFECTED (CBE) NOTICE. Labeling changes to improve product safety may be made by holders of NDAs through a notice to FDA of a "Change Being Effected," or CBE. Such a notice allows label changes without prior approval by the FDA. Generic drug manufacturers (ANDA holders) are not able to use the CBE notice, but are expected to propose changes to FDA when new safety information is discovered.

ABBREVIATED NDAS (ANDA) are filed by manufacturers who wish to market generic versions of approved drugs after patent rights expire. (See drug product selection section.)

NEW DRUG APPLICATIONS ARE CLASSIFIED by the FDA using a rating scheme, which is indicated in information announcing the drug's approval. A number indicates the chemical type and a letter (P, S, or O) indicates the priority assigned to the review. The FDA considers 1P (New Molecular Entity that is a Priority review drug) the most important kind of new drug:[229] Information on NDAs is found at Drugs@FDA.

CHEMICAL TYPE	REVIEW TYPE
1 – New Molecular Entity (NME)	P - Priority review drug
2 – New salt or ester of a previously-approved drug	S – Standard review drug
3 – New dosage form	O – Orphan drug
4 – New combination of previously-approved drugs	
5 – New formulation or new manufacturer	
6 – New indication [no longer used]	
7 – Drug already marketed without approved NDC	
8 – OTC switch	
9 – New indication submitted as distinct NDA, consolidated with original NDA after approval	
10 – New indication submitted as distinct NDA, not consolidated	

FOODS

Under the FDCA, "food" means articles used for food or drink for *man*[230] or other animals, chewing gum, and articles used for components of any such article. (21 USC § 321(f))

The FDA regulates labeling of foods, and has powers to seize foods that are adulterated or misbranded. Foods do not require premarketing approval, although certain food additives (colorings, preservatives, etc.) do.

The FDA Food Safety Modernization Act of 2010 was signed into law by President Obama on January 4, 2011. Among its many sweeping reforms is a grant of authority to FDA to initiate a recall of foods that present safety issues.[231]

COSMETICS

Cosmetics are defined under the FDCA to include (1) articles intended to be rubbed, poured, sprinkled, or sprayed on, introduced into, or otherwise applied to the human body or any part thereof for cleansing, beautifying, promoting attractiveness, or altering the appearance, and (2) articles intended for use as a component of any such articles; except that such term shall not include soap. (21 USC § 321(i))

FDA control over cosmetics is primarily restricted to assuring safety. The FDA does not regulate claims made for cosmetics.

PRODUCTS WHICH MAKE THERAPEUTIC CLAIMS are regulated as drugs, or as both cosmetics and drugs. Examples include dandruff shampoos, antiperspirant deodorants, cosmetics claiming sun-protection, and fluoride toothpaste.[232]

Cosmetic manufacturers are not required to register with FDA, but may choose to do so under the Voluntary Cosmetic Registration Program (VCRP).[233]

MEDICAL DEVICES

The FDCA defines **devices** as follows:

The term "device" ... means an instrument, apparatus, implement, machine, contrivance, implant, in vitro reagent, or other similar or related article, including any component, part, or accessory, which is -

- recognized in the official National Formulary, or the United States Pharmacopeia, or any supplement to them,
- intended for use in the diagnosis of disease or other conditions, or in the cure, mitigation, treatment, or prevention of disease, in *man* or other animals, or
- intended to affect the structure or any function of the body of *man* or other animals, and which does not achieve its primary intended purposes through chemical action within or on the body of *man* or other animals and which is not dependent upon being metabolized for the achievement of its primary intended purposes. (21 USC § 321(h)) [Note: the equivalent definitions in Washington's statutes were revised in 2009 to replace *man* with *human beings*.[234]]

MEDICAL DEVICE AMENDMENTS. Significant authority over medical devices was granted to the FDA in 1976, with the passage of the Medical Device Amendments. The publicity concerning deaths and injuries from the Dalkon Shield[235] intrauterine device is considered one of the factors leading to the passage of these amendments. The problems with the Dalkon Shield led to the bankruptcy of the A.H. Robins Co., formerly one of America's most respected drug firms, and the outcomes of the second largest class action lawsuit (after asbestos) in American history are still unfolding.

The 21st Century Cures Act includes several amendments to the medical device requirements, including easing reporting requirements for certain class I and class II devices, and improvements to the requirements for obtaining CLIA waivers for office-based laboratory tests. (See below)

DEVICE CLASSIFICATIONS. The Device Amendments modified the FDCA to provide, among other provisions, the following classification of devices:[236]

- CLASS I – Common and simple devices needing to conform to general standards (e.g., tongue depressors, bandages, neck braces)
- CLASS II – Devices needing to meet specific performance standards (e.g., thermometers)
- CLASS III – Devices that pose risk of injury if not properly used or produced, that require pre-market approval (e.g., defibrillators, pacemakers, IUDs, laboratory tests)

RESTRICTED DEVICES. Some devices require a prescription or order of a prescriber to sell or dispense. These are labeled "Caution: Federal law restricts this device to sale by or on the order of a physician."

SYRINGES AND NEEDLES. Syringes and needles are not restricted devices under federal law. However, many states place restrictions on the sale of injection devices, and may require a prescription before a pharmacist may make a sale.

NEEDLE EXCHANGE PROGRAMS ARE LEGAL IN WASHINGTON. PHARMACISTS MAY SELL SYRINGES AND NEEDLES TO ADULT IV DRUG USERS. Washington law allows pharmacists to sell needles and syringes without prescription, subject to the requirement that "On the sale at retail of any hypodermic syringe, hypodermic needle, or any device adapted for the use of drugs by injection, the retailer shall satisfy himself or herself that the device will be used for the legal use intended." (RCW 70.115.050) SHB 1759, passed in 2002, modified the state's drug paraphernalia law, and added the following provisions:

- Making it lawful for "any person over the age of eighteen to possess sterile hypodermic syringes and needles for the purpose of reducing blood borne diseases" (RCW 69.50.412(5)).
- Specifying that nothing in the Drug Paraphernalia Act "prohibits legal distribution of injection syringe equipment through public health and community based HIV prevention programs, and pharmacies." (RCW 69.50.412(3))
- Specifying that "Nothing contained in [the Drug Paraphernalia Act] shall be construed to require a retailer to sell hypodermic needles or syringes to any person." (RCW 70.115.060)

Under these provisions, needle exchange programs are legal in Washington, and pharmacists may sell syringes and needles to persons over the age of eighteen, even if those persons are believed to be using the devices to inject illegal drugs, providing that the purpose of the sale is to prevent spread of blood borne pathogens, such as HIV, HBV, or HCV.

A summary of state laws regulating syringe sales is available on the internet at http://www.temple.edu/lawschool/phrhcs/otc.htm.

POSSESSION OF TRACES OF CONTROLLED SUBSTANCES ILLEGAL. Although it is legal for an IV drug user to possess syringes and needles, controlled substance residue in the syringe may still be used as evidence of illegal possession of controlled drugs. Under Washington law, unlawful possession of even a trace amount of controlled substance is punishable by up to 5 years in prison, a fine of up to $10,000, or both (RCW 69.50.140(d), *State v. Malone*, 864 P.2d 990 (Wash.App.Div. 1994)).

LABORATORY TESTS. Clinical laboratory tests are regulated as devices, and generally must be performed in a qualified clinical laboratory registered under the Clinical Laboratory Improvement Amendments (CLIA).[237] Laboratories must meet requirements for calibration of tests, quality and training of personnel, proficiency testing, records and specimen retention, quality assurance, and other requirements for Good Laboratory Procedures. Pharmacists and other health professionals performing point-of-care-based laboratory tests must obtain a waiver from these requirements, which is called a CLIA Waiver. This allows them to perform tests using certain laboratory testing devices that have also been certified by the FDA as CLIA-waived devices. In many states, the CLIA waiver for a health professional is obtained from the CMS website[238] using federal form CMS-116, but in Washington, CLIA waivers are obtained from the Department of Health's Laboratory Quality Assurance Program.[239]

MERCURY-CONTAINING DEVICES. Concerns with the buildup of mercury in the environment led the Legislature in 2006 to prohibit the sale of thermostats and other devices containing mercury, including medical thermometers and manometers. Exceptions are:

- Prescribed thermometers, such as low-temperature reading devices or basal temperature thermometers;
- Electronic thermometers with mercury-containing batteries;
- Thermometers or manometers used to calibrate other devices;
- Devices sold to hospitals or hospital-controlled health care facilities that have adopted a plan for mercury reduction in accordance with state law. (RCW 70.95M.050)

Additional information is available from the DOH,[240] and from the Department of Ecology.[241]

ANIMAL DRUGS

This textbook, unless otherwise specified, discusses drugs for use in *humans*. The FDA also regulates drugs used to treat other animal species, and shares with the Department of Agriculture responsibility for drugs and other chemicals used in animal feed or in the production of foods. The FDCA makes a distinction between a "new drug" and a "new animal drug" and enforces specific regulations for both types of drugs. In general, veterinarians may prescribe human drugs for animals, and pharmacies may fill them. It should be noted that many human drugs are toxic to specific species, such as lincomycin's gastrointestinal toxicity in horses, and other drugs are less toxic in other animal species than in humans, such as chloramphenicol in dogs. Animal drugs may not be used in humans, and there are species-specific restrictions on their use in other animals. Also, animal drugs used in feed may pose environmental and other dangers, and there are a number of animal drugs that may not be administered in feed. The regulations also treat non-food animals (e.g., cats and dogs) differently from animals intended for human food (e.g., cattle, pigs, chickens, etc.). Veterinarians increasingly refer to "pets" as companion animals, whose proper care is worthwhile in itself, but frequently important to the health of their human companions as well.

The FDA's Center for Veterinary Medicine[242] administers the FDCA as it pertains to drugs used in animals and in animal feed. The veterinary equivalent to the "Orange Book" is the "Green Book"[243] (FDA Approved Animal Drug Products).

Two federal laws are of interest to pharmacists involved in veterinary pharmacy or in supplying drugs to veterinarians.

THE ANIMAL MEDICINAL DRUG USE CLARIFICATION ACT OF 1994 (AMDUCA), which provides for veterinarian prescribing of extra-label drug use (ELDU) for non-food animals.

THE MINOR USES AND MINOR SPECIES HEALTH ACT OF 2004 (MUMS), which provides for legal use of non-approved drugs in minor animal species such as ornamental fish, zoo animals, ferrets, and even sheep and goats, among others. Minor uses are off-label uses of drugs for uncommon diseases in major species.

Many pharmacists compound drugs for use in animals, with creating flavored dosage forms for companion cats being a particularly significant activity. The FDA has attempted to enforce its view that AMDUCA prohibits compounding animal drugs from bulk ingredients, and sought an injunction against a Florida pharmacy. The federal district court ruled against FDA, holding that its Compliance Policy Guide on animal compounding was contrary to prior enforcement and was not the subject of notice-and-comment rule-making.[244] (See compounding) The government and the pharmacy ultimately reached a settlement following the suit and jointly moved to vacate the decision as moot, which was granted. So, although the Court found against the FDA, its decision is no longer in force.[245]

The FDA's position in 2019 is that it has withdrawn the policy guidance documents at issue in the lawsuit, and is in the process of issuing a new guidance document on compounding of animal drugs pursuant to veterinarians' prescriptions: "In developing the new draft, the FDA will carefully consider the issues that are specific to compounding of animal drugs, including the significance of using compounded drugs as a treatment option in various veterinary settings and animal species. Until we publish final guidance on this issue, FDA intends to look at the totality of the circumstances when determining whether to take enforcement action for unlawful animal drug compounding activities."[246]

DRUGS – GENERALLY

The FDCA was enacted in 1938, at a time when the concept of prescription-only drugs (other than narcotics) was over a decade in the future. Thus, the original view of the Act was that all drugs would be marketed only if the manufacturer could show they were safe for use by humans in accordance with the labeling that would be available to the user or consumer. As with other categories of articles regulated under the Act, whether a substance is a "drug" depends on its INTENDED USE.

For example, earlier we saw that whether an article was a device depends in part on whether it is *intended* to diagnose or treat conditions in humans or animals, and for an article to be a cosmetic required that it be *intended* only for application to the skin to cleanse or beautify. Drugs differ from devices in that they depend upon some form of chemical action to affect body function.

FDCA DEFINITION OF "DRUG"

21 USC § 321 (g) (1) - The term "drug" means

(A) articles recognized in the official United States Pharmacopoeia [*sic*], official Homoeopathic Pharmacopoeia of the United States, or official National Formulary, or any supplement to any of them; and

(B) articles INTENDED FOR USE IN THE DIAGNOSIS, CURE, MITIGATION, TREATMENT, OR PREVENTION OF DISEASE IN MAN* OR OTHER ANIMALS; and

(C) articles (other than food) intended to affect the structure or any function of the body of man* or other animals; and

(D) articles intended for use as a component of any article specified in clause (A), (B), or (C). A food or dietary supplement for which a claim, subject to sections 343(r)(1)(B) and 343(r)(3) of this title or sections 343(r)(1)(B) and 343(r)(5)(D) of this title, is made in accordance with the requirements of section 343(r) of this title is not a drug solely because the label or the labeling contains such a claim. A food, dietary ingredient, or dietary supplement for which a truthful and not misleading statement is made in accordance with section 343(r)(6) of this title is not a drug under clause (C) solely because the label or the labeling contains such a statement.

*As noted above, equivalent Washington definitions of "drug" have been amended to replace "man" with "human beings."

As a result of the history of the FDCA, there are two major types of drugs that are regulated differently based on whether they may be sold directly to the general public or require a prescription. However, all drugs must meet the tests in the FDCA of SAFETY, EFFECTIVENESS, and freedom from ADULTERATION or MISBRANDING.

NON-PRESCRIPTION (OTC) DRUGS

ADULTERATION AND MISBRANDING

The 1938 Act retained two key requirements for marketing of drugs in the US that were in the Wiley Law: they may neither be adulterated nor misbranded. Drugs that fail either of these requirements may be seized and removed from the marketplace by the FDA, and marketers or sellers of the products may be subject to criminal or civil penalties.

ADULTERATION. A drug is *adulterated* if it CONTAINS ANY ADDED DELETERIOUS SUBSTANCES, HAS BEEN STORED IMPROPERLY, OR IS PACKAGED IN SUCH A WAY AS TO ALLOW DETERIORATION. (21 USC § 351)

Any article listed in the official compendium (i.e., the USP/NF) must conform to compendial standards for purity, quality, strength, and appropriate assays.

Drugs must be stored in accordance with USP standards, and any special requirements specified on the manufacturer's label.

The USP defines the following temperature ranges for storing drugs:

- Controlled room temperature – 68 °F to 77 °F (20 °C to 25 °C), subject to requirements for the maximum "mean kinetic temperature" and limited excursions and "spikes."
- Cool place – between 46 °F and 59 °F (8 °C and 15 °C)
- Cold place – a "refrigerator," between 36 °F and 46 °F (2 °C to 8 °C)
- Freezer – a place maintained between -13 °F and 14 °F (-25 °C to -10 °C)

Pharmacies must maintain their drug storage areas within a controlled range, which requires air conditioning in most areas of the US. Refrigerators or freezers used to store drugs may not be used to store food or non-drug products.

MISBRANDING. A drug is *misbranded* if it's LABELING IS INCOMPLETE OR MISLEADING. Repackaging an OTC drug without supplying all the information contained on the original bottle is a form of misbranding. (21 USC § 352)

The "LABEL" of a drug is the actual label affixed to the bottle or box containing the medication. The "LABELING" includes the label, and any other printed or written material accompanying the drug. Labeling also includes statements made by the manufacture or seller in promotional materials, advertisements, or other communications to patients or health professionals.

OTC drugs must bear adequate directions so that lay persons can use the product safely and effectively. If a product cannot be labeled in such a way that the consumer can use it just by reading the label, it will be restricted to sale by prescription.

REQUIRED OTC LABELING. Specific elements are required by the FDCA on the labels of OTC drugs. The "7-point label" must contain:

- Name of Product
- Name and address of manufacturer, packager, distributor
- Net contents
- Active ingredients and quantity of certain other ingredients
- Name of any habit forming drug
- Cautions and warnings
- Adequate directions for use

STANDARDIZED "DRUG FACTS" OTC LABELS. FDA regulations[247] that require the same format for all OTC labels. Information about the OTC product must be in plain language and provide the following in the order shown:

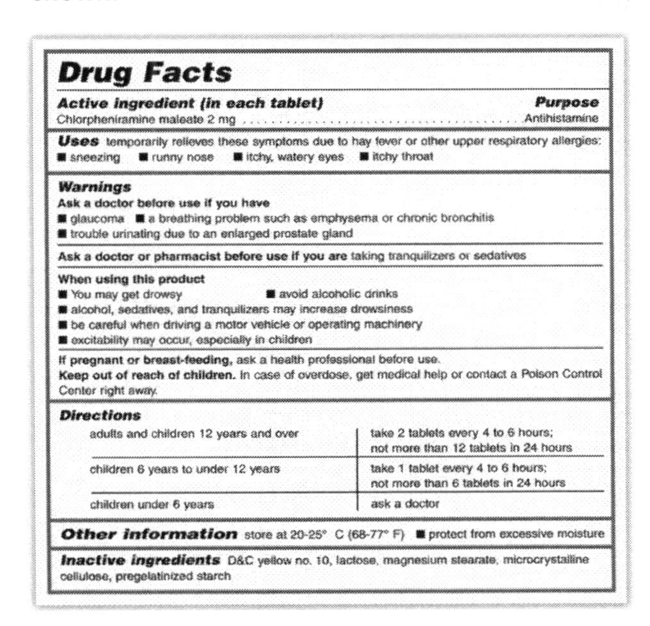

Drug Facts

Active ingredient (in each tablet) — **Purpose**
Chlorpheniramine maleate 2 mg .... Antihistamine

Uses temporarily relieves these symptoms due to hay fever or other upper respiratory allergies:
■ sneezing ■ runny nose ■ itchy, watery eyes ■ itchy throat

Warnings
Ask a doctor before use if you have
■ glaucoma ■ a breathing problem such as emphysema or chronic bronchitis
■ trouble urinating due to an enlarged prostate gland

Ask a doctor or pharmacist before use if you are taking tranquilizers or sedatives

When using this product
■ You may get drowsy ■ avoid alcoholic drinks
■ alcohol, sedatives, and tranquilizers may increase drowsiness
■ be careful when driving a motor vehicle or operating machinery
■ excitability may occur, especially in children

If pregnant or breast-feeding, ask a health professional before use.
Keep out of reach of children. In case of overdose, get medical help or contact a Poison Control Center right away.

Directions

adults and children 12 years and over	take 2 tablets every 4 to 6 hours; not more than 12 tablets in 24 hours
children 6 years to under 12 years	take 1 tablet every 4 to 6 hours; not more than 6 tablets in 24 hours
children under 6 years	ask a doctor

Other information store at 20-25° C (68-77° F) ■ protect from excessive moisture

Inactive ingredients D&C yellow no. 10, lactose, magnesium stearate, microcrystalline cellulose, pregelatinized starch

The product's active ingredients, including the amount in each dosage unit.

The purpose of the product.

The uses (indications) for the product.

Specific warnings, including when the product should not be used under any circumstances, and when it is appropriate to consult with a doctor or pharmacist. This section also describes side effects that could occur and substances or activities to avoid.

Dosage instructions--when, how, and how often to take the product.

The product's inactive ingredients, important information to help consumers avoid ingredients that may cause an allergic reaction.

IMPRINTS REQUIRED ON SOLID ORAL DOSAGE FORMS. Washington requires that all OTC solid oral dosage forms sold in the state must be imprinted with a distinctive symbol or code. (RCW 69.60) Subsequent FDA regulations (21 CFR 206) require imprints on virtually all US OTC products.

ENGLISH LANGUAGE REQUIRED. All required label elements must be in English (21 CFR 201.15(c)(1)). This requirement is implemented in WA regulations in WAC 246-869-150(4).[248]

SPANISH-SPEAKING US TERRITORIES. However, drugs distributed in Puerto Rico, or a US Territory where the predominant language is other than English, the label elements may be in the predominant language. (21 CFR 201.15(c)(1) Drugs labeled in English that include any representations in the label or labeling in a foreign language (e.g., Spanish or French) must also include all the other required information in the same foreign language (21 CFR 201.15(c)(2,3).

POISON-PREVENTION PACKAGING. Selected OTC products must be packaged in "special packaging," otherwise known as child-resistant containers (CRCs), as required by the Poison Prevention Packaging Act (15 USC §§ 1471-1474). Regulations implementing the act are developed by the Consumer Product Safety Commission, which publishes "Poison Prevention Packaging: A Guide for Healthcare Professionals."[249] Rules for non-prescription drugs are contained in 16 CFR § 1700.14.

POISON-PREVENTION PACKAGING

- NOT REQUIRED FOR MOST OTC PRODUCTS, with specific exceptions
- REQUIRED FOR MOST RX PRODUCTS, with some exceptions

OTC Drugs Requiring Child-Resistant Containers include:

- ASPIRIN (ASA) OR ACETAMINOPHEN (APAP): any formulation containing ASA in any amount or containing APAP > 1 g/package.
  Exceptions: Effervescent tablets/granules ≤ 15% ASA or APAP, if the oral LD_{50} of the granules ≥ 5 g/Kg or unflavored APAP or ASA-containing powders (not intended for pediatric use) packaged in unit doses providing ≤ 13 *grains* APAP or ≤ 15.4 *grains* ASA per unit dose. (What would these quantities be in *milligrams*?)
- NSAIDS: Ibuprofen > 1 g/package; Naproxen > 250 mg/package; Ketoprofen > 50 mg/package
- IRON preparations (including dietary supplements) > 250 mg elemental iron per package
- DIPHENHYDRAMINE > 66 mg/package
- FLUORIDE > 50 mg fluoride ion (F^-)/package or > 0.5% w/v of fluoride ion
- LIDOCAINE > 5 mg/package or DIBUCAINE > 0.5 mg/package
- LOPERAMIDE > 0.045 mg/package
- MINOXIDIL > 14 mg/package
- METHACRYLIC ACID (in liquid bandage) > 5% w/v
- METHYL SALICYLATE – any quantity
- ETHYLENE GLYCOL – any quantity
- METHYL ALCOHOL – any quantity
- MOUTHWASH containing 3 g or more ethanol/package; however a pump container with non-removable pump, containing 7% w/w or more cinnamon or mint flavoring, and < 15 g of ethanol per container, and dispensing < 0.03 g of ethanol per pump is exempt.
- HYDROCARBONS, SOLVENTS, HOUSEHOLD FUELS; drugs and cosmetics containing low-viscosity hydrocarbons (e.g., certain light mineral oil, NF)
- NAOH, KOH – any quantity
- H_2SO_4 – any quantity
- PERMANENT WAVE NEUTRALIZERS (> 600 mg $NaBrO_3$ or >50 mg $KBrO_3$)
- PREVIOUS RX-ONLY PRODUCTS - other OTCs containing any active ingredient that was previously available for oral administration only by prescription (e.g., omeprazole, ranitidine)
- OTC CONTROLLED SUBSTANCES – any quantity
- LIQUID NICOTINE PRODUCTS – added to the PPPA requirements by the Child Nicotine Poisoning Prevention Act of 2015.[250] Certain forms of packaging for e-cigarette refills may be exempted.

Packages for Households without Small Children. For OTC drugs, each manufacturer must make at least one package size with a CRC. A manufacturer may make one size only that is intended for households without small children. It must bear the caution "This Package for Households without Young Children." For small packages, the manufacturer may substitute the wording, "Package Not Child-Resistant."

Dispensing covered OTCs by prescription. Washington law requires pharmacists who dispense any of the above-listed OTC drugs on prescription to use a CRC. (RCW 18.64.246 and WAC 246-869-230) These regulations can be read to require CRCs on all prescriptions in which OTC drugs are dispensed, even if the CPSC has not listed the product, but in at least one state court case the judge ruled to the contrary.

PREVENTING PRODUCT TAMPERING. Problems with product tampering have led to requirements in the 1983 Federal Anti-Tampering Act (18 USC § 1365). Most OTC drugs, devices, and cosmetics require the following elements (dentifrices, dermatologicals, lozenges, and insulin are exempted):

- An indicator of tampering or barrier to entry, that
- If breached or missing provides visible evidence of tampering; and
- A label statement must describe the barrier or indicator.

An OTC product that is on a pharmacy shelf whose packaging is damaged is MISBRANDED and in violation of the anti-tampering act. The responsible pharmacist manager within the store may be held liable for not assuring that such products are removed from the shelves, even in establishments where the pharmacist doesn't stock or order OTC products.

RECALLS OF OTC PRODUCTS are handled in the same manner as for legend drugs (see below).

UNLABELED USES OF OTC DRUGS. Sellers are responsible for any false, misleading, or unapproved claims they or their employees make concerning OTC products that are not consistent with the approved labeling. Pharmacists are allowed to make recommendations to customers about the hazards and benefits of medications, consistent with their knowledge, training, experience, and good judgment. Specific assurances ("this is perfectly safe for your baby") may create a warranty of fitness for a particular purchase that can lead to liability to the consumer if the product does not perform as stated or is harmful (see Chapter 7).

CONTROLLED OTC SUBSTANCES (see also Chapter 5).

The Controlled Substances Act permits the sale of certain products without a prescription. However, unlike most other OTC products, these products may only be sold by pharmacists pursuant to state and federal laws.

METHAMPHETAMINE PRECURSOR-CONTAINING PRODUCTS

At various times it has been permissible to sell cough-and-cold or diet-control preparations containing ephedrine, phenylpropanolamine (PPA), or pseudoephedrine as OTC formulations. Each of these ingredients has been a source of illegal production of methamphetamine.

PPA was found to be associated in OTC doses of 75 mg or greater with increased risk of hemorrhagic stroke, and the FDA requested all manufacturers to voluntarily recall PPA-containing OTC products in November, 2000. On December 22, 2005, the FDA published a proposed final rule that would permanently place OTC formulations of PPA in Category II, i.e., not approved for use OTC, and has established a 90-day comment period. (70 FR 75988-98, December 22, 2005.)

Drug products containing EPHEDRA or its alkaloids may not be promoted for weight loss, enhancement of athletic performance, or as stimulants. In July 2005, the FDA published a proposed final rule allowing the continued use of ephedrine alkaloids with enhanced warnings and label requirements (70 FR 40237-49, July 13, 2005). Subsequently, the FDA has proposed to reclassify ephedrine *combinations* as not GRASE for OTC use,[251] but will continue to allow single-ingredient products. Certain ephedrine salts may be used in ophthalmic preparations or nasal sprays and in rectal products used to treat hemorrhoids; in all cases as topical vasoconstrictor. Single-ingredient ephedrine/ephedra products are further restricted to sale behind the counter by DEA rules (see Chapter 5). Washington law classifies all ephedrine containing products, except certain combinations which have been removed from the market, as prescription-only drugs.

Pseudoephedrine containing products are now restricted by both federal and state laws which limit the quantity that can be sold at any one time and/or require the product to be kept behind the counter. (See also Chapter 5) Manufacturers are reformulating many nasal decongestant products with phenylephrine to allow their brand to be continued to be sold without restriction.

NON-PHARMACY SALES OF OTC DRUGS. The requirement that pharmacies must be owned by pharmacists gained acceptance early in the 20th century, but was later abandoned in most states. A US Supreme Court decision in 1928 (*Liggett v. Baldridge*, 278 U.S. 105 (1928)) overturned state laws restricting ownership of pharmacies and was seen as binding until 1973, when the Supreme Court reversed its decision in *Liggett* and allowed state legislatures the right to pass such laws (*North Dakota Board of Pharmacy v Snyder's Drug Stores*, Inc., 414 U.S. 156 (1973)). Few state legislatures have chosen to restrict ownership of pharmacies to pharmacists, instead to require that a registered pharmacist be placed in charge of every pharmacy. At the same time, states allow OTCs to be sold in non-pharmacy outlets. Most states require registration of these sellers, as does Washington, where they must be registered as Shopkeepers or Itinerant Vendors (see Chapter 3).

ADVERTISING OF OTC DRUGS is regulated, not by the FDA, but by the Federal Trade Commission (FTC).

DIETARY SUPPLEMENTS

Dietary supplements are regulated by the Dietary Supplement Health and Education Act of 1994 (DSHEA). The Act was passed to allow certain health-related claims to be made for dietary supplements without violating the FDCA or causing the supplements to be regulated as if they were drugs.

DIETARY SUPPLEMENTS are defined under the DSHEA as articles containing one or more of the following: VITAMIN, MINERAL, HERB or other botanical, or AMINO ACID.

To be considered dietary supplements, a product must be

- INTENDED TO SUPPLEMENT THE DIET BY INCREASING TOTAL DIETARY INTAKE OF THE ABOVE, OR A CONCENTRATE, EXTRACT, METABOLITE, CONSTITUENT OR COMBINATION OF THE ABOVE.
- INTENDED FOR INGESTION
- NOT REPRESENTED FOR USE AS A CONVENTIONAL FOOD OR SOLE ITEM OF A MEAL OR DIET
- LABELED AS A DIETARY SUPPLEMENT

If the article meets all of the above requirements, it is deemed to be a FOOD, and is regulated by the FDA as a food, subject to some specific labeling requirements.

ALLOWABLE LABELING for a dietary supplement can

- Claim benefit related to a CLASSIC NUTRITIONAL DEFICIENCY DISEASE (e.g., scurvy, beri-beri)
- DESCRIBE THE ROLE of a nutrient intended to affect the structure or function of the body
- Characterize the MECHANISM OF ACTION
- Describe GENERAL WELL-BEING gained from consuming a nutrient
- Must state that the FDA HAS NOT EVALUATED any labeling claims

The FDA can take action against false statements, adulterated or misbranded products, or remove from market products that are shown to be harmful. Dietary supplements containing ephedra or ephedrine alkaloids (ephedrine, ephedrine HCl, ephedrine sulfate, and racephedrine HCl) were banned in the US by FDA rulemaking in February 2004 (69 FR 6788-6853) that declared such products adulterated (21 CFR 119).

SELLERS MAY NOT ADD PROMOTIONAL INFORMATION THAT IS NOT ALLOWED IN LABELING. Sellers (such as pharmacies) of dietary supplements may not juxtapose non-complying material (books, advertisements, etc.) with dietary supplements in such a way as to make health claims not allowed in the labeling. Sellers may sell or display articles, books, and abstracts of peer-reviewed scientific publications. However, any such books, etc., must be reprinted in their entirety, must be presented with other publications to present a balanced view, and must be physically separate from the product. Sellers may not apply information to the product by sticker, shelf-talker, etc., that would make claims not allowed in labeling.

CONSUMER PRODUCTS ADVERTISING

Regulation of advertising of products sold directly to consumers is placed under the authority of the Federal Trade Commission (FTC); this includes OTC drugs, homeopathic products, and dietary supplements. The FTC generally sets truth-in-advertising standards that apply to all consumer products. These standards, according to the FTC, "can be boiled down to two common-sense propositions: 1) advertising claims must be truthful and not misleading; and 2) before disseminating an ad, advertisers must have adequate substantiation for all objective product claims." The FTC evaluates claims about safety and efficacy of foods, dietary supplements, and drugs based on "competent and reliable scientific evidence." Significant actions by FTC relating to OTC health claims have included:

- $30 million settlement with makers of Airborne™ - a vitamin C supplement
- $2.6 million judgment against makers of "Zyladex Plus" – the "New Skinny Pill"
- Order prohibiting Nestlé Healthcare Nutrition, Inc., from promoting its BOOST Kid Essentials as reducing duration of acute diarrhea in children or reducing absences from school or daycare due to illness

HOMEOPATHIC DRUGS. In December 2016, the FTC announced a new enforcement policy regarding claims made for homeopathic remedies.[252] The FTC noted that "for the vast majority of OTC homeopathic drugs, the case for efficacy is based solely on traditional homeopathic theories and there are no valid studies using current scientific methods showing the product's efficacy. Accordingly, marketing claims that such homeopathic products have a therapeutic effect lack a reasonable basis and are likely misleading in violation of Sections 5 and 12 of the FTC Act." The FTC policy has the following elements:

- An advertising claim for a homeopathic product may not be misleading if it has a prominent disclaimer that "effectively communicates to consumers that (1) There is no scientific evidence that the product works and (2) the product's claims are based only on theories of homeopathy from the 1700s that are not accepted by most modern medical experts."
- Any disclaimers should "stand out and be in close proximity to the efficacy message"
- Marketers should not undercut qualifications with additional positive statements or consumer endorsements
- The inherent contradiction in asserting a product is effective and yet there is no evidence for such an assertion may mean that the disclaimer is not effective; marketers should be able to demonstrate that consumers do understand the limited proof of any claims
- If the FTC finds that "despite a marketer's disclosures, an ad conveys more substantiation than the marketer has, the marketer will be in violation of the FTC Act."

Deceptive advertising for consumer products, including homeopathic drugs may also lead to lawsuits by consumers or consumer groups under state laws, such as consumer protection acts (see Chapter 7). Numerous lawsuits have been filed and in some cases settlements were reached. Most recently, in June 2018, a public interest group sued CVS pharmacies in the District of Columbia under its consumer protection law alleging false and deceptive marketing of homeopathic products.[253]

LEGEND DRUGS (PRESCRIPTION ONLY DRUGS)

FDA DETERMINES A DRUG'S STATUS ON A CASE-BY-CASE BASIS. Unless the drug can be marketed as an OTC product in accordance with the various approved monographs, a new entity will be evaluated on a case-by-case basis to determine whether it can be marketed OTC or must be prescription only.

WASHINGTON DESIGNATION OF PRESCRIPTION ONLY DRUGS. For the purposes of the state Legend Drug Act, the Pharmacy Commission is charged with determining by regulation the drugs covered by the Act. (RCW 69.41.010(12)). The Commission has traditionally done this by specifying a nationally-recognized list of drugs requiring a prescription under federal law, i.e., the *Drug Topics Red Book*. As of January 2019, the reference for this purpose is the 2009 edition of the Red Book.[254] (WAC 246-883-020)

Marketed products that are in fact legend drugs under federal law, but not listed in the *Red Book*, may or may not constitute legend drugs under the Legend Drug Act. This is usually a technical issue when a person is charged with a violation of RCW 69.41. For pharmacists, however, dispensing such a product without prescription would violate federal law, in any case, which is a basis for discipline.

Washington's Intrastate Commerce in Food, Drugs and Cosmetics Act (RCW 69.04) contains another source of a prescription-only requirement: "A drug or device shall be deemed to be misbranded if it is a drug which by label provides, or which the federal act or any applicable law requires by label to provide, in effect, that it shall be used only upon the prescription of a physician, dentist, or veterinarian, unless it is dispensed at retail on a written prescription signed by a physician, dentist, or veterinarian, who is licensed by law to administer such drug." (RCW 69.04.540) The legislature has not attempted to update this statute to reflect the authority it has granted to other practitioners to prescribe legend drugs.

"RX" SYMBOL ON LABEL. (FDCA – 21 USC §502). Formerly, prescription drugs were required to bear the *legend*, "Caution: Federal Law prohibits dispensing without a prescription." Now they may merely bear the "Rx" symbol.

BAR CODING REQUIREMENTS FOR INSTITUTIONAL USE DRUGS. Although most bulk packages of prescription drugs have a bar code on the label, unit-dose items often do not. The lack of bar coding on individual packages of prescription drugs has hampered the implementation of bar code scanning systems in hospitals, which are seen as an essential element for improving patient safety. The FDA adopted regulations in 2004, which became effective in April 2006, requiring certain human drug and biological product labels to contain a bar code consisting of the NDC number in a readily scanned format. (21 CFR 201.25) Exemptions can be sought for selected products. Covered products include:

- Versions of prescription drug products that are sold to or used in hospitals, except:
- Prescription drug samples
- Allergenic extracts
- IUDs treated as drugs
- Medical gases
- Radiopharmaceuticals
- Low-density polyethylene (LDPE) form fill and seal containers not packaged with an overwrap
- Biological products

- OTC products that are dispensed pursuant to an order and are commonly used in hospitals

PHARMACIST LABELING OF DISPENSED PRESCRIPTION DRUGS. As with OTC drugs, a legend drug is MISBRANDED if the labeling is incomplete or misleading. The "LABEL" of a legend drug is the actual label affixed to the bottle or box containing the medication. The "LABELING" includes the label, and any other printed or written material accompanying the drug. Labeling also includes statements made by the manufacture in promotional materials, advertisements, or other communications to patients or health professionals. Dispensing a legend drug pursuant to a prescription without a prescription label is a form of misbranding.

USP GUIDELINES ON PRESCRIPTION CONTAINER LABELING. The USP published General Chapter <17>, Prescription Container Labeling, which became official on May 1, 2013. The goal of the standards is to reduce variability in the way that prescription labels are organized, and to encourage a "patient-centered" approach to prescription container labeling. The National Association of Boards of Pharmacy has recommended making changes to the Model State Pharmacy Act to incorporate these guidelines, but as of January 2019, Washington law or regulations have not adopted the USP guidelines. Elements of the guidelines include:

- Emphasizing instructions and other information important to patients
- Improving readability
- Giving explicit instructions
- Including a purpose for use
- Addressing limited English proficiency
- Addressing visual impairment

LABELS ON AMBULATORY PRESCRIPTIONS. Table 4-1 summarizes FDCA and state law requirements for the label of a prescription dispensed by a pharmacist to a patient.

TABLE 4-1. ELEMENTS REQUIRED ON A PRESCRIPTION LABEL DISPENSED TO A PATIENT (AMBULATORY PHARMACY, HOSPITAL OUTPATIENT)			
		Rx Bottle	**Custom Packaging**
	FDCA	**RCW 18.64.246**	**WAC 246-869-255**
Name and address of the pharmacy	✓	✓	✓
A serial number	✓	✓	✓
Name of prescriber	✓	✓	✓
Name of patient, if on the prescription	✓		
Name of patient		✓	✓
Directions for use, if on the prescription	✓		
Complete directions for use		✓ "As directed" prohibited (WAC 246-875-020(1)(h))	✓
Date of filling or refilling	✓	✓	✓
Name and strength of drug		✓*	✓
Quantity dispensed		✓ WAC 246-869-210(2)	✓ Max. 31 day supply
An expiration date. Often called a "use before" or "discard after" date		✓ (See factors required in WAC 246-869-210(1))	
A TRANSFER CAUTION LABEL containing the statement, "Warning: State or Federal law prohibits transfer of this drug to any person other than the person for whom it was prescribed"		✓ WAC 246-869-210(3)	
Identity of pharmacist responsible for dispensing.		✓**	✓
Supplemented by additional oral or written information as required by regulation. Includes auxiliary labels.		✓ WAC 246-869-210(4); See WAC 246-869-220	
A Side Effects Statement: "Contact your doctor for medical advice about side effects. You may report side effects to FDA at 1-800-FDA-1088."	✓*** 21 CFR Parts 201, 208, 209		

*May be omitted if prescriber requests.
** May be omitted if tracked in the patient record system.
*** May be omitted if present on container cap, a Medication Guide, PIL, or other printed matter presented to patient with each prescription.

LABELING REQUIREMENTS FOR NON-AMBULATORY PRESCRIPTION MEDICATIONS

Drugs supplied to hospitals, nursing homes, and physician offices must meet the general labeling requirements of the FDCA. How those drugs are labeled in these settings when they are being prepared for administration to patients is left primarily to state law or, for Medicare and Medicaid patients, to regulations issued by CMS. The Pharmacy Commission in Washington has developed specific regulations for several settings (see also Chapter 3), which are summarized in the Table 4-2.

TABLE 4-2. ELEMENTS REQUIRED ON NON-AMBULATORY PRESCRIPTION DRUG LABELS IN WASHINGTON

	Hospital, Parenteral	Hospital, Inpatient	Non-hospital, Parenteral	ECF, Non-unit Dose	ECF, Unit Dose
WAC	246-873-080(5)c	246-873-080(5)a	246-871-050	246-865-060(4)a	246-865-040(4)b
Phcy Name			✓	✓	
Phcy Address			✓	✓	
Phcy Phone			✓		
Rx Number			✓	✓	
24-hr Phone			✓		
Pt Name	✓		✓	✓	On cassette
Pt Location	✓				On cassette
Prescriber			✓	✓	
Drug Name	✓	✓	✓	✓	✓
Drug Conc. or Strength	✓	✓	✓	✓	✓
Dosage					✓
Lot No.			In profile		✓
Directions for use			✓		
Infusion rate			✓		
CSA Sched.				✓	✓
Quantity				✓	
Date Prepared or Dispensed			✓	✓	
Exp. Date	✓ ("appropriate dating")	✓	✓	✓	
Expiration Time	✓ ("appropriate dating")		✓		
Storage instructions		✓ ("appropriate")	✓		
RPh Initials	✓		✓	✓	
Preparer Initials	✓		In Profile		
Auxiliary Labels		✓ ("appropriate")	✓ (see WAC)		
Transfer Caution Label			✓		

PRESCRIPTION DRUG CONTAINER LABELING FOR PERSONS WHO ARE BLIND, VISUALLY-IMPAIRED, OR ELDERLY. In 2012 Congress directed the FDA (in §904(a)(1) of FDASIA) to convene a working group to develop best practices on access to information on prescription container labels for individuals who are blind or visually impaired. The group shall consider the use of braille, auditory means (e.g., "talking bottles"), and enhanced visual means such as high contrast printing.

The recommendations resulting from the working group were published by the United States Access Board in July 2013 (https://www.access-board.gov/guidelines-and-standards/health-care/about-prescription-drug-container-labels/working-group-recommendations). The recommendations were developed in part from the guidelines in USP <17>.

Several options are available for delivery of prescription label information to visually-impaired patients:

- Hard copy braille and/or large print
- Electronic methods are now available including
  - Digital voice or text-to-speech recorder may be affixed to the container
    - AccessaMed offers a Digital Audio Label[255] (www.accessamed.com) that adheres to the side of the prescription container
    - Walgreens' proprietary Talking Pill Reminder[256] adheres to the cap
  - Radio frequency identification device (RFID) is affixed to container, and container is placed on a reader device (e.g., ScripTalk® - www.envisionamerica.com)
  - Patient-owned smart devices that respond to RFID tag or QR code

Provision of these labeling services is becoming a standard of practice, particularly among national pharmacy chains and mail-order pharmacies. National chains or providers that have implemented these recommendations include Caremark, CVS, Express Scripts, H-E-B, Humana, Kaiser Permanente, Rite Aid, Walgreens, and Walmart, according to a March 2016 update by the law firm of Lainey Feingold, available at http://www.lflegal.com/2016/03/talking-label-2016update/.[257] In many cases, the availability of enhanced labeling is the result of structured negotiation between the provider and the American Council of the Blind and one or more ACB state affiliates.[258]

Patients may locate pharmacies using the En-Vision America ScripTalk program on the ScripAbility webpage; the site also allows them to indicate if they prefer large print or braille labels. (http://www.envisionamerica.com/products/scripability/)

PROFESSIONAL LABELING AND PRESCRIBING INFORMATION. Labeling of a prescription drug includes prescribing information, which is often called the package insert. The law does not prohibit the patient from receiving the package insert.

STRUCTURED PRODUCT LABELING. In 2006 the FDA issued revised regulations to standardize the package insert and make it more useable by prescribers and pharmacists. A tutorial on the required product labeling is available at CDERLearn.[259] The rule is applicable to: all new legend drugs approved on or after the effective date; drugs approved within 5 years prior to the effective date; and older drugs when there is a major change in the prescribing information.

"HIGHLIGHTS OF PRESCRIBING INFORMATION" must be the first section of the insert. It must summarize the following:

- Recent Major Changes

- The Drug Approval Date
- Adverse Event Reports
- Table of Contents

THE MAJOR SECTIONS are now numbered, and referred to in the Highlights and Table of Contents. The new regulations put information on use, dosage, and precautionary statements first, whereas the descriptive information was first in older inserts.

1. Indications and usage
2. Dosage and administration
3. Dosage forms and strength
4. Contraindications
5. Warnings and precautions
6. Adverse reactions
7. Drug interactions
8. Use in specific populations
9. Drug use and dependence
10. Overdosage
11. Description
12. Clinical pharmacology
13. Nonclinical toxicology
14. Clinical studies
15. References
16. How supplied, storage, and handling
17. Patient counseling information

"CONTRAINDICATION" CLARIFIED. In a guidance document, the FDA makes it clear that a "contraindication" is a reason not to use the drug: *"A drug should be contraindicated only in those clinical situations for which the risk from use clearly outweighs any possible therapeutic benefit. Only known hazards, and not theoretical possibilities, must be listed. If there are no known contraindications for a drug, this section must state 'None'* [*emphasis* added]."[260] The phrase, "relative contraindication" has no useful meaning in evidence-based medication use. A "relative contraindication" is more properly called a "precaution."

USE IN PREGNANCY AND LACTATION.

In December 2014, the FDA published a final rule[261] that changes how information will be presented on use of prescription drugs during pregnancy and lactation. Prior to this final rule, labeling regarding pregnancy and lactation was contained in 3 subparts of section 8 (Use in Specific Populations) of the professional labeling: 8.1 Pregnancy, 8.2 Labor and Delivery, and 8.3 Nursing Mothers. New labeling will consist of 3 relabeled sections: 8.1 Pregnancy (including labor and delivery), 8.2 Lactation (includes nursing mothers), and 8.3 Females and Males of Reproductive Potential.

A more substantial change under the new guidelines will be the elimination of alphabetical letter categories related to use in pregnancy (A, B, C, D, and X). Instead, each subsection will be required to provide more detailed information from trials and current literature, and, if available, data from any existing pregnancy exposure registry concerning the drug.

The rule became effective on June 30, 2015. NDAs submitted on or after the effective date must provide labeling consistent with the revised rule. Manufacturers of other products will have 3 or 4 years (depending upon the approval date for their NDA) after the effective date to revise their labeling.

"DAILYMED" The FDA has instituted a service in cooperation with the National Library of Medicine to electronically disseminate up-to-date and comprehensive information for use with information systems that support patient care. This site (http://dailymed.nlm.nih.gov) is a source of the most current labeling for the drugs that are listed. As of January 2019, nearly 106 thousand product labels were available.

PATIENT PACKAGE INSERTS, PILS, AND MEDICATION GUIDES.

Many products also contain additional patient package inserts (PPIs), which are intended to be included with the dispensed prescription. Failure to dispense a patient package insert or Medication Guide, unless specifically directed to withhold it by the prescriber, is considered misbranding. However, if a patient requests a PPI or Medication Guide, it must be provided, even if the prescriber has directed otherwise (21 CFR 208.26(b))

PPIS REQUIRED BY REGULATION. Two specific parts of the CFR deal with patient package inserts for oral contraceptives and with estrogens.

ORAL CONTRACEPTIVE INSERTS consist of a complete insert and a brief insert. Both must be dispensed to ambulatory patients each time the drug is dispensed. In hospitals, these must be provided to the patient at the first dispensing, and once every 30 days.

ESTROGENS also require a single patient information leaflet be dispensed with each prescription and each refill. In hospitals, these must be provided to the patient with first use of the drug, and every 30 days.

PATIENT INFORMATION LEAFLETS (PILS). PILs are supplementary information sheets provided by pharmacies as part of the prescription process. These are generally written by 3rd party providers, of which FirstDataBank and MediSpan are among the largest. Washington requires that written information accompany prescriptions that are delivered outside the confines of the pharmacy, and it is a national standard of practice to provide written material to patients that expands and reinforces the information they need to properly use their drugs, which should also be communicated during patient counseling. These same vendors provide the underlying data for drug interaction screening and alerts. Pharmacies have options for use of this data in their software, and are ultimately responsible for its proper use and review (see Chapter 6).

MEDICATION GUIDES. The FDA has authority under 21 CFR 208 to require a "Medication Guide" in a specific format to accompany a particular drug product. The FDA has become active in requiring Medication Guides, which replace PILs when they are required. Each dispenser – which may be a practitioner dispensing the product to a patient – must provide a required guide to the patient each time the drug is dispensed (i.e., for new and refill prescriptions).[262] The FDA relies heavily on Medication Guides as key elements of newly-developed REMS plans (see above). The FDA has indicated it will exercise enforcement discretion concerning the requirement that a medication guide must always be provided, depending on the setting, and 5 specific situations; the following table summarizes the FDA's requirements: [263]

TABLE 4-3. FDA REQUIREMENTS FOR DISTRIBUTION OF MEDICATION GUIDES

Setting	**Patient or Agent Requests**	**Each time medication dispensed**	**Provided at time of first dispensing**	**When Medication Guide materially changed**	**Drug is subject to a REMS that requires guide**
Inpatient	Must provide	Need not provide	Need not provide	Need not provide	Must provide as specified in REMS
Outpatient when dispensed to professional for administration to patient (e.g., clinic, infusion center, ED)	Must provide	Need not provide	Must provide	Must provide	Must provide as specified in REMS
Outpatient when dispensed directly to patient or caregiver (e.g., retail pharmacy, hospital outpatient pharmacy, patient samples)	Must provide	Must provide	Must provide	Must provide	Must provide as specified in REMS

DRUGS REQUIRING MEDICATION GUIDES. A list of drugs requiring Medication Guides is posted on the FDA website (http://www.fda.gov/Drugs/DrugSafety/ucm085729.htm), and the site has a link allowing interested persons to sign up for email notifications when the list changes. Particular classes of drugs for which Medication Guides have been developed that are frequently overlooked by pharmacists, resulting in potential legal liability, include

- Anticoagulants
- Anticonvulsants
- Antidepressants
- Antidiabetic agents
- NSAIDS – pay particular attention to warnings about rashes, SJS, and TEN
- Opiates
- Benzodiazepines and "Z-drugs," (e.g., zolpidem, zaleplon)

The FDA sends email alerts when the Medication Guides page is updated; a link on the page allows individuals to subscribe to the list.

FDA INDEX TO DRUG-SPECIFIC INFORMATION. The FDA provides an index to currently marketed drugs for which specific FDA information materials have been published. These include HealthCare Professional, Patient, or Consumer Information Sheets, Medication Guides, or Information Pages. The index can be accessed at http://www.fda.gov/Drugs/DrugSafety/PostmarketDrugSafetyInformationforPatientsandProviders/ucm111085.htm.

EXPIRATION DATES

Manufacturers must place an expiration date on the containers of legend drugs, as well as a lot number. As pharmacists know from their education in pharmaceutics, these dates generally reflect a time when at least 95% of the drug's labeled potency is still available, and no undesirable degradation has taken place. These dates are usually assigned very conservatively by manufacturers. If the expiration date is specified in the form of a month, day, and year, the drug may not be dispensed after that date. If the date is specified as a month and year only, then the drug is considered expired after the last day of the month indicated. Pharmacists should not dispense a quantity of drug that cannot be used by the patient prior to the expiration date.

"USE BEFORE" OR "DISCARD AFTER" DATES. Washington regulations (WAC 246-869-210(1)) specify that in determining a Use Before (or "Discard After") date to place on a dispensed prescription, the pharmacist must consider several factors, including

- THE NATURE OF THE DRUG;
- THE CONTAINER IN WHICH IT WAS PACKAGED BY THE MANUFACTURER AND THE EXPIRATION DATE THEREON;
- THE CHARACTERISTICS OF THE PATIENT'S CONTAINER, if the drug is repackaged for dispensing;
- THE EXPECTED CONDITIONS TO WHICH THE ARTICLE MAY BE EXPOSED;
- THE EXPECTED LENGTH OF TIME OF THE COURSE OF THERAPY; and
- OTHER RELEVANT FACTORS.

It is permissible to dispense medications in the manufacturer's original container, and the expiration date and lot number may be left visible to the patient. Many states impose a one-year limit on the "Use Before" date, but there is no such limit in Washington. MANY COMPUTER SYSTEMS USED BY RETAIL PHARMACIES DEFAULT TO A ONE-YEAR "USE BEFORE" DATE. Care should be taken to OVERRIDE THIS DEFAULT IF THE ACTUAL MANUFACTURER'S DATE IS EARLIER than one year from the date dispensed.

REGULAR INSPECTION OF DRUG STOCKS REQUIRED. Pharmacists are required by regulation in WA to regularly inspect drugs in the pharmacy and remove products from their stock when the merchandise has exceeded its expiration date. (WAC 246-869-150(2)) Outdated drugs are considered adulterated.

PRESCRIBERS WHO DISPENSE DRUGS must label the prescriptions in accordance with the same standards that are required for pharmacists. (RCW 69.41.050)

THE LABEL must contain the name of the patient, name, strength of the drug, the date, the name of the prescriber, and complete directions for use. The drug name and directions may be omitted on the basis of a considered judgment by the prescriber.

SAMPLE PACKAGES need to contain the name of the prescriber and the name of the patient. This is very seldom actually done, however. It is particularly for prescribers handing out samples of controlled substances to follow this rule; their patients may be charged with unlawful possession of the drugs if their names are not on the package.

NURSES OR MEDICAL ASSISTANTS MAY NOT DISPENSE LEGEND DRUGS, so if a prescriber dispenses a drug he or she must do it personally. Prescribers may not dispense drugs for other prescribers.

The Nursing Commission in 2016 issued an advisory opinion in which it declared that "a registered nurse (RN) may distribute, deliver, or dispense prescriptive medications/devices for reproductive care and prevention and treatment of communicable diseases according to a written or standing order of an authorized prescriber." The advisory opinion applies to "RNs employed by public health programs," subject to specific guidelines expressed in the advisory opinion.[264] Labels are required to contain the same elements, including directions for use, as are required on outpatient pharmacy labels.

VETERINARIANS are required by their disciplinary board to include complete directions for use, the name of the client or identification of the animal, the name of the drug and strength, and name of prescribing veterinarian. No exception is made for samples in this rule. (WAC 246-933-340(5)(b))

Prescribers are equally subject to the USP REQUIREMENTS for storage and DISPENSING CONTAINERS, for to store or dispense drugs in violation of compendial standards is to subject the drugs to adulteration under the FDCA.

Prescribers must also adhere to the POISON PREVENTION PACKAGING RULES, except that they may specify non-CRC containers on a case-by-case basis for individual patients.

ELEMENTS OF A PRESCRIPTION

All of the following conditions must be present to authorize a pharmacist to dispense a legend drug in WA. (RCW 69.41.040)

ELEMENTS NEEDED FOR A VALID PRESCRIPTION

- SPECIFIC PATIENT
- AUTHORIZED PRESCRIBER
- DUE COURSE OF PRACTICE
- MEDICAL PURPOSE

WRITTEN FOR A SPECIFIC PATIENT.

Each prescription should be written for a specific, named patient. In order to fulfill the obligations to prevent adverse drug reactions and conduct drug use review, the pharmacist must be able to match the prescription order with a particular patient's profile. Some patients have requested that they be allowed to use a code name to shield their identity (e.g., HIV-positive patients), but the Board of Pharmacy at the time rejected the request. HIPAA requirements should be sufficient to assure confidentiality to those patients. Sometimes prescriptions are written for all the members of a family, or are written for one spouse who has insurance to provide drug for the uninsured spouse. These are challenges for the pharmacist, and these prescriptions are technically invalid.

Naloxone may be prescribed for caregivers of patients receiving or our using opioids under WA law. (See chapter 5) In addition, "partner therapy" for STDs is an exception to the requirement for a specifically-named patient (see below).

Washington rules require that drugs be delivered directly "to the patient, person picking up the prescription for the patient, or person delivering the prescription to the patient at his residence or similar place." (WAC 246-869-020(4)). DEA rules require delivery of controlled substance prescriptions only to the ultimate user or a member of his or her "household." (See Chapter 5)

WRITTEN BY AUTHORIZED PRESCRIBERS (RCW 69.41.030)

All states allow physicians, podiatrists, dentists, and veterinarians to prescribe legend and controlled substances. Other practitioners may or may not have prescriptive authority for one or more classes of drugs

All states honor prescriptions from out of state physicians, podiatrists, dentists, and veterinarians.

Washington allows full or partial prescriptive authority to a variety of practitioners. Table 4-3 summarizes prescriptive authority and scope of practice in WA. This table also includes academic and other abbreviations commonly used by professionals who practice in health care settings.

PRACTITIONERS – out of state prescriptions are acceptable. WA allows the following prescribers who are licensed in any state or US territory, or in British Columbia, to issue prescriptions for legend drugs that are valid in WA. (Note: Canadian prescribers cannot issue prescriptions for controlled substances unless they are also licensed in the US and registered with the DEA.)

- Physicians (MD) and Osteopathic Physicians (DO)
- Dentists (DMD, DDS)
- Podiatrists (PodD, DPM)
- Veterinarians (DVM)
- Nurse Practitioners (ARNP)
- Physician's Assistants (PA, PA-C)

MID-LEVEL PRACTITIONERS – out of state prescriptions are *not* allowed from these practitioners.

- Nurse Anesthetists (CRNA)
- Optometrists (OD)
- Naturopaths (ND) – in December 2014, the Department of Health has submitted a "Sunrise Review" of the Naturopathic scope of practice, recommending changes in the statute to permit expanded, but still limited, prescribing of controlled substances.[265]
- Midwives (very limited)
- Pharmacists (R.Ph., Pharm.D.) under collaborative practice agreements
- Physical therapists (R.P.T., Dr.P.T.) and Occupational Therapists (O.T., Dr.O.T.) – may not prescribe, but may order and use certain legend drugs.
- East Asian Medicine Practitioners (acupuncturists) – may prescribe, order and use certain sterile injectable drugs (e.g., sterile saline, water for injection, vitamins) as part of point injection therapy "as defined by rule by the department. Point injection therapy includes injection of substances, limited to saline, sterile water, herbs, minerals, vitamins in liquid form, and homeopathic and nutritional substances, consistent with the practice of East Asian medicine. Point injection therapy does not include injection of controlled substances ... or steroids ..." (RCW 18.06.010 (1)(j))[266]

PRESCRIBING BY PHARMACISTS. The Pharmacy Commission has limited authority to review or approve collaborative practice agreements for pharmacists. The statute (RCW 18.64.011(11)) defines the practice of pharmacy to include "initiating or modifying of drug therapy in accordance with written guidelines or protocols previously established and approved for his or her practice by a practitioner authorized to prescribe drugs." The phrase, "initiating or modifying drug therapy" is tantamount to saying "prescribing." Since this authority is inherent in the license to practice pharmacy, the statute does not authorize restriction of prescriptive authority to pharmacists with particular levels of training or experience. As long as the protocol or guideline is in writing, and approved by an authorized prescriber, the pharmacist may proceed.

CDTAS ARE NOT THE ONLY MEANS BY WHICH A PHARMACIST MAY EXERCISE PRESCRIPTIVE AUTHORITY; the statute calls for "written guidelines or protocols," approved by a practitioner for the pharmacist's practice. The use of a written agreement between individual pharmacists and individual prescribers emerged in other states after the Washington statute was enacted. Thus, a "Collaborative Drug Therapy Agreement" is one format for recording protocols or guidelines approved for an individual pharmacist's practice, but it is also appropriate for statewide protocols, or protocols issued by a county health medical director, or by a pharmacy and therapeutics committee to be the basis for a pharmacist's prescriptive practice. In the following material, when I refer to a CDTA, I am also including other written guidelines or protocols, unless it is clear otherwise from the context.

The 2013 legislature repaired an omission in RCW 69.41.030 by adding pharmacists to the list of persons who could prescribe legend drugs. The exact language used included " ... a pharmacist under chapter 18.64 RCW to the extent permitted by drug therapy guidelines or protocols established under RCW 18.64.011 and authorized by the board of pharmacy[267] and approved by a practitioner authorized to prescribe drugs ..." The import of the phrase "authorized by the board of pharmacy" may be subject to further interpretation, but as of January 2017, the Commission has not interpreted this to allow it to "approve" CDTAs.

WAC 246-863-100 requires that a written copy of the approved protocol must be on file in the pharmacy and on file with the Board of Pharmacy. The protocol must contain:

- The identity of the authorizing practitioner and the pharmacist(s) authorized must be stated. The guideline may authorize a pharmacist or a group of pharmacists.
- A time period, not to exceed 2 years, during which the protocol will be in effect.
- A statement of the type of prescriptive authority authorized, that includes:
- Types of diseases, drugs, or drug categories included, and the type of authority (i.e., initiating or modifying) allowed for each type.
- A general statement of the procedures, decision criteria or plan the pharmacist will follow when making therapy decisions.
- A statement of the activities the pharmacist is to follow when exercising prescriptive authority, including documentation of decisions made, and a plan for communication or feedback to the authorizing prescriber concerning decisions made. The regulation allows documentation on the prescription, in a patient chart, patient medication profile, or separate logbook. The Commission has struggled with the process for receiving and recording collaborative practice agreements, particularly as the number of authorized pharmacists grew exponentially due to immunization protocols. In July, 2014, the Commission adopted a policy to clarify the process (see sidebar). No change was made to the existing rule.

At its September 30, 2016 meeting, the Commission recognized that a "CDTA is an agreement between a pharmacist and the delegating provider," and removed its internal process requirement that the Commission staff review the CDTA and send a letter of acknowledgement to the pharmacist when a CDTA is filed with the Commission. It adopted the proposed revised practice for handling CDTAs: "(1) a pharmacist procures a CDTA with a practitioner; (2) The pharmacist or employer fills out a CDTA review form that aids credentialing in providing tracking (a numbering system); (3) the paperwork is recorded with credentialing for the licensee; (4) ... a copy is then on file with DOH and a copy is on file at the pharmacist's place of practice."[268]

Duties of a Pharmacist in a Prescribing Role

The pharmacist who undertakes to prescribe or modify therapy under protocol assumes all the duties of any other prescriber, and is no longer just dispensing medications based on the prescribing decisions of others. The prescribing process involves at least the following elements:

- *ADHERING TO A PATIENT CARE PROCESS.* All major US pharmacy organizations have joined together to adopt and endorse a standardized "Pharmacists' Patient Care Process." As noted by the JCPP, "the Pharmacists' Patient Care Process uses a patient-centered approach that depends first and foremost on the pharmacist having an established relationship with the patient. This relationship supports engagement and effective communication with the patient, family, and caregivers throughout the process. The process also involves the pharmacist working with prescribers and other practitioners to optimize patient health and medication outcomes."[269] While this process applies in all settings and to all pharmacists' roles, it is particularly relevant to collaborative drug therapy management. At the heart of the process is the use of evidence-based practice. The plan for any new or modified therapy must result as a result of collection of relevant patient information and assessment of drug-therapy-related problems.

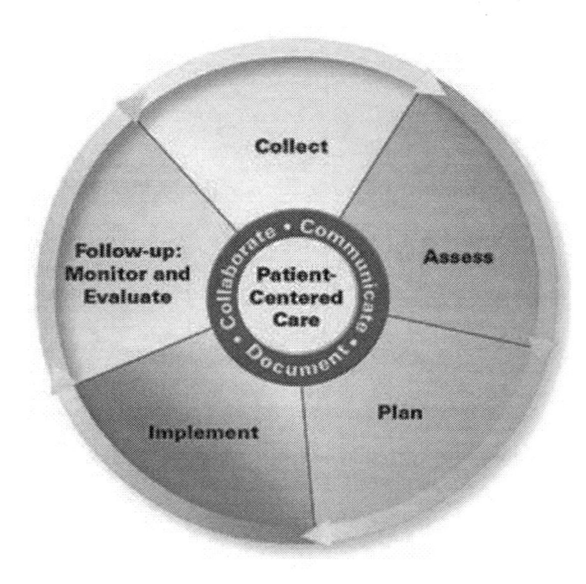

- *IDENTIFYING AN INDICATION OR DIAGNOSIS.* In a collaborative setting, the pharmacist may be relying on another provider to make the diagnosis, and collaborative drug therapy management is often called "post-diagnosis primary care." However, the pharmacist must be clear on the nature of the diagnosis or indication that necessitates the therapy he or she is prescribing or modifying. The indication for therapy must be documented in the patient record.
- *OBTAINING INFORMED CONSENT TO THERAPY.* The patient has a right to refuse any proposed treatment, and his or her agreement to a treatment must be based on being provided with information necessary to make that consent an informed one. The elements of patient counseling that apply to the pharmacist's dispensing role are not sufficient to obtain informed consent. This subject is covered in more detail in Chapter 7. All prescribing by a pharmacist should be based on the pharmacist's documentation that the patient has an understanding of the risks and benefits of therapy and has agreed to the treatment. If another practitioner has clearly documented that consent – which is common in clinic settings – the pharmacist may be able to rely on that documentation.
- *PROPER DOCUMENTATION.* Documentation of dispensing decisions is generally quite limited, with pharmacists making specific notes only in non-routine transactions, such as when a DUR alert has been responded to. The expectation for prescribers is that the patient encounter is fully documented, using SOAP notes or other standardized formats, and making it clear in the patient record who formulated the plan and the prescription or order modifying therapy. Communicating the decision to other health care providers involved in the patient's care is a critical aspect of the prescribing process. In settings where pharmacists are billing for services to third party payers, the documentation must include all the information necessary to provide the proper diagnostic and procedure codes on the claim. Miscoding can result in significant penalties (see Chapter 8).
- *FOLLOW UP.* The prescriber is responsible for monitoring the results of his or her prescribing decisions, and the pharmacist engaged in collaborative practice bears the responsibility of following up with the patient or with others who will implement the prescribed treatment. In a recent case, a pharmacist issued an order to modify the morphine dosing rate for a patient-controlled analgesia (PCA) pump. The pharmacist never returned to follow up on the change and, due to a nursing error, the patient was

overdosed. Neither the pharmacist doing the dosing nor the pharmacist who supplied an early cartridge change caught the error, and the patient died.

ISSUING THE PRESCRIPTION OR ORDER BY A PHARMACIST

The pharmacist who initiates or modifies therapy must generate a prescription or order, just as would any other prescriber. A physician who dispenses medication to his or her patients must record the order in the patient's chart as well as maintaining a dispensing record. In Washington, the pharmacist must sign the prescription or order just as any other prescriber would do. It is not appropriate to issue a prescription under the name of the prescriber approving the CDTA, protocol, or guideline. Thus, the pharmacist issuing an order that will be administered or dispensed by another provider must indicate his or her NPI on the prescription, and, if it is for a controlled substance, his or her DEA number. A pharmacist changing a prescription or issuing a refill to a patient based on a protocol should record his or her name as the authorizing prescriber, not the prescriber who issued the original prescription. As with other prescribers, prescriptions written by pharmacists and given to patients must be on prescription blanks that conform to state tamper-resistant rules.

The Commission issued an "Interim Guidance on Collaborative Drug Therapy" in December 2018. The guidance confirms that a CDTA is required when the pharmacist is initiating or modifying drug therapy, and in such cases it is the pharmacist who must sign the resulting order. The Commission did discuss some hypothetical situations in which a CDTA might not be required when the pharmacist is operating under certain standing orders or protocols. Pharmacists involved in collaborative practice should review this guidance, which is available on the Policies and Procedures page of the Commission's website.[270]

PITFALLS IN COLLABORATIVE PRACTICE AND PHARMACIST PRESCRIBING

The following are some examples that have led to difficulties for pharmacists engaged in collaborative practice.

- *NOT HAVING TRULY READ THE CDTA.* Pharmacists may come into a practice where certain protocols are in place, and "learn by doing" the protocols, without having actually completely read the protocol or even knowing for sure that they are named in the protocol.
- *FAILING TO ADHERE TO THE CDTA.* In some immunization settings, pharmacists have failed to follow protocol guidelines on sanitation, privacy, or knowing where the emergency kit is to be found. In another case, the pharmacists involved in monitoring aminoglycoside therapy failed to follow the monitoring guidelines for the type of therapy ordered, and failed to require documentation of the indication for treatment as specified in the protocol.
- *NOT EXPLAINING TO THE PATIENT* that the pharmacist is operating under a protocol or guideline. This may lead to unnecessary misunderstandings, and also misses an opportunity to educate the patient on the broader range of services now available from pharmacists.
- *RELYING ON A LOOSELY-WRITTEN OR AMBIGUOUS CDTA.* A recent case involved a pharmacist whose CDTA very broadly described the drugs he could prescribe. When a patient was injured by poor prescribing decisions of the physician (not the pharmacist), the pharmacist was also sued on the grounds that the CDTA allowed him to prescribe the drugs in question – even though neither he nor the prescriber intended those drugs to be covered. It is not a good idea for a pharmacist to have authority beyond what he or she is trained or prepared to deliver.
- *FAILURE TO DOCUMENT OR COMMUNICATE.* In a case where the pharmacist worked in a clinic, the pharmacist's prescribing decisions were entered into the patient chart, but one could not tell whether the physician or pharmacist had done so. The pharmacist never reviewed or signed the entries, only the physician did so. This led to challenges when the physician's poor prescribing was blamed on the pharmacist. Pharmacists in another case "managed" a patient's treatment with gentamicin for over 21

days without ever assuring that the risks of vestibular toxicity from prolonged treatment had been documented as having been discussed with the patient.

- *EXTENDING PROTOCOL AUTHORITY* to other pharmacists or student pharmacists. In one case, a pharmacist allowed his resident to call the pharmacy and issue the prescription, using the resident's name as the prescriber, but the resident was not named in the protocol (and, coincidentally, the protocol had expired). In another case, student pharmacists on APPE rotations at the site were allowed to calculate and write dosing instructions for pain therapy and aminoglycoside therapy, signing their own names in the chart. While this was okay for the students to do under the supervision of the preceptor, the orders were invalid without the pharmacist's review and signature.
- *USING A CDTA TO ORDER MEDICAL DEVICES.* The statute authorizing pharmacists to initiate or modify therapy only applies to drugs, not devices, so the order of an authorized prescriber other than a pharmacist is required to authorize the dispensing of prescription-only devices. This is not to say that a pharmacist may not instruct, demonstrate, or administer a device, but they cannot be authorized to prescribe it. (Note that a drug-delivery system, such as a prefilled syringe, is treated as a drug, not a device.)
- *MANAGING POORLY DESIGNED THERAPY.* When drugs are prescribed by another practitioner with "pharmacists to dose," under protocol, or similar means of having the pharmacist manage the dosing and administration of a drug, the pharmacist carrying out the management is doing more than just dispensing. Authority to prescribe a different dose truly encompasses the need to decide if any dose is appropriate for the patient, and to decline to dose a poorly-prescribed drug. Another way of expressing this issue is that when a pharmacist takes over the dosing of a drug he or she "takes ownership" of the underlying decision to use the drug in the first place.
- *FAILING TO ANTICIPATE PROBLEMS*. In other courses in pharmacy programs, student pharmacists are trained in patient safety and in the use of tools such as FMEA. When the CDTA is developed, a reasonable forward-looking assessment of how things could go wrong should be undertaken.

TABLE 4-4. PRACTITIONER AND PROFESSIONAL DESIGNATIONS AND PRESCRIBING LIMITS IN WASHINGTON.

This table provides descriptions of common academic degrees and/or professional designations commonly encountered in the health care environment. It also discusses drug-related dispensing, use, or prescribing authority issued to credentialed health care providers in Washington.

Designation*	Indicates	Law Ref.**	Prescribing Limits
A.R.N.P. (also CNP – clinical nurse practitioner; FNP – family nurse practitioner, etc.)	Advanced Registered Nurse Practitioner	RCW 18.79.250; WAC 246-840-410 et seq.; RCW 69.50.100(w)(3); WAC 246-840-4657	Drugs necessary for treatment of patients within specialty; C-5 controlled substances. May prescribe C-2, 3, and 4 if within scope of specialty. Must place initials, "ARNP" or "NP" on Rx. Example specialty areas: family practice (children and adults); psychiatric; pediatric; women's health; nurse midwife. Prescriptions for legend drugs and controlled substances may be filled when issued by out-of-state ARNPs. Prescriptions for opioids must include diagnosis or ICD code.
C.Ph.T.	Certified Pharmacy Technician	RCW 18.64A; WAC 246-869-060	A pharmacy technician who has passed a certifying examination provided by the Pharmacy Technicians Certification Board (the PTCE) or the Institute for Certification of Pharmacy Technicians (the ExCPT). As with other pharmacy technicians, may assist pharmacists by performing non-discretionary tasks related to dispensing. No authority to prescribe or administer drugs.
C.P.M.	Certified Professional Midwife		See midwives
C.R.N.A.	Certified Registered Nurse Anesthetist	RCW 18.79.240(r)	Drugs used in anesthesia practice; scope of practice established by American Association of Nurse Anesthetists. May prescribe drugs, including C-2 to C-5 for anesthesia in accordance with protocols approved within the facility. This is a specialty area practiced by ARNPs in Washington.
D.C.	Doctor of Chiropractic	RCW 18.25	No prescriptive authority
D.D.S., D.M.D.	Doctor of Dental Surgery, Doctor of Dental Medicine	RCW 18.32	Same scope as MD as long as treating diseases of the head and neck.
D.N.P.	Doctor of Nursing Practice; see R.N.		A clinical doctorate awarded to nurses; it is intended to become the primary credential for nurse clinicians and nurse practitioners. Same scope as A.R.N.P.
D.O.	Doctor of Osteopathy	RCW 18.57	Osteopathic Physician and Surgeon; same scope as MD
D.P.M	Doctor of Podiatric Medicine, see also Pod.D.	RCW 18.22	Podiatry is the diagnosis and treatment of diseases of the foot. Podiatrists may not amputate feet, administer spinal or general anesthesia, or treat systemic conditions. May prescribe all drugs and controlled substances necessary in the practice of podiatry. Prescriptions may be filled from out-of-state podiatrists in WA.
Dr.O.T., O.T.	Doctor of Occupational Therapy, Occupational Therapist	RCW 18.59.160	"may purchase, store, and administer topical and transdermal medications such as hydrocortisone, dexamethasone, fluocinonide, topical anesthetics, lidocaine, magnesium sulfate, and other similar medications for the practice of occupational therapy as prescribed by a health care provider with prescribing authority ... Administration of medication must be documented in the patient's medical record. Some medications may be applied by the use of iontophoresis and phonophoresis. An occupational therapist may not purchase, store, or administer controlled substances. A pharmacist who dispenses such drugs to a licensed physical therapist is not liable for any adverse reactions caused by any method of use by the occupational therapist."

Designation*	Indicates	Law Ref.**	Prescribing Limits
Dr.P.T., R.P.T.	Doctor of Physical Therapy, Registered Physical Therapist	RCW 18.74.160	"May purchase, store, and administer medications such as hydrocortisone, fluocinonide, topical anesthetics, silver sulfadiazine, lidocaine, magnesium sulfate, zinc oxide, and other similar medications, and may administer such other drugs or medications as prescribed by an authorized health care practitioner for the practice of physical therapy. A pharmacist who dispenses such drugs to a licensed physical therapist is not liable for any adverse reactions caused by any method of use by the physical therapist."
D.V.M.	Doctor of Veterinary Medicine	RCW 18.92; WAC 246-933-340(5)b	Unlimited scope as long as treating animals. May prescribe for animals and prescriptions may be filled by pharmacists. May dispense drugs for prescribed by other veterinarians, subject to certain limits. Veterinarians are not able to obtain an NPI, so the pharmacy must be able to record some other identifier when dispensing veterinary prescriptions.
E.A.M.P.; M.Ac., M.Ac.O.M.; *D.A.C.M.*	East Asian Medicine Practitioner; Masters in Acupuncture; Masters in Acupuncture and Oriental Medicine; Doctor of Acupuncture and Chinese Medicine	RCW 18.06; WAC 246-803	Revised name for acupuncturist in Washington. May perform acupuncture and other therapies including point injection therapy. May purchase and administer certain injectable products as part of point injection therapy. May recommend or sell herbs, vitamins, minerals, dietary or mineral supplements. May use "superficial heat and cold therapies."
J.D.	Juris Doctor (doctor of law)		Attorney. No prescriptive authority. By convention, within legal circles attorneys who hold the J.D. do not use the title "doctor," but are referred to as "Mr.," "Ms.," etc.
L.Ac.	Licensed acupuncturist	RCW18.06	See East Asian Medicine Practitioner
L.P.N.	Licensed Practical Nurse	RCW 18.79	May administer prescribed drugs.
M.D.	Doctor of Medicine, Physician and Surgeon	RCW 18.71	All drugs needed for his or her patients. No limits on controlled substances unless restricted for a given practitioner by the board of medical examiners.
Midwife, CPM	Licensed Midwife (not a nurse midwife); Certified Professional Midwife	WAC 246-834-250	Permitted to order and use drugs needed in delivery and immediately post-partum. May prescribe a limited list of products, and pharmacists may fill their orders for diaphragms and other listed devices issued for post-partum women.
Nurse Midwife	ARNP		A specialty area of practice for ARNPs, same authority as ARNPs.
N.D.	Doctor of Naturopathy	RCW 18.36A; WAC 246-836-210	All legend drugs with the exception of Botulinum toxin (e.g., Botox®) and inert substances used for cosmetic purposes. Non-drug contraceptive devices. Controlled substances are limited to codeine and testosterone products that are contained in Schedules III, IV, and V in chapter 69.50 RCW. May not treat malignancies except in collaboration with a physician (MD or DO). See note in text concerning the 2014 Sunrise Review.
O.D.	Doctor of Optometry	RCW 18.53; WAC 246-851-580, 590	Prescribes eye glasses and contact lenses, and treats minor eye conditions. May order and use topical ophthalmic products for diagnosis and refraction and may prescribe topical ophthalmic and prescribe certain oral drugs including C-3, 4, and 5 drugs, and may also order and administer epinephrine injection for anaphylactic shock. May prescribe hydrocodone products only in schedule 2. Allowed drugs are listed in WAC 246-851-580 and -590. Limits: Benzodiazepines for anti-anxiety associated with procedures – single doses per Rx; CSA not more than 7 days; C-3 or C-4, not more than 30 dosage units/Rx. Notation of purpose required on Rx.
PA PA-C	Physician's Assistant Physician Assistant-Certified Osteopathic Physician's Assistant Osteopathic PA - Certified	RCW 18.57A; 18.71A; WAC 246-854-030; WAC 246-918-030, 035.	Washington does not distinguish between PA and PA-C, all physicians' assistants must have national certification. May prescribe legend drugs and controlled substances. Limited to a list of drugs approved by supervising physician.. Needs own DEA number if prescribing CSAs. Out-of-state Rx for legend and CS drugs may be filled in WA. No major distinctions in scope exist between allopathic and osteopathic physician assistants, except osteopathic PA-Cs may do osteopathic manipulations
Pharm.D., B.S. Pharm., B.Pharm., R.Ph.	Doctor of Pharmacy; Bachelor of Science in Pharmacy; Bachelor of Pharmacy[271]; Registered Pharmacist	RCW 18.64; WAC 246-863-100	May prescribe ("initiate or modify therapy") in accordance with approved protocol as part of collaborative practice agreement. Same limits for his or her protocol as the authorizing prescriber. Must have DEA number to prescribe CSAs. May administer prescribed drugs and devices.
Pod.D.	Doctor of Podiatry – see D.P.M.	RCW 18.22	Same scope as M.D. if treating or performing surgery on feet or ankles.

Designation*	Indicates	Law Ref.**	Prescribing Limits
R.D.H.	Registered Dental Hygienist	RCW 18.29	May apply topical prophylactic agents (e.g., fluorides), topical antimicrobials, or topical anesthetics to teeth and gums. No prescriptive authority. Must practice under supervision of a dentist.
R.N., *B.S.N., M.N., M.S.N., D.N.P.*	Registered Nurse; Bachelor of Science in Nursing, Master of Nursing; Master of Science in Nursing; Dr. of Nursing Practice	RCW 18.79	No prescriptive authority unless also an ARNP. May administer drugs ordered for his or her patients. The Nursing Care Quality Assurance Commission has determined that nurses may restock remote drug dispensing devices.[272] Public health RNs may dispense certain drugs, according to NCQAC. Many ARNPs hold either the M.N. or M.S.N. degrees, and the D.N.P. (Doctor of Nursing Practice) degree is intended to become the primary graduate degree for nurse practitioners and nurse clinicians. Nurses who are not ARNPs or CRNAs may convey a prescriber's order but cannot be delegated to prescribe or authorize refills.
R.T., R.R.T., Respiratory Care Practitioner	Respiratory Therapist; Registered Respiratory Therapist	RCW 18.89	Now licensed as Respiratory Care Practitioners in Washington. May administer prescribed respiratory drugs.
R.V.M.C.; R.V.T.	Registered Veterinary Medication Clerk; Registered Veterinary Technician	RCW 19.92.30; WAC 246-935, 937	R.V.M.C. may perform dispensing tasks under direct supervision of a veterinarian, and may deliver verified drugs to a client. R.V.T. may administer veterinary drugs under direct or indirect supervision of veterinarian.
*Academic degrees are in *ITALIC*. ** See also RCW 69.41.030 and RCW 69.50.101(w)			

PRESCRIBING OF CONTRACEPTIVES BY PHARMACISTS – SIGN NOTIFYING PUBLIC OF AVAILABILITY

A growing number of states have determined to make oral contraceptives more readily available by authorizing pharmacists to prescribe them, including California and Oregon. Washington legislators introduced legislation similar to the Oregon statute in the 2016 session; pharmacists convinced legislators that no specific statutory authorization was needed because the current ability of pharmacists to prescribe under protocol was meeting the objective of the legislation. The Legislature required the Pharmacy Commission to develop a sign to be placed in prescribing pharmacies (RCW 18.64.008). The sign was approved in June 2017.

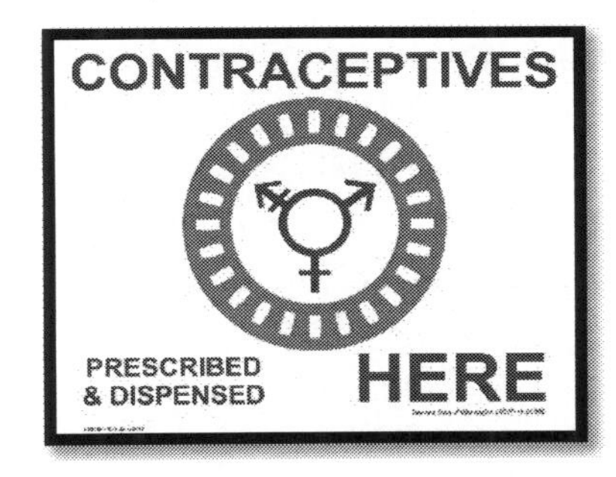

PRESCRIBING AUTHORITY MAY NOT BE "DELEGATED," UNLESS SPECIFICALLY PROVIDED IN STATUTE. As the Board of Pharmacy noted in 2009, "Valid prescriptions must be 'signed,' either manually or electronically, by a practitioner with prescriptive authority ... the act of 'signing' a prescription cannot be delegated. A registered nurse may 'prepare' a prescription for manual or electronic signature, but the prescribing practitioner is always responsible for ensuring that the prescription conforms in all the essential elements to the law and regulations."[273]

It is important to recognize that a pharmacist prescribing under protocol in Washington has not been "delegated" any authority by the practitioner who approves the protocol. The authority to prescribe under protocol is part of the scope of practice of a pharmacist (see above discussion of how the pharmacist should issue a prescription).

WHERE OTHERWISE ALLOWED BY LAW, A NURSE OR STAFF MEMBER MAY "COMMUNICATE" A PRESCRIPTION TO THE PHARMACIST AT THE PRESCRIBER'S REQUEST. When a telephoned prescription or refill reauthorization is allowed, a nurse or designated staff member may communicate the order to the pharmacist at the direction of the prescriber.

A pharmacist engaged in practice at a clinic may communicate orders on behalf of a prescriber just as can any other staff member. As noted above, it is important that a pharmacist doing so clearly distinguish his or her role as an "agent" as opposed to a "prescriber" under protocol. The pharmacist who is communicating the order does have an opportunity to review the order prior to its transmission, and it would be reasonable to assume that his or her responsibilities in this case are similar to those of the pharmacists receiving the order (of course, the receiving pharmacist may have additional knowledge about prescriptions from other prescribers that the transmitting pharmacist does not have).

As noted in Chapter 3, a pharmacist or nurse in a long-term care facility or hospice may act as the agent of the prescriber in entering verbal orders in a chart and/or in communicating orders to a pharmacy, without any prior formal agency relationship with the prescriber.

DECEASED OR DISCIPLINED PRESCRIBER. What becomes of his or her prescriptions when a prescriber loses his or her license or dies? Obviously, no prescriptions written after the loss of a license could be valid, and prescribers cannot issue prescriptions from the grave (there have been cases where a deceased physician's widow continued to try to operate his practice after his death). In Washington, however, it appears that prescriptions, when written by an authorized prescriber, are valid until they legally expire, even if the prescriber subsequently loses his or her license to practice. Because a patient can no longer obtain care from a practitioner when that practitioner is not licensed, but a prescription previously-written by that practitioner is still valid, then, by extension, there is also no basis to invalidate the previously-issued prescriptions of a practitioner who dies.

A former executive director of Washington's Board of Pharmacy was publicly on record that "prescriptions die with the prescriber," and that when a prescriber loses his or her license, the prescriptions she or he previously wrote now become invalid. However, when the executive director provided testimony in a state court criminal trial that a physician's previously-written prescriptions become invalid when that physician loses his or her license, the Washington Appeals Court subsequently opined that "The State concedes that this opinion 'does not appear to be explicitly supported in statutory law,' and indeed, there is no Washington authority for [the executive director's] statement." (*State v. Clausing*, 104 Wn. App. 75, 86, 15 P.3d 203 (2001)) The Washington Supreme Court subsequently declared that the executive director's opinion "was an erroneous one ..." (*State v. Clausing*, 149 Wn.2d 620, 629, 56 P.3d 550 (2002)). (Be aware that other states, such as Oregon, do deal with this issue explicitly in regulation.)

However, IF A PATIENT PRESENTS A NEW OR REFILL PRESCRIPTION, AND THERE ARE PROBLEMS WITH THE PRESCRIPTION THAT PRECLUDE DISPENSING THE MEDICATION UNTIL THEY ARE RESOLVED, the pharmacist cannot consult with a dead or unlicensed prescriber, and will need to locate a licensed practitioner currently caring for the patient to resolve them.

If a patient has a new or refillable prescription that is not expired under Washington law, and there are no problems related to the prescription that need to be resolved in order to provide the patient with pharmaceutical care, the pharmacist may consider the prescription valid.

In every case, the best practice for a pharmacist to follow is one that ASSURES CONTINUITY OF PATIENT CARE; making sure that patients remain in appropriate relationships with currently-licensed practitioners, but at the same time not causing the patient to go without necessary medication.

ISSUED IN THE DUE COURSE OF MEDICAL PRACTICE (RCW 69.41.040)

Legend drugs must be prescribed in the context of a BONA FIDE PRESCRIBER-PATIENT RELATIONSHIP. Prior to issuing a prescription, for example, the prescriber must have conducted an appropriate examination and maintained proper records, and made a professional judgment.

PRESCRIPTIONS THAT ARE "SOLD" TO PATIENTS ARE NOT VALID. For example, Internet prescribing seldom involves a bona fide patient-prescriber encounter. Likewise, prescription "mills" where patients pay to have prescriptions written (often for CSAs) do not produce valid prescriptions that a pharmacist can lawfully dispense.

INTERNET PRESCRIPTIONS ARE GENERALLY INVALID. Prescriptions written by physicians on the basis of an Internet questionnaire filled out by the patient are generally invalid, because there is no actual examination of the patient involved.

RYAN HAIGHT ONLINE PHARMACY CONSUMER PROTECTION ACT OF 2008. In October 2008, Congress passed Public Law 110-425, named after Ryan Haight, a high school senior in La Mesa, CA, who died in 2001 following ingestion of Vicodin obtained from an online pharmacy in Oklahoma. The act prohibits the delivery dispensing or distribution of a controlled substance via the Internet unless it is pursuant to a prescription issued by a practitioner who has conducted at least one in person physical examination and evaluation of the patient within the prior 24 months. It also requires Internet pharmacies to register with the DEA prior to engaging in Internet pharmacy involving controlled substances (see chapter 5).

TREATMENT OF PARTNERS FOR SEXUALLY-TRANSMITTED DISEASES – EXPEDITED PARTNER THERAPY. A physician may prescribe antibiotics to treat a patient with Chlamydia or gonorrhea, and issue a prescription for the patient's partner, even though the partner has not been examined. This activity is known as "Expedited Partner Therapy (EPT)",[274] and is considered acceptable and ethical medical practice, because without treatment of the partner, the patient is likely to become reinfected. The benefits of treating the partner may be seen to outweigh the risk of adverse effects arising from a less-than-ideal prescribing and dispensing situation. The Washington Medical Commission has issued a policy statement acknowledging the appropriateness of such prescribing under certain circumstances.[275] Under this policy, the bona fide physician-patient relationship is considered established, so the prescriptions are valid. The MC has also allowed a "special prescribing protocol" whereby partner packs may be distributed by public health clinic staff without a prescription, provided the individual case is reviewed by a licensed prescriber within 7 days.[276]

In accordance with this policy, public health clinics in Washington distribute "partner packs" which may or may not contain the partner's name on the label. County Health Departments in many counties distribute these partner packs free through participating community pharmacies. Not all county health departments provide these services, however. As of January 2019, distribution of partner packs through pharmacies or health departments is available in all counties except Ferry County. In Columbia County, Klickitat County, and Skamania County the packs are available from the Health Department only. A website is available for patients and physicians to locate participating pharmacies.[277] The Pharmacy Commission has provided input to the Department of Health on this program and has encouraged pharmacist to contact their local public health clinic for more specific information on the special prescribing protocol for partner packs.[278]

Even when prescriptions are written for EPT outside of such a protocol, the pharmacist is justified in dispensing these prescriptions in outpatient pharmacies if certain steps are taken.

- Importantly, unless the patient's 3rd party payer specifically allows it, do not charge a 3rd party for the partner's medication.
- Determine as best as possible whether the partner has any conditions or allergies which would preclude use of the drug.
- Advise the patient to tell the partner to confer with a pharmacist or physician before taking the drug if the partner has drug allergies or is on any medication.
- In many cases, the prescriber does not know or indicate the partner's name on the prescription. This creates a problem under Washington law, which requires that the name of the person receiving the drug must be on the prescription. However, the Pharmacy Commission has given tacit approval to the Department of Health's protocol using partner packs. A reasonable policy would mirror one previously approved in Colorado:
  - Prepare a separate container for the partner's medication.
  - Label the patient's prescription with the patient's name
  - Label the partner's prescription with the partner's name, if known, or with the patient's name followed by "Partner" (e.g., Jordan Smith's Partner).
  - Issue a separate prescription number for each prescription.

MUST BE WITHIN THE SCOPE AND AUTHORITY OF THE PRESCRIBER. A podiatrist cannot prescribe medications for congestive heart failure, even though ankle edema may be a result of CHF. A dentist cannot normally prescribe birth control pills. Likewise, some practitioners, such as optometrists, are not able to prescribe Schedule II drugs in most states (except, as in Washington, hydrocodone products). Veterinarians cannot prescribe drugs for humans, and MDs cannot prescribe drugs for cats or dogs. A pharmacist who knows, or should know, that a particular prescription is not within the scope or authority of the issuing prescriber has a corresponding responsibility not to fill the prescription. The pharmacist must be aware, however, of current trends in use of drugs by the various practitioners who normally prescribe for his or her clients. If in doubt, ask the prescriber to fill you in on how they intend the drug to be used, so you can help the client understand its use better.

ISSUED FOR A LEGITIMATE MEDICAL PURPOSE

Drugs used for non-medical purposes include stimulants for "recreational use" or androgens for weight training. Non-legitimate drug use is a greater problem with controlled substances than with legend drugs. Nevertheless, if a pharmacist knows or should know that the drug is being used for a non-medical purpose, he or she is not authorized to dispense the product.

ANABOLIC STEROID RESTRICTIONS. Specific statutory prohibitions exist against prescribing, administering, or dispensing "steroids," or any form of autotransfusion, for the purpose of manipulating hormones to increase muscle mass, strength, or weight, or to enhance athletic ability unless medically necessary (e.g., runner's anemia). Steroids include

- "Anabolic steroids"
- "Androgens"
- "Human growth hormone" (RCW 69.41.300-310)
- The Pharmacy Commission has listed by regulation particular drugs that constitute steroids (WAC 246-883-040).

RESTRICTIONS ON SCHEDULE II STIMULANTS – SEE CHAPTER 5.

FEDERAL RESTRICTIONS ON HUMAN GROWTH HORMONE. A specific federal statute establishes criminal penalties for off-label dispensing of human growth hormone (HGH, rhGH, somatropin). 21 U.S.C. §333(e)) makes it a crime to knowingly distribute HGH for use in humans "other than the treatment of a disease or other recognized medical condition, where such use has been authorized by the Secretary of Health and Human Services under section 355 of [Title 21] and pursuant to the order of a physician." Although the FDA may not initiate action against prescribers, dispensers have been subject to prosecution and at least one specialty pharmacy is subject to a deferred prosecution agreement with the Justice Department related to its dispensing of somatropin for off-label uses. The approved indications are: Pediatric patients – GH deficiency leading to short stature or growth failure, Turner syndrome, idiopathic short stature, SHOX deficiency, failure to catch up in height after small for gestational birth; Adults – childhood-onset or adult-onset GH deficiency. A 2015 Indiana court opinion held that specialty pharmacies had no "duty to dispense" somatropin prescriptions when they refused from a good faith belief that the prescriptions were not for approved indications.[279] Pharmacists are entitled to know the diagnosis or indication for a somatropin prescription before dispensing.

OFF-LABEL USES. Drugs may be prescribed for uses not included in their package insert; this is not the same as issuing a prescription for other than a legitimate medical purpose. The FDCA prohibits manufacturers from promoting drugs for off label use, but does not restrict the practice of medicine under state law, with certain exceptions such as HGH (see above). When dispensing a prescription written for a non-FDA approved indication, the pharmacist should be aware of the intended use, and the literature supporting it. The pharmacist must distinguish between use of the drug for a condition not listed in the package insert and prescribing of doses that are outside the normal range for the drug when making professional judgments about the appropriateness of the prescription for the patient. Resources available to evaluate off label uses include the American Hospital Formulary Service (AHFS) and the USP-DI. (See chapter 8 regarding off label uses and Medicaid or Medicare prescriptions.)

The FDA has filed criminal and civil lawsuits against manufacturers or their employees who have promoted prescription drugs for off-label uses. However, the successful criminal misdemeanor prosecution of a pharmaceutical sales representative for promoting Xyrem® (gamma hydroxybutyrate) for off-label uses was overturned by the US Court of Appeals for the Second Circuit on the basis that the salesman's statements were free speech protected by the First Amendment.[280]

LEGIBLE. Written prescriptions in Washington must be "legible." RCW 69.41.120 requires written prescriptions to be legible. RCW 69.41.010(13) defines a "legible prescription" as "capable of being read and understood by the pharmacist filling the prescription or the nurse or other practitioner implementing the medication order. A prescription must be hand printed, typewritten, or electronically generated." This statute is interpreted to declare prescriptions or drug orders written in cursive to be legally "illegible." Pharmacists who fill illegible prescriptions without verifying the prescription are liable for damages caused to their patients. The best strategy for dealing with a prescription in cursive handwriting is to call the prescriber to verify it, and indicate on the prescription the verified order.

TAMPER-RESISTANT PRESCRIPTION PADS.

FOR MEDICAID RECIPIENTS. A provision in an omnibus Iraq War and Katrina Recovery appropriations bill[281] requires WRITTEN PRESCRIPTIONS ISSUED FOR MEDICAID RECIPIENTS to be executed on tamper-resistant prescription pads. CMS has published a fact sheet for pharmacists.[282]

A qualifying prescription pad contains the following elements:

- One or more industry-recognized features designed to prevent copying;

- One or more industry-recognized features designed to prevent erasure or modification; and
- One or more industry-recognized features designed to prevent use of counterfeit forms.

The rule does not apply to oral prescriptions, faxed prescriptions, or electronic prescriptions, or to refills of prescriptions which were issued prior to the effective date (June 2006).

TRANSFERRED MEDICAID PRESCRIPTIONS. When receiving transferred prescriptions for Medicaid patients, the receiving pharmacist must confirm from the transferring pharmacist that the prescription was written on tamper-resistant pad or was exempt.

NON-COMPLYING PRESCRIPTIONS. Pharmacists may fill non-complying prescriptions in emergencies as long as confirmation from the prescriber is received by fax, phone, or e-mail within 72 hours. Pharmacist should document the time of day dispensed in the time of day that confirmation is received.

Pharmacists may confirm noncomplying prescriptions with the prescriber, either verbally or by fax, if the confirmation is received before the product is dispensed to the patient. The exact time of day that the confirmation is received, and that the product is dispensed, should be documented.

Pharmacies that dispense Medicaid prescriptions pursuant to non-qualifying prescriptions are subject to rejection of the related Medicaid claim and sanctions imposed under federal law.

ALL PRESCRIPTIONS ISSUED TO PATIENTS IN WASHINGTON STATE must conform to the same tamper-resistant prescription pad (TRPP) requirements as Medicaid prescriptions.[283] However, the pads must printed on approved paper and must bear a Pharmacy Commission "seal of approval." (RCW 18.64.500(7)) The Board announced in January 2010 that the seal will consist of a map of the State of Washington with a mortar and pestle in the center." The process for approval of paper is available on the Commission's website.[284] The Commission has since 2016 redesigned the seal, and to make changes including no longer requiring green thermo-chromic ink, and allowing "approved plain paper printing technology/solutions." Prescriptions written on pads using the 2010 version of the seal are still valid.[285] The seal must be on the lower right corner of the prescription form and the mortar and pestle must be 1.125" x 1.125".

TRPPs are required for *all* prescriptions that are hand written by the prescriber (for both legend drugs and controlled substances) for delivery to a pharmacy, **except** for:

- Prescriptions that are transmitted to the pharmacy by telephone, fax, or e-prescribed; or
- Prescriptions written for patients in hospitals (inpatient or outpatient), residents of LTC facilities or hospice programs, inpatients or residents of mental health facilities, or incarcerated individuals, where:
    - The order is written by the prescriber or authorized agent (in the case of LTC facilities or hospice programs) into the patient's medical or clinical record,
    - The order is given directly to the pharmacy, and
    - The patient never has the opportunity to handle the written order. (RCW 18.64.500(9))

The statute specifies that "All acts related to the prescribing, dispensing, and records maintenance of all prescriptions shall be in compliance with applicable federal and state laws, rules, and regulations." (RCW 18.64.500(10)). The statute gives the Commission authority to issue regulations to implement its requirements.

Prescriptions written outside of the state of Washington by authorized prescribers are not covered by these rules, but must conform to rules in the state where written.

TIME LIMITS ON PRESCRIPTIONS. Prescriptions must have been written no more than one year prior to the date of filling or refilling, and no more than six months prior in the case of prescriptions for controlled substances in schedules II, III, IV or V. The general one-year limit on legend drugs found in Pharmacy Commission regulations that specify that no prescription in Washington may be refilled beyond one year from the date written. (WAC 246-869-100(2)(d)) This rule necessarily means that a prescription may not be initially filled more than one year after the date it was written. A specific rule placing a "12-month" limit on prescriptions applies to home IV therapy drugs. (WAC 246-871-050(1)) The limit on controlled substances is found in the federal Controlled Substances Act and in RCW 69.50.308(d) and (f) (see Chapter 5).

OTHER REQUIRED ELEMENTS. Other elements that must be on the prescription or available to the pharmacist are described in the following paragraphs.

DATE WRITTEN

The prescriber must place on the prescription the date he or she actually issued the prescription. Pre-dating or post-dating prescriptions renders the prescriptions invalid. When the date is inadvertently entered improperly, the pharmacist may contact the prescriber to correct the date. For example, prescriptions issued in January often inadvertently indicate the previous year. The pharmacist may not simply assume this is an error, however, but must confirm with the prescriber the actual date the prescription was issued. In the case of legend drugs, a confirmation with the prescriber's office or agent should be sufficient, but to correct dates on a controlled substance prescription requires a direct conversation with the issuing prescriber (see Chapter 5).

THE PATIENT'S ADDRESS must be on the prescription or available in patient medication record, a record book, or hospital or clinic record. (WAC 246-869-100(2)(a)) The definition of "address" as it applies to the patient is not clear under federal law. And, frankly, some patients don't have a home. The only description under federal law of an "address" is contained in the US Postal Service Domestic Mail Manual, which indicates that "the delivery address specifies the location to which the USPS is to deliver a mailpiece." The DMM indicates that for "street and number" the sender shall "Include the apartment number, or use the post office box number, or general delivery, or rural route or highway contract route designation and box number, as applicable." Thus, it appears that under federal law the patient may provide any location to which the USPS could deliver mail. It is a common practice for the Medicaid program to use a physician's office address as the address for a homeless Medicaid recipient.
The WA patient medication record regulations define the "address" to be used in the medication profile as "the place of residence of the patient," but a similar definition is not set forth for WAC 246-869. (WAC 246-876-010)

PMP ADDRESSES. Washington's rules for data entered in the Prescription Monitoring Program (see chapter 5) require the following for "patient address."

- Patient address – the current geographic location of the patient's residence, or, if the patient address is in care of another person or entity, that person's or entity's address is the "patient address." If more than one is possible, they should be recorded in the following order of preference:
    - Geographical location of residence, as would be identified by a 9-1-1 locator;
    - An address listed by the US Postal Service; or
    - The common name of the residence and town (WAC 246-470-010(6))

DIRECTIONS FOR USE. WAC 246-875-020(h) requires that the pharmacist record in an automated patient medication record system, "The complete directions for use of the drug. The term "as directed" is prohibited pursuant to RCW 18.64.246 and 69.41.050." Thus, Washington does not allow a pharmacist to record "UD" (from the Latin, *ut dictum* – as directed) instructions as the directions for a prescription in an automated patient medication record system. (Note, however, that this requirement is not specified for manual record systems in WAC 246-875-030). Thus, for the pharmacist to satisfy this rule, the prescription must contain complete directions. If not, the pharmacist must ascertain the directions from the prescriber.

Other laws and rules are more specific concerning directions for use, including the statutory requirements for prescriptions dispensed from emergency departments (see Chapter 3).

DEALING WITH SPECIFIC LABELING SITUATIONS:
PRODUCTS WITH CONSUMER LABELING. Some products are clearly labeled on the container, such as birth control pills. In these cases, "UD" should be interpreted to read "as directed on the container."

COMPLICATED DOSAGE REGIMENS. Some directions are for complicated doses. The prescriber may have given a written schedule to the patient, such as in step-down dosing of prednisone. In such a case, the pharmacist needs to know what those instructions were, to determine compliance. The pharmacist should make a copy of the instructions and attach them to the original prescription, and use them to estimate a days' supply. The directions would then be interpreted as "Take according to written sheet provided by physician." If appropriate, a "not to exceed" limit should be specified on the label.

DRUG REQUIRING DOSAGE ADJUSTMENT. Sometimes the patient is given the drug, and told to confirm the dosage with the prescriber, or will take differing doses in accordance with monitoring of therapy, as in treatment with Coumadin®. In such cases, the directions should be interpreted as "take on a [daily] basis in accordance with consultation with [provider]." Maximum dosing should be specified if appropriate. Pharmacists who manage warfarin therapy in anticoagulation clinics routinely provide the patient with a printed sheet showing specific doses on specific days to be taken until the next appointment or other change.

INSTRUCTIONS REGARDING GENERIC SUBSTITUTION. This is automatic with two-line prescription blanks, but the information needs to be gathered specifically on telephoned orders, and recorded on the face of the prescription by the pharmacist. (RCW 69.41.120).

Prescriptions written by generic name (or telephoned by generic name) do not come under the requirements of the substitution law.

RX NUMBER, DATE OF FILLING, PHARMACIST ID. The pharmacist must place a serial number, the date of dispensing, and the initials of the responsible pharmacist on the face of the prescription. (WAC 246-869-100(2)(c)).

NDC OF DRUG PRODUCT DISPENSED. In all cases where product interchange has occurred (see below), the pharmacist must record the identity of the actual drug dispensed on the prescription and in the patient record. (RCW 69.41.120) This is most easily and clearly done by recording the National Drug Code (NDC) of the product dispensed. Note that for purposes of identifying the drug product and dosage form, only the first 2 NDC fields (manufacturer and drug product) must be recorded. The third field, which records the package size is required to submit claims to third party payers, and must match the actual package dispensed (see Chapter 8).

TELEPHONED OR ORAL PRESCRIPTIONS. Pharmacists may receive oral or telephoned prescriptions for legend drugs. A copy of an oral prescription must be maintained in the pharmacy records. (RCW 69.41.120 (4), RCW 69.50.308(2)(d), 21 CFR § 1306.21(a)) It is important for the pharmacist to record the full name of the person communicating the prescription, with enough detail to unambiguously identify the person in case of later inquiry. (See also Chapter 7 section on risk-management).

VOICE MESSAGE SYSTEMS. Commission rules allow for recording of prescribers' verbal prescriptions in pharmacies with approval for differential hours (see Chapter 3), subject to the requirement that the pharmacist must be the one to play back the message, and the voice message system must inform the caller of the pharmacy's hours of operation.[286] The FDA has published a compliance policy guide that considers a recorded oral prescription as meeting the requirements in the FDCA of an "oral prescription," "if the pharmacist plays back the recording and concludes that the voice he or she hears is that of a physician known to the pharmacist, and there is no obvious reason for suspecting the authenticity of the recorded prescription."[287] This CPG, issued in 1980, seems based on an archaic model of community pharmacy practice.

BEST PRACTICES FOR VERBAL PRESCRIPTIONS. Pharmacy Commission and other Department of Health staff have developed guidelines for transmission of verbal prescriptions to a pharmacist (see side bar).[288]

2ID NATIONAL PATIENT SAFETY GOAL. National patient safety standards now advocate that key patient care record elements use at least 2 unique means of identifying ("2ID") the patient, such as the patient name, telephone number, date of birth, and/or medical record number. This is included in The Joint Commission's National Patient Safety Goals for 2019 (NPSG 01.01.01).[289] As the Commission suggested in its guidelines, obtaining at least 2 identifiers when receiving verbal orders should be standard of practice for pharmacists.

FACSIMILE TRANSMISSION (FAX). In general, faxes of legend drugs were traditionally treated as if they were telephoned orders. Recently, however, state law has begun to treat faxes as a separate entity from verbal orders, and faxes are specifically not considered a form of "electronic communication of prescription information." See RCW 69.41.010(10) and RCW 69.50.101(n).[290]

The legislature[291] has revised RCW 18.64.245 to specify that "when a pharmacy receives a prescription in digital or electronic format through facsimile equipment transmitting an exact visual image of the prescription, ... the digital or electronic record of every such prescription dispensed at the pharmacy constitutes a suitable record of prescriptions, provided that the original or direct copy of the prescription is electronically or digitally numbered or referenced, dated, and filed in a form that permits the information required to be readily retrievable." (RCW 18.64.245 (2)). This suggests that a fax copy of a written prescription for legend drugs is to be treated as if it were the valid record of the written prescription, and that an electronic file copy of a fax may be stored in the computer.

DEPARTMENT OF HEALTH GUIDELINES: BEST PRACTICE GUIDELINES FOR VERBAL PRESCRIPTIONS

When calling in a prescription to a pharmacist, the following information should be provided:

Patient Information

- Name, including middle initial (spell last name if unusual)
- Date of birth
- Phone number

Drug Information

- Drug name
- Strength
- Dosage
- Directions (dose & frequency of administration)
- Route of administration
- Quantity
- Refills, if any
- Notation of purpose, if appropriate
- If generic substitution is permitted

Prescriber Information

- Name (whole name, with identifier, if a common name)
- Name of clinic or practice
- DEA number if appropriate
- Name and role of caller, if other than practitioner
- Phone number where pharmacist can check back with the prescriber if there are any questions about the prescription

Information concerning each prescription must include all the information specified below for electronic prescriptions generally, as applicable.

The Commission has specified the following requirements for faxes for legend drugs prescriptions or refill authorizations sent *directly from the prescriber* to the pharmacy. (WAC 246-870-050):

- Must contain the **date, time, and telephone** number and location of the transmitting fax machine.
- The pharmacist is responsible for assuring that the fax will be **legible for two years** (i.e., not printed on thermal paper).

See Chapter 5 for rules for faxing controlled substances prescriptions.

Transmission of refill information from PHARMACY TO PHARMACY may be faxed.

What if the fax is a copy of a prescription on a TAMPER-RESISTANT PAD that when faxed displays "VOID" or "ILLEGAL"? Such a fax effectively renders the prescription unfillable and will require follow up and, if possible, conversion to an oral prescription. The Commission has recommended that pantographs on tamper-resistant pads should state "COPY" or "COPY/fax" instead of VOID or ILLEGAL.

Electronic prescriptions.

The law allows for electronic transmission of prescriptions, (RCW 69.41.055) and permits the Board to adopt specific rules (WAC 246-870). The law requires the following:

- Transmission is directly from the prescriber to a pharmacy of the patient's choice, with no intervening person having access to the information. (This prohibits orders being transmitted through an insurance company.) An agent of the prescriber in a long-term care facility or hospice program is not "an intervening person" under this rule.
- The Commission must approve the systems for sending and receiving the information.
- The information must include an "explicit opportunity" for prescribers to communicate preferences regarding generic substitution, but does not limit the ability of practitioners or pharmacies to permit substitution by default under a prior-consent authorization.
- The pharmacist in charge (responsible pharmacy manager) shall establish or verify procedures and policies to ensure integrity and confidentiality of the prescription information.
    - All managers, employees, and agents of the pharmacy must read, sign, and comply with the established procedures.
- The pharmacist must exercise professional judgment regarding the accuracy, validity and authenticity of the drug orders transmitted electronically.
- Electronic storage of digital or electronic prescriptions meets the record keeping requirements of RCW 18.64.245, provided that such records are "electronically or digitally numbered or referenced, dated, and filed in a form that permits the information required to be readily retrievable."

The Commission publishes a list of APPROVED SYSTEMS[292] on its website. Rules governing these systems are contained in WAC 246-870-060.

COMMISSION RULES FOR ELECTRONIC PRESCRIPTIONS. The Commission has adopted additional rules in WAC 246-870. An electronically-transmitted prescription must include the following elements. Electronic prescriptions lacking these should be verified with the prescriber and treated as telephoned prescriptions after verification.

- Prescriber's name and address
- Prescriber's DEA number for CSA prescriptions

- Date of issuance
- Patient's name and address
- Drug name, dose, route, form, directions for use, quantity
- Electronic, digital, or manual signature of the prescriber
- Refills or renewals authorized, if any
- A place to note allergies and a notation of purpose for the drug
- Indication of a preference for generic substitution.
- Other requirements of the law
- Identification of the electronic system readily retrievable for Pharmacy Commission inspection.
- The **pharmacist is responsible for verifying** that each electronic prescription is valid and shall verify the authenticity of the prescription with the prescriber if there is a question.
- There cannot be an exclusive agreement concerning faxed orders between the pharmacy and the prescriber.

DRUG PRODUCT SELECTION

The policy issues related to the selection of a drug product to meet a physician's prescription are almost entirely economic, and related to balancing the need for new drugs, and hence the need for incentives for innovation, with the goal of making drug therapy affordable. However, modern policy has emerged from earlier policy that was concerned with protecting the public against pharmacists' mistakes in compounding, as well as the possibility that a pharmacist would substitute an inferior ingredient instead of the one intended by the prescriber.

ACCURATE DISPENSING. The pharmacist is required to dispense the product and strength called for in the prescription. The Commission may discipline a pharmacist or intern who has "compounded, dispensed, or caused the compounding or dispensing of any drug or device which contains more or less than the equivalent quantity of ingredient or ingredients specified by the person who prescribed such drug or device." (RCW 18.64.160(5))

When a drug is prescribed by its official or "generic" name (e.g., ibuprofen tablets 800 mg), the prescriber has left it to the pharmacist to determine the particular manufacturer or source of the product, *secundum artem* ("according to the art [of the apothecary]").

When a drug is prescribed by brand name (e.g., Motrin tablets 800 mg), it is understood that the prescriber intends a particular product from a particular manufacturer.

Most states allow generic substitution, and many provide for therapeutic substitution. These two activities fall in the category of drug product selection, sometimes called product interchange. When allowed, product interchange does not expose pharmacists to charges of misfilling prescriptions when they use a different manufacturer's product.

BRAND VERSUS GENERIC DRUGS.

THE INNOVATOR PRODUCT. All "new drugs" marketed in the US must be subject to an approved NEW DRUG APPLICATION (NDA) approved by the FDA The manufacturer who is first granted an NDA is said to be the "innovator" of the drug, and generally has patent rights granting it exclusive privileges to sell the drug for a defined period of time (typically 17 years from the date the patent is filed). Since it may take seven to ten years to develop a patented "New Chemical Entity" (NCE) after a patent is obtained, the marketing exclusivity may last for as little as seven years after the NDA is approved. Certain provisions of the Prescription Drug Marketing Act (PDMA) and the Orphan Drug and Patent Right Extension Act allow for extension of market exclusivity.

When, as a result of Phase IV experience, a manufacturer wishes to change information in the package insert (e.g., new indications, changed directions, additional warnings, etc.), a SUPPLEMENTAL NEW DRUG APPLICATION (SNDA) is filed with the FDA. To the extent that these changes result from patentable innovations, the innovator may gain additional market exclusivity for the new claims.

OFFICIAL NAME. All approved new drugs are given a non-proprietary name, which in the US is officially called the UNITED STATES ADOPTED NAME (USAN), approved by the USAN Commission, a division of the Department of Commerce. The manufacturer's label of all approved drugs must include the USAN, and the manufacturer may also market the drug under a proprietary, or trade name.

TRADE NAMES are the property of the manufacturer who coins them, subject to filing with the Patent Office. The trade name may be either "registered" as indicated by the ® symbol, or "trademarked," as indicated by the ™ symbol. The manufacturer's label must present the non-proprietary name in letters at least half as high as the trade name. Pharmacists labeling prescription containers may always use the nonproprietary name, and may also use the trade name as long as the product in the container is made by the manufacturer who owns the trade name.

ENFORCEMENT OF COPYRIGHT. The manufacturer is required by copyright law to enforce its rights to a trade name by challenging in court any inappropriate use of the trade name by others. From time to time, drug companies have filed lawsuits against pharmacists who used their trade names on packages of drugs containing a generic product, challenging phrases such as "ibuprofen – same as Motrin" or "ibuprofen – generic Motrin." Some pharmacy law experts recommend the following language on prescription labels to avoid trademark infringement suits: "ibuprofen – substituted for Motrin."

CAPITALIZATION OF DRUG NAMES

BRAND NAMES are proper nouns, and should be Capitalized (unless the manufacturer has chosen to do otherwise, as in "ella®").

GENERIC NAMES are not proper nouns and are not capitalized, unless the term is the beginning of a sentence or list.

EXAMPLES:

Soma (carisoprodol)
Pradaxa (dabigatran etexilate)
Lantus (insulin glargine [rDNA origin] injection)
ella (ulipristal acetate)

Example chart note: "Current drugs: hydrochlorothiazide 25 mg qd, Pradaxa 150 mg bid, ramipril 10 mg qd, omeprazole 20 mg qd, Centrum Silver 1 qd"

PATENT EXPIRATION. After the patent rights expire on a particular drug product, other manufacturers may market generic products that are the same chemical entity as indicated in the NDA, provided they meet requirements for bioavailability and bioequivalence. Primarily, the generic equivalent must provide the same pharmacokinetic parameters, Cp, Tp and AUC, as the innovator's product, as demonstrated by *in vivo* testing. The generic manufacturer does not need to repeat the innovator's Phase I through Phase III testing, but only the more limited proof of bioavailability and bioequivalence. These are documented in an Abbreviated New Drug Application (ANDA). After the FDA approves the ANDA, the generic manufacturer may distribute the product under its non-proprietary ("generic") name, and/or may develop a brand name of its own for the product.

HATCH-WAXMAN ACT. In 1984, Congress passed the DRUG PRICE COMPETITION AND PATENT TERM RESTORATION ACT[293] with the intention of speeding the adoption and approval of generic drugs. It is commonly called the Hatch-Waxman Act, after its congressional sponsors, Sen. Orrin Hatch (R-Utah) and Rep. Henry Waxman (D-Cal). The title of the Act suggests it was a matter of compromise: it hoped to increase competition yet at the same time extended patent protections to certain drugs. Two major sections of the Act deal with these goals:

ANDAS. The Act clarified and standardized the process by which a generic manufacturer may seek to market a generic drug, by filing an ANDA.

PATENT ISSUES.
The Act provides for up to 5 years of patent extension for certain categories of new drugs to cover time spent in drug development after the patent was issued. The Act also provided a means by which a generic manufacturer could challenge the patent status of the innovator's product without running the risk of lengthy post-marketing patent infringement lawsuits.

Each innovator must file with the FDA a list of the patents it claims protect its right to market the product. These patents are listed by the FDA in *The Orange Book* (see below).

The first generic competitor to file an ANDA may, under section 505(j)(5)(B)(IV) of the Act, file a so-called Paragraph IV notice that it is contesting the innovator's patent. This triggers two provisions:

- If the innovator files a suit within 45 days to challenge the generic application, then the innovator is awarded a 30-month extension of its patent.
- The first generic manufacturer to file a successful ANDA gains a 180-day exclusive right to market the drug, and the FDA will not approve another ANDA for the same product during that period of exclusivity.

ALLEGED ABUSE OF HATCH-WAXMAN PROVISIONS. By the early 2000s it became apparent to many that innovators were taking advantage of the Paragraph IV provisions to unduly extend their marketing exclusivity, largely by protecting their drugs with "extra patents of poor quality, filing lawsuits to protect the patents even when the lawsuit will be lost, but getting the extra market exclusivity anyway."[294] In addition, manufacturers have begun to enter into a variety of schemes with potential generic competitors. Strategies used to avoid generic competition have included:

- Filing of additional patents based on such things changes in the crystalline structure of the active pharmaceutical ingredient.
- Filing last-minute changes to the innovator's product labeling.
- Entering into agreements for "authorized generics" and/or "pay for delay" contracts where the generic manufacturer agrees to delay bringing its product to market in return for "reverse payments" from the innovator.

IMPACT ON PHARMACIES. In general, these issues affect manufacturers only, and do not affect pharmacists who dispense or distribute generic drugs that are subject to an ANDA. The major exception is when pharmacists attempt to prepare by extemporaneous compounding a product that is subject to an existing patent. (See section on compounding.)

BIOSIMILARS VERSUS GENERICS. The major difference between "generics," which are therapeutically equivalent and chemically identical small molecules, and "biosimilars," is that biosimilars are typically not molecularly identical, but have been shown to be "highly similar" to the reference product, with only minor differences in the clinically inactive components of the molecule, and no clinically meaningful differences between the biosimilar and the reference drug.

NONPROPRIETARY NAMES. In addition, where generics all have exactly the same nonproprietary name, the nonproprietary name of a biosimilar product may contain a suffix designating the manufacturer. For example, Neupogen® is the reference filgrastim product, while the nonproprietary name for Zarxio® is "filgrastim-sndz." Similarly, the biosimilar for Remicade® (infliximab) is Inflectra® (infliximab-dyyb).

RELATED BIOLOGICAL PRODUCTS. Some potentially interchangeable biosimilars may not be approved via the biosimilar approval process; Granix® (tbo-filgrastim) was approved using the NDA process; it is considered a "related biological product" to Neupogen, and its non-proprietary name includes a prefix (e.g., "tbo-").

GENERIC AND BIOSIMILAR SUBSTITUTION

DRUG VERSUS BIOLOGIC. In this discussion, I will use "drug" to refer to a small-molecule drug approved by an NDA or ANDA, and "biosimilar" to refer to a biologic drug product approved by an NDA, a BLA, or a 351K interchangeability application.

Virtually all states provide for "generic substitution," whereby the pharmacist may or must dispense the generic drug, even when the prescriber prescribes the product by its trade name. The purpose of all these laws is to provide savings to consumers, or to third party payers (such as state Medicaid programs). Many states, including Washington, require that all or a significant part of the savings arising from generic substitution be passed on to the purchaser. Generally, the pharmacist must have some evidence that the generic product is an approved drug product that has been found bioequivalent to the innovator's product. Similarly, pharmacists must have evidence that a potential biosimilar product is approved for interchange.

In Washington (RCW 69.41.100-180), the pharmacist may use any information regarding generic equivalency he or she considers reliable. Other states specify one or more of several resources or lists that the pharmacist can or must consult.

To determine biosimilar interchangeability, Washington requires that pharmacists consult a positive formulary or listing provided by FDA, or a copy of the list that is posted on the Commission website. However, the current listing on the Commission website has typically lagged behind the postings by FDA (see Purple Book, below).

PHARMACIST'S GENERIC SUBSTITUTION REFERENCE SOURCES

In all states, a prescription written by generic (nonproprietary) name permits the pharmacist to choose the source of the product, whether it is bioequivalent to a brand name drug or not.

ORANGE BOOK

The "Orange Book" is officially entitled "Approved Drug Products with Therapeutic Equivalents[295] and is published by the FDA. The only products listed are drugs with NDAs and/or ANDAs. None of the unapproved drugs discussed above are listed. The Orange Book does not include listings for authorized generics, since they are the same drug as the brand-name (see below).

EQUIVALENCY DETERMINATIONS. Drugs are considered equivalent if they are approved drugs with the same ingredient and dosage form, and generally produce the statistically equivalent AUC and C_{max} when compared to the reference drug. If for various reasons a comparison between a generic and the reference product cannot be done, the products cannot be rated. Thus, an Orange Book rating of AB can be taken as evidence of therapeutic equivalence, but other ratings do not prove non-equivalence.

EQUIVALENCY RATINGS. Drugs that are considered therapeutically equivalent are given an "A" rating; those that are not are rated "B." A second letter is appended to indicate the basis for the rating, and all generically equivalent products are rated "AB." In every case, the rating of a generic drug is related to a specific innovator's product. In some cases, two innovator's products have the same chemical ingredient, but are not, themselves, bioequivalent. This is most often the case with sustained-release preparations that use different formulations to achieve their release characteristics. For example, Adalat CC™ and Procardia XL™ each contain nifedipine HCl. However, they use different formulations, and are not interchangeable as generics. Adalat CC is rated AB1 and Procardia XL is rated AB2. Generic nifedipine formulations that are interchangeable with Adalat CC are rated AB1, and those that can be substituted for Procardia XL are rated AB2.

LEVOTHYROXINE products have posed a special problem, and the FDA uses four ratings AB1, AB2, AB3, and AB4. Some products are rated in more than one category. For example, here are the November 2014 ratings for 25 mcg levothyroxine products:

- Synthroid® is rated AB1 and AB2
- Levoxyl® is rated AB1 and AB3
- Levo-T® is rated AB2 and AB3
- Levothroid® is rated AB4
- Unithroid® is rated AB1, AB2, and AB3
- Levothyroxine (Merck KGAA) is rated AB2, AB3
- Levothryroxine (Mylan) is rated AB1, AB2, AB3, and AB4
- Currently, Mylan's levothyroxine in 25 mcg strength may be substituted for any of the other named products, and careful matching of the remaining products shows that they may all be interchanged for one another, with the exception of Levothroid®.

POSITIVE FORMULARIES. Some states do not allow the pharmacist to substitute any equivalent generic, but require the pharmacist to choose from drugs on a specific list. This list is often called a "positive formulary." Some states specify the Orange Book as their positive formulary, while others have a special commission that develops the list. Washington allows the pharmacist to choose from sources in addition to the Orange Book, so Washington does not *require* a positive formulary. However, the Orange Book is referred to in WAC 246-899-030(b) as a "board approved reference for a positive formulary of therapeutically equivalent products within the limits stated in that publication."

NEGATIVE FORMULARIES. A few states have lists of drugs that cannot be substituted. Many of these lists include so-called "narrow therapeutic index drugs," such as levothyroxine, warfarin, digoxin, and furosemide. The drugs placed on these lists are often placed there as a result of a political process in which manufacturers and physicians have lobbied to limit generic substitution. Washington does not specifically preclude generic substitution by use of a negative formulary.[296]

BIOSIMILAR INTERCHANGEABILITY REFERENCE – THE PURPLE BOOK: The equivalency evaluation guide for biological products that corresponds to the Orange Book is the Purple Book, officially entitled "Lists of Licensed Biological Products with Reference Product Exclusivity and Biosimilarity or Interchangeability Evaluations." This listing, which is updated quarterly by FDA, consists of a table showing all licensed biological products, and whether they are biosimilar (designated by a "B") and/or interchangeable (designated by an "I"). As of January 2017, the FDA has not yet designated any products as "interchangeable." As noted above, new reference biological products are granted 12 years of data exclusivity before an interchangeable biosimilar may be approved. A draft guidance for industry on how to demonstrate to FDA that a biological product is interchangeable with a reference product was issued for comment on January 17, 2017.[297]

PHARMACIST COMMUNICATION TO PRESCRIBER WHEN INTERCHANGING BIOSIMILARS. Until August 1, 2020, RCW 69.41.193[298] requires that a pharmacist interchanging a biological product must assure creation within 5 days of an electronic record accessible to the patient's practitioner that provides the exact biosimilar dispensed, using the name of the product and manufacturer, or the NDC code. The record may be placed in a system that is accessible through:

- An interoperable electronic medical records system;
- An electronic prescribing technology;
- A pharmacy benefit management system; or
- A pharmacy record accessible to the practitioner

Such a record is "presumed to provide notice to the practitioner." Alternatively, the pharmacist may communicate this information directly to the practitioner using fax, phone, electronic transmission, or other "prevailing means."

These communications are not required when:

- The prescribed product has no interchangeable biological product equivalent; or
- The dispensing was a refill with no change in product from the prior filling; or
- The pharmacist or "the pharmacist's designee" and the practitioner communicated before dispensing and the communication included the required information.

"DAW" INSTRUCTIONS AND SPECIAL PRESCRIPTION BLANKS.

Most states allow prescribers to prevent drug product selection or interchange on a per-prescription basis. Some will allow the prescriber to indicate "Dispense As Written" or "DAW" in writing on the prescription. Others allow a check-box (☑ DAW). Washington, like several other states, requires a two-line prescription blank, with one signature line indicating "Substitution Permitted" and the other indicating "Dispense As Written." In Washington, manufacturer's successfully lobbied to have the DAW line be on the right hand side of the blank, reasoning that many right-handed physicians would, by force of habit, preferentially sign that line. Under Washington law, a prescription that is written by a Washington prescriber is not valid unless it is written on a two-line prescription blank. In Washington, pharmacists are required to obtain and record specific instructions regarding substitution when receiving telephoned prescriptions, and to indicate this on the permanent record (WAC 246-899-020 (a))

DEALING WITH OUT-OF-STATE PRESCRIPTIONS. According to the statute, Washington pharmacists may substitute the generic product or interchangeable biosimilar on an out-of-state prescription written by brand name unless "otherwise instructed by the prescriber through the use of the words 'dispense as written', words of similar meaning, or some other indication." However, the Commission has qualified this requirement in WAC 246-899-050. If the practitioner has not clearly provided instructions regarding substitution, the pharmacist may substitute a generic only if the pharmacist has determined substitution is permitted by one of the following means:

- The pharmacist has personal knowledge of the rules in the state of origin; or
- The pharmacist has obtained authorization from the prescriber; or
- The pharmacist obtains current information on the rules in the other state from
    - The Washington Pharmacy Commission
    - The Board of Pharmacy in the other state
    - Some other reliable professional means.

GENERIC SUBSTITUTION IS REQUIRED IN WASHINGTON. Washington does not allow the pharmacist to dispense a brand name if substitution is permitted except when:

- The pharmacy does not have a generic product in stock which is, in the pharmacist's professional judgment, bioequivalent to the drug prescribed; or
- The patient or the patient's agent requests the branded product, and the product is not being paid for by public funds.

BIOSIMILAR INTERCHANGE IS REQUIRED IN WASHINGTON.

RCW 69.41.125 specifies that the pharmacist must substitute an interchangeable biological drug product that he or she has in stock if "substitution permitted" is indicated on the prescription, unless:

- the prescribed biological product is requested by the patient or the patient's agent, or
- the wholesale cost of the interchangeable biological drug product is not less than the prescribed biological product.

SAVINGS MUST BE PASSED ON TO PURCHASER IN WASHINGTON.

Washington law requires that 60% of savings resulting from generic substitution (but not biosimilar interchange) be passed on to the consumer. Washington is one of 17 states with some requirement to pass on at least some of the savings.[299] The calculation should be made as follows:

$$SAVINGS = Pharmacy's\ Cost\ of\ Brand\ Name\ Drug - Pharmacy's\ Cost\ of\ Generic\ Drug$$

$$MAXIMUM\ PRICE\ TO\ CONSUMER = Normal\ Price\ of\ Brand\ Name\ Drug - (SAVINGS\ \times 0.6)$$

I am not aware of any enforcement of this rule by the Commission or any other group in Washington. However, attorneys for consumers in other states have filed class action suits for consumer fraud when pharmacists have failed to follow specific regulations and they can show economic damages.[300] One of the collateral issues that arises is how to calculate the pharmacy's usual and customary price for the drug. If the pharmacy has a "discount program" that is generally open to the public, the discounted price for the brand name drug will determine its usual price.

PHARMACY CALCULATIONS IN A LAW TEXTBOOK!

EXAMPLE: Your pharmacy's normal cash price for a brand-name drug is $85.00 for 90 tablets. The Average Wholesale Price (AWP) for this product is $83.00 per 100. Your Actual Acquisition Price (AAC) from the wholesaler is AWP less 18% for this drug (or 82% of AWP). Your AAC for the generic equivalent is $41.00 per 100. What is the maximum price you can charge the patient for 90 tablets under WA law?

$$Savings = \left[\left(\frac{\$83}{100\ tabs} \times 90\ tabs\right) \times 0.82\right] - \left[\frac{\$41}{100\ tabs} x\ 90\ tabs\right] = \$24.35$$

$$Maximum\ Price = \$85.00 - (\$24.35\ \times 0.6) = \$70.39$$

As long as your pharmacy's charge for the generic is less than $70.39, your pharmacy will be in compliance with this statutory requirement.

For this example, the pharmacy's gross margin on the brand name drug is 27.9% ($23.75/$85.00 × 100%); the margin on generic drug is 47.5% ($33.49/$70.39 × 100%),

NOTICE TO PUBLIC. RCW 69.41.160 requires the following notices to be displayed to the public in every pharmacy (the content of this sign was revised in 2015 to include biological products):

"Under Washington law, a less expensive interchangeable biological product or equivalent drug may in some cases be substituted for the drug prescribed by your doctor. Such substitution, however, may only be made with the consent of your doctor. Please consult your pharmacist or physician for more information."

PHARMACIST JUDGMENT PROTECTED. Pharmacists are protected by RCW 69.41.170 from being coerced by employers to dispense a particular generic drug or to substitute a generic drug for another drug. Interchangeable biosimilars are not included in this section of the statute.

NO GREATER LIABILITY. Physicians and pharmacists are protected from liability for authorizing or dispensing generic drugs. (RCW 69.51.150)

- A practitioner who authorizes a prescribed drug shall not be liable for any side effects or adverse reactions caused by the manner or method by which a substituted drug product is selected or dispensed.
- A pharmacist who substitutes a therapeutically equivalent drug product pursuant to RCW 69.41.100 through 69.41.180 as now or hereafter amended assumes no greater liability for selecting the dispensed drug product than would be incurred in filling a prescription for a drug product prescribed by its established name.
- A pharmacist who substitutes a preferred drug for a nonpreferred drug pursuant to RCW 69.41.190 [i.e., under the Preferred Drug List] assumes no greater liability for substituting the preferred drug than would be incurred in filling a prescription for the preferred drug when prescribed by name.
- A pharmacist who selects an interchangeable biological product to be dispensed pursuant to RCW 69.41.100 through 69.41.180, and the pharmacy for which the pharmacist is providing service, assumes no greater liability for selecting the interchangeable biological products than would be incurred in filling a prescription for the interchangeable biological product when prescribed by the same name. The prescribing practitioner is not liable for a pharmacist's act or omission in selecting, preparing, or dispensing an interchangeable biological product under this section.

AUTHORIZED GENERIC DRUG PRODUCTS

An "authorized generic" is a product that is marketed by the brand-name manufacturer under the NDA for the brand-name drug, or by a firm authorized by the brand-name manufacturer. An authorized generic, according to the FDA, is identical to the brand name drug in dosage form, strength, all ingredients including inactive ingredients, and labeling, except that it may appear different, and marketed under a different NDC and name. Authorized generics are not listed in the Orange Book, because they are the same drug as the brand name drug listed by the same NDA number. Instead, the FDA publishes a "List of Authorized Generic Drugs" that is updated quarterly.[301]

For each listed authorized generic, the FDA assures that, as related to the brand-name drug, "an authorized generic is considered to be therapeutically equivalent to its brand-name drug because it is the same drug."

Under Washington law, it is not an illegal substitution to dispense the authorized generic when its brand-name drug is prescribed. First, as the FDA notes, the authorized generic is the same drug as the brand-name drug. Thus, even if the prescriber indicates "DAW," dispensing the authorized generic is dispensing the drug written for. Second, even if one insists otherwise, the authorized generic is a therapeutic equivalent. Because Washington allows pharmacists to use any reliable source to learn whether a drug is a therapeutic equivalent, the FDA listing of authorized generics provides that information.

Because the authorized generic may have a different name or appearance, it is desirable to explain to the patient that this version of the drug is identical in every way to the drug prescribed, only cheaper. It is also desirable to communicate to the prescriber – particularly with newly-released authorized generics – the action the pharmacist has taken and the name of the authorized generic dispensed.

THERAPEUTIC SUBSTITUTION

Therapeutic substitution involves dispensing a drug in the same therapeutic class as the brand prescribed, but not of the same chemical entity; this would also apply to dispensing a biosimilar that has not been declared interchangeable. A common example would be use of atorvastatin (Lipitor™) when the prescription was issued for simvastatin (Zocor™). Therapeutic substitution could also include dispensing of a generic equivalent that is not of the same dosage form or delivery system as the drug prescribed, such as using Adalat CC™ in place of Procardia XL™. The key element is that the control of the patient's symptoms is equivalent once adjustments have been made for dosage and/or dosing intervals. It is normally assumed that therapeutic interchanges are made in such a way as to avoid additional adverse effects. Therapeutic interchange is often performed to provide the "drug of choice," as in dispensing amoxicillin when ampicillin has been prescribed (to improve absorption and avoid GI effects). The driving force behind most therapeutic interchange, however, is to achieve drug cost savings. Washington law allows therapeutic substitution whenever the pharmacist has obtained "prior authorization" from the prescriber, and is not explicit about how this authorization must be obtained, in contrast to the rules regarding generic substitution. The pharmacist may exercise therapeutic substitution under the following circumstances:

WITH PRIOR AUTHORIZATION (Washington requires documentation to be available in the pharmacy records – WAC 246-899-030(3).) If a pharmacy has received permission from a prescriber, or group of prescribers, to perform therapeutic substitution for a given class of drugs, and has a record of that permission, then they may undertake that substitution for all of the prescribers' patients unless instructed otherwise on an individual basis. There is no requirement under Washington law that the prior authorization be in writing, although it must be documented in the pharmacy records. A "prior authorization log," recording the dates and times when individual prescribers granted prior authorization, would be one approach to meeting the required documentation. In general, however, written approval will be preferred for many reasons.

SPECIFIC AUTHORIZATION ON AN INDIVIDUAL PRESCRIPTION

Any time the prescriber has indicated on the prescription that substitution of another drug in the same therapeutic class may be undertaken, that will allow the pharmacist to perform the substitution for that prescription.

VIA COLLABORATIVE PRACTICE AGREEMENT (in this case, the pharmacist is not performing therapeutic interchange as much as is prescribing a different drug.)

IN ACCORDANCE WITH THE THERAPEUTIC INTERCHANGE PROGRAM AND PREFERRED DRUG LIST (RCW 69.41.190; WAC 182-50-200.)

A Therapeutic Interchange Program (TIP) is required, using a Preferred Drug List (PDL), in all state-funded drug programs, including Apple Health (Medicaid), Labor and Industries, and the Uniform Medical Plan (UMP) for state employees. The Washington Health Care Authority (HCA) administers the program. The current Preferred Drug List[302] is updated frequently on the Rx Washington web site. Pharmacists should note that the Apple Health program has its own PDL for its fee-for-service clients, which is an extension of the statewide PDL.[303]

The Pharmacy & Therapeutics Committee that determines the PDL is composed of 10 members (4 physicians, 4 pharmacists,[304] 1 PA, 1 ARNP).

A THERAPEUTIC INTERCHANGE PROGRAM (TIP) is established by the legislation. This program went into effect in mid-2004, and pharmacists dispensing prescriptions that are paid for by a state program are authorized and required to perform therapeutic substitution using drugs on the PDL, where a non-preferred drug has been ordered. The statute was significantly revised in 2009,[305] and again in 2011 when all state drug programs were moved to the HCA.

ELIGIBLE PRESCRIPTIONS MUST BE HAVE BEEN WRITTEN BY AN "ENDORSING PRACTITIONER." HCA maintains a database[306] to identify endorsing practitioners. The endorsing practitioner may indicate "DAW" – the drug will NOT be subject to him prior authorization, but will for UMP recipients (see below) be subject to Tier-3 pricing. This "DAW" does not relate to generic substitution, which is indicated by a signature on a two-line blank, but must be specifically written on the prescription.

A UMP recipient may request DAW, and pay the Tier-3 price, if the drug is covered.

PRESCRIPTIONS WRITTEN BY NON-ENDORSING PRACTITIONERS are treated as follows by each state-funded program:

- Uniform Medical Plan (PPO): The pharmacist cannot make a substitution, even for a generic equivalent. The patient would receive the non-preferred drug as prescribed, at a higher cost.
- L&I: A non-endorsing practitioner does not qualify for the "dispense as written" exemption and the non-preferred drug would not be payable unless the pharmacist or practitioner calls with medical justification.
- Medicaid: The pharmacist is required to contact ACS to request the non-preferred drug and show medical justification.

SUBSTITUTIONS ARE TO BE MADE FROM WITHIN THE SAME THERAPEUTIC CLASS.

REFILLS OF CERTAIN TYPES OF DRUGS ARE NOT SUBJECT TO SUBSTITUTION

- Antipsychotics
- Antidepressants
- Antiepileptics
- Chemotherapy
- Antiretrovirals
- Immunosuppressives
- Immunomodulator/antiviral treatment for hepatitis C for which an established, fixed duration of therapy is prescribed for at least twenty-four weeks but no more than forty-eight weeks.

NOTIFICATION TO PRESCRIBER. When a substitution is made, the pharmacist shall notify the prescriber of the specific drug and dose dispensed (can be by fax, etc.)

CONTROLS ON EXCESSIVE EXCEPTIONS TO ENSURE ECONOMIC DRUG USE.

Programs may impose limited **restrictions on endorsing prescribers' authority to write DAW prescriptions**, under the following conditions:

- There is clear data or statistical evidence that the prescriber's pattern of use of DAW differs from his or her peers;
- The program director has
    - Presented data to the endorsing practitioner indicating his or her deviation from peer norms,
    - Provided the endorsing practitioner with an opportunity to explain the variation, and

 - If the variation has not been explained, has given the practitioner sufficient time to change his or her prescribing patterns.
- The restrictions must be limited to the extent necessary to reduce variation, and only until the practitioner can demonstrate a reduction in variation in line with his or her peers.
- Refills of antipsychotics and other listed drugs may not be restricted.

Agencies may immediately **designate an available generic as the preferred drug** in a previously reviewed therapeutic class without P&T committee review. Programs may **designate an available equally effective OTC alternative** as a preferred drug.

Limited restrictions may be imposed on endorsing practitioners' options to specify DAW for a **patient's first course of therapy** within a therapeutic class, when:

- There is a less expensive equally effective therapeutic alternative generic product available to treat the condition;
- The DUR board has reviewed and provided recommendations as to the appropriateness of the limitation;
- The endorsing practitioner retains the opportunity to request the brand drug as a medically necessary first-course treatment;
- The program may provide available prescription, emergency room, diagnosis and hospitalization history to the endorsing practitioner; and
- For any antipsychotic restrictions, the program shall effectively guide good practice without interfering with the timeliness of clinical decision making. DSHS prior authorization programs must provide for responses within 24 hours and at least a 72-hour emergency supply of the requested drug.

Off-label use of brand name drugs may be subject to restrictions on use of DAW by endorsing practitioners when:

- There is a less-expensive, equally effective on-label product available to treat the condition;
- The DUR board has reviewed and provided recommendations to the appropriateness of the limitation;
- The endorsing practitioner shall retain the ability to request the off-label drug as medically necessary.

REFILLING AND PARTIAL FILLING OF PRESCRIPTIONS, AND OTHER DEVIATIONS FROM QUANTITY REQUIREMENTS

HOW PRESCRIBERS INDICATE REFILLS. Refills may be authorized by the prescriber at the time the prescription is written. The prescriber may indicate refills in a number of ways:

- MAY BE REFILLED X TIMES. In this case, the pharmacist may refill the drug up to X times, in the same quantity as the original.
- MAY BE REFILLED THROUGH A CERTAIN DATE. In this case the pharmacist may refill the drug as often as needed in an appropriate quantity until the date shown.
- MAY BE REFILLED "PRN." "PRN" is an abbreviation of the Latin phrase, *pro re nata,* which may be interpreted "as the occasion arises," "according to circumstances," or "as needed." In Washington, PRN is defined by the Commission to indicate authorization for up to one year from the date the prescription

was written. No prescription in Washington may be refilled beyond one year from the date written. (WAC 246-869-100(2)(d)) This rule necessarily means that a prescription may not be initially filled more than one year after the date it was written.

- REFILLS MAY BE AUTHORIZED BY THE PRESCRIBER AFTER THE PRESCRIPTION IS WRITTEN, typically upon a call or electronic request from the pharmacist. The Commission requires pharmacies to treat a refill authorization occurring more than a year after the prescription is written as a new prescription, with a new prescription number.

DISPENSING OF REFILLS MUST BE CONSISTENT WITH DIRECTIONS. In all cases of refills, the pharmacist must issue refills and quantities that are consistent with the directions on the prescription. The pharmacist is responsible for noting and dealing with both overuse and under use. An early refill at one point must be considered when reviewing the appropriate time for refill at a later date. It is good practice to communicate to the prescriber unusual circumstances such as when a patient reports the loss of drug so that both the pharmacist and prescriber may become aware of patterns potential of misuse.

EARLY REFILLS OF TOPICAL OPHTHALMIC PRODUCTS. Variations in how patients self-administer eye drops may cause a patient to use drops at a faster rate than would be predicted. The 2015 Legislature[307] amended RCW 18.64 to allow for "one early refill of a prescription for topical ophthalmic products" without contacting the prescriber, if all of the following conditions exist.

- Refill is requested by patient at or after 70% of the predicted days of use based on the date of the original fill or the last refill;
- The prescriber has indicated on the original prescription that a specific number of refills will be needed (i.e., other than "PRN"); and
- The refill does not exceed the number of authorized refills. (RCW 18.64.530)

EFFECT OF TIME LIMIT ON REFILLS. When a refill is time-limited, the pharmacist may dispense the full original quantity at any time prior to the expiration date of the authorization.

EMERGENCY SUPPLY. In Washington, a pharmacist may dispense an "emergency supply" of legend drugs: "if the prescriber is not available and in the professional judgment of the pharmacist an emergency need for the medication has been demonstrated, the pharmacist may dispense enough medication to last until a prescriber can be contacted but not to exceed 72 hours' supply. The prescriber shall be promptly notified of the emergency refill." (WAC 246-869-100(2)(f)).

Note that this particular regulation applies to all legend drugs in Washington, but because there is no equivalent provision under federal rules for controlled substances, this provision DOES NOT APPLY TO PRESCRIPTIONS FOR CONTROLLED SUBSTANCES.

In determining how many doses to give the patient, the pharmacist must estimate how soon the prescriber will be available, and dispense enough to last until the prescriber is available, but not more than a 72 hours' supply. In some cases, an emergency supply of a unit-of-use package may involve dispensing more than 72-hours' worth of drug, such as with a bronchodilator inhaler. If clearly needed by the patient on an emergency basis, it is unlikely that the Commission will discipline the pharmacist. However, in the event that the physician determines that continued use of the drug dispensed would be not in the patient's interest, the pharmacist must be prepared to recover the excess supply from the patient or to take other steps to minimize the risk to the patient. A better solution: develop a prescriptive authority protocol with local physicians to allow the pharmacist to prescribe these emergency supplies to patients of the pharmacy.

The pharmacist, when finally contacting the prescriber, DOES NOT NEED TO OBTAIN THE PRESCRIBER'S PERMISSION TO HAVE DISPENSED THE EMERGENCY SUPPLY – the pharmacist needs merely to inform the prescriber that the supply was given. However, THE PRESCRIBER MUST AUTHORIZE ANY ADDITIONAL REFILLS.

DECLARED EMERGENCY – CONTINUITY OF CARE REFILL AUTHORITY

In addition to the provisions of WAC 246-869-100(2)(f), a pharmacist may refill medications when the Governor has declared an emergency "for an event which prevents continuity of health care for persons and animals because their prescribed medications due to the emergency event." During the period of the declared emergency event, pharmacists and pharmacies may provide:

- An initial supply of up to 30 days of current prescriptions for legend drugs
- An initial supply of up to 7 days of current prescriptions for controlled substances in schedules III, IV, or V. The Commission has determined that under a declared emergency, controlled substances other than Schedule II may also be supplied.

To dispense an emergency supply, the following conditions are required:

- Presentation of a valid prescription container complete with legible label indicating there are remaining refills, or
- Confirmation of the prescribed medication and available refills by review of the patient's current medical records or pharmacy records; or
- In the professional judgment of the pharmacist; or
- If the prescription is expired or has no refills and the pharmacist is unable to readily obtain refill authorization from the prescriber, up to a 72-hour supply as described in WAC 246-869-100(2)(f) or up to a 30-day supply of maintenance medication may be supplied.

When dispensing an emergency supply under a declared emergency, the pharmacist shall:

- Document the dispensing as a prescription, noting the source of medication information (i.e., container, prescriber, or pharmacy records);
- Inform the patient's provider and the pharmacy dispensing the original supply as soon as possible following dispensing; and
- Mark the face of the prescription as an "emergency" prescription. (WAC 246-869-105)

PRESCRIBERS CANNOT DELEGATE REFILL AUTHORITY TO STAFF. Sometimes a local physician may be planning a vacation and wishes to tell his or her office staff to "okay all refills till I come back." This is an unlawful delegation of authority to his or her staff, and prescriptions or refills authorized based on this delegation are not valid. A pharmacist who knows or should know of the situation may be disciplined for dispensing pursuant to these authorizations. The physician is responsible to provide alternative physician coverage for his or her patients. However, it is possible for the physician to establish a collaborative practice agreement with a pharmacist to allow the pharmacist to review requests for refills and to authorize them in accordance with a protocol. This protocol could allow the pharmacist to review requests from pharmacies other than his or her own site.

The Washington Nursing Quality Assurance Commission received a request in 2007 to allow registered nurses at a clinic to approve refill requests in accordance with a protocol approved by the clinic physicians. The Commission denied the request, recognizing the inability of prescribers to delegate such authority to nurses.[308] The Nursing Commission has not completely given up on expanding the role of nurses related to drug authorizations under protocol, and in 2016 issued an opinion that RNs in public health settings may determine the need for drugs and engage in dispensing them to patients under protocol.[309]

PARTIAL FILLING.

Generally, when the patient's interests require, pharmacists are allowed to dispense *less* than the prescribed quantity of medication, as long as each dosage form is of the correct strength. There are special requirements for partial filling of controlled substances, but for legend drugs, it is generally sufficient for pharmacists merely to track the quantities dispensed. Partial filling often occurs when:

FOR FINANCIAL REASONS (including insurance coverage) the patient doesn't want to purchase the full amount. A prescription written for levothyroxine 100 mcg, #90, can be filled for any quantity less than 90, e.g., 30 tablets. It may be refilled in quantities of 30 until a total of 90 have been dispensed.

WHEN THE PATIENT HAS NOT RECEIVED THE DRUG BEFORE and is unsure whether he or she will tolerate it or if it will meet the patient's needs.

WHEN THE PHARMACY DOES NOT HAVE SUFFICIENT MEDICATION IN STOCK.

BILLING TO 3RD PARTY PAYERS FOR PARTIAL FILLING. Handling of out-of-stock creates problems when third parties (especially government payers) are to be billed for the drug. These parties do not want to pay for unused drug or drug that is not delivered to patients. When partial fills have been made with the expectation that patients will pick up the remainder, and the third party is billed for the full amount due to transaction requirements, the third party will feel defrauded if the patient forgets to pick up the drug. The US government sued a major chain over this issue and the settlement was in the millions of dollars. (See also Chapter 8)

IF POSSIBLE, 3RD PARTIES SHOULD NOT BE BILLED UNTIL THE FULL QUANTITY HAS BEEN DISPENSED.
The pharmacy cannot legally reuse drugs that have been sold to a patient, even if the patient "abandons" the drug by not returning. Most states, including Washington, have "abandoned property" statutes that require that the abandoned property belong to the state.

DELIVERING REMAINING QUANTITY TO THE PATIENT. If the pharmacy wants to deliver or mail the remainder of the product to the patient, that may raise problems of making drugs available to children or others without the knowledge of the patient that the drug was to be mailed.

If possible, OBTAIN THE PATIENT'S WRITTEN PERMISSION TO MAIL THE REMAINDER OF THE DRUG TO THEIR HOME in the event that they have not picked up the drug in a certain length of time. Some states other than Washington have rules specifically prohibiting mailing of drugs to patients without their prior permission.

SCHEDULED REFILLS AND MEDICATION SYNCHRONIZATION PROGRAMS

Scheduling of patient's refills of chronic medications – with their permission – is seen as a means to improve patient adherence, and to provide medications in a more cost-effective manner that also minimizes the amount of inventory a pharmacy must keep on hand. However, concerns have been raised about "automatic refill" systems that simply send patients a monthly supply every 30 days, both as a source of fraud, waste and abuse, and of potential error.[310] Medicare established new policies for 2014 requiring Medicare Part D plans to assure that the patient actually needs a given drug before an automatic refill is sent. The policies were directed particularly at Part D plans that use mail order delivery. If the pharmacy cannot demonstrate that the patient actually needed the refill, it may be exposed to liability under state or federal false claims acts (see Chapter 8).

Medication synchronization, although similar to automatic refills, does more than simply send refills. The pharmacy using a system such as the NCPA-sponsored "Simplify My Meds" program,[311] or the "Align My Refills" initiative under an appointment-based model promoted by the APhA Foundation,[312] works to schedule all the patient's currently-needed chronic medications to require refills on the same date – either monthly or every 90 days. Prior to dispensing any refills, the patient is contacted to determine any non-compliance or changes in medications since the last refill. A key element of the APhA program's effectiveness is that under most circumstances, patients are scheduled to make an appointment with the pharmacist at the time they pick up their medications. Medicare requires that Part D recipients be able to pay a "partial co-pay" when needed to obtain less-than-30-day supplies, such as when starting on new medications or coordinating refill schedules.[313]

COMBINING REFILLS TO DISPENSE A LARGER QUANTITY. It is a long-standing standard of practice that the pharmacist may dispense more than the amount specified in the prescription when refills have been allowed, and the patient's interests warrant it. For example, the physician prescribes Lipitor 10 mg, #30, and labels the prescription "Refill PRN." It is known and obvious that if the patient tolerates the initial prescription, he or she will be continuing to take the drug chronically. If the insurance allows a 90-day supply, the patient will want to obtain the drug in the larger quantities on refills. Using good judgment, the pharmacist may reasonably refill the Lipitor in quantities of 90, without consulting the physician. If no refills were allowed, however, this would not be possible. Generally, controlled substance prescriptions cannot be refilled in larger amounts than specified on the original prescription.

JUDGMENT IS IMPORTANT. Just because a drug is not a controlled substance does not justify refilling in larger quantities than originally specified. For example, a patient with a history of attempted suicide may be placed on tricyclic antidepressants in quantities of 10 to 30 tablets per refill. Even if additional refills are allowed, the pharmacist must be cognizant of the reality that dispensing 100 tablets at a single time provides the patient with the opportunity of taking a fatal overdose. Excessive early refills of carisoprodol have led the Board of Pharmacy to discipline a pharmacist,[314] and, in at least one case, to the death of the patient.

It is important to note, however, that nothing in law **requires** a pharmacist to refill in larger quantities than originally ordered without confirming it with the prescriber.

It is also important to note that 3rd party contracts may require specific prescriber authorization of the quantity in order to receive payment.

The Pharmacy Practice Act allows for dispensing of 90-day quantities of non-controlled substances, using judgment as outlined above.[315] Under these provisions (RCW 18.64.520), a pharmacist may dispense up to a 90-day supply "pursuant to a valid prescription that specifies an initial quantity of less than a ninety-day supply followed by periodic refills of that amount" subject to the following

- The patient has completed an initial 30-day supply of the drug, unless the prescription continues the same medication as previously dispensed in a 90-day supply;
- The total quantity dispensed does not exceed the total quantity authorized by the prescriber, including refills;
- The prescriber has not specified on the prescription that dispensing the prescription exactly as written is medically necessary; and
- The pharmacist is exercising his or her professional judgment.

Dispensing a greater quantity is not allowed if the prescriber has personally indicated, orally or in writing, "no change to quantity," or words of similar meaning. A prescriber checking a box marked "no change in quantity," must initial the box or the check mark.

The pharmacist dispensing the increased supply must notify the prescriber.

The law does not create an obligation on any insurer or 3rd party to allow coverage for the increased supply.

DISPENSING DIFFERENT STRENGTHS TO ACHIEVE THE PRESCRIBED DOSE. Pharmacists may also reasonably deviate from the prescription by providing alternate strengths if the patient's interests require.

A prescription written for prednisone 10 mg tablets #50, ½ tablet daily, may be filled with prednisone 5 mg #100, provided the label directions correctly specify **1** tablet instead of ½ tablet as the dose. The patient must clearly understand what has been done, and it is best practice to notify the prescriber.

A prescription written for levothyroxine 225 mcg per dose cannot be dispensed as such because no manufacturer makes a 225-mcg tablet. The pharmacist may wish to verify the dose to be sure an error was not made, but otherwise has the choice of dispensing the prescription as follows:

> levothyroxine 113 mcg, with directions of 2 tablets per dose
>
> or
>
> levothyroxine 200 mcg, 1 tablet per dose, plus
> levothyroxine 25 mcg, 1 tablet per dose, as two separate prescriptions

In either situation, the best practice is to notify the prescriber what was actually dispensed. Also, if the second option is used, each container should be explicit that the dose should be taken along with the dose from the other container, so that the patient understands he or she must take 2 different strengths of levothyroxine to achieve the necessary dose.

TABLET SPLITTING PROGRAMS. Many insurers or third party payers encourage patients to split tablets to achieve cost savings. For example, Crestor® 10 mg tablets were available at one point from DrugStore.Com for $474.39 for 100 tablets, while the 20-mg tablets were $475.55 for 100, or nearly half as expensive per mg. Many pharmacists consider a request by a patient to adjust the dose on the prescription to be within the general reasonable deviation from the prescription discussed here. Not all patients are good candidates for tablet-splitting programs, however. Because the primary interest served by tablet splitting is cost savings, not patient care issues, the pharmacist should probably proceed with tablet splitting programs only when based on prior consultation with or approval of the prescriber.

IT IS IMPORTANT THAT THE PRESCRIBER'S RECORDS OF WHAT IS DISPENSED ARE CONSISTENT WITH THE PHARMACIST'S ACTIONS TO AVOID CONFUSION AND POSSIBLE OVERDOSE**.** Confusion over a tablet splitting program led to a federal lawsuit when a patient suffered rhabdomyolysis after he was instructed by a nurse practitioner to increase his simvastatin dose to "1 whole tablet." The nurse practitioner believed he was inappropriately taking only 20 mg per day, when in fact he was taking half of an 80-mg tablet as part of a tablet splitting program.

TRANSFERS OF PRESCRIPTIONS BETWEEN PHARMACIES

There are many times when a patient requests that his or her prescription be filled at a different pharmacy, or wishes to take a copy of the prescription to another prescriber or pharmacy.

"COPIES." The original of every prescription must be retained in the pharmacy. Sometimes patients will request a "copy" of their prescription for informational purposes. Such copies may be made, but must be clearly labeled as such. (WAC 246-869-100(e)).

Prescriptions may be photocopied and provided to the patient or others to whom the patient has authorized, stamped with "COPY".

Pharmacists may hand copy the prescription on the pharmacy's prescription form, indicating a COPY.

CODING PRICES ON COPIES NO LONGER ACCEPTABLE. It was the practice of pharmacists in past years to include pricing information on the prescription, often in coded fashion. One popular code was called the NARD Code, developed by the National Association of Retail Druggists, now known as NCPA. This code used the word "PHARMOCIST' where each letter represented the digits, 1-2-3-4-5-6-7-8-9-0, respectively. The letters NA preceded the code and it was followed by RD. For example, "NA-PHM-RD" would indicate a price of $1.25. This practice is uncommon now, in part because of challenges to its use as a means of price fixing among competitors.

These COPIES ARE NOT VALID FOR FILLING, so the pharmacist receiving such a copy must contact the prescriber and obtain a new oral prescription.

TRANSFER OF REFILL INFORMATION. Pharmacies are allowed under WAC 246-869-090 to transfer prescriptions, along with available refills, to another pharmacy. It is important for the pharmacist or intern involved in the process to follow the steps listed in the regulation. In Washington, pharmacists or interns may transfer and receive transferred prescriptions.

THE ORIGINATING PHARMACIST ("transferor pharmacist") must perform the following steps:

- Record that the prescription has been transferred in the medication record system.
- Record in the medication record system the
- Name and address of the pharmacy to which it has been transferred
- The name of the pharmacist (or intern) that received the information.

  Note: it is usage that a person's "name" for legal purposes is the **full name** that the person normally would use to conduct business. Thus, simply recording the first name of the other pharmacist is not generally appropriate. A Pharmacy Commission consultant pharmacist has stated that *"Neither WAC 246-869 nor CFR 1306.25 define the word 'name' as it is used in each respective passage. However, both the law and rule require both transferring pharmacists to be identified when transferring a prescription. This may (or may not) be achieved by recording the first name only. The extent of required information depends on ... your ability to unequivocally identify the other pharmacist if required to do so at a later time."*[316]

- In addition, for controlled substances (schedule III, IV, and V), the originating pharmacist must follow the procedures specified in 21 CFR § 1306.25, which include the following:
  - Locate the original hard copy of the transferred prescription.
  - Write the word "VOID" on the face of the prescription
  - Record the name, address, and DEA number of the pharmacy receiving the information on the reverse of the original prescription, along with the name of the pharmacist receiving the information.

THE RECEIVING PHARMACIST treats the prescription as an oral prescription, and must perform the following steps:

- Reduce the prescription to writing on a prescription blank, including patient name, address, prescriber's name and address, and other information required to be on the prescription.
- Write the word "TRANSFER" on the face of the prescription.

- Also record the following:
- The date the prescription was originally written (cannot be refilled for a year after that.)
- When processing a transferred prescription, it is important to override the current date in the computer, and record the original date written
- Number of refills remaining
- Date of last refill
- The name and address of the transferring pharmacy, and the serial number of the original prescription at that pharmacy
- The name of the transferring (transferor) pharmacist. As noted above, this should normally be the full legal name of the individual.
- For controlled substances, the receiving pharmacist must also record the following:
    - Number of original refills allowed on the prescription
    - Dates (and locations) of all previous refills
    - Number of valid refills remaining
    - DEA number of transferring pharmacy
    - Name, address, serial number and DEA number of pharmacy at which prescription was originally filled (if different from transferring pharmacy).

For MEDICARE OR MEDICAID prescriptions originally *issued in writing* after April 1, 2008, the receiving pharmacist must

- Obtain and record from the transferring pharmacist verification that the original prescription, if a written prescription, was issued on a tamper-resistant pad, or that the transferring pharmacy had obtained verification of the prescription by fax, phone, or e-mail.

MULTIPLE TRANSFERS. Refill information and prescriptions for legend drugs may be transferred, and re-transferred as often as needed until all refills are used. If a patient has had a prescription transferred to another pharmacy, and now wants to have it refilled at the original pharmacy, the original pharmacy must contact the other pharmacy and receive the prescription back as a transferred prescription. At this point, it should be given a new prescription number.

According to DEA rules, controlled substances may be transferred on a "one-time" basis, unless the transferring pharmacies share a common electronic database. (See further discussion in Chapter 5.)

Pharmacies with a common electronic database may track refills for non-controlled substances at any outlet in this common database, without going through the prescription transfer process. Many chains (e.g., Rite-Aid and Walgreens) have these databases.

WAC 246-870-030 specifically allows transfer of refill information between pharmacies via fax. The proposed 2015 revision of WAC 246-870 retains this provision.

MAY A TECHNICIAN TRANSFER REFILL INFORMATION TO ANOTHER PHARMACY VIA FAX? Just as an agent of the prescriber can communicate information about a prescription, there is no rule that prohibits the technician completing the fax transmission of refill information to another pharmacy, provided that a pharmacist has reviewed the information on the fax before the technician sends it. The fax should bear the name of the transferring pharmacist, and also the identity of the technician who is communicating that information on behalf of the approving pharmacist.

MAY A PHARMACIST "TRANSFER" A NEW PRESCRIPTION? It is not clear that the rules as written permit transfer of a prescription that has not been actually filled at the transferring pharmacy. However, it is hard to see why this would be much different than transferring information on an already filled prescription. Indeed, if the original prescription was a verbal or electronic prescription, the pharmacist cannot really create a written prescription to hand to the patient. To conform with the letter of the rule, the transferring pharmacy should enter the prescription into the patient medication record, indicate that it was never filled, then record the transfer as indicated above, keeping the original prescription on file. The Pharmacy Commission essentially agrees with this approach, indicating that using good judgment a pharmacist can transfer an unfilled or on hold prescription provided an audit trail is maintained and the transferred prescription is assigned a number and retained in the originating pharmacy's system.[317]

Alternatively, if the patient has presented a written prescription, the pharmacy may merely refer the patient to another pharmacy, and return the written prescription to the patient to take to the other pharmacy.

PACKAGING

USP CONTAINERS. All drugs that are repackaged for dispensing to patients must meet USP requirements. Multi-dose containers of solid dosage forms must meet USP requirements for "tight" containers that are sealed to be air- and water-resistant, and must be either opaque or light-resistant. The USP also provides recommendations for materials used in unit-dose or "Bingo Card" packaging.

CHILD-RESISTANT CONTAINERS REQUIRED FOR PRESCRIPTION DRUGS. Washington law requires that the cap of every prescription container meet safety standards adopted by the pharmacy commission (RCW 18.64.246). The Commission, in turn, has incorporated by reference Chapter 16, part 1700 of the CFR (WAC 246-869-230). Prescription drugs are included among "household substances" that must be packaged in "special packaging" as specified in the Poison Prevention Packaging Act (PPPA, 15 USC 1471). These containers are commonly-called Child-Resistant Containers (CRCs). The PPPA is implemented by rules promulgated by the Consumer Products Safety Commission (CPSC). The CPSC has published a guide for pharmacists and other health professionals.[318]

UNIT OF USE PACKAGING FOR RETAIL PHARMACIES. Products packaged by manufacturers in unit-of-use retail units (e.g., Z-packs, OTC omeprazole 20 mg) are in packages that have been designed and tested to meet the requirements for child-resistant containers.

ALL PRESCRIPTIONS FOR ORAL DOSAGE FORMS OF LEGEND DRUGS IN WA MUST BE DISPENSED IN CRCS, EXCEPT FOR DRUG PRODUCTS EXEMPTED BY THE CPSC. Exempted products are listed in 16 CFR § 1700.14 (a) (10), and include:

- Nitroglycerine sublingual tablets
- Sublingual and chewable isosorbide tablets ≤ 10 mg
- Erythromycin ethylsuccinate, measured as erythromycin equivalent
    - Granules for suspension and suspensions containing ≤ 8 g
    - Tablets containing ≤ 16 g per package
- Oral contraceptives in memory aid packages
- Cholestyramine and colestipol powder
- K^+ supplements ≤ 50 mEq/dose in unit dose packaging

> PHARMACY CALCULATIONS IN A LAW TEXTBOOK!
> Exercise: how many tablets of Chewable Vitamins with Fluoride containing 0.5 mg of fluoride ion per tablet may be dispensed in a container without a child-resistant closure? (Hint: 1 mg F^- is contained in 2.21 mg of NaF.)

- NaF ≤ 110 mg per package (tablets and liquids, must be ≤ 0.5% elemental fluoride w/w or w/v)
- Oral cortisteroid tablets in manufacturer's dispenser packages ("Dosepak," etc.)
    - Prednisone containing ≤ 105 mg per package
    - Betamethasone containing ≤ 12.6 mg per package
    - Methylprednisolone containing ≤ 84 mg per package
- Pancrelipase sole-ingredient products
- Mebendazole tablets ≤ 600 mg per package
- Aerosols for inhalation
- Hormone products
    - Conjugated estrogens in mnemonic packages containing ≤ 32 mg per package
    - Norethindrone acetate in mnemonic packages containing ≤ 50 mg per package
    - Medroxyprogesterone acetate tablets
- Sacrosidase (sucrase) in glycerol and water.
- Hormone Replacement Therapy Products relying solely on one or more estrogens or progestogens for activity.
- Colesevelam hydrochloride powder in packages containing ≤ 3.75 g per package
- Sevelamer carbonate powder in packages containing ≤ 2.4 g per package

USE OF NON-CRC CONTAINERS. Pharmacists may dispense legend drugs in non-CRCs if:

- THE PATIENT OR THE PATIENT'S AGENT REQUESTS. Such a request may be a "blanket" request that all drugs dispensed to the patient be in non-CRCs; or
- THE PRESCRIBER REQUESTS IT ON THE PRESCRIPTION AT THE TIME IT IS WRITTEN. Prescribers may not issue "blanket" requests, either for all drugs dispensed to a particular patient, or for all of his or her patients.

REQUESTS FOR NON-CRCS MUST BE IN WRITING IN WASHINGTON. Under federal law, requests for non-CRC containers may be oral or in writing. Washington incorporates the federal rules into its pharmacy regulations, but requires in addition, that requests for non-CRC containers are IN WRITING, by the patient or the patient's agent, or in writing by the prescriber. Authorization by the patient or agent shall be verified in one of the following ways:

- A statement on the back of the prescription signed by the patient or agent;
- A statement on the medication record requesting non-child resistant containers, or;
- A signed statement on any other permanent record requesting non-CRC containers. (WAC 246-869-230(2))

The date of the request should be included in the documentation kept in the pharmacy. At various times, Pharmacy Commission investigators have insisted that such requests be renewed after some "reasonable" length of time, such as one year. This is a good practice, but it is NOT required by current Washington pharmacy regulations.

NON-CRC REQUESTS MUST BE IN PATIENT RECORD. An indication that a non-CRC has been requested must be made in the patient medication record system. (WAC 246-875-020(1)(j))

LEGAL LIABILITY FOR USE OF NON-CRCs.

If a pharmacist dispenses a covered drug in a non-CRC, and a child is injured as a result of gaining access to the drug, the child, his or her guardian, or the child's estate (in case the child dies), may file a lawsuit against the pharmacist for damages. In an Iowa case[319] the pharmacist was found liable for the death of a child who ingested Tedral SA (containing theophylline) prescribed for her father that was dispensed in a non-CRC. The pharmacy argued that the father had requested a non-CRC on the prescription, but didn't have a written record to substantiate this, and the parents claimed otherwise. Normally, being able to document that the parent or guardian of the child authorized the use of the non-CRC will serve as a defense against liability. However, most childhood poisonings from legend drugs now occur as a result of children obtaining access to grandparents' drugs. Because grandparents are not normally the legal guardians of their grandchildren, their request for non-CRCs may not provide an adequate defense. Pharmacists should consider including statements covering the following elements in the form used by patients to request a non-CRC.

1. CRCs are required by law unless specifically requested otherwise by the patient.
2. The purpose of these regulations is to prevent childhood poisoning from prescription drugs.
3. As few as one or two tablets of some drugs may be fatal to young children.
4. The CPSC has reported one study which found that 36% of childhood ingestions related to a prescription vial involved a grandparent's medication.[320]
5. Over 90% of elderly persons can successfully open CRCs if shown how. The pharmacy is willing to provide demonstrations and instructions to the patient on how to open a CRC. There are alternative CRCs that can be used by patients with arthritis or lack of hand strength, and the pharmacy is willing to obtain and provide these at cost to the patient.
6. The patient agrees that it is his or her responsibility to keep medications out of children's reach, especially when using a non-CRC container.
7. Having read and understood the above, the patient nevertheless requests that non-CRCs be used on his or her prescription, and agrees to indemnify and hold harmless the pharmacy for any injuries that might occur to a child as a result of the patient's request to use non-CRCs.

An example request form implementing these recommendations is provided at the end of the chapter as Appendix 4A.

FIXED CONTAINER SIZE FOR SUBLINGUAL NITROGLYCERINE. Sublingual nitroglycerin tablets (e.g., Nitrostat®) are now only available for dispensing in bottles of 25 tablets, to preserve stability. FDA rules indicate that these products may not be repackaged, so pharmacists should not undertake to do so.

MEDISETS AND COMPLIANCE PACKAGING. Medisets, pharmacy-packaged blister cards ("Bingo Cards"), and similar packages have not met federal standards for CRCs, thus, pharmacists must obtain requests from the patients to use non-CRC packaging.

HELPING PATIENTS IN THEIR HOMES TO FILL COMPLIANCE PACKAGING. The Commission has indicated that "A pharmacist, like a family member, may fill a patient's medication planner/pillbox [in the patient's home]. Keep in mind a patient may not bring a prescription bottle filled by Pharmacy A into Pharmacy B and ask for the pills [sic] to be repackaged into something else (such as a bubble pack) as Pharmacy B did not fill the prescription. This is considered repackaging."[321]

PHARMACIST ADMINISTRATION OF DRUGS TO PATIENTS

IS CERTIFICATION REQUIRED TO ADMINISTER DRUGS? No. Pharmacists may administer drugs ordered for a patient by an authorized prescriber, by any route, by virtue of their license to practice. Certification programs for immunizations are part of the process by which pharmacists in Washington may easily gain documented competence and adhere to the terms of a prescriptive authority protocol developed by WSPA and endorsed by the Commission in order to prescribe vaccines. However, a pharmacist may develop a prescriptive authority protocol to prescribe and inject drugs without certification, as long as an authorized prescriber agrees to the protocol. Clearly, pharmacists should not undertake procedures unless they are adequately skilled in them.

Note that some 3rd party payers (e.g., Medicaid) will not reimburse pharmacists for administration of vaccines unless they have a collaborative practice agreement on file with the Commission (see Chapter 8).

AVOID PRE-FILLING VACCINE SYRINGES. The Pharmacy Commission has alerted pharmacists involved in flu shot clinics that the Centers for Disease Control strongly recommends that providers do not pre-fill individual syringes because of risks of administration and dosing errors and concerns over stability.[322]

MERCURY-CONTAINING VACCINES AND INJECTIONS. Washington law prohibits injection of a vaccine (or other product) containing greater than 0.5 mcg of mercury (present in thimerosol) per 0.5 mL dose into a person KNOWN TO BE PREGNANT or a CHILD UNDER 3 YEARS of age. (RCW 70.95M.115).

EXCEPTION FOR FLU VACCINES. Influenza vaccines (seasonal and H1N1) may contain up to 1 mcg of mercury per 0.5 mL dose.

EXCEPTION FOR EMERGENCY. The secretary of the DOH may suspend these restrictions upon declaration of a public health emergency (i.e., an outbreak or vaccine shortage), for the duration of the emergency. A woman known to be pregnant or lactating, and the parent or guardian of any minor who be vaccinated with a product containing mercury above the limits, must be informed of the fact.

ADMINISTRATION OF DRUGS TO PATIENTS BY OTHER PERSONS

OTHER HEALTH PROFESSIONALS WHO MAY ADMINISTER DRUGS

Anyone who may prescribe drugs may administer drugs.

NURSES, BOTH RNs AND LPNs

STUDENT NURSES, when part of their academic program under faculty oversight (unlike student pharmacists, student nurses are not individually registered, except when they are employed as nursing technicians)

NURSING TECHNICIANS, under direct supervision of nurse – a nursing technician is a student nurse who is employed by a hospital outside of his or her academic program. MAY NOT ADMINISTER chemotherapy, blood or blood products, IV meds, scheduled drugs, or carry out procedures on central lines

RESPIRATORY CARE PRACTITIONERS may administer prescribed or ordered respiratory drugs

MEDICAL ASSISTANTS. Four type of medical assistants are credentialed by the Department of Health:

MEDICAL ASSISTANT – CERTIFIED. May administer medications if they are

- Administered by unit or single dosage, or by a dose calculated and verified by a practitioner
- Limited to legend drugs, vaccines, or schedule III-V controlled substances authorized by a practitioner in accordance with DOH rules
- May not be experimental drugs or chemotherapy agents.
- DOH may by rule further limit allowable drugs
- Administered pursuant to a written order by a practitioner
- May administer intravenous diagnostic agents or drugs as delegated and supervised by practitioner, subject to qualifications established by DOH rule
- DOH rules prohibit MA-Cs from administering
    - Schedule II controlled substances, chemotherapy agents, or experimental drugs
    - Medications through a central venous line
- The MA-C may not start an IV line, but may interrupt an IV line, administer an injection, and restart at the same rate.

Allowed categories of drugs are set forth in a table in the regulation (WAC 246-827-0240(5):

Drug Category	Routes Permitted*	Level of Supervision Required
Controlled substances, schedule III, IV, and V	Oral, topical, rectal, otic, ophthalmic, or inhaled routes	Immediate supervision
	Subcutaneous, intradermal, intramuscular, or peripheral intravenous injections	Direct visual supervision
Other legend drugs	All other routes	Immediate supervision
	Peripheral intravenous injections	Direct visual supervision

MEDICAL ASSISTANT – HEMODIALYSIS TECHNICIAN.
May administer drugs and oxygen to a patient when delegated and supervised by a practitioner, subject to DOH rules.

MEDICAL ASSISTANT – PHLEBOTOMIST. No authority to administer drugs.

MEDICAL ASSISTANT – REGISTERED.
Extent of activities and procedures must be set forth by supervising practitioner. An MA-R cannot transfer his or her authorized duties to another setting without authorization from the new practitioner

Under the delegation and supervision of a practitioner, may administer eye drops, topical ointments, and vaccines, including combination or multidose vaccines.

LICENSED MIDWIVES (may be designated C.P.M. for Certified Professional Midwife) may purchase and administer prophylactic ophthalmics, postpartum oxytocics, vitamin K, Rho immune globulin, and local anesthetics; pharmacists dispensing such drugs to a midwife are not liable for any adverse reactions caused by any method or use by the midwife. (RCW 18.50.115) In addition to the statutory medications, midwives may administer certain IV fluids (LR, D5LR, heparin, NS), intradermal sterile water, magnesium sulfate, epinephrine, MMR vaccine, HBIG or HBV, terbutaline, antibiotics for intrapartum prophylaxis, antihemorrhagic post-partum drugs (misoprostol, methylergonovine maleate, PG F2 alpha. (WAC 246-834-250)

OCCUPATIONAL THERAPISTS AND PHYSICAL THERAPISTS may purchase, use, and administer modalities and certain other drugs used in physical therapy.

DENTAL HYGIENISTS may administer local anesthetics, topical antimicrobials, and topical fluorides for dental patients

EMERGENCY MEDICAL SYSTEM PERSONNEL. The state licenses or certifies 4 categories of EMS personnel:

- ADVANCED EMERGENCY MEDICAL TECHNICIANS (AEMTS) – certified as an "intermediate life support technician" as defined in RCW 18.71.200, which includes advanced cardiac and trauma life support.
- EMERGENCY MEDICAL RESPONDER (EMR) - certified as a first responder to provide prehospital EMS care (ambulance attendants)
- EMERGENCY MEDICAL TECHNICIAN (EMT) – certified to render prehospital EMS care according to rules set by DOH
- PARAMEDIC – a "physician's trained emergency medical service paramedic" who is trained to perform all phases of prehospital emergency medical care, including advanced life support, under written or oral authorization of Medical Program Director or a physician designate.

In general, the scope of practice of these individuals is specified by the Medical Program Director (MPD) of the county Emergency Medical Services department. EMTs, AEMTs, and Paramedics may administer prescribed drugs within the protocols established by the MPD per verbal or written orders of a MD or DO credentialed by the MPD.

PROVISION OF DRUGS BY HOSPITAL PHARMACIES TO AMBULANCE OR AID SERVICES. Hospital pharmacies may provide drugs to "ambulance or aid services" licensed under RCW 18.73.130 for use associated with providing emergency medical services, when:

- The hospital is located in the same or an adjacent county as the ambulance service;
- A medical program director of the ambulance or aid service has requested drugs from the hospital per an agreed protocol;
- Drugs requested must be (a) relevant to the level of service provided and the training of its emergency personnel; and (b) are approved as part of prehospital patient care protocols approved for use by emergency personnel in the county in which the ambulance or aid service is located
- The provision of drugs by the hospital pharmacy is not contingent upon arrangements for transport of patients to the hospital for reasons other than the consideration of patients' medical needs (RCW 18.64.540)

RADIOLOGICAL ASSISTIVE PERSONNEL

RADIOLOGIC TECHNOLOGISTS – may administer diagnostic and therapeutic agents under the direct supervision of a physician.

RADIOLOGIST ASSISTANTS – may administer imaging and non-imaging agents parenterally, administer prescribed oxygen, and administer oral medications. Oral medications and parenteral administration require direct supervision by a physician.

NON-HEALTH CARE PROFESSIONALS WHO MAY ADMINISTER DRUGS

SCHOOL PERSONNEL – including trained paraeducators – may administer drugs to students in accordance with school district policies and state regulations.[323]

States that give trained school personnel authority to administer epinephrine have preference regarding certain federal asthma grants.[324]

NONPRACTITIONER JAIL PERSONNEL may provide medication assistance to inmates and administer drugs via oral route or inhalation. (See Chapter 3, Correctional Facilities)

SHIP CAPTAINS ON OCEAN-GOING VESSELS, when a health care practitioner is not stationed on the ship (e.g., large fishing vessels), may stock and administer drugs in case of emergencies.

ENTITIES AUTHORIZED TO STORE AND USE EPINEPHRINE AUTOINJECTORS. Organizations or entities where allergens capable of causing anaphylaxis may be present may obtain, store, and administer epinephrine autoinjectors. Such entities include, but are not limited to, restaurants, recreation camps, youth sports leagues, amusement parks, colleges, universities, and sports arenas, in accordance with the provision of RCW 70.54.440:[325]

- Authorized health care providers my prescribe epinephrine autoinjectors (EAs) in the name of an authorized entity.
- Pharmacists, ARNPs, or physicians may dispense EAs pursuant to such prescriptions.
- An authorized entity must
  - Store EAs in a location readily accessible during an emergency in accordance with the EAs labeling and any regulations promulgated by the DOH
  - Designate employees or agents to be responsible for storage, maintenance, and general oversight of EAs acquired by the entity

  - Designated employees must have undergone training specified in the statute (RCW 70.54.440(4))
  - Submit a report to the DOH of each incident in which EAs are used
- Designated trained agents or employees may
  - Provide an EA to any individual believed to be experiencing anaphylaxis for immediate self-administration, or administer an EA to such an individual, regardless of whether the individual has been diagnosed with an allergy or has a prescription for an EA
- The statute limits liabilities of authorized entities and delegated agents for injuries resulting from administration or self-administration of EAs in good faith in compliance with the statute.
- Administration of an EA in compliance with the statute is not "the practice of medicine."

DELIVERY OF DRUGS TO PATIENTS, CAREGIVERS, OR PRESCRIBERS.

In general, pharmacies have traditionally acquiesced to requests from patients to deliver their prescriptions to their office, their home, their physician, or some other place convenient for the patient. However, a variety of federal and state laws and rules create limitations on how, and where, and to whom, a pharmacist may deliver a patient's prescription.

Also in general, the pharmacy may use pharmacy employees (registered at least as pharmacy assistants) to deliver drugs to patients, or may use common carriers (FedEx, UPS, etc.), or special carriers such as couriers or taxicabs, or the United States Postal Service, to deliver drugs. "Volunteers" are more problematic, and may or may not be used depending on special circumstances. Other health professionals who are not employees of the pharmacy are "volunteers." Whenever non-pharmacy personnel are utilized, care must be taken to preserve the security and stability of the drugs, and to package the drug in such a way as to avoid disclosing protected health information.

PHARMACY COMMISSION RULES for community pharmacies indicate that the prescription may not leave the pharmacy unless it is delivered directly to the patient, an agent of the patient, or the "patient's home or similar place." (WAC 246-869-020(5)) This appears to apply to NON-COMPOUNDED PRESCRIPTIONS FOR LEGEND DRUGS.

CONTROLLED SUBSTANCES. The federal CSA and Washington's parallel statute, however, restrict delivery of controlled substances unless they are directly delivered to the "ULTIMATE USER." The ultimate user is the patient, or a member of the patient's household. (21 U.S.C. §802 (27)) This technically prevents a pharmacist from delivering a controlled substance to a relative of the patient who does not live with the patient. The DEA's *Pharmacist Manual* does contemplate delivering to the patient via common carrier, or the US Postal Service. (See Chapter 5)

COMPOUNDED PRESCRIPTIONS. The Pharmacy Practice Act allows compounded prescriptions to be delivered "to locations other than a patient's home when requested by the patient; or the prescriber to be administered to the patient; or to another pharmacy to dispense to the patient." (RCW 18.64.011(15)(d))

Given the potential conflict between the Pharmacy Commission rule and the Pharmacy Practice Act, it can be expected that the Commission will harmonize its rule with the Act. However, the DEA has been fairly strict in applying its regulations to pharmacies, and has treated delivery of controlled substances to the prescribing physician for later delivery to the patient as a violation. (See Chapter 5)

RETURN OR EXCHANGE OF DRUGS FROM CONSUMERS.

Generally, PHARMACIES MAY NOT ACCEPT RETURNS OR EXCHANGES OF DRUGS, items of personal hygiene, or sick room supplies, after the items have left the pharmacy. (WAC 246-869-130) (The FDA issued a compliance policy guide in 1980 in which it stated that "a pharmacist should not return drug products to his stock once they have been out of his possession. ... The pharmacist or doctor dispensing a drug is legally responsible for all hazards of contamination or adulteration that may arise, should he mix returned portions of drugs to his shelf stocks."[326]) Controlled substances may be returned to pharmacies for destruction only in accordance with DEA rules.

While consumers may not return drugs to a pharmacist, they may dispose of drugs by taking them to a secure disposal site, which may include a disposal box located at a pharmacy that complies with DEA rules for disposal of controlled substances (21 CFR Part 1317 – see also Chapter 5). The Commission has published a guidance document interpreting the DEA rules and to provide steps by which retail pharmacies, hospitals and clinics with onsite pharmacies, and any LTC facilities that the pharmacies choose to register as collection sites with the DEA.[327]

UNIT DOSE PACKAGING EXCEPTION. Unit dose packages or full or partial multiple dose medication cards may be accepted from hospitals or long-term care facilities, if

- the pharmacist can determine that the package is intact;
- the pharmacist determines that the unit dose package or a multiple dose medication card meets USP standards for storage including temperature, light sensitivity chemical and physical stability;
- the drug has been stored in such a manner as to prevent contamination by means that would affect the efficacy or and toxicity of the drug;
- the pharmacist knows that the drug has always been under the control of a third party trained and knowledgeable in the storage and administration of drugs;
- the labeling or packaging has not been altered or defaced so that the identity of the drug, it is potency, lot number, and expiration date is retrievable; and,
- if the drug had been prepackaged, it was not mixed with drugs of different lot numbers and/or expiration dates, unless the specific lot numbers were retrievable and expiration dates accompany the drug. If the drug is extemporaneously packaged, it shall not be mixed with drugs of different expiration dates unless the earliest expiration date appears on the label.

DURABLE MEDICAL EQUIPMENT, including mobility aids and wheelchairs, which may be cleaned and sanitized, may generally be returned.

See also the section on disposal of drugs, below.

RECALLS

The FDA may seize actual packages of drugs that are adulterated or misbranded. To preclude seizure, manufacturers may "voluntarily" recall adulterated or misbranded drugs. (Note: the FDA may initiate a recall of non-complying infant formulas or for medical devices.)

RECALLED DRUGS CANNOT BE DISPENSED. Any drug for which a recall is announced must be assumed to be either misbranded or adulterated, and thus may not be sold or dispensed without violating the FDCA. Dispensing a recalled drug has led to civil lawsuits when the patient was injured by the continued use of the recalled drug.[328]

LEVELS OF RECALLS. Recalls may extend to one of the following levels (in increasing order of severity):

- WHOLESALER LEVEL – only products in the inventory of a wholesale distributor need to be returned to the manufacturer.
- RETAIL LEVEL – only products still in the inventory of a pharmacy (or a wholesaler) must be returned to the manufacturer.
- CONSUMER LEVEL – MOST SERIOUS – IN ADDITION TO WHOLESALERS AND PHARMACIES, CONSUMERS ARE INSTRUCTED TO RETURN OFFENDING PRODUCTS TO THE MANUFACTURER

CLASSES OF RECALLS. When the FDA approves a voluntary recall, it determines and publishes a classification of the recall to indicate its severity.

CLASS I – MOST SERIOUS – there likelihood of injury or death from the use of the product; may include a public warning. The manufacturer may, in its recall notice, request retail distributors to notify consumers of the recall.

THE FDA'S COMPLIANCE POLICY GUIDE ON CLASS I RECALLS OF DRUGS[329] requires that pharmacies, hospitals and nursing home pharmacists review their prescription files to determine which patients may have received the specific lot numbers involved in any Class I recall, and must then notify the patients' physicians of the specific problem, and keep a record of the notification. If the pharmacy cannot separate out lot numbers to identify patients who received the specific product involved in the recall, they must notify the physicians of all customers who received the drug. The FDA will also under most circumstances issue a warning to the general public.

> **Comment:** I can find no record of any pharmacy being subject to discipline or prosecution for failing to comply with this guidance. However, pharmacies have been sued in civil cases, alleging that the notification was not made or was made too late during the 2008 recall of Digitek®.[330]

THE JOINT COMMISSION requires accredited institutions to adhere to Policy MM.4.70 regarding medication management, which states, "The pharmacy must retrieve medications recalled or discontinued by the Food and Drug Administration (FDA) or the manufacturer."

- Staff retrieve medications according to the organization's policy when the FDA or the manufacturer informs the hospital of the recall.
- The hospital must notify all staff ordering, dispensing, and giving out medications when the FDA issues a recall order.
- Staff identify and notify patients who may have received the recalled medication.[331]

CLASS II – health problems, if any, are expected to be temporary or reversible

CLASS III – use of the product is NOT likely to cause health problems

MARKET WITHDRAWAL – minor health risk or minor FDA violation

SAFETY WARNINGS AND LABEL REVISIONS FROM FDA

WHAT SHOULD PHARMACISTS DO WHEN THE FDA ISSUES SAFETY ALERTS OR REVISED DOSAGE GUIDELINES? Because the FDA has authority to force manufacturers to make label revisions as a result of safety concerns, the best approach to dealing with announcements, such as the recent reduced dosage limits for zolpidem[332] and citalopram,[333] is to consider them as a type of "recall" of the approved labeling. Once the FDA has publicized through a "Drug Safety Communication" a significant revision of the maximum dosage of a product, for example, this would seem to trigger the pharmacist's identification of possible clinical misuse of the drug, and, at the very least, would require contacting the prescriber to discuss the revisions when a new prescription or request for refill is for a dose that exceeds the new maximums. It is easy for every pharmacist to learn of these Drug Safety Communications by subscribing to MedWatch.[334]

A recent lawsuit in Washington arose when a health care system took several months to issue warnings directly to patients about the revised dosing of citalopram, and the estate of a deceased patient alleged that her death resulted from failure to promptly reduce her citalopram dose. The case settled without the health system admitting any liability.

DRUG SHORTAGES

In recent years, the US drug supply chain has experienced a spate of drug shortages, particularly critical drugs used in institutional practice. According to the FDA, there were 178 drug shortages reported in 2010 (132 were for injectable drugs), and 251 shortages (183 injectables) reported in 2011.[335] The FDA maintains a website on drug shortages[336] and the American Society of Health-system Pharmacists operates a drug shortage resource center.[337] Anticipating shortages and assisting other providers and patients in dealing with shortages of critical drugs are becoming important professional responsibilities for pharmacists, particularly in hospitals.

Congress gave FDA additional power to manage drug shortages and track shortages and threatened shortages in its 2012 enactment of FDASIA.[338] By 2017, the number of shortages reported by FDA had declined to 35.

MANUFACTURERS MUST REPORT DISRUPTIONS.

Manufacturers of all drugs that are LIFE-SUPPORTING, LIFE-SUSTAINING, or are "INTENDED FOR USE IN THE PREVENTION OF A DEBILITATING DISEASE OR CONDITION, INCLUDING ANY SUCH DRUG USED IN EMERGENCY MEDICAL CARE OR DURING SURGERY," must notify FDA of permanent discontinuance of the drug or of an interruption in the manufacture of the drug that is likely to lead to a meaningful disruption in supply, and the reasons for the discontinuation or interruption.

Notices must be made 6 months prior to the date of discontinuance or disruption, or as "soon as practicable"

FDA must notify appropriate organizations of discontinuations or interruptions, and must provide a means for organizations or providers to notify FDA of shortages

A notice of a controlled substance disruption or shortage may generate a request from FDA to DEA to alter production quotas as necessary to help overcome shortages. The Attorney General must provide reasons for rejecting the request, which must be made public.

Pharmacists must work to assure, particularly in institutional settings, that an impending drug shortage triggers careful assessment and planning to minimize the impact of the shortage on patients, and to assure that alternative drugs, packages, and dosage forms are utilized in such a manner as to avoid patient safety risks.[339]

Federal and state statutes enacted in 2013 provide for compounding of drugs subject to shortages by outsourcing facilities and/or compounding pharmacies. (See section on Compounding).

DISPOSAL OF OUTDATED DRUGS OR OTHER DANGEROUS WASTE

Pharmaceutical wastes have been regulated for many years, but recent publicity in the national press in 2008 has increased attention on the issue. The Associated Press reported in March 2008 that drugs had been detected in the drinking water supplies of 24 major metropolitan areas. In September, the AP reported that an

EPA survey revealed that the majority of 5,700 hospitals and 45,000 long-term care facilities flush unwanted drugs down the drain and do not document amounts. Data from 14 facilities in Minnesota extrapolates to over 250 million pounds of drug waste annually, including packaging. Congressional hearings were held in 2008 as well.

WASTE MANAGEMENT COMPANIES. Under state and federal laws, each non-household waste generator (such as a pharmacy, clinic, or hospital) is required to handle its waste to assure that dangerous and hazardous wastes are disposed appropriately. Several national companies now provide a suite of programs combining reverse distribution with waste management to help pharmacies comply with the law. Some, like Waste Management, primarily handle non-viable pharmaceutical waste. Others are primarily reverse distributors, such as Guaranteed Returns and National Pharmaceutical Returns, and some, like Stericycle, offer both waste management and reverse distribution.

WASTE CATEGORIES. The four major categories of waste are liquid, gaseous, radioactive, and solid waste. Waste may be hazardous or non-hazardous. Most pharmacies (other than nuclear pharmacies) produce primarily liquid and solid waste, and most pharmaceutical waste is a form of solid waste.

WASTE STREAMS. At one time, pharmacies dumped all their waste in a single trash receptacle, which was then picked up by the garbage collector and most commonly trucked to a land fill (or dump). The operations of a pharmacy create, however, several distinct streams of unwanted materials. Each facility must have a plan and process for dealing with each of these streams, and must train staff to handle waste safely and appropriately. Protections for individual workers handling dangerous or hazardous products and materials are subject to regulations issued by the Occupational Safety and Health Administration (OSHA) or its state counterpart (WISHA in Washington).

RETURNABLE PRODUCTS. Depending on the nature of the sales contract between the pharmacy and its suppliers, unsold, overstocked, defective, recalled, or outdated products may be returned for credit. In many instances, these products cannot be resold or reused, and the manufacturer will need to determine how to dispose of them. Most pharmacies now utilize the services of REVERSE DISTRIBUTORS who collect returnable products, separate them by manufacturer, obtain available credits, and return credit payments to the pharmacy, less the service fee. Reverse distributors who handle returns of controlled substances must be registered with the DEA, and these firms can handle controlled substances that are intended for destruction.

RECYCLABLES. A significant portion of the waste generated by pharmacies can be recycled. Paper packaging, cardboard, paper records, labels, glass and metal packages, batteries, electric lighting elements, and many other items need to be separated into a recycling stream at the source in most municipalities.

MEDICAL BIOHAZARD WASTE needs to be segregated and stored to avoid human exposure prior to its destruction, and most of it is ultimately incinerated. Sharps disposal is a part of medical waste management.

DANGEROUS AND HAZARDOUS SOLID WASTE produced by pharmacies differs from biohazard waste in that it consists primarily of chemical compounds that must be kept out of air and water.

NON-HAZARDOUS SOLID WASTE THAT CANNOT BE READILY RECYCLED includes food items and materials for which a recycling market doesn't currently exist.

FEDERAL REGULATION OF PHARMACEUTICAL WASTE is governed by the Resource Conservation and Recovery Act of 1976 (RCRA),[340] the principal federal statute dealing with solid waste disposal. The statute is enforced by the Environmental Protection Agency (EPA), with regulations in 40 C.F.R. parts 238-282. Congress amended the RCRA by the Hazardous and Solid Wastes Amendments of 1984,[341] which added small quantity generators (e.g., pharmacies) and established requirements for hazardous waste incinerators. The federal Clean Water Act (CWA)[342] also has implications for pharmaceutical waste, because it sets goals for elimination of toxic substances from drinking water. The CWA is also enforced by the EPA.

LISTED CHEMICALS. The EPA currently maintains lists of specific chemical substances, some of which are pharmaceuticals. In particular there are "P-listed" and "U-listed" chemicals.

EXAMPLE P-LIST PHARMACEUTICALS

- Arsenic trioxide – P012
- Epinephrine base – P042 (salts exempted federally, but not in WA)
- Nicotine – P075
- Phentermine (C-4) – P046
- Physostigmine – P204
- Physostigmine salicylate – P188
- Warfarin > 0.3% - P001

EXAMPLE U-LIST PHARMACEUTICALS

- Chloral hydrate (C-4) – U034
- Chlorambucil – U035
- Cyclophosphamide – U058
- Daunomycin (daunorubicin) – U059
- Melphalan – U150
- Lindane – U129
- Warfarin < 0.3% - U248

CONTAINERS that have held listed chemicals are treated as hazardous waste. P-list containers are not considered "empty" unless they have been triple washed and the washing solution treated as hazardous waste. U-list containers are considered empty if all contents are removed that can be removed through normal means, and no more than 3% by weight remains.

CHARACTERISTICS OF HAZARDOUSNESS. A waste is hazardous if it has one or more of the following *characteristics*

IGNITABLILITY

- Solutions with flashpoints < 140° F
    - Aqueous with > 24% alcohol
    - Nonaqueous
- Oxidizers
- Flammable aerosols
- Rubbing Alcohol
- Topical preparations (e.g., clindamycin phosphate topical solution)
- Injections (e.g., paclitaxel injection)

CORROSIVITY - Aqueous solution with pH ≤ 2 or ≥ 12.5

- Glacial acetic acid
- Sodium hydroxide

TOXICITY – 40 chemicals included in P or U lists

HEAVY METALS – selenium, chromium, and silver

- Selenium injection
- Chromium injection
- Silver sulfadiazine cream

PRESERVATIVES – thimerosol and m-cresol

- Influenza vaccines
- Insulin injections

REACTIVITY – explosive and water reactive wastes. Nitroglycerin formulations are excluded federally and in most states unless they exhibit ignitability

CHEMOTHERAPY AGENTS are not fully regulated by EPA. About 100 agents are not federally regulated under the RCRA, but most are state-regulated. Chemotherapy wastes that are regulated fall into three categories:

- TRACE WASTE (YELLOW LABEL/CONTAINER), including empty vials, syringes, iv's, gowns, gloves, zip lock bags. These are treated as infectious medical waste and incinerated as medical waste.
- "BULK" CHEMO WASTE (BLACK CONTAINER) – if not empty, should be placed into RCRA hazardous waste container
- SPILL CLEANUP (BLACK CONTAINER) – managed as RCRA hazardous waste

UNIVERSAL WASTE. "Universal waste" is a general category of RCRA waste that allows combining into a single waste stream. P-listed and U-listed waste must be "designated" (segregated and labeled separately) by the waste designator, whereas universal waste does not. The EPA published a proposed rule that would place pharmaceutical waste generated by health care entities into the Universal Waste category.[343,] Based on comments received, the agency withdrew the proposal and has issued a revised proposal in 2015.[344] On December 11, 2018, the final rule, "Management Standards for Hazardous Waste Pharmaceuticals ..." was signed by the EPA Administrator. The rule becomes effective 6 months following publication in the Federal Register. As of January 28, 2019, the final rule has not been published.

Major features of the rule include:

- Federal nationwide ban on flushing hazardous waste pharmaceuticals into sewer or waste water streams.
- Protection for healthcare facilities from being classified as large quantity generators (LQGs).
- Healthcare facilities are exempted from "satellite accumulation area" regulations
- Healthcare facilities will not need to specify hazardous waste codes on manifests
- Healthcare facilities may accumulate hazardous waste pharmaceuticals for up to 365 days without a permit
- Healthcare facilities will have basic training requirements

2017 EPA Waste Generator Rule. The EPA administrator signed a final rule in November 2016 that alters definitions of hazardous waste generators and allows flexibility, including reducing the burden on very small quantity generators. The rule goes into effect on May 30, 2017.[345]

WASHINGTON STATE REGULATION OF PHARMACEUTICAL WASTE. The Department of Ecology regulates disposal of dangerous wastes. Described here are rules as of January 2019; the DOE will need to revise its rules in accordance with the new EPA final rule.

Solid waste (such as drugs or medical devices) may be designated as dangerous, and if so, it must be disposed of in accordance with the Department's regulations and/or federal regulations. The Department has established a 4-step process by which a "waste generator" can determine if a solid waste is designated as a DANGEROUS WASTE:

> (a) To determine whether or not a solid waste is designated as a dangerous waste a person must:
>
> (i) First, determine if the waste is a listed discarded chemical product, WAC 173-303-081;
>
> (ii) Second, determine if the waste is a listed dangerous waste source, WAC 173-303-082;
>
> (iii) Third, if the waste is not listed in WAC 173-303-081 or 173-303-082, or for the purposes of compliance with the federal land disposal restrictions as adopted by reference in WAC 173-303-140, determine if the waste exhibits any dangerous waste characteristics, WAC 173-303-090; and
>
> (iv) Fourth, if the waste is not listed in WAC 173-303-081 or 173-303-082, and does not exhibit a characteristic in WAC 173-303-090, determine if the waste meets any dangerous waste criteria, WAC 173-303-100.
>
> (b) A person must check each section, in the order set forth, until they determine whether the waste is designated as a dangerous waste. Once the waste is determined to be a dangerous waste, further designation is not required except as required by subsection (4) or (5) of this section. If a person has checked the waste against each section and the waste is not designated, then the waste is not subject to the requirements of chapter 173-303 WAC.
>
> Any person who wishes to seek an exemption for a waste which has been designated DW or EHW must comply with the requirements of WAC 173-303-072

Generally, DRUGS ARE NOW CONSIDERED TO BE DANGEROUS WASTE, and in Washington MAY NOT BE DISPOSED OF IN SEWERS (e.g., by flushing down the toilet) or in SANITARY LANDFILLS or OTHER WASTE DISPOSAL SITES. Upon input from the Board of Pharmacy, the DOE has exempted controlled substances, legend drugs, and OTC drugs from most of its regulations when they are disposed of by a person or entity licensed to possess them, provided they are disposed of in an approved incinerator or a facility approved to incinerate municipal waste. WAC 173-303-071(3)(nn)(i)

STATE-ONLY HAZARDOUS WASTE. These regulations affect only "state-only" hazardous substances. Some drugs are classified under federal law as hazardous waste and the state cannot exempt these drugs from federal requirements. (See above).

INCINERATORS. Hospitals may operate approved incinerators, and hospital pharmacists may be able to use these facilities.

REVERSE DISTRIBUTORS. Pharmacies are increasingly relying on "reverse distributors" to handle pharmaceutical returns. Any product that can be returned to the manufacturer for credit is called a "viable pharmaceutical." A product disposed of without receiving credit is "non-viable." The DOE rules indicate that pharmacies may return viable pharmaceuticals using a reverse distributor, and may also use a DEA-registered reverse distributor to dispose of non-viable controlled substances. (See also chapter 5) Other pharmaceutical waste must be sent to a properly-registered incinerator. The Board has advised pharmacists to make sure that they obtain confirmation from their "reverse distributor" that it will dispose of drugs in accordance with WA law, since the person who "arranges" for the disposal of hazardous waste is ultimately responsible if the waste is not disposed of properly.

CONDITIONAL EXCLUSION – The DOE considers "special wastes" to be those wastes that pose a relatively low hazard. Under DOE guidelines, certain pharmaceuticals are considered "special wastes" that can be handled under the Conditional Exclusion.

INTERIM ENFORCEMENT POLICY – In April 2008, the DOE published an "Interim Enforcement Policy for Pharmaceutical Waste in Healthcare"[346] under which it will "refrain from enforcing portions of the *Dangerous Waste Regulations* ... at facilities meeting the conditions of this policy." The policy is to remain in effect until EPA finalizes its proposed Universal Waste Rule for Pharmaceuticals. Eligible facilities include patient care facilities and retail pharmacies. The policy was revised in October 2016, and the Department anticipates promulgating revised rules in 2017. The policy allows covered entities to accumulate waste and forward them to a reverse distributor. Steps in using the policy include:

- Create a waste profile by characterizing waste accumulated over a minimum of 90 days. List each waste type (e.g., warfarin, silver nitrate, cyclophosphamide, etc.) by its waste code and estimate its minimum and maximum percentage by weight of the total waste. Include "conditionally excluded state-only pharmaceutical waste" (i.e., all other non-listed pharmaceutical waste) as a single total. The waste profile must be updated every 3 years.
- Notify DOE that your facility is managing waste under the policy, including a copy of your completed profile.
- Train staff in proper handling of pharmaceutical waste.
- Accumulate waste in accordance with DOE guidelines. Waste may be accumulated for up to 180 days.
- Dispose of Waste by following DOE guidelines.
- Viable waste and non-viable controlled substances may be returned using a reverse distributor
- Non-viable non-controlled substances may be submitted to a registered waste transporter.

HIPAA REGULATIONS apply to any PHI contained within the waste stream. Waste that contains patient information on labels must be stored and handled so as not to breach a patient's privacy. (See also Chapter 6)

The Department of Ecology has established a "PHARMACEUTICALS" WEBSITE to assist medical facilities in management of dangerous wastes, including pharmaceuticals, IV admixtures, and sharps. It can be found at http://www.ecy.wa.gov/programs/hwtr/pharmaceuticals/index.html. Specific "Best Management Practices" are listed for various categories of pharmaceutical waste at http://www.ecy.wa.gov/programs/hwtr/pharmaceuticals/pages/bmp.html.

PATIENT DISPOSAL OF DRUGS

The hazardous substances rules applying to drugs in the possession of waste generators (e.g., pharmacies and hospitals) do not apply to private citizens.

FEDERAL LEGISLATION. In 2010, Congress passed S. 3397 – the Secure and Responsible Drug Disposal Act of 2010 – which amended the CSA to allow an authorized user to return to an approved agent his or her unused controlled substances for disposal, under regulations to be developed by DEA.[347]

The DEA issued a final rule on September 9, 2014, which became effective 30 days later. The rule allows pharmacies to register as "collectors" of drugs and controlled substances deposited by patients into approved containers, and/or to provide such containers to nursing homes for the disposal of residents' drugs. Pharmacies may also participate in mail-back programs.[348] (See also Chapter 5)

The Pharmacy Commission allows pharmacies to comply with DEA-approved drug return programs. As noted above, the Commission's web page has a guidance document that pharmacies should read and adhere to.

Extended Producer Responsibility (EPR) Laws

Extended Producer Responsibility (EPR) is a policy by which a product's producer continues to bear financial and/or physical responsibility for a product during the post-consumer stage of a product's life cycle. In other words, the producer is made responsible for the environmentally-safe disposal of a product after its useful life is over. Passage of EPR laws by states began in 2000, primarily with statutes concerned with electronic products. EPR laws for pharmaceuticals became nationally prominent in 2012, when Alameda County, CA, passed an ordinance requiring drug producers to pay for the collection and disposal of unwanted medications from consumers. A legal challenge was brought by manufacturers, and the ordinance was upheld in the 9th Circuit, with the U.S. Supreme Court denying review.[349] Similar laws in other counties in California and other states followed.

LOCAL LEGISLATION. King County (WA) – In June 2013 the King County Board of Health passed a regulation to create a drug take-back program for county residents. Based on the Alameda County, ordinance, the regulation requires producers of prescription drugs sold in King County to create a producer-funded take-back program, which is now in effect. Other counties in Washington that have followed suit include Kitsap County, Whatcom County, Pierce County, and Snohomish County.

INDUSTRY RESPONSE – MED-PROJECT™ In response to the success and growth of EPR laws in California and Washington, an industry-wide organization, the Pharmaceutical Product Stewardship Work Group, was formed from among over 400 producers to meet their new obligations; its operational subsidiary is called MED-Project. Consumers may go to the MED-Project website (med-project.org) and enter their ZIP code to identify medicine return kiosks near them.

STATE LEGISLATION. Washington became the 3rd state in the nation to pass an EPR law – related to electronic products – in 2006. A second statute, dealing with mercury-containing products (see below) was passed in 2010. The 2009 Washington Legislature also considered, but did not pass, HB 1165, which would establish a pharmaceutical product stewardship program (i.e., a consumer take-back program) funded and provided by drug producers. The 2018 Legislature, following on the lead taken by King, Snohomish, Pierce, Kitsap, and Whatcom counties, enacted a statewide EPR law for pharmaceuticals (see below).[350]

Until the statewide program is in place in late 2019, Washington residents will have different options, depending on their city or county of residence:

> RESIDENTS OF SPOKANE, WA may discard drugs and syringes in their residential garbage, because Spokane incinerates all its municipal waste in its unique Waste-to-Energy Facility.
>
> RESIDENTS OF KING, SNOHOMISH, PIERCE, KITSAP, or WHATCOM COUNTIES may go to the MED-Project web page for their county.
>
> Residents of most other communities may normally take medications to the hazardous-waste area of their local landfill or transfer station, or to a pharmacy that operates a return program. They should be advised to call their local waste management authority for instructions.

WASHINGTON DRUG TAKE-BACK PROGRAM. The Washington drug take-back program statute is encoded as RCW 69.48, with regulatory authority assigned to the Department of Health. Regulations, under development as of January 2019, will be found in WAC 246-480. Covered producers have until July 1, 2019 to submit programs for approval by the DOH. It seems likely that the program to be adopted will be a MED-Project statewide program, since MED-Project is already operating all of the county programs in the state. DOH has 120 days after a program submission to approve or reject the proposal.

Collection sites will take back prescription and OTC medications except for (1) Schedule I drugs; (2) exposed sharps or emptied devices; and (3) vitamins, minerals, supplements, cosmetics, shampoos, lip balm, toothpaste, antiperspirants and similar non-drug OTC products.

Pharmacies may serve as collection sites, but are not required to do so. Pharmacies that seek to become collections sites must be granted permission by the take-back program within 90 days. Other sites may include LTC facilities with a pharmacy, hospitals or clinics with on-site pharmacies, or substance use disorder treatment programs. Collection sites must accept all covered drugs during normal business hours.

The existing county programs are grandfathered and may continue for 12 months following approval of the state-wide program.

The statute will face a sunset review in 2030, or when an equivalent federal program is approved.

HANDLING OF HAZARDOUS DRUGS IN PHARMACIES AND OTHER PATIENT CARE FACILITIES

WORKPLACE SAFETY RULES ARE DESIGNED TO PROTECT EMPLOYEES FROM WORKPLACE HAZARDS.

Washington employers are required to provide employees a workplace free from recognized hazards that are causing, or likely to cause, serious injury or death. (WAC 296-800-11005). Among these many rules are a number that affect pharmacies. Employers must

- Prohibit employees from working who are under the INFLUENCE OF ALCOHOL OR NARCOTICS. (WAC 296-900-11025)
- CONTROL CHEMICAL AGENTS in a manner that they will not present a hazard to your workers; or protect workers from the hazard of contact with, or exposure to, chemical agents. (WAC 296-800-11040)
- Protect employees from exposure to hazardous concentrations of BIOLOGICAL AGENTS that may result from processing, handling, or using materials or waste. (WAC 296-800-11045). This applies to exposure to biologic agents during cleanup, or other tasks, where employees handle ANIMALS OR ANIMAL WASTE or body fluids.
- Employers must WARN EMPLOYEES OF BIOHAZARDS using appropriate tags or signage

SPECIFIC RULES EFFECTIVE IN 2015 FOR HEALTH CARE SETTINGS RELATING TO HANDLING OF HAZARDOUS DRUGS.

A statute passed in 2011[351] requires the Department of Labor & Industries to adopt rules implementing the 2004 NIOSH Safety Alert on safe handling of hazardous drugs. Washington was the first state in the nation to enact protection for health care workers.[352] Considerable input by health care providers has been made to the Department, which published final rules in January of 2014.

Enforcement of these rules (WAC 296-62-500 and following) was delayed until January 2015.[353] The rules apply to all employers in health care facilities regardless of the setting. Only the hazardous drugs being used in the workplace are covered by the rule.

COVERED OCCUPATIONS. The Department believes that the following occupations may involve exposures to hazardous drugs.

- Pharmacists and pharmacy technicians
- Physicians and physician assistants
- Nurses
- Patient care assistive personnel
- Operating room personnel
- Home health care workers
- Veterinarians and veterinary technicians
- Environmental services employees
- Employees in health care facilities who ship or receive hazardous drugs from the manufacturer or distributor.

COVERED DRUGS. Hazardous drugs covered in the rule are those on the NIOSH list, found at www.cdc.gov/niosh/docs/2012-150/pdfs/2012-150.pdf.

Drugs were placed on the list due to potential:

- Carcinogenicity
- Teratogenicity or other developmental toxicity
- Reproductive toxicity
- Organ toxicity at low doses
- Genotoxicity
- New drugs with structure and toxicity profiles that mimic existing hazardous drugs

The drugs on the 2012 list include many obvious agents, such as chemotherapy and antineoplastic agents (eg, azathioprine, carboplatin, dactinomycin, and methotrexate). Other drugs include carbamazepine, clonazepam, paroxetine, risperidone, and zoledronic acid.

WRITTEN HAZARDOUS DRUGS CONTROL PROGRAM. Each facility must establish a hazardous drug control program, consisting at least of the following:

- A WRITTEN INVENTORY of covered hazardous drugs in the workplace
- A completed HAZARD ASSESSMENT FOR EACH DRUG which anticipates "reasonably anticipated occupational exposure(s)" to the drug. Specific requirements for conducting a hazard assessment are found in WAC 296-62-50020.
- HAZARDOUS DRUG POLICIES AND PROCEDURES designed to prevent employee exposure to hazardous drugs (WAC 296-62-50015). The policies should consider
    - Engineering controls
    - Provision of personal protective equipment (PPE) when necessary
    - Safe handling practices during

        - Receiving
        - Storage
        - Labeling
        - Preparing
        - Administering
        - Disposal
    - Cleaning, housekeeping, and waste handling
    - Spill control
    - Personnel issues (eg, exposure of pregnant workers)
    - Training
- ANNUAL REVIEW AND UPDATE of the program, and update when changes occur
- Employers must seek and CONSIDER INPUT FROM EMPLOYEES
- AVAILABILITY OF ADEQUATE FACILITIES, INCLUDING VENTILATED CABINETS

Detailed rules relating to engineering controls, PPE, safe handling practices, cleaning and housekeeping, spill control, and training are in WAC 296-62-50025 through 50050.

Specific guides have been developed for different professions, including one for pharmacy, and are available at http://www.lni.wa.gov/safety/topics/atoz/hazardousdrugs/programguides.asp

USP <800> - HANDLING OF HAZARDOUS DRUGS IN HEALTHCARE SETTINGS. The United States Pharmacopeia (USP) has adopted a chapter on handling of hazardous drugs (HDs) in health care settings, which is designed in part to supplement the requirements of USP <797> on compounding of sterile products. The implementation date of the chapter has been delayed to December 1, 2019,[354] at which time a revision of USP <797> will also become official. The chapter applies to all health care personnel who handle hazardous drug preparations, not just pharmacy personnel. As noted above, the essential elements of USP <800> are already applicable to pharmacies in Washington state.

COVERED SUBSTANCES.

- A hazardous drug is a drug on the NIOSH list discussed above that is:
    - Any HD API (active pharmaceutical ingredient)
    - Any antineoplastic requiring HD manipulation
- Drugs on NIOSH list are not included if an assessment of risk is performed and implemented, and the drug is found to be:
    - A final dosage form of compounded HD preparations; or
    - A final dosage form of conventionally manufactured HD products; and
    - Do not require any further manipulation other than counting or repackaging

COVERED INDIVIDUALS AND ENTITIES.

- All healthcare personnel who handle HD preparations, including but not limited to:
    - Pharmacists
    - Pharmacy technicians
    - Nurses
    - Physicians
    - Physician assistants
    - Home healthcare workers
    - Veterinarians
    - Veterinary technicians

- All entities that store, prepare, transport, or administer HDs, including but not limited to:
  - Pharmacies
  - Hospitals and other healthcare institutions
  - Patient treatment clinics
  - Physician's practice facilities
  - Veterinarians' offices
- Not covered by USP <800> are manufacturers, wholesale personnel, researchers, or family members of covered individuals.

MAJOR PROVISIONS. The introduction and another 17 sections of the chapter outline the "practice and quality standards for handling hazardous drugs to promote patient safety, worker safety, and environmental protections." Covered individuals and entities should review the chapter directly. Each covered entity must develop a program covering the following elements:

- Introduction and scope
- List of HDs
- Types of exposure
- Responsibilities of personnel handing HDs
- Facilities and engineering controls, including designated areas for receipt and unpacking, storage, non-sterile compounding (must follow USP <795>), and sterile compounding (must follow USP <797>)
  - HDs must be received and unpacked in neutral/negative pressure area
  - Must be stored so as to prevent spillage or breakage
  - Containment – Primary Engineering Controls (C-PEC) includes the cabinet types needed for compounding – may include
    - Class II Biological Safety Cabinets (Type A2, B1, or B2)
    - Compounding Aseptic Containment Isolators (CACI)
    - Containment Ventilated Enclosures/Powder Hoods
  - Containment – Secondary Engineering Controls (C-SEC) relates to the room in which compounding is done
    - Externally vented
    - Physically separated
    - Negative pressure
    - Sink
    - Eyewash station
  - Supplemental engineering controls include closed system transfer devices (CSTDs), which are required for administration and recommended for compounding
  - Must follow C-PEC standards for manipulation, including crushing of dosage forms
- Environmental quality and control – includes initial sampling and routine sampling (every 6 months recommended)
- Personal Protective Equipment (PPE)
  - Head covers
  - Beard covers
  - Eye protection for spill protection
  - Face mask – limited safety protection
  - Powered air-purifying respirator for spills
  - Disposable gowns, must be polyethylene or laminate
  - 2 pairs of gloves

  - 2 pairs of anti-skid shoe covers, don 2 pairs prior to entry, discard outer pair when leaving
- Hazard communication program
  - Written plan
  - All containers of HDs must be labeled
  - Must have safety data sheet for each HD
  - SDS must be readily available to personnel
  - Information and training must be provided before job
  - Personnel capable of reproduction must confirm in writing they understand reproductive risks of handling HDs
- Personnel training –
  - All personnel must be trained
  - All personnel must be assessed every 12 months
  - Must be trained on new HDs and equipment
  - Must document competencies
- Receiving HDs –
  - Must be a neutral or negative pressure area
  - Gloves worn for unpacking HDs
  - Spill kit available
  - Visual inspection for HDs
  - Any damaged packages considered a spill
- Labeling, packaging, transport & disposal
  - All transported HDs must be labeled with HD precaution
  - Must not transport HD liquids via pneumatic tubes
- Dispensing final dosage forms
  - Any counting or packaging equipment must be cleaned after each use for an HD
  - **NO ANTINEOPLASTIC DRUGS IN AUTOMATED COUNTING OR PACKAGING MACHINES**
  - May put antineoplastic drugs in automated dispensing cabinets
- Compounding
  - Follow USP <795> or <797>
  - Should use CSTD for sterile compounding
  - Should use chemo mat
  - Must dedicate special equipment for HDs
- Administering
  - Must use CSTDs or protective medical devices and techniques
  - Must pre-prime IV tubing with non-HD solution
  - Must wear PPE
  - Must avoid manipulation (splitting, crushing, opening capsules)
- Deactivating, decontaminating, cleaning and disinfecting
  - 2% sodium hypochlorite solution for deactivation
  - Physical surface wipe with sodium thiosulfate solution for decontamination
  - Clean with tri- or quadrivalent detergent or ready-to-use (RTU) peroxide
  - Disinfection with sterile 70% isopropyl alcohol and/or UV light
- Spill control
  - Proper training in use of PPE, respirators, and spill kits
  - Spill signs posted
  - Readily available spill kits

- Dispose of spill kits as hazardous waste
- Policies and training must address spill size

- Documentation and SOPs – reviewed every 12 months
- Medical surveillance
  - Individual personnel should be identified as to risk of exposure at time of hire and routinely thereafter
  - Provide for post-exposure examination
  - Conduct environmental sampling
  - Verify engineering controls are working
  - Conduct FMEA of processes and policies
  - Develop action plan
  - Ensure confidential 2-way communication
  - Provide continuing medical surveillance

EXTEMPORANEOUS COMPOUNDING OF DRUG PRODUCTS BY PHARMACISTS

PHARMACIES EXEMPT FROM REGISTRATION WITH FDA. Extemporaneous compounding of medications is a long-standing aspect of the practice of pharmacy. When the FDCA was adopted in 1938, manufacturers were required to register with the FDA.

§ 510(b) requires annual registration by every person engaging in the "manufacture, preparation, propagation, compounding, or processing of drug[s] ..."

However, § 510(g) exempts from registration "pharmacies ... regularly engaged in dispensing drugs and devices ... and which do not ... compound ... drugs other than in the regular course of their dispensing or selling drugs at retail ..."

COMPOUNDING PHARMACIES MAY STILL BE VIEWED AS MANUFACTURERS UNDER STATE PRODUCT LIABILITY LAWS.

Although compounding pharmacies are not treated as manufacturers under the FDCA, they remain liable for defects in the products they produce. Unlike laws regarding suits for professional negligence, product liability laws may impose liability on the entity that introduces the product into the stream of commerce for any product defect, whether it was foreseeable or not. (See also Chapter 7)

PHARMACIES MUST BE ENGAGED IN *BONA FIDE* PHARMACY OPERATIONS.

Until the 1980s, the FDA and most commentators believed that pharmacists could compound any medication ordered by a physician without violating the FDCA. Some pharmacies began to expand their compounding business greatly, and a few used the excuse that they were compounding drugs to shield them from regulation for some potentially or actually harmful practices.

For example, the Seven Freedoms Pharmacy in Florida compounded a product called "GH-8," and shipped the product around the United States via the mail. GH-8 consisted of a formulation of procaine, and it was alleged to retard aging reduce or eliminate many of the symptoms of aging. GH-8 was the only product compounded or sold by Seven Freedoms Pharmacy, and the "patients" joined Club Sene-X to receive prescriptions for GH-8, or to receive instructions for their own physician to prescribe GH-8. In a landmark lawsuit,[355] the US Court of Appeals ruled that Seven Freedoms Pharmacy was not engaged in the bona fide practice of pharmacy, that GH-8 was a new drug that had not been approved by the FDA, and that its distribution violated the FDCA.

Injuries from poorly compounded prescriptions included overdoses of pediatric medications, blindness from non-sterile compounded eye drops, and deaths due to meningitis caused by non-sterile betamethasone injection. FDA surveys in 2001 discovered several problems in a random selection of compounded products.

CHANGES IN FDA'S VIEW OF COMPOUNDING. In response to these events, the FDA reexamined its position that compounding was exempt from FDA oversight. It determined that, although pharmacies do not need to register, §510(g) does not exempt pharmacies from the new drug requirements of the Act, which include the following three sections:

- § 501(a)(2)(b) – A drug is adulterated if it is not manufactured in accordance with Current Good Manufacturing Practices (GMPs).
- § 502(f)(1) – A drug is misbranded if it lacks adequate directions for use.
- § 505 – An approved New Drug Application is required before a new drug can be marketed or introduced into the stream of commerce.

Thus, the FDA determined, compounded products are new drugs, which come under its jurisdiction. Over nearly 2 decades, litigation and legislation unsuccessfully clarified the role of compounded pharmaceuticals in the US, and compounding largely was regulated by states and sporadic FDA action.

FDA GUIDANCE ON POSSIBLE MELAMINE CONTAMINATION. The presence of melamine contamination in Chinese-produced components used in animal food gained significant publicity in 2008. In August 2009, the FDA issued a guidance[356] to alert pharmaceutical manufacturers and pharmacy compounders to the possible contamination by melamine of pharmaceutical components. It suggests that compounders should independently test components for possible melamine contamination, or purchase such components only from reliable suppliers who have performed such testing. Because the testing involves liquid or gas chromatography combined with mass spectrometry (LC-MS/MS and/or GC-MS), the most practical response of pharmacy compounders is to purchase only components that are certified melamine free by a reputable supplier. Example at-risk components listed by the FDA include certain amino acids, gelatin, guar gum, and lactose, among other items. The advice in the guidance is generally non-binding. Failure of a compounding pharmacy to act in response to this announcement, however, could be seen as evidence of negligence if a patient were injured.

CHALLENGES TO "BIO-IDENTICAL" HORMONE REPLACEMENT THERAPY.

In early 2008, Wyeth filed a citizen's petition asking the FDA to take enforcement actions, including seizures, injunctions and/or warning letters, against pharmacies engaged in compounding of so-called bio-identical hormone replacement therapy (BHRT). Among the requested actions were that pharmacies compounding BHRT must provide a patient package insert, noting that BHRT is not FDA approved, is not manufactured according to good manufacturing practices, and that the BHRT has not been demonstrated to be safe for effective for any use. Wyeth also requested that the FDA issue an alert or talk paper directed to consumers, health care providers and the compounding industry. FDA limited its actions in response to the citizen's petition to developing a consumer awareness campaign, publishing an article on its web site, issuing a press release, and arranging calls with media and stakeholders to discuss the issues.[357]

At the same time, the FDA independently sent warning letters to 7 compounding pharmacies that were promoting BHRT on their web sites. In general the FDA raised three types of issues relating to the pharmacies' website claims:

- unsubstantiated therapeutic claims, such as "bio-identical estrogen replacement therapy can benefit a woman by ... reducing risk of heart disease, reducing the risk of Alzheimer's ...";
- unsubstantiated superiority claims, such as "bio-identical hormones differ from synthetic hormones in that synthetics are not identical in either structure or function to the natural hormones they emulate ..."; and
- unsubstantiated "bio-identical claims", which suggests that compounded hormone therapy drugs are natural or identical to the hormones made by the body.

It seems clear that the pharmacies came to the FDA's attention primarily because of their websites, and the claims made therein. The FDA was careful to note that this action did "not target pharmacist who practice traditional pharmacy compounding and do not make false or misleading claims about compounded products."[358]

NEW ENGLAND COMPOUNDING CENTER INCIDENT. In early September 2012, patients began arriving in US hospitals with a rare variety of fungal meningitis. A Tennessee physician, Dr. April Pettit, contacts the Tennessee Health Department after identifying fungus in a patient's CSF, seeking to see if there were other reports. Dr. Pettit thus uncovered an outbreak of fungal disease that by February 2013 would sicken 696 patients and cause 45 deaths.[359] The disease was traced to lots of preservative-free methylprednisolone acetate injection prepared and sold to physicians for intrathecal injection by the New England Compounding Center in Framingham, Massachusetts, and was primarily due to *Exserohilum rostratum,* a common mold that rarely causes disease in humans. NECC operated under a pharmacy license, but investigations revealed that it did not appear to comply with the requirement of a pharmacist-patient-physician relationship, nor did it adhere to USP <797> quality control requirements. Some commentators on the situation suggested that the *Western States* decision had the effect of weakening FDA oversight and federal-state cooperation.[360] APhA, as well as other pharmacy organizations, noted that compounding in the recognized context of a patient-pharmacist-physician relationship is a needed professional service regulated under state law, and that both the USP standards as well as accreditation standards support safe and effective pharmacy compounding; nevertheless, APhA expressed a need for improved state and federal regulation of illegal manufacturers who do not compound within professional standards.[361]

DRUG QUALITY AND SECURITY ACT. Congress responded to the NECC incident by enacting legislation in 2013. The first part of the DQSA dealt with issues related to pharmacy compounding as discrete from large volume compounding of unapproved sterile drugs.

SECTION 503A REENACTED. The Act reinstates the former §503A in full except for the previous prohibitions on advertising and/or solicitation of prescriptions, as it applies to "traditional pharmacy compounders" (See FDAMA in Chapter 2).

COMPARISON OF COMPOUNDING PHARMACY VS. OUTSOURCING FACILITY		
	COMPOUNDING PHARMACY (§503A)	OUTSOURCING FACILITY (§503B)
INDIVIDUAL PRESCRIPTION	Required	Optional
SUBJECT TO GMPS	No	Yes
WHOLESALING	Subject to state laws	Prohibited by federal law
REGISTRATION WITH FDA	No	Yes
REPORTING	No	Yes
FEES	None	$18,375 annual registration ($5,461 small business); $16,382 reinspection

SECTION 503B REGARDING "OUTSOURCING FACILITIES." Congress established a mechanism by which entities engaged in large volume compounding of sterile products (or other drugs not otherwise approved for marketing) could "voluntarily register" with FDA and be exempt from NDA or adequate labeling requirements of the FDCA. These entities, however, would be subject to current GMP regulations developed to apply to their activities. The outsourcing facility must be under the supervision of a licensed pharmacist, but would not necessarily need to be a pharmacy.

The FDA has reiterated that under current law, the only source of compounded products for "office use" without compounding pursuant to individual prescriptions is an outsourcing facility. The FDA further notes that an outsourcing facility must do some sterile compounding to qualify for registration, but may do non-sterile compounding as well.

The FDA's website on compounding is a useful resource for pharmacists regarding the federal law (www.fda.gov/drugs/GuidanceComplianceRegulatroyInformation/PharmacyCompounding).

SECTION 503A REQUIREMENTS

Pharmacies duly licensed by a state, and engaged in the good faith practice of pharmacy, may compound prescribed drug products that are not "new drugs" subject to §501(a)(2)(B), §502(f)(1), or §505 of the FDCA, if they follow all of the following requirements.

RECEIPT OF A PRESCRIPTION FOR AN INDIVIDUAL IDENTIFIED PATIENT REQUIRED. §§ 501(a)(2)(b), 502(f)(1), and 505 do not apply to drugs that are compounded ... for an individual identified patient, based on the receipt of a valid prescription. The FDA issued a guidance[362] in December 2016 stating that a valid prescription order includes

- A prescription issued by an authorized prescriber;
- Valid order or notation made in a patient's health record in an institutional setting; or
- A valid order or notation made by a physician who compounds a drug for his or her own patient and noted in the patient's medical record.
- The order must identify the specific patient. An order specifying a compounded prescription naming the prescriber as the patient is only valid if the compounded product is to be administered to the prescriber, rather than some other patient.
- Notwithstanding state laws which may allow compounding of prescriptions that do not name a particular patient, or that allow compounding for general physician office use, the FDA reiterated in its 2016 guidance that compounding for office use may only be done by outsourcing facilities, unless the compounding is done for a specific-named patient.

LIMITED QUANTITIES MAY BE COMPOUNDED PRIOR TO RECEIVING A PRESCRIPTION, based on a history of the pharmacist receiving valid orders within an established relationship between the pharmacist, physician, and patient. In its 2016 guidance, the FDA specified that "this means that anticipatory compounding ... is done in limited quantities, based on an expectation that the licensed pharmacist ... will receive a patient-specific prescription for the particular drug product, written for a patient or by a prescriber with whom the compounder has a relationship." The FDA will not assert that the compounder is compounding excessive quantities in violation of the Act if:

- The compounder holds for distribution not more than an estimated 30-day supply of a particular compounded product; i.e., the amount the compounder reasonably expects to need to fill orders received over a 30-day period; and
- The amount of a particular compounded product needed is based on the number of valid prescriptions received over a 30-day period selected by the compounder from the prior year.

COMPONENTS AND METHODS used to compound the product

- Must comply with USP or NF monographs, if they exist, and the USP Chapters on Pharmacy Compounding.
- If no monographs exist, the products must be made from components of approved drugs, or
- Must be components that appear on a bulk ingredients list developed by FDA. In December 2016, the FDA issued a proposed rule on this topic, containing the following 6 ingredients:[363]
    - Brilliant Blue G, a/k/a Coomassie Brilliant Blue G-250
    - cantharadin (for topical use only)
    - diphenylcyclopropenone (topical use)
    - N-acetyl-D-glucosamine (topical use)
    - squaric acid dibutyl ester (topical use)
    - thymol iodide (topical use)

  It is not clear if this proposed rule is subject to an executive order issued by President Trump relating to regulations promulgated in the final 60 days of the Obama administration.

- Must be manufactured in an FDA registered facility

PROHIBITED PRODUCTS. Pharmacists are prohibited from compounding certain products:

- May not compound products that are listed by FDA as having been removed from market due to lack of safety or efficacy [current final rule published October 7, 2016; 21 CFR 216.24].
- May not compound "regularly or in an inordinate amount" products that are essentially copies of commercially available drug products.
- May not compound products that are listed by FDA as having demonstrable difficulties in compounding [list to be developed].

USP CHAPTER REVISIONS. The USP has developed three chapters related to compounding, including chapter <800>, discussed above.

COMPOUNDING OF NONSTERILE PRODUCTS – CHAPTER <795>. Chapter <795> of USP 27, relates to general standards of compound and to compounding of nonsterile products, and covers most compounding activities of community pharmacies.

CHAPTER <795> STANDARDS.

Among the standards of chapter <795> are the following general requirements.

STABILITY AND EXPIRATION DATING

"Appropriate stability evaluation is performed or determined from the literature for establishing reliable beyond-use dating."

"... Beyond-use dates are to be assigned conservatively."

"In the absence of stability information that is applicable to a specific drug and preparation, the following maximum beyond-use dates are recommended for nonsterile compounded drug preparations that are packaged in tight, light-resistant containers and stored at controlled room temperature unless otherwise indicated:

- For **Water-Containing Formulations** (prepared from ingredients in solid form) – The beyond-use date is not later than 14 days for liquid preparations when stored at cold temperatures between 2º and 8º (36º to 46º F)." (27 USP 2347)
- For **nonaqueous liquids and solid formulations**
    - Where the **manufactured drug product is the source of the active ingredient** – the beyond-use date is not later than 25% of the time remaining until the product's expiration date or 6 months, whichever is earlier.
    - **Where a USP or NF substance is the source** of the active ingredient – the beyond-use-date is not later than 6 months.
    - For **all other formulations** – the beyond-use date is not later than the intended duration of therapy or 30 days, whichever is earlier.

LABELING. The USP specifies that, as part of the compounding process, the compounder should "label the prescription containers to include the following items: a) the name of the preparation; b) the internal identification number; c) the beyond-use date ...; d) the initials of the compounder who prepared the label; e) any storage requirements; and f) any other statements required by law."

COMPOUNDING OF STERILE PRODUCTS – CHAPTER <797>. The second monograph, chapter <797> of USP 39, details good practices for compounding of sterile products, which includes home IV admixtures, eye drops, and similar products. The standards in these chapters were incorporated by reference in §503A. Every pharmacy engaged in sterile compounding must maintain a current version of chapter <797> and adhere to its requirements. With the adoption of USP <800>, USP <797> was significantly revised to focus primarily on maintaining the quality and sterility of the compounded product, and the revised version will become effective when USP <800> becomes effective. Until that time (July 2018), the older version of USP <797> details many of the elements to protect personnel involved in compounding from hazardous drugs. The revised chapter contains the following major elements:

- Introduction and scope
- Personnel qualifications – training, evaluation, requalification
- Personal hygiene and PPEs
- Building and facilities
- Environmental monitoring
- Cleaning and disinfecting compounding areas
- Equipment and components
- Sterilization and depyrogenation
- SOPs and Master Formulation and Compounding records

- Release testing
- Labeling
- Establishing beyond-use dates and in-use times
- Quality assurance and quality control
- CSP storage, handling, packaging and transport
- Complaint handling and ADR reporting
- Documentation
- Radiopharmaceuticals as CSPs

PHARMACY COMPOUNDING ACCREDITATION BOARD. In 2006, 8 national organizations (ACA, APhA, IACP, NABP, NCPA, NASPA, NHIA, and USP) established the Pharmacy Compounding Accreditation Board (PCAB). In a manner similar to the Joint Commission's review of hospitals, PCAB evaluates compounding pharmacies' compliance with over 35 standards and certifies qualified pharmacies as meeting its standards. In particular, pharmacies that undertake any forms of sterile compounding will likely need to become accredited in order to obtain liability insurance in the future. Since 2014, PCAB has been a service of the Accreditation Commission for Health Care (ACHC).

The PCAB has adopted labeling guidelines for products intended for specific patients to take or use at home:

Notification to the patient that the product is compounded, including the notice that "This medicine was specially compounded in our pharmacy for you at the direction of your prescriber."

All labels should contain the following elements:

- Patient's name, and/or species, if applicable;
- Prescriber's name;
- Name, address, phone number of the pharmacy preparing the medicine;
- Prescription number;
- The medication's established or distinct common name;
- Strength;
- Statement of quantity;
- Directions for use;
- Date prescription filled;
- Beyond-use date
- Storage instructions; and
- All state labeling requirements

An extended statement must accompany all compounded prescriptions:

This medicine was compounded specifically for you in our pharmacy to fill the prescription your prescriber wrote for you. It was specially made to meet your individual needs. For this reason, no standardized information or literature is available with your prescription. If you have not done so, please discuss this medicine with your pharmacist or prescriber to assure that you understand (1) why you have been prescribed a compounded medicine, (2) how to properly take this medicine, and (3) the interactions, if any, this medicine may have with any other medicines you are taking.

Compounding is a long-standing pharmacy practice that allows prescribers to treat their patients' individual needs without being restricted only to off-the-shelf medicines or devices. This medicine was prepared in our compounding pharmacy to meet the specifications ordered by your prescriber.

1. *Call your pharmacist or prescriber if:*

    ♦ *You experience any side effects.*

    ♦ *You are taking additional medicines that may interact with this compounded medicine.*

    ♦ *You have allergies or other medical conditions that should be noted.*

2. *Call our pharmacists if:*

    ♦ *Information on the label is not clear to you.*

    ♦ *You have any concerns regarding precautions, ingredients, or proper storage.*

Our pharmacists are available to address any additional questions or concerns.

If the medicine is compounded for use in the practitioner's office, the primary label must contain the statement, *"This medicine was compounded in our pharmacy for use by a licensed practitioner only. This compounded preparation may not be resold."*[364]

WASHINGTON COMPOUNDING STATUTE

The 2013 legislature also responded to the NECC debacle by amending the Pharmacy Practice Act regarding Drug Compounding and Distribution.[365] The Act clarifies the definition of "manufacturing."

COMPOUNDING IS NOT MANUFACTURING. Distribution of a compounded product by a pharmacy for "resale" is "manufacturing," not compounding. However, it allows compounding of a specific product for resale subject to approval by the Pharmacy Commission. Under the Act, "Manufacturing" does not include:

- Compounding by a pharmacy on, or in anticipation of, an order of a licensed practitioner for use in the course of their professional practice for administration to patients;
- Repackaging commercially available medication in "small, reasonable quantities" for office use by a practitioner;
- Distribution of a compounded product to other appropriately licensed entities under the ownership or control of the facility in which the compounding takes place; or
- The delivery of finished and appropriately compounded products dispensed pursuant to a valid prescription to "alternative delivery locations, other than the patient's residence, when requested by the patient, or the prescriber to administer to the patient, or to another licensed pharmacy to dispense to the patient." (RCW 18.64.011(15))

USP <795> AND <797> INCORPORATED INTO WASHINGTON LAW. The statute incorporates USP chapters <795> and <797> as standards for compounding of nonsterile or sterile products pursuant to a prescription. When USP <800> becomes effective, it will be applicable in Washington, because USP <797> specifies compliance with USP <800>. (RCW 18.64.270(2))

Washington-registered entities desiring to be "outsourcing facilities" under federal law will need to be licensed as manufacturers; the Commission requires out-of-state outsourcing facilities to register as nonresident wholesalers.

WASHINGTON COMPOUNDING RULES. Washington Pharmacy Commission regulations regarding compounding generally follow the NABP Model Act, and specify that pharmacists may extemporaneously compound products ordered for a patient in the context of a physician-pharmacist-patient relationship. (WAC 246-878-020).

CURRENT WAC 246-878. The Commission has not successfully promulgated revisions to its compounding rule in response to the changes to federal law. A CR-101 notice of proposed rulemaking on "Safe Compounding Practices"[366] was withdrawn in 2018.[367] The Commission intends to consider changes to compounding rules in its ongoing rules re-write project. The current rules specify the following:

DOCUMENTATION OF PHYSICIAN AND PATIENT ACCEPTANCE OF COMPOUNDED ALTERNATIVE. If a commercially available product is being replaced by a compounded equivalent, records must indicate that the patient and physician agree to the use of the compounded product, and this shall be documented on the prescription or in the prescription records. An example compounding worksheet is provided at the end of the chapter as Appendix 4B.

SOURCE OF INGREDIENTS. The first choice for compounded products is to use ingredients meeting USP or NF requirements; however, pharmacists may use judgment if compendial products are not available.

LIMITED QUANTITIES. Products should be compounded in limited quantities, based on a history of receiving prescriptions for the product, or upon anticipated need for refills of existing products. Compounding of excessively large amounts is considered manufacturing.

WHOLESALING PROHIBITED. The regulation prohibits sale of compounded products to other licensed persons or commercial entities. However, it is permitted in WA to sell compounded products to a prescriber for administration to a patient. Under federal law, such products must be compounded pursuant to a prescription for the specific patient to whom the drug will be administered.

PROMOTION RESTRICTED, BUT THIS RESTRICTION NOT ENFORCEABLE. The regulation allows promotion of the compounding service, but states that they "they shall not solicit business (e.g., promote, advertise, or use salespersons) to compound specific drug products." (WAC 246-878-020(4)). As a result of legal challenges to an earlier version of §503A in the 9th Circuit, which was affirmed by the Supreme Court, this prohibition is unconstitutional and unenforceable.[368]

PERSONNEL REQUIREMENTS. The regulation specifies requirements for pharmacists and ancillary personnel involved in compounding (WAC 246-878-030):

- The pharmacist is responsible for inspecting all supplies, processes, and equipment, and for making sure of the accuracy of the compounding process.
- Pharmacists and ancillary personnel involved in compounding must keep up to date with training and continuing education, and be aware of the requirements of WAC 246-878.
- Clean clothing and appropriate protective apparel are required.
- Compounding areas are limited to personnel involved in compounding, and the pharmacist shall exclude persons with lesions or other illnesses that may compromise the product.

FACILITIES. Requirements for facilities used in compounding are specified in WAC 246-878-040:

> There shall be adequate space and facilities, and non-sterile compounding shall be separate from sterile compounding facilities.

Bulk containers shall be properly stored, including under refrigeration if necessary.

Adequate water and other supplies must be available for compounding and cleaning.

Facilities must be maintained in clean and sanitary condition.

STERILE PRODUCTS. Compounding of sterile products must conform to WAC 246-871 (Parenteral Products for Nonhospitalized Patients – see Chapter 2).

Pharmacy Commission Guidance. The Commission has also published a guidance on its website entitled "Standards for Pharmacist/Pharmacies Compounding Drug Products," which largely reiterate WAC 246-878.[369] As of January 2017, no proposed rules relating to compounding are listed on the Commission website.

PRESCRIPTION DRUG SAMPLES

The PRESCRIPTION DRUG MARKETING ACT (PDMA) placed restrictions on the distribution of drug samples by manufacturers. In essence, the law requires that samples of legend drugs be distributed only to authorized prescribers pursuant to a request by the receiving prescriber. Written records must be retained by manufacturers' representatives of the samples they have distributed.

DISTRIBUTION OF SAMPLES BY HOSPITAL PHARMACIES OR AT DIRECTION OF PRESCRIBER. Section 503(d)(1) of the act states that, for purposes of this subsection, the term "distribute" does not include the providing of a drug sample to a patient by a practitioner licensed to prescribe such drug, by a health care professional acting at the direction and under the supervision of such a practitioner, or the pharmacy of a hospital or of another health care entity acting at the direction of such a practitioner who received the drug sample in accordance with the act and regulations.

FDA GUIDANCE FOR INDUSTRY ON DISTRIBUTION OF SAMPLES TO "FREE CLINICS." The FDA adopted regulations in 1999 to allow samples to be distributed to a charitable organization, which is defined as "a nonprofit hospital, health care entity, organization, institution, foundation, association, or corporation" which has received exemption under section 501(c)(3) of the Internal Revenue Code. Included in these proposed regulations were the requirements that such samples must be inspected by a licensed practitioner or registered pharmacist, and drug sample receipt and distribution records must be kept by the institution for a minimum of 3 years. (21 CFR 203.39) Numerous free clinics asserted that these regulations were overly burdensome, and a study of the matter commissioned by the FDA found that clinics with total revenues under $200,000 per year were, in fact, over burdened by the rules. While awaiting rulemaking to revise the regulations, the FDA adopted a "Guidance for Industry"[370] on samples in free clinics in March 2006. The guidance indicates that the FDA will exercise enforcement discretion when free clinics are not in full compliance with sections of the regulations related to receipt, disposal, and record keeping.

GUIDANCE REQUIREMENTS FOR FREE CLINICS. However, the clinics are expected to comply with certain requirements, including

- The sample must be received in its original unopened container with intact labeling.
- The sample may not be distributed or administered to a patient unless it has been inspected by a licensed practitioner or registered pharmacist to assure it is not adulterated or misbranded. The FDA will allow registered pharmacist or licensed practitioner to designate a staff member of the clinic to perform the inspection.
- The clinic must store samples properly to assure they do not become adulterated or misbranded.

- The clinic shall notify the FDA within 5 days if it becomes aware of known theft or significant loss of drug samples from the clinic.

WASHINGTON RESTRICTIONS ON SAMPLES. The Washington statute corresponding to federal law is RCW 69.45.050:

- Drug samples are defined as "any ... products requiring prescriptions in this state, which [are] distributed at no charge to a practitioner by a manufacturer or a manufacturer's representative ..."
- Drug samples may be distributed only to authorized prescribers, or, at their request, to a hospital pharmacy or health care facility.
- The written request shall contain:
  - The name and address of the receiving practitioner, and professional designation.
  - Name, strength, and quantity of samples delivered.
  - Name of manufacturer and individual delivering the samples.
  - Dated signature of practitioner requesting the sample.
- No fee or charge may be imposed for distribution of samples within this state.
- Manufacturers' representatives may only possess sample drugs distributed by the manufacturer they represent. This does not preclude any individual from possessing drug samples that have been prescribed for that individual.

LABELING ON SAMPLES DISPENSED BY PRESCRIBERS. As noted earlier in this chapter, the Legend Drug Act requires that practitioners who dispense samples to patients must label the sample package with the name of the patient and the name of the prescriber. (RCW 69.41.050(1))

The Pharmacy Commission has promulgated a parallel regulation in WAC 246-877-020:

- The possession, distribution, or dispensing of legend drug samples by a pharmacy is prohibited.
- This does not apply to any pharmacy of a licensed hospital or health care entity which has received samples by the direction of an authorized prescriber as specified in RCW 69.045.050.
- A health care entity under this rule is one that does not include a retail pharmacy licensed under state law.

IMPACT OF RCW 69.70. It appears now that RCW 69.70, the 2013 statute dealing with donations of drugs and distribution of donated drugs by community pharmacies, has overturned any general prohibition on the possession of samples in community pharmacies. The statute clearly allows community pharmacies to receive donated drug supplies from drug manufacturers, and does not exclude drugs in packages marked "sample." Because these drugs are "donated" they are clearly distributed at no charge. The chapter includes a section stating that "nothing in this chapter restricts the use of samples by a practitioner during the course of a practitioner's duties at a medical facility or pharmacy." As long as the pharmacy is obtaining these samples for distribution pursuant to a prescription in accordance with the terms of the statute, the community pharmacy cannot be summarily prohibited from possessing samples.

Furthermore, pharmacists with CDTAs are now "practitioners" under the legend drug law, and are entitled to receive samples of drugs they would be authorized to prescribe under the CDTA.

For the requirements relating to donated drugs in community pharmacies, see the discussion in Chapter 3.

ACCOMMODATION SALES AND TRANSFERS TO OTHER PRACTITIONERS

ACCOMMODATION SALES. There is a long tradition of pharmacists loaning or borrowing drugs – or purchasing them outright – from other pharmacists to meet urgent needs. These exchanges are often called "accommodation sales," and are generally excluded from the definitions of either wholesale or retail sales. As a result, these sales or trades are not subject to wholesale or retail sales taxes, or to business and occupation taxes.

TRANSFERS TO OTHER PRACTITIONERS. Pharmacists may also sell legend drugs directly to authorized practitioners (see Table 4-3) for use in their practices, but those sales are subject to applicable taxes. In addition, sales to pharmacists or other practitioners do not require the pharmacist who is providing the drug to register as a wholesaler if they do not constitute more than 5% of total sales as measured during any 12 consecutive months (WAC 246-879-010(10)(e)). However, the receiving practitioner is also limited to no more than 5% of his or her purchases coming from a given pharmacy.

Pharmacies may also sell legend drugs to certain other individuals for use in their practice or occupation. The following is a partial list, and other individuals may assert a right to purchase legend drugs, subject to verification (e.g., with the Pharmacy Commission). As noted in Chapter 3, the Pharmacy Commission has recently emphasized that transfers to other practitioners must be to meet an "emergency need," and should not be a routine – only a wholesaler can routinely sell drugs to practitioners. In general, these occasional sales are recorded on an invoice, not a prescription (see also chapter 5).

ANIMAL CONTROL AGENCIES and humane societies may purchase drugs in accordance with Commission rules.[371]

MASTERS OF OCEAN-GOING VESSELS (i.e., ship captains and/or first officers) may purchase legend drugs and controlled substances to be used in case of an emergency. To purchase controlled substances, the master must appear in person at the pharmacy, and the pharmacy must maintain a record of "Sale of Controlled Substances to Vessels."[372] There is nothing specific in the FDCA about use of prescription drugs on vessels, but the FDA only suggests that "the pharmacist ... supplying prescription drugs for use on ships should exercise reasonable care and assure themselves that the prescription drugs are in fact going to a ship's medicine chest and are not being diverted to improper channels."[373]

TEACHING INSTITUTIONS may register with the DEA to order and use controlled substances in research and/or instruction. A separate application is used for teaching and for research. Individual teachers do not need to register, but use the institution's DEA number when ordering products, which may be supplied by a community pharmacy in accordance with the rules for distribution to other registrants. The educational institution[374] and individual researchers must also register with the Board of Pharmacy. (See Chapter 5).

REPACKAGING IS MISBRANDING. However, the long-accepted practice of pharmacists repackaging or relabeling drugs that are loaned, borrowed, or sold to other practitioners is unacceptable under the FDCA or most state laws unless the repackaged product has all of the required labeling. Incomplete relabeling renders the product misbranded.

In order to avoid creating a misbranded product, PHARMACISTS SHOULD LOAN, BORROW, SELL, OR TRADE PRODUCTS WITH OTHER PHARMACIES OR PRACTITIONERS ONLY IN THE MANUFACTURER'S ORIGINAL PACKAGE WITH ALL OF THE ACCOMPANYING LABELING, INCLUDING THE PACKAGE INSERT.

Distribution of legend drugs to other pharmacists or practitioners must be documented in the pharmacy's records; this is done by preparing an invoice and retaining a copy. (See Chapter 5 for requirements related to sales of controlled substances to other registrants.) Pedigrees may need to be provided for certain transfers (see below).

When the drugs in question are purchased at a special price (e.g., by hospitals, or pharmacies eligible for 340B pricing), they may not be resold to any entity that is not eligible for the same pricing. To do so places the seller in possible violation of federal antitrust laws, or, in the case of 340B drugs, federal fraud statutes. In emergencies, these drugs may only be loaned, and the borrower must repay with the same quantity of the same drug product.

DRUG SUPPLY CHAIN INTEGRITY

THE DRUG SUPPLY CHAIN is generally thought of as the series of individuals or firms who engage in the distribution of a drug from the point of manufacture of the active pharmaceutical ingredient (API) to the point of receipt of the finished dosage form by the ultimate user. It consists of a complex array of chemical manufacturers, drug product manufacturers, repackagers, wholesalers, pharmacies, hospitals, clinics, and reverse distributors. Particularly since 2004, there has been increased concern about the integrity of the US drug supply chain and ways to protect it from counterfeit, subpotent, adulterated, or expired drug products.

THE PRESCRIPTION DRUG MARKETING ACT OF 1987 was one of the first attempts to minimize the presence of counterfeit drugs in the US. It was amended in 1992 by the Prescription Drug Act. It required in part that certain wholesalers or redistributors provide a statement, also known as the drug's PEDIGREE, prior to each wholesale delivery or sale of prescription drugs. The Act excludes the drug's manufacturer, and "authorized distributors of record (ADR)," from the pedigree requirement. An "authorized distributor" must have an "ongoing relationship" with the manufacturer. In 1999, the FDA published proposed rules defining "ongoing relationship," but delayed enforcement of these rules as a result of concerns raised by affected companies. In 2006, these rules were finally enforced, and the FDA published a "guidance," to answer questions concerning the implementation of these rules.[375] Issues of particular interest to pharmacists include:

Pharmacists should be able to find list of ADRs for a particular product or manufacturer on the manufacturer's website.[376]

Non-ADRs must supply pedigrees to physicians' offices.

A pharmacy transferring a drug to another pharmacy will have to provide a pedigree for that drug except for

- Intra-company transfers
- Transfers for a documented medical emergency to another pharmacy
- Sale of minimal quantities by retail pharmacies to licensed practitioners for office use
- Chain pharmacy warehouses do not need to supply a pedigree for transfers to its own retail outlets

VERIFICATION OF PEDIGREES. Pharmacies are not expressly required to verify the accuracy or authenticity of a pedigree under the PDMA, but according to FDA, "they are encouraged to perform due diligence in verifying the accuracy of the information and integrity of the source of the drug product."

RETENTION OF PEDIGREES. Pedigrees must be retained by all wholesale distributors involved in the distribution of the drug product for 3 years. "If the pharmacy receiving the pedigree will not itself engage in further distribution of the product to persons other than a consumer or a patient, then the pharmacy is not required to maintain that pedigree ... However, consistent with the PDMA, FDA encourages pharmacies and other end users to retain the pedigree for 3 years."

PEDIGREES WHEN RETURNING DRUGS. Pharmacies and physician's offices are technically required to provide a pedigree when they return drugs to a wholesaler. However, finding that this would be very hard for pharmacies to do, particularly when they purchased the drug from an ADR in the first place, the FDA will exercise discretion when enforcing this provision:

> Pharmacies and physician's offices may return drugs that are expired, damaged, recalled, or in some other non-salable condition without having to provide a pedigree, providing they return the drug to the wholesaler or manufacturer from whom they purchased the drugs, or to a licensed reverse distributor for destruction, and maintain for 3 years a record that documents "each return and the source from which [they] originally purchased the drugs."

Returns from hospitals, health care entities, and charitable institutions are excluded from the definition of wholesale distribution, so they would not normally need to provide a pedigree.

SALE OR PURCHASE OF A PHARMACY. "The purchase of a pharmacy by another pharmacy would not be considered wholesale distribution, provided that the drugs purchased by the second pharmacy are dispensed or distributed by that pharmacy in the normal practice of retail pharmacy." However, pedigrees retained by the first pharmacy as part of its inventory records should be provided and retained for the remaining retention period by the purchasing pharmacy.

STATE PEDIGREE LAWS. As of January 2011, all but 20 states had some form of distributor licensing statute with pedigree requirements that went beyond the requirements of the PDMA. These state-level greater requirements were preempted starting in 2015 by the Drug Quality and Security Act (see below).

STANDARDS AND TECHNOLOGIES FOR IDENTIFYING, VALIDATING, AUTHENTICATING, TRACKING, AND TRACING OF PRESCRIPTION DRUGS. The FDAAA (see above) requires FDA to develop standards and validate effective technologies to secure the drugs supply chain. The Act requires the establishment of a standard numerical identifier (SNI) to be used for tracing and identifying the drug, as well as investigation of technologies, such as radio-frequency identification (RFID) to help track and validate a drug's identity.

SERIALIZED NATIONAL DRUG CODE (SNDC). In March 2010, FDA published a guidance for industry indicating that the package-level SNI for most prescription drugs should be the "serialized NDC," consisting of the NDC followed by a unique serial number for each package of the drug.[377] The serial number can contain up to 20 characters. The FDA believes this sNDC should be in both machine-readable and human-readable format. Ultimately, pharmacies should be able to scan an sNDI and obtain information about the production date, expiration date, and prior transfers of the individual package from a national database.

Certain prescription drugs, such a blood products, do not use NDCs; the FDA recommends use of a system known as ISBT 128 for determining the SNI for this type of product.

DRUG QUALITY AND SECURITY ACT OF 2013. Title II of the DQSA enacted the "Drug Supply Chain Security Act of 2013," (DSCSA) which puts the US on a 10-year track to develop a fully interoperable electronic drug track and trace system. The track and trace system will ultimately incorporate the elements, such as a sNDC, described above in the final system. In the interim, pharmacies need to meet the first set of deadlines that apply to dispensers.[378]

DOCUMENTATION OF DISTRIBUTED DRUGS' AUTHENTICITY. Starting in 2014, 3 types of documentation regarding a drug product became essential to lawful distribution of the drug from manufacturer to wholesaler to pharmacy:

TRANSACTION HISTORY – a statement in paper or electronic form that includes the transaction information for each prior transaction going back to the manufacturer of the product.

TRANSACTION INFORMATION – information concerning the product transferred during a given sale, which includes:

- The propriety or established name or names of the drug
- Strength and dosage form
- NDC number
- Container size
- Number of containers
- Lot number of the product
- Date of transaction
- Date of shipment, if more than 24 hours after the transaction date
- Business name and address of the person from whom the ownership is being transferred
- Business name and address of the person to whom ownership is being transferred

TRANSACTION STATEMENT – a statement in paper or electronic form that the entity transferring ownership in a transaction

- Is authorized under the DSCSA;
- Received the product from a person that is authorized as required under the DSCSA;
- Received transaction information and a transaction statement from the prior owner of the product;
- Did not knowingly ship a suspect or illegitimate product;
- Had systems and processes in place to comply with verification requirements under § 582;
- Did not knowingly provide false transaction information; and
- Did not knowingly alter the transaction history

PHARMACIES' RESPONSIBILITIES. Dispensers (pharmacies) must fulfill the following responsibilities, which apply to hospitals, chain pharmacies, independent pharmacies, and other dispensers:

- Dispensers may not accept ownership of a product unless the prior owner provides a transaction history, transaction information, and a transaction statement.
- Dispensers must maintain transaction histories, information, and statements for 6 years "as necessary to investigate a suspect product."
- Dispensers transferring products to other owners must provide a transaction history, information and statement to the subsequent owner, except for:
    - Returns of a saleable product to a trading partner from whom it was obtained
    - Returns of a non-saleable product to a manufacturer, wholesaler, or returns processor
    - Dispensing to a patient
    - Accommodation sales to other pharmacies or physicians
- Dispensers must have in place systems to quarantine, investigate and notify the Secretary of cleared suspect products.

- Dispensers must have a means for assisting in the disposal and analysis of illegitimate products and for notifications within 24 hours to the Secretary and trading partners of discovery of illegitimate products.
- Notifications to FDA are made using Form 3911; findable by "Googling" "FDA Form 3911."

TIME LINE IN 2017 AND AFTER. Future events in the DSCSA implementation timeline that affect pharmacies will include the following:

2017 – A 2-dimensional (2D) bar code with the unique serialized NDC will be required on each drug package. Pharmacies will be able (but not required) to check these numbers and verify the product's authenticity.

2020 – Pharmacies will only be allowed to purchase bar coded, serialized products, and must verify the serial numbers of a certain percentage of suspect medicines when "conducting investigations into products that appear potentially compromised or unsafe."

2023 – Pharmacies must participate in a fully electronic traceability system that uses the serialized NDCs to help detect illegitimate products.

IMPORTATION OF DRUGS FROM OUTSIDE OF THE UNITED STATES

Because other countries, particularly Canada, have regulatory systems that control the prices charged for prescription drugs, and for other marketing reasons, US-made brand name drugs sell for less outside of the United States than the same products do in the US. Manufacturers cite many reasons for this, not the least of which includes the regulatory costs associated with marketing drugs in the US, as well as other facets of the US economic system that justify different pricing strategies. Critics of the cost of drugs have suggested a fairly simple solution: allow US citizens to purchase drugs from other countries at the lower prices. Practical objections to this proposal include real questions about the ability of a small nation like Canada to be able to meet the needs of the US, and about the ability of the US to regulate drugs that may be shipped from Canada, for example, as a "way station" from China or other sources.

FDCA PROHIBITIONS ON IMPORTATION. At any rate, the major current impediment to the plan is the Food, Drug, and Cosmetic Act, which prevents such importation. The FDA has cited 3 major legal and regulatory bases for denying the importation of drugs from other countries:

NO DRUG MAY BE IMPORTED INTO THE US EXCEPT BY A FIRM REGISTERED WITH THE FDA, and the particular drug product must be an approved drug with a current NDA.

ONLY US LICENSED DRUG FIRMS MAY REIMPORT US-MADE FDA-APPROVED DRUGS into the US for marketing and distribution within the US (21 U.S.C. § 381(d)(1)).

DRUGS IMPORTED FROM OUTSIDE THE US MAY ALSO VIOLATE THE FDCA FOR OTHER REASONS. They may be:

- Unapproved (21 U.S.C. § 355)
- Labeled incorrectly (21 U.S.C. § 353(b)(2)), and/or
- Dispensed without a valid prescription (21 U.S.C. § 353(b)(1))

PERSONAL TRANSPORT OF PRESCRIBED DRUGS. The FDA has adopted as a regulatory policy[379] that it will not generally take action against individuals who bring small amounts of drugs (generally not more than a 3-month supply) into the US from abroad (especially Canada) for THEIR PERSONAL USE AS PRESCRIBED BY THEIR

PERSONAL PHYSICIAN. This was originally an enforcement policy, not a provision that legalized such importation. However, Congress has apparently given legal status to this policy in 2018 – see below.

NO PERSONAL TRANSPORT OF CONTROLLED SUBSTANCES. Neither the FDA nor the DEA will knowingly permit importation of CONTROLLED SUBSTANCES by individuals for their own use, and the 2018 changes do not legalize personal importation of controlled substances.

Congress passed legislation in 2002 (the Medicine Equity and Drug Safety (MEDS) Act), which was revised in 2003 by the Medicare Prescription Drug, Improvement and Modernization Act (MMA) that modified the FDCA to potentially allow for reimportation of US-made FDA-approved drugs from Canada by pharmacists, wholesalers, and individuals. This ONLY BECOMES EFFECTIVE FOLLOWING A CERTIFICATION from the Secretary of Health and Human Services that implementation of these programs would (1) pose no additional risk to public health and safety, and (2) result in a significant reduction in the cost of drugs to the American consumer (21 USC § 384). An HHS Task Force on Drug Importation issued a report to Congress (required by the MMA) in December 2004 that essentially concluded that reimportation would pose significant risks and would not result in a correspondingly significant reduction in drug costs to American consumers. Two HHS Secretaries have declined to provide the certification provided for by either the MEDS Act or the MMA.

DEPARTMENT OF HOMELAND SECURITY PROHIBITED FROM PREVENTING INDIVIDUALS FROM BRINGING IN 90-DAY PERSONAL SUPPLIES OF DRUGS FROM CANADA. Congress in 2006 adopted §535 of the Homeland Security Appropriations Act (PL 109-295) which provides that US Customs and Border Protection may not use appropriated funds for the purpose of preventing individual patients from bringing up to a 90-day personal supply of FDA-approved drugs into the US from Canada. This provision does not apply to biological products or controlled substances.

IMPORTATION OF DRUGS FOR PERSONAL OR HOUSEHOLD USE DECRIMINALIZED BY CONGRESS IN 2018. The 2018 Opioid statute (H.R. 6 – SUPPORT for Patients and Communities Act of 2018)[380] includes a provision that defines illegal importation to exclude "import[ing] ... a drug ... in an amount that is inconsistent with personal or household use of the importer."[381] This applies to drugs under the FDCA, but not to controlled substances as defined by the CSA.

STATE WAIVER REQUESTS. Numerous state and local governments have requested waivers from the FDA to allow various schemes for importing drugs from Canada. The FDA has routinely denied these waiver requests from a wide variety of states including Oregon, California, Nevada, Texas, Minnesota, Illinois, New Hampshire, and Wisconsin. Of particular interest is the denial of the request for a waiver from Montgomery County, Maryland, the county in which the FDA's Headquarters is located.

A 2004 request from Vermont was denied by the FDA, and Vermont filed suit to compel approval of their request. In September 2005, the federal district court for the District of Vermont dismissed the Vermont lawsuit and affirmed the FDA's position that, as a matter of law, granting the waiver is prohibited by the FDCA. (*State of Vermont v. Leavitt*, 405 F. Supp. 2d 466 (D. Vt., 2005)).

WASHINGTON IMPORTATION WAIVER REQUEST. The Washington request for a waiver to allow for the licensing of Canadian pharmacies as Non-resident Pharmacies in Washington, and for the licensing of Canadian wholesalers, was denied by FDA on March 17, 2006.

MAINE STATUTE. In 2013 the State of Maine passed legislation that removed restrictions in the state's pharmacy practice act against sales of drugs from outside the US to Maine citizens by foreign pharmacies, and foreign pharmacies are shipping drugs into the state under the law. According to press reports, shipments are coming not only from Canada and Great Britain, but from other nations as well – mostly via Internet sales. The statute is being challenged in state court, but it has stimulated introduction of legislation in Congress to modify the FDCA to allow importation under state laws.

In January 2015, the FDA began refusing shipments of prescription drugs into Maine from Great Britain, and, while it doesn't typically take action against individuals, it can take action against companies such as FedEx or UPS to require them to embargo shipments until the FDA has cleared them. A press report described how a Maine citizen paid for drugs from Great Britain, only to have them denied entry by the FDA.[382]

In February 2015, a federal district court judge struck down the Maine statute as being preempted by the requirements of the FDCA. [383]

Appendix 4A: Example Request for Non-Child Resistant Container

Request to Dispense Prescription Medication in **Non-child-resistant** Container and Release, Hold Harmless and Agreement to Indemnify

I understand that all prescription medications are required to be dispensed in a child-resistant container unless the patient or the patient's agent authorizes the pharmacist to dispense the medication in a regular (non-child-resistant) container.

I certify that I am the patient or the patient's authorized representative and agent and that I request that all medications, now and in the future, for the below-named patient be dispensed in a non-child-resistant container.

I understand that **prescription medications may be dangerous, especially to children**, and **that use of a regular (non-child-resistant) container increases the risk that a child may gain access to the medicine** in the container. I understand that this may cause serious injury or even death to a child or other person gaining access to this medication.

I acknowledge that the pharmacist and the pharmacy have offered to provide additional training to me or the patient on how to use child-resistant containers, and have offered to provide alternative types of containers at a nominal fee that will are designed for persons with arthritis or other conditions to make them easier to open.

I hereby release the pharmacist and the pharmacy from all liability which may be caused by the lack of a child-resistant container for any medications for the below-named patient.

I hereby agree to hold harmless and indemnify the pharmacy and its agents and pharmacists from any loss or damage to any and all third parties, including children and their relatives, which may result, in whole or in part, from the lack of a child-resistant container for any medications for the below-named patient which have been dispensed in a regular (non-child-resistant) container as authorized and requested in this Release, Hold Harmless and Agreement to Indemnify.

Dated this ______________day of ________20_____.

____

Patient

____

Authorized Agent of Patient

(Adapted by William E. Fassett, Ph.D., R.Ph., for instructional purposes only, from a form developed by Craig A. Ritchie, R.Ph., J.D., Sequim, WA. No recommendation is made respecting the use of this form, nor is any warranty of its fitness for a particular situation made, express or implied. All responsibility for the utility or applicability of this form is expressly disclaimed. Pharmacists should consult an attorney for advice on the applicability of this or any other form to their particular circumstances.)

Appendix 4B: Sample Compounding Workup Form

ABC Pharmacy **Extemporaneously Compounded Dosage Forms** **Patient Care Workup**		
Patient:	DOB:	SSN:
Address:	Gender:	Carrier:
Phone:	Formula #	Plan:
Prescriber:	Associated Rx #	
Allergies:		
Medical Conditions:		

Prescriber agreement to use a compounded alternative to the marketed product was
□ obtained by the pharmacist in consultation with the prescriber on ____/____/____
□ indicated on the prescription □ not applicable Pharmacist Initials: ________

Problem	**Objective**	**Indicators**
1.		
2.		

Marketed product alternative:

Reason why marketed product is undesirable:

Extemporaneously compounded alternative:

Rationale for use or evidence of effectiveness:

Planned Follow Up

Date	**Comments**	**Next Follow Up**

Patient Certification

I understand that the extemporaneously compounded alternative indicated above is to be prepared specifically for my use to meet my medical needs as determined by me and my prescriber. I have received information from my prescriber and pharmacist concerning the purpose and effects of this product. I understand that it is not an FDA-approved dosage form. I have requested this product because I believe it represents the best alternative to me at the present time.

Patient Signature ______________________________ Date ____________

Note: This example is for instructional purposes only. This should be reviewed with an attorney to determine the applicability to any particular setting.

REFERENCES

[185] http://www.fda.gov
[186] http://www4.law.cornell.edu/uscode/html/uscode21/usc_sup_01_21_10_9.html
[187] http://www.fda.gov/oc/history/default.htm
[188] Although claims made by the manufacturer's representative about a drug may render the product misbranded, a 2012 decision by the 2nd Circuit Court of Appeals overturned a criminal conviction of a sales representative for making off-label claims. See below concerning off-label uses of drugs. U.S. v. Caronia, No. 09-5006-cr, 2nd Cir., 703 F.3d 149, December 3, 2012.
[189] Lamb, Ruth deForest. *American Chamber of Horrors; the Truth about Food and Drugs*. New York: Farrar & Rinehart; 1936.
[190] http://en.wikipedia.org/wiki/Elixir_Sulfanilamide
[191] Unlike the USP, which has officially adopted the modern spelling of pharmacopeia, the HPUS retains the older spelling, including the older form of "homoeopathic;" on its website it even uses the ligature, i.e., "Homœopathic Pharmacopœia"
[192] USDHHS, FDA. Zicam Fact Sheet, June 16, 2009; http://www.fda.gov/Drugs/DrugSafety/ucm166927.htm
[193] Named for the statute's sponsors, both of whom were pharmacists: Representative Carl Durham (D-NC) and Senator (and later Vice-President) Hubert Humphrey Jr (D-MN).
[194] Also known as the Drug Efficacy Amendment, named for its sponsors, Sen. Estes Kefauver (D-TN) and Rep. Oren Harris (D-AR).
[195]http://en.wikipedia.org/wiki/Thalidomide#cite_note-Bren-76
[196] Hecht A. A long reach back to assure drug quality - Drug Efficacy Study Implementation program. FDA Consumer 1984 Dec.
[197] The chapter headings for the 1st edition of APhA's *Handbook of Nonprescription Drugs* were largely drawn from the monograph categories used by the OTC review panels.
[198] Approved Drug Products with Therapeutic Evaluations, 34th Ed. USDHHS, FDA, CDER 2014; iv.
[199]http://www.fda.gov/downloads/Drugs/GuidanceComplianceRegulatoryInformation/Guidances/ucm070290.pdf, accessed 1/31/17
[200]http://www.fda.gov/Drugs/GuidanceComplianceRegulatoryInformation/EnforcementActivitiesbyFDA/SelectedEnforcementActionsonUnapprovedDrugs/ucm238675.htm, accessed 1/23/15.
[201] http://en.wikipedia.org/wiki/KV_Pharmaceutical, accessed 1/23/15.
[202] As of January 2014, K-V Pharmaceutical was maintaining an action in federal court seeking to force FDA to take action to remove pharmacy-compounded hydroxyprogesterone caproate products from the market. *K-V Pharm. Co. v. United States FDA*, No. 12-5349, D.C. Cir., 2014 U.S. App. LEXIS 670, January 7, 2014.
[203] http://supct.law.cornell.edu/supct/html/01-344.ZS.html
[204] *Medical Center Pharmacy et al. v. Mukasey,* Case No. 06-51583, 5th Cir., July 18, 2008.
[205] Pub. L. 110-85.
[206]https://www.accessdata.fda.gov/scripts/cder/rems/index.cfm
[207] https://www.ipledgeprogram.com/
[208] See, e.g., *Alexis v. GlaxoSmithKline*, 2002 U.S. Dist. LEXIS 9654 (E.D. La., 2002), *Stanley v. Wyeth,* 2006 U.S. Dist. LEXIS 64037 (E.D. La., 2006)
[209] Pub. L. 112-144, 126 Stat. 993 (2012)
[210] H.R. 2430, Pub. L. 115-52, 8/8/17.
[211] http://en.wikipedia.org/wiki/New_England_Compounding_Center_meningitis_outbreak, accessed 2/24/14.
[212] Pub. L. 113-54.
[213] Pub. L. 114-146.
[214] 42 U.S.C. chapter 6A.
[215] 72 Fed Reg 56769, October 4, 2007.
[216] ACP Statement to Commissioner Eschenbach, November 12, 2007; http://www.acponline.org/hpp/eschenbach.pdf, accessed 12/31/07.
[217] 72 Fed Reg 66180, November 27, 2007.
[218] Pray WS, Pray GE. Behind-the-counter products: a third class of drugs. U.S. Pharm. 2011;36(9): 11-15.
[219] http://www.fda.gov/drugs/newsevents/ucm289290.htm
[220] 70 Fed Reg 40232, July 13, 2005.
[221] Title VII, Subtitle A, Patient Protection and Affordable Care Act, Pub. L. 111-148 §§7001-03, 124 Stat. 119 (2010).

[222] http://www.fda.gov/downloads/Drugs/GuidanceComplianceRegulatoryInformation/Guidances/UCM459987.pdf
[223] 2015 c 242
[224] Note that dilute acids and bases are generally expressed in w/v concentrations, whereas concentrated acids, such as 38% HCl are expressed as w/w.
[225] Anhydrous acetic acid (e.g., 100% w/w) is also commonly called "Glacial Acetic Acid"
[226] With the replacement of strychnine as a rodenticide by warfarin-based products, there are now no pharmacies in WA who have obtained a poison distributor license. When strychnine was used as a rodenticide, its sale was limited to pharmacies under RCW 16.52.193. According to Board of Pharmacy staff in January 2009, a handful of distributors are licensed and the most common purpose is for the distribution of cyanide to be used in gold mining.
[227] 2013 c 3; most of I-502's substantive provisions are to be found in RCW 69.50.325 - .369
[228] H.R. 34, §§ 3001, 3021, 3022.
[229] http://www.fda.gov/Drugs/InformationOnDrugs/ucm075234.htm#chemtype_reviewclass
[230] The equivalent Washington statutes were revised in 2009 to use "human beings" wherever "man" was stated. 2009 c 549.
[231] H.R. 2751, Pub. L. 111-353
[232] http://www.fda.gov/Cosmetics/ResourcesForYou/Consumers/CosmeticsQA/ucm136560.htm
[233] 21 CFR Parts 710 and 720 (http://www.fda.gov/Cosmetics/GuidanceComplianceRegulatoryInformation/VoluntaryCosmeticsRegistrationProgramVCRP/default.htm
[234] 2009 c 549.
[235] http://www1.umn.edu/scitech/dalkfina.htm
[236] http://www4.law.cornell.edu/uscode/21/360c.html
[237] Pub. L. 100-578
[238] https://www.cms.gov/Regulations-and-Guidance/Legislation/CLIA/index.html
[239] http://www.doh.wa.gov/LicensesPermitsandCertificates/FacilitiesNewReneworUpdate/LaboratoryQualityAssurance/Licensing/Applications
[240] http://www.doh.wa.gov/CommunityandEnvironment/Contaminants/Mercury.aspx
[241] http://www.ecy.wa.gov/mercury/mercury_containing_products.html
[242] http://www.fda.gov/cvm/default.html
[243] http://www.accessdata.fda.gov/scripts/animaldrugsatfda/
[244] U.S. v. Franck's Lab, No. 5:10-cv-147-Oc-32TBS, M.D. Fla. Ocala Div., September 12, 2011.
[245] Karst KR, Gibbs JN. The end of the road: Franck's compounding case is moot. FDA Law Blog 2012 Oct 16; http://www.fdalawblog.net/fda_law_blog_hyman_phelps/2012/10/the-end-of-the-road-francks-compounding-case-is-moot.html
[246] https://www.fda.gov/AnimalVeterinary/ResourcesforYou/ucm268128.htm#compounding, accessed 1/28/19.
[247] http://www.fda.gov/Drugs/ResourcesForYou/Consumers/ucm143551.htm
[248] The Washington Pharmacy Commission once charged a pharmacist with violating these requirements when a European herbal product, "Doktor Mom," which is labeled in Ukrainian but with ingredients described using Linnaean nomenclature, was sold to a Russian-speaking consumer allegedly without any supplemental labeling in English.
[249] http://www.cpsc.gov//PageFiles/114277/384.pdf
[250] Pub. L. 114-116.
[251] 70 Fed Reg 40232, July 13, 2005.
[252] Federal Trade Commission. Enforcement policy statement on marketing claims for OTC homeopathic drugs. 81 Fed. Reg. 90122-90123, December 13, 2016.
[253] *Center for Inquiry, Inc. v. CVS Health Corp.,* D.C. Super. Ct.; complaint available at https://bit.ly/2B4fpsz.
[254] WSR 10-02-081, January 2010. [This rule is unchanged as of 1/22/15]
[255] http://www.accessamed.com
[256] https://www.walgreens.com/store/c/walgreens-talking-pill-reminder/ID=prod6211860-product
[257] Talking Prescription Labels: Spring 2016 Update. Law Office of Lainey Feingold; www.lflegal.com/2016/03/talking-label-2016update/
[258] See, e.g., Humana talking prescription label and accessible information settlement agreement. 2015 Sep 30; http://www.lflegal.com/2015/09/humana-agreement/
[259] http://www.fda.gov/Training/ForHealthProfessionals/ucm090590.htm
[260] Guidance for Industry: Warnings and Precautions, Contraindications, and Boxed Warning Sections of Labeling for Human Prescription Drug and Biological Products —

Content and Format. http://www.fda.gov/downloads/Drugs/GuidanceComplianceRegulatoryInformation/Guidances/ucm075096.pdf, October 2011.
[261] 79 Fed. Reg. 72063-72103, December 14, 2014.
[262] 21 CFR 208.24(e).
[263] USDHHS, FDA. Guidance: Medication Guides – Distribution requirements and inclusion in risk evaluation and mitigation strategies (REMS), 2011 Nov; http://www.fda.gov/downloads/Drugs/Guidances/UCM244570.pdf
[264] Washington State Department of Health, Nursing Care Quality Assurance Commission. Dispensing medications/devices for prophylactic and therapeutic treatment of communicable diseases and reproductive health by public health nurses. Advisory Opinion No. NCAO 9.0, November 18, 2016.
[265] Washington State Department of Health Publication No. 631-052, Naturopathic Scope of Practice Sunrise Review, December 2014.
[266] 2016 c 97
[267] The revision did not say "Pharmacy Commission" because the change from Board to Commission status was contained in a separate bill.
[268] Minutes and supporting documentation, Pharmacy Quality Assurance Commission, September 30, 2016.
[269] https://jcpp.net/patient-care-process/, accessed 1/25/17
[270] WSDOH, PQAC. Interim Guidance on Collaborative Drug Therapy, 2018 Dec.; https://www.doh.wa.gov/Portals/1/Documents/Pubs/690327.pdf
[271] This degree was offered in the US only for the 5-year baccalaureate program at Washington State University. It was formerly the entry-level degree for pharmacists offered in Australia, India, Ireland, and the United Kingdom.
[272] Board of Pharmacy meeting minutes, October 25, 2007, p. 5.
[273] Article No. 997, Washington State Board of Pharmacy Newsletter 2009 Apr; 30(4):4.
[274] http://www.cdc.gov/std/ept/default.htm
[275] http://www.doh.wa.gov/portals/1/Documents/Pubs/MD2008-03.pdf May 23, 2008.
[276] http://www.doh.wa.gov/Portals/1/Documents/Pubs/MD2008-03.pdf
[277]http://www.doh.wa.gov/YouandYourFamily/IllnessandDisease/SexuallyTransmittedDisease/ExpeditedPartnerTherapy/EPTPharmacies.aspx
[278] Article No. 972, Washington State Board of Pharmacy Newsletter. 2008 Jul;30(1):4.
[279] *Kadambi et al. v. Express Scripts, Inc. et al.* No. 1:13-CV-321 JD, N.D. Ind., February 5, 2015]
[280] U.S. v. Caronia, 2nd Cir., 703 F.3d 149, December 3, 2012.
[281] U.S. Troop Readiness, Veteran's Care, Katrina Recovery and Iraq Accountability Appropriations Act of 2007, § 7002(b).
[282]http://www.cms.hhs.gov/FraudAbuseforProfs/Downloads/pharmacisfactsheet.pdf
[283] 2009 c 328 §1; RCW 18.64.500
[284] http://www.doh.wa.gov/portals/1/Documents/2300/ApprovalProcess.pdf
[285]https://www.doh.wa.gov/LicensesPermitsandCertificates/ProfessionsNewReneworUpdate/PharmacyCommission/TamperResistantPrescriptions
[286] WAC 246-869-020(7),(8)
[287] FDA. CPG § 460.425, Prescription Status when Telephoned to Recording Machine (CPG 7132b.08), October 1, 1980.
[288]http://www.doh.wa.gov/Portals/1/Documents/2300/BestPracticeGuidelines_For_VerbalPrescriptions.pdf
[289] https://www.jointcommission.org/assets/1/6/2019_AHC_NPSGs_final.pdf
[290] 2014 c 192 § 1.
[291] 2016 c 148 §17
[292]http://www.doh.wa.gov/LicensesPermitsandCertificates/ProfessionsNewReneworUpdate/PharmacyCommission/ElectronicRxTransmissionSystems
[293] Pub. L. 98-417; 21 USC 355(j)
[294] The Hatch-Waxman Act and New Legislation to Close Its Loopholes. http://www.cptech.org/ip/health/generic/hw.html, accessed 1/6/10.
[295] http://www.fda.gov/Drugs/InformationOnDrugs/ucm129662.htm
[296] Vivian J. Generic-substitution laws. US Pharm 2008;33(6)(Generic Drug Review):30-34; http://www.uspharmacist.com/content/t/generic_medications/c/9787/, accessed 2/5/13.
[297] USDHHS, FDA. Considerations in demonstrating interchangeability with a reference product: guidance for industry [draft guidance], 2017 Jan; http://www.fda.gov/downloads/Drugs/GuidanceComplianceRegulatoryInformation/Guidances/UCM537135.pdf
[298] 2015 c 242 §4

[299] Vivian J., *ibid.*
[300] See, e.g., *West Virginia v. Rite Aid of West Virginia, Inc.,* No. 2:09-0956, S.D. W.Va., remanded, 2/1/10; also, *State of Michigan ex rel. Gurganus v. CVS Caremark Corp. et al.; City of Lansing et al. v. Rite Aid of Michigan, Inc. et al.; City of Lansing v. CVS Caremark Corp., et al.*; Nos. 29997, 29998, 29999, Mich. App., 2013 Mich. App. LEXIS 113, January 22, 2013 (unpublished opinion).
[301] FDA Listing of Authorized Generics; https://www.fda.gov/AboutFDA/CentersOffices/OfficeofMedicalProductsandTobacco/CDER/ucm126391.htm
[302] http://www.hca.wa.gov/about-hca/prescription-drug-program
[303] http://www.hca.wa.gov/assets/billers-and-providers/ah-ffs-pdl-20170301.pdf
[304] In 2017, the committee chair is Michael Johnson, who holds both the PharmD and DO degrees.
[305] 2009 c 575
[306]https://www.modahealth.com/EndorsingPractitioner/faces/pages/public/practitionerSearch.xhtml
[307] 2015 c 85 §1
[308] Article No. 997, Washington State Board of Pharmacy Newsletter 2009 Apr; 30(4):4.
[309] Washington Department of Health, Nursing Care Quality Assurance Commission, Advisory Opinion No. NCAO 9.0, November 18, 2016.
[310] Thompson T. Prescription for error? Auto refills. News 4 Washington (DC) 2014 Feb 26; http://www.nbcwashington.com/news/local/Prescription-for-Error-Auto-Refills-247159401.html
[311] http://www.ncpanet.org/innovation-center/adherence-simplify-my-meds/simplify-my-meds/preview-of-simplify-my-meds-
[312] http://www.aphafoundation.org/appointment-based-model
[313] Schweers K. Medicare addresses mail order waste, refill synchronization for 2014. The Dose (NCPA), 2013 Oct 3; https://ncpanet.wordpress.com/2013/10/03/medicare-addresses-mail-order-waste-refill-synchronization-for-2014/
[314] In the Matter of the License to Practice Pharmacy of [S.E.], R.Ph., Stipulated Findings of Fact, Conclustions [sic] of Law, and Agreed Order, State of Washington, Department of Health, Board of Pharmacy, Docket No.04-08-A-1052PH, December 1, 2004.
[315] 2013 c 262 § 1
[316] Mecca A. "Prescription transfers," e-mail correspondence, 5/17/2006.
[317] https://www.doh.wa.gov/Portals/1/Documents/2300/2018/TransferUnfilledOnHoldRX.pdf
[318] Poison Prevention Packaging: a Guide for Health Professionals. http://www.cpsc.gov/cpscpub/pubs/384.pdf
[319] Baas v. Hoye, 766 F.2d 1190 (8th Cir., 1985)
[320] Grandparents! Prevent your grandchildren from being poisoned: Safety Alert!, CPSC Document #5041; http://www.cpsc.gov/cpscpub/pubs/5041.html (accessed 2011)
[321]https://www.doh.wa.gov/LicensesPermitsandCertificates/ProfessionsNewReneworUpdate/PharmacyCommission/GeneralPharmacyPracticeFAQs
[322] Article No. 961, Washington State Board of Pharmacy Newsletter 2008 Apr; 29(4):1.
[323] http://www.k12.wa.us/HealthServices/pubdocs/b034-01.pdf
[324] Pub. L. 113-48. School Access to Emergency Epinephrine Act of 2013.
[325] 2016 c 10 §1
[326] FDA. CPG Section 460.300, Return of Unused Prescription Drugs to Pharmacy Stock (CPG 7132.09), October 1, 1980.
[327] Washington Department of Health, Pharmacy Quality Assurance Commission, Secure and responsible drug disposal program; guidance document No. DOH 690-294, March 2016; http://www.doh.wa.gov/portals/1/Documents/Pubs/690294.pdf
[328] *Downing v. Hyland Pharmacy*, No. 20060771, Utah Supr. Ct., 194 P.3d 944, 2008.
[329] FDA. Compliance Policy Guide § 400.900, Class I Recalls of Prescription Drugs (CPG 7132.01), October 1, 1980 ;http://www.fda.gov/ICECI/ComplianceManuals/CompliancePolicyGuidanceManual/ucm074365.htm
[330] See, e.g., *Yarbrough et al. v. Actavis Totowa et al.,* No. 4:10-cv-129, S.D. Ga., 2010 US Dist. LEXIS 95127, Sept. 13, 2010.
[331] Prep staff on drug recalls before your next JCAHO survey. Accreditation Connection, 2004 Mar 8; http://www.hcpro.com/ACC-38144-851/Prep-staff-on-drug-recalls-before-your-next-JCAHO-survey.html
[332] http://www.fda.gov/drugs/drugsafety/ucm352085.htm
[333] http://www.fda.gov/drugs/drugsafety/ucm297391.htm
[334] http://www.fda.gov/Safety/MedWatch/
[335] FDA. Frequently Asked Questions About Drug Shortages, http://www.fda.gov/Drugs/DrugSafety/DrugShortages/ucm050796.htm#q1, accessed 1/30/17.
[336] http://www.fda.gov/Drugs/DrugSafety/DrugShortages/ucm050796.htm, accessed 1/30/17.

[337] http://www.ashp.org/menu/DrugShortages/CurrentShortages, accessed 1/30/17.
[338] Title X, FDASIA, Pub. L. 112-144 (2012).
[339] Fox E, Birt A, James KB, Kokko H, Salverson S, Soflin D. ASHP guidelines on managing drug product shortages in hospitals and health systems. Am J Health-syst Pharm. 2009;66:1399-406.
[340] Pub. L. 94-580; 42 U.S.C. § 6901 et seq.
[341] Pub. L. 98-616
[342] 33 U.S.C. § 1251 et seq.
[343] 73 Fed. Reg. 73520, December 2, 2008
[344] http://www.epa.gov/waste/hazard/generation/pharmaceuticals.htm, accessed 2/10/15
[345] https://www.epa.gov/hwgenerators/final-rule-hazardous-waste-generator-improvements#rule-summary
[346] http://www.ecy.wa.gov/pubs/0704024.pdf
[347] Pub. L. 111-273, October 12, 2010.
[348] DOJ, DEA. 21 CFR Parts 1300, 1301, 1304 et al. Disposal of controlled substances; final rule. 79 Fed. Reg. 53520, 2014 Sep 9.
[349] Pharmaceutical Research and Manufacturers of America et al., v. County of Alameda, California. Petition denied. No. 14-751, S.Ct., May 26, 2015.
[350] 2018 c 196; ESHB 1047, effective June 7, 2018.
[351] 2011 c 39; ESSB 5594
[352] Massoomi F. It's official, but what's next? USP 800 Safe Handling of Hazardous Drugs, 2016 Apr 19; visanteinc.com.
[353] Washington Department of Labor & Industries, Division of Occupational Safety & Health. DOSH Directive 13.20, 2013 Apr 10.
[354] USP. Compendial Notices: General Chapter <800> Hazardous Drugs – Handling in Health Care Settings; Notice of intent to revise; 2017 Sep 29; http://bit.ly/2DjVWXg
[355] *United States v Sene-X Eleemosynary Corp.,* 479 F.Supp. 970 (S.D. Fla. 1979), aff'd, 697 F.2d 1093 (11th Cir. 1983)
[356]http://www.fda.gov/downloads/Drugs/GuidanceComplianceRegulatoryInformation/Guidances/UCM175984.pdf
[357] www.fda.gov/ohrms/dockets/dockets/05p0411/BHRTletter.html
[358] http://www.fda.gov/downloads/ForConsumers/ConsumerUpdates/ucm049312.pdf
[359] Centers for Disease Control and Prevention, Multistate Fungal Meningitis Outbreak – Current Case Count, http://www.cdc.gov/hai/outbreaks/meningitis-facilities-map.html, accessed 2/5/15.
[360] Outterson K. Regulating compounding pharmacies after NECC. NEJM 2012;367(21):1969-72.
[361] APhA. American Pharmacists Association statement on rare meningitis outbreak. 2012 Oct 11; http://www.pharmacist.com/node/66241.
[362] USDHHS, FDA. Prescription requirements under section 503A of the Federal Food, Drug, and Cosmetic Act; Guidance for Industry, December 2016; http://www.fda.gov/downloads/Drugs/GuidanceComplianceRegulatoryInformation/Guidances/UCM496286.pdf
[363] http://www.fda.gov/Drugs/DrugSafety/ucm532474.htm
[364] Pharmacy Compounding Accreditation Board, Standard 7.30 Labeling; http://www.pcab.org/cms/wp-content/themes/pcab/img/PCAB-Accreditation-Manual.pdf
[365] 2013 c 46
[366] WSR 13-11-096
[367] WSR 18-21-147
[368] *Thompson et al. v. Western States Medical Center et al.,* 535 U.S. 357 (2002); in 2017 the Commission began an investigation of a pharmacy under this provision, but later withdrew all charges when the attorney for the pharmacy pointed out the Supreme Court ruling.
[369]http://www.doh.wa.gov/LicensesPermitsandCertificates/ProfessionsNewReneworUpdate/PharmacyCommission/PharmacyCompoundingStandards
[370] FDA. Guidance for Industry. Prescription Drug Marketing Act – Donation of Prescription Drug Samples to Free Clinics. March 2006 (Compliance). http://www.fda.gov/downloads/Drugs/GuidanceComplianceRegulatoryInformation/Guidances/ucm070317.pdf
[371] RCW 69.41.080; WAC 246-886
[372] 21 CFR § 1301.25; http://www.deadiversion.usdoj.gov/21cfr/cfr/1301/1301_25.htm
[373] FDA. Compliance Policy Guide § 460.500. Prescription Drugs for Ship's Medicine Chests (CPG 7132.11), October 1, 1980.
[374] WAC 246-887-200(2)
[375] FDA. Guidance for Industry – Prescription Drug Marketing Act (PDMA) Requirements: Questions and Answers, 2006 Nov.; http://www.fda.gov/downloads/Drugs/GuidanceComplianceRegulatoryInformation/Guidances/UCM134399.pdf

[376] See, e.g., Pfizer Authorized Distributors,
http://www.pfizer.com/products/hcp/pfizer_authorized_distributors.jsp#undefined
[377] FDA. Guidance for Industry – Standards for Securing the Drug Supply Chain – Standardized Numerical Identification for Prescription Drug Packages, 2010 March;
http://www.fda.gov/downloads/RegulatoryInformation/Guidances/UCM206075.pdf
[378] Fassett WE. Key January 1, 2015 deadline for pharmacies under the Drug Supply Chain Security Act. *Rx Ipsa Loquitur* 2013 (Nov/Dec); 6(3).
[379] FDA Regulatory Procedures Manual, Chapter 9, Part 2, March 2009.
http://www.fda.gov/downloads/ICECI/ComplianceManuals/RegulatoryProceduresManual/UCM074300.pdf
[380] Pub. L. 115-271, 10/24/18
[381] Pub. L. 115-271, §3022 b(5).
[382] Farwell J. Bangor man caught in conflict between Maine mail-order pharmacy laws, federal government. Bangor Daily News (online) 2015 Jan 20; http://bangordailynews.com/2015/01/20/health/bangor-man-caught-in-conflict-between-maine-mail-order-pharmacy-laws-federal-government/
[383] *Ouellette et al. v. Mills et al.,* No. 1:13-cv-00347-NT, D. Me., February 23, 2015

5 – CONTROLLED SUBSTANCES

STATUTORY SCHEMES FOR CONTROLLING SUBSTANCES OF ABUSE

> COMPETENCY AREAS IN THIS CHAPTER
>
> 2016 MPJE COMPETENCY STATEMENTS – Areas 1.1.1, 1.3.1, 1.3.2, 1.3.4, 1.3.5, 1.3.6, 1.4.1, 1.4.2, 1.4.3, 1.4.10, 1.4.11, 1.4.12, 1.4.14, 1.6.3, 1.7.1, 1.7.2, 2.1.1, 2.1.4, 2.2.1, 2.3.2, 3.1.1
>
> 2016 ACPE REQUIRED ELEMENTS – Pharmacy Law & Regulatory Affairs; Medication Dispensing, Distribution, and Dispensing; History of Pharmacy

EARLY FEDERAL INTEREST IN REGULATING NARCOTICS arose primarily from American dealings abroad. As a result of the Spanish-American War, the US acquired possession of the Philippines, which had a pre-existing system of licensing opium addicts. At the same time, Great Britain was attempting to deal with significant problems with opium trade from China. A US commission established to propose an alternative to the licensing system in the Philippines recommended that international control of opium trafficking was essential. In 1906 – the year of the passage of the US Pure Food and Drug Law – President Roosevelt called for an international conference on opium, which was held in Shanghai in 1909. A second conference in 1911 was held at The Hague, Netherlands, and the resulting Hague Convention became the first international compact governing narcotics. Congress passed the Harrison Narcotic Act in 1914 as a means of controlling narcotic distribution, and limiting its possession and use to medical purposes.

The scheme of the HARRISON ACT was similar to the scheme for controlling alcohol, and, later, marijuana – a federal tax was imposed on sales of narcotics, and each sold package had to bear a narcotics tax stamp. Dealing in narcotics which were not under this scheme became a tax law violation. As with alcohol, the "revenuers" (Department of Treasury agents) became the enforcers of narcotic control law. The Act remained the principal US controlled drug law until the 1960s.

In the 1960s, the law identified 4 categories of "narcotics": A, B, X, AND M. Class A narcotics required a written prescription that was not refillable. Class B narcotics could be telephoned. Classes X and M were "exempt narcotics" because no tax was collected on them. They could be dispensed pursuant to a telephoned prescription, and some forms could be sold OTC by pharmacists if the sales were recorded in a register.

The statute required the pharmacist who filled a prescription for a Class A narcotic to sign his name across the face of the filled prescription and indicate the date filled. Pharmacists often called this "cancelling" the prescription. Many pharmacists continue to sign their name on Schedule II drugs, but this is NOT a requirement of federal or Washington law, and very few states still require this.

NEW DRUGS OF ABUSE. The Harrison Act defined "narcotics" to include opiates and certain stimulants, including cocaine. However, the 1960s saw the development of newer drugs, not controlled by the Act, which were subject to abuse. Barbiturates, amphetamines, carbamates, and benzodiazepines were not covered. Non-medical agents, such as LSD, phencyclidine, and psilocybin, were likewise not controlled, except that their distribution was a violation of the FDCA.

With the repeal of Prohibition in 1933, many of the agents formerly in the Bureau of Prohibition were moved to the new FEDERAL BUREAU OF NARCOTICS, which was created in 1930 and placed under the direction of Harry Anslinger, former assistant director of the Bureau of Prohibition. Anslinger undertook a sustained campaign against marijuana, which previously had not been seen as a significant problem to the US government. In 1937, THE MARIHUANA TAX ACT was passed, classifying marijuana as a narcotic, and bringing it within the ambit of the FBN. The medical product, cannabis, became subject to federal narcotic control, at a tax rate of $1 per ounce for persons registered under the Act who would pay a special tax of $24 per year; largely removing it from the medical armamentarium because of cost, in spite of over 100 years of use by physicians in the US.

The average income of a US physician in 1933 was $3,600 (Paul Starr, *The Social Transformation of American Medicine*, New York: Basic Books, 1982, p. 270). In today's terms, an equivalent registration fee as a percentage of his or her annual income for a family physician to prescribe marijuana (distinct from the general narcotics registration) would be over $1,500.

The growth of substance misuse in the late 1950s and early 1960s led to adoption of a new international compact, the SINGLE CONVENTION ON NARCOTIC DRUGS,[384] in 1961, which incorporated controls on all psychoactive drugs of abuse, including narcotics, marijuana, stimulants, and psychedelic drugs. The United States ratified the Single Convention in 1967. The United Nations Economic and Social Council (ECOSOC) enforces the Single Convention through the Commission on Narcotic Drugs and the International Narcotics Control Board (INCB). The INCB is independent of ECOSOC, except that its members are elected by ECOSOC: 3 members from a list nominated by the World Health Organization, and 10 members nominated by government members of the UN. Under Article VI of the US Constitution, treaties are superior to federal and state laws, and many proposals to alter federal or state controlled substances laws may be challenged as not complying with the Single Convention (see discussion of marijuana, below.)

Congress passed the DRUG ABUSE CONTROL AMENDMENTS OF 1965 which added "stimulant, depressant, or hallucinogenic" agents to federal control as if they were narcotics. A BUREAU OF NARCOTICS AND DANGEROUS DRUGS (BNDD) was created in 1968 as a successor to the Narcotics Bureau, and placed, for the first time, in the Department of Justice. The DACA continued to use a tax scheme to control substances.

THE CONTROLLED SUBSTANCES ACT. In 1970, Congress passed a completely revised scheme, the Controlled Substances Act, to replace previous controlled substances law. Rather than a tax act, THE CSA IS A CRIMINAL STATUTE, establishing criminal penalties for unlawful possession, manufacturer, distribution or diversion of controlled substances. The new scheme is described more fully below.

In 1973, THE DRUG ENFORCEMENT ADMINISTRATION, A DIVISION OF THE JUSTICE DEPARTMENT, was created to administer the CSA. The CSA is found in the US Code in Title 21, starting at section 801, and the corresponding DEA regulations implementing the Act are found in 21 CFR § 1301 et seq.

PRESCRIBING AND DISPENSING CONTROLLED SUBSTANCES

WASHINGTON CONTROLLED SUBSTANCES ACT. The CSA (21 USC § 801 et seq.) serves as a model for Washington's laws and regulations regarding controlled substances, which closely follow federal rules. The

Washington Controlled Substances Act, RCW 69.50, is the principal law dealing with controlled substances, and, like the federal CSA, requires registration of prescribers, dispensers, manufacturers, and wholesalers of controlled substances. This section will discuss the Washington statute, except where the federal statute differs, or where the DEA has issued interpretations of the federal statute that are not covered by state law.

The Act's fundamental rule is that no person may possess a controlled substance unless it is for a specific purpose allowed in the Act, and this principally means that for most persons they must be an ultimate user of the substance and that they obtained it as a result of a prescription issued in accordance with the statute.

A "controlled substance" includes marketed drug products approved by FDA and designated by the FDA in collaboration with the DEA as controlled substances based upon their POTENTIAL FOR ABUSE. The substances are placed in one of 5 schedules (Schedule I through Schedule V – see below), again based on their use in medicine and propensity for abuse. It also includes precursors of controlled substances and certain chemicals which are routinely necessary for the production of controlled substances.

PRESCRIPTIONS. WA requirements for controlled substances prescriptions are contained in RCW 69.50.308.

The CSA requires that prescriptions be issued to individual patients, by a practitioner authorized to prescribe in Washington, in the due course of that prescriber's practice, and in good faith for a legitimate medical purpose.

4 REQUIREMENTS FOR A VALID CONTROLLED SUBSTANCES PRESCRIPTION

- ✓ Issued to an INDIVIDUAL PATIENT (or animal)
- ✓ By an AUTHORIZED PRESCRIBER
- ✓ IN THE DUE COURSE of the prescriber's practice
- ✓ Issued in GOOD FAITH for a LEGITIMATE MEDICAL

DUE COURSE OF PRACTICE requires that the prescription be issued in the context of a BONA FIDE PRESCRIBER-PATIENT RELATIONSHIP, and within the SCOPE OF PRACTICE of the prescriber.

LEGITIMATE MEDICAL PURPOSES are those which are consistent with the generally recognized standards of the prescriber's profession, with due consideration of the prescriber's specialty. Prescriptions for legitimate medical purposes do *NOT* include the following:

- PRESCRIPTIONS ISSUED "FOR OFFICE USE," i.e., as a means of obtaining controlled substances for the prescriber to use in his or her office, without specifying a specific patient. Purchases of controlled substances by a practitioner for office use are accomplished by order forms or purchase orders.
- FRAUDULENT OR FORGED prescriptions.
- PRESCRIPTIONS ISSUED SOLELY TO MAINTAIN AN ADDICTION (other than issued in office-based narcotic maintenance programs – see below). Prescriptions issued to an addicted person to treat pain or another indication are permissible. Prescriptions issued to habitual users for naloxone or other opioid overdose drugs are valid, notwithstanding RCW 69.41.040(1).
- SELF-PRESCRIBING OR SELF-DISPENSING of controlled substances prohibited in Washington.

    Washington restricts self-prescribing or self-dispensing of controlled substances. It is an act of unprofessional conduct to prescribe any controlled substances for oneself in RCW 18.130.180(6). This prevents a pharmacist from dispensing such prescriptions since prescriptions issued as an unprofessional act cannot be considered issued in the due course of practice. This does not prohibit practitioners from prescribing controlled substances for a family member.

It is also a violation of the WA Controlled Substances Act for practitioners (including pharmacists) to dispense Schedule II, III, or IV substances for oneself (RCW 69.50.308(l)). This, again, does not prohibit a practitioner from dispensing controlled substances for family members, nor does it apply to self-dispensing of Schedule V substances.

- PRESCRIPTIONS FOR CONTROLLED SUBSTANCES THAT ARE FOR USES NOT WITHIN THE APPROVED INDICATIONS (or those that are contraindicated) in the package insert. The DEA takes the somewhat controversial position that certain non-approved uses cannot normally be legitimate, but generally does not rest a decision to prosecute on this factor alone. It has disclaimed this position with regards to treatment of pain with methadone or buprenorphine.

USE OF CONTROLLED SUBSTANCES FOR AID-IN-DYING. The DEA in 2001 issued an "interpretive rule" that use of controlled substances in accordance with Oregon's Death with Dignity Law would violate the CSA since using these drugs to cause death would not be for a "legitimate medical purpose" within the normal course of a practitioner's practice, and physicians who wrote – or pharmacists who filled – prescriptions for this use could lose their DEA number.

This rule was challenged in court, and in January 2006 the US Supreme Court ruled in *Gonzales v. Oregon* that "The CSA does not allow the Attorney General to prohibit doctors from prescribing regulated drugs for use in physician-assisted suicide under state law permitting the procedure."[385] The Court ruled that Congress has not given the Attorney General authority to promulgate rules other than those to register or deregister individual registrants, and to determine which schedule into which a controlled substance will be placed.

The Court's opinion is consistent with the notion that Congress has not yet chosen to regulate the practice of medicine or pharmacy, but has deferred that role to the states.

WASHINGTON'S DEATH WITH DIGNITY ACT was presented to Washington voters as Initiative 1000 in November 2008.[386] A 58% majority approved the law, which took effect on March 4, 2009. It closely parallels the Oregon Death with Dignity Act, and the fundamental effect of the law is to exclude from the definition of "assisted suicide" (which remains a crime) the prescribing and dispensing of a drug that will aid a qualified patient in dying.

QUALIFIED PATIENTS are mentally competent adults who reside in Washington who have been certified by two independent physicians as being terminally ill with a life expectancy of six months or less. If either physician believes that the patient's judgment may be affected by depression or other mental conditions, he or she is required to seek a psychological evaluation before issuing the request of prescription.

WRITTEN AND ORAL REQUESTS REQUIRED. The law requires the patient to make a written and oral request to the physician, and then must make a second oral request for the prescription. A minimum of 15 days must elapse between the first and second oral requests. The written request must be witnessed by two individuals, and at least one witness must not be related to the patient, entitled to share in the patient's estate, or employed by an institution in which the patient is receiving care. At least 48 hours must elapse following the second oral request and issuance of the prescription.

DISPENSING OR PRESCRIBING. The physician may dispense the medication directly to the patient, or, with the patient's permission contact a willing pharmacist and inform the pharmacist of the prescription and then deliver the prescription to the pharmacist personally by mail or by fax.

PHARMACIST'S ROLE. The pharmacist, upon agreeing to participate, must prepare the prescription and dispensing directly to the patient, the attending physician, or an agent of the patient specifically named in the prescription. Within 30 days, the pharmacist must mail a copy of the "dispensing record and such other administratively required documentation" to the Department of Health in accordance with DOH regulations. The Department proposed these regulations in January 2009 as WAC 246-978.

Prescriptions must be written for medications that the patient may self-administer by ingestion, i.e., orally, without help from another person. The most common oral prescriptions written in Oregon consist of 24 hours of pre-medication with metoclopramide (20 mg q 8 h) to minimize vomiting, followed by 9 g of secobarbital or pentobarbital in 100 mL of oral suspension.[387]

No pharmacist is required to participate in dispensing prescriptions written under this Act.

A pharmacy may not discipline, suspend, or otherwise penalize a pharmacist for "participating or refusing to participate in good faith compliance" with the law. The law does not permit a pharmacy to prohibit its employee pharmacists from dispensing prescriptions issued under the act.

The Pharmacy Commission's regulation on Pharmacies' Professional Responsibilities (WAC 246-869-010) is not applicable to prescriptions written under the act, primarily because of the law's requirement that only willing providers shall participate in the provision of medication to the qualified patient, but also because the regulation only mandates prompt dispensing of FDA-approved products. The compounded barbiturate prescriptions will not meet this test.

Comment: The law is explicit that only licensed physicians (MD or DO) may be involved in the process of issuing prescriptions to aid in dying, and that only licensed pharmacists may be involved in the dispensing of those prescriptions. Our interpretation of this specificity is that pharmacy technicians or interns should not participate in dispensing prescriptions issued under the law.

PROHIBITED USES OF SPECIFIC CONTROLLED SUBSTANCES. Specific prohibitions exist under the law for the use of certain substances. For example:

ANABOLIC STEROIDS for weight training. WAC 246-919-610 prohibits physicians from prescribing, administering, or dispensing anabolic steroids, growth hormones, testosterone or its analogs, HCG, other hormones, or any form of autotransfusion for the purpose of enhancing athletic ability. Federal statute makes it a crime to dispense HGH (somatropin) for non-approved uses.

SPECIFIED CNS STIMULANTS FOR WEIGHT CONTROL. These include amphetamines, dextroamphetamine salts, methamphetamine (desoxyephedrine), phenmetrazine, lisdexamfetamine, or methylphenidate. (WAC 246-887-040; RCW 69.50.402(1)(c)(ii))

INDICATIONS FOR USE must be included in certain prescriptions under federal or state law:

- XYREM® – Federal rules require indications for use to be specified on prescriptions for Xyrem® (sodium oxybate; GHB) (21 CFR 1306.05(c))
- AMPHETAMINES AND STIMULANTS – Washington law limits approved indications for Schedule II stimulants; these include amphetamines or Schedule II stimulants designated as such by DEA. The pharmacist is entitled to know the indication for use and most prescribers indicate this use on the prescription. The approved indications are in RCW 69.50.402(1)(c)(ii) and in WAC 246-887-045:
    - Narcolepsy
    - Hyperkinesis (e.g., ADHD)
    - Drug-induced brain dysfunction
    - Epilepsy
    - Differential diagnostic psychiatric evaluation of depression

  - Treatment of depression shown to be refractory to other modalities
  - Multiple sclerosis
  - Moderate to severe binge eating disorder in adults
- OPTOMETRISTS' prescriptions in Washington must include a "notation of purpose." (WAC 246-851-590(10))
- NURSE PRACTITIONERS' prescriptions for opioids shall include the diagnosis or ICD code. (WAC 246-840-4657)

NALOXONE FOR EMERGENCY USE is specifically allowed under Washington law. The 2010 legislature passed the "Good Samaritan 911 Law" to help reduce the number of deaths due to narcotic overdoses,[388] noting that in 2007 more Washingtonians died of drug overdose than died in car accidents, and that fear that calling 9-1-1 will result in prosecution was a significant barrier to seeking help for drug overdoses. Pharmacists may fill naloxone prescriptions written for a caregiver or friend of a patient taking opiates, subject to certain privacy concerns when the patient is in a narcotics treatment program.[389] (Note: Naloxone is not a controlled substance, but is included in this chapter because its use is related to treating opiate overdose.)

The statute modified RCW 69.50[390] by providing, in part:

- Immunity from prosecution for possession of controlled substances for a person acting in good faith who seeks medical assistance for someone experiencing a drug-related overdose.
- A person suffering an overdose will be immune from prosecution if the evidence for the charge of possession of a controlled substance results from the overdose and the need for medical assistance.

The Act also modified RCW 18.130 to provide that administering, dispensing, prescribing, or other use or delivery of naloxone shall not constitute unprofessional conduct if the conduct results from a good faith effort to assist

- a person experiencing or likely to experience an opiate related overdose; or
- a family member, friend , or other person in a position to assist a person experiencing, or likely to experience, an opiate-related overdose.[391] This subsection was replaced by the provisions of RCW 69.41.095 in 2015.

PROCEDURES FOR PRESCRIBING, DISTRIBUTION, AND ADMINISTRATION OF OPIOID OVERDOSE MEDICATION. The 2015 Legislature added a new section RCW 69.41.095 to explicitly provide for access to naloxone (or other opioid overdose medication) by (1) persons at risk of experiencing an opioid overdose; (2) first responders, family members, or other persons or entities in a position to assist a person at risk.

- Opioid overdose medications are defined as "any drug used to reverse an opioid overdose that binds to opioid receptors and blocks or inhibits the effects of opioids acting on those receptors. It does not include intentional administration via the intravenous route."
- Opioid-related overdose is "a condition including, but not limited to, extreme physical illness, decreased levels of consciousness, respiratory depression, coma, or death that: (i) results from the consumption or use of an opioid or another substance with which an opioid was combined; or (ii) a lay person would reasonably believe to be an opioid-related overdose requiring medical assistance."
- Practitioners (including pharmacists with prescriptive authority for opiate overdose drugs) may prescribe, dispense, distribute, and deliver opioid overdose medications directly to a person at risk;
- Practitioners may by collaborative drug therapy agreement, standing order, or protocol deliver to a first responder, family member or other persons in a position to assist a person at risk;

- When prescribing, dispensing, distributing, or delivering the opioid overdose medication, the practitioner shall inform the recipient that the person at risk should be transported to a hospital or a first responder summoned as soon as possible after administration of the overdose medication.
- Pharmacists (with or without prescriptive authority) may
    - dispense opioid overdose medications pursuant to prescriptions issued under the statute, or
    - may administer (with or without a prescription) an overdose medication to a person at risk of experiencing an opioid overdose
- Pharmacists dispensing overdose therapy must provide written instructions for seeking medical attention, with the instructions to seek immediate attention "conspicuously displayed."
- A practitioner, including a pharmacist authorized by CDTA, may distribute opioid overdose drugs to other persons or entities who will use the drugs in accordance with a standing order or protocol, which is defined as "written or electronically recorded instructions, prepared by a prescriber, for distribution and administration of a drug by designated and trained staff or volunteers of an organization or entity, as well as other actions and interventions to be used upon the occurrence of clearly defined clinical events in order to improve patients' timely access to treatment."

The statute reiterates that the following individuals, acting in good faith and with reasonable care shall not be subject to criminal or civil liability, or discipline under RCW 18.30, when acting in compliance with RCW 69.41.095:

- Practitioner who prescribes, dispenses, distributes, or delivers an opioid overdose medication;
- Pharmacist who dispenses an opioid overdose medication;
- Any person who possesses, stores, distributes, or administers an opioid overdose medication.

OTC NALOXONE

On January 17, 2019, the FDA Commissioner published a statement on efforts by the FDA to speed the development of and approval of non-prescription naloxone products. According to the announcement, FDA has been working to make naloxone products available without prescription, and has determined that the development of an approved Drug Facts label is a necessary step towards achieving this goal. For the first time in its history, FDA has on its own initiative developed and tested a model Drug Facts label for two forms of naloxone: (1) a nasal spray, and (2) an autoinjector. Potential drug sponsors may download the model forms and populate them with their own product-specific information.[392] OTC naloxone products may well be available in the US sometime in 2019.

CORRESPONDING RESPONSIBILITY OF THE PHARMACIST. While the prescriber bears the primary responsibility for the legitimacy of his or her prescriptions, the law holds the pharmacist to a "corresponding responsibility" for recognizing invalid prescriptions, when the pharmacist "knew or should have known" from the circumstances that the prescription was not issued in the due course of practice for a legitimate medical purpose. (RCW 69.50.308(e); 21 CFR §1306.04(a)) (See Reporting of Violations, below)

EXCESSIVE ISSUANCE OF OTHERWISE APPROPRIATE PRESCRIPTIONS. It is not uncommon for a pharmacist to receive prescriptions for a controlled substance that, on their face, are appropriate. However, what should the pharmacist do when the patient brings in a subsequent prescription, written by the same prescriber, which is prescribed exceedingly early given the quantity and directions on the prior prescription? It is the primary author's opinion that anything prescribed in excess of the prescriber's own dosage instructions is no longer for a legitimate purpose. Certainly, when early prescribing has become an obvious pattern, the DEA and/or the Commission has held the pharmacist responsible for failing to recognize or report the situation.

PRESCRIBERS AND FIRMS MUST REGISTER WITH THE DEA. The federal law requires registration of practitioners, and defines practitioners as a physician, dentist, podiatrist, veterinarian, mid-level practitioner, or other registered practitioner who is authorized to prescribe controlled substances by the jurisdiction in which he or she is licensed to practice.

INTERNET PHARMACIES. Special registration requirements were established by the RYAN HAIGHT ONLINE PHARMACY CONSUMER PROTECTION ACT OF 2008[393] for pharmacies that distribute or dispense controlled substances via the Internet.

An "online pharmacy" is defined as "a person, entity, or Internet site, whether in the United States or abroad, that knowingly or intentionally delivers, distributes, or dispenses, or offers or attempts to deliver, distribute, or dispense, a controlled substance by means of the Internet."

Exempted from the definition of "online pharmacy" are

- Manufacturers or distributors registered with the DEA;
- Nonpharmacy practitioners registered with the DEA;
- Hospitals or other medical facilities operated by an agency of the United States that are registered with the DEA;
- Health care facilities owned or operated by an Indian tribe or tribal organization which is carrying out a contract or compact under the Indian Self-Determination and Education Assistance Act;
- Mere advertisements that do not attempt to facilitate an actual transaction involving a controlled substance;
- Pharmacies registered with the DEA whose dispensing of controlled substances via the Internet consist solely of
- Refilling prescriptions for controlled substances in schedule III, IV, or V; or
- Filling new prescriptions in schedule III, IV, or V where the pharmacy had previously filled a non-Internet prescription for the same patient and at the patient's request contacts the prescriber for a new prescription which is issued in the due course of that prescriber's practice for a legitimate medical purpose.

Note that any dispensing of schedule II controlled substances via the Internet appears to make a pharmacy an online pharmacy.

Online pharmacies must register with the DEA 30 days prior to engaging in Internet pharmacy involving controlled substances. Monthly reports must be made to the DEA of the quantity of each controlled substance dispensed by the pharmacy, if, during the month in question, the pharmacy has dispensed at least 100 prescriptions or at least 5,000 dosage units.

A statement must be placed on the pharmacy's home page that includes:

- A statement that the pharmacy complies with the Act;
- The name, address, e-mail address, and telephone number of the pharmacy;
- The name, professional degree, and states of licensure for the pharmacist-in-charge, and a telephone number at which the PIC may be contacted;
- A list of states in which the pharmacy is licensed;
- A certification that the pharmacy is registered with the DEA as an Internet pharmacy; and
- The name, address, telephone number, professional degree, and states of licensure of any practitioner who has a contractual relationship with the pharmacy.

- The following statement must also be posted: "This online pharmacy will only dispense a controlled substance to a person who has a valid prescription issued for a legitimate medical purpose based upon a medical relationship with a prescribing practitioner. This includes at least one prior in-person medical evaluation or medical evaluation via telemedicine in accordance with applicable requirements of Section 309 of the Controlled Substances Act."

The Act gives states authority to bring complaints against Internet pharmacies seeking injunctions or damages for violations of the law. The Attorney General is authorized to issue a special registration for prescribers of controlled substances engaged in telemedicine.

EMPLOYEE SCREENING REQUIRED. Registrants may not employ any person who will have access to controlled substances if that person has been previously convicted of a felony involving controlled substances or has had an application for registration denied, revoked, or surrendered for cause.[394] DEA regulations, however, permit an employer to seek a waiver of this exclusion in specific cases. The waiver procedure is described in Section V of the *DEA Pharmacists Manual.*[395]

PRE-EMPLOYMENT INQUIRIES. Pre-employment interview questions must be designed to avoid discrimination under federal and state laws. The federal agency enforcing antidiscrimination laws is the Equal Employment Opportunity Commission (EEOC). The EEOC guidelines regarding pre-employment inquiries point out that "federal law does not prohibit employers from asking about your criminal history, but do prohibit employers from discriminating when they use criminal history information." In general, inquiries about arrests and convictions must be related to essential functions and security requirements of the job. Inquiries about arrests may be restricted by state law, and generally employers are cautioned that an arrest is not proof of guilt. However, convictions that are related to job requirements are permitted.[396]

WASHINGTON'S RULES CONCERNING PRE-EMPLOYMENT INQUIRIES state the following concerning arrests and convictions:[397]

- Arrests – "Because statistical studies regarding arrests have shown a disparate impact on some racial and ethnic minorities, and an arrest by itself is not a reliable indication of criminal behavior, inquiries requiring arrests must include whether charges are still pending, have been dismissed, or led to conviction of a crime involving behavior that would adversely affect job performance, and the arrest occurred within the last ten years. Exempt from this rule are law enforcement agencies and *state agencies, school districts, businesses and other organizations that have a direct responsibility for the supervision, care, or treatment of children, mentally ill persons, or other vulnerable adults [emphasis added.]*"
- Convictions – "Statistical studies on convictions and imprisonment have shown a disparate impact on some racial and ethnic minority groups. Inquiries concerning convictions (or imprisonment) will be considered to be justified by business necessity if the crimes inquired about relate reasonably to the job duties, and if such convictions (or release from prison) occurred within the last ten years. *Law enforcement agencies, state agencies, school districts, businesses and other organizations that have a direct responsibility for the supervision, care, or treatment of children, mentally ill persons, developmentally disabled persons, or other vulnerable adults are exempt from this rule [emphasis added]."*

DEA REQUIREMENTS FOR PRE-EMPLOYMENT SCREENING. The DEA has suggested specific language that it expects is included in "an employer's comprehensive employee screening program:"[398]

- Question. Within the past five years, have you been convicted of a felony, or within the past two years, of any misdemeanor or are you presently formally charged with committing a criminal offense? (Do not include any traffic violations, juvenile offenses or military convictions, except by general court-martial.) If the answer is yes, furnish details of conviction, offense, location, date and sentence.
- Question. In the past three years, have you ever knowingly used any narcotics, amphetamines or barbiturates, other than those prescribed to you by a physician? If the answer is yes, furnish details.

AUTHORIZED PRESCRIBERS are specified in RCW 69.50.101(dd)(1) to include the following. The various authorizing statutes specify the levels of authority shown. [Also see Table 4-3 in Chapter 4]

- A PHYSICIAN [MD] under chapter 18.71 RCW – all schedules
- An OSTEOPATHIC PHYSICIAN AND SURGEON [DO] under chapter 18.57 RCW – all schedules
- A PHYSICIAN ASSISTANT [PA, PA-C] under chapter 18.71A RCW, or OSTEOPATHIC PHYSICIAN ASSISTANT under chapter 18.57A RCW who is licensed under RCW 18.57A.020, subject to limitations in RCW 18.57A.040. All PA applicants in Washington must be nationally certified. So the use of "PA" is now archaic. There are no significant differences between allopathic and osteopathic PA rules.
    - Allopathic PA/PA-C (under supervision of MD) – all schedules as permitted by the supervising physician
    - If the supervising physician's prescribing privileges are restricted, such restrictions apply to a PA under his or her supervision, unless the Medical Commission or Osteopathic Medicine Board approves otherwise in writing
- An OPTOMETRIST [OD] licensed under chapter 18.53 RCW who is certified by the optometry board under RCW 18.53.010 subject to any limitations in RCW 18.53.010 – Rules for optometrists are found in WAC 246-851-580 through -610.
    - Drug list is limited to specific products or classes of products
    - May only prescribe allowed controlled substances in Schedule III, IV, and V, and hydrocodone products in Schedule II
    - Benzodiazepines are limited to single doses per prescription for anti-anxiety related to procedures.
    - No more than a 7-day supply of controlled substances may be prescribed.
    - Schedule III and IV have a maximum prescribed quantity of 30 dosage units per prescription.
    - A "notation of purpose" shall be included on all prescriptions (WAC 246-851-590 (9))
    - May not prescribe oral drugs within 90 days following ophthalmic surgery unless in consultation with the treating ophthalmologist.
- A DENTIST [DDS, DMD] under chapter 18.32 RCW – all schedules
- A PODIATRIC PHYSICIAN AND SURGEON [DPM, Pod.D.] under chapter 18.22 RCW – all schedules
- A VETERINARIAN [DVM] under chapter 18.92 RCW – all schedules (for non-human animals)
- A NATUROPATHIC PHYSICIAN [ND] under chapter 18.36A RCW and 246-836 WAC – codeine and testosterone products in schedules III through V. Note that synthetic opiates (e.g., hydrocodone) or synthetic anabolic steroids (e.g., oxandrolone) may not be prescribed by a naturopath in Washington. (The 2015 Legislature has been presented with a Sunrise Review by the Department of Health that recommended limited prescribing of Schedule II drugs, i.e., hydrocodone combinations; as of January, 2019, this has not resulted in legislation.)

- An ADVANCED REGISTERED NURSE PRACTITIONER [ARNP] under chapter 18.79 RCW – Schedule V; Schedule II, III, and IV within scope of specialty. The diagnosis or ICD code must be placed on all prescriptions for opioids.
- A PHARMACIST [R.Ph., Pharm.D.] under chapter 18.64 RCW – all schedules if authorized by a protocol approved for his or her practice by a practitioner authorized to prescribe, consistent with the scope of that authorizing practitioner.[399]

MID-LEVEL PRESCRIBING AUTHORITY IN OTHER STATES. The DEA maintains an interactive guide to CSA prescribing authority of midlevel practitioners in each state on its website at http://www.deadiversion.usdoj.gov/drugreg/practioners/index.html.

OUT-OF-STATE PRESCRIPTIONS ALLOWED. Controlled substances prescriptions may be also be filled in Washington when prescribed by "A physician licensed to practice medicine and surgery, a physician licensed to practice osteopathic medicine and surgery, a dentist licensed to practice dentistry, a podiatric physician and surgeon licensed to practice podiatric medicine and surgery, a licensed physician assistant or a licensed osteopathic physician assistant specifically approved to prescribe controlled substances by his or her state's medical quality assurance commission or equivalent and his or her supervising physician, an advanced registered nurse practitioner licensed to prescribe controlled substances, or a veterinarian licensed to practice veterinary medicine in any state of the United States." (RCW 69.50.101(dd)(3)) Note: "State" includes DC, Puerto Rico, or territory or possession of US that is subject to US jurisdiction. (RCW 69.50.101(ii)).

REGISTRATION PROCEDURES. Registration with the DEA is required in order to exercise prescribing authority for controlled substances. The Drug Enforcement Administration now utilizes an online application (https://www.deadiversion.usdoj.gov/webforms/jsp/regapps/common/newAppLogin.jsp) procedure to submit DEA Form 224 – Application for Retail Pharmacy, Hospital/Clinic, Practitioner, Teaching Institution, or Mid-Level Practitioner.

HOW TO VALIDATE A DEA NUMBER

ONLINE VALIDATION. An apparently valid DEA number may still be invalid, particularly if the prescriber's registration has lapsed or been suspended or revoked. The DEA now maintains a current database of all valid DEA numbers in the United States on its website: https://www.deadiversion.usdoj.gov/webforms/validateLogin.jsp. (This can be accessed from the Quick Links on the DEA Diversion Control Website by clicking on "Registration Validation.")

The DEA encourages all pharmacists to verify the prescriber's DEA unless they are certain of the prescriber and his or her continued registration status. In 2012 and 2013, the DEA has included use of this service in terms of consent agreements with pharmacies that have experienced loss of controlled substances due to fraudulent prescriptions.

The user must enter his or her DEA number and social security number to log in. Pharmacists without their own DEA number use the DEA number of their employer and their employer's federal Employer Identification Number (EIN).

USING THE CHECK DIGIT. Registered practitioners (or pharmacies) are issued a DEA Number, in the form, AA1234567

- The first letter is usually "A," "B," or "F" for physicians, dentists, etc., and "M" for mid-level practitioners (MLPs, e.g., P.A.s, ARNPs, and pharmacists). "X" is used for DATA-waived practitioners prescribing buprenorphine maintenance.
- The second letter is usually the first letter of the registrant's last name. (May be a former last name, or may be a number, under certain circumstances).
- The numbers consist of a 6-digit registration number and a "check digit."
- Note, however, that a "valid" number may still have been suspended or revoked, so the check-digit is just a quick first step assessment. DEA numbers should be validated online for any prescriber not actually known to the pharmacist.

VALIDATING A DEA NUMBER USING THE CHECK DIGIT

1. Add the 1st, 3rd, and 5th digits of the registration number.
2. Add the 2nd, 4th, and 6th digits of the registration number and multiply that sum by 2
3. Add the sum of (1) to the product of (2); the check digit is the right most digit in the resulting sum.

EXAMPLE: MJ 2034685:

$$\begin{aligned} 2+3+6 &= 11 \\ \underline{(0+4+8)\times 2} &\underline{= 24} \\ \textit{Check sum} &= 35 \\ \textit{Check digit} &= 5 \end{aligned}$$

HOSPITAL-BASED PRESCRIBERS. Any practitioner (including a pharmacist with prescriptive authority for controlled substances) who works in a hospital may use the hospital's DEA number, plus a hospital-assigned internal code, when PRESCRIBING ONLY FOR HOSPITAL PATIENTS, without registering with the DEA. The prescriptions issued for hospital patients may be filled at community pharmacies.

It is important for hospitals to regularly update their list of authorized users of the institution's DEA number and communicate these to pharmacists in the community.

Federal Employees Exempt

PUBLIC HEALTH SERVICE OR BUREAU OF PRISONS employees do not need to register – use Social Security number as DEA number.

MILITARY PRACTITIONERS DO NOT NEED TO REGISTER. They indicate their branch of service plus their service identification number; however, DEA will issue DEA numbers to military personnel, so they can use a DEA number as well. Military MLPs must be specifically licensed or authorized to prescribe in the state where they are stationed to receive a DEA number. To prescribe "off base," they need a separate DEA registration.

MULTIPLE DEA NUMBERS. Some practitioners may have multiple DEA numbers.

SEPARATE PRACTICE SITES. A separate DEA registration is required for each location at which controlled substances are stored or administered. Practitioners, who prescribe in multiple locations, but store or administer controlled substances at only one location, do not need a separate registration number for locations where they only prescribe.

REGISTRANTS PRACTICING IN MORE THAN ONE STATE must obtain a separate DEA registration number for each state.[400]

BUPRENORPHINE MAINTENANCE PRESCRIBING. A provider registered to prescribe buprenorphine for office-based narcotic maintenance is issued a separate DEA number for those prescriptions (see below).

Pharmacists dispensing prescriptions issued by prescribers with more than one DEA number must record the DEA number that is on the prescription, but should make sure that it relates to the type of prescription or to the site whose address is on the Rx.

LOSS OR THEFT OF CONTROLLED SUBSTANCES MUST BE TRACKED AND REPORTED. Any "significant loss" or theft must be reported immediately to the DEA, by telephone, fax, or brief written message to the local DEA office. The DEA encourages an immediate notification to the local police. Non-significant losses must be accounted for in the pharmacy's records. The immediate notification is followed up by submission of a DEA Form 106 (see below), with a copy to the Pharmacy Commission.

WHAT IS A "LOSS?" A loss generally includes any reduction in inventory of a controlled substance that is not due to a lawful transfer, administration, or dispensing of the drug. Pharmacists may incur a loss through normal dispensing activities when:

- A controlled substance is dispensed in error to the wrong person, or dispensed in error instead of another drug; or
- A controlled substance is dispensed pursuant to a fraudulent prescription, whether or not the prescription is recognized as fraudulent at the time.

WHAT IS "SIGNIFICANT?" It is up to the pharmacy to determine whether a loss or shortage is significant. The DEA cites the following factors to be considered:

- The actual quantity of controlled substances lost in relation to the type of business;
- The specific controlled substances;
- *Whether the **loss** of the controlled substances can be associated with access to those controlled substances by specific individuals*, [*emphasis* added] or whether the **loss** can be attributed to unique activities that may take place involving the controlled substances;
- A pattern of losses over a specific time period, whether the losses appear to be random, and the results of efforts taken to resolve the losses; and, if known
    - Whether the specific controlled substances are likely candidates for diversion; and
    - Local trends and other indicators of the diversion potential of the missing controlled substances.

INSIGNIFICANT LOSSES should not be reported on a Form 106. According to the Pharmacist's Manual, "If it is determined that the loss is not significant, the registrant should place a record of the occurrence in a theft and loss file for future reference. Miscounts or adjustments to inventory involving clerical errors on the part of the pharmacy should not be reported on a DEA Form 106, but rather should be noted in a separate log at the pharmacy management's discretion."

LOSSES IN-TRANSIT. Suppliers are responsible for reporting in-transit losses. Pharmacies are responsible for reporting items missing from a shipment they have signed for.

BREAKAGE OR SPILLAGE IS NOT "LOSS," and can be accounted for as breakage or spillage in the pharmacy's CS records.

PHARMACIES MUST FOLLOW UP INITIAL REPORT OF LOSS WITH DEA FORM 106. Following an investigation, pharmacies must file a DEA Form 106 with the DEA. The DEA now has an on-line version of DEA Form 106, available at https://www.deadiversion.usdoj.gov/webforms/app106Login.jsp

- A COPY OF FORM 106 MUST BE PROVIDED TO THE PHARMACY COMMISSION. (WAC 246-887-020 (3)(c))
- IF LOSS IS NOT CONFIRMED. If, after further investigation, it is found that the loss did not occur, no Form 106 needs to be filed, but the DEA (and the Commission) must be informed that the investigation was conducted and that no Form 106 is forthcoming.
- FEDERAL INVESTIGATION OF THEFTS AND ROBBERIES is provided for by the Controlled Substances Registration Protection Act of 1984 (18 U.S.C. §2118) when
  - The replacement cost of the controlled substances if $500 or more;
  - Interstate or foreign commerce was involved in the crime; OR
  - A person was killed or significantly injured as a result of the crime

REQUIRED RECORDS

PHARMACY RECORDS. All pharmacies must maintain in their files for inspection by the DEA or Commission the following controlled substances records.

- DEA Registration Certificate.
- Official Order Forms (Form 222)
- Power of Attorney authorization to sign order forms.
- Initial inventory upon opening of pharmacy.
- Biennial inventory records.
- Reports of Theft or Loss (DEA Form 106)
- Inventory of Drugs Submitted for DEA Disposal (Form 41)
- Records of transfers between pharmacies*
- Inventory Transaction Records. A pharmacy must maintain records of receipt, dispensing, and destruction of controlled substances.*
- Schedule II records must include copies of Form 222, copies of requisitions for order forms, and copies of powers of attorney documents related to order forms, plus invoices and filled prescriptions. Invoices* and Forms 222 are stored separately from other controlled substances records.
- Schedule III, IV, and V records include copies of invoices* and filled prescriptions. These are stored separately from records of purchase of non-controlled substances (see below for prescription filing requirements), or may be stored in such a way as to make them readily retrievable from non-controlled substance records.
- Threshold amounts of List 1 Chemicals. These are precursor chemicals. Few pharmacies are involved in threshold level sales, except as otherwise provided by rules for sales of EPP OTC products (see below).
- Central Record Storage: Financial and shipping records (including invoices and packing slips) – the records indicated above with an asterisk (*) – may be stored at a central location, provided that the registrant has notified the regional DEA Special Agent in Charge in writing (see 21 CFR §1304.04) at least 14 days prior to beginning centralized storage, and has not been denied by the SAC. Centralized storage cannot include required inventories, completed form 222s, or prescriptions, which must be at the location where applicable.
  - Records relating to remote dispensing systems at long-term care facilities may be kept centrally

CENTRAL FILL PHARMACY RECORDS. Retail pharmacies that utilize the services of central fill pharmacies must keep a record of all central pharmacies that are authorized to fill prescriptions on its behalf: name, address, and DEA number. The registration of each central fill pharmacy must be verified by the retail pharmacy. Likewise, each central fill pharmacy must verify the registration of any retail pharmacy it provides services to, and record the name, address, and DEA number of those retail pharmacies.

MID-LEVEL PRACTITIONER RECORDS. Pharmacists and other mid-level practitioners who prescribe or administer controlled substances pursuant to their prescriptive authority must maintain "in a readily retrievable manner those documents required by the state in which he/she practices which describe the conditions and extent of his authorization" to prescribe controlled substances, including any protocols, practice guidelines, or practice agreements. (21 CFR §1304.03(e))

Generally, practitioners are not required to keep records of controlled substances prescribed in the lawful course of professional practice, unless such substances are prescribed for maintenance or detoxification of an individual. The major exception to this rule relates to requirements for electronic prescribing.

Records of controlled substances administered in the lawful course of professional practice are only required if "the practitioner regularly engages in the dispensing or administering of controlled substances and charges patients, either separately or together with charges for other professional services, for substances so dispensed or administered." Records of drugs administered during maintenance or detoxification are required.

Note: this regulation and state law presume that the prescribing practitioner is maintaining patient records in accordance with the usual standards of practice.

RECORD RETENTION: the federal and state statutes require that all records required under the Acts be maintained for 2 years.

PHARMACIES MUST CONDUCT PERIODIC PHYSICAL INVENTORIES (COUNTS) OF CONTROLLED SUBSTANCES. These include an initial inventory upon opening of a pharmacy, or upon change of ownership, and a biennial inventory thereafter. Many wholesalers provide pharmacies with pre-printed forms for completing these inventories.

REQUIRED ELEMENTS OF THESE INVENTORIES INCLUDE:

- The inventory date
- Time of inventory (i.e., opening or closing of business)
- Drug name
- Drug strength
- Drug form
- Number of units/volume
- Total quantity

RECOMMENDED ELEMENTS INCLUDE:

- Name, address, and DEA number of registrant
- Signature of person or persons responsible for taking the inventory.

HOW TO COUNT DOSAGE UNITS FOR INVENTORIES

SCHEDULE II – ACTUAL PHYSICAL COUNT required

SCHEDULE III, IV, AND V - An ESTIMATED COUNT may be made. An ACTUAL COUNT must be made for Schedule III, IV, or V drugs if the container contains more than 1,000 dosage units and has been opened.

A BIENNIAL INVENTORY must be completed at least every 2 years after the initial inventory. If a drug changes its status, as tramadol changed on August 18, 2014, stocks of the drug must be added to the inventory on that day. If a drug changes status at the state level, and then later at the federal level, a second inventory will be needed for the federal change.

REQUIREMENTS FOR PRESCRIPTIONS are essentially identical between RCW 69.50 and the federal CSA. The major difference is that all prescriptions for Schedule II and Schedule V drugs expire after 6 months from date written, whereas the federal CSA does not place an expiration date on Schedule II or Schedule V prescriptions. Washington also limits Schedule V prescriptions to 5 refills, but the federal law does not.

HARD COPY (WRITTEN) PRESCRIPTIONS must conform to the following DEA requirements (21 CFR § 1306.05):

- Dated as of and signed on the day when issued
- Shall bear the full name and address of the patient
- The drug name
- The drug strength
- The dosage form
- Quantity prescribed
- Directions for use
- Name, address, and registration number of the practitioner

In at least some criminal or administrative prosecutions, the DEA has asserted that all of these elements must be placed on the prescription *at the time* the practitioner issues it, and that a pharmacist cannot be the agent of the prescriber in filling in any missing elements. The Pharmacy Commission subsequently reiterated its position that a pharmacist may change or correct elements of controlled substances after consultation with the prescriber (see below), and that a pharmacist may add the DEA number or the patient's address without consulting the prescriber if he or she already knows it.[401]

ELECTRONIC PRESCRIBING OF CONTROLLED SUBSTANCES is allowed subject to a DEA rule designed to assure that the electronic signature of the prescriber is valid.[402] However, before an e-prescription for controlled substances is valid, the prescriber's computer system and the pharmacy's computer system must both be certified to comply with the rule.

PHARMACIES will be able to process electronic prescriptions only if all the following conditions are met:

- The pharmacy computer application must comply with the requirements of the rule; and
- The prescription was issued in conformity with the requirements of the rule and all other requirements for prescriptions in the CSA.
- All of the pharmacist's responsibilities to assure the validity of the prescription apply to e-prescriptions as well as other prescriptions.
- The prescriber's e-signature must be verified by 2 of the following forms of authentication:
    - a *biometric* – something the practitioner *is* (e.g., iris scan, fingerprint);
    - a *knowledge factor* – something only the practitioner *knows* (e.g., password or response to a challenge question); or
    - a *device separate from the computer* – something the practitioner *has* (e.g., a hard token)

Pharmacies Must:

- Determine that the pharmacy application has been certified by a third-party auditor or certification organization to accurately and consistently
- Import, store, and display information required for prescriptions under 21 CFR § 1306.5(a);
- Import, store, and display the indication of signing as required by the e-prescribing rule;
- Import, store, and display the number of refills as required by 21 CFR § 1306.22;
- Import, store, and verify the prescriber's digital signature, as provided in the rule, when applicable.
- Discontinue processing of e-prescriptions for controlled substances if the auditor or certification organization has found that the application does not function as required or no longer qualifies, or if notified that the application is not in compliance.
- Determine which employees are authorized to enter information regarding dispensed prescriptions, and annotate or alter records of those prescriptions. Logical access controls for the application must be set so that only authorized employees are granted access.

Pharmacists' Responsibilities:

- When a pharmacist fills a prescription in a manner that would require a notation if the prescription were a paper prescription (e.g., partial filling under 21 CFR 1306), the application must allow the pharmacist to make and retain such notations electronically.
- Prescriptions received electronically must be retained electronically.
- When a pharmacist receives a paper or oral prescription that indicates it was originally transmitted electronically to the pharmacy, he or she must check the pharmacy's records to ensure the e-version was not received. If both prescriptions were received, one must be marked void.
- When a pharmacist receives a paper or oral prescription indicating that it was originally e-transmitted to another pharmacy, he or she must contact that pharmacy to determine whether that pharmacy received and/or dispensed the prescription. The pharmacy that did not dispense the received prescription must mark the prescription void.
- The pharmacist retains the corresponding responsibility to insure that all prescriptions dispensed were issued for a legitimate medical purpose in the due course of the prescriber's practice.

Washington's CSA defines "electronic communication of prescription information" as the "transmission of a prescription or refill authorization for a drug of a practitioner using computer systems. *This term does not include a prescription or refill authorization verbally transmitted by telephone nor a facsimile manually signed by the practitioner."* (RCW 69.50.101(n))

RCW 69.50.312 sets for the rules for e-prescribing and permits the Commission to adopt additional rules. Information concerning prescriptions (schedule II-V) or refills (for schedule III-V) may be communicated electronically to a pharmacy of the patient's choice subject to the following conditions:

- The information communicated electronically complies with all applicable statutes and rules regarding the form, content, recordkeeping, and processing of a prescription for a legend drug.
- The system used must be approved by the Commission and in accordance with federal rules. *This does not apply to currently used facsimile equipment transmitting an exact visual image of the prescription.*
- An explicit opportunity must exist for practitioners to communicate their preferences for generic substitution.
- Prescription drug orders are confidential health information, and may only be released to the patient or the patient's authorized representative, the prescriber or other authorized practitioner caring for the patient, or other persons specifically authorized by law to receive PHI.

- Adequate security and systems are required to maintain confidentiality. (See RCW 69.50.312(e))
- The pharmacist shall exercise professional judgment regarding the accuracy, validity, and authenticity of the prescription drug order received electronically, consistent with federal and state laws and rules and guidelines of the Commission.

At its January 2015 meeting, the Commission adopted revisions to its rule on electronic prescribing, to conform to the statutory changes. As of January 2019, the rule remains unchanged from its last version in 2011 and the previously filed CR-101 has been withdrawn.

See below for specific prescription requirements for various schedules.

DELIVERY OF CONTROLLED SUBSTANCES TO PATIENTS OR PRESCRIBERS

DELIVERY TO PATIENTS. Under federal law, to "'dispense' means to deliver a controlled substance to an ultimate user or research subject by, or pursuant to a lawful order of, a practitioner..." (21 USC 802(10))

AN ULTIMATE USER is "a person who has lawfully obtained a controlled substance for his own use or for the use of a member of his household or for administering to an animal owned by the individual or a member of his household." (21 USC 802(27); RCW 69.50.101(kk)[403])

The CSA does not define "household," but the federal definition of a household is "... all the persons who occupy a housing unit as their usual place of residence." Thus, a daughter who does not live with her parents is not a member of the parents' household, but an unrelated college student who rents a room in the parent's house is a member of that household. In 2016, the Washington Court of Appeals reversed a conviction and held that an affirmative defense to the charge of possession of controlled substances without a prescription is available to a member of the household of the person for whom drug was prescribed. In the case, a mother was charged with illegal possession of what turned out to be a dose of controlled substances for her adolescent daughter.[404]

The DEA has held that it is inappropriate for a pharmacist to deliver a prescription to the patient's physician for administration or later delivery to the patient.[405] The DEA and the Pharmacy Commission have charged pharmacies and pharmacists with violation of this rule.

It is permitted for the pharmacist to use an employee of the pharmacy, or a common carrier (e.g. UPS or FedEx), or a taxicab or other delivery service, or the postal service to deliver a controlled substance directly to the patient. Section 453 of USPS Publication 52 provides instructions for mailing drugs and controlled substances.[406]

DELIVERY TO PRESCRIBERS. The DEA has held that pharmacies who wish to compound or prepare controlled substances for use in a physician's office must be registered as manufacturers, repackagers, or wholesalers. Section X of the *Pharmacist's Manual* states that "... a pharmacist who receives a prescription for a controlled substance must dispense that prescription to a patient or a member of the patient's household. To provide the controlled substance to anyone other than the patient or a member of the patient's household is distribution, not dispensing."

Controlled substances in their original manufacturer's container may be transferred to a physician for office use subject to the use of Form 222 for schedule II drugs or based on an invoice for other controlled substances (subject to the 5% limit) without registering as a wholesaler. The DEA has held that breaking up a manufacturer's package (such as taking 1 vial out of package of 25) constitutes repackaging and requires registration as a repackager.

CONTROLLED SUBSTANCE SCHEDULES. The Act sets forth FIVE SCHEDULES OF CONTROLLED SUBSTANCES based on likelihood of abuse and/or medical use. Only substances in schedule II through V are available for medical use. Table 5-1 summarizes the requirements of these schedules. The specific requirements related to each schedule are discussed below.

TABLE 5-1. CONTROLLED SUBSTANCES SCHEDULES AND REQUIREMENTS

Schedule	Basis for Inclusion	Examples	How Prescribed	Prescriptions Expire		Refill Limits	
				Federal Law	WA	Federa l Law	WA
I	**No medical use,** high potential for abuse	heroin, LSD, psilocybin, marijuana	May not be prescribed	N/A	N/A	N/A	N/A
II	High potential for abuse	cocaine, meperidine, morphine, oxycodone, methylphenidate, am-phetamines, propoxyphene powder, codeine, hydrocodone and hydrocodone combinations, fentanyl, tapentadol	Written	Never	6 months from date written	No refills	No refills
III	Moderate potential for abuse; mostly narcotic combos, anabolic steroids	codeine ≤ 90 mg/dose with ASA, APAP or NSAID, e.g. ibuprofen; buprenorphine; anabolic steroids, including testosterone; sodium oxybate (Xyrem®); Fiorinal®; "new" Fioricet® (300 mg APAP)[407]	Written or oral	6 months from date written	6 months from date written	5 refills	5 refills
IV	Moderate potential for abuse; Non-narcotics mostly	Benzodiazepines; chloral hydrate; phenobarbital; meprobamate; carisoprodol; "Z-drugs": zolpidem, zaleplon, zopiclone; modafinil; sibutramine; butorphanol; tramadol[408]	Written or oral	6 months from date written	6 months from date written	5 refills	5 refills
V	Agents with low abuse potential, eg, codeine ≤10 mg/dose plus other ingredients	Lomotil®; Tylenol® with Codeine Elixir; codeine cough syrups; Lyrica® (pregabalin); Epidiolex® (cannabidiol); some products may be OTC	Written or oral	Never	6 months from date written	No limit	5 refills

SCHEDULE II REQUIREMENTS

C-II DRUGS ARE EXCHANGED BETWEEN REGISTRANTS (MANUFACTURERS, WHOLESALERS, PHARMACIES, PRESCRIBERS) BY USE OF ORDER FORMS (DEA FORM 222).

CSOS – ELECTRONIC ORDERING. The DEA has published standards by which registrants may order CSA drugs electronically, using the Controlled Substances Ordering System (CSOS). Registrants must apply for a CSOS Certificate, and adapt their computer system to work within the specifications of the DEA. Currently, this is voluntary, but it is the DEA's intention to eliminate paper order forms over time. Information on CSOS is available at www.deaecom.gov.

TRANSFER TO PHYSICIANS to meet "emergency needs" is limited to FDA-approved drugs in their original containers if transfers do not exceed 5% of total controlled substances.

POWER OF ATTORNEY ISSUED TO EMPLOYEES. The individual who signed the original registration application for the pharmacy is the person who can sign DEA form 222, or sign the requisition to obtain additional DEA 222 forms. To allow other employees of the pharmacy to sign order forms or requisitions, the applicant must execute a LIMITED POWER OF ATTORNEY**,** which is kept on file in the pharmacy. A person does not have to be a pharmacist to have authority to order controlled substances or order forms. A person authorized by a power of attorney must obtain his or her own digital signature certificate from the CSOS to participate in electronic ordering.

WRITTEN PRESCRIPTIONS. C-II prescriptions must be in writing, signed by the prescriber in his or her hand.

FAXES are allowed for C-II drugs for patients in LTC facilities, hospice patients, and for home IV products for injectable C-IIs.

- Faxes must be a copy of a written prescription that is signed by the prescriber in his or her hand (a "wet signature"); faxes may not be computer generated and "electronically signed."
- Faxes may serve as the "Authorization for an Emergency Supply" of a C-II drug under federal law. (See below.)
- Faxes may be a reference for filling a C-II prior to the patient's arrival, if compared to the original before dispensing.

Under WA law, "LTC facilities" include nursing homes, boarding homes, hospice facilities, and adult family homes. (RCW 69.50.308(ii)) Federal regulations define LTC facilities to mean a nursing home, retirement care, mental care or other facility or institution which provides extended health care to resident patients. (21 CFR § 1300.01(b)(25))

The federal rule requires a fax for a C-II to be made directly from the prescriber to the pharmacy. This has led to confusion over whether the fax may come from the LTC to the pharmacy, with the LTC nurse acting as the prescriber's agent. Initially, the DEA said the LTC employee could not be an agent of the prescriber, but in October 2010, the agency issued a policy allowing physicians to appoint agents who are not employees of the prescriber to transmit fax or verbal orders on behalf of the prescriber.[409]

> The core responsibilities of prescribing may not be delegated, but "an individual practitioner may authorize an agent to perform a limited role in communicating ... prescriptions to a pharmacy in order to make the prescription process more efficient."
>
> Where faxes of controlled substance prescriptions are allowed, "an authorized agent of the prescribing practitioner may transmit the practitioner-signed prescription by facsimile on behalf of the practitioner."

When the authorized agent is not an employee of the prescriber, the authority of the agent must be made in writing by the prescriber. The DEA has a sample agreement on its website for prescribers to use to authorize non-employees (e.g., nurses employed by LTC facilities) to transmit prescriptions on their behalf.

The 2016 Legislature addressed this concern in part by amending RCW 69.50.308(f) to specify that "A written, oral, or electronically communicated prescription for a substance included in Schedule III, IV, or V, which is a prescription drug as determined under RCW 69.04.560,[410] for a resident in a long-term care facility or hospice program may be communicated to the pharmacy by an authorized agent of the prescriber. *A registered nurse, pharmacist, or physician practicing in a long-term care facility or hospice program may act as the practitioner's agent for purposes of this section, without need for a written agency agreement.*" Although the first part of the paragraph refers only to Schedule III, IV, or V drugs, "this section" is the entire RCW 69.50.308, which permits transmission of Schedule II faxes to a pharmacy in an LTC setting.

Washington's Uniform Controlled Substances Act in RCW 69.50.308 allows faxing of Schedule II drugs "by a practitioner to a pharmacy," ... when "the practitioner or the practitioner's agent notes on the facsimile prescription that the patient is a long-term care or hospice agent."

The most likely interpretation of the interplay between federal rules and Washington statute is that a facsimile that transmits an exact visual image of a Schedule II prescription may be transmitted by an LTC employee acting as agent of the practitioner as established in RCW 69.50.308(f); the original must be "wet signed" by the practitioner.

The DEA appears to require that all the information required for prescriptions be present on a faxed order for C-IIs – in both community and LTC settings. Thus, a copy of the physician's order sheet would need to be supplemented with the prescriber's printed name, office address, and DEA number, at the very least.

AUTHORIZATION FOR EMERGENCY SUPPLY. If an urgent need exists and the prescriber cannot supply a written prescription to the pharmacy in sufficient time to meet the patient's needs, the pharmacy may accept a telephoned or faxed "Order for an Emergency Supply" of C-II meds, provided the prescriber delivers a written prescription to the pharmacy within 7 days (or postmarks it within 7 days). The oral order must be communicated directly by the prescriber to the pharmacist. Note: the relevant WA regulation still says "72 hours," and the Commission did not propose to change it when it published its notice to amend the rule, but it doesn't seem to be enforcing that requirement. (WAC 246-887-020(6))

There is no actual limit on the quantity that can be prescribed, except that it should be "sufficient ... to last until a written Rx can be supplied." The following procedures are required when dispensing an emergency supply:

- The pharmacist must place "Authorization for an Emergency Supply" on the face of the prescription, and the same wording must be on the original written Rx
- The quantity authorized on the two orders must be identical.
- If the written prescription is not delivered within 7 days, the pharmacy must notify the Board and the DEA.

The pharmacist staples the written prescription to the telephoned or faxed order.

According to the DEA's October 2010 policy statement, *AN AGENT OF THE PRESCRIBER "MAY NOT CALL IN AN ORAL PRESCRIPTION FOR A SCHEDULE II CONTROLLED SUBSTANCE ON BEHALF OF A PRACTITIONER EVEN IN AN EMERGENCY CIRCUMSTANCE."*[411]

The 2013 changes to Washington's electronic prescribing law appear to have inadvertently omitted faxes as a means of authorizing an emergency supply of a schedule II drug, since it excluded facsimiles as a means of electronic prescribing and failed to specifically mention faxes in the wording allowing for emergency prescriptions: "In emergency situations, as defined by rule of the commission, a substance included in Schedule II may be dispensed upon an oral prescription of a practitioner, reduced promptly to writing and filed by the pharmacy." (RCW 69.50.308(c))

However, as noted in Chapter 4, the 2016 legislature[412] revised RCW 18.64.245 to specify that "when a pharmacy receives a prescription in digital or electronic format through facsimile equipment transmitting an exact visual image of the prescription, or through electronic communication of prescription information, the digital or electronic record of every such prescription dispensed at the pharmacy constitutes a suitable record of prescriptions, provided that the original or direct copy of the prescription is electronically or digitally numbered or referenced, dated, and filed in a form that permits the information required to be readily retrievable." (RCW 18.64.245 (2)). This suggests that a fax copy of a written prescription for legend drugs is to be treated as if it were the valid record of the written prescription, and that an electronic file copy of a fax may be stored in the computer. This also suggests that a fax for an emergency supply can be treated as a written temporary prescription.

PRESCRIPTIONS ARE INVALID IF THEY ARE "POST-DATED," I.E., DATED ON A DATE LATER THAN THE DAY ACTUALLY WRITTEN. However, nothing in the law prohibits a prescriber from indicating in the directions to the pharmacist a date before which the prescription should not be filled.

C-II PRESCRIPTIONS ARE NOT REFILLABLE.
The DEA considers the requirement that Schedule II prescriptions may not be refilled to be one of the more sacrosanct requirements of the Act. It has allowed for "partial filling," of controlled substances (see below), but has worked hard to distinguish "partial fills" from "refills."

MULTIPLE PRESCRIPTIONS FOR THE SAME PATIENT MAY BE WRITTEN ON ONE DATE TO BE FILLED AT LATER DATES. As a result of its heightened concern about refills of Schedule II drugs, the DEA for a period of time was opposed to a practice that emerged – primarily among physicians treating attention deficit disorders – as a result of insurance company limitations on prescriptions to 30-day supplies. Because the patients with ADDs were being treated with chronic dosing of methylphenidate or other stimulants in Schedule II, they were having to return to the prescriber monthly just to obtain new prescriptions. The prescribers began to issue 3 prescriptions at a time, each for a 30-day supply. In some cases, the prescribers mistakenly thought they should "post-date" the prescriptions. After considerable pressure from the states and practitioner organizations, the DEA adopted a final rule that became effective on December 19, 2007[413] allowing, where otherwise permitted by state law (21 CFR §1306.12 and 21 CFR §1306.14), multiple prescriptions for a single substance and patient, written and signed on the same day under the following circumstances and requirements:

- No more than a 90-day supply is authorized;
- Each prescription after the first includes instructions indicating the earliest date on which the pharmacy may fill the prescription; and
- The prescriber concludes that this does not create an undue risk of diversion or abuse.
- Pharmacists may not fill prescriptions prior to the date indicated in the prescriber's instructions.
- This rule does not create a 90-day limit on the amount of a schedule II drug that can be prescribed on a single prescription.

The Pharmacy Commission has indicated that Washington laws allow this procedure. This is not available to prescribers in states, such as Idaho, which place a 30-day expiration date on Schedule II prescriptions.

PARTIAL FILLING OF C-II PRESCRIPTIONS. Washington and Federal law (21 CFR § 1306.13) allow for partial filling of C-II prescriptions.

- *IF THE PHARMACY IS UNABLE TO SUPPLY ENOUGH DRUG TO FILL THE PRESCRIPTION*; the remainder must be filled within 72 hours or not at all. If the remainder cannot be filled within 72 hours, the prescriber must be notified. (This is the statutory specification.)
- *IF THE PATIENT INITIALLY DOESN'T WANT OR CAN'T PAY FOR THE FULL QUANTITY*; the remainder must be filled within 72 hours or not at all.[414] If not filled, the prescriber must be notified.
- *IF THE PHARMACY IS ATTEMPTING TO CONFIRM THE VALIDITY OF THE PRESCRIPTION*, may fill a small amount to start the patient's therapy, then, if the prescription is verified, fill the rest within 72 hours.[415]
- *IF THE PHARMACIST IS INFORMED BY THE PRESCRIBER THAT THE PATIENT IS TERMINALLY ILL*, may partially fill for up to 60 days from date written. A notation must be made on the prescription that the patient is terminally ill.
- *IF THE PATIENT IS IN A NURSING HOME* (see definition, above), may partially fill for up to 60 days from date written
- *WHEN REQUESTED BY THE PATIENT OR PHYSICIAN AND FILLED WITHIN 30 DAYS*
  The Comprehensive Addiction and Recovery Act (CARA) has amended the Controlled Substances Act by adding the following paragraph to 21 U.S.C. 829:

(f) Partial fills of Schedule II Controlled Substances –

(1) Partial fills – A prescription for a controlled substance in schedule II may be partially filled if –

(A) it is not prohibited by State law;

(B) the prescription is written and filled in accordance with this title, regulations prescribed by the Attorney General, and State law;

(C) the partial fill is requested by the patient or the practitioner that wrote the prescription; and

(D) the total quantity dispensed in all partial fillings does not exceed the total quantity prescribed.

(2) Remaining portions –

(A) In general. – Except as provided in subparagraph (B), remaining portions of a partially filled prescription for a controlled prescription in schedule II –

(i) may be filled; and

(ii) shall be filled not later than 30 days after the date on which the prescription is written.

(B) Emergency situations – In emergency situations, as described in subsection (a), the remaining portions of a partially filled prescription for a controlled substance in schedule II –

(i) may be filled; and

(ii) shall be filled not later than 72 hours after the prescription is issued.

(3) Currently lawful partial fills. – Notwithstanding paragraph (1) or (2), in any circumstance in which, as of the day before the date of enactment of this subsection, a prescription for a controlled substance in schedule II may be lawfully partially filled, the Attorney General may allow such a prescription to be partially filled.

Under this change, a pharmacist would be able to comply with a prescriber's request to dispense weekly supplies, for example, of a schedule II drug, based on a new prescription issued each month. The Commission has explained that WA law does not prohibit partial fills and that WA pharmacists may partially fill C-II prescriptions in accordance with CARA.[416] As of January 2019, the DEA has not modified the CFR, but the statute is in effect.

It is important to note that the prescriber or the patient must request the partial filling under the CARA statute. The pharmacist should document whether the request came from the patient or the prescriber.

There is no apparent prohibition on the pharmacist informing the patient of his or her right to request a partial fill when it would be in the patient's interest.

TRANSFER LABEL REQUIRED. Federal law requires C-II Rx containers to bear the label: "Warning: Federal law prohibits transfer of this medication to any person other than the person for whom it was prescribed." *WASHINGTON* regulation requires ALL prescription containers, including those containing CSA drugs, to bear, instead, the label*: "WARNING: STATE OR FEDERAL LAW PROHIBITS TRANSFER OF THIS MEDICATION TO ANY PERSON OTHER THAN THE PERSON FOR WHOM IT WAS PRESCRIBED."* (WAC 246-869-010(3))

6-MONTH TIME LIMIT ON C-II PRESCRIPTIONS IN WASHINGTON. Federal law does not impose a time limit on the filling of C-II prescriptions; once written, they do not expire under federal law. *UNLIKE UNDER FEDERAL LAW, C-II PRESCRIPTIONS ARE INVALID AFTER 6 MONTHS FROM THE DATE WRITTEN IN WA* (RCW 69.50.308 (d))

ELEMENTS OF A COMPLETED C-II PRESCRIPTION. A completed written C-II prescription must bear all of the following elements:

- Patient name
- Patient address
- Date written
- Drug, quantity, directions
- Prescriber address
- Prescriber DEA number
- Prescriber Written Signature
- Indication in Washington of substitution status, using a 2-line Rx blank
- Tamper resistant features and the Pharmacy Commission seal indicating that the prescription meets the requirements of Washington law (unless prescription was written by out-of-state prescriber)
    - Faxed prescriptions do not require tamper-resistant features. But they must be a visual image of a hand-signed prescription form that meets Washington requirements, including 2 signature lines to indicate substitution preferences.

FAXES MARKED "VOID" MAY NOT BE FILLED
A faxed copy of a prescription issued on a tamper-resistant prescription will display a "pantographic image," such as "VOID", "ILLEGAL," "COPY", or "FAX/COPY." If the image says "void" or "illegal," then the fax is not capable of serving as the original prescription for a schedule II drug. However, the words "copy" or "FAX/Copy" only indicate that the Rx is a facsimile and are valid whenever faxed prescriptions may be filled.

WHAT MAY A PHARMACIST CHANGE OR EDIT ON A C-II PRESCRIPTION? The DEA has amended its policy on edits to a C-II prescription several times in recent years. Its current website no longer has a FAQ on the subject. The Pharmacy Commission has reiterated its policy that a pharmacist may make the following changes to a controlled substance prescription:[417,418]

- Add or change the *PATIENT'S ADDRESS* after verification with patient
- Add the prescriber's *DEA REGISTRATION NUMBER*, either after consultation with prescriber or, if already known to the pharmacist, without contacting the prescriber
- After consultation with the prescriber, may change or add
    - *DOSAGE FORM*
    - *DRUG STRENGTH*
    - *DRUG QUANTITY*
    - *DIRECTIONS FOR USE*

- *ISSUE DATE – IN 2009, THE BOARD INDICATED THAT THE DATE MAY BE CHANGED OR ADDED; A PHARMACIST WAS REPRIMANDED IN 2017 FOR REFUSING TO FILL A C-II PRESCRIPTION WITHOUT CONSULTING THE PRESCRIBER SOLELY BECAUSE THE DATE WAS WRONG.*
- *BRAND-GENERIC CHANGES*

- PHARMACISTS MAY NOT CHANGE the patient's name, or the controlled substance prescribed (other than brand/generic).[419]

> **Fassett's Comment:** Under the US Supreme Court decision in *Gonzales v. Oregon*, it seems likely that the DEA does not have authority to overrule state regulations interpreting what the nature of a valid prescription is or whether changes may be made to written prescriptions once issued. Given the DEA's wavering position on this issue, however, pharmacists should make changes to C-IIs based on verbal instructions only when clearly needed in the patient's best interest, and document the changes carefully, adhering to state rules.

ELECTRONIC PRESCRIBING USING NON-APPROVED SYSTEMS. Until the prescriber's system has been certified to comply with the DEA e-prescribing rule, the prescriber using an electronic system must print a copy of the prescription and sign it in his or her own hand (see above).

FILING OF PRESCRIPTION RECORDS. Prescriptions for C-II prescriptions may not be filed by the pharmacist in the same file as prescriptions for legend drugs. The federal law allows 3 options:

- Option 1 – Three separate files (one for C-II, one for C-III, C-IV, and C-V, and one for legend drugs)
- Option 2 – Two separate files (one for C-II, and one for all other drugs)
- Option 3 – Two separate files (one for Controlled Substances and one for legend drugs)

"OPTION 3" NOT ALLOWED IN WA. UNLIKE FEDERAL LAW, Washington regulations (WAC 246-887-020(4)) do NOT permit filing of C-II prescriptions in the same file as non-schedule II drugs.

AMPHETAMINE SALTS AND OTHER SCHEDULE II NON-NARCOTIC STIMULANTS are restricted in WA to use for only limited medical indications. Pharmacists are entitled to know the indication before dispensing.

The Board of Pharmacy has identified the following substances as subject to these limitations (WAC 246-887-040)

- Amphetamine and its salts or combinations
- Dextroamphetamine and its salts or combinations
- Methamphetamine
- Phenmetrazine (Preludin®)
- Methylphenidate (Ritalin®, etc.)
- Lisdexamfetamine (Vyvanse®, etc.)

RCW 69.50.402 specifies these indications by statute as follows:

- Narcolepsy
- Hyperkinesis (a synonym for ADHD)
- Drug-induced brain dysfunction
- Epilepsy
- Differential diagnostic psychiatric evaluation of depression
- Depression refractory to other modalities
- Multiple sclerosis
- Other indications specifically approved by FDA

The Pharmacy Commission, in consultation with medicine and osteopathic boards, may designate additional medical uses by rule. WAC 246-887-045 adds the following indication to the above list:

- Moderate to severe binge eating disorder in adults

SCHEDULE III, IV, AND SCHEDULE V LEGEND DRUG REQUIREMENTS are similar under Washington law to federal law, *EXCEPT THAT SCHEDULE V SUBSTANCES MAY NOT BE REFILLED MORE THAN 5 TIMES OR MORE THAN 6 MONTHS AFTER THE DATE WRITTEN*. As noted above, the 2013 revisions to Washington law removed facsimiles as a form of electronic prescribing, and this appears to have inadvertently affected schedule III through V prescribing (see below).

PRODUCTS ARE EXCHANGED BETWEEN REGISTRANTS USING AN INVOICE with the address and DEA number of each registrant contained on the invoice.

ORAL OR FAXED PRESCRIPTIONS ARE ALLOWED UNDER FEDERAL LAW, BUT WASHINGTON LAW MAY HAVE CHANGED IN 2013. Prior to 2013, Washington also allowed facsimile prescriptions for schedule III through V because facsimiles were considered a form of allowed electronic prescribing for these drugs. The revised definition of electronic prescribing excludes facsimiles (RCW 69.50.101(p)) as a form of electronic prescribing. The current language regarding schedule III through V prescriptions says that these drugs "may not be dispensed without a written, oral, or electronically communicated prescription of a practitioner," and doesn't mention facsimiles as it does for schedule II drugs. (RCW 69.50.308(e)) However, as noted above, the 2016 Legislature has established that a fax transmitting an exact image of the written prescription can serve as the record of the original prescription.

ELECTRONIC PRESCRIBING FOR C-III THROUGH C-V ARE ALLOWED WHEN PRESCRIBER AND PHARMACY SYSTEMS ARE COMPLIANT WITH THE DEA E-PRESCRIBING RULE.

ELECTRONIC PRESCRIPTIONS FROM NON-COMPLYING SYSTEMS MUST HAVE A "WET SIGNATURE" OR BE ORALLY VERIFIED AND TREATED AS AN ORAL PRESCRIPTION. In January 2011, the Commission indicated that the prescribers must print the e-prescription, sign it, and give it to the patient, fax a copy to the pharmacy, or orally prescribe it. "Pharmacists must call to verify and then take as an oral prescription, any prescription for a controlled substance [in schedule III through V] that is not manually signed by the prescribing practitioner."[420]

AUTHORIZED AGENTS OF THE PRESCRIBER (see above) may fax or communicate oral prescriptions for schedule III through V drugs to the pharmacy at the prescriber's direction.

Prescribers may authorize *UP TO 5 REFILLS FOR C-III, C-IV, OR C-V DRUGS IN WASHINGTON*. There is no refill limit for C-V legend drugs under federal law.

Prescriptions for C-III, C-IV, or C-V drugs may *BE FILLED OR REFILLED UP TO 6 MONTHS* after the date written. There is no time limit under federal law for filling or refilling C-V legend drugs under federal law.

MAY TRANSFER PRESCRIPTIONS AND REFILL INFORMATION ON A ONE-TIME BASIS TO ANOTHER PHARMACY. The Commission's rules allow the transfer of information concerning refills of prescriptions between pharmacies, thus allowing a patient to have his or her refillable prescription dispensed at a different pharmacy without needing to obtain a new prescription from the prescriber. The rule (WAC 246-869-090) requires that the "transfer is communicated directly between two licensed pharmacists," but elsewhere (WAC 246-870-030) the Commission specifically allows fax transfers of refills information between pharmacies (see below).

TRANSFERRING PHARMACIST. The transferring pharmacist must record the following information *ON THE HARD COPY OF ORIGINAL* prescription. This differs under federal law from the state law for transferring refill information on legend drugs.

- The word "VOID"
- Name, address, and DEA number of receiving pharmacy
- Date of transfer
- Name of receiving pharmacist (should be full name!)
- Name or ID of transferring pharmacist.

RECEIVING PHARMACIST. The receiving pharmacist must record the following information on the hard copy of the transferred prescription:

- Name, address, and DEA number of the transferring pharmacy.
- Prescription number of the prescription at the transferring pharmacy.
- Name of the transferring pharmacist (should be full name!)
- Date the prescription was originally written.
- Complete dispensing history:
  - Date of original dispensing
  - Date of each refill dispensed
  - Prescription number and pharmacy name of each dispensing
- Original number of refills ordered.
- Number of refills remaining.

The following illustrates the information needed on the original and transferred controlled substances prescription. (Note how old the dates are on this example – the rules haven't changed in 20 years!)

"DIRECTLY BETWEEN TWO LICENSED PHARMACISTS." The Commission has expressed concern over instances where technicians have been the sole pharmacy personnel involved in the transfer of prescription information – typically by fax, and has cited the requirement of "directly between two licensed pharmacists" as precluding technician-to-technician fax transfers.

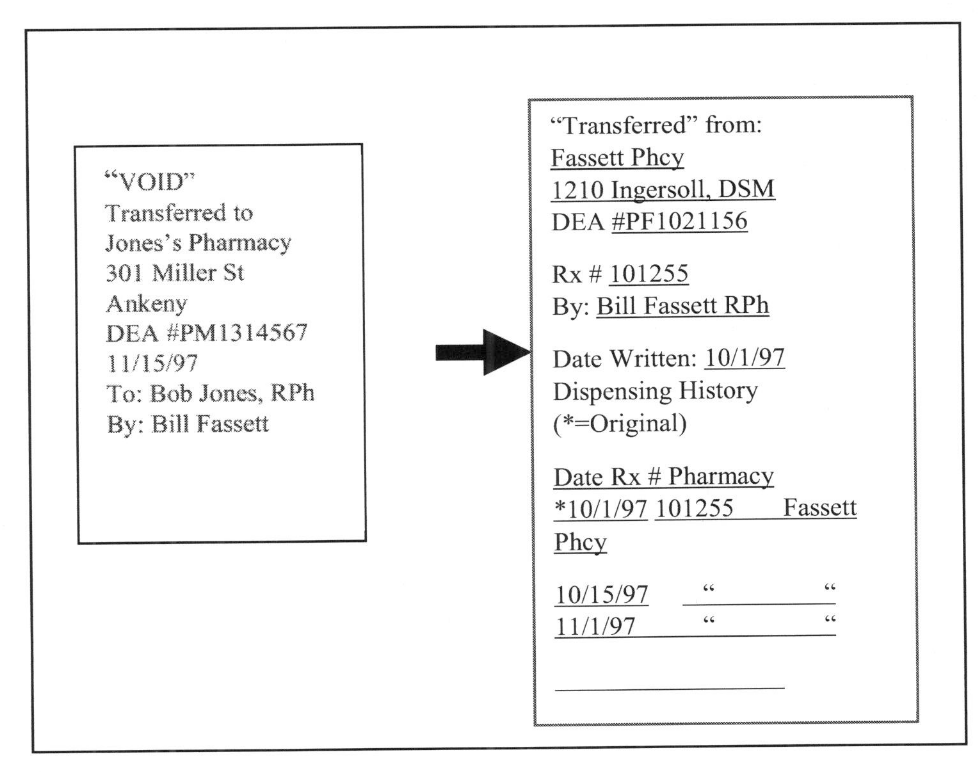
"VOID"
Transferred to
Jones's Pharmacy
301 Miller St
Ankeny
DEA #PM1314567
11/15/97
To: Bob Jones, RPh
By: Bill Fassett

"Transferred" from:
Fassett Phcy
1210 Ingersoll, DSM
DEA #PF1021156

Rx # 101255
By: Bill Fassett RPh

Date Written: 10/1/97
Dispensing History
(*=Original)

Date	Rx #	Pharmacy
*10/1/97	101255	Fassett Phcy
10/15/97	"	"
11/1/97	"	"

However, there is no actual prohibition of allowing a technician to prepare a request by one pharmacist to another pharmacy for prescription transfer information. Nor is there a prohibition of allowing a technician to prepare information for review by the transferring pharmacist prior to transfer, or of performing the nonjudgmental function of faxing the approved transfer information on behalf of the pharmacist or intern.

To be compliant with the regulation, key elements of the faxes must include: the name of the pharmacist or intern issuing or authorizing the request (signature would be a good idea, also), the name (and perhaps signature) of the pharmacist or intern reviewing and authorizing the communication of the information, and the name on the fax with the transferred information of the requesting pharmacist, who must review the transferred information before dispensing the transferred prescription.

COMPUTER RECORDS FOR C-III OR C-IV MUST BE KEPT ON-LINE FOR 24 MONTHS AFTER THE LAST POSSIBLE REFILL OF A GIVEN PRESCRIPTION. In practice, this means that 2½ years' worth of data must be available on line for refillable prescriptions.

PHARMACISTS USING COMPUTER RECORDS MUST SIGN A DAILY LOG SHEET, OR A BOUND BOOK, at the end of each shift or day, indicating the correctness of the computer records. (See *Pharmacists Manual* for more details.)

THE STATE TRANSFER WARNING LABEL must be affixed.

PARTIAL FILLING OF C-III, C-IV, OR C-V PRESCRIPTIONS. Pharmacists may partially fill C-III or C-IV prescriptions in quantities less than the original prescription, and these partial fills do not count as "refills" within the 5-refill limit, provided that:

- No partial fills are dispensed after 6 months
- The total quantity dispensed by the original and all partial fills does not exceed the total quantity authorized on the prescription.[421]

SCHEDULE V OTC DRUGS

A small number of OTC products – primarily those marketed under the cough and cold monograph – contain codeine in a dose of 10 mg/5 mL, which qualifies them as Schedule V drugs that do not require a prescription under federal law, and the labels of these products do not bear the "Rx Only" legend. RCW 69.50.308(e), as revised in 2013, specifies that "Except when dispensed directly by a practitioner authorized to prescribe or administer a controlled substance, other than a pharmacy, to an ultimate user, a substance included in Schedule III, IV, or V, which is a prescription drug *as determined under RCW 69.04.560*, may not be dispensed without a written, oral, or electronically communicated prescription of a practitioner." This statute has been interpreted by a staff attorney at the Pharmacy Commission, reading "which is a prescription drug," as defining all C-V drugs as Rx only. This interpretation reads out of the statute the qualifying phrase, "as determined under RCW 69.04.560."

One challenge to interpreting paragraph (e) is that it contains an error. RCW 69.04.560 does not deal with the definition of a prescription drug, but rather with exemptions for drugs dispensed by practitioners to patients. The reference should have been to RCW 69.04.540, which states:

> **RCW 69.04.540 Drugs-Misbranding by sale without a prescription of drug requiring it.**
> A drug or device shall be deemed to be misbranded if it is a drug which by label provides, or which the federal act or any applicable law requires by label to provide, in effect, that it shall be used only upon the prescription of a physician, dentist, or veterinarian, unless it is dispensed at retail on a written prescription signed by a physician, dentist, or veterinarian, who is licensed by law to administer such a drug.

This statute has not been revised since 1945, and obviously predates the Durham-Humphrey amendments to the FDCA, but it clearly indicates that a drug requires a prescription only when some applicable federal or state law defines it as a prescription-only drug. A Schedule V drug that is federally OTC remains OTC in Washington under this statute in the absence of state law to the contrary. The only state law otherwise dealing with Schedule V is RCW 69.50.308(i), requiring that "A substance included in Schedule V must be distributed or dispensed only for a medical purpose." This section predates 2013, and the Legislature in amending RCW 69.50.308(e) did not deem it necessary to disallow "distribution" of a Schedule V OTC drug.

In spite of receiving testimony and comment to the contrary, the Commission accepted the input of its staff attorney, and repealed all of WAC 246-887-030, effective July 15, 2015,[422] which previously regulated C-V OTC sales in a manner different than federal law. If the Commission's critics (including the primary author and a former chief investigator) are correct, then **Washington now has no specific rules regarding sale of C-V OTC products**, except a statutory requirement that they are distributed for medical purposes only, and the following federal rules apply.

FEDERAL RULES FOR SALE OF OTC SCHEDULE V PRODUCTS. Under federal law, certain products that satisfy the monograph requirements promulgated by the FDA for OTC antidiarrheal products, cough and cold products, and oral analgesics, may be sold by pharmacies without a prescription. The products specified in federal regulations are:

- Opium-containing antidiarrheal products – not more than 240 mL or 48 solid doses within a 48-hour period.*
- Codeine containing pain relievers – not more than 24 solid doses within a 48-hour period.*
- Codeine containing cough syrups (e.g., guiafenesin and codeine) – not more than 120 mL within a 48-hour period

*As a practical matter, only a limited number of generic cough syrup versions of the now-discontinued Robitussin AC® (guiafenesin plus codeine), are still available on the market.

The purchaser must be at least 18 years of age.

The pharmacist (or pharmacy intern in Washington) selling the C-V substance must:

- Require each purchaser who is not otherwise known to him or her to provide "suitable identification (including proof of age where appropriate)"
- Maintain a bound book containing the following information for each sale:
  - Name and address of the purchaser
  - Name and quantity of controlled substance purchased
  - Date of the purchase
  - The name or initials of the pharmacist who dispensed the medication.

Maintain the C-V OTC sales book along with other controlled substances records.

Fassett's Comment: Although I am confident in my scholarship regarding OTC Schedule V medications and Washington law, I cannot prevent the Pharmacy Commission from acting in reliance on its own set of "alternative facts."[423] I cannot predict what the best answer would be to a question on the Washington MPJE about whether OTC C-V drugs can be sold without a prescription, but I suspect the Commission's question writers would rely on the Commission's current interpretation of the law. I also recommend that any pharmacy thinking about selling OTC C-V preparations without a prescription under the federal rules engage their attorney in a careful analysis of the option.

DEA RULE CLARIFICATIONS. The DEA issues clarifications of its rules in response to inquiries from pharmacists or other registrants at http://www.deadiversion.usdoj.gov/faq/

COMPOUNDING PRODUCTS WITH CONTROLLED SUBSTANCES. Pharmacists may use controlled substances to compound lawfully-issued prescriptions. The schedule into which a compounded product is placed depends on the composition of the finished product, not the schedule of ingredients used. For example, codeine powder (schedule II) mixed with other active non-narcotic ingredients to make a cough syrup, will produce a product in schedule III if the codeine content is 90 mg or less per 5 mL dose, or a product in schedule V if the codeine content is 10 mg or less per 5 mL dose. It is wise to place a copy of the prescription in the schedule II prescription files, however.

The DEA does not allow compounding with controlled substances for sale directly to a physician (i.e., for office use), unless the pharmacy is registered as a manufacturer.

Although some jurisdictions limit the concentration of a controlled substance in a compounded prescription distributed by a pharmacy to no more than 20% of the complete solution, compound, or mixture,[424] this is **not** a restriction under Washington law.

WASHINGTON RULES ON PRESCRIBING OF OPIOIDS FOR CHRONIC NON-CANCER PAIN

Engrossed Substitute House Bill 1427[425] required new opioid prescribing practices for nurse practitioners, physicians, physician assistants, podiatrists, and dentists. With the exception of dentists, all prescribers writing opioid prescriptions for non-cancer pain will take a three tiered approach to care starting January 1, 2019. Pain treatment is based upon acute (0-6 weeks), subacute (6-12 weeks) and chronic phases. The Washington Department of Health has created a guide to pharmacists with the new requirements which can be found on their website.[426]

In general, prescribers are limited to a 7 day supply of opioids for acute non-surgical pain and 14 days post-surgery. In the subacute phase, a 14 day supply is limited. These limitations can be exceeded if the prescriber documents a need in the medical record. The PMP must be checked by the prescriber, under a personal or employer based system (WAC 246-919-985). In the chronic phase, written agreement plans are required. Naloxone should either be co-prescribed or documented in high risk patients (WAC 246-919-980). Nurse practitioners are required to include the International Classifications if Disease (ICD) code or diagnosis on the prescription (WAC 246-840-4657). These rules do not apply to end of life patients, those in hospice care, with cancer related pain or those who are hospitalized.

MEDICAL COMMISSION RULES EXAMPLE

Using the MC rules for physicians as an example, the adopted rules provide for the following:

PHYSICIANS ARE TO COMPLETE A ONE-TIME, AT LEAST ONE HOUR LONG, CONTINUING EDUCATION ON opioid prescribing best practice includes details describing the practice in Washington state. (WAC 246-919-875)

PATIENTS ARE TO BE ADVISED OF THE RISKS ASSOCIATED WITH OPIOID USE, ALTERNATIVES FOR TREATING PAIN, PROPER STORAGE AND DISPOSAL (WAC 246-919-865, WAC 246-919-870)

WHEN TREATING PAIN WITH OPIOIDS, PRESCRIBERS WILL

For Acute nonoperative pain (WAC 246-919-880)

- Obtain a past medical history including previous pain treatments, screening for overdose risk factors and evaluate the patient's pain needs
- Nonopioids should be considered. If opioids are prescribed, the PMP shall be checked. A maximum of 7 days be prescribed unless a greater quantity is justified by clinical documentation. (WAC 246-919-885).
- Pain that exceeds the initial therapy is to be reevaluated for change in
    - pain level
    - physical function
    - psychosocial function
    - additional indicated diagnostic evaluations may be obtained
- Opioid prescribing in combination with a benzodiazepine, barbiturate, sedative, carisoprodol or nonbenzodiazepine hypnotic shall be documented. If the prescriber, adds an opioid to an existing sedative therapy managed by another provider, the other prescriber shall be consulted. (WAC 246-919-970.)
- Extended release opioids should be avoided

For Acute perioperative pain. (WAC 246-919-890)

- The prescriber should follow the rules listed above
- A maximum of 14 days of the opioid can be prescribed unless a greater quantity is justified by clinical documentation

For Subacute pain (WAC 246-919-895)

- The prescriber shall assess the need for continued therapy
- In addition to physical examination, pain evaluation and review of the PMP the prescriber shall
    - Screen for overdose risk and the potential for misuse
- "If the patient's functional status is deteriorating or if pain is escalating"
    - Complete a biologic drug screening
    - Evaluate for psychosocial factors
    - Continued therapy shall be properly documented.
- A maximum of 14 days of the opioid can be prescribed unless a greater quantity is justified by clinical documentation

For Chronic Pain (WAC 246-919-905)

- The prescriber shall evaluate and reassess the patient's ongoing opioid medication needs, order appropriate laboratory monitoring, imaging, and offer complementary treatments
- Continued treatment shall include an opioid treatment plan including a written patient agreement for treatment outlining the patient's responsibilities (WAC 246-919-910, WAC 246-919-915)
- Based upon a patient's risk category for substance abuse disorder determined by a standardized risk assessment tool, ongoing review of the physical evaluation, PMP, and treatment plan is assessed on an quarterly to annual basis
- Consultation for pain management (WAC 246-919-930)

- Recommendations and requirements for consultation include the following:
    - Special attention and consideration of referral should be given for patients less than 18 years of age, or who are at risk for misuse, abuse, or diversion

- *MANDATORY CONSULTATION THRESHOLD:* 120 mg morphine equivalent dose per day (MEDD) oral.
- Mandated consultation shall consist of at least one of the following:
  - Office visit by patient to pain-management specialist
  - Telephone consultation between pain-management specialist and physician
  - Electronic consultation between pain-management specialist and physician
  - Audio-visual evaluation conducted remotely by pain-management specialist "where the patient is present with either the physician or *A LICENSED HEALTH CARE PRACTITIONER DESIGNATED BY THE PHYSICIAN OR THE PAIN-MANAGEMENT SPECIALIST."*
- Exemptions to the mandatory consultation requirement include (WAC 246-919-935):
  - The patient is following a tapering schedule
  - The patient requires treatment for acute pain, which may or may not include hospitalization, with the expectation that the patient will return to baseline after a temporary dosage escalation
  - The patient's pain and function is documented as stable and is on a non-escalating dosage of opioids.
- Prescribers are exempted when one or more of the following apply (WAC 246-919-940):
  - He or she is a pain management specialist. Pain management specialists are practitioners who meet the requirements of WAC 246-919-945
  - Has completed 12 Category I CME hours on chronic pain management with at least hours devoted to substance abuse disorder, within the prior 4 years
  - He or she is a pain management practitioner working within a multidisciplinary chronic pain treatment center or academic research facility
  - Has a minimum of 3 years of clinical experience in chronic pain management and at least 30% of his or her current practice is the direct provision of pain management care.

PHARMACIST'S RESPONSIBILITIES UNDER THE RULES.
The rules do not directly apply to pharmacists, nor do they modify pharmacists' other responsibilities under the law, but they do create some expectations for pharmacists' monitoring and review of prescriptions issued to chronic pain patients, and should apply to pharmacists with prescriptive authority to treat chronic pain patients

The Guide for Pharmacists published by DOH in 2018 suggests:

- Practitioners must provide patients with education on safe storage and disposal of opioids. Pharmacists are encouraged to include similar education in their patient counseling.
- Practitioners may exceed the prescribing limits if they have documented the clinical necessity. "This should be an exception rather than the norm. A pharmacist should use professional judgment to determine if further actions such contacting the prescriber, checking the PMP, or others are appropriate."
- Pharmacists have a corresponding responsibility "for patient safety" and should use PMP checks when indicated in their professional judgment to verify that the prescription is for a legitimate medical purpose and a legitimate patient.
- Partial filling is allowed under the new rules.

ONE PHYSICIAN – ONE PHARMACY. Note that the rules strongly recommend that patients go to one prescriber and one pharmacy. A pharmacist who knows that the patient is seeing multiple prescribers should notify the primary care provider.

DESIGNATED PROVIDER DURING CONSULTATIONS. Pharmacists could be designated to be the provider present during a remote A-V consultation with a pain specialist.

PHARMACIST PRESCRIBERS. Pharmacists operating under collaborative practice agreements and initiating or modifying therapy for chronic non-cancer pain patients should follow the same standards as for the authorizing prescriber, and should revise their protocols, guidelines, or CDTAs to reflect their adherence to these standards.

CONTROLLED SUBSTANCES IN INSTITUTIONAL PRACTICE

HOSPITALS

The Director of Pharmacy is responsible for developing policies and procedures to assure accountability and compliance with state and federal laws.

WRITTEN ORDERS RATHER THAN PRESCRIPTIONS. Controlled substances (and other drugs) are administered to patients based on written orders in the patient charts, rather than by individual prescriptions, except for outpatient distribution. Note that when a written order forms the basis for an outpatient prescription, all the additional information required for the prescription must be placed on the order.

HOSPITAL OUTPATIENT PHARMACIES are treated just like community pharmacies.

SPECIFIC SCHEDULE II REQUIREMENTS IN WA include (WAC 246-873-080 (7)):

PERPETUAL INVENTORY OF SCHEDULE II DRUGS. The pharmacy must maintain a perpetual inventory of C-II controlled substances that are in the pharmacy and have not been distributed to patients or patient care areas.

DRUGS DISTRIBUTED TO OTHER UNITS. The pharmacy must maintain a record of drugs distributed to other units (e.g., nursing unit) which includes:

- Date
- Name of the drug
- Amount of drug issued
- Name and/or initials of pharmacist who dispensed the drug
- Name of the patient and/or unit to whom the drug was issued.

ADMINISTRATION AND DISPOSITION OF SCHEDULE II DRUGS. Hospital units must maintain records of administration and disposition of Schedule II drugs. These are usually maintained in the MAR or patient chart, and must include:

- Date
- Time of administration
- Name of the drug (if not already indicated on the records
- Dosage of the drug which was used which shall include both the amount administered and any amount destroyed.
- Name of the patient to whom the drug was administered
- Name of the practitioner who authorized the drug
- Signature of the licensed individual who administered the drug.

"WASTAGE" MUST BE WITNESSED. When nurses must "waste" small amounts of controlled substances in any schedule, the destruction shall be noted and witnessed by a second nurse, who must sign the record.

POLICIES FOR DESTRUCTION OF CONTROLLED SUBSTANCES that conform to state and federal law must be developed by the Director of Pharmacy. (See Chapter 4 on environmental rules for drug waste.) A copy of the policies must be provided to DEA and the Board of Pharmacy. At a minimum, the policies must assure that:

- Destruction renders the drugs unrecoverable.
- Destruction is by a pharmacist and one other licensed health professional.
- Records of destruction are maintained in the pharmacy, and quarterly summary reports are mailed to the DEA with copies to the Board of Pharmacy.
- Note that hospitals must comply with state Department of Ecology rules for pharmaceutical waste in formulating these policies (see Chapter 4).

PERIODIC MONITORING OF CHART RECORDS by a nurse or a pharmacist is performed to assure that chart records are accurate.

USE OF MULTIPLE DOSE VIALS of controlled substances is DISCOURAGED.

SCHEDULE II OR III DRUGS – PHYSICAL COUNTS AT CHANGE OF SHIFT ARE REQUIRED for floor stocked Schedule II or III drugs. These counts must be made by two individuals licensed to administer drugs.

CONTROLLED SUBSTANCES RECORDS MUST BE KEPT FOR 2 YEARS; this includes records of destruction. Hospital pharmacies may apply for approval to use innovative record keeping systems.

SIGNIFICANT LOSSES OR DISAPPEARANCES OF CONTROLLED SUBSTANCES MUST BE REPORTED to the pharmacy department, the DEA, the Board of Pharmacy, the hospital CEO, and other appropriate officials.

LONG-TERM CARE

(WAC 246-865-060) Extended care facilities are subject to specific requirements for storage and administration of controlled substances. These differ in many instances depending on whether the facility uses unit-dose distribution or stores patients' drugs in" traditional" outpatient containers.

LABELING BY PHARMACIES FOR LTC USE

- PHARMACIES MUST INCLUDE THE CSA SCHEDULE NUMBER ON LABELS of drugs dispensed to LTC patients. (WAC 246-865-060 (4))
- COMPOUNDED DRUGS containing Schedule II or III substances must show the quantity of drug per mL or teaspoonful on the label.

NON-UNIT DOSE SYSTEMS must handle controlled substances as follows:

- *SCHEDULE II DRUGS MUST BE STORED SEPARATELY* in an individually keyed and locked area or cabinet.
- *SCHEDULE III DRUGS MUST BE STORED SEPARATELY* from other drugs, but may be stored with Schedule II drugs.
- *A BOUND LOG BOOK MUST BE MAINTAINED FOR SCHEDULE II AND III DRUGS,* which records all receipts and withdrawals of these drugs.
- *PHYSICAL COUNTS* by two individuals licensed to administer drugs must be made
    - at least *EVERY 24 HOURS FOR SCHEDULE II* drugs, and
    - at least *WEEKLY FOR SCHEDULE III* substances.
- *UPON DISCHARGE* of a resident, a record of release of Schedule II or III drugs shall be kept in the log book.

- *DISCONTINUED OR REMAINING SCHEDULE II DRUGS* must be destroyed, with proper documentation, within 30 days of discontinuance or discharge by
    - A pharmacist or the director of nursing services (DNS) or a RN-designee, plus an RN employee of the facility; or
    - By a representative of the Pharmacy Commission.
- DISCONTINUED SCHEDULE III, IV, AND V DRUGS (as well as legend drugs) remaining after discontinuance or discharge must be destroyed within 90 days.

UNIT DOSE DISTRIBUTION SYSTEMS may follow the rules for non-unit dose systems, or may develop an alternative system which maintains equivalent records of the receipt and disposition of Schedule II and III drugs.

- Schedule III drugs may be stored with other unit dose medications.
- Discontinued unit dose drugs other than Schedule II may be returned to the pharmacy.

CHALLENGES FOR DESTRUCTION/RETURN OF SCHEDULED DRUGS. Because nursing homes are not registered with the DEA, current rules do not allow them to transfer drugs to other registrants. The Secure and Responsible Drug Disposal Act of 2010[427] required DEA to develop a rule that would allow consumers and other non-registrants to return or cause the destruction of controlled substances.[428] The final rule was issued in late 2014.

LTCFs are restricted under the rule to the disposal of discontinued or outdated resident's controlled substances by use of a qualifying collection receptacle maintained in the facility by a community pharmacy authorized under the rule. (See discussion in Chapter 4)

Washington law allows return and reuse of unit-dose schedule III-V controlled substances from nursing homes; the DEA rule allows this only if the controlled substances are distributed in the facility by an automated dispensing device properly registered with the DEA (see below). Unused unit doses are, under the DEA scheme, not actually "returned" to the pharmacy, since the remote device is considered the pharmacy's property and its contents are inventoried by the pharmacy until the drugs are actually withdrawn from the device.

- The nursing home regulation (WAC 246-865-060 (5)(f)) allows returns of unit dose drugs to pharmacies
- The rule on Return or Exchange of Drugs (WAC 246-869-130) extends the authority of the pharmacy to accept returns from nursing homes to *modified unit dose* packaging (e.g., bingo cards).
- State Medicaid rules on unit dose distribution systems apply to unit dose and modified unit dose and require pharmacies to take back C-III through C-V medications. (WAC 388-530-5100(5))

Notwithstanding the above, the DEA in 2011 sought to revoke or suspend a pharmacy's DEA registration in part for accepting returns of C-III through C-V controlled substances from nursing homes. Long-term care pharmacies in Washington are typically not accepting returns of any controlled substances from LTC facilities.

AUTOMATED DISPENSING SYSTEMS (ADS) are defined by the DEA as mechanical systems performing storage, dispensing, packaging, counting, and labeling of medications. A pharmacy may place one or more ADS in a LTC facility, but each ADS must be registered with the DEA. The pharmacy must have a current DEA number, and a separate fee is required for each ADS location.

- A pharmacy may install ADS at any LTCF, and may operate one or more ADS under the one DEA number at the same LTCF.
- One or more pharmacies may install ADS at the same facility.
- The pharmacy must submit an application for registration (DEA-224) with an affidavit, which is a sworn statement that the ADS operation is authorized by the state.

- The ADS application is exempt from the registration fee (but not the original DEA number for the parent pharmacy).
- An ADS approval is location-specific, and the ADS cannot be moved to another facility without an approved request to modify the location.
- The affidavit must be notarized and contain the following information:[429]
    - Name and complete address of the parent pharmacy and LTCF;
    - Name, title, and signature of corporate officer or official signing the affidavit;
    - The name of the corporation operating the retail pharmacy;
    - The state license number of the pharmacy (and state CSA number if issued – not applicable in WA);
    - The date of state approval of the ADS;
    - The following statement:
      "This affidavit is submitted to obtain a DEA registration number. If any material information is false, the Administrator may commence proceedings to deny the application under section 304 of the Act (21 U.S.C. 8224(a)). Any false or fraudulent material information contained in this affidavit may subject the person signing this affidavit and the named corporation/partnership/business to prosecution under section 403 of the Act (21 U.S.C. 843)."

PRESCRIBING CHALLENGES IN LONG-TERM CARE FACILITIES

AGENT OF THE PRESCRIBER – as noted above, the DEA has expressed concerns that nurses or others who are not directly employed by a prescriber can only be called "agents of the prescriber" if a formal agency agreement has been established. The DEA has provided an example written agreement that would satisfy its need for documentation of the relationship, and the DEA policy requires the agent to acknowledge the appointment. The policy position also states the following regarding notification of pharmacists concerning the agent's appointment:

> A signed copy should also be provided to the practitioner's designated agent, the agent's employer (if other than the practitioner), and any pharmacies that regularly receive communications from the agent pursuant to the agreement. Providing a copy to pharmacies likely to receive prescriptions from the agent on the practitioner's behalf may assist those pharmacies with their corresponding responsibility regarding the dispensing of controlled substances. It is important to reiterate that a pharmacist always has a corresponding responsibility to ensure that a controlled substance prescription conforms with the law and regulations, including the requirement that the prescription be issued for a legitimate medical purpose by a practitioner acting in the usual course of professional practice, and a corresponding liability if a prescription is not prepared or dispensed in a manner consistent with the CSA or DEA regulations. Even where the pharmacist has a copy of an agency agreement, the pharmacist may also have a duty to inquire further depending upon the particular circumstances. Because the agency agreement may be revoked at any time by the practitioner or by the agent, the party terminating the agreement should notify the other party immediately upon termination. The practitioner should notify those pharmacies that were originally made aware of the agency agreement of the termination of that agreement.[430]

Washington law now makes it clear – at least for Schedule III, IV, and V drugs – that a nurse or pharmacist at the facility may serve as an agent of the prescriber without a formal agreement (see Chapter 4).

OMNICARE SETTLEMENT IN 2012. One of the nation's largest providers of pharmacy services to LTC facilities reached a $50 million settlement with the DEA in 2012 over allegations related to dispensing of controlled substances. Among the claims made by DEA and settled by the agreement were the following acts:

- Routinely dispensing controlled substances to residents of long-term facilities without a prescription signed by a practitioner.

- In a limited emergency situation, dispensing controlled substances without an oral prescription called in by a practitioner.
- Dispensing controlled substances to residents of long-term facilities from prescriptions missing essential elements, such as drug name, dosage, strength, quantity, DEA registration number and practitioner's name.
- Not properly documenting partially filled prescriptions thus preventing DEA from conducting an audit.

Many of these claims appear to have arisen in part from the DEA's position on designation of nurses as agents, and others involved DEA's assertion that LTC "orders" are not conforming "prescriptions" in that they lack the prescriber's name, address, DEA number, etc., on their face. According to the announcement of the settlement, "Omnicare has routinely accepted facility medical chart orders, oral orders from facility staff and other substitute documents and procedures as bases to dispense controlled substances, instead of requiring signed prescriptions or oral prescriptions directly from the prescribing physician."[431]

RESIDENTIAL TREATMENT FACILITIES in Washington are licensed to provide 24-hour per day health care to persons receiving services for a mental disorder or substance abuse. Categories of care include the following: Chemical Dependency (acute detoxification, subacute detoxification, intensive inpatient care, long-term care, or recovery house); or Mental Health (adult residential treatment, inpatient evaluation and treatment, child long-term inpatient treatment, or child inpatient evaluation and treatment).

The DEA has stated a position on provision of drugs to patients in RTFs by a pharmacy:

- Option 1 – the pharmacy that serves the RTF remains the DEA registrant for that facility, and provides drugs using a "smart" automated dispensing system. The pharmacist must review each order, then releases the drug to the nurse via the ADS.
- Option 2 – the ARNP or physician provides a patient-specific prescription and transmits the order to the pharmacy. The pharmacy dispenses and then delivers the prescription to the facility.
- Option 3 – the ARNP or physician obtains a DEA registration for the facility and order the prescriptions manually or electronically.[432]

CONTROLLED SUBSTANCE USE BY EMERGENCY MEDICAL SERVICES (EMS)

The Protecting Patient Access to Emergency Medications Act (PPAEMA)of 2017[433] amended an omission in the CSA which had previously forced EMS to operate without a DEA registration. Under PPAEMA, EMS agencies can register with the DEA as an entity or utilize an existing hospital registration to carry opioids and benzodiazepines for administration under a standing order from an authorized prescriber. Inventory receiving and use of the controlled substances must be tracked by the registrant. Where appropriate arrangements are made, EMS vehicles may restock controlled substances from a hospital without completing CSA order forms.[434]

CONTROLLED SUBSTANCE USE BY NON-PRACTITIONERS

DEPARTMENT OF FISH AND WILDLIFE OFFICERS AND BIOLOGISTS may use the following controlled substances for chemical capture programs (WAC 246-887-280):

- Butorphanol
- Diazepam

- Diprenorphine
- Carfentanil (Wildnil®)
- Fentanyl
- Ketamine
- Midazolam
- Tiletamine and zolazepam (Telazol®)

ANIMAL CONTROL AGENCIES AND HUMANE SOCIETIES may use legend drugs and controlled substances for sedation prior to euthanasia and for chemical capture programs.

Veterinary grade sodium pentobarbital may be used by humane societies and animal control agencies to euthanize animals (WAC 246-886-035).

Additional sections of WAC 246-886 set requirements under which humane societies and animal control agencies may use legend drugs or controlled substances.

WASHINGTON PRESCRIPTION MONITORING PROGRAM (PMP).[435]

As of December 2013, 48 states and 1 territory (Guam) were operating programs to track prescriptions, generally limited to controlled substances; 3 additional jurisdictions had passed legislation, but had not yet begun to operate the programs.[436] The goals of these programs vary among the states, but in general, these programs seek to monitor prescribing of controlled substances and/or legend drugs for purposes of education and information, public health initiatives, early intervention and prevention, and/or investigation and enforcement, and all seek to protect the confidentiality of the data collected. Washington has had a PMP in place for a number of years by which disciplined prescribers have been required to use triplicate prescription forms. In 2007, the Legislature enacted a statute authorized the Department of Health to expand this program statewide, subject to available funding, which is now established. (RCW 70.225.020) The enabling statute was amended in 2015 and 2016 to provide access to PMP information to additional persons and entities.

THE CORE ELEMENTS of the PMP include the following:

- The program is to monitor the prescribing and dispensing of covered drugs by "all professionals licensed to prescribe or dispense such substances in this state."
- Drugs to subject to monitoring include Schedule II, III, IV, and V substances and "any additional drugs identified by the board of pharmacy as demonstrating a potential for abuse."
- Program goals include improving health care quality and effectiveness by reducing abuse of controlled substances, reducing duplicative prescribing and overprescribing of controlled substances, and improving controlled substance prescribing practices.

DISPENSERS OTHER THAN VETERINARIANS (pharmacists and dispensing prescribers other than veterinarians) are required to electronically submit the following information for each prescription dispensed for more than immediate one day use:[437]

- Patient identifier
- Drug dispensed
- Date of dispensing
- Quantity dispensed
- Prescriber ID

- Dispenser ID

These requirements do not apply to

- inpatient hospitals and related settings
- pharmacies operated by the Department of Corrections for prescriptions dispensed to inmates, except for the offender's current prescriptions for controlled substances issued upon release from a correctional facility

PROGRAM RULES. Program rules are placed in WAC 246-470.

Key definitions. In addition to easily understood terms, the rules are specific as to the following:

PATIENT ADDRESS – the current geographic location of the patient's residence, or, if the patient address is in care of another person or entity, that person's or entity's address is the "patient address." If more than one is possible, they should be recorded in the following order of preference:

- Geographical location of residence, as would be identified by a 9-1-1 locator;
- An address listed by the US Postal Service; or
- The common name of the residence and town

VALID PHOTOGRAPHIC IDENTIFICATION means:

- A driver's license or instruction permit issued by any US state or province of Canada. If the license has expired, must show a valid temporary license along with the card
- A state identification card issued by any US state or province of Canada
- An official passport issued by any nation
- A US armed forces ID card
- A US Coast Guard-issued merchant marine ID card
- A state liquor control ID card issued by the liquor control authority of any US state or province of Canada
- An enrollment card issued by the governing of a federally recognized Indian tribe located in Washington if it contains features implemented by the DOL and recognized by the liquor control board.

DISPENSER ID. Dispensers (including prescribers who dispense) must use NPI and DEA numbers.

REQUIRED INFORMATION. The following information must be submitted for each dispensing, not later than one business day following dispensing (if no dispensing occurs on a business day, must report within 7 days that no report was required for that day):

- UNIQUE PATIENT IDENTIFIER: a unique identifier assigned to a particular patient by the dispenser – this would be the medical record number or a number assigned by the pharmacy information system. The rule does not specify that the patient must supply an ID number to serve this purpose.
- NAME OF PATIENT: first, middle initial, last, suffixes (Jr., II, etc.)
- PATIENT DATE OF BIRTH
- PATIENT ADDRESS
- PATIENT GENDER AND CODE FOR SPECIES (IF ANIMAL)
- DRUG DISPENSED
- DATE OF DISPENSING
- QUANTITY AND DAYS' SUPPLY DISPENSED
- REFILL AND PARTIAL FILL INFORMATION

- PRESCRIBER IDENTIFIER – MUST INCLUDE NPI AND DEA NUMBER WITH ANY SUFFIXES
- PRESCRIPTION ISSUED DATE
- DISPENSER IDENTIFIER – MUST INCLUDE DEA NUMBER AND NPI
- PRESCRIPTION FILL DATE AND NUMBER
- SOURCE OF PAYMENT:
    - Private pay (cash, check, credit card, etc.)
    - Medicaid
    - Medicare
    - Commercial insurance
    - Military or Veterans Affairs
    - Worker's compensation
    - Indian nations
    - Other;
- NAME OF PATIENT'S AGENT. When practicable, the name of person picking up or dropping off the prescription, as verified by valid photographic identification. Note: nothing in the rule appears to require that the ID number be recorded.
- PRESCRIBER'S AND DISPENSER'S BUSINESS PHONE NUMBERS

VETERINARIANS

Veterinarians are required to report much of the same information, however:

- The dispenser ID is the veterinarian's DEA number; veterinarians are not eligible for NPIs
- Reports must only be made quarterly
- Reports must only be made if the quantity dispensed is for more than a 14-day supply
- The report must report the name of animal including pet name, species, and owner's name (first, last, middle initial, generational suffixes)
- The owner's name and address must be reported, but the owner's ID number from a valid photo ID is to be obtained only "when practicable."

ACCESS TO PMP INFORMATION

PATIENTS or their personal representative may gain access to their own information in accordance with procedures specified in WAC 246-470-040

PHARMACISTS, PRESCRIBERS, OR LICENSED PRACTITIONERS authorized by a prescriber or a pharmacist may gain access to information on their patients for the purpose of providing medical or pharmaceutical care

- Prior registration by the pharmacist or other practitioner with the Department is required.
- The department will verify the identity and authority of the registrant, and will issue authentication that may be used to access PMP data electronically
- Alternatively, the registrant may submit a written request to the department
- The registrant is required to notify the Department immediately by phone and in writing if the authentication is lost or stolen.

LAW ENFORCEMENT OFFICIALS (federal, state, tribal, or local) may obtain information from the PMP for a bona fide specific investigation involving a designated person.

CERTAIN EMPLOYEES OF DOH, DSHS, HCA, OR DOC

MEDICAL EXAMINERS OR CORONERS may obtain information on a specific individual to determine the cause of death. Procedures for access are specified in WAC 246-470-060.

PERSONNEL OF DRUG TEST SITES

HEALTH CARE FACILITIES OR HEALTH CARE ENTITIES UNDER DEFINED CIRCUMSTANCES

OTHER PRESCRIPTION MONITORING PROGRAMS may obtain information as specified in WAC 246-470-070.

REQUESTS FROM RESEARCHERS for PMP information are subject to WAC 246-470-080.

CONFIDENTIALTY. Information disclosed to a health care provider by the PMP is considered health care information under the Washington Health Care Information Act and federal privacy rules (e.g., HIPAA). Such information may be retained by providers within other patient health care records that are protected by state and federal law.

METHAMPHETAMINE PRECURSOR DRUGS

RCW 69.43 deals with precursors to controlled substances. Sections relevant for retail pharmacies are aimed at limiting the availability of OTC products containing ephedrine, phenylpropanolamine, and pseudoephedrine, or their salts or isomers (EPP), which are used to make methamphetamine. This law was significantly revised by the 2005 Legislature and again revised in 2010 to bring it into conformance with federal law, and to establish a statewide electronic tracking system.[438]

PHARMACIES, SHOPKEEPERS, ITINERANT VENDORS, AND CHINESE HERBAL PRACTITIONERS may sell lawful EPP-containing products only under the following restrictions (RCW 69.43.105):

- THEY MUST OBTAIN PHOTO ID OF THE PURCHASER SHOWING DATE OF BIRTH, and the purchaser is required to provide such ID.
- EPP PRODUCTS MUST BE KEPT IN A CENTRAL LOCATION in the licensed premises that is not accessible by customers without assistance of an employee of the seller.
- THE PURCHASER MUST BE AT LEAST 18 years of age.

EXCEPTIONS: These restrictions do not apply to the following:

- Combination products (i.e., EPP plus non-EPP ingredients) in LIQUID, LIQUID CAPSULE, OR GEL CAPSULE FORM.
- LEGEND DRUGS SOLD PURSUANT TO A PRESCRIPTION.
- Sale by a traditional CHINESE HERBAL PRACTITIONER to a patient.
- WHEN THE DETAILS OF THE TRANSACTION ARE RECORDED IN A PHARMACY PROFILE INDIVIDUALLY IDENTIFIED WITH THE RECIPIENT AND MAINTAINED BY A LICENSED PHARMACY.

Fassett's Comment: It appears this allows pharmacies to sell to persons under age18 if the transaction is recorded in the pharmacy computer system as a patient record.

POLICE ORGANIZATIONS MAY PETITION TO ADD DRUGS. The law allows for a petition from the Washington Association of Police Chiefs, or the Washington State Patrol, asking the Commission to place particular combination products within the ambit of the log requirements based upon a showing that EPP within the product can be effectively converted into meth and evidence that the product is being converted into meth or other controlled substance.

LIMITS are specified in RCW 69.43.110 through .130. Individuals may not

- PURCHASE more than 3.6 g of EPP, at any one time within 24 hours, or 9 g of EPP in any 30-day period.
- POSSESS more than 15 g of EPP, except in their home as consistent with typical household use.

  A PEDIATRIC FORMULATION containing EPP is exempted if its label indicates it is intended for administration to persons less than 12 years of age and if each dose is less than 15 mg; or if it is a liquid intended for children less than 2 years of age, for which the dose does not exceed 2 mL and the total quantity in the package is not more than 1 fluid ounce.

FEDERAL LIMITS

The Combat Methamphetamine Epidemic Act of 2005 – as part of the extension of the USA PATRIOT Act (PL 109-177) is the federal law governing sales of EPP. These apply to non-liquid dosage forms of EPP sold OTC. Key differences between the federal requirements and WA are:

- As with WA law a maximum quantity of EPP is 3.6 g/day and 9 g/month, but the federal law sets a maximum of 7.5 g/month if ordered via the mail or common carrier.
- EPP must be sold only in blister packs containing 2 or fewer doses per blister.

SALES RECORDS. Until October, 2008, federal law did not permit electronic tracking of EPP retail sales. A new federal statute, the Methamphetamine Production Prevention Act of 2008, now allows retailers to use one of the following options:

- A written logbook
- An electronic logbook by which the purchaser's signature is captured
- By a device that captures signatures in an electronic format. The device must display the required notice of penalties, and clearly links the signature to other electronically captured required information relating to the sale.
- Signing a bound paper book to which the seller affixes a printed sticker displaying the required information regarding the sale or a unique identifier linked to that information, or in which the seller writes the unique identifier and the purchaser signs an adjacent line. The bound book must display the required penalty notices.
- Signing a printed document produced by the seller at the time of sale that displays the required penalty notices and the required information related to the sale. The signed page is immediately placed into a binder or other secure means of document storage.

PRODUCT INFORMATION may be captured through electronic means including barcode reader technology.

FEDERAL PENALTY NOTICE. The log book must contain "a notice to purchasers that entering false statements or misrepresentations in the logbook, or supplying false information or identification that results in the entry of false statements or misrepresentations, may subject the purchaser to criminal penalties under section 1001 of title 18, United States Code, which notice specifies the maximum fine and term of imprisonment under such section."

NO FEDERAL AGE MINIMUM. The federal law does not specify an age minimum.

TRAINING OF EMPLOYEES. Each seller must train all employees in the law and procedures, must maintain records of this training, and must certify to the DEA on a website,[439] that it has met these requirements.

TABLE 5-2. SUMMARY OF STATE AND FEDERAL EPP REQUIREMENTS: SALES LIMITS

	WA	Federal
Sales/day	3.6 g	3.6 g
Sales/month	9 g	9 g (**7.5 g** for Internet or mail order)
Possession	**15** g	n/s
Package size	n/s	3.6 g
Package type	n/s	**Blister, 2** units/blister

TABLE 5-3. SUMMARY OF STATE AND FEDERAL EPP REQUIREMENTS: LOG BOOK

	WA	Federal
Purchaser Name	Yes	Yes
Address	Yes	Yes
Date of birth	**Yes**	n/s
Type of ID	**Yes**	n/s
Signature	Yes	Yes
Name of drug	Yes	Yes
Quantity sold	Yes	Yes
Date of purchase	Yes	Yes
Time of purchase	Yes	Yes
Notice of penalties	n/s	**Yes**

STATE EXEMPTIONS LIST. The Commission has authority to exempt certain products or packages from the statutory sales limits upon application from the manufacture in accordance with specific guidelines in the statute. A list of exempted products is maintained on the Commission web site.

WHOLESALERS MUST REPORT SUSPICIOUS TRANSACTIONS. Methamphetamine precursors are called "regulated products" in RCW 69.43.010(1), and the statute requires reports of sales by wholesalers, and gives the Pharmacy Commission authority to regulate these products and sales. Any person who sells or transfers precursor chemicals (which could include pharmacies selling regulated product in bulk form rather than prepared dosage forms) must make certain reports under this statute. In particular, any manufacturer or wholesaler that sells a regulated product to any licensee must report to the Commission in writing any suspicious transactions. The Commission has adopted by rule the following definitions of suspicious transactions:

- Sales that would lead a reasonable person to believe that the substance would be used for illegal manufacture of controlled substances, based on such factors as
    - The amount of the substance involved
    - The method of payment
    - The method of delivery
    - Past dealings with the participant

  - Sales of regulated product paid for by cash or money orders in a total amount of more than $200
- Sales meeting criteria for suspicious transactions set by the DEA
- Where the dollar value of regulated products exceeds 10% of the dollar value of the total order of non-prescription products.
- An order containing only regulated products and no other non-prescription products.

ELECTRONIC PSEUDOEPHEDRINE TRACKING PROGRAM. The Commission has established an electronic point-of-sale tracking system under a memorandum of understanding with the National Precursor Log Exchange (NPLEx™).[440] NPLEx is sponsored by manufacturers of OTC pseudoephedrine, with technology supplied by the National Association of Drug Diversion Investigators. Rules for this program are contained in WAC 246-889.

EARLIER LOG BOOK REQUIREMENTS REPLACED. The NPLEx system replaces other forms of the transaction log that were set forth prior to 2011 in Washington. However, small retailers may seek an exemption to the electronic system and use a written logbook.

REQUIREMENTS FOR SELLERS. Retailers must verify the purchaser's ID, ensure the purchaser is at least 18 years of age, submit the required information regarding the sale.

Acceptable forms of ID include:

- Current foreign, federal, state, or tribal government-issued ID which includes the person's photograph, name, date of birth, signature, and physical description. These include the following:
  - Valid driver's license or instruction permit issued by any US state or foreign government; if the card is expired, must be accompanied by a valid temporary permit
  - US armed forces ID card
  - Merchant marine ID card issued by US Coast Guard
  - Official US passport or unexpired foreign passport containing a temporary I-551 stamp.
  - Federally-registered tribal enrollment card that has security features similar to Washington driver's licenses

PHARMACY AND RETAILER SUBMISSION REQUIREMENTS: At the time of sale, pharmacies or other sellers do the following:

- Enter the customer's ID number (e.g., Driver's License), and the system populates the customer's information.
- Address information must be the address as it appears on the photo ID, or the current address if not on the photo ID; must include house number, street, city, state, and zip code
- The customer's signature is either captured in a manual signature log, or via scanner.
- Click on a drop-down menu to select the product sold.
- Submit the data.

NPLEx will indicate whether the sale is compliant with federal and state rules.

DENIAL OF SALE. If NPLEx recommends DENIAL, the pharmacy employee provides customer with a printout directing the customer to the NPLEx website.

- The employee may attempt another transaction with a reduced quantity.

- The employee may select a SAFETY OVERRIDE if he or she feels threatened or that there is a danger to others, and complete the sale. The selection of a safety override will trigger a report to local law enforcement.

Penalty. The Pharmacy Commission may impose a civil penalty not to exceed $10,000 for each violation of RCW 69.43; each day of a continuing violation constitutes a separate violation. The Commission may waive suspension, revocation, or penalties upon a finding of good faith intentions to comply with the chapter, and that the violation occurred despite the registrant's or licensee's exercise of due diligence.

OTHER PRECURSORS

RCW 69.43.135 restricts sales and possession of iodine or methylsulfonylmethane. Chemical wholesalers must record sales or transfers on a form developed by the Washington State Patrol.

TREATMENT PROGRAMS FOR OPIOID ADDICTION

NARCOTIC TREATMENT PROGRAMS

The NARCOTIC ADDICT TREATMENT ACT OF 1974 allows for the establishment of narcotic treatment programs (NTPs) which may administer certain controlled substances, particularly methadone and levomethadyl (LAAM), to narcotic addicts being treated in the programs. Administration of narcotic treatment programs is vested in the SUBSTANCE ABUSE AND MENTAL HEALTH SERVICES ADMINISTRATION (SAMHSA), a part of the U.S. Department of Health and Human Services. No prescribing of methadone or LAAM can be done by NTPs, and community pharmacies may not fill prescriptions for methadone used to prevent withdrawal (levomethadyl is not available in the US outside of NTPs). These rules do not affect the use of methadone for treatment of pain.

USE OF METHADONE FOR MAINTENANCE OUTSIDE OF AN NTP. A PRACTITIONER who is not part of an NTP may administer methadone to an addict to relieve acute withdrawal symptoms while that practitioner is making arrangements to refer the addict to an NTP. No more than one day's drug may be administered at a time, and no more than three days' treatment may be provided.

A HOSPITAL which does not have an NTP may administer methadone to prevent withdrawal symptoms while the hospital is treating the patient for a medical condition other than narcotic addiction.

USE OF METHADONE FOR TREATMENT OF PAIN. Pharmacists receiving prescriptions for methadone should generally question prescriptions that are prescribed for obvious maintenance doses (e.g., once daily), rather than multiple daily doses which would be appropriate for treatment of actual pain.

Methadone 40 mg dispersible (Methadone Disket®) tabs are not available to community pharmacies, but are restricted for distribution to SAMHSA-certified opioid treatment programs.[441]

Pharmacists should be alert when patients present with initial prescriptions for methadone. In opiate-naïve patients, starting doses are typically 2.5 mg every 8 to 12 hours, and as low as 2.5 mg daily in frail elderly. Methadone dosed at 10 mg q 8 h is roughly equivalent to 120 mg of morphine per day or greater. Conversions from other opiates to methadone are not straight-forward, and at higher chronic doses methadone is progressively more potent.[442] Failure to consult with prescribers concerning obviously high methadone conversion doses is a growing source of negligence lawsuits against pharmacists.

OFFICE-BASED NARCOTIC MAINTENANCE PROGRAMS. Congress passed the DRUG ADDICTION TREATMENT ACT OF 2000 (DATA) (21 USC 823(g)), which allows for office-based narcotic maintenance programs using buprenorphine as an alternative to methadone maintenance in NTPs. Physicians wishing to prescribe outpatient buprenorphine for maintenance must apply for a waiver with the SAMHSA's Center for Substance Abuse Treatment. SAMHSA's buprenorphine web page can be found at http://buprenorphine.samhsa.gov/. Nurse practitioners or PAs became eligible as a result of the CARA act to apply for DATA waivers starting in 2016;[443] SAMHSA has announced training guidelines on its website for the 24 hours of required training. CARA also has a provision by which the DHHS Secretary can approve other practitioners – possibly pharmacists – to be eligible providers.

Each authorized practitioner is given a unique DATA waiver identification number. Prescribers are encouraged to include their DATA Waiver Number on prescriptions for buprenorphine, and SAMHSA has proposed rules that will require this in the future. Pharmacists may use the Buprenorphine Physician Locator page on the SAMHSA web site (http://buprenorphine.samhsa.gov/bwns_locator/index.html), which includes a link to information on how to verify a waiver for a physician who is not listed in the locator. The DEA issues qualified prescribers an additional DEA number with "X" as the first letter, which, like other DEA registrations, may be site-specific.

Authorized practitioners initially are waived for up to 30 patients, and later may be approved for up to 100 patients; after treating 100 patients for at least one year, a practitioner may seek to be approved for up to 275 patients.

PRESCRIPTIONS FOR BUPRENORPHINE MAINTENANCE. Pharmacists may fill prescriptions for buprenorphine issued by prescribers who have DATA waivers. The DATA waiver specific DEA number should be the number shown on the prescription for buprenorphine maintenance, and should be recorded when the prescription is dispensed.

Pharmacists who plan on filling prescriptions for buprenorphine should review SAMHSA's "Clinical Guidelines for the Use of Buprenorphine for the Treatment of Opioid Addiction: A Treatment Improvement Protocol," available on their website at http://buprenorphine.samhsa.gov/Bup_Guidelines.pdf.

AVAILABLE DRUG PRODUCTS. Only buprenorphine SL tablets and buprenorphine-naloxone SL film or tablets in a 4:1 buprenorphine-to-naloxone ratio are FDA-approved for narcotic maintenance or withdrawal treatment. The DEA could consider dispensing of buprenorphine injection for maintenance as diversion, since it would not serve a "legitimate medical purpose."

Available buprenorphine SL tablets are provided as 2 mg or 8 mg doses; manufacturers with approved ANDAs include Hi-Tech Pharmacal, Roxane, and Teva. Because Reckitt Benckisler has withdrawn Subutex® tablets from the US market, Roxane's 8-mg tablet is the RLD (reference listed drug) for the other generics, all of which are AB rated.

Reckitt Benckisler removed Suboxone® SL tablets from the US market in 2013, and now provides only Suboxone® SL film, in 2-mg or 8-mg dosages. Amneal Pharmaceuticals and Actavis Elizabeth produce 2-mg and 8-mg buprenorphine-naloxone SL tablets, with Actavis Elizabeth's product designated as the RLD; they are AB rated against each other. Another sublingual product, Zubsolv®, containing 1.4 mg or 5.7 mg of buprenorphine is manufactured by Orexo. The manufacturer claims that these doses are equivalent to the 2-mg or 8-mg combination products because of the greater bioavailability of the dosage form. Biodelivery Sciences produces Bunavail® (buprenorphine/naloxone buccal film) in the following strengths of buprenorphine and naloxone (mg): 2.1/0.3; 4.2/0.7; and 6.3/1.0, which it considers equivalent to the 4-mg, 8-mg, or 12-mg strengths of Suboxone.

In Washington, because the dosage forms are different, there is no generically-substitutable product for Suboxone SL film, nor, at present are there generic alternatives for Zubsolv or Bunavail.

All buprenorphine products are subject to REMS which require distribution of a Medication Guide to patients.

BUPRENORPHINE PRESCRIBED FOR PAIN. Although the use of buprenorphine or buprenorphine-naloxone combinations for treatment of pain is an off-label use, these products may be prescribed for treatment of pain, typically in doses given 3 or 4 times a day, by prescribers authorized to prescribe Schedule III drugs. No DATA waiver is required to prescribe buprenorphine for treatment of pain.[444]

PRIVACY CONSIDERATIONS UNIQUE TO TREATMENT PROGRAMS

Federal rules governing privacy in treatment programs require that any party disclosing information about the treatment must obtain a signed release from the patient before the information is transmitted.[445] The permission to disclose must also be possessed by the recipient before the information may be received. The treatment program privacy rule is found in 42 CFR Part 2, and are known as the "Part 2 rule." The Part 2 rule is separate from and in addition to protections in HIPAA. Whereas HIPAA allows transmission of PHI for treatment to other providers known to be providing care without the patient's explicit consent, the Part 2 rule does not. Therefore, NTPs do not disclose information to other caregivers who are treating patients enrolled in NTPs, absent the patient's written consent on a case-by-case basis.

Prescriptions transmitted from a DATA-waived prescriber to the pharmacist fall under the Part 2 requirements. Thus, pharmacists filling prescriptions for buprenorphine written by a physician with a DATA waiver are advised to require the patient to bring a written prescription to the pharmacy, since information released directly by the patient is not subject to the need for a release.

COMPREHENSIVE ADDICTION AND RECOVERY ACT (CARA)

In July 2016, Congress passed the Comprehensive Addiction and Recovery Act (CARA),[446] a major piece of federal legislation designed to address the opioid epidemic, and addressing six major elements of a coordinated effort: prevention, treatment, recovery, law enforcement, criminal justice reform, and overdose reversal. As with all major legislation, the full impact on health care providers and the public will not be felt immediately, while rules are promulgated and other elements of the program are completed. Some of the major initiatives spawned by the act include the following that should be of interest to pharmacists include:

- PAIN MANAGEMENT BEST PRACTICES. Create a federal "Pain Management Best Practices Inter-Agency Task Force" including representatives of major agencies – DHHS, VA, DoD, ONDCP – and representatives from the private and state government sectors, including physicians and other prescribers, pharmacists and pharmacies, addiction researchers, and major professional and consumer groups. The goal is to review current practices and recommend and disseminate best practices for treating acute and chronic pain in the US. (§ 101)
- YOUTH SPORTS INJURIES LEADING TO ADDICTION. DHHS shall develop informational materials designed to prevent addiction related to treatment of youth sports injuries (§ 104)
- EXPANDING ACCES TO NALOXONE AND OPIOID OVERDOSE DRUGS
    - Grants will be made to eligible entities to expand access to opioid overdose drugs (e.g., naloxone). Eligible entities include federally qualified health centers, opioid treatment programs, or "any practitioner dispensing narcotic drugs," or other entities deemed appropriate by HHS. Grants may be up to $200,000. Up to 20% of the grant funds may be used to purchase overdose agents or offset copays; other uses include training and providing resources for health care providers and pharmacists on the prescribing of opioid overdose drugs or devices. (§ 107)
    - Grants will be made available to States to (1) implement strategies for pharmacist dispensing of naloxone and similar agents; (2) encourage pharmacists to dispense naloxone and similar drugs

pursuant to a standing order; (3) develop training materials that naloxone dispensers may use to educate the public. $5 million is appropriated for FY 2017 through 2019. (§ 110)

- PRESCRIPTION MONITORING PROGRAMS. Changes were made to the National All Schedules Prescription Electronic Reporting Act of 2005 to further promote the development of a nationwide PMP, and funding of $10 million per year from 2017 to 2021 was provided to support this initiative. (§109)
- OFFICE-BASED NARCOTIC TREATMENT PROGRAMS. Two major changes to DATA-waived office-based narcotic treatment programs (see above) are made: (1) DHHS was allowed by regulation to increase the number of patients seen by a given DATA-waived prescriber – prescribers now may be approved for up to 275 patients; and (2) nurse practitioners and physicians' assistants are added to the list of qualifying practitioners starting in 2016 and continuing through October 21, 2021. (§ 303)
- PARTIAL FILLS OF SCHEDULE II DRUGS. CARA amends the Controlled Substances Act to allow for partial fills of schedule II drugs when requested by patient or prescriber, all partial fillings are completed within 30 days, and total quantity dispensed does not exceed the amount originally prescribed. (See discussion above under Schedule II prescriptions) (§ 702)
- MEDICARE PART D PLANS MAY RESTRICT BENEFICIARY TO ONE PHARMACY. Medicare Part D plan sponsors will be allowed to establish "at-risk beneficiary drug management programs," which may include restricting access to a single pharmacy or a single pharmacy chain with real-time data sharing, subject to several conditions and restrictions and provision for notice to beneficiary. (§ 704)
- FRAUD AUDIT METHODS PROTECTED FROM FOIA DISCLOSURES. A not-so-nice change is protection for federally-funded health programs from disclosing any of the metrics or approaches used for predictive modeling or other analytic techniques used in audits and investigations of waste, fraud and abuse, and creates protections for this information from release under the Freedom of Information Act. (§ 706)
- MANDATED PROGRAM CHANGES FOR VETERANS AFFAIRS BENEFICIARIES. CARA includes a major section – Title IX – which enacts the "Jason Simcakoski Memorial and Promise Act," and directs the Department of Veterans Affairs to implement a major set of programs across all VA medical facilities to improve the care of veterans and implement opioid safety measures. The scope of Title IX is too extensive to summarize in this text, but VA pharmacists will be significantly affected by its provisions as the VA rolls out compliance. (Title IX, §§ 901-951)

IMPAIRED HEALTH PROFESSIONALS

The current trend in health profession regulation is to treat impairment due to alcohol or substance abuse as an illness, and to encourage treatment that will return the impaired professional to practice. Some states, such as Michigan, have developed recovery assistance programs that deal with all or most health professions in the state. Others have tended to deal with each profession individually. The Uniform Disciplinary Act (RCW 18.130) authorizes disciplinary boards to establish programs for monitoring professionals whose practice has been restricted, and to contract with organizations and licensees to undertake such monitoring. Washington has adopted rules to allow for referral of impaired pharmacists (and students and other licensees) to an approved recovery network. In Washington, this recovery program is called the Washington Recovery Assistance Program for Pharmacy (WRAPP).

HISTORY AND GOALS. WRAPP was established in 1983 by the Washington State Pharmacists Association and the Washington State Society of Hospital Pharmacists (now merged into the Washington State Pharmacy Association). It is supported by the Pharmacy Quality Assurance Commission, WSU, UW, and WSPA. Its goals are to:

- Protect the health and safety of the public.

- Provide a health resource and rehabilitation support for the impaired pharmacist.

There is no fee for WRAPP services, but costs for assessment and treatment (including drug screens) are borne by the participant or by programs covered by employers or third party payers.

REFERRALS TO WRAPP. Referral can be by self, with intervention by a concerned individual, or by Commission. Recovery program rules apply to any licensee of the Commission: pharmacists, interns, and ancillary personnel.

SELF-REFERRALS.
Details of participation are confidential for self-referrals. No notification is made to the Commission as long as participant is compliant with monitored treatment program. Practice restrictions may be required by program during early phases of treatment.

SELF-REFERRAL CONTACT: 800-446-7220.

INVOLUNTARY, DUE TO INTERVENTION by a concerned individual. WRAPP will not notify the Pharmacy Commission of an involuntary referral due to intervention as long as participant is compliant with monitored treatment program. However, if the impairment was discovered in connection with a drug theft, the Commission may be notified.

COMMISSION REFERRAL.
The Pharmacy Commission may refer a licensee to WRAPP as an alternative to discipline, in which case, a CONTRACT is developed with the licensee, and no discipline is instituted if the contract is completed. Participation in this case is kept confidential.

Alternatively, the Commission may include referral to WRAPP for monitoring of compliance with COMMISSION ORDER that may be part of discipline, which disciplinary record is not confidential.

Commission rules are found in WAC 246-871.

REQUIRED REPORTING. Licensees are required to report known or suspected impairment of another licensee, and may choose to report to WRAPP or to the Commission (see Chapter 2). Reporting to WRAPP satisfies the reporting requirement.

A licensee who is required to report known or suspected impairment, and who makes good faith reporting of known or suspected impairment to WRAPP or the Commission, is immune from civil liability arising from that report. This is specified in WAC 246-867-030, but stems from the statutory protection afforded by RCW 4.24.500-510 (see next section).

PHARMACISTS' REPORTING OF SUSPECTED VIOLATIONS OF THE CSA

The corresponding responsibility of the pharmacist that is imposed by the CSA, requires that the pharmacist independently determine for each controlled substance prescription whether the prescription is legitimate. If the prescription is not legitimate, it may not be dispensed, and the prescriber should be notified. In addition, pharmacists have been encouraged by law enforcement officials to report incidents of forged or altered prescriptions to them. Because the pharmacist is first a primary care provider, and not a law enforcement officer, these determinations must always be made with the needs of the patient in mind.

"RED FLAGS" are characteristics that should alert a pharmacist to the possibility of a problem with the prescription. The DEA has suggested that the following are red flags, and that the more of these characteristics found in a given prescription, the greater is the possibility that the prescription is not legitimate or there is need for caution in dispensing addicting drugs to a particular patient:

- The prescription looks "too good."
- The directions, quantity, or dosage differs from usual medical usage.
- Abbreviations used differ from standard medical abbreviations.
- Directions are written in full with no abbreviations. (This is actually a desirable practice, to minimize error, but it is unusual.).
- Different handwriting, and/or different colored inks are used in the prescription.
- The patient appears to be "doctor shopping" by visiting multiple prescribers to obtain multiple prescriptions for the same or similar drugs.
- The patient appears to be altering elements on the prescription, such as the quantity or the date written.
- The pharmacist has evidence that the patient is selling or sharing his or her controlled substances.
- The patient insists on specific brand-name narcotics and refuses generics in situations where the use of generics is appropriate.
- The patient insists on paying cash for controlled substances, which could be covered under insurance.
- The patient has a history of frequent reports of "lost," "stolen" or accidentally destroyed prescriptions and/or drugs.

"WHITE FLAGS" may be thought of as signals to the pharmacist that he or she needs to assure patient care. When a pharmacist, delays or refuses to dispense a prescription in response to a red flag, patient care is delayed or denied. If the pharmacist's judgment is in error, the patient suffers unnecessarily. Sometimes this leads to a lawsuit. Before deciding to delay, refuse to fill, or report the patient to the police, the pharmacist should engage in direct conversation with the prescriber about his or her concerns. The following are questions a pharmacist should ask when deciding about the legitimacy of a prescription:

- Did the pharmacist's information about the validity of the prescription come directly from the prescriber? If not, did the party providing the information state unequivocally that the prescription was a fraud, and that his or her information is not based solely on a lack of information in the patient record?
- Did the pharmacist discuss with the prescriber that he or she was intending to call the police? If yes, did the prescriber agree that action was appropriate?
- Does the patient have a pre-existing relationship with the pharmacist or the pharmacy? If so, has the pharmacist carefully reviewed the patient profile to see if this prescription represents a pattern of reasonable treatment?
- Did the pharmacist ask the patient specifically about his or her concerns? If so, did the patient have a reasonable explanation for any discrepancies?
- Does the pharmacist expect the police to further investigate before deciding to arrest or charge the patient with a crime? If no, as the pharmacists believe the police can rely on his or her information to conclude that the prescription is fraudulent?
- Is the pharmacist prepared to defend his or her actions in court?

IMMUNITY FROM CIVIL LAWSUITS FOR REPORTING SUSPECTED VIOLATIONS. When pharmacists exercise their duties as citizens to report crimes or apparent crimes to the police, the Pharmacy

Commission or the DEA, in Washington they may be protected against civil suits arising from these reports by a Washington statute, RCW 4.24.510:[447]

> **Communication to government agency or self-regulatory organization -- Immunity from civil liability.** A person who communicates a complaint or information to any branch or agency of federal, state, or local government, or to any self-regulatory organization that regulates persons involved in the securities or futures business and that has been delegated authority by a federal, state, or local government agency and is subject to oversight by the delegating agency, is immune from civil liability for claims based upon the communication to the agency or organization regarding any matter reasonably of concern to that agency or organization. A person prevailing upon the defense provided for in this section is entitled to recover expenses and reasonable attorneys' fees incurred in establishing the defense and in addition shall receive statutory damages of ten thousand dollars. Statutory damages may be denied if the court finds that the complaint or information was communicated in bad faith.

TO AVOID COMMON LAW LIABILITY for libel, defamation, or false arrest, pharmacists should follow these guidelines (see also Chapter 7):

- In making reports to police of suspicious prescriptions, pharmacists must TAKE REASONABLE CARE TO BE SURE OF THEIR FACTS
  - Follow the DEA's guidelines for identifying a forged or suspicious prescription
  - Remember that reports from medical offices based on lack of records or absence of the prescriber may be unreliable
  - Record the specific names and contact information of any individuals who have provided information used in the pharmacist's decision. If possible have them fax you any documentation.
- DO NOT COMMUNICATE SUSPICIONS TO ANYONE OTHER THAN THE POLICE OR ANOTHER PERSON WHO HAS A NEED TO KNOW the information (e.g., the prescriber, store management, other pharmacy staff)
- DO NOT UNREASONABLY DETAIN THE PATIENT. If you have obtained an address, the police can follow up on your report even if the patient has left the pharmacy.
  - Do not restrict the patient from leaving
  - Do not threaten or intimidate the patient
  - Do not physically restrain the patient

IS THE PRESCRIBER'S OVERALL PRACTICE SUBJECT TO QUESTION?

The "context" in which the patient brings prescriptions to the pharmacist may alert the pharmacist to PRESCRIBERS WHOSE PRACTICE EXCEEDS RECOGNIZED NORMS, and the DEA has revoked the registration of pharmacists who fill multiple prescriptions from prescribers under obviously suspicious circumstances. In revoking the DEA registration of East Main Street Pharmacy of Columbus, Ohio, the DEA cited circumstances that should have alerted the pharmacist that the prescriptions were probably not issued in good faith for a legitimate medical purpose:

- VERY LARGE VOLUMES OF PRESCRIPTIONS FROM A SINGLE PHYSICIAN. In a 5-month period, the pharmacy filled 6,619 controlled substance prescriptions, of which 4,979 (75%) were from one physician, Dr. Volkman, whose office was in Portsmouth, Ohio, 92 miles from the pharmacy.
- PATIENTS COMING FROM OUTSIDE THE PRIMARY TRADE AREA OF THE PHARMACY. 98% of Dr. Volkman's patients that came to the pharmacy lived outside of the Columbus area. Some patients were coming from Kentucky, or were driving more than 100 miles past dozens of other pharmacies to get to East Main Street Pharmacy.
- LARGE PERCENTAGE OF PRESCRIPTIONS PAID FOR IN CASH.

- FREQUENT PRESCRIBING FOR A SET COMBINATION OF DRUGS, WITHOUT ADJUSTING DOSES OR DRUGS USED FOR INDIVIDUAL PATIENTS. 75% of Dr. Volkman's patients were issued the same set of prescriptions: Xanax, 2 narcotics, and Soma.
- PRESCRIBING CONSISTENTLY HIGH DOSES. Most of the Xanax prescriptions were for 2 mg; narcotics were uniformly prescribed at the top of the dosage range
- MULTIPLE NARCOTIC PRESCRIPTIONS ON THE SAME DAY
- OTHER PHARMACIES WERE KNOWN TO REFUSE TO FILL DR. VOLKMAN'S PRESCRIPTIONS. The pharmacist was aware from patients that other pharmacies had refused to fill the prescriptions they were bringing to him, but never discussed with his neighboring pharmacists their reasons for refusing to fill the prescriptions.[448]

As with patient-specific "red flags," these indicators are only that; but the higher the number of indicators, the greater the potential concern for the prescriber's practices. Suspect practices should be reported to the Pharmacy Commission, and, where appropriate to the DEA.

In the last 2 years, widely-publicized revocation of the licenses of nurse practitioners in the Vancouver area, Whitman County, and a physician in Poulsbo have led to lawsuits against the prescribers in which the pharmacies were also named as defendants. The plaintiffs have almost uniformly alleged that the pharmacies should have been aware that the prescribers' practices were unprofessional and should have taken action to protect the patients from harm. (See also Chapter 7)

WHEN PRESCRIBER OR NURSE SEEKS TO PICK UP PRESCRIPTION FOR PATIENT. Several recent cases in Washington have resulted in discipline or DEA action against pharmacies when physicians or, in one case a nurse, sought to pick up prescriptions for delivery to patients and it was later discovered that the physicians and nurse were diverting the drugs. As noted above, the state and federal controlled substances act require delivery to the ultimate user, or a member of the ultimate user's household.

CANNABIS (MARIJUANA)

For the purposes of the Controlled Substances Act, "marihuana" is defined as "all parts of the plant Cannabis sativa L., whether growing or not; the seeds thereof; the resin extracted from any part of such plant; and every compound, manufacture, salt, derivative, mixture, or preparation of such plant, its seeds or resin. Such term does not include the mature stalks of such plant, fiber produced from such stalks, oil or cake made from the seeds of such plant, any other compound, manufacture, salt, derivative, mixture, or preparation of such mature stalks (except the resin extracted therefrom), fiber, oil, or cake, or the sterilized seed of such plant which is incapable of germination." (21 USC §802(16))

Federal law criminalizes the possession or use of marijuana (*Cannabis spp.*) for any purpose – marijuana is a Schedule I controlled substance under federal (and Washington) law. This criminalization is required by the United States' participation as a signatory to the Single Convention on Narcotic Drugs (see above). Also in schedule I are extracts of marijuana including various forms of tetrahydrocannabinol (THC, Δ9-THC, THCA, etc.) Cannabidiol (CBD) derived from marijuana is in schedule I, but CBD in hemp oil (see below), is not. THC and its related forms constitute the psychoactive components of marijuana, and CBD is not considered psychoactive but is said to have health benefits, including anticonvulsant effects and is thought to have therapeutic value in brain injuries.

In October 2009, Attorney General Holder announced formal guidelines for federal prosecutors in states that allow medical use of marijuana. In relevant part, the guidelines state:

> The prosecution of significant traffickers of illegal drugs, including marijuana, and the disruption of illegal drug manufacturing and trafficking networks continues to be a core priority in the Department's efforts against narcotics and dangerous drugs, and the Department's investigative and prosecutorial resources should be directed towards these objectives. **As a general matter, pursuit of these priorities should not focus federal resources in your States on individuals whose actions are in clear and unambiguous compliance with existing state laws providing for the medical use of marijuana.** For example, prosecution of individuals with cancer or other serious illnesses who use marijuana as part of a recommended treatment regimen consistent with applicable state law, or those caregivers in clear and unambiguous compliance with existing state law who provide such individuals with marijuana, is unlikely to be an efficient use of limited federal resources. [**Emphasis added**][449]

Of course, because this is an act of prosecutorial discretion, a future Attorney General under a different administration might take a different approach. President Trump's Attorney General Jeff Sessions was regarded as being generally opposed to the tolerance policy; how his replacement will act is not yet known.

Various states have chosen to eliminate criminal sanctions for various forms of marijuana use. In January 2010, an ABC news poll revealed that 81% of Americans believe that "doctors should ... be allowed to prescribe marijuana for medical purposes to treat their patients," and 46% of Americans "favor ... legalizing the possession of small amounts of marijuana for personal use."[450] In 2014, the INCB further complained that legalization in Alaska, Oregon, and the District of Columbia "put the United States even further in breach of its international treaty obligations." It is likely that some opponents of marijuana decriminalization or legalization will continue to point to our obligations under the Single Convention, one commentator has noted that the INCB was equally concerned when Uruguay legalized marijuana in 2013, but the UN and INCB "did not announce any repercussions for Uruguay's violation of its international commitments." This same author concluded that serious consequences for the US for "flexibility in interpreting drug treaties" are unlikely.[451]

DECRIMINALIZATION allows for possession of small amounts for personal use; according to the National Organization for Reform of Marijuana Laws (NORML), "typically, decriminalization means no prison time or criminal record for first-time possession of a small amount for personal use."

MEDICAL MARIJUANA programs do not decriminalize marijuana, but do exempt medical use from the criminal sanctions imposed by state law. Some states do not allow use of marijuana for medical purposes, but do allow possession and use of extracts that are low in THC and high in cannabidiol (CBD) for treatment of certain condition, particularly epilepsy. Pure hemp oil, which has negligible THC, is legal to possess and consume and is regulated by FDA as a food.

LEGALIZATION typically affirmatively allows for possession and consumption of marijuana and also sets requirements for the legal growing and sale of marijuana products. As with alcohol, restrictions apply and there are penalties for exceeding legal limits.

As of January 2019, NORML reports that only Idaho, Wyoming, South Dakota, Kansas, Iowa, Wisconsin, Indiana, Kentucky Virginia, So. Carolina, Georgia, Tennessee, Texas and Alabama do not authorize either medical or recreational use of marijuana. Of those states, only Idaho and Kansas do not allow for medical CBD.

HEMP. Industrial hemp is derived from cultivars of *Cannabis sativa* that contain less than 1% THC by dry weight, and is made from the mature stalks of the plant. It is specifically excluded from the CSA because it is the fiber from those stalks. However, since 1937, cultivation of industrial hemp in the US was illegal under federal law in the absence of a permit from the DEA, which was rarely, if ever, granted. In 2014, hemp cultivation for "research" purposes was legalized in states that permit its cultivation;[452] the "research" is designed to rebuild the US hemp seed crop. 27 states, including Washington, permit cultivation of industrial hemp. The 2018 Farm Bill legalized cultivation and interstate transfer of cultivated hemp products for commercial or other purposes, with several restrictions. First, hemp must contain less than 0.3% THC, plants with greater concentration are marijuana. Second, USDA must consult with state officials to formulate a state-specific plan for cultivation and distribution of hemp. Violations of the hemp law, such as cultivating hemp without a license or producing marijuana may be punished.

HEMP OIL is typically derived from the seeds of the hemp plant, and itself is not a controlled substance. Hemp oil contains various amounts of cannabidiol (CBD), and CBD in hemp oil is not a controlled substance, whereas CBD extracted from marijuana is. The FDA regulates hemp oil as a food, and in 2015 and 2016 issued a number of warning letters to hemp oil marketers who were making therapeutic claims for hemp oil, which would make it a new drug; in addition, some of these marketers were claiming concentrations of CBD in the oil that were significantly greater than the actual measured CBD concentration in samples tested by FDA.[453] In its 2016 letters, FDA explained that CBD-based claims are not eligible for treatment as dietary supplements under the DSHEA, because CBD has been authorized for investigation as a new drug, and CBD-containing products were not marketed as dietary supplements prior to authorization of the new drug investigations. In June 2018, the FDA approved Epidiolex (cannabidiol), a CBD-based product for treatment for of two rare seizure disorders.[454] Epidiolex has since been placed in Schedule V.

APhA has placed recommendations for pharmacists who are considering stocking and selling OTC CBD oil on its website.[455] Among the considerations are investigation and selection of products for quality and potency. Reports in the media indicate that the WSLCB has stated that it only controls CBD oil derived from marijuana.

WASHINGTON CANNABIS LAWS

INITIATIVE 692. The voters passed Initiative 692[456] in 1998, which found "that some patients with terminal or debilitating illnesses, under their health care professional's care, may benefit from the medical use of marijuana." The Legislature amended the statute in 2007,[457] in 2010,[458] in 2011[459] and again in 2015,[460] to harmonize the medical cannabis statute with the passage of Initiative 502.

INITIATIVE 502. By a 56% majority, and with a voter turnout of 82%, Washington voters in November 2012 approved Initiative 502,[461] intended to "license and regulate marijuana production, distribution, and possession for persons over twenty-one, remove state-law criminal and civil penalties for activities that it authorizes, tax marijuana sales, and earmark marijuana-related revenues." The initiative modified multiple sections of the Controlled Substances Act.

With the passage of this initiative, which did not alter the medical marijuana provisions, conflicts and uncertainties became apparent, including continued arrests of medical marijuana users, problems with "community marijuana gardens," and the ability of medical marijuana users to obtain marijuana that was not subject to the purity and conformity requirements in place for recreational users. The Legislature responded in 2015 with changes to the medical marijuana law (RCW 69.51A) to harmonize the two statutes and create one scheme for the cultivation and distribution of marijuana.[462] Among its provisions were changes to the controlled substances act to remove marijuana from Schedule I, a provision which the Governor vetoed. The statute required the Department of Health to develop reports on creation of specialty marijuana clinics and scheduling of marijuana. As to the specialty clinics, the Department recommend against doing so; as regards to scheduling marijuana, the Department came up with no clear recommendation but its discussion suggested that rescheduling out of schedule I and/or into schedule II would create numerous unintended consequences and is probably unnecessary.

OVERALL CONTROL OF MARIJUANA PRODUCTION AND DISTRIBUTION rests with the Washington State Liquor and Cannabis Board (WSLCB). The Board consists of 3 members appointed by the Governor to 6-year terms. The Board hires a Director who oversees Board operations among its divisions, which include Education and Education, and Licensing and Regulation. Individuals seeking licenses to cultivate, distribute, or sell marijuana deal with the WSCLCB; individuals and health care professionals who are involved in medical use will interact with the Department of Health.

PERSONAL (RECREATIONAL) USE OF MARIJUANA.

POSSESSION AND USE. Persons age 21 and over may possess:

- Up to 1 ounce of usable marijuana
- Up to 7 g of marijuana concentrate/extract for inhalation
- Up to 16 ounces of marijuana infused product in solid form
- Up to 72 ounces of marijuana infused product in liquid form
- Marijuana-related drug paraphernalia

PENALTIES. Possession in excess of these amounts or any possession by a person under age 21 is a crime and is punishable (unless within the provisions of medical use). Public consumption is a civil infraction.

- Public consumption of 1 oz or less – civil infraction, $100 maximum fine.
- Possession > 1 oz up to 40 g – Misdemeanor, 24 hours minimum confinement (up to 90 days), $1,000 maximum fine
- Possession > 40 g – Felony, maximum 5 years confinement, $10,000 maximum fine

PRODUCTION AND DISTRIBUTION OF MARIJUANA.

COMMERCIAL ENTITIES. The statute creates 3 types of commercial licenses; each of which has a $266 application fee and a $1,062 annual renewal fee:

- Marijuana producer: produces marijuana for sale at wholesale to marijuana processors; allows production, possession, delivery, and distribution.
- Marijuana processor: processes, packages, and labels marijuana/marijuana infused product for sale at wholesale to marijuana retailers; allows for processing, packaging, possession, delivery, and distribution.
- Marijuana retailer: allows for sale of usable marijuana/marijuana infused products at retail outlets regulated by the WSLCB. Retailers may obtain a medical marijuana endorsement (see below).
    - Retail outlets originally authorized by Initiative 502 were limited to 334 licenses by the WSLCB, but with the 2015 revisions to the medical marijuana laws, formerly-registered dispensaries may now transfer to become retail outlets and the Board has set the total number at 556.
    - Retailers may not employ any persons under the age of 21, and may not allow any person under the age of 21 to be on the premises, unless the retailer has a medical marijuana endorsement
    - Retailers may only sell marijuana products or paraphernalia
    - Retailers may display up to 2 signs identifying the business or trade name, not to exceed 1,600 square inches
    - Marijuana products or paraphernalia may not be displayed in a manner visible to the general public
    - The Board has established a number of rules on advertising designed to prevent advertising to minors, promotion of curative effects of marijuana, and to assure that warnings on adverse effects are included. Retails sales may not be made by internet websites, but only at the physical location of the retailer

- All retail sales of marijuana products for recreational use are subject to a 37% excise tax. Medical marijuana users who are in a registry are exempted from the tax, as are sales of CBD (see below). Most retailers are required to remit the tax electronically – the Board will allow some retailers to pay by cash, but charges a 10% penalty for paying in cash!
- All sales of paraphernalia (even to medical users) are subject to state and local sales tax.

CBD PRODUCTS as defined by RCW 69.50 are any product containing or consisting of cannabidiol that has been derived from the marijuana plant. In recent years, the use of CBD products have been promoted to treat alignments ranging from headaches to inflammation without cause the psychoactive effects of THC. Unlike hemp derived CDB oil which is OTC, marijuana CDB oil remains a schedule I substance and is regulated by the Washington State Liquor and Cannabis Board.

MEDICAL MARIJUANA COOPERATIVES. Growing of marijuana by "community collective gardens," is no longer allowed. Rather, up to 4 patients or their designated providers who are entered into the Medical Marijuana Authorization Database (see below) may form a "cooperative" to cultivate marijuana for the use of the patients. Cooperatives apply for registration with the WSLCB.

- Membership
  - No more than 4 members are allowed in one cooperative
  - All members must be at least 21 years old
  - All members must hold valid recognition cards
  - May grow the total number of plants authorized for the patients; up to 60 plants
  - A member may belong to only one cooperative
  - A member may grow their plants only in the cooperative, not anywhere else
  - Members may not sell or give away marijuana to anyone not in the cooperative
- Location
  - Not within 1 mile of a licensed retailer
  - Not within 1,000 feet of schools, playgrounds, recreation centers, child care centers, public parks, public transit centers, libraries, or game arcades that admit persons under 21; or where prohibited by a city, town, or county zoning provision
  - Must be located at the domicile of one of the members
  - May not be more than one cooperative per tax parcel
  - If plants are grown out of doors, must be obscured from public view and enclosed by an 8-foot high fence
- Lead member must keep proper records in accordance with traceability requirements, notify the WSLCB within 15 days of adding a member, and may not add a replacement member prior to 60 days after departure of a former member
- Plants must be purchased from a licensed marijuana producer

MEDICAL USE OF MARIJUANA. Medical use of marijuana in Washington is governed by the provisions of RCW 69.51A, regulations of the WSLCB, and regulations of the Department of Health. DOH rules cover marijuana product compliance (246-70 WAC), the Medical Marijuana Authorization Database (246-71 WAC), and certification of Cannabis Consultants (246-72 WAC).

PROTECTION FROM PROSECUTION, ARREST, OR OTHER LEGAL CONSEQUENCES.
Qualifying patients with terminal or debilitating illnesses, who, in the judgment of their health care professionals, may benefit from the medical use of marijuana, shall not be arrested, prosecuted, or subject to other criminal sanctions or civil consequences under state law based solely on their medical use of marijuana;

Persons who act as designated providers to such patients shall not be arrested, prosecuted, or subject to other criminal sanctions or civil consequences under state law based solely on their assisting with the medical use of marijuana; and

Health care professionals shall not be arrested, prosecuted, or subject to other criminal sanctions or civil consequences under state law for the proper authorization of medical use of marijuana by qualifying patients for whom, in the health care professional's professional judgment, the medical use of marijuana may prove beneficial.

Compliance requires a preexisting provider-patient relationship, completion of a physical examination, documentation of the debilitating or terminal condition, informing the patient of other treatment options, documenting other measures attempted to treat the terminal or debilitating condition.

The law prohibits the health care practitioner from engaging in a variety of business-practices related to the provision of marijuana to patients.

TERMINAL OR DEBILITATING ILLNESSES include:

- Cancer, HIV, MS, epilepsy or other seizure disorders, spasticity;
- Intractable pain, i.e., pain unrelieved by standard medical treatments and medications;
- Glaucoma, acute or chronic, i.e., increased intraocular pressure unrelieved by standard treatments and medications;
- Crohn's disease with debilitating symptoms unrelieved by standard treatments or medications;
- Hepatitis C with debilitating nausea or intractable pain unrelieved by standard treatments or medications;
- Diseases, including anorexia, which result in nausea, vomiting, wasting, appetite loss, cramping, seizures, muscle spasms, or spasticity, when these symptoms are unrelieved by standard treatments or medications;
- PTSD; or
- Traumatic brain injury

DESIGNATED PROVIDERS are persons who

- Are 21 or over; and
    - Is the parent or guardian of a qualifying patient under the age of 18 and has a recognition card; or has been designated in writing by a qualifying patient to serve as the designated provider for that patient;
    - Has an authorization from the qualifying patient's health care professional; or has been entered into the medical marijuana authorization database as being the designated provider, and has been provided a recognition card;
- Is prohibited from consuming marijuana obtained for the personal medical use of the qualifying patient;
- Provides marijuana to only the qualifying patient; and
- Is the designated provider to only one patient at any one time
- May not become a designated provider to a different patient until 14 days have elapsed since serving the previous patient

QUALIFYING PATIENTS are individuals who

- Is a patient of a health care professional;

- Has been diagnosed by that professional as having a debilitation or terminal medication;
- Is a resident of Washington at the time of the diagnosis;
- Has been advised of the risks and benefits of medical use of marijuana by that professional;
- Has been advised by the professional that they may benefit from medical marijuana use;
- Has an authorization from his or her health care professional; or has been entered into the medical marijuana authorization database and has been provided a recognition card
- Are not persons who are actively being supervised for a criminal conviction by a corrections agency that has determined that the terms of the chapter are inconsistent with that supervision

MEDICAL MARIJUANA RETAILER ENDORSEMENTS

- Are required for a marijuana retailer to distribute marijuana for medical use and for the sale to be exempt from the excise tax
- Endorsed retailers must maintain computer equipment required to access the authorization database and to issue recognition cards
- Endorsed retailers must employ certified Cannabis Consultants who
  - Have completed a 20-hour training course approved by DOH
  - Are the only employees allowed to handle patient's or provider's authorization form
  - Are required to enter patients and providers into the database
  - Have their certificate conspicuously displayed at the place of business
- Other employers of endorsed retailers must be trained on identifying persons under age 21 and recognizing recognition cards
- Allow the endorsed retailer to display a Medical Marijuana logo on their business
- Allow the endorsed retailer to admit persons between 18 and 21 years of age who have a recognition card; or under age 18 with a valid recognition card when accompanied by the designated provider.

CERTIFIED MEDICAL MARIJUANA CONSULTANTS are not medical providers and are subject to rules adopted by DOH. They must complete a 20-hour training program, be 21 years or older, and have a current certificate showing completion of CPR training. Certifications must be renewed annually on the consultant's birthday.

Consultants may:

- Enter information into the authorization database and generate recognition card
- Assist patient with selecting products
- Describe risks and benefits of methods for using products
- Give advice on proper storage of products and keeping products safe from children and pets
- Show how to properly use products
- Answer questions about the medical marijuana law

Consultants may not:

- Provide medical advice
- Diagnose any conditions
- Recommend changing current treatment(s) in place of marijuana
- Open or use actual products when demonstrating how to use

MEDICAL MARIJUANA AUTHORIZATION DATABASE.

The AUTHORIZATION DATABASE is a voluntary registry that allows

- A retailer with a medical marijuana endorsement to add a qualifying patient or designated provider and include the amount of marijuana plants or products that are authorized for the patient;
- Practitioners or pharmacists to access health care information on their patients when providing medical or pharmaceutical care; pharmacists seeking access must comply with the following requirements in WAC 246-71-070:
    - Register with the Department of Health to receive access credentials;
    - Notify the department if the credentials are lost or missing in writing within one business day;
    - Notify the department and the database vendor immediately when they no longer have authority to prescribe or dispense controlled substances;
    - Adhere to the requirements of 69.51A RCW
- Qualifying patients or their designated providers to access their own information or information on anyone who has queried the database concerning them;
- Other entities, persons or agencies to have access: appropriate local, state, tribal, or federal law enforcement officials; marijuana retailer with medical marijuana endorsements; department of revenue; department of health and its disciplinary authorities
- Authorizations to expire after 6 months for a minor qualifying patient or 12 months for an adult qualifying patient

RECOGNITION CARDS are provided via the database to qualifying patients or their designated providers.

- Recognition cards for qualifying patients who are 18 years or older or their designated providers are valid for 12 months
- Recognition cards for qualifying patients who are under 18 years of age or their designated providers are valid for 6 months

BENEFITS OF VOLUNTARY REGISTRATION. Qualifying patients and their designated providers obtain several benefits from voluntary registration in the authorization database:

- May purchase up to 3 times the recreational limits at any one time (non-cardholders restricted to recreational limits
- May possess 6 to 15 plants if authorized (non-cardholders restricted to 4 plants)
- May purchase high-THC products (> 10 mg THC per serving or application)
- Purchases at endorsed stores not subject to excise tax
- Registration card protects against arrest (non-cardholders if arrested must plead an affirmative defense)
- May participate in a cooperative

HEALTH PROFESSIONALS who may authorize medical marijuana use include physicians, physician assistants, naturopaths, and advanced registered nurse practitioners. The disciplinary authorities for these professionals are required to develop continuing education programs based on practice guidelines developed by the boards.

VALID DOCUMENTATION of the authorization must be retained by the patient, and provided to their designated provider and/or any law enforcement officer on request. The documentation must include:

- A form developed by the DOH and completed by the qualifying patient's health care professional written on tamper-resistant paper; or

- A recognition card generated by the authorization database system.

Purchase and Possession Limits. Patients or designated providers with recognition cards may

- Purchase from an endorsed retailer a combination of the following:
    - 48 oz of marijuana-infused product in solid form;
    - 3 oz of usable marijuana;
    - 216 oz of marijuana-infused product in liquid form; or
    - 21 g of marijuana concentrates
- Grow in his or her domicile up to 6 plants, and possess up to 8 oz of usable marijuana produced from his or her plants
- The authorizing health care professional may specify in the authorization form up to 15 plants grown at the patient's or provider's domicile and possession of up to 16 oz of usable marijuana produced from those plants

Non-card holders are limited to growing up to 4 plants and possession of up to 6 oz of usable marijuana produced from those plants. They may purchase and possess other marijuana products up to the same limits as recreational users.

A person who is a qualifying patient and a designated provider for another person may possess no more than twice the limits above.

OTHER CONTROLLED SUBSTANCES LAWS IN WASHINGTON include the following.

These laws are rarely of importance to pharmacy practice. RCW 69.43 – Precursor Substances; RCW 69.51 – Controlled Substances Therapeutic Research Act; RCW 69.52 – Imitation Controlled Substances; RCW 69.53 – Use of Buildings for Unlawful Drugs.

REFERENCES

[384] United Nations. Single Convention on Narcotic Drugs, 1961 (amended by the 1972 protocol); https://www.unodc.org/pdf/convention_1961_en.pdf
[385] *Gonzales v. Oregon*, 546 U.S. 243, January 17, 2006.
[386] 2009 c 1 (Initiative Measure No. 1000, Approved November 4, 2008); RCW 70.245
[387] Seventh Annual Report on Oregon's Death with Dignity Act, Oregon Department of Human Services, 2005.
[388] 2010 c 9.
[389] See discussion below concerning privacy issues for patients in certain narcotic treatment programs. See also Chapter 8 discussion regarding provision of naloxone to caregivers of clients in Washington Medicaid.
[390] RCW 69.50.315
[391] RCW 18.130.345
[392] USDHHS, FDA. Statement from FDA Commissioner Scott Gottlieb, MD, on unprecedented new efforts to support development of over-the-counter naloxone to help reduce opioid overdose deaths. 2019 Jan 17; https://www.fda.gov./NewsEvents/Newsroom/PressAnnouncements/ucm629571.htm
[393] Pub. L. 110-425, effective April 15, 2009.
[394] 21 CFR § 1301.76(a)
[395] 21 CFR § 1307.03
[396] USEEOC, Laws, Regulations & Guidance; Prohibited Practices; http://www.eeoc.gov/laws/practices/inquiries_arrest_conviction.cfm
[397] WAC 162-12-140(3) b, d
[398] 21 CFR §1301.90
[399] The CSA must be read in conjunction with the requirements for a prescription for a legend drug under RCW 69.41.030(1), which was revised in 2013: "... a pharmacist licensed under chapter 18.64 RCW to the extent permitted by drug therapy guidelines or protocols established under RCW 18.64.011 and authorized by the board of pharmacy and approved by a practitioner authorized to prescribe drugs ..." See Chapter 4.
[400] 71 FR 69478, Dec. 1, 2006
[401] Article No. 1074. Changes to controlled substances prescriptions. Washington Board of Pharmacy News 2011 Jul; 33(1):4.
[402] 21 CFR § 1311, Part C.
[403] The WA language differs slightly to avoid use of gender-specific terms: "... an individual who lawfully possesses a controlled substance for the individual's own use or for the use of an member of the individual's household ..."
[404] State of Washington v. Yokel, No. 47847-4-II, Wash. App. Div. II, Wash. App. LEXIS 2527, October 18, 2016]
[405] However, a 2007 decision by the DC Circuit challenged DEA's holding that a veterinarian could not be an agent of the pharmacy for "constructive transfer" of the prescribed drug to the ultimate user. See Wedgewood Village Pharmacy v. DEA, No. 06-1156, D.C. Cir., December 11, 2007
[406] USPS, Publication No. 52, Hazardous, Restricted, and Perishable Mail, §453; http://pe.usps.com/text/pub52/pub52c4_019.htm
[407] In 2013, Fioricet (butalbital, acetaminophen & caffeine) and Fioricet with Codeine® were reformulated to reduce the APAP dose to 300 mg; this occasioned a new ANDA and at that time the DEA placed the new formulation in Schedule III.
[408] The DEA placed tramadol in Schedule IV effective August 18, 2014.
[409] DEA. Role of authorized agents in communicating controlled substance prescriptions to pharmacies. 75 Fed. Reg. 61613-61617, 2010 Oct 10; http://www.deadiversion.usdoj.gov/fed_regs/rules/2010/fr1006.htm
[410] This reference perpetuates an error contained elsewhere in RCW 69.50. The actual section defining a prescription drug is RCW 69.04.540.
[411] 75 Fed. Reg. 61615
[412] 2016 c 148 §17
[413] 72 Fed Reg 64921
[414] Letter from DEA to Prof. David Brushwood in 2001
[415] Personal communication, V. Seeger, R.Ph., DEA, 4/4/05
[416] WSDOH, PQAC. Policy/Procedure No. 55. Partial fill of a schedule II controlled substance prescriptions under the Comprehensive Addiction and Recovery Act 2016, Pub. L. No. 114-198. May 12, 2017
[417] Article No. 991, Washington State Board of Pharmacy Newsletter, 2009 Jan;30(3):4.
[418] Article No. 1042, Washington State Board of Pharmacy Newsletter, 2010 Jul; 32(1):4.
[419] Article No. 1074. Changes to controlled substances prescriptions. Washington Board of Pharmacy News 2011 Jul; 33(1):4

[420] Article No. 1058, Washington State Board of Pharmacy Newsletter, 2011 Jan; 32(3):4.
[421] http://www.deadiversion.usdoj.gov/faq/general.htm#prescrip
[422] WSR 15-13-086, June 15, 2015
[423] Conway, K. Meet the Press January 22, 2017. See "Alternative Facts," https://en.wikipedia.org/wiki/Alternative_facts
[424] See, e.g., DC Mun. Regs. tit. 22 § 1323.1;
[425] 2017 c 297, effective 7/3/2017
[426]https://www.doh.wa.gov/ForPublicHealthandHealthcareProviders/HealthcareProfessionsandFacilities/OpioidPrescribing/HealthcareProviders/Toolkits
[427] Pub. L. 111-273
[428] 77 Fed. Reg. 75784-75817, December 21, 2012
[429] Article No. 1039. Washington State Board of Pharmacy Newsletter, 2010 Jul; 32(1):1,4.
[430] 75 Fed. Reg. 61613, October 6, 2010; http://www.deadiversion.usdoj.gov/fed_regs/rules/2010/fr1006.htm
[431] US Attorney, N.D. Ohio, US DOJ News. Omnicare to pay $50 million to resolve allegations of improper dispensing of controlled substances at nursing homes." 2012 May 11; http://www.justice.gov/usao/ohn/news/2012/11mayomnicare.html
[432] Article No. 1055, Washington State Board of Pharmacy Newsletter, 2011 Jan; 32(3):1.
[433] Pub. L. 115-83, 2017
[434]https://www.cdc.gov/phlp/publications/topic/briefs/ema/index.html
[435] In most other states and generally nationwide, these programs are called PMPs.
[436] Finklea KM, Sacco LN, Bagalman E. Prescription Drug Monitoring Programs. Washington DC: Congressional Research Service; 2014 Mar 24; http://www.fas.org/sgp/crs/misc/R42593.pdf
[437] SSB 6105 (2012) clarified that one-day use does not have to be "immediate" to be exempt from reporting
[438] ESSHB 2961; 2010 c 182.
[439] http://www.deadiversion.usdoj.gov/meth/index.html
[440] www.nplexservice.com; accessed 2/14/11.
[441] http://www.deadiversion.usdoj.gov/pubs/advisories/methadone_advisory.htm, accessed 2/19/15.
[442] Toombs JD, Kral LA. Methadone treatment for pain states. Amer Fam Phys. 2005 Apr 1; 71(7):1353-8; http://www.aafp.org/afp/2005/0401/p1353.html
[443] This is a provision of CARA, Pub. L. 114-198 §303, which sunsets on October 1, 2021
[444] http://buprenorphine.samhsa.gov/bwns_locator/physician_faq.htm#A21
[445] 42 CFR Part 2; see also USDHHS, SAMHSA. The confidentiality of alcohol and drug abuse patient records regulation and the HIPAA privacy rule: implications for alcohol and substance abuse programs, June 2004; http://www.samhsa.gov/sites/default/files/part2-hipaa-comparison2004.pdf
[446] Pub. L. 114-198.
[447] Note, however, that this protection does not extend to civil actions against the person who was the subject of the report, when the plaintiff is the person who engaged in the protected communication with the agency. See *Saldivar v. Momah*, No. 34891-8, Wa App Div II, June 24, 2008.
[448] Dept. of Justice, Drug Enforcement Administration. East Main Street Pharmacy; Affirmance of Suspension Order. 75 Fed. Reg. 66149, 2010 Oct 27.
[449] Dept. of Justice, Memorandum for selected United State[s] Attorneys on investigations and prosecutions in states authorizing the medical use of marijuana. 2009 Oct 19; http://www.justice.gov/opa/documents/medical-marijuana.pdf
[450] ABC News/Washington Post Poll: Medical Marijuana, 2010 Jan 18; http://abcnews.go.com/images/PollingUnit/1100a3MedicalMarijuana.pdf
[451] Quinn M. *Op cit.*
[452] Pub. L. 113-79
[453] http://www.fda.gov/NewsEvents/PublicHealthFocus/ucm484109.htm
[454] https://www.fda.gov/newsevents/newsroom/pressannouncements/ucm611046.htm
[455] https://www.pharmacist.com/article/selling-cbd-oil-implications-pharmacy-owners
[456] Initiative 692, 1999 c 2
[457] 2007 c 371
[458] 2010 c 284
[459] 2011 c 181
[460] 2015 c 70
[461] 2013 c 3
[462] The Cannabis Patient Protection Act, 2015 c 70

6 – PATIENT INFORMATION: COLLECTION, USE, QUALITY ASSURANCE, AND CONFIDENTIALITY

INFORMATIONAL RESPONSIBILITIES OF PHARMACISTS

In general, pharmacists have six major responsibilities regarding patient information, under both federal and state laws and regulations. Pharmacists must:

> COMPETENCY AREAS IN THIS CHAPTER
>
> 2016 MPJE COMPETENCY STATEMENTS – Areas 1.4.4, 1.5.1, 1.5.2, 1.7.2, 1.7.3, 2.1.2, 3.1.1
>
> 2016 ACPE REQUIRED ELEMENTS – Pharmacy Law & Regulatory Affairs; Cultural Awareness; Medication Dispensing, Distribution, and Administration; Health Informatics; Patient Assessment; Professional Communication; History of Pharmacy; Patient Safety

MAINTAIN PATIENT RECORDS FOR EVERY PATIENT which will aid them in documenting the distribution of drugs and devices to the patients and in providing pharmaceutical care services to their patients (*Where pharmacists are engaged in initiating and modifying therapy or other complex drug therapy management activities, the content of their patient records will need to go beyond the minimum requirements for dispensing records and encompass the types of notes, including subjective and objective patient assessments, assessment of drug therapy related problems, and recording the plan of treatment that has been agreed to by the patient following informed consent.*);

USE THESE RECORDS TO REVIEW THERAPY PRIOR TO DISPENSING – this is known as PROSPECTIVE DRUG USE REVIEW (P-DUR);

ACT TO CORRECT ANY PROBLEMS that are discovered as a result of the P-DUR;

PROVIDE INFORMATION TO THEIR PATIENTS NECESSARY TO INSURE APPROPRIATE USE OF THEIR MEDICATIONS and promote the attainment of desired therapeutic outcomes;

ASSURE THE CONFIDENTIALITY OF PROTECTED HEALTH INFORMATION (PHI) under their control; and

CONTINUOUSLY IMPROVE THE QUALITY OF THEIR PATIENT CARE using information concerning patient outcomes and adverse events.

TABLE 6-1. REQUIREMENTS FOR PATIENT INFORMATION COLLECTION, USE, QUALITY ASSURANCE AND CONFIDENTIALITY

RESPONSIBILITY	STATE LAW OR REGULATION	FEDERAL LAW OR REGULATION/NATIONAL ACCREDITATION STANDARDS
MAINTAIN PATIENT RECORDS	RCW 18.64.245, 69.41.042; WAC 246-875-020	Omnibus Budget Reconciliation Act of 1990 (OBRA-90)
CONDUCT P-DUR	WAC 246-875-040	OBRA-90
ACT ON P-DUR FINDINGS	WAC 246-875-040; WA case law (*McKee v American Home Products*, 782 P2d 1045, 1989)	OBRA-90
PROVIDE INFORMATION TO PATIENTS	WAC 246-869-220	OBRA-90; Title VI Civil Rights Act
ASSURE CONFIDENTIALITY OF PHI	RCW 70.02; RCW 18.64.245; 69.41.044, 69.41.055; WAC 246-875-070(2)	Health Information Portability and Accountability Act of 1996 (HIPAA); Health Information Technology for Economic and Clinical Health Act of 2009 (HITECH); Patient Protection and Affordable Care Act of 2010 (ACA); 21st Century Cures Act
ENGAGE IN QUALITY IMPROVEMENT ACTIVITIES	RCW 43.70.510; WAC 246-50-001 thru 990	Patient Safety and Quality Improvement Act of 2005 (PSQIA); Joint Commission standards; Center for Pharmacy Practice Accreditation (CPPA) standards

MAINTAINING PATIENT RECORDS

HISTORY OF THE PATIENT RECORDS REQUIREMENT. The requirement to maintain a record of all prescriptions dispensed has been in WA law since at least 1939. However, maintenance of individual prescription records for each patient was not a standard of practice nationally well into the 1980s. The first state to actually require pharmacists to maintain patient profiles was New Jersey, whose administrative rule was sustained by the New Jersey Supreme Court in 1973.[463] The Washington Board of Pharmacy, at about the same time, adopted a regulation requiring the pharmacist to maintain such records as would enable him or her to "attempt" to detect drug-drug interactions, multiple prescribing of similar drug classes by different physicians, and the like. The Board adopted more specific regulations setting forth the requirements of patient records systems in 1984. Among the changes in practice needed to bring about patient record systems were the following, which were reflected in the 1984 regulations:

- Allowing refill information to be recorded on the patient record, rather than on the back of hardcopy of the prescription.
- Allowing (prior to computerization) pharmacists to refill prescriptions without going back to the original prescription each time, if the patient record contained a correct copy of the original.

- Recognition that a system of records could be used to meet needs for patient information as well as records of distribution of drugs. This included understanding that in some facilities, the patient's chart or medical records could be used as part of a system accessible to the pharmacist to fulfill the needs of a patient medication record system.

WASHINGTON'S REGULATIONS REQUIRE EVERY PHARMACY AND OTHER PLACE WHERE DISPENSING OF DRUGS TAKES PLACE TO MAINTAIN A "PATIENT MEDICAL RECORD SYSTEM." The patient medical record system must assure the pharmacist the means to retrieve all new and refill prescription information relevant to patients of the pharmacy. (WAC 246-875-001) The purpose of the system is to "insure that the information it contains will be reviewed by the pharmacist in a manner consistent with sound professional practice when each prescription is filled."

INDIVIDUAL RECORDS REQUIRED. The regulation does not explicitly require that an individual record is maintained for each patient. However, the same chapter (WAC 246-875-070) sets forth a requirement that information in the patient medication record which identifies the patient shall be deemed confidential. Thus, the Commission has held for many years that a "family medication record" cannot be maintained, because it creates a record that, when shared with any patient in the record, reveals protected information about other patients. Standards under newer state and federal laws (RCW 70.02 and HIPAA/HITECH/ACA) clearly preclude non-individual patient records.

TABLE 6-2. REQUIRED ELEMENTS: PATIENT MEDICATION RECORD SYSTEMS IN WA

Element	**Automated Ambulatory**	**Manual Ambulatory**	**Automated Institutional**	**Manual Institutional**	**Home IV Therapy**
Required by WA Regulation	WAC 246-875-020(1)	WAC 246-875-030(1)	WAC 246-875-020(2)	WAC 246-875-030(2)	WAC 246-871-050(2)
Patient's full name	✓	✓	✓	✓	✓
Patient's address†	✓	✓			*
Unique Patient Identifier			✓	✓	
Patient's age or DOB	Required for PMP**	Required for PMP**			✓
Patient's weight (if applicable)					✓
Patient's gender (if applicable)	Required for PMP**	Required for PMP**			✓
Patient location			✓	✓	
Patient status (on leave, discharged, etc.)			✓	✓	
Serial number of Rx	✓	✓			✓
Date of dispensing	✓	✓			✓
ID of dispenser	✓	✓			✓
ID of preparing tech (if applicable)					✓

†See discussion in chapter 4. *Must be on face of the prescription ** WAC 246-470-030 – see Chap. 5

TABLE 6-2, CONTINUED

Element	Automated Ambulatory	Manual Ambulatory	Automated Institutional	Manual Institutional	Home IV Therapy
Required by WA Regulation	WAC 246-875-020(1)	WAC 246-875-030(1)	WAC 246-875-020(2)	WAC 246-875-030(2)	WAC 246-871-050(2)
Drug dispensed (name, strength, dosage form, quantity)	✓	✓			✓
Drug name, dose, route, form, quantity when appropriate			✓	✓	
Name of mfr and lot numbers of components used					✓
Refill instructions	✓				
Start and stop dates and time when appropriate			✓	✓	
Prescriber (name, address, DEA number if required)	✓	✓	✓	✓	*
Complete directions for use ("as directed" not allowed)	✓		✓	✓	✓
Patient allergies, idiosyncrasies, or chronic condition which may relate to drug utilization. If no allergy data, indicate "none" or "NKA"	✓	✓	✓	✓	✓
Authorization for non-CRC use	✓				
Special status (on hold, dc'd, self-administration, etc.)			✓	✓	
Other drugs used by patient					✓
Any cautionary alerts to be placed on labeling			✓	✓	

TABLE 6-2, CONTINUED

Element	Automated Ambulatory	Manual Ambulatory	Automated Institutional	Manual Institutional	Home IV Therapy
Required by OBRA-90 (see below)					
Patient's age or DOB	✓	✓			✓
Patient's gender	✓	✓			✓
Patient's phone number	✓	✓			✓
Other drugs and devices used by patient	✓	✓			✓
Pharmacist's comments regarding therapy	✓	✓			✓
Required for e-prescribed controlled substances					
Indication of signing or practitioner's digital signature	✓	✓			✓
Pharmacist notations required by 21 CFR § 1306; e.g., "terminally ill," partial filling information	✓	✓			✓

MINIMUM REQUIRED INFORMATION. The regulation sets forth minimum information that must be maintained in the patient medication record. It specifies this slightly differently depending upon whether a manual or computer system is used for ambulatory patients. The requirements for an automated system are specified in WAC 246-875-020. The manual system requirements are set forth in WAC 246-875-030. The requirements are the same for institutional patients whether a manual or automated system is used, and are repeated for each section.

As seen from Table 6-2 above, it is assumed that REFILL INSTRUCTIONS IN A MANUAL SYSTEM may be maintained on the original prescription, but they may be maintained in the manual system/card itself. Likewise, although INFORMATION ON USE OF NON-CRCS DOES NOT NEED TO BE ON THE MANUAL PATIENT MEDICATION RECORD, it may be, or it may be maintained in a separate file or on the original prescription. Note that OBRA-90 also requires outpatient pharmacies to maintain the patient's age or date of birth, the patient's gender, and telephone number in medication record systems. SOME BELIEVE THAT THE WA REGULATION DOES REQUIRE GENDER AS A "CHRONIC CONDITION" THAT MAY RELATE TO DRUG UTILIZATION; in any case, recording age and gender can be considered a standard of practice, or at least a practical necessity in an age of third party payers. OBRA-90 also requires "pharmacist's comments relevant to an individual's therapy."

OMNIBUS BUDGET RECONCILIATION ACT OF 1990 (OBRA-90) PATIENT RECORD REQUIREMENTS

The sections of OBRA-90 that relate to Medicaid prescription drug programs were enacted by Congress primarily to take advantage of certain pharmaceutical care services that were expected to result in more appropriate utilization of outpatient prescription drugs by Medicaid patients, and that, in turn was expected to produce savings in the federal government's share of the cost of these drugs. The Act mandated that federal and state Medicaid programs perform or require the following activities:

- Establish a system of MANDATORY REBATES FROM MANUFACTURERS of prescription drugs purchased for use by Medicaid recipients.
- Fund DEMONSTRATION PROJECTS among one or more states to establish the value of
    - ON-LINE PROSPECTIVE DRUG USE REVIEW (OPDUR). These systems involve use of centralized computer systems to screen for patient drug related problems prior to authorization of payment for a proposed claim. A project was conducted in Iowa. These systems are commonly used in all states and by almost all third-party payors and pharmaceutical benefits managers (PBMs).
    - PAYMENT FOR PHARMACIST'S COGNITIVE SERVICES. This project was funded and conducted in Washington. Overall, it showed that in the mid-1990s, for an average payment of around $5, each cognitive service provided by participating pharmacists saved approximately $13.
- Mandate states to conduct RETROSPECTIVE DRUG USE REVIEW, whereby overall utilization of various drugs or classes of drugs is reviewed by the Medicaid agency to determine population-based approaches to improving drug use.
- Require pharmacists in community pharmacies to conduct PROSPECTIVE DRUG USE REVIEW prior to filling prescriptions for Medicaid recipients
- Require pharmacists to OFFER COUNSELING TO MEDICAID RECIPIENTS.

The PATIENT RECORD REQUIREMENTS arose because without an adequate patient medication record, pharmacists cannot conduct prospective drug use review. OBRA-90 calls these records "Patient Drug Use Histories," and requires that the pharmacist make a "reasonable effort to obtain" the following information for each patient (note the *EMPHASIZED REQUIREMENTS* that are not in Washington rules):

- Name, address, *PHONE, AGE/DOB, AND GENDER OF EACH PATIENT*
- Significant disease states that the patient has that may affect drug therapy
- Known allergies or drug reactions
- A list of all drugs and devices previously used by the patient (*FROM ANY SOURCE, NOT JUST THE DISPENSING PHARMACY)*
- *PHARMACIST COMMENTS RELEVANT TO AN INDIVIDUAL'S THERAPY*.

STATES WERE REQUIRED TO MODIFY THEIR OWN REGULATIONS AS THEY RELATED TO MEDICAID PATIENTS TO COMPLY WITH OBRA-90. Washington had both patient record system and patient counseling requirements in place that applied to ALL patients well before OBRA-90, so THE FEDERAL GOVERNMENT DEEMED OUR STATE TO BE IN SUBSTANTIAL COMPLIANCE without further rule changes.

Pharmacies that provide services to Medicaid patients agree to abide by OBRA-90 as part of their contract with the Health Care Authority, which is Washington's Medicaid agency. Technically, these pharmacies do not need to maintain OBRA-90-only data elements for all patients, since the Commission has not amended its regulations, but they do need to maintain them for Medicaid patients. Obviously, they must perform a review of the record and provide counseling to ALL patients in Washington.

MAY THE PATIENT REFUSE TO PROVIDE CERTAIN INFORMATION? Those elements that are only required by OBRA-90 are subject to the "reasonable effort" qualification of OBRA-90, so it seems that a patient may decline to provide them, which would include age/DOB, gender, and telephone number. Washington's rule is not so qualified, however, it is clear that a pharmacist can't collect information that is inapplicable or unavailable from a given patient. If a pharmacist requests that the patient inform him or her of other medications he or she is taking, and the patient omits some drugs, the pharmacist will only be held responsible for knowing what the patient revealed. The patient cannot decline to provide an address, particularly for controlled substance prescriptions, but presumably may give an alternative address of their choice. Note that patients who are eligible for Washington's address confidentiality program may use the address provided by the Secretary of State.

The obligation to inquire about the patient's drug use history and their current allergies is clearly now a national standard of practice; as with other health care providers, this type of information must be up to date and patients should be asked on a regular basis if their drug history or allergy information has changed since the last visit. It should be clear by now that a patient's history of use of alcohol, nicotine products, or cannabis is relevant to drug therapy and should be collected either as part of their drug use history or as conditions that should be tracked.

DATA SECURITY

Washington's pharmacy regulations require that information in patient records be maintained for a minimum of two years, and that security codes must be imposed in automated systems to prevent unauthorized modification of data. (WAC 246-875-070)

Each pharmacy must have an auxiliary record system for use when the automated system is inoperative due to system interruption, with provisions for prompt entry of information into the system – within two working days – after the system is again functioning. (WAC 246-875-050)

Pharmacies are also subject to the requirements of Washington's Health Care Information Act, RCW 70.02, which specifies in RCW 70.02.150 that:

> A health care provider shall effect reasonable safeguards for the security of all health care information it maintains.
> Reasonable safeguards shall include affirmative action to delete outdated and incorrect facsimile transmission or other telephone transmittal numbers from computer, facsimile, or other data bases. When health care information is transmitted electronically to a recipient who is not regularly transmitted health care information from the health care provider, the health care provider shall verify that the number is accurate prior to transmission.

FEDERAL RULES GOVERNING SECURITY of patient information have been promulgated under authority of the HEALTH INFORMATION PORTABILITY AND ACCOUNTABILITY ACT OF 1996 (HIPAA).[464]

THE SECURITY STANDARDS REQUIRE PHARMACIES TO PROVIDE BASIC SAFEGUARDS that will "protect electronic PHI from unauthorized access, alteration, deletion, and transmission." Much of the summary in this section is based on Bell's presentation to the NACDS Foundation HIPAA Security Conference.[465] CMS has published an understandable summary of its 2003 security rule entitled "Security 101 for Covered Entities."[466]

The standards apply to ELECTRONIC PHI ONLY, or PHI that is maintained or transmitted using electronic media. These systems include

- Computers and computer networks;
- Optical and magnetic storage;
- Telephone voice response and "faxback" systems; and
- The Internet
- Information transmitted via telephone is NOT included in these standards.

It is the purpose of the standards to protect the INTEGRITY, CONFIDENTIALITY, and AVAILABILITY of electronic PHI

- INTEGRITY – the data has not been altered or destroyed in an unauthorized manner
- CONFIDENTIALITY – data or PHI is not disclosed to unauthorized persons or processes
- AVAILABILITY – data is accessible on demand by an authorized requestor

The standards allow for each entity to develop approaches appropriate to their own systems, scope of operations, and capabilities. This does mean that each entity needs to assess its own system, size, and capabilities, and identify specific risks applicable to its systems as it develops its safeguards. They require each covered entity (e.g., pharmacy) to establish or have in place

- ORGANIZATIONAL PRACTICES:
  - Establishment of information security officer
  - Establishing security policies
  - Providing for education and training for each employee in security practices
  - Sanctions for violation of policies
- TECHNICAL PRACTICES AND PROCEDURES:
  - Individual authentication of users of health information systems
  - Access controls
  - Audit trails
  - Physical security and disaster recovery
  - Protection of remote access points
  - Protection of external electronic communications
  - Software discipline
  - System assessment

The federal rule sets forth "IMPLEMENTATION SPECIFICATIONS" that describe how the entity is to undertake to fulfill the standard in specific areas. These specifications may be "addressable" or "required."

- *ADDRESSABLE STANDARDS* -- The entity needs to assess whether an addressable specification is reasonable and appropriate for its situation, and
  - Implement the specification if it is reasonable and appropriate, or
  - If the specification is not reasonable and appropriate to the entity's situation,
    - Document in its plan why the specification is inappropriate and
    - Implement an equivalent alternative measure if appropriate.
- *REQUIRED STANDARDS* -- The entity must implement the specification as written in the rules. For example, according to Bell, all pharmacies must adhere to the "Security Management Process" specified in the rules.

Ultimately, each pharmacy should take advantage of resources provided by various professional organizations, such as the National Association of Chain Drug Stores (NACDS), the National Community Pharmacists Association (NCPA), or their state pharmacy association, all of whom provide access to implementation manuals or guides. Larger pharmacy firms may well have in-house expertise, but smaller firms should work with their system vendors or other experts to help develop their implementation plan.

MAJOR IMPACT ON PHARMACISTS. The major impact of the security standards on individual practicing pharmacists includes

- *STRINGENT AUTHENTICATION PROCESSES*, such as requiring re-logging on to the terminal after a minimum timeout and use of positive ID requirements, such as thumb print, retinal scan, or key card access to terminals;
- *HIERARCHY OF SYSTEM USERS,* such that, for example, pharmacy assistants will not be able to access prescription entry or editing functions of the computer system;
- *RESPONSIBILITY FOR OVERSEEING SECURITY* – pharmacists and pharmacy department managers are responsible for overseeing security issues and knowing how to report and respond to security incidents

As noted in Chapter 7, security breaches and unauthorized disclosures may lead to civil lawsuits under state privacy statutes or common law invasion of privacy claims.

REQUIRED NOTIFICATION TO PATIENTS AND CUSTOMERS OF SECURITY BREACHES. The HITECH Act of 2009 was contained in the American Recovery and Reinvestment Act of 2009[467] (ARRA – the "stimulus package"). A major subtitle of the Act amends HIPAA to strengthen its privacy and security requirements. The Act sets forth requirements for covered entities to notify their customers or patients if the security of their protected health information has been breached. The Act also strengthens enforcement provisions and restricts sales of certain information for marketing purposes.

ENFORCEMENT OF THE SECURITY RULE is the responsibility of the Office of Civil Rights, DHHS. Complaints to the OCR are usually resolved by settlements with the offenders, which may include monetary penalties. Recent cases involving pharmacies include:[468]

- Failure by a pharmacy chain to enter into a business provider agreement with a law firm representing the chain in an administrative hearing, resulting from a claim that the law firm had released PHI concerning an individual patient during the hearing. The investigation revealed no wrong-doing, but the Chain was required to amend its policies to require business associate agreements with law firms or other consultants.
- A pharmacy chain revealed information containing PHI for individual patients to law enforcement officials without obtaining written requests as required under the Privacy Rule.
- A grocery chain maintained pseudoephedrine log books in a manner such that subsequent purchasers could see the identities of previous purchasers. The chain erroneously believed that the information in the log books did not contain PHI.
- A pharmacy technician placed a patient's insurance card in a bag containing another patient's prescriptions. OCR ruled that patient insurance cards contain PHI. (Consider the impact of placing a patient's prescription container in another patient's bag!)

USE OF PATIENT INFORMATION IN DISPENSING

MINIMUM PROCEDURES FOR USE OF PATIENT INFORMATION

Washington pharmacy regulations have required prospective drug use review since at least 1984. WAC 246-875-040 sets forth the "Minimum procedures for utilization of a patient medication record system:"

ON RECEIPT OF A PRESCRIPTION OR DRUG ORDER, a dispenser must
EXAMINE THE PATIENT'S MEDICATION RECORD, visually or via an automated data processing system
to DETERMINE THE POSSIBILITY OF

- A clinically significant DRUG INTERACTION;
- A clinically significant DRUG REACTION;
- A clinically significant THERAPEUTIC DUPLICATION; or
- IMPROPER UTILIZATION of the drug

AND CONSULT WITH THE PRESCRIBER if needed

> 2 KEY DUTIES OF PHARMACISTS IN USING PATIENT INFORMATION:
>
> - REVIEWING THE INFORMATION AT EVERY ENCOUNTER
> - TAKING ACTION WHEN PROBLEMS ARE FOUND

The Pharmacy Commission has challenged pharmacists who fail to consult with prescribers over doses of drugs – whether for approved or off-label indications – when the doses prescribed are considerably greater than the dose recommended in the official labeling; the charges have been brought citing 2 major requirements of law: (1) failing to consult concerning improper utilization of the drug; and (2) failing to assure the safety of patients.

ORDERS MODIFIED IN THE SYSTEM must carry in the audit trail the unique identifier of the person who modified the order.

ANY CHANGE IN DRUG NAME, DOSE, ROUTE, DOSE FORM OR DIRECTIONS which occurs after an initial dose has been given must

- result in a new order entered into the system and the old order discontinued; or
- accurately document changes in the system in such a manner that the original record or its audit trail is not destroyed.

NO DISTINCTION BETWEEN "NEW" AND "REFILL" PRESCRIPTIONS

Although Washington rules require the review "on receipt of" an order, which might imply only when the order is first received, it also requires that the review must consider improper utilization of the drug, which involves looking at the patient's history of use as revealed by prior dispensing of the drug; thus, one should consider the "receipt of an order" to include the patient's request for a refill of that order. Furthermore, the Commission's rules regarding use of pharmacy technicians require that each prescription – new or refill – prepared for dispensing by a technician, must be verified by a pharmacist who "has examined the patient's drug profile, and has approved the drug order after taking into account pertinent drug and disease information to insure the correctness of the order for a specific patient." (WAC 246-901-010(10))

WASHINGTON REQUIRES THE DISPENSER TO EXAMINE THE MEDICATION RECORD EACH TIME (for new and refill requests) an order or prescription is processed.

- THIS INVOLVES "INTERPRETATION OF THE DATA IN A PATIENT MEDICATION RECORD SYSTEM" which is a professional responsibility that cannot be delegated to ancillary personnel (WAC 246-863-095(e)).
- THIS IS PART OF THE "VERIFICATION" defined in WAC 246-901-010(10). "'Verification' means the pharmacist has ... examined the patient's drug profile ..."

REQUIRES EVALUATION OF THE PATIENT'S "UTILIZATION OF THE DRUG" – this includes early and late refills or other evidence that the drug is not being utilized properly

APPLIES TO BOTH INPATIENT AND OUTPATIENT SETTINGS. The rule uses the phrase "prescription or drug order" so that this rule covers inpatient and ambulatory care settings.

CIVIL LIABILITY FOR FAILURE TO REVIEW AND TAKE ACTION. The Supreme Court of Washington has concluded that A "PHARMACIST HAS A DUTY TO TAKE CORRECTIVE MEASURES WHEN CONFRONTED WITH A PRESCRIPTION CONTAINING AN OBVIOUS OR KNOWN ERROR, SUCH AS AN OBVIOUSLY LETHAL DOSAGE, INADEQUACIES IN THE INSTRUCTIONS, KNOWN CONTRAINDICATIONS, OR INCOMPATIBLE PRESCRIPTIONS."[469]

OBRA-90'S PROSPECTIVE DRUG USE REVIEW RULES closely parallel Washington's regulation. They require that all prescriptions are "screened against the patient's drug use history" to identify

- Therapeutic duplication
- Drug-disease contraindications
- Drug-drug interactions (including interactions with OTC drugs)
- Incorrect dosage or duration of treatment
- Drug allergies
- Clinical abuse or misuse

OBRA-90 rules specify that the review be manual and/or computer-assisted, and may take advantage of "on-line" PDUR.

ADDITIONAL FEDERAL P-DUR REQUIREMENTS. OBRA-90 rules impose at least three additional requirements on pharmacists beyond those that are imposed by Washington regulation

- They explicitly require the PDUR to CONSIDER INTERACTIONS WITH OTC DRUGS the patient is taking
- They are BASED ON THE ASSUMPTION THAT THE PATIENT'S DRUG USE HISTORY IS CURRENT and contains information concerning ALL THE DRUGS THAT THE PATIENT IS TAKING, WHETHER OR NOT THEY HAVE BEEN DISPENSED BY THE PHARMACY CONDUCTING THE REVIEW
- They anticipate that PHARMACISTS WILL RECORD THEIR OBSERVATIONS CONCERNING THERAPY and the decisions they have made in the patient record

THE PHARMACIST IS NOT REQUIRED TO CONTACT THE PRESCRIBER IN EVERY CASE WHERE A POTENTIAL PROBLEM IS IDENTIFIED. WAC 246-875-040 only requires contacting the prescriber "if needed." However, it is clear that the pharmacist must "take corrective measures" when problems are discovered. A couple of obvious possibilities include

CONSULTING WITH THE PATIENT to gain more information that helps resolve the problem.

Example: a prescription is written for Tylenol with Codeine 30 mg tablets, with directions to "Take 1-2 tabs q4-6h prn infection." This suggests a possible error in the product that is specified, or at least "inadequacies in the directions." However, the pharmacist notes that the patient also has a prescription for an antibiotic, which is also labeled "for infection." She asks the patient what the physician told her the Tylenol with Codeine was for, and the patient responds, "The pain of my sinus infection." This clarifies the order, and the pharmacist may resolve the problem by augmenting the directions to read, "Take 1 or 2 tablets every 4 to 6 hours if needed for pain of sinus infection."

EXERCISING HIS OR HER JUDGMENT and subsequently informing the prescriber of the decision

Example: a prescription is received for a 3-year old for 30 Amoxicillin 250 mg capsules, to be taken q8h. The dose is appropriate for the child's weight, but the child cannot swallow capsules. The prescriber is not immediately available for consultation. The pharmacist discusses with the mother the choice of liquid or chewables, which the child can ingest, and they agree on the use of chewables. This is not technically allowed by the generic substitution rules, but it is arguably a form of "secundum artem" that effectively solves the problem. This will allow the resolution of the problem promptly and get the mother and sick child on their way. The pharmacist can notify the prescriber of the decision, which will normally be acknowledged without any problems.

PROVIDING INFORMATION TO PATIENTS

WASHINGTON WAS THE FIRST STATE IN THE US TO REQUIRE ALL PHARMACISTS TO PROVIDE PATIENT CONSULTATION. The original rule (WAC 360-16-250), promulgated in 1973, specified that "With each new prescription dispensed after January 1, 1974, the pharmacist, in addition to labeling the prescription in accordance with preexisting requirements, must orally explain to the patient or the patient's agent the directions for use and any additional information, in writing if necessary, to assure the proper utilization of the medication or device prescribed. For those prescriptions delivered outside the confines of the pharmacy, the explanation shall be by telephone or in writing. PROVIDED, that this shall not apply to those prescriptions for patients in hospitals or institutions where the medication is to be administered by a nurse or other individual licensed to administer medications, or to those prescriptions for patients who are to be discharged from a hospital or institution."

This regulation, although it set a national precedent, was limited to requiring information on new prescriptions only. In addition, in its actual application, pharmacists tended to limit their "counseling" to fairly superficial issues. Also, the Commission has, over the years, been disappointed with the extent of compliance with this requirement by pharmacists.

WHAT ARE THE 3 GREATEST FALSEHOODS BELIEVED BY PHARMACISTS AND PHARMACY TECHNICIANS IN WASHINGTON?

1. No counseling is needed if the patient has had the drug before.
2. Counseling is not required on refills.
3. Washington technicians may ask the patient "Do you have any questions for the pharmacist?" instead of the pharmacist providing counseling.

CURRENT RULE. In 2001, the Board promulgated a REVISED PATIENT COUNSELING REGULATION, WAC 246-869-220, which sets forth its purpose as "educate the public in the use of drugs and devices dispensed upon a prescription."

- THE PHARMACIST SHALL DIRECTLY COUNSEL THE PATIENT OR THE PATIENT'S AGENT on the use of drugs or devices.
- FOR PRESCRIPTIONS DELIVERED OUTSIDE OF THE PHARMACY, the pharmacist shall offer in writing to provide direct counseling and information about the drug, including information on how to contact the pharmacist.
- For each patient, THE PHARMACIST SHALL DETERMINE THE AMOUNT OF COUNSELING THAT IS REASONABLE AND NECESSARY under the circumstance
  - to promote safe and effective administration of the medication, and
  - to facilitate an appropriate therapeutic outcome for that patient from the prescription.
- THIS RULE APPLIES TO ALL PRESCRIPTIONS EXCEPT WHERE A MEDICATION IS TO BE ADMINISTERED BY A LICENSED HEALTH PROFESSIONAL authorized to administer medications.

DIFFERENCES BETWEEN CURRENT RULE AND OLD RULE. Note that the current WAC 246-869-220 differs from the old rule in several significant ways

- It is NOT LIMITED TO NEW PRESCRIPTIONS only
- It REQUIRES AN OFFER TO COUNSEL, NOT JUST WRITTEN INFORMATION, ON DRUGS DISPENSED OUTSIDE OF THE PHARMACY
- It REQUIRES THE PHARMACIST TO EVALUATE what is needed to promote safe and effective use of the drug and facilitate an appropriate therapeutic outcome and to tailor the counseling to the specific patient
- It DOES NOT EXEMPT HOSPITAL OR INSTITUTIONAL DISCHARGE MEDICATIONS from its requirements

PHARMACY COMMISSION CONCERNS on issues in pharmacy compliance with counseling requirements were published in January 2012.[470] In particular, the Commission was concerned with improper use of point-of-sale (POS) systems that captured patients' signatures concerning the dispensing of drugs and delivery of counseling, and with failure to counsel on refills in accordance with pharmacist judgment. Among the major positions made in the article were the following:

- While pharmacies may use POS systems, they "must not interfere with a pharmacist's interaction with the patient."
- It is inappropriate for ancillary personnel to guide patients to select a check box to decline counseling
- IT IS A COMMON MISCONCEPTION THAT ALL REFILLS MAY BE AUTOMATICALLY DISPENSED WITH NO PHARMACIST INTERVENTION
- While pharmacists may exercise judgment regarding counseling on refills, the Board "clarified that patients with NEW PRESCRIPTIONS, including those that are issued new prescription numbers, MUST be counseled by the pharmacist.
- A patient or agent must COMMUNICATE TO THE PHARMACIST any refusal to receive counseling

The Commission reiterated its key concerns when it adopted a formal policy statement in 2017 to guide its investigators in enforcing counseling requirements and the need for the full-time presence of a pharmacist in a retail pharmacy.

> **Background:** The pharmacist accessible to the patient or patient's when a prescription requires counseling or counseling is requested.

Guidelines: No new prescription *or medication that requires counseling* shall be delivered without immediate and direct access to a pharmacist, excluding prescriptions delivered outside the pharmacy premises. ... [*Emphasis added*]

If a pharmacist is readily available but not within direct and immediate access, the pharmacy may continue with dispensing, non-discretionary functions and delivery of prescriptions that do not require counseling.[471]

The Commission's current policy that clarifies its expectations on patient counseling includes the following guidelines:

1. Pharmacists must counsel patients, or their agents, on all new and renewed prescriptions and devices (i.e. where there is a new prescription number).
2. Pharmacists must counsel on refill prescriptions if the pharmacist determines counseling is necessary.
3. Pharmacies may develop policies and procedures to identify when counseling is required as long as the policies and procedures do not conflict with WAC 246-869-220 and any other applicable law.
4. A pharmacy's drive-through window(s) is considered part of the continuous pharmacy space.[472]

Numerous lawsuits in Washington have been filed in Washington in recent years where the pharmacy and its technicians regularly operated on the assumption that little or no pharmacist intervention is needed on refills, or that counseling is not required if "the patient has had the medication before." Where a patient was injured as a result, these cases have routinely resulted in damages paid to the patient or his or her estate. (See also Chapter 7)

OBRA-90 REQUIREMENTS

Under the requirements of OBRA-90, pharmacies providing services to Medicaid patients must

- Make an "OFFER TO COUNSEL" Medicaid patients; and
- If the offer is accepted, OBRA-90 sets forth the following "SIGNIFICANT ITEMS" THAT THE PHARMACIST SHOULD BE PREPARED TO DISCUSS WITH PATIENTS:
    - Name and description of the medication
    - Dosage form, dose, route, and duration of therapy
    - Special directions for preparation, administration, or use by the patient
    - Common severe side effects, adverse effects, interactions, or contraindications that the patient can detect and deal with
    - Self-monitoring techniques
    - Storage and refill information
    - What to do if a dose is missed

Federal Medicaid rules promulgated under OBRA-90 allow for an "offer to counsel," which some states allow to be communicated by a sign in the pharmacy or by a technician. However, as made clear above, WASHINGTON'S RULES MAKE NO MENTION OF AN "OFFER TO COUNSEL" except as part of the written information included when a prescription is delivered outside the confines of the pharmacy.

To state it one more time, it is not lawful in Washington for a technician to make an offer to counsel. On every new prescription, the pharmacist must attempt to counsel the patient, and on each refill the pharmacist must determine if additional counseling or follow up is necessary. The following scenario is illegal in Washington when dispensing a newly-numbered prescription:

Tech: "Have you had this medication before?"

Patient: "Yes, I think so."

Tech: "Oh, OK. Do you have any questions for the pharmacist?"

Patient: "No, I can't think of any."

In addition, such a conversation in no way constitutes a patient refusing to be counseled, and cannot be used as a defense in subsequent litigation where the issue of failing to counsel has been appropriately raised.

PHARMACISTS MAY ALLOW THE PATIENT TO REFUSE TO BE COUNSELED. "Nothing in this clause shall be construed as requiring a pharmacist to provide consultation when an individual ... or caregiver of such individual refuses such consultation." (42 USC § 1396r-8(g)(2)(A)(ii)(II)) Nor does OBRA-90 require that refusal be documented, although some states have placed such a requirement in their rules.

PATIENT REFUSAL OF COUNSELING IN WASHINGTON. Currently, there is no requirement in Washington that counseling must be documented or that refusal to be counseled must be documented. Given the continued concern by the Board that pharmacists are not as fully compliant with these rules as they should be, the Board at its October, 2004, meeting voted to establish a stakeholders group to advise the Board on a rule to require documentation of counseling. However,

PATIENT REFUSAL FOR COUNSELING SHOULD BE COMMUNICATED DIRECTLY BY THE PATIENT OR AGENT TO A PHARMACIST. The Commission determined in 2016 that "any refusal to receive counsel from the pharmacist by a patient or patient's agent must be directly solicited by and communicated to the pharmacist." This policy was omitted in 2017 when the Patient Counseling procedure was revised, but since the offer of counseling is not to be made by technicians in Washington, it is up to the pharmacist to deal with patients who do not wish counseling.

VOLUNTARY SIGN IN PHARMACY. After much deliberation, the Board decided not to proceed with further rule making, but in January 2006 developed a notice to patients that could be voluntarily placed in the pharmacy. This form cannot be readily found on the Commission website as of January 2019.

Ask questions. It's your health.

Take an active part in your health care. Talk with your pharmacist about your medicines.

Pharmacists have a duty to counsel you on your medicines. Questions? Contact the Washington State Board of Pharmacy at 800-896-0522.

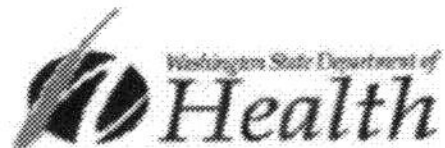

LEGAL IMPACT OF OBRA-90

STATES HAVE IMPLEMENTED OBRA-90 PATIENT COUNSELING REQUIREMENTS IN DIFFERENT WAYS. SOME allow an offer to counsel to be made by other than the pharmacist; some, like Washington, simply require counseling and make no provision for an "offer." (Washington requires an "offer" only when the drug is delivered outside the pharmacy.) In a few states, these rules apply *only* to Medicaid patients, but most states chose to apply the requirements to all patients.

CREATION OF FEDERALLY SPECIFIED STANDARDS

- OBRA-90 rules, however, do establish an objective standard for the STRUCTURE needed to support patient counseling and prospective drug use review (ie, patient drug use histories, on-line or pharmacy-based computer systems)
- OBRA-90 rules also establish an objective standard for the PROCESS of patient counseling and prospective drug use review.
- Finally, OBRA-90 rules establish an objective standard for the CONTENT of patient counseling

In a state with a rule like Washington's, OBRA-90 RULES PROVIDE EVIDENCE OF A MINIMUM, OBJECTIVE STANDARD OF HOW THE PHARMACIST SHOULD HAVE IMPLEMENTED PATIENT COUNSELING IN HIS OR HER PRACTICE.

TO THE EXTENT THAT PHARMACISTS CAN DOCUMENT THEIR COMPLIANCE WITH OBRA-90 STANDARDS, THEY ARE PROVIDING EVIDENCE OF PROPER PROFESSIONAL PRACTICE.

PATIENTS WITH LIMITED ENGLISH PROFICIENCY (LEP)

Title VI of the Civil Rights Act of 1964 prohibits discrimination against persons based on national origin.[473] Recipients of federal financial assistance, which includes pharmacies receiving federal funds under Medicaid or Medicare, are covered by this prohibition. The U.S. Supreme Court in 1974 held that Title VI prohibits conduct that has a disproportionate effect on LEP persons because such conduct constitutes national-origin discrimination.[474] Information on federal requirements is available on the HHS Office of Civil Rights website at http://www.hhs.gov/ocr/civilrights/resources/specialtopics/lep/.

EXECUTIVE ORDER 13166 was signed by President Clinton on August 11, 2000; its title is "Improving Access to Services for Persons with Limited English Proficiency."[475] The order requires every federal agency that provides financial assistance to non-federal entities publish guidance on how their recipients can provide meaningful access to LEP persons.

HHS LEP GUIDANCE. The Department of Health and Human Services published its current guidance document affecting Medicaid and Medicare providers in 2003.[476]

ARE PHARMACISTS AND PHARMACIES COVERED? Yes, if they participate in Medicare, Medicaid, or other federally funded programs (e.g., SCHIP).

WHO IS AN LEP INDIVIDUAL PROTECTED BY TITLE VI? LEP persons are individuals who "do not speak English as their primary language and who have a limited ability to read, write, speak or understand English." LEP persons seeking health care services are eligible to receive "language assistance" during health care encounters.

LANGUAGE ASSISTANCE may be either oral assistance (by use of interpreters or by providers who are multilingual) or written assistance (printing materials in the LEP person's primary language).

AMOUNT OF ASSISTANCE REQUIRED OF A PHARMACY VARIES according to a four-factor test:

- The number or proportion of LEP persons served or encountered in the pharmacy's patient population.
- The frequency with which LEP persons come into contact with the pharmacy.
- The nature and importance of the care provided.
- The resources available to the pharmacy and the cost of adaptation.

EACH COVERED ENTITY IS REQUIRED TO ASSESS its compliance in light of the four-factor test and develop a written compliance plan. Pharmacies that serve "very few" LEP persons are exempt from this requirement.

ENFORCEMENT OF THESE RULES AGAINST PHARMACIES has been limited, but it is expected to increase. In 2008, the state of New York entered into a consent agreement with Rite Aid and CVS by which these chains will provide language assistance to LEP persons.

AT A MINIMUM, PHARMACIES SHOULD DEVELOP DUAL LANGUAGE LABELING FOR PRESCRIPTIONS FOR COMMONLY ENCOUNTERED LEP PATIENTS. For example, many pharmacies in Eastern Washington regularly provide prescriptions to Spanish-speaking patients. Computer software readily exists to print Spanish-language prescription labels and should be used by these pharmacies.

RESOURCES AND ADDITIONAL INFORMATION may be found at a federal government interagency web site: www.lep.gov

PATIENT INFORMATION FOR BLIND OR VISUALLY-IMPARED INDIVIDUALS

As discussed in Chapter 4, the FDA Safety and Innovation Act of 2012 required the United States Access Board to develop guidelines on best practices for making prescription labeling information available to persons with low-vision, who are blind, or for seniors. These guidelines are not mandatory, but, again as noted in Chapter 4, advocacy groups for the blind were successful in structured negotiations with major chains to achieve their adoption of recommended practices. In 2016, it has now become a national standard of practice to provide for these services.[477]

IMPROVING USE AND AVAILABILITY OF PATIENT CARE DATA

The Health Information Portability and Accountability Act of 1996 (HIPAA) – provisions to improve use and availability of patient care data. (Note: the proper acronym is "HIPAA", not "HIPPA.") The Act was passed by Congress with three major goals:

PORTABILITY

The first objective of the Act was to IMPROVE THE ABILITY OF EMPLOYEES TO TAKE INSURANCE COVERAGE WITH THEM WHEN THEY CHANGE JOBS. These portability provisions add to those that are generally known as "COBRA" provisions

- COBRA (Consolidated Omnibus Budget Reconciliation Act of 1986) provided that employees who leave one employer may keep their health care benefits in force for up to 18 months by paying premiums
- A problem arose with the ability of COBRA beneficiaries to convert their old coverage to new coverage with a new employer, since the new employer's plan would often not cover "preexisting conditions."

- HIPAA establishes that the maximum time period during which a new employer's plan can refuse coverage for preexisting conditions is 12 months, after which these conditions must be covered, unless the condition is not covered for any employee

Many issues related to portability that were initially dealt with by HIPAA were further subject to provisions of the Affordable Care Act (ACA). Where these have significant importance for pharmacists, they are discussed below.

ACCOUNTABILITY

Congress was also concerned with improving access to patients' health information to improve care, and it also responded to considerable public concern over health information privacy. The accountability provisions of HIPAA were designed to deal with the following, which will be discussed further below.

- INTEGRITY of health care information
- CONFIDENTIALITY of health care information
- AVAILABILITY of health care information

ADMINISTRATIVE SIMPLIFICATION. The Act recognized considerable health care costs in the US associated with administrative complexity – some estimates are that over 20% of the health care dollar is spent on claims processing costs. Thus HIPAA dealt with "Administrative Simplification" involving electronic transmission of health care data among providers and payers. It established five major areas of new federal regulation:

- TRANSACTION STANDARDS – creating a common set of standards for sharing claims among providers and payers
  - Pharmacy claims must be transmitted using NCPDP D.0 transmission standards.
  - Developed by the National Council on Prescription Drug Programs
  - All Medicare claims must be submitted electronically.
  - Other transaction data, such as claim status, denials, referrals, and remittances are subject to HIPAA X12 version 5010 transaction and code set standards.
  - NCPDP's SCRIPT 10.6 standard applies to e-prescribing transactions.
  - NCPDP's Formulary and Benefits standard 3.0 applies to transactions related to formularies and benefit limits. [478,479]
- STANDARD IDENTIFIERS – establishing a single set of identifiers for health care providers
  - NPI. Rules (45 CFR 162.402-414) established a National Provider System which assigns a unique *NATIONAL PROVIDER IDENTIFIER (NPI)* to each health care provider and covered entity. Elements of the NPI include the following:
    - 10-digit number, which for some uses will be expressed in conjunction with an international prefix of 80840 (80 = health care, 840 = United States)
    - The NPI replaces all other provider identifiers (CHAMPUS, UPIN, Blue Cross/Blue Shield, etc.)
    - The NPI is assigned for the provider's lifetime
    - Address, name, and other changes will be made on-line, and must be made within 30 days.
  - EVERY PROVIDER TO RECEIVE AN NPI. Each individual provider – including pharmacists – is eligible to receive an NPI

- NPI APPLICATIONS. The application is online, through the National Plan & Provider Enumeration System (NPPES) website.[480]
  - There is no charge to individuals to apply
- NPI REQUIRED FOR ALL PROVIDERS. All health care providers who are covered entities under HIPAA must obtain an NPI whenever they first become a covered entity.
  - Veterinarians are not covered entities and are not able to obtain an NPI. Pharmacy computer systems must allow for some unique identifier to be entered for veterinary prescribers in place of the NPI or the DEA number, if they are to be able to process prescriptions for non-human patients.
- NPI REQUIRED FOR ALL CLAIMS. Pharmacists will need to know NPI of the prescriber to submit prescription claims
- FINDING A PROVIDER'S NPI. The NPPES website has a search option to find the NPI for any individual provider

- CODE SETS FOR DATA ELEMENTS – establishing a common data set to simplify communications among providers and payers
- SECURITY STANDARDS – providing for integrity and security of health care information (see discussion above)
- ELECTRONIC SIGNATURES – allowing for a paperless health care information system

COVERED ENTITIES – with regards to the accountability requirements, HIPAA applies to all entities that

- Render care to individuals
- Collect and maintain Protected Health Information (PHI)
- Exchange electronic records

Virtually all pharmacies fit these requirements and are "covered entities"

BUSINESS ASSOCIATES – entities that contract with covered entities to perform such services as claims review, accounting, batch billing, reimbursement for MTM services, 340B resupply, or legal services, and who may receive PHI from the covered entity for treatment, payment, or health care operations, are subject to the same security and privacy requirements as the covered entity. The covered entity must have in place a conforming business associate agreement advising the business associate of its responsibilities, and must reasonably monitor compliance with that agreement. Pharmacists who plan to consult with covered entities, or with business associates of covered entities (such as attorneys or accountants), must be prepared to adhere to privacy and security requirements of HIPAA.

ASSURING THE CONFIDENTIALITY OF PATIENT INFORMATION

WASHINGTON'S PRIVACY LAWS ARE AS IMPORTANT AS HIPAA. HIPAA has been the center of recent national attention regarding protection of the privacy of patient information. However, Washington Supreme Court jurisprudence has required confidentiality of patient information since early in the 20th century,[481] has mandated confidentiality for records in pharmacy regulations at least since the inception of mandatory patient records, and the Washington Legislature passed a comprehensive Health Care Information Act in 1994 (RCW 70.02), prior to HIPAA. Other state rules affecting privacy of medical records include the AIDS Omnibus Act of 1988 (RCW 70.24) and various statutes and regulations regarding mental health (RCW 71.05.390). Federal laws (PL 104-193 § 407) also govern confidentiality in substance abuse treatment programs. The privacy rules of each state are important for practitioners to understand, since HIPAA does not preempt any state or other federal privacy rules which are more stringent than the HIPAA requirements. Thus, in each state, what is actually required will be a combination of federal and state rules.

HIPAA was amended in 2009 by the HITECH Act,[482] final rules under the HITECH Act were published in 2013. Major changes to HIPAA, reflected in the discussion below, related to notification of breaches of PHI, requirements for business associates of covered entities, and various restrictions on marketing, use of genetic information by insurers, and easing of rules for access to juvenile immunization records by parents.

HIPAA PRIVACY RULE – MAJOR FEATURES. The HIPAA Privacy Rule is encoded at 45 CFR 160 and 45 CFR 164. Its principal features are:

- PROTECTED HEALTH INFORMATION (PHI) is that which
  - Relates to a health condition (past, present, or future); and
  - Identifies the patient (45 CFR 164.501)
- COVERED ENTITIES MAY USE PHI FOR TPHCO:
  - TREATMENT;
  - PAYMENT; or
  - HEALTH CARE OPERATIONS.
- PATIENT CONSENT IS NOT REQUIRED to use information for TPHCO
- PATIENT CONSENT IS REQUIRED for all other disclosures or dissemination of PHI
  - Use of PHI for marketing, research, and other non TPHCO functions requires permission
  - Data may be shared for marketing or research if it is "de-identified"
- STRICTER PROVISIONS OF ANY STATE LAW must be followed
- BUSINESS ASSOCIATES must assure compliance with the rules and are subject to the same penalties.
  - Business associates include firms who perform payment or health care operations functions on the entity's behalf
- CONSENT FROM MINORS is subject to state law
- NOTICE OF PRIVACY PRACTICES. Each patient must be provided with a Notice of Privacy Practices (NOPP) at first point of contact; receipt of the NOPP must be documented

USE OF PHI FOR TREATMENT. Pharmacies may use PHI to provide treatment to patients. The NOPP of the pharmacy must include a description of how it will use PHI for treatment, which would typically include the following activities:

- Processing prescriptions and dispensing drugs
- Maintaining and reviewing patient profiles
- Consulting with prescribers relative to the patient's care
- Providing emergency information necessary for the patient's care
- Consulting with the patient or caregiver regarding the patient's medications
- Transferring refill information to or from other pharmacies

USE OF PHI FOR PAYMENT. Typical pharmacy activities involving payment would include:

- Determining eligibility or coverage
- Preauthorization of prescriptions and on-line prospective drug use review
- Billing 3rd party payers, justifying charges

- Collecting payment from the patient, or collecting past-due charge accounts
- Providing certain information to consumer reporting agencies
- Transmitting credit card charges
- Refunding charges or payments

USE OF PHI FOR HEALTH CARE OPERATIONS. Typical pharmacy HCO activities would include:

- Quality assurance within the pharmacy
- Quality assurance activities with external organizations
- Contacting providers or patients with information on treatment alternatives and related functions that do not include treatment
- Medical review, legal services, auditing, and fraud and abuse detection
- Employee training and development
- Complying with regulatory agencies and complying with other provisions of HIPAA
- Inventory control and planning

MINIMUM NECESSARY DATA SET. Disclosures of PHI between covered entities for TPHCO are now limited to the minimum information necessary to accomplish the intended purpose of the request or release. It does not apply to requests from the patient for his or her own information, nor to releases to another provider for treatment. Under the rule, the REQUESTING PARTY is to determine the needed elements, and specify those to the entity releasing the information. For example, a request to a pharmacy for certain information from a payer may indicate that only the prescription number, NDC, and patient's date of birth are to be supplied. If the pharmacy sends more information than requested, it may be in violation of the rule.

DEIDENTIFIED DATA. If a covered entity deidentifies an individual's PHI by removing the following identifiers, the information is no longer individually identifiable health information: Identifiers of individuals or of relatives, employers, or household members of the individual must all be removed, including but not limited to, name, address, zip code, city, birth date, admission date, discharge date, age, telephone number, fax number, electronic mail address, social security number, medical record numbers, vehicle identifiers, and pictures. (45 CFR § 164.502).
Such deidentified data is not subject to the privacy rule and may be used for research or studies, and can be electronically transmitted.

NOTICE OF PRIVACY PRACTICES. Each patient of a covered entity must be provided with a Notice of Privacy Practices adopted by the covered entity when they first become a patient. A conforming NOPP has the following elements:

- Advises patients that you will use their PHI for TPHCO
- Spells out what that means for your pharmacy
- Advises patients of their rights
- Advises patients that you do need written permission to release PHI for non-TPHCO purposes
- Identifies the pharmacy's Privacy Officer and how to contact that person
- Describes business associate relationships
- Describes applicable state laws and regulations. It is critical that the NOPP is specific to each state, and that "turnkey" NOPPs developed for a national audience are adapted to local laws. Wherever a local or state law confers greater privacy or security protections than HIPAA, the local or state law or regulation prevails.
- Describes how you will notify of changes

- Most pharmacies will take advantage of the option to notify of changes to the NOPP by posting them in the pharmacy
- Requires patient to acknowledge receipt of the NOPP
    - The covered entity may use a signature log to capture this acknowledgement
    - Pharmacies should place an indication in the computer record that notice was provided

THE TITLE OF THE NOTICE must be printed exactly as stated in the regulation:

> "THIS NOTICE DESCRIBES HOW MEDICAL INFORMATION ABOUT YOU MAY BE USED AND DISCLOSED AND HOW YOU CAN GET ACCESS TO THIS INFORMATION"

POSTING, DISTRIBUTION, AND CHANGES.

- The pharmacy must post a notice announcing the availability of this information
- The pharmacy must provide a copy of the NOPP to any person who requests it
- The pharmacy must track changes to the NOPP

PATIENTS HAVE A RIGHT TO SEE A COPY OF THEIR RECORD

Patient may see records, and may request changes in the record to correct any errors

THE PHARMACY MUST RESPOND TO THE REQUEST IN A TIMELY MANNER. This is treated differently under Washington law than under HIPAA, so the shorter time limits apply in Washington. Table 6-3 summarizes these requirements.

TABLE 6-3. COMPARISON OF HIPAA AND WASHINGTON REQUIREMENTS FOR PATIENT RECORD REQUESTS

Type of Request	**Limits under HIPAA**		**Limits under Washington law**
Access to records			
Time for Initial Response	If information is available on site	30 days	15 days
	If information is off-site	60 days	
One time extension		30 days (total of 60 or 90 days)	6 days (total of 21 days)
Corrections to Records			
Initial response		60 days	10 days
One time extension		30 days (total of 90 days)	11 days (total of 21 days)

WHEN A PATIENT REQUESTS COPIES OF HIS OR HER RECORDS, the pharmacy must either deliver the copies within the time limit for an initial response, or provide the patient with an explanation that it will take additional time to provide the records; the pharmacy then can take advantage of a one-time extension as specified in the law. In Washington, the maximum time if 21 days, including the extension, and the initial response must be made within 15 days. Washington law, unlike HIPAA, does not distinguish between on-site and off-site records.

WHEN A PATIENT REQUESTS CHANGES TO HIS OR HER RECORDS, the pharmacy must respond within 10 days in Washington, which may include a notice that additional time is needed, which will provide an extra 11 days in which to

- Amend the record as requested by the patient; or
- Deny the request to amend the record.
- If the pharmacy denies the requested change, the patient may provide a statement to be inserted into the record.

FEES FOR COPYING RECORDS. HIPAA and Washington law allow providers to charge a reasonable fee for searching and copying records. (If there is a fee to be charged, it should probably be set forth in the NOPP.) Washington law sets forth maximum amounts that can be charged in WAC 246-08-400:

- Copying charges
  - 1st 30 pages, not more than $1.17 per page.
  - Beyond 30 pages, not more than $0.88 per page
- Other charges
  - Up to a $26 clerical fee for searching and handling records
  - If the provider personally edits confidential information, may charge his or her usual and customary fee for a basic office visit. (Pharmacists may be able to establish a UAC office visit fee based on charges for disease management services, such as diabetic counseling, etc.)

These fees are updated each biennium; the current fees are approved through June 30, 2019.

HIPAA RESTRICTIONS. If the individual requests a copy of the protected health information or agrees to a summary or explanation of such information as part of a formal HIPAA request then the following federal rule applies: the covered entity may impose a reasonable, cost-based fee, provided that the fee includes only the cost of:

- Copying, including the cost of supplies for and labor of copying, the protected health information requested by the individual;
- Postage, when the individual has requested the copy, or the summary or explanation, be mailed; and
- Preparing an explanation or summary of the protected health information, if agreed to by the individual as required by paragraph (c)(2)(ii) of this section.[483]
- The pharmacy will need to determine its actual costs, and may charge the lesser of its actual costs or the Washington maximum fee. The "office visit fee" probably cannot be assessed for formal HIPAA disclosures.

The fee must be determined in relationship to the individual request, not by a blanket fee. A Pennsylvania appeals court held that patients could sue a pharmacy chain that charged a flat $50 fee for copying patients' records, contrary to a Pennsylvania statute that is similar to Washington's Health Care Information Act. In that case, the Court also ruled that pharmacy records were "medical records" within the meaning of the Pennsylvania Medical Records Act.[484] However, the chain appealed on the basis that under language of the

Pennsylvania law, pharmacy customers were not "patients," and this assertion was upheld by the Pennsylvania Supreme Court based on its interpretation of the intent of the legislature when the law was enacted in 1998.[485] It is unlikely that the Washington statute could be interpreted in a similar vein.

PATIENTS MAY REQUEST AN ACCOUNTING OF DISCLOSURES. The patient may request that the provider provide a listing of all disclosures of PHI made during the six years prior to the request.

The provider is NOT REQUIRED to account for disclosures

- Made directly to the patient
- Made to carry out TPHCO
- Made pursuant to an authorization granted by the patient
- Made to persons involved in the patient's care
- Made for national security or intelligence purposes if an accounting of disclosures is not permitted by law
- To correctional institutions or law enforcement officials if an accounting of disclosures is not permitted by law
- Of a limited data set that excludes direct identifiers of the patient or relatives, employers, or household members of the patient.[486]

If the provider maintains a qualifying Electronic Health Record (EHR) as provided in the HITECH Act, then the patient may request a listing, in electronic form, of all disclosures made during the prior 3 years. *THE EXCEPTIONS ABOVE DO NOT APPLY*. It is not clear whether current retail pharmacy medication record systems constitute EHR systems under the HITECH Act.

The provider may not charge for the first accounting provided to the patient within any 12-month period; a reasonable cost-based fee may be charged for additional requests within 12 months.

Some disclosures made to law enforcement agencies or as a result of a court order may not be subject to the accounting. The pharmacist should consult legal counsel in these cases, since the rules are complex and involve both state and federal restrictions.

Certain required notices regarding individuals who have been committed for mental health reasons are exempt from disclosure to the patient, and are exempt from restrictions on disclosure of any PHI incidental to the required notice.[487] Pharmacists providing services to such patients committed for care will need to become familiar with these requirements.

THE PATIENT MAY REQUEST THAT COMMUNICATION OF PHI TO THE PATIENT BE RESTRICTED to confidential channels, such as:

- A particular address
- A particular telephone number
- A particular electronic address

If they choose one of these options, they must acknowledge that this may restrict communications with family members or caregivers.

THE PATIENT MAY REQUEST THAT A PHI DISCLOSURE NOT BE REPORTED TO HIS OR HER HEALTH PLAN IF:

- The purpose of the disclosure is for payment or operations, and not for treatment; and

- The disclosure pertains solely to a healthcare item that the provider has been paid for in full out of pocket.

WASHINGTON'S RULES ARE MORE STRINGENT THAN HIPAA IN THE FOLLOWING WAYS, and must be followed

- TIME LIMITS TO RESPOND TO REQUESTS to see or amend records
- CONSENT BY CERTAIN MINORS (see below)
- CONSENT BY PATIENTS WITH STDS OR HIV FOR CERTAIN OTHERWISE PERMITTED DISCLOSURES (e.g., oral communications with family member)
- WASHINGTON LAW DOES NOT ALLOW REPORTS TO THE MILITARY WITHOUT CONSENT, in contrast to HIPAA which allows reports to the military concerning military personnel
- ABUSE OF A VULNERABLE ADULT OR CHILD MUST BE REPORTED

DISCLOSURE WITHOUT PATIENT'S CONSENT. Washington law – in ways that are consistent with HIPAA – allows disclosure without the patient's consent under the following circumstances (RCW 70.02.050):

- To a person who is reasonably believed to be providing health care to the patient
- To any person if it is reasonably believed to be needed to avoid or minimize imminent danger to the health or safety of the patient or another individual (this is allowed but not required). NOTE THAT THIS TYPE OF DISCLOSURE IS NOT PERMITTED REGARDING ADMISSIONS FOR MENTAL HEALTH CARE, UNLESS SPECIFICALLY ALLOWED IN RCW 70.02.230.
- To a provider who is successor in interest to the provider maintaining the information (e.g., on the sale of the pharmacy).

  Additional conditions are listed in RCW 70.02.050

- Disclosure of PHI related to treatment or testing for SEXUALLY-TRANSMITTED DISEASES is subject to specific restrictions listed in RCW 70.02.220. Disclosures may be made without the patient's permission to a person WITH A NEED TO KNOW such information, in the following circumstances:
  - To the subject of a test for STD or to the subject's legal representative for health care decisions, except the representative of a minor 14 years of age or older who is otherwise competent;
  - To state or local public health officers, or to the CDC, in compliance with requirements for reporting diagnoses of STDs; or
  - For other purposes specified in the RCW, few of which apply to pharmacists.

DISCLOSURES RELATING TO MENTAL HEALTH TREATMENT. It was noted in Chapter 5 that certain requirements of Part 2 of 42 CFR limit disclosures concerning patients in treatment programs for alcohol or substance abuse in ways that may conflict with the types of disclosures allowed under HIPAA. In early 2016, SAMHSA proposed major revisions to Part 2 of 42 CFR to "increase opportunities for individuals with substance abuse disorders to participate in new and emerging health and health care models and health care information technology (IT). Our intent is to facilitate sharing of information within the health care system to support new models of integrated health care which, among other things, improve patient safety while maintaining or strengthening privacy protections for individuals seeking treatment for substance disorders." Among the changes will be to allow patients being treated in both methadone-maintenance programs and office-based buprenorphine programs to allow disclosure to other entities, such as their treating pharmacies, in a "general designation." Congress recognized this proposed update to 42 CFR Part 2 in the 21st Century Cures Act, and provided that DHHS must convene relevant stakeholders to "determine the effect of such regulations on patient care, health outcomes, and patient privacy" within 1 year after finalizing its updates of 42 CFR 2. As a result of this review, DHHS is directed to revise the Privacy Rule under HIPAA to "ensure that health care providers, professionals, patients and their families have adequate, accessible, and easily comprehensible resources relating to appropriate uses and disclosures of protected health information ..." Pharmacists and pharmacy associations will need to monitor this activity during 2017 to contribute to and become aware of likely significant revisions.[488]

OBTAIN APPROVAL FOR DISCLOSURE BEFORE THE DISCLOSURE IS NEEDED. Disclosures of information to known caregivers or to health providers that have previously treated the patient are not currently allowed under Washington law without the patient's specific consent. Prior to July 2014, these disclosures were allowed, so many providers have become accustomed to making such disclosures without specific permission from their patients. IT IS NOW IMPORTANT FOR PHARMACISTS TO OBTAIN FROM EACH PATIENT THE NAMES OF INDIVIDUALS TO WHOM ORAL OR WRITTEN DISCLOSURES ARE PERMITTED AND RECORD THOSE PERMISSIONS IN THE PATIENT'S PHARMACY RECORD. This should be done when the patient first establishes a relationship with the pharmacy, and should be updated periodically (the patient's birthday is a good trigger for obtaining updated profile information annually).

DISCLOSURES FOR LAW ENFORCEMENT PURPOSES. HIPAA allows disclosures to law enforcement officials under a restricted set of circumstances. An oral request from a police officer is normally not sufficient to justify release of PHI. Release of PHI without the patient's permission may be justified in the following circumstances:

- When a court issues an order, a warrant, a subpoena, or other formal summons, or when a grand jury issues a subpoena for the information containing PHI.[489]
- In response to certain *written* administrative requests by federal or state agencies authorized by law to issue such requests, including administrative subpoenas or investigative demand. Such requests, under HIPAA, must include written statement that "the information requested is relevant and material, specific and limited in scope, and de-identified information cannot be used."[490,491, 492,493]
- To respond to a request for PHI for the purposes of identifying or locating a suspect, fugitive, material witness, or missing person.

Such disclosures must be limited to name, address, place of birth, social security number, date and time of treatment, distinguishing physical characteristics, and certain other information not normally found in pharmacy records.[494]

The same limited information may be supplied to law enforcement when the covered entity is

- Providing information about a suspected perpetrator when the crime is reported by a victim who is a member of the covered entity's workforce; or
- The information is provided to identify an individual who has admitted participation in a violent crime, subject to limitations when the admission was made during the course of certain treatment or therapy
- When making required reports, such as of child abuse or abuse of a vulnerable individual, or to alert law enforcement to emergency situations, to report a crime against the covered entity, or, when ethically appropriate, to prevent possible imminent injury to another person.

PHARMACY COMMISSION RULE IS OBSOLETE. WAC 246-875-070(2) specifies that information in the patient medication record is confidential, and restricts its disclosure more stringently than the HCIA. This rule was promulgated in 1992, prior to the adoption of RCW 70.02.050; to the extent that it conflicts with the RCW, it is probably not enforceable.

REGISTERED DOMESTIC PARTNERS. State-registered domestic partners have same rights as family members or spouses. The Marriage Equality Act (Referendum 74) eliminated domestic partnerships between parties after 2014 unless at least one partner is 62 or older. Same-sex couples in which neither member is 62 or over must be married to obtain the rights of spouses or domestic partners.

PURPOSE. "It is the intent of the legislature that for all purposes under state law, state registered domestic partners shall be treated the same as married spouses."

Under current Washington law, domestic partnerships may be entered into by two individuals who

- are 18 years or older, and one of the members is at least 62 years of age;
- share a common residence;
- not be married or in a domestic partnership with a third person;
- be capable of consenting;
- not be nearer in kinship than second cousins, nor be a sibling, child, grandchild, aunt, uncle, niece, or nephew to the other person;
- be members of the same sex or opposite sex.

Among the powers and rights granted to domestic partners are the following:

- Health care facility visitation rights
- Ability to grant informed consent for health care for a patient who is not competent
- Authority of health care providers to disclose information to the domestic partner under the same conditions that such disclosure to a spouse would be allowed
- Domestic partners who are residents of long-term-care facilities may share the same room.
- Insurance policies that cover spouses must also cover domestic partners, including rights under group policies, policy rights after death of partner, continuing coverage rights
- Right to use sick leave to care for a domestic partner
- The right to disability insurance benefits
- Workers' compensation coverage
- Other non-healthcare-related rights extended by the statute include:
    - Spousal testimony privilege
    - Ability to share a bank account
    - Community property rights
    - Divorce rights
    - Child-custody provisions
    - Domestic partners of public officials must submit financial disclosure forms
    - The right to wages and benefits when a partner is injured, and to unpaid wages upon death of a partner.

Providers may confirm the existence of a specific state-registered domestic partnership via a website for the Office of the Secretary of State.[495] After June 30, 2014, same-sex domestic partnerships between persons under age 62 are being discontinued or converted to marriages.

SAME-SEX MARRIED COUPLES IN WASHINGTON are guaranteed equal treatment under the law by the Marriage Equality Act,[496] which was approved by voters in November 2012 pursuant to Referendum 74, by a

52% favorable vote. The law amends RCW 26.04.010 to define marriage as "a civil contract between two persons who have each attained the age of eighteen years, and who are otherwise capable."

AGE OF CONSENT – CONTROL OF PHI BY MINORS. As with most other legal issues, persons who are 18 years of age or older a considered adults and must consent to medical treatment for themselves; they control the disclosure of PHI as it pertains to them, and have a right to see their medical records. A notable exception to this rule relates to medical marijuana. Persons under 21 who are authorized to purchase medical marijuana must do so through the actions of a designated provider. (See Chapter 5)

A key issue deals with whether parents or minors have control of PHI for the minor. HIPAA defers to state rules on this issue. GENERALLY, PARENTS OR LEGAL GUARDIANS HAVE CONTROL OVER HEALTH CARE DECISIONS FOR MINORS. IMPORTANT EXCEPTIONS INCLUDE:[497]

- EMANCIPATED MINORS. Minors over age 16 may petition the court to become emancipated, and if successful may consent to health care services. (RCW 13.64.060)
- MINORS MARRIED TO A PERSON WHO IS NOT A MINOR. (RCW 26.28.020)
- MINORS WHO MAY HAVE COME IN CONTACT WITH AN STD AND ARE 14 YEARS OF AGE OR OLDER MAY consent to treatment. (RCW 70.24.110). As noted above, after July 1, 2014, PHI concerning testing or treatment of STDs in otherwise competent minors age 14 or older may not be disclosed without the minor's permission (RCW 70.02.220).
- MINORS SEEKING CONTRACEPTIVE OR PREGNANCY TERMINATION SERVICES AT ANY AGE may consent to treatment. (State v. Koome, 84 Wn.2d 901; 530 P.2d 260, 1975)
- MINORS 13 YEARS OF AGE OR OLDER MAY CONSENT TO INPATIENT (RCW 71.34.500) OR OUTPATIENT (RCW 71.34.530) MENTAL HEALTH TREATMENT. Note that for inpatient consent, the minor must be a "child in need of services (CHINS)," as determined by DSHS.
- MINORS 13 YEARS OF AGE OR OLDER MAY CONSENT TO OUTPATIENT TREATMENT FOR CHEMICAL DEPENDENCY. (RCW 70.96A.095)
- MINORS CAPABLE OF UNDERSTANDING OR APPRECIATING THE CONSEQUENCES OF THE MEDICAL PROCEDURE UNDER THE MATURE MINOR DOCTRINE may consent to NON-EMERGENCY MEDICAL PROCEDURES based on the health care provider's evaluation of the child's
    - age
    - intelligence
    - maturity
    - training
    - experience
    - economic independence
    - general conduct as an adult
    - freedom from the control of parents

  The mature minor doctrine was noted by the Washington Supreme Court in 1967, holding that an 18-year old (a legal minor at the time) could consent to a vasectomy.[498] The Court cited this decision in 1975 when it concluded that a 16 year old female had a constitutionally-protected interest in consenting to an abortion without parental consent. As noted above, the legislature has also specifically extended to minors the right to consent to mental health therapy and treatment for sexually transmitted diseases. In many other settings, where the benefits to the minor are obvious, and the risks remote, such as in immunizations, providers should not hesitate to undertake the analysis required under the mature minor doctrine.

POWER TO CONSENT TO DISCLOSURE OF PHI IS VESTED IN THE MINOR FOR ANY INFORMATION RELATING TO TREATMENT FOR WHICH THE MINOR WAS ALLOWED TO CONSENT. (RCW 70.02.130). Thus, the pharmacist should presume that the minor can control disclosure of treatment with contraceptives, psychotropics, or drugs used for STDs or pregnancy. Treatment for other conditions could be disclosed with permission of the parent or guardian, but the safest approach is to consult the minor prior to disclosure if any part of the PHI is related to matters over which the minor has control. Minors who are clearly "on their own" should be given the opportunity to determine to whom their PHI should be disclosed.[499]

DISCLOSURE TO DIVORCED PARENTS. Washington law specifically protects health care providers from liability when they disclose PHI for a minor (other than when the minor has control of the record) based on permission of either parent or any legal guardian, as long as the parent or guardian represents to the health care provider that they are authorized to give consent. (RCW 70.02.130) This protects the health care provider from disputes when parents are divorced or separated.

RELATIVES OF MINORS MAY CONSENT FOR MINORS UNDER CERTAIN CIRCUMSTANCES. So-called "kinship caregivers" may consent to health care for a child even if they do not have a court order and if the parents are not available. The individuals include any adult with signed authorization, and adult relatives. The law does not define "relatives" but general usage would suggest that grandparents, aunts/uncles, sisters/brothers would be among adult relatives covered by the law. In addition to the parent(s) of the minor, court-appointed legal guardians, or a court-authorized person caring for the minor in an out-of-home placement, the following adults may consent to care for a minor when the minor cannot consent for himself or herself:

- An individual who has a signed authorization from the child's parent to make health care decisions for the child;
- An adult representing himself or herself to be a relative responsible for the health care of the child; or
- A relative caregiver who has signed and dated a declaration that says the caregiver is an adult relative responsible for the health care of the minor child.[500]

PREVENTING INCIDENTAL RELEASE OF PHI. Under federal regulations implementing HIPAA, each pharmacy is responsible to assure that it provides administrative, technical, and physical safeguards to prevent the intentional or unintentional disclosure of its patients' PHI. An important element is proper training of staff, monitoring of staff to assure that they comply, and discipline of staff who do not. Many state laws also protect the privacy of patients, and either the federal government or state governments may be able to prosecute pharmacies for failure to prevent release of PHI. In January 2009, CVS entered into a settlement with the Office of Civil Rights, DHHS, for $2.5 million over charges that CVS employees were dumping pharmacy records, labels, and other PHI into unsecured dumpsters. In July, 2008, Seattle's Providence Health & Services agreed to a fine of $100,000 arising from thefts of employees' laptops and other media containing unencrypted PHI. Enhanced provisions of the HITECH Act require covered entities to notify customers and patients of any security breaches that have caused the release of their PHI, and empowers State Attorneys General to bring cases under HIPAA.

ENFORCEMENT. Civil penalties for willful neglect of the privacy rule are mandatory under the law, and can be as much as $250,000 per violation, with repeated/uncorrected violations extending up to $1.5 million. Civil and criminal penalties may extend to Business Associates of covered entities. Individual patients may not bring an action to enforce HIPAA or HITECH, but either the federal government or state attorneys general may bring actions. To discover violations, the Department of Health and Human Services is required to undertake periodic audits of covered entities and business associates beginning in 2010.

CIVIL LEGAL LIABILITY FOR UNAUTHORIZED DISCLOSURE OF PHI.

HIPAA does not provide for a "private right of action" by a patient against a provider who discloses his or her PHI without permission. However, state privacy laws and common law trespass jurisprudence do provide a means to sue for invasion of privacy. HIPAA and state laws also may be held by courts to establish a set of expected privacy practices, and, therefore, a duty on the part of the provider. See also Chapter 7.

QUALITY ASSURANCE ACTIVITIES

IOM REPORT. The 1999 publication of *To Err is Human* by the Institute of Medicine generated significant national attention concerning medical errors, of which medication errors constitute a significant segment.

REQUIRED CQI PROGRAMS. In general, hospitals are now required by state law and/or JCAHO accreditation requirements to have a continuous quality improvement process in place by which quality-related events (QREs) are reported, investigated, tracked, and efforts made to improve the system of care so as to reduce the incidence and impact of these events. Washington's laws requiring all hospitals to maintain a Coordinated Quality Improvement Program (CQIP) are RCW 70.41.200 (relating to hospital CQIPs) and RCW 43.70.510 (relating to CQIPs for non-hospital entities).

REQUIRED REPORTING OF ADVERSE EVENTS. The Washington Medical Malpractice Act of 2006 (2006 c 8 § 106) requires medical facilities to notify the Department of Health of adverse events using an on-line reporting system.

- ADVERSE EVENTS are those events found on the list of serious reportable events adopted by the National Quality Forum in 2002.[501]
- THE REPORT SHALL IDENTIFY THE FACILITY, but not any health care professionals, employees, or patients involved.
- A ROOT CAUSE ANALYSIS shall be conducted and included as part of the report.

HOSPITAL NOTIFICATION OF UNINTENDED OUTCOMES. Washington hospitals must have in place policies to assure that, when appropriate, information about unanticipated outcomes is provided to patients or their families or any surrogate decision makers. (RCW 70.41.380)

STATE-MANDATED OR ENCOURAGED QUALITY ASSURANCE PROGRAMS. Most states have now enacted legislation to encourage continuous quality improvement programs, including Washington. Under Washington law, entities other than hospitals (for whom CQIPs are required) wishing voluntarily to develop CQIPs may apply to the Department of Health to be recognized, in accordance with RCW 43.70.510. The DOH CQIP website provides information needed to develop CQIPs (http://www.doh.wa.gov/PublicHealthandHealthcareProviders/HealthcareProfessionsandFacilities/CoordinatedQualityImprovement.aspx). Regulations governing CQIPs are contained in WAC 246-50. Eligible entities may be developed by

- Professional societies or organizations
- Health care service contractors
- Health maintenance organizations
- Health carriers
- Health care institutions and medical facilities, other than hospitals

- Provider groups of ten or more. This may take many forms, as long as its members are practitioners regulated under the state's laws for health professionals (Title 18)
  - A group might consist of providers sharing treatment modalities and perspectives.
  - A community of providers which cross-disciplinary lines.
  - Solo practitioners may form a group to create a Coordinated Quality Improvement Program.

A LIST OF APPROVED CQIPS in Washington is available on the DOH website at http://www.doh.wa.gov/PublicHealthandHealthcareProviders/HealthcareProfessionsandFacilities/CoordinatedQualityImprovement/ApprovedPlans.aspx. The Washington State Pharmacy Association participates in the governance and advising of the Washington Patient Safety Coalition, which is a state-approved CQIP.

THE GOAL OF THE CQIP or similar organization is to provide structures and processes that:

- Measure, retrospectively and prospectively, key characteristics of services such as effectiveness, accuracy, timeliness and cost.
- Review categories of services and methods of service delivery to improve health care outcomes.
- Ensure information gathered for the program is reviewed and used to revise health care policies and procedures.

PROTECTIONS AGAINST DISCOVERY IN CIVIL ACTIONS.

COORDINATED QUALITY IMPROVEMENT PROGRAMS APPROVED BY THE STATES ARE PROVIDED DISCOVERY LIMITATIONS. Once approved by Department of Health, information and documents specifically created for, collected, and maintained by an approved program are exempt from discovery during lawsuits in most cases.

To assure the same protection to quality improvement programs that transcend state lines, Congress enacted the PATIENT SAFETY AND QUALITY IMPROVEMENT ACT OF 2005.[502] The information used in these programs is defined in the Act as "PATIENT SAFETY WORK PRODUCT" (PSWP), and as with most of the state laws, is protected from being discovered or used in civil lawsuits, administrative hearings, and most criminal proceedings.

These protections are found in Washington law in RCW 4.24.250. In addition to protecting quality review or provider review information from discovery, it immunizes providers who in good faith file charges or provide evidence to review bodies concerning incompetence or gross negligence of other members of their profession.

TO QUALIFY AS PSWP, the protected information must be gathered for patient safety purposes, kept separate from other health care information collected by the provider, and communicated to a Patient Safety Organization (PSO) that is registered with the Department of Health and Human Services (through the Agency for Healthcare Research and Quality – AHRQ). Information on PSOs and related regulations are available at the AHRQ website (http://www.pso.ahrq.gov/index.html)

The protections for PSWP are creatures of statute that operate as exceptions to general rules concerning discovery of materials in civil lawsuits. As such, the requirements of the statute must be followed closely. A 2014 North Carolina decision allowed discovery of root cause analysis records in a civil lawsuit because the hospital failed to properly structure its peer review process and define the RCA team as part of a medical review process under the North Carolina statute, which is similar to Washington's law.[503]

In December 2016, the Federal District Court in Kansas held that pharmacy "incident reports," which detailed reported dispensing errors or near misses, were protected from disclosure in an employment discrimination suit because they were in fact collected for and reported to the Alliance for Patient Medication Safety, a qualified PSO, even though they were subsequently retained in "error log books" because Kansas pharmacy rules required retention of error logs.[504]

DISCLOSURE OF PROVIDER ID IN PSWP PROHIBITED. In general, state and federal laws prohibit unauthorized disclosure of PSWP that contains the identity of any provider (including individual practitioners as well as provider entities). This identifiable PSWP may only be used for patient safety activities. In a way, these laws protect the identity of practitioners in the same way as HIPAA protects the privacy of patients.

RETALIATION PROHIBITED. The federal law specifically protects employees of a provider from retaliation for reporting errors, either to the provider or to a PSO.

PHARMACISTS MUST BECOME ADEPT AT PATIENT SAFETY. Increasingly, pharmacists will need to understand the operation of patient safety programs, including patient safety tools such as Root Cause Analysis (RCA)[505] and Failure Mode Effects Analysis (FMEA).[506] Excellent resources on FMEA available from the Institute for Healthcare Improvement.[507]

QUALITY IMPROVEMENT ACTIVITIES NEEDED FOR PHARMACY PRACTICE ACCREDITATION. The Center for Pharmacy Practice Accreditation (CPPA) announced the first group of accredited pharmacy practice sites in 2014. The accreditation standards of CPPA include requirements designed to "Facilitate the delivery of high-quality care, medication safety, and efficient patient care by requiring (1) a continuous quality improvement process that focuses on safe medication distribution processes, internal operations, and quality in pharmacy practice; and (2)The use of patient care data to advance patient care, enhance medication safety, and improve delivery of care."[508]

REFERENCES

[463] Gibson JT. Medication Law & Behavior 1976; New York: Wiley-Interscience, 298-301.
[464] 68 FR 8334, February 23, 2003.
[465] Bell M. Administrative and physical safeguards and recent developments in electronic security law. NACDS Foundation HIPAA Security Conference. http://www.nacdsfoundation.org/user-assets/Documents/PDF/Bell_Presentation.pdf (Last accessed 1/5/07).
[466] USDHHS, CMS. Security 101 for covered entities, 2007; http://www.hhs.gov/ocr/privacy/hipaa/administrative/securityrule/security101.pdf
[467] Pub. L. 111-5.
[468] USDHHS, OCR. HIPAA Privacy – Case Examples Organized by Covered Entity; http://www.hhs.gov/ocr/privacy/hipaa/enforcement/examples/casebyentity.html#2pharmacies, accessed 3/26/14.
[469] *McKee v American Home Products*, 113 Wn.2d 701, 782 P.2d 1045 (1989)
[470] Article No. 1087, Washington State Board of Pharmacy News 2012 Jan; 33(3): 1.
[471] Washington State Pharmacy Quality Assurance Commission Procedure No. 49: Absence of a pharmacist in a community/retail practice setting. February 17, 2017.
[472] WSDOH, PQAC. Procedure No. 52, Patient Counseling, March 30, 2017
[473] 42 U.S.C. 2000d: No person shall "on the ground of race, color, or national origin, be excluded from participation in, be denied the benefits of, or be subjected to discrimination under any program or activity receiving Federal financial assistance."
[474] Lau v. Nichols, 414 U.S. 563 (1974).
[475] 65 FR 50121 (August 16, 2000).
[476] Guidance to Federal Financial Assistance Recipients Regarding Title VI Prohibition Against National Origin Discrimination Affecting Limited English Proficient Persons, DHHS, 68 FR 47311 (August 8, 2003). Revised 2006 at http://www.hhs.gov/ocr/civilrights/resources/specialtopics/lep/hhslepguidancepdf.pdf
[477] https://www.access-board.gov/guidelines-and-standards/health-care/about-prescription-drug-container-labels/working-group-recommendations
[478] http://www.emdeon.com/5010/pdfs/HIPAA_Simplified_FAQ-NCPDP_D%200_and_5010_Version_1-0.pdf, accessed 4/1/2014
[479] http://www.cms.gov/Medicare/E-Health/Eprescribing/index.html?redirect=/eprescribing, accessed 4/1/2014
[480] https://nppes.cms.hhs.gov/NPPES/Welcome.do
[481] *Smith v. Driscoll,* 94 Wash. 441 (1917)
[482] Pub. L. 111-5, February 17, 2009.
[483] 45 CFR § 164.524(c)(4)
[484] *Landay et al. v. Rite Aid*, 40 A.3d 1280 (Pa. Super., 2012)
[485] *Landay et al. v. Rite Aid*, 2014 Pa. LEXIS 3086 (S. Ct. Pa., 2014)
[486] RCW 70.02.0210(3)(i)
[487] RCW 71.05.425
[488] Pub. L. 114-255 §§ 11001-11003
[489] 45 C.F.R. 164.512 (f)(1)(ii)(A)-(B).
[490] 45 C.F.R. 164.512 (f)(1)(ii)(C).
[491] However, a federal district court ruled in 2014 ruled that Fourth Amendment privacy rights are violated when the DEA uses administrative subpoenas to obtain PHI from Oregon's Prescription Drug Monitoring Program, and that such requests must be backed by court orders. If this ruling is sustained on appeal, it could have wide impact on law enforcement requests for PHI from any source. In January 2017, the 9th Circuit noted that the appeal was withdrawn pending a Supreme Court ruling in Town of Chester v. Laroe Estates, Inc. and that enforcement of Oregon's statutory requirements against the DEA are stayed pending the resolution of the Supreme Court case.
[492] *Oregon Prescription Drug Monitoring Program v. U.S. DEA*, No.3:12-cv-02023-HA, D. Or., 2014 U.S. Dist. LEXIS 17047, February 11, 2014
[493] Town of Chester v. Laroe Estates, Inc., No. 16-605, S.Ct.
[494] 45 C.F.R. 164.512(f)(2)
[495] http://www.secstate.wa.gov/corps/domesticpartnerships/
[496] 2012 c 3; SSB 6239

[497] A good summary of Washington laws regarding provision of health care to minors is available at http://www.washingtonlawhelp.org/resource/providing-health-care-to-minors-under-washing?ref=WyGRG, accessed 3/4/2015.
[498] *Smith v. Seibly*, 72 Wn.2d 16 (1967), cited in *State v. Koome*, 84 Wn.2d 901,911-912 (1975): "The common law requires that a physician subjectively evaluate the capacity of a minor to give informed and meaningful consent to any type of medical care."
[499] See the website for the Everett Clinic for a succinct, well-written explanation to parents why the clinic does not allow parents to access the on-line medical records for children age 13 to 17: https://www.myeverettclinic.com/default.asp?mode=stdfile&option=faq#PA_teen, accessed 3/4/2015.
[500] RCW 7.70.065
[501] http://www.qualityforum.org/projects/completed/sre/
[502] Fassett WE. Patient Safety and Quality Improvement Act of 2005. Ann Pharmacother. 2006 May; 40(5):917-24. Epub 2006 Apr 25.
[503] *Hammond v. Sanai et al.,* No. 492PA13, S. Ct. N.C., December 19, 2014.
[504] Taylor v. Hy-Vee, Inc., No. 15-9718-JTM, D. Kans., 2016 U.S. Dist. LEXIS 177784, December 22, 2016.
[505] Wichman K, Greenall J. Using root cause analysis to determine the system-based causes of error. CPJ/RPC 2006 May/Jun; 139(3):63;
http://www.ismp-Canada.org/download/CPJ2006MayJun.pdf
[506] Fassett WE. Key performance outcomes of patient safety curricula: root cause analysis, failure mode and effects analysis, and structured communications skills. Amer J Pharm Educ. 2011; 75(8): Article 164; https://doi.org/10.5688/ajpe758164.
[507] http://www.ihi.org/ihi
[508] http://www.pharmacypracticeaccredit.org/accreditation/program-overview, accessed 3/4/2015.

7 – AVOIDING DISCIPLINE, CIVIL LAWSUITS, AND EMPLOYER/EMPLOYEE DIFFICULTIES

DISCIPLINE

> COMPETENCY AREAS IN THIS CHAPTER
> 2016 MPJE COMPETENCY STATEMENTS – Areas 2.1.2, 2.1.3, 2.1.4, 2.2.4
> 2016 ACPE REQUIRED ELEMENTS – Pharmacy Law & Regulatory Affairs; Ethics; Medication Dispensing, Distribution, and Administration; Patient Safety; Practice Management

UNIFORM DISCIPLINARY ACT

Individuals licensed or registered by the Department of Health, including the Pharmacy Commission, are subject to the provisions of WASHINGTON'S UNIFORM DISCIPLINARY ACT (UDA, RCW 18.130).* The conduct of disciplinary actions by the Department of Health and its Boards is governed by a set of Model Procedural Rules for Boards contained in WAC 246-11. The UDA establishes the bases for discipline and the Model Rules describe how the various stages of the disciplinary process are carried out. The conduct of hearings and discipline by state agencies is governed by the Administrative Procedures Act (APA, RCW 34.05). The major features of the UDA of interest to pharmacists, pharmacy technicians, and pharmacy assistants are:

ESTABLISHMENT OF THE PHARMACY QUALITY ASSURANCE COMMISSION as the DISCIPLINARY AUTHORITY for pharmacists (RCW 18.130.040(viii))

COMMISSION POWERS. The UDA grants the following powers to disciplinary authorities:

- Discipline licensees
  - The licensure of pharmacy assistants starting in 2017 places them, along with pharmacy technicians, pharmacy interns, and pharmacists, under the provisions of the UDA
- Grant or deny licenses based on the provisions of the Act
- Adopt, amend, or rescind rules needed to carry out the Act
- Investigate all complaints or reports of unprofessional conduct and to hold hearings
- Issue subpoenas or administer oaths in conjunction with hearings or proceedings authorized by the Act

---

* Note that *facilities*, such as pharmacies, are not subject to several provisions of the Uniform Disciplinary Act dealing with discipline, but only to penalties prescribed in statutes governing such facilities; for pharmacies these statutes include the Pharmacy Practice Act, the Legend Drug Act, and the Uniform Controlled Substances Act. The reporting requirements of the UDA apply to facilities, however. The Commission investigates pharmacies under procedures specified in the APA.

- Take or cause depositions to be taken
- Compel the attendance of witnesses at hearings
- To conduct practice reviews in the course of investigating complaints
- To take emergency action ordering summary suspension of a license pending further proceedings
- Commission members may be used to direct investigations; however, such members may not participate in the hearing
- Adopt standards of professional conduct or practice
- Establish panels of three or more members to carry out any functions allowed in the Act

MANDATORY REPORTING BY LICENSEES. All licensees are required to report knowledge of discipline or unfitness to practice of colleagues. The legislature in 2006 (2006 c 99 § 1(6) and § 2 (1)(a)) amended RCW 18.130.070 to require the Secretary of the Department of Health to "adopt rules requiring EVERY LICENSE HOLDER TO REPORT TO THE APPROPRIATE DISCIPLINING AUTHORITY ANY CONVICTION, DETERMINATION, OR FINDING THAT ANOTHER LICENSE HOLDER HAS COMMITTED AN ACT WHICH CONSTITUTES UNPROFESSIONAL CONDUCT, OR TO REPORT INFORMATION to the disciplining authority, an impaired practitioner program, or voluntary substance abuse monitoring program approved by the disciplining authority, WHICH INDICATES THAT THE OTHER LICENSE HOLDER MAY NOT BE ABLE TO PRACTICE HIS OR HER PROFESSION WITH REASONABLE SKILL AND SAFETY TO CONSUMERS AS A RESULT OF A MENTAL OR PHYSICAL CONDITION." Previously, these rules did not extend to individual practitioners, but only to organizations and employers. There are exceptions to these requirements related to peer review and quality assurance activities, and to recovery programs. Additional legislation in 2008 further modified these reporting requirements. (See also the discussion in Chapter 2)

REPORTING OF UNPROFESSIONAL CONDUCT BY ANOTHER LICENSEE. Every licensee (this includes pharmacists, interns, pharmacy assistants, and technicians) must report to the DOH when they have knowledge that another licensee has been convicted of any gross misdemeanor or felony. Licensees must also report when they become aware that another licensee has been determined by an employer or institution to have committed unprofessional conduct. These reports are made to the DOH in accordance with WAC 246-16-220.

The requirement to report UNPROFESSIONAL CONDUCT is triggered by PERSONAL KNOWLEDGE on the part of the licensee, not by rumors or second-hand reports. Consider the following example:

> Pharmacist A works with pharmacist B. One day pharmacist B is terminated from her employment by pharmacist C, the regional pharmacy manager. Pharmacist B is told by pharmacist C that she is being fired because the pharmacy security staff has evidence that she has been filling prescriptions for herself for controlled substances. Pharmacist B tells pharmacist A that she's been fired.
>
> Pharmacist A knows only that pharmacist B has been fired; she doesn't have first-hand knowledge of the reason why.
>
> Pharmacist C, as the person who terminates pharmacist B, has first-hand knowledge that a determination has been made that pharmacist B has committed unprofessional conduct.
>
> Pharmacist C has a duty to report; it is unlikely under these facts that pharmacist A has such a duty.

REPORTING OF IMPAIRMENT OF ANOTHER LICENSEE. Licensees are required to report impairment of another licensee. If the impairment has not resulted in harm to a patient, the report may be made to WRAPP or to the DOH. If a patient has been harmed, the report must be made to the DOH.

The duty to report POSSIBLE IMPAIRMENT is triggered by a REASONABLE BELIEF on the part of the licensee that another licensee MAY BE impaired or unable to practice safely. Consider the following example:

> Pharmacist A frequently returns from lunch with the smell of alcohol on her breath and often is inattentive and forgetful, and technician B and assistant C have noticed this and even discussed it with each other. Assistant D, however, normally works only as a delivery person for 3 hours in the late afternoon, and doesn't interact much with pharmacist A.
>
> Under these circumstances, technician B and assistant C are required to notify the Pharmacy Commission (and should also notify management). Assistant D would not likely be found to have a duty to report pharmacist A.

SELF-REPORTING REQUIRED. Pharmacy licensees are also required to report to the Pharmacy Commission any

- CONVICTION, DETERMINATION, OR FINDING that he or she has committed an act which constitutes unprofessional conduct; or
- DISQUALIFICATION FROM PARTICIPATION IN FEDERAL MEDICAID OR MEDICARE PROGRAMS. Among the reasons a pharmacist might be disqualified are:
  - Conviction (or plea of guilty or *nolo contendere*[509]) of misdemeanor fraud;
  - License suspension or revocation in any jurisdiction;
  - Default on federal student loans; or
  - Felony conviction relating to the Controlled Substances Act

> **Fassett's Comment**: Because these requirements may implicate licensees' Fifth Amendment or state constitutional rights against self-incrimination, I believe that licensees should seek advice from an attorney before making a self-report.

UNPROFESSIONAL CONDUCT is defined in RCW 18.130.180 to include the following – these are the bases by which pharmacists may be disciplined. The criteria set forth in SMALL CAPS are probably the most common reasons for pharmacist discipline:

- Commission of any act involving moral turpitude, dishonesty, or corruption relating to the practice of the person's profession, whether or not the act constitutes a crime.
- Conviction of a relevant crime may be used in a disciplinary hearing as conclusive evidence that the crime was committed; pleas of nolo contendere or deferred sentencing are considered as convictions for this purpose.
- Misrepresentation or concealment of a material fact in obtaining a license or in reinstatement of a license
- All advertising which is false, fraudulent, or misleading
- INCOMPETENCE, NEGLIGENCE, OR MALPRACTICE WHICH
  - RESULTS IN INJURY TO A PATIENT, OR
  - WHICH CREATES AN UNREASONABLE RISK THAT A PATIENT MAY BE HARMED
- Suspension, revocation, or restriction of the person's license to practice any health care profession in any state, federal, or foreign jurisdiction

- Note: legislation in 2006 now requires the Department to immediately suspend a license – pending resolution of departmental investigation and proceedings – when the holder of that license has had his or her license suspended or revoked in another jurisdiction. (RCW 18.130.370, 2006 c 99 §§ 3-4)
- POSSESSION, USE, PRESCRIPTION FOR USE, OR DISTRIBUTION OF CONTROLLED SUBSTANCES in any way other than for legitimate or therapeutic purposes, DIVERSION OF CONTROLLED SUBSTANCES OR LEGEND DRUGS, the VIOLATION OF ANY DRUG LAW, or PRESCRIBING CONTROLLED SUBSTANCES FOR ONESELF.
- VIOLATION OF ANY STATE OR FEDERAL STATUTE OR ADMINISTRATIVE RULE REGULATING THE PROFESSION IN QUESTION, INCLUDING ANY STATUTE OR RULE DEFINING OR ESTABLISHING STANDARDS OF PATIENT CARE OR PROFESSIONAL CONDUCT OR PRACTICE (Note – see discussion in Chapter 6 regarding how OBRA '90 sets objective standards of the structure, process, and content of patient counseling.)
- Failure to cooperate with the disciplinary authority
    - Not furnishing any papers or documents
    - NOT FURNISHING IN WRITING A FULL AND COMPLETE EXPLANATION COVERING THE MATTER CONTAINED IN THE COMPLAINT FILED WITH THE DISCIPLINING AUTHORITY
    - Not responding to subpoenas issued by the disciplining authority
    - Not providing reasonable and timely access for the disciplinary authority to perform practice reviews
- FAILURE TO COMPLY WITH AN ORDER OF THE COMMISSION
- Aiding or abetting an unlicensed person to practice when a license is required
- Violations of rules established by any health agency
- Practice beyond the scope of practice defined by law or regulation
- Misrepresentation or fraud in the conduct of the business or profession
- FAILURE TO ADEQUATELY SUPERVISE AUXILIARY STAFF to the extent that the consumer's health or safety is at risk
- Engaging in a profession involving contact with the public while suffering from a contagious or infectious disease involving serious risk to public health
- Promotion for personal gain of any unnecessary or inefficacious drug, device, treatment, procedure or service
- Conviction of any gross misdemeanor or felony relating to the practice of the person's profession.
- Procuring, or aiding and abetting in procuring, a criminal abortion
- The offering, undertaking, or agreeing to cure or treat disease by a secret method, procedure, treatment, or medicine
- Willful betrayal of a practitioner-patient privilege as recognized by law
- Violation of Chapter 19.68 RCW – The Anti-Kickback Statute (see also Chapter 8)

    It shall be unlawful for any person, firm, corporation or association, whether organized as a cooperative, or for profit or nonprofit, to pay, or offer to pay or allow, directly or indirectly, to any person licensed by the state of Washington to engage in the practice of medicine and surgery, drugless treatment in any form, dentistry, or pharmacy and it shall be unlawful for such person to request, receive or allow, directly or indirectly, a rebate, refund, commission, unearned discount or profit by means of a credit or other valuable consideration in connection with the referral of patients to any person, firm, corporation or association, or in connection with the furnishings of medical, surgical or dental care, diagnosis, treatment or service, on the sale, rental, furnishing or supplying of clinical laboratory supplies or services of any kind, drugs, medication, or medical supplies, or any other goods, services or supplies prescribed for medical diagnosis, care or treatment.

    The Washington Supreme Court has held that charging patients for medications dispensed or administered directly to them by an authorized prescriber was not a violation of RCW 19.68.[510]

- Willful interference with a Commission investigation
- CURRENT MISUSE OF ALCOHOL, CONTROLLED SUBSTANCES, OR LEGEND DRUGS
- Abuse of a client or patient, or sexual contact with a client or patient
- Acceptance of more than a nominal gratuity from a representative of a manufacturer or vendor of medical or health-related products or services intended for patients, where a recognized conflict of interest is presented

SEXUAL MISCONDUCT

The Department has worked with each disciplinary board to develop additional regulations regarding sexual misconduct by licensees. The Pharmacy Commission rules were adopted as WAC 246-860-100, and revised most recently in December 2016. Among other requirements,

THE RULES PROHIBIT

- Romantic or sexual relationships with a patient, client, or key party (a key decision maker related to the patient or client);
- A variety of acts that are sexual or seductive in nature;
- Unpermitted touching of a sexual nature not required by legitimate health care purposes;
- Soliciting a date with a patient, client or key party;
- Making statements regarding the patient, client, or key party's body, appearance, sexual history, or sexual orientation other than for legitimate health care purposes;
- Sexually demeaning behavior including any verbal or physical contact which may be reasonably interpreted as demeaning, humiliating, embarrassing, threatening or harming a patient, client or key party;
- Photographing or filming the body or any body part or pose of a patient, client, or key party, other than for legitimate health care purposes;
- Showing a patient, client, or key party sexually explicit photographs, other than for legitimate health care purposes.
- Sexual misconduct also includes sexual contact with *any person* involving force, intimidation, or *lack of consent*; or a conviction of a sex offense as defined in RCW 9.94A.030.
    - Note that this embraces a wide variety of sexual misconduct that is not necessarily carried out within a health care setting or relationship.
    - This means that a pharmacy student, for example, charged with date rape or similar violations of the college's or school's conduct code could be subject to his or her intern's license being disciplined.

THE RULES PERMIT

- Provision of health care services to a person with whom the provider is in a romantic relationship in case of emergency where the services cannot or will not be provided by another health care provider;
- Contact that is necessary for a legitimate health care purpose and that meets the standard of care appropriate to the profession; and
- Providing health care services for a legitimate health care purpose to a person who is in a preexisting, established personal relationship with the health care provider where there is no evidence of, or potential for, exploiting the patient or client.

PHARMACIST'S PROFESSIONAL RESPONSIBILITIES

The Commission has defined by rule in WAC 246-853-095 those responsibilities which a pharmacist may not delegate to a technician or pharmacy assistant. To do so is considered unprofessional conduct. The Commission amended this rule in response to issues related to pharmacist conscientious objection to dispensing certain drugs. The rule operates in conjunction with WAC 246-869-010 (Pharmacies' Responsibilities – see Chapter 3).

A PHARMACIST'S PRIMARY RESPONSIBILITY IS TO ENSURE PATIENTS RECEIVE SAFE AND APPROPRIATE MEDICATION THERAPY.

A PHARMACIST SHALL NOT DELEGATE THE FOLLOWING PROFESSIONAL RESPONSIBILITIES:

- Receipt of a verbal prescription other than refill authorization from a prescriber.
- Consultation with the patient regarding the prescription, both prior to and after the prescription filling and/or regarding any information contained in a patient medication record system; provided that this shall not prohibit pharmacy ancillary personnel from providing to the patient or the patient's health care giver certain information where no professional judgment is required such as dates of refills or prescription price information.
- Consultation with the prescriber regarding the patient and the patient's prescription.
- Extemporaneous compounding of the prescription, however, bulk compounding from a formula and IV admixture products prepared in accordance with chapter 246-871 WAC may be performed by a pharmacy technician when supervised by a pharmacist.
- Interpretation of data in a patient medication record system.
- Ultimate responsibility for all aspects of the completed prescription, such as: Accuracy of drug, strength, labeling, proper container and other requirements.
- Dispense prescription to patient with proper patient information as required by WAC 246-869-220.
- Signing of the poison register and the Schedule V controlled substance registry book at the time of sale ... and any other item required by law, rule or regulation to be signed or initialed by a pharmacist.
- Professional communications with physicians, dentists, nurses and other health care practitioners.
- Decision not to dispense lawfully prescribed drugs or devices or to not distribute drugs and devices approved by the U.S. Food and Drug Administration for restricted distribution by pharmacies.

UTILIZING PERSONNEL TO ASSIST THE PHARMACIST.

The responsible pharmacist manager shall retain all professional and personal responsibility for any assisted tasks performed by personnel under his or her responsibility, as shall the pharmacy employing such personnel. The responsible pharmacist manager shall determine the extent to which personnel may be utilized to assist the pharmacist, and shall assure that the pharmacist is fulfilling his or her supervisory and professional responsibilities.

This does not preclude delegation to an intern or extern.

IT IS CONSIDERED UNPROFESSIONAL CONDUCT FOR ANY PERSON AUTHORIZED TO PRACTICE OR ASSIST IN THE PRACTICE OF PHARMACY TO ENGAGE IN ANY OF THE FOLLOWING:

- Destroy unfilled lawful prescription;
- Refuse to return unfilled lawful prescriptions;
- Violate a patient's privacy;
- Discriminate against patients or their agent in a manner prohibited by state or federal law; and

- Intimidate or harass a patient.

Although portions of this rule were challenged in federal courts, it was ultimately upheld by the 9th Circuit Court of Appeals, and a further appeal to the US Supreme Court was not accepted.[511,512]

DISCIPLINE PROCESS. The general ORDER IN WHICH DISCIPLINE IS CARRIED OUT can be outlined as follows

RECEIPT OF A WRITTEN COMPLAINT charging unprofessional conduct or unfitness to practice by a licensee, or, without a formal complaint, the Commission has reason to believe that the licensee may be unfit to practice or have engaged in unprofessional conduct (for example, during the course of investigating an unrelated complaint at the same pharmacy) (RCW 18.130.080)

- Complaints may come from individuals, other agencies, other licensees, corporations or treatment programs
- In communicating with the complainant in writing, the Commission may not include the address or telephone number of the licensee (RCW 18.130.085)

INVESTIGATION BY THE BOARD

- INITIAL COMMISSION REVIEW BY A 3-MEMBER PANEL. In 2005, the Washington Appeals Court ruled in *Client A & B et al. v. Yoshinaka* that the Uniform Disciplinary Act requires that "an investigation should not be conducted, and records should not be obtained, until the [relevant Board or Commission] determines that the complaint merits investigation."[513] Three members of the Commission, sitting in various panels, review complaints and determine whether an investigation shall be begun.[514]
- A DOH INVESTIGATOR then follows up on the complaint, which may include meeting with the licensee and asking the licensee to provide a written explanation of the circumstances related to the complaint

  The licensee may at this point wish to contact an attorney to assist in preparing his or her response to the Commission.

- THE INVESTIGATOR WILL PROVIDE A MEMORANDUM TO THE COMMISSION, which may recommend closure or further investigation
- A REVIEWING COMMISSION MEMBER will examine the case; he or she may recommend
  - Closure
  - A Notice of Correction – which is not considered discipline
  - A Statement of Charges and Proposed Settlement

  The RCM is typically advised by this point by an attorney from the Attorney General's Office who is assigned to work with the Department and Commission on disciplinary matters.

- THE RCM WORKS WITH THE ASSISTANT ATTORNEY GENERAL assigned to the Commission to develop any charges and proposed settlement
- IF A STATEMENT OF CHARGES IS PREPARED, THE ATTORNEY GENERAL'S OFFICE NOTIFIES THE LICENSEE AND PROVIDES THEM WITH A PROPOSED AGREEMENT that
  - Stipulates to the matters of fact and law involved
  - Sets forth a settlement of the matter which may involve various forms of discipline
- THE LICENSEE MAY AGREE TO THE SETTLEMENT, in which case the settlement is taken to the Commission for approval and issue of a Commission Order approving the settlement. In some cases, the Commission does not accept the proposed settlement.
- THE LICENSEE MAY, INSTEAD OF AGREEING TO THE SETTLEMENT, DEMAND A HEARING BEFORE THE COMMISSION, at which he or she may call witnesses and present a case to the Commission.

HEARINGS BY THE BOARD

Hearings are quasi-judicial proceedings that are somewhat less formal than court proceedings, but adhere to the rules of evidence inherent in a court proceeding. Witnesses are sworn, as in a court hearing, and both the State and the licensee may present witnesses and cross-examine them.

The hearings of the Pharmacy Commission generally consist of a panel of five Commission members,[515] (excluding the Reviewing Board Member), and are presided over by an Administrative Law Judge from the Office of Administrative Hearings.

Pharmacists and other licensees are entitled to be REPRESENTED BY AN ATTORNEY in all matters before the Commission. Because of the complexity of legal issues, procedures, and the implications for the future practice of the licensee, I believe it is generally a good idea to consult with an attorney when a pharmacist first learns of a complaint. A licensee should choose an attorney with specific knowledge and experience in dealing with administrative law.

- Some professional liability insurance policies will reimburse pharmacists for some of their costs in retaining an attorney to deal with complaints filed by the Commission. This protects the interests of the licensee, as well as the insurance company, since discipline of a pharmacist may affect the likelihood and outcome of civil suits filed as a result of the incident that prompted the complaint.

The STANDARD OF EVIDENCE needed to discipline a PHARMACIST in Washington is a clear and convincing evidence standard – this standard requires the hearing panel to find with a high degree of probability that the licensee committed the charged conduct, as a result of the Supreme Court ruling in *Nguyen v. State, Dep't of Health*, 144 Wn.2d 516, 29 P.3d 689 (2001). The Court held that the Department of Health had failed to use a clear and convincing standard of evidence in the suspension of a physician's license. The factors requiring a heightened standard when disciplining physicians have been applied to lawyers, to professional engineers, and in an unpublished opinion in a disciplinary case involving a pharmacist.

- A 2009 Supreme Court decision in *Ongom v. Dep't of Health,* 159 Wn.2d 132 (2009) case extended the clear and convincing standard to licensed nursing assistants, a class of licensees similar to pharmacy technicians or assistants. This appeared to set a precedent by which the Commission must use a clear and convincing evidence standard for disciplinary actions involving pharmacy ancillary personnel.
- However, the Court overturned *Ongom* in July 2011, in a case involving the license of a child day care provider. The lead opinion held that *Ongom* was decided in error because it focused on "Ongom's desire to work as a nurs[ing assistant] compared with Nguyen's desire to practice medicine. ... This is not the proper inquiry. The proper inquiry should focus on objective measures to determine the value of the property interest the State seeks to take away – i.e., the license. It is therefore relevant to consider the time, expense and education invested to obtain the license."

  Four justices would have overturned *Nguyen*, as well, but the 9th, dissenting justice argued that *Nguyen* should continue to apply to all licensees. Therefore, the clear and convincing standard of evidence should still apply when pharmacists are disciplined, but it might no longer be applied in the case of pharmacy technicians or pharmacy assistants.[516]

THE HEARING PANEL WILL REACH A DECISION, which the Commission will ultimately apply as a final order. Discipline may take one or more of several forms:

- Fines
- Suspension of a license

- Revocation of a license for a specific period (typically 10 years), after which time the person may seek to be licensed
- Permanent revocation, if the board finds that the licensee can never be rehabilitated or regain the ability to practice with reasonable skill or safety.
- Probation
- Limitations on practice; such as requiring work under supervision, or prohibition against being an RPM or preceptor
- A requirement for additional continuing education, internship, or retaking of the law exam, or participation in a recovery or treatment program
- Staying of the imposition of the discipline during a probationary period, with abeyance of the discipline at the end of the probationary period

APPEALS. Licensees may petition for a reconsideration of the final order, and/or may appeal the decision to the Superior Court. A decision of the Superior Court may be appealed to the Appellate Court, and, subject to Supreme Court rules, to that body.

DISCIPLINARY STATUS INDICATED ON LICENSE COPY. The Department indicates on the printed license certificate whether the holder is on probation or has restrictions on his or her practice. The notice will read "ACTIVE ON PROBATION," or "ACTIVE WITH RESTRICTIONS."[517] The "Provider Credential Search" link on the Department or Commission website allows a person to determine if a given licensee or firm has had disciplinary action taken against its license.

SANCTIONING GUIDELINES. In 2006 and 2007 the DOH developed its first attempt at standardizing the imposition of sanctions against licensees who are disciplined by one of the boards or commissions within the department. The goal was to treat similar cases similarly, assure protection of the public, and the approach is similar to that used to discipline lawyers. Certain of the independent boards or commissions were reluctant to abandon their own sanctioning rules and resisted implementing the DOH guidelines. The 2008 Legislature required joint review by the health boards and commissions of the 2007 guidelines, and establishment of a uniform sanctioning schedule by emergency regulation by January 1, 2009.[518] (RCW 18.130.390). The resulting regulation is found at WAC 246-16-800.

- The sanctioning rules apply to active or expired credentials, not to applicants.
- Selection of sanctions by disciplinary authorities must adhere to the following:
- Sanctions selected must PROTECT THE PUBLIC, and, if possible, REHABILITATE the license holder.

SUSPENSION OR REVOCATION will be imposed when the license holder cannot practice with reasonable skill or safety.

PERMANENT REVOCATION may be imposed when the disciplining authority finds the license holder can never be rehabilitated or can never regain ability to practice safely.

SURRENDER OF CREDENTIAL may be accepted when the license holder is at the end of his/her effective practice and surrender alone is enough to protect the public. The license holder must agree to retire and not resume practice.

INDEFINITE SUSPENSION may be imposed in default orders.

Deviation from these rules is allowed when the disciplining authority determines that the schedule does not adequately address the facts in a case. Disciplining authorities will use their judgment to determine appropriate sanctions if the sanction schedules do not address the misconduct.

SANCTIONING PROCESS. When the disciplining authority has determined that a violation of the uniform disciplinary act has occurred. It shall follow a four-step process in determining the sanction to be applied.

STEP 1. The nature of the misconduct is described in the findings of fact in an order or in the allegations in an informal disposition. The disciplining authority uses the misconduct described as select the appropriate sanction schedule.

- If the act of misconduct falls in more than one sanction schedule, the greater sanction imposed.
- If different acts of misconduct fall in the same sanction schedule, the highest sanction is imposed and the other acts of misconduct are considered aggravating factors.

STEP 2. The disciplining authority identifies the severity of the misconduct and identifies a tier using the sanction schedule tier descriptions.

STEP 3. The disciplining authority identifies aggravating or mitigating factors using the list in WAC 246-16-890. The disciplining authority describes the factors in the order or stipulation.

STEP 4. The disciplining authority selects sanctions within the identified tier.

SANCTION SCHEDULES. Six separate sanctioning schedules were created by DOH.

PRACTICE BELOW STANDARD OF CARE (WAC 246-16-810)

PRACTICE BELOW STANDARD OF CARE				
Severity	**Tier / Conduct**	**Sanction Range In consideration of Aggravating & Mitigating Circumstances**		**Duration**
		Minimum	Maximum	
least	A – Caused no or minimal patient harm or a risk of minimal patient harm	Conditions that may include reprimand, training, monitoring, supervision, probation, evaluation, etc.	Oversight for 3 years which may include reprimand, training, monitoring, supervision, evaluation, probation, suspension, etc.	0-3 years
	B – Caused moderate patient harm or risk of moderate to severe patient harm	Oversight for 2 years which may include suspension, probation, practice restrictions, training, monitoring, supervision, probation, evaluation, etc.	Oversight for 5 years which may include suspension, probation, practice restrictions, training, monitoring, supervision, probation, evaluation, etc. OR revocation.	2 years - 5 years unless revocation
greatest	C – Caused severe harm or death to a human patient	Oversight for 3 years which may include suspension, probation, practice restrictions, training, monitoring, supervision, probation, evaluation, etc. In addition - demonstration of knowledge or competency.	Permanent conditions, restrictions or revocation.	3 years - permanent

SEXUAL MISCONDUCT OR CONTACT (WAC 246-16-820)

SEXUAL MISCONDUCT OR CONTACT (including convictions for sexual misconduct)				
Severity	**Tier / Conduct**	**Sanction Range In consideration of Aggravating & Mitigating Circumstances**		**Duration**
		Minimum	Maximum	
least	**A** –Inappropriate conduct, contact, or statements of a sexual or romantic nature	Conditions that may include reprimand, training, monitoring, probation, supervision, evaluation, etc.	Oversight for 3 years which may include reprimand, training, monitoring, supervision, evaluation, probation, suspension, etc.	0-3 years
	B – Sexual contact, romantic relationship, or sexual statements that risk or result in patient harm	Oversight for 2 years which may include suspension, probation, practice restrictions, training, monitoring, supervision, probation, evaluation, etc.	Oversight for 5 years which may include suspension, probation, practice restrictions, training, monitoring, supervision, probation, evaluation, etc. OR revocation.	2 years - 5 years unless revocation
greatest	**C** – Sexual contact, including but not limited to contact involving force and/or intimidation, and convictions of sexual offenses in RCW 9.94A.030.	1 year suspension AND oversight for 5 additional years which may include suspension, probation, practice restrictions, training, monitoring, supervision, probation, evaluation, etc. AND demonstration of successful completion of evaluation and treatment.	Permanent conditions, restrictions, or revocation.	6 years - permanent

ABUSE – PHYSICAL AND EMOTIONAL (WAC 246-16-830)

ABUSE -- Physical and/or Emotional				
Severity	**Tier / Conduct**	**Sanction Range In consideration of Aggravating & Mitigating Circumstances**		**Duration**
		Minimum	Maximum	
least	**A** – Verbal or nonverbal intimidation, forceful contact, or disruptive or demeaning behavior, including general behavior not necessarily directed at a specific patient or patients	Conditions that may include reprimand, training, monitoring, probation, supervision, evaluation, etc.	Oversight for 3 years which may include reprimand, training, monitoring, supervision, evaluation, probation, suspension, etc.	0-3 years
	B – Abusive unnecessary or forceful contact or disruptive or demeaning behavior causing or risking moderate mental or physical harm, including general behavior not directed at a specific patient or patients.	Oversight for 2 years which may include suspension, probation, practice restrictions, training, monitoring, supervision, probation, evaluation, etc.	Oversight for 5 years which may include suspension, probation, practice restrictions, training, monitoring, supervision, probation, evaluation, etc. OR revocation.	2 years - 5 years unless revocation
greatest	**C** – Severe physical, verbal, or forceful contact, or emotional disruptive behavior, that results in or risks significant harm or death	1 year suspension AND oversight for 5 additional years which may include suspension, probation, practice restrictions, training, monitoring, supervision, probation, evaluation, etc. AND demonstration of successful completion of evaluation and treatment.	Permanent conditions, restrictions, or revocation.	6 years - permanent

DIVERSION OF CONTROLLED SUBSTANCES OR LEGEND DRUGS (WAC 246-16-840)

DIVERSION OF CONTROLLED SUBSTANCES OR LEGEND DRUGS				
Severity	**Tier/Conduct**	**Sanction Range In consideration of Aggravating & Mitigating Circumstances**		**Duration**
		Minimum	Maximum	
least	**A** – Diversion with no or minimal patient harm or risk of harm	Conditions that may include reprimand, training, monitoring, probation, supervision, evaluation, treatment, etc.	Oversight for 5 years which may include reprimand, training, monitoring, supervision, evaluation, probation, suspension, treatment etc.	0-5 years
	B – Diversion with moderate patient harm or risk of harm or for distribution	Oversight for 2 years which may include suspension, probation, practice restrictions, training, monitoring, supervision, probation, evaluation, treatment, etc.	Oversight for 7 years which may include suspension, probation, practice restrictions, training, monitoring, supervision, probation, evaluation, treatment, etc. OR revocation.	2 - 7 years unless revocation
greatest	**C** – Diversion with severe physical injury or death of a patient or a risk of severe physical injury or death or for substantial distribution to others	1 year suspension AND oversight for 5 additional years which may include suspension, probation, practice restrictions, training, monitoring, supervision, probation, evaluation, etc. AND demonstration of successful completion of evaluation and treatment.	Permanent conditions, restrictions OR revocation.	6 years - permanent

SUBSTANCE ABUSE (WAC 246-16-850)

SUBSTANCE ABUSE				
Severity	**Tier / Conduct**	**Sanction Range In consideration of Aggravating & Mitigating Circumstances**		**Duration**
		Minimum	Maximum	
least	**A** – Misuse of drugs or alcohol with no to minimal patient harm or risk of harm	Conditions that may include reprimand, training, monitoring, probation, supervision, evaluation, treatment, etc.	Oversight for 5 years which may include reprimand, training, monitoring, supervision, evaluation, probation, suspension, treatment, etc.	0-5 years
↓	**B** –Misuse of drugs or alcohol with moderate patient harm or risk of harm	Oversight for 2 years which may include suspension, probation, practice restrictions, training, monitoring, supervision, probation, evaluation, treatment, etc.	Oversight for 7 years which may include suspension, probation, practice restrictions, training, monitoring, supervision, probation, evaluation, treatment, etc. OR revocation.	2 - 7 years unless revocation
greatest	**C** –Misuse of drugs or alcohol with severe physical injury or death of a patient or a risk of significant physical injury or death	1 year suspension AND oversight for 5 additional years which may include suspension, probation, practice restrictions, training, monitoring, supervision, probation, evaluation, etc. AND demonstration of successful completion of evaluation and treatment.	Permanent conditions, restrictions OR revocation.	6 years - permanent

CRIMINAL CONVICTIONS (WAC 246-16-860)

CRIMINAL CONVICTIONS (excluding sexual misconduct)				
Severity	**Tier / Conviction**	**Sanction Range In consideration of Aggravating & Mitigating Circumstances**		**Duration**
		Minimum	Maximum	
least	**A** – Conviction of a Gross Misdemeanor except sexual offenses in RCW 9.94A.030	Conditions that may include reprimand, training, monitoring, probation, supervision, evaluation, etc.	Oversight for 5 years which may include reprimand, training, monitoring, supervision, evaluation, probation, suspension, etc.	0-5 years
↓	**B** – Conviction of a Class B, C, OR Unclassified Felony, except sexual offenses in RCW 9.94A.030	Oversight for 2 years which may include suspension, probation, practice restrictions, training, monitoring, supervision, probation, evaluation, etc.	Oversight for 5 years which may include suspension, probation, practice restrictions, training, monitoring, supervision, probation, evaluation, etc. OR revocation.	2 years - 5 years unless revocation
greatest	**C** – Conviction of a Class A Felony, except sexual offenses in RCW 9.94A.030	5 years suspension	Permanent revocation	5 years - permanent revocation

AGGRAVATING FACTORS move the appropriate sanctions towards the maximum end of the tier.

MITIGATING FACTORS move the appropriate sanctions towards the minimum and of the tier.

Mitigating or aggravating factors may result in the determination of a sanction outside the range of the tier. Table 7-1 summarizes aggravating or mitigating factors set forth in the regulation.

TABLE 7-1. AGGRAVATING AND MITIGATING FACTORS listed in WAC 246-16-890:

FACTORS RELATED TO THE MISCONDUCT	• Gravity of the misconduct; • Age, capacity and/or vulnerability of the patient, client, or victim; • Number and frequency of the acts of misconduct; • Injury caused by the misconduct; • Potential for injury to be caused by the misconduct; • Degree of responsibility for the outcome; • Abuse of trust; • Intentional or inadvertent act(s); • Motivation is criminal, immoral, dishonest or for personal gain; • Length of time since misconduct occurred.
FACTORS RELATED TO THE LICENSE HOLDER	• Experience in practice; • Past disciplinary record • Previous character; • Mental and/or physical health; • Personal circumstances; • Personal problems having a nexus with the misconduct.
FACTORS RELATED TO THE DISCIPLINARY PROCESS	• Admission of key facts; • Full and free disclosure to the disciplining authority; • Voluntary restitution or other remedial action; • Bad faith obstruction of the investigation or discipline process or proceedings; • False evidence, statements or deceptive practices during the investigation or discipline process or proceedings; • Remorse or awareness that the conduct was wrong; • Impact on the patient, client, or victim.
GENERAL FACTORS	• License holder's knowledge, intent, and degree of responsibility; • Presence or pattern of other violations; • Present moral fitness of the license holder; • Potential for successful rehabilitation; • Present competence to practice; • Dishonest or selfish motives; • Illegal conduct; • Heinousness of the misconduct; • Ill repute upon the profession; • Isolated incident unlikely to reoccur.

As indicated above, most discipline of pharmacists arises from a limited number of possible charges. A review of Commission reports over the last several years indicates that two major areas account for most discipline:

- Substance or alcohol abuse, and charges of diversion arising from that abuse. See Chapter 5 for a discussion of impaired pharmacist recovery programs.
- Dispensing errors, particularly where
  - The pharmacist failed to counsel the patient and counseling would likely have revealed the error;
  - The pharmacist mislead the patient or otherwise dealt improperly with a patient's report of an error; or
  - A repeated pattern of errors over time.

> **Fassett's Comment:** The increased specificity and complexity of the sanctioning process seems to me to increase the importance of obtaining competent advice from an attorney experienced in administrative law and applications of sanctions whenever a pharmacist, intern, assistant, or technician is faced with potential discipline.

CIVIL LAWSUITS BASED ON CONTRACTS OR WARRANTIES

A person may file a civil lawsuit against a pharmacist when the pharmacist has a contractual or professional obligation to that person, and by some failure on the pharmacist's part, has cause the person to suffer an injury or loss. Two broad categories of civil lawsuits are those based on contracts, and those based on intentional wrongdoings, also known as torts.

CONTRACTS are voluntary agreements between two or more parties that are enforceable under the law.

TO BE A VALID CONTRACT, it must meet certain tests:

- It must be VOLUNTARY (a contract obtained by force or threats is not enforceable)
- It must be for a LEGAL PURPOSE
- It must be the result of an OFFER AND AN ACCEPTANCE OF THAT OFFER
- It must have resulted in EXCHANGE OF MUTUAL CONSIDERATION, that is, each party must have given up something and gained something in return

Contracts can be established either VERBALLY OR IN WRITING. Certain contracts, such as real estate, must be in writing.

The parties must be COMPETENT to enter into the contract

- LEGALLY COMPETENT generally means adult status (18 or over)
- MENTALLY COMPETENT means that the person is mentally capable of understanding the nature of the contract
- MINORS CAN ENTER INTO CERTAIN CONTRACTS, such as a promise to pay for medical care, when it is in the interest of the minor to have done so. As noted in Chapter 6, minors can consent to care in certain circumstances, which may create a contract that can be enforced against either the minor or the responsible parent or guardian.

CONTRACTS CAN BE EXPRESS, OR IMPLIED

- EXPRESS contracts specifically set forth what the terms are of the contract. This can be done in verbal as well as written contracts.

- IMPLIED contracts are established by the actions of the parties.

BREACH OF CONTRACT

If one party BREACHES, or fails to fulfill the contract, the other can sue for damages.

BREACHES OF CONTRACT usually involve one of two acts

- Failure to perform or fulfill the contract
- Negligent performance of the contract causing damages

LEGAL REMEDIES for breaches of contracts may include

COMPELLED PERFORMANCE

The party in breach may be forced to complete the service or deliver the goods as promised. For example, a person who has promised to buy a car, and then changes his mind, might be compelled to actually purchase the vehicle.

MONETARY DAMAGES

Alternatively, the person in breach may be forced to pay the other party the losses incurred as a result of the breach. These can include *ACTUAL LOSSES*, such as decline in value of a piece of property as a result of the contract breach, or *INCIDENTAL LOSSES*, such as the cost of opportunities foregone

"PROMISSORY ESTOPPEL"

Sometimes an actual contract doesn't exist, but the courts will treat a situation AS IF there were a contract

- One party must have made REPRESENTATIONS to the other
- The second party must have ACTED IN REASONABLE RELIANCE on those representations
- The second party SUFFERED A LOSS as a result of that reliance
- The court will act as if an actual contract existed

This is called "promissory estoppel;" estoppel is Latin for an action to stop; the courts will "estop" the first party from claiming that a contract did not exist.

> An example: A pharmacy chain manager contacts you in Spokane and asks you to come to Wenatchee to work in a new store. In reliance on the manager's representations, you incur the cost of moving to Wenatchee, and also turn down a similar offer of employment in Spokane. However, the store does not open as planned, and you are now stuck in Wenatchee without a job. As seen below from employment law, most employment of pharmacists is "at will" and no employment contract actually exists. But because you reasonably relied on the manager's representations that a job was waiting for you, and because you suffered direct costs of moving and also opportunity losses from turning down the Spokane job, you may have a valid claim for damages against the chain, based on the promissory estoppel doctrine.

WARRANTIES ARE "CONTRACTS" THAT ARE ATTACHED TO THE SALE OF PRODUCTS.

Like contracts, WARRANTIES MAY BE EXPRESS OR IMPLIED.

Some products, such as power tools, come with written warranties that are usually specifically limited in nature, and seek to establish exactly what the manufacturer is promising the product will do, and what will the manufacturer do if the product fails to perform. This limits the remedies available to the purchaser if the product is defective.

Under common law, every sale of goods carries with it two IMPLIED WARRANTIES

- MERCHANTABILITY or a warranty that the product meets the normal standards of goods of its type. For example, a pharmacy selling aspirin tablets should only sell tablets that are not decomposed into acetic acid.
- FITNESS FOR A PARTICULAR PURPOSE. This warranty comes into play if the purchaser makes it clear to the seller that he or she intends to use the product for a particular purpose and the seller completes the sale. A pharmacist was approached by a group of high school students who had formed a "rocket club," and were seeking potassium chlorate, sulfur, and charcoal to make the fuel. The pharmacist sold these ingredients to the boys. After one of the boys was injured in the resulting explosion, the pharmacist was sued, successfully. Although this particular case was decided on a negligence basis, it illustrates a situation where a lawsuit might also be grounded in warranty law, since the pharmacist knew the purpose of the supplies was to make an explosive mixture. (*Krueger v Knutson*, 111 N.W.2d 526 (Minn. 1961))

Often, manufacturers that provide written limited warranties specifically disclaim both of these common law implied warranties.

SALES OF COMMERCIAL PRODUCTS IN THEIR OWN PACKAGING. Normally, when a pharmacist sells a commercial product (such as Tylenol PM™) in its original package, the only warranties implied are those of the manufacturer, not the seller. However, IF THE PHARMACIST MAKES A CLAIM FOR THE PRODUCT, he or she may create a warranty of fitness for a particular purpose, and become liable from any damages arising from the product's use. Generally, this isn't a problem for pharmacists, since they are knowledgeable about the products they sell and generally correct in the claims they make. However, the pharmacy can be bound by the representations of any of its employees, and a sales clerk or pharmacy assistant can create a warranty by the statements they make to purchasers of OTC drug products. To avoid this, pharmacies should have strong policies about who can make recommendations to patients.

LAYAWAYS. Many retailers, including pharmacies, sell non-pharmacy merchandise to customers on "lay-away plans." These plans have been less used in recent years owing to the use by customers of credit cards. With the recent credit crunch and decreased availability of consumer credit, lay-away plans are becoming an import option to help convince customers to buy in a store rather than on-line. The Federal Trade Commission has published a guide to retailers to help them avoid misunderstandings and legal actions relating to lay-away programs. There are no specific federal laws regarding lay-away programs, but the FTC Act prohibits deceptive trade practices, and the Truth-in-Lending Act may affect retailers who require customers to make all payments until the lay-away item is paid in full. Full and fair disclosure of your policies is the best approach to dealing with customers regarding layaways.[519]

WASHINGTON LAYAWAY LAW. A few states have specific layaway laws, but Washington is not among them; however, certain unfair actions in dealing with consumers' layaways might be grounds for suit under the state's consumer protection laws. Specific guidance exists under Washington's sales tax rules for when the sales tax must be collected on a layaway item. In general, the tax is reported when the customer collects the layaway item. A forfeited item is not considered a retail sale for tax purposes.

RENT TO OWN. Legally known as "lease-purchase agreements," commonly known as "rent-to-own" plans, are regulated by state laws in 47 jurisdictions, including Washington. Although the most common examples are rent-to-own establishments that provide appliances or furniture to consumers, some consumer transactions engaged in by pharmacies may come under these laws. For example, a pharmacy may have a rental rate for crutches, wheel chairs, walkers, and other durable medical equipment, with a provision that when the rent totals a certain amount, the patient will own the equipment. Washington's lease-purchase agreement statute is found at RCW 63.19.

DEFINITION. A lease-purchase agreement is defined as "an agreement for the use of personal property by a natural person primarily for personal, family, or household purposes for an initial period of four months or less that is automatically renewable with each payment after the initial period, but does not obligate or require the consumer to continue leasing or using the property beyond the initial period, and that permits the customer to become the owner of the property."

Among other requirements, the lessor (i.e., pharmacy) must provide disclosure of the total amount, and number and timing of payments needed to own the item, and a statement that the consumer will not own the property until the total payment necessary is made. The lessor must also disclose the *CASH PRICE* of the property, and inform the consumer that he or she is responsible for the fair market value of the property as of the time it is lost, stolen, damaged, or destroyed. Other requirements and restrictions are contained in RCW 63.19.040, and must be followed to comply with the statute.

Unlike some states (e.g., California), Washington's law does not set a maximum amount, as a multiple of the cash price, that may be collected from the consumer. In 2010, the Washington Attorney General settled with Rent-A-Center over claims arising from aggressive techniques use to collect from Rent-A-Center customers, under the Consumer Protection Act.

CIVIL LAWSUITS BASED ON TORTS.

Torts (from the Latin word for "twisted") include a wide range of civil wrongs committed by one person against another. Conduct that creates a tort is called "tortious" conduct.

Some of the MAJOR TORTS are

- Libel, slander, and defamation of character.
- Assault or battery
- False imprisonment or false arrest
- Intentional infliction of emotional distress or outrage
- Invasion of privacy
- Negligence

LIBEL, SLANDER AND DEFAMATION

DEFAMATION – written or spoken words that FALSELY AND NEGATIVELY REFLECT ON A LIVING PERSON'S CHARACTER. In Washington law, there are not separate offenses of libel or slander – both are treated as defamation. In jurisdictions that make a distinction, the two offenses are characterized as follows:

LIBEL – WRITTEN OR BROADCAST defamation;

SLANDER – SPOKEN defamation

DEFENSES.

A person accused of defamation may assert the following defenses.

TRUTH OF THE STATEMENTS – to be defamation, the offending statement must be false.

Statements were NOT MADE TO OTHER PERSONS. Defamation only arises from communications to third parties concerning the defamed individual.

Statements were made in circumstances which afford a CONDITIONAL PRIVILEGE. Some statements may be made that would otherwise be defamatory, if they are:

- Made in the public interest;
- Made without malicious intent; and
- Made without actual knowledge of their falsity or in reasonable reliance on the source of the information

Several lawsuits have been filed against pharmacies arising out of pharmacists' refusal to fill controlled substance prescriptions and comments made to patients in explaining the reasons for refusal. Pharmacies have lost these actions where the statements made were made to more than just a patient, and/or were unsupported by evidence. In one case, the pharmacist allegedly stated about the prescribing physician that "He is bad news," "He writes too much pain pills and it's against the law," and "Your doctor won't be in business much longer." In another case, the pharmacists allegedly told the patient that the prescriber "operates a pill mill," "is a murderer," and has been or soon will be arrested." In the second case, which resulted in a $1 million damages award against the pharmacy, none of the statements were found to be supported by any facts. Experts recommend that a prescription that is denied based on a professional review might be explained to the patient by saying, "We can't honor this prescription based on company policy."[520] Note that under Washington rules, unless the prescription is proven to be a forgery or otherwise invalid, it must be returned to the patient on request. A copy of the prescription can certainly be retained as part of a record of the reasons for refusal.

ASSAULT OR BATTERY

ASSAULT – an "assault" is an act which fulfills the following criteria:

- An intentional, unlawful THREAT or "offer" to cause bodily injury to another by force;
- Under circumstances which create in the other person a WELL-FOUNDED FEAR OF IMMINENT PERIL;
- Where there exists the apparent present ABILITY TO CARRY OUT the act if not prevented.

BATTERY –

A battery is the WILLFUL OR INTENTIONAL TOUCHING OF A PERSON AGAINST THAT PERSON'S WILL BY ANOTHER PERSON, or by an object or substance put in motion by that other person. Any offensive touching can constitute a battery even if it does not cause injury, and could not reasonably be expected to cause injury. A defendant who emphatically pokes the plaintiff in the chest with his index finger to emphasize a point may be culpable for battery (although the damages award that results may well be nominal). A defendant, who spits on a plaintiff, even though there is little chance that the spitting will cause any injury other than to the plaintiff's dignity, has committed a battery.

PRIVILEGE – to be assault or battery, the defendant must have lacked "privilege" to commit the act. Some bases for privilege are:

- *CONSENT* -- if the person consents to the assault, as in football, or the touching, as in authorized medical procedures or physical exams, there is no offense. However, *LACK OF INFORMED CONSENT TO A MEDICAL PROCEDURE CREATES A BATTERY.*
- POLICE CONDUCT – police are authorized to use reasonable force in the performance of their duties
- SELF-DEFENSE OR DEFENSE OF OTHERS – a pharmacist who physically restrained a customer who was about to attack another customer could be found to have privilege on the grounds of defense of others
- MERCHANT'S PRIVILEGE -- Most jurisdictions grant merchants the right to apply reasonable force to detain shoplifters, or other persons who the merchant reasonably believes are attempting to steal the merchant's property. This privilege might justify a pharmacist detaining a person who is caught trying to walk off with controlled substances from the pharmacy.

AVOIDING ASSAULT OR BATTERY BY PHARMACISTS OR PHARMACY STAFF. UNLESS they enjoy one of the above privileges, pharmacists and pharmacy employees need to AVOID PHYSICAL TOUCHING OF CUSTOMERS OR PATIENTS WITHOUT THEIR PERMISSION, OR THREATENING FORCE. If needed, it is best to call police and allow them to exercise their authority.

FALSE IMPRISONMENT OR FALSE ARREST

These torts involve physically or by threat of force detaining a person without a legal reason. Pharmacies are often involved in claims of false arrest when dealing with shoplifters, or WHEN THE PHARMACIST DELAYS DELIVERING A PRESCRIPTION TO A PATIENT WHILE WAITING FOR THE POLICE TO ARRIVE TO INVESTIGATE A SUSPICIOUS PRESCRIPTION. The use of subterfuge to detain a patient constitutes a potential form of unlawful arrest. Unless the pharmacist has personally used force or intimidation, these claims rarely prevail, but they do require defending. To avoid liability, the pharmacist should not imply to the person that they aren't free to leave the pharmacy. If the police cannot arrive in a reasonable time, it is better to let the patient leave with the medication or their prescription and the police have the option of following up later.

The "merchant's privilege" may be a bar to false arrest claims in some jurisdictions.

INTENTIONAL INFLICTION OF EMOTIONAL DISTRESS

The tort of intentional infliction of emotional distress has four elements:

- the defendant must act INTENTIONALLY OR RECKLESSLY;
- the defendant's conduct must be EXTREME AND OUTRAGEOUS; and
- the conduct must be the CAUSE of
- SEVERE EMOTIONAL distress

Examples of claims that have been filed against pharmacists include

- charges of sexual harassment in the work place (the pharmacist supervisor being sued by an employee);
- charges that a pharmacist revealed a patient's HIV status to his family

These claims are often alleged following a dispensing error, for example, by the parents of a child who died while they were administering the drug that was dispensed wrongly. These claims are often a means to seek damages for a family member who was not the one directly injured by a pharmacist's negligence.

INVASION OF PRIVACY may be alleged when the pharmacist reveals confidential information to others.

RECORDS SUBPOENAED IN LAWSUITS. Many cases arise from release of medical records to a spouse, particularly in relationship to divorce proceedings and child custody cases. A party to a lawsuit may issue a subpoena to obtain records, but it is important to recognize that a civil subpoena is not the same as a court order. Even when the pharmacy has received a subpoena from a party in a civil lawsuit, the records should not be released until the patient has been informed of the subpoena and given an opportunity to have it "quashed," or invalidated by a court, unless the subpoena is accompanied by a release from the patient. A 1977 Rhode Island case illustrates this issue.[521] In response to a subpoena by the patient's estranged husband, the pharmacy mailed the records without first informing the patient or obtaining her consent. The Rhode Island Supreme Court found that there was a legal basis for the patient to sue the pharmacy for violation of the state's confidentiality act as well as for violating her rights of privacy.

In a Washington case, a county sheriff was obtaining controlled substances from multiple physicians and multiple pharmacies. A pharmacist in the community notified the then Board of Pharmacy, who then examined the records of the other pharmacies and ultimately filed a report with the County Prosecutor that led to charges filed against the sheriff. He ultimately sued the Board for invasion of privacy. In this case, the courts ultimately held that the Board had the right to inspect pharmacy records and the sheriff had no expectation that his records could not be so examined.[522]

Some bizarre behavior has been reported in which pharmacists have been sued for invasion of privacy, for example an independent pharmacy owner who installed cameras in the restrooms of the pharmacy – ostensibly to protect against shoplifting.

Suits for invasion of privacy are also arising as a result of violations of HIPAA, although HIPAA itself does not confer a private right of action on individual patients. See the discussion in Chapter 6.

NEGLIGENCE

The most common tort cases against pharmacies involve allegations of malpractice, or professional negligence.

To establish a case of negligence, the plaintiff must prove FOUR ELEMENTS:

- That the pharmacist owed a DUTY to the plaintiff.
- That the pharmacist BREACHED the duty.
- That the plaintiff was INJURED.
- That the PROXIMATE CAUSE of the injury was the pharmacist's breach of his or her duty.

DUTY OF CARE

A pharmacist must use the degree of care of a reasonable and prudent person under similar circumstances. The "reasonable and prudent person" is a properly educated pharmacist considered competent to practice in the same jurisdiction. In general, the existence of a duty arises from a relationship to the patient or injured party, so that the pharmacist would have been aware of a responsibility to the injured party. Finally, the scope of a pharmacist's duty arises from foreseeability of harm,[523] or that the pharmacist would reasonably have known that a failure to use care could result in the type of injury sustained by the patient. The existence of a duty is a matter of law; the scope of a duty is a matter to be determined by the finder of fact (jury or judge in a bench trial) based on evidence provided at trial.

BREACH OF DUTY

It is a breach of duty when the pharmacist's conduct falls below the standard of practice. The standard of practice is a national or statewide standard, not local, and arises in part from the reasonable expectations of the patient as expressed publicly by the profession.

Courts may impose a higher standard than current practice, if they believe an entire profession has failed in a duty. For example, a Washington case held that physicians (and, by extension, optometrists) need to test intraocular pressure in all persons, not just those aged 35 and over, in spite of the prevailing practice to limit the test to persons above that age.[524]

The standard of care is usually established by expert witness testimony. Because the jury or fact finder will not fully understand the standards of a pharmacist, the plaintiff must provide testimony by an expert, who is qualified by experience and training to state what the standard of care actually is. This normally will be another pharmacist.

The standard of care may be set by a law or regulation under certain circumstances, but in general a regulation standing alone does not necessarily define the standards of the profession.

TRADITIONAL DUTIES owed by pharmacists to patients include the following:

- Accurate dispensing
- Interpretation of Rx
- Skilled compounding
- Correct product
- Correct label
- Detect obvious errors, particularly lethal overdoses
- Give package to the correct patient
- Don't fill/refill beyond instructions
- Recognize false/fraudulent prescriptions

NEGLIGENCE PER SE

A pharmacist may be found to have fallen below the standard of care owed to the patient, without any expert testimony, when the following is established from the facts of the case:

- Pharmacist clearly violates a statute or regulation, and
- Plaintiff is member of class of persons the statute or regulation was intended to protect, and the
- Harm that resulted was the type of harm the statute or regulation was intended to prevent

The Court may adopt the statute or regulation as the standard of care, and the plaintiff need only prove causation and damages. This is a rare occurrence in today's legal environment.

CAUSATION

The plaintiff must prove that the pharmacist's breach was the proximate cause of the injury. This involves proving that unless the pharmacist had breached the duty the injury would not have occurred, and also that no subsequent act or omission of another – unforeseeable by the pharmacist – was a more direct cause of the injury.

DAMAGES

The goal of an award of damages (or monetary compensation) is to return plaintiff to the position in which the plaintiff would have been were it not for the pharmacist's negligence. Damages may include the following:

ACTUAL DAMAGES

- Dollar losses (care, lost wages, etc.) – these are known as "economic damages," and are the most easily quantified form of damages.
- Non-economic damages are harder to quantify, and, of course, not fully compensated for by money alone. These include compensation for
    - Pain and suffering
    - Emotional and relational losses

Some states have established limits or "caps" on non-economic damages. Washington has not done so.

PUNITIVE (EXEMPLARY) DAMAGES

Punitive damages are designed to punish defendant or set an example to discourage similar conduct when the plaintiff can convince the jury that the defendant exhibited wanton and reckless disregard of patient's rights, or morally culpable behavior. If they may be awarded, they may often be "treble damages" or equal to 3 times the amount of actual damages. Punitive damages, unlike actual damages, are not taxed.

One of the goals of "tort reform" at the state and federal level is to either eliminate punitive damages or place a "cap" on how much can be awarded. Washington does not allow punitive damages in medical negligence lawsuits.

INFORMED CONSENT. One of the duties a prescriber owes to a patient is the duty to obtain the informed consent of the patient to the treatment. Providing treatment without consent is an assault under common law. This obligation grew in importance during the latter half of the 20th century, with the recognition of the legal and ethical obligation to allow patients to participate in decisions concerning their care.

INFORMED CONSENT IN HUMAN SUBJECTS RESEARCH. A specific body of rules has developed regarding the ethical conduct of research, including the need to obtain informed consent for human subjects research. Pharmacists participating in clinical trials, academic pharmacists engaged in clinical or social and behavioral research, and their students or residents must become aware of these requirements, and generally their institutional research boards (IRBs) will require training appropriate to their roles. The DHHS Office of Research Integrity has educational resources, and an "Introduction to the Responsible Conduct of Research" document on its website.[525]

"HUMAN SUBJECTS RESEARCH," consists of

- *SYSTEMATIC INVESTIGATION* that is
    - Conducted with *THE INTENTION OF DRAWING CONCLUSIONS* that have some general applicability, and uses
    - *A COMMONLY-ACCEPTED SCIENTIFIC METHOD*, and which is
- Conducted so as to obtain *DATA* or *IDENTIFIABLE PRIVATE INFORMATION* about *A LIVING INDIVIDUAL*, when the investigator
    - *INTERACTS OR INTERVENES DIRECTLY WITH THE INDIVIDUAL* OR
    - *COLLECTS* identifiable private information about the individual.

UNDERLYING BASIS OF THE INFORMED CONSENT DOCTRINE. The great American jurist, Benjamin Cardozo, when he was a Justice of the New York Court of Appeals, characterized the underlying basis of informed consent in a famous opinion: "Every human being of adult years and sound mind has a right to determine what shall be done with his own body, and a surgeon who performs an operation without his patient's consent commits an assault, for which he is liable in damages."[526]

PATIENTS MAY REFUSE TREATMENT. It is generally recognized that if competent patients must give consent to care, they can also refuse it; this applies to even life-saving therapy or life-sustaining treatments, including food and hydration.[527] One of the exceptions to this rule is that mentally ill prison inmates may be forced to take psychotropic medications if necessary to reduce their danger to others as long as it is medically in their interest as well.[528]

Sometimes the duty to obtain informed consent is characterized as a "DUTY TO WARN" OF THE HAZARDS OF TREATMENT. In general, courts have found this duty to fall on the prescriber, not the dispenser, of prescription drugs. The Washington Supreme Court has held that a pharmacist, who is dispensing medications pursuant to a lawful prescription, has no duty to warn patients of all dangers of prescription drugs: "Nothing in RCW Ch. 18.64 nor in WAC 360-16 [now WAC 246-869] requires pharmacists to disclose all contraindications or warnings."[529] This opinion in the landmark *McKee* case, was written before the passage of OBRA-90, but it was reasserted in an appellate decision in 1999.[530]

However, this was based on the Court's holding that THE DUTY TO WARN RESTED WITH THE PRESCRIBER OF THE DRUG. It seems clear, though there has yet to be a case to test the assumption, that IF THE PHARMACIST IS THE PRESCRIBER OF A DRUG, HE OR SHE HAS THE SAME OBLIGATION TO OBTAIN INFORMED CONSENT FROM THE PATIENT THAT ANY OTHER PRESCRIBER OBTAINS.[531]

In general, the FOLLOWING ELEMENTS MUST BE INCLUDED in the information provided to patients when obtaining their consent to therapy.

- The nature and purpose of the therapy.
- The likely benefits.
- The material risks of therapy.
- The alternatives which are available, including the alternative of doing nothing.

(See the section below discussing Washington's codification of these requirements in RCW 7.70.050.)

CONSENT MAY BE OBTAINED ORALLY OR IN WRITING. The use of a consent form, signed by the patient or other person competent to give consent for the patient, is evidence that consent was obtained.

MINORS MAY CONSENT TO CARE IN WASHINGTON STATE. Both statute and court decisions in Washington have made it legally viable for minors to consent to necessary medical care (see Chapter 6). The same consent procedures are necessary for a qualified minor as for adults.

PHARMACISTS WHO ARE IMMUNIZERS in Washington are already experienced in obtaining informed consent when they discuss the VIS with the patient and obtain agreement to be immunized.

DEFENSES TO NEGLIGENCE CLAIMS

As with other torts, the defendant may assert certain defenses to claims of negligence:

- CONTRIBUTORY OR COMPARATIVE NEGLIGENCE – the plaintiff contributed to the harm by his or her own actions. For example, the pharmacist may have dispensed an incorrect dose, but the patient took twice the dose on the label, thus further adding to the adverse result.

  In most states, the jury can assign some percentage of the damages to the plaintiff, thus reducing the damage award imposed on the defendant, however, the defendant will still be liable for a portion of the damages.

- STATUTE OF LIMITATIONS
  A statute of limitations sets in law a certain time during which the injured party must file or the case cannot be brought. The time to file starts when the injury occurs, but if the patient could not reasonably have discovered the injury, then the time can begin when the injury was actually discovered through normal diligence on the plaintiff's part. The time may be extended if the defendant undertook to prevent discovery or hide the fact of injury from the patient.

  In Washington, the statute of limitations on health care negligence lawsuits is 3 years from the date of the injury (see below).

  The time to file may be extended in the case of injury to minors (see below for current WA law).

- STATUTE OF REPOSE
  A statute of repose is another limit on the time in which a plaintiff must file a negligence claim. Regardless of any unavoidable delay in discovering the injury, no claim may be filed after a certain time since the injury. Washington has an 8-year statute of repose for health care negligence lawsuits (see below).

  Statutes of repose are very common in negligence suits related to building or home construction; no claim relating to negligent construction of a building may be filed after 6 years from substantial completion of construction.

WASHINGTON LAWS GOVERNING NEGLIGENCE LAWSUITS AGAINST PHARMACISTS.

STATUTE OF LIMITATIONS FOR HEALTH CARE NEGLIGENCE LAWSUITS. The state of Washington has enacted statutory limits on the time to file claims of negligence against health professionals, in RCW 4.16.350.

WHO'S COVERED? The chapter applies to lawsuits alleging professional negligence against "A person licensed by this state to provide health care or related services, including, but not limited to, a physician, osteopathic physician, dentist, nurse, optometrist, podiatric physician and surgeon, chiropractor, physical therapist, psychologist, *PHARMACIST*, optician, physician's assistant, osteopathic physician's assistant, nurse practitioner, or physician's trained mobile intensive care paramedic." Also covered are suits against employees of the foregoing or employers of the foregoing.

> ESSENTIAL ELEMENTS OF A NEGLIGENCE CLAIM AGAINST PHARMACISTS
> - Duty owed to patient by pharmacist
> - Breach of duty
> - Injury to the patient
> - Cause of the injury was the breach of the duty

TIME LIMIT FOR FILING.

- 3 years from date of the act or omission alleged to have caused the injury; or
- 1 year from the time at which the patient discovered or should have discovered that the act caused the injury, whichever is later; but
- No more than 8 years in any case (the statute of repose).

EXCEPTION: proof of fraud, concealment, or presence of a foreign body not intended to have a therapeutic effect, in which case the time limit is 1 year from the plaintiff's actual knowledge

This 8-year "statute of repose" was challenged in a 1998 Supreme Court case[532] on the basis that the legislature had failed to articulate a rationale for the limit. The 2006 Legislature re-enacted this 8-year limit, with a statement of its rationale, which applies to actions commenced on or after June 7, 2006.[533]

Washington law relating to health care malpractice suits has imputed knowledge of the custodial parent or guardian of a minor to the minor, so there has been no extension of these limits for minors; they have been treated since the re-enactment of the tort reform statute in 2006 as if adults were injured. HOWEVER, IN 2014, THE WASHINGTON SUPREME COURT OVERTURNED THE PORTION OF THIS LAW THAT FAILS TO "TOLL" THE STATUTE FOR MINORS. A minor may now be able to file a suit up to 1 year after he or she turns 18 years of age.[534] (The Court did not deal with the 8-year statute of repose in this case.)

Given the current law regarding medical negligence lawsuits by minors, pharmacists who are aware that they may have injured a minor (e.g., by dispensing an incorrect dose or drug) should be sure to discuss the situation with their insurer and/or corporate risk manager as soon as possible.

The ELEMENTS NECESSARY TO ESTABLISH A NEGLIGENCE CLAIM AGAINST A PHARMACIST are specified in RCW 7.70.

No award shall be made in any action or arbitration for damages for injury occurring as the result of health care which is provided after June 25, 1976, unless the *PLAINTIFF ESTABLISHES ONE OR MORE OF THE FOLLOWING PROPOSITIONS:*

(1) That injury resulted from the failure of a health care provider to follow the accepted standard of care;

(2) That a health care provider promised the patient or his representative that the injury suffered would not occur;

(3) That injury resulted from health care to which the patient or his representative did not consent.

Unless otherwise provided in this chapter, the plaintiff shall have the burden of proving each fact essential to an award by a preponderance of the evidence. (RCW 7.70.030)

The following shall be *NECESSARY ELEMENTS OF PROOF THAT INJURY RESULTED* from the failure of the health care provider to follow the accepted standard of care:

(1) The health care provider failed to exercise that degree of care, skill, and learning expected of a reasonably prudent health care provider at that time in the profession or class to which he belongs, in the state of Washington, acting in the same or similar circumstances;

(2) Such failure was a proximate cause of the injury complained of. (RCW 7.70.040)

CLAIMS FOR FAILURE TO OBTAIN INFORMED CONSENT.

(1) The following shall be necessary elements of proof that injury resulted from health care in a civil negligence case or arbitration involving the issue of the alleged breach of the duty to secure an informed consent by a patient or his representatives against a health care provider:

(a) That the health care provider failed to inform the patient of a *MATERIAL FACT OR FACTS* relating to the treatment;

(b) That the patient *CONSENTED TO THE TREATMENT WITHOUT BEING AWARE OF OR FULLY INFORMED* of such material fact or facts;

(c) That a *REASONABLY PRUDENT PATIENT UNDER SIMILAR CIRCUMSTANCES WOULD NOT HAVE CONSENTED* to the treatment if informed of such material fact or facts;

(d) That the treatment in question *PROXIMATELY CAUSED* injury to the patient.

MATERIAL FACTS TO BE DISCLOSED WHEN OBTAINING INFORMED CONSENT

- Nature an purpose of proposed treatment
- Expected results of proposed treatment
- Recognized possible alternatives to the proposed treatment
- The recognized serious possible risks, complications, and anticipated benefits involved in the treatment and in recognized alternative forms of treatment, including non-treatment.

(2) Under the provisions of this section a fact is defined as or considered to be a material fact, if a reasonably prudent person in the position of the patient or his representative would attach significance to it deciding whether or not to submit to the proposed treatment.
(3) Material facts under the provisions of this section which must be established by expert testimony shall be either:
(A) THE NATURE AND CHARACTER OF THE TREATMENT PROPOSED AND ADMINISTERED;
(B) THE ANTICIPATED RESULTS OF THE TREATMENT PROPOSED AND ADMINISTERED;
(C) THE RECOGNIZED POSSIBLE ALTERNATIVE FORMS OF TREATMENT; OR
(D) THE RECOGNIZED SERIOUS POSSIBLE RISKS, COMPLICATIONS, AND ANTICIPATED BENEFITS INVOLVED IN THE TREATMENT ADMINISTERED AND IN THE RECOGNIZED POSSIBLE ALTERNATIVE FORMS OF TREATMENT, INCLUDING NONTREATMENT.
(4) If a recognized health care emergency exists and the patient is not legally competent to give an informed consent and/or a person legally authorized to consent on behalf of the patient is not readily available, his consent to required treatment will be implied. (RCW 7.70.050)

USE OF CONSENT FORMS. Washington specifies that the use of a consent form with certain required elements is sufficient to prove that the patient consented.

If a patient while legally competent, or his representative if he is not competent, signs a consent form which sets forth the following, the signed consent form shall constitute prima facie evidence that the patient gave his informed consent to the treatment administered and the patient has the burden of rebutting this by a preponderance of the evidence:
(1) A description, in language the patient could reasonably be expected to understand, of:
(a) The nature and character of the proposed treatment;
(b) The anticipated results of the proposed treatment;
(c) The recognized possible alternative forms of treatment; and
(d) The recognized serious possible risks, complications, and anticipated benefits involved in the treatment and in the recognized possible alternative forms of treatment, including nontreatment;
(2) Or as an alternative, a statement that the patient elects not to be informed of the elements set forth in subsection (1) of this section.
Failure to use a form shall not be admissible as evidence of failure to obtain informed consent. (RCW 7.70.060)

As noted above, minors may also consent to several types of medical care as a result of statute or court decision. It is likely that a minor's signature on a consent form for a procedure that he or she has a legal right to consent to will be treated under this statute as if an adult had consented. Where the minor is consenting based on a provider's determination that they meet the requirements of the Mature Minor Doctrine, it is probably advisable that the consent form or related record document the provider's evaluation and determine of the minor's status under the doctrine. (See Chapter 6)

MEDICATION GUIDES. In many situations where pharmacists are initiating therapy, a medication guide may be a useful resource for obtaining informed consent when one is available for the drug. However, merely distributing the medication guide is not sufficient; the pharmacist should have a plan for specifically reviewing the medication guide's description of the known risks of the drug, explaining them to the patient, and making sure the patient is aware of alternatives. This discussion and the patient's response should be documented in the patient record.

LEARNING MORE ABOUT INFORMED CONSENT. A complete discussion of best practices in obtaining informed consent is beyond the scope of this textbook, and is more properly covered in clinical coursework or courses on patient safety. Individual pharmacists – particularly those participating in prescribing activities – must maintain and improve their competence in this area. One guide that may be helpful is "A Practical Guide to Informed Consent," published by Temple University.[535]

QUALIFICATIONS OF EXPERTS. The Washington Supreme Court has held that expert testimony concerning the standard of practice of a given health profession must be provided by a member of that profession, and, more particularly, that a "licensed pharmacist is not competent to testify as an expert regarding the standard of care that a physician must meet when prescribing medication."[536] This holding has led the courts in Washington to be highly restrictive in allowing non-physician testimony in negligence cases. For example, the Washington Appeals court decided that nurses could never testify to causation in a medical malpractice action.[537] This same court, however, had decided a year previously that a physician with extensive experience supervising nurses could testify to the standard of care of a nurse.[538] More recently, though, the same appellate division concluded that "we now question that decision," and opined that "the scope of the expert's knowledge, not his or her professional title, should govern 'the threshold question of admissibility of expert medical testimony in a malpractice case.'"[539] The same Court held in the same year that under the specific facts of a case, the physician expert (a radiologist) did not demonstrate actual expertise sufficient to testify to the standard of care owed by nurses or other hospital employees.[540] Nevertheless, unless the specific facts of the case demand, most of the time when a pharmacist is sued for malpractice, the expert who is providing a conclusion about the quality of the defendant's practice will be a pharmacist.

MALPRACTICE INSURANCE

Malpractice insurance is essential for every pharmacist and technician, and policies are widely available from state and national associations, such as the WSPA, which provide protection to employed pharmacists and technicians for very reasonable premiums.

The typical employed pharmacist coverage is known as a supplemental policy, which provides indemnity benefits that are not otherwise covered by the employer's policy. However, specific benefits for the employed pharmacist include the insurance company's obligation to defend the individual. A typical policy:

- Pays damages awarded against insured, up to policy limits
- In addition, pays costs of defending insured and providing services of an attorney
- Does not pay for defending against damages due to illegal acts committed by the insured

Because the policy provides the insured with his or her own attorney, it avoids conflicts when the interests of employer and employee differ. For example, settlement may be desired by employer, but not employee, in part because a settlement could possibly be used as evidence by a board of pharmacy in a hearing. Also, it is not unheard of for employers to sue an employee to recover their insurance losses.

Some insurers also provide a defined level of coverage to defend the insured in proceedings before a pharmacy board or other regulatory body. They do so, in part, because adverse results from a regulatory hearing can have negative consequences in related civil litigation. One company's current policy for pharmacists provides reimbursement for attorney's fees at 90% of out-of-pocket costs, with a limit of $10,000. While successful defense of a licensee before a hearing could well exceed that amount, it is a considerable benefit at little cost.

STUDENT PHARMACIST INSURANCE

Student pharmacists are typically required by their academic programs to purchase school-arranged insurance that covers them and the school for liability arising from IPPEs and APPEs. Individual coverage is also available to student pharmacists through ASP, other student organizations, and WSPA. Student pharmacists should be aware that the school-required policy may only provide coverage while they are engaged in school-sponsored activities, and may not cover them while working as interns or in other settings. As with any insurance, individuals should read the coverage certificate and be aware of who is covered, what is covered, and what is excluded.

PRODUCTS LIABILITY

NEGLIGENCE BY THE MANUFACTURER. Generally, manufacturers may be held liable if they are NEGLIGENT IN THE DESIGN OR MANUFACTURE OF A PRODUCT, and the injured consumer can demonstrate that the injury was proximately caused by the product.

STRICT LIABILITY. When products, such as drugs, are "unavoidably unsafe," the manufacturer may be held liable for untoward effects of the product even if the injured party cannot show defective design or defective manufacture. This type of liability is called "strict liability." One way of avoiding this type of liability is to clearly warn the user of the unavoidable dangers of the use of the product.

LEARNED INTERMEDIARY DOCTRINE. For prescription drugs, the manufacturer historically does not have a direct relationship with the patient, and is thus not in a position to warn of the known dangers of the drug as they apply to that particular patient. Thus, the manufacturer is held free from liability for failure to warn of the product's dangers if it has adequately warned the prescriber, who serves as a "learned intermediary" between the manufacturer and patient.

Because manufacturers have increasingly turned to direct-to-consumer advertising of prescription drugs in magazines, on radio, and on ubiquitous TV commercials, some jurisdictions are starting to find that this activity may create a direct relationship with the consumer that would invalidate the learned intermediary doctrine.[541]

PHARMACISTS ARE INSULATED FROM LIABILITY FOR DISPENSING A MANUFACTURED PRODUCT when the injury was caused by a defect that the pharmacist could not foresee or be aware of at the time of sale or dispensing, rather, the liability will be on the manufacturer. Exceptions to this immunity may arise when:

- PHARMACISTS ARE THE MANUFACTURER OF A PRODUCT, such as when they have promoted and compounded the product, may bear any liability that would normally attach to the manufacturer, and
- PHARMACISTS MAY ALSO BE HELD LIABLE WHEN THEY ALTER THE MANUFACTURER'S PRODUCT in such a way as to make it defective. For example, a pharmacist in Oregon was held liable for damage from the use of Lindane lotion when he dispensed the product without including the instructions and warnings provided by the manufacturer of the product.

Washington law (RCW 18.64.275) limits exposure of pharmacists for lawsuits based on strict liability, or implied warranties under the Uniform Commercial Code WHEN THEY DISPENSE A MANUFACTURER'S PRODUCT PURSUANT TO A PRESCRIPTION WITHOUT ALTERING THE PRODUCT. Claims against pharmacists under these circumstances are limited to (1) negligence, (2) breach of an express warranty issued by the pharmacist, or (3) intentional misrepresentation about the product or intentional concealment of information about the product.

CONSUMER PROTECTION LAWS

Whereas much of the jurisprudence involving contracts and torts arises from common law principles, protections for consumers and enforcement of fair trade practices are primarily creatures of statute. These statutes often operate in tandem with antitrust laws, which are also designed to provide consumers with a competitive market for goods and services. In Washington, the panoply of consumer protection laws is overseen by the Office of the Attorney General (OAG). On the OAG's Consumer Protection Division website's [542] "A-Z" list of consumer issues can be found a wide variety of concerns: antitrust/unfair competition, cancellation rights, cars (Lemon Law), cellular phones, charities, contractors, credit, foreclosure, health clubs, identity theft, junk mail, landlord-tenant, prescription drug prices, pyramid schemes, spam, sweepstakes, and telemarketing. Several major areas affect pharmacists and pharmacies. See also Chapter 8 for a discussion of consumer protection related to third party payers and health plans.

FEDERAL ANTITRUST LAWS

THE SHERMAN ANTITRUST ACT (1890) is a federal law that prohibits

> "Every contract, combination, in the form of trust or otherwise, or conspiracy, in restraint of trade or commerce among the several States, or with foreign nations."
>
> Efforts to "monopolize . . . attempt[s] to monopolize, or . . . conspir[acies] . . . to monopolize any part of the trade or commerce among the several States , or with foreign nations."

The FEDERAL TRADE COMMISSION ACT (1914) established the Federal Trade Commission and gave it power to enforce the antitrust laws.

The CLAYTON ANTITRUST ACT (1914) prohibits conduct, such as "mergers and acquisitions where the effect may substantially lessen competition," and gave state attorneys general the right to enforce federal antitrust laws.

The ROBINSON-PATMAN ACT (1936) amended the Clayton Act to prohibit certain forms of discriminatory conduct, including discriminatory pricing.

The HART-SCOTT-RODIN ACT (1976) requires companies intending to merge to notify the FTC before the merger to allow a review of the effects of the merger on competition.

WASHINGTON CONSTITUTIONAL ANTITRUST PROVISIONS

Article XII, § 22 of the Washington Constitution prohibits monopolies and trusts:

> Monopolies and trusts shall never be allowed in this state, and no incorporated company, copartnership, or association of persons in this state shall directly or indirectly combine or make any contract with any other incorporated company, foreign or domestic, through their stockholders, or the trustees or assignees of such stockholders, or with any copartnership or association of persons, or in any manner whatever for the purpose of fixing the price or limiting the production or regulating the transportation of any product or commodity. The legislature shall pass laws for the enforcement of this section by adequate penalties, and in case of incorporated companies, if necessary for that purpose, may declare a forfeiture of their franchises.

WASHINGTON'S UNFAIR BUSINESS PRACTICES AND CONSUMER PROTECTION ACT

Statutory requirements governing unfair trade practices, anti-trust, and consumer protection are found in one major statute in Washington – the Unfair Business Practices & Consumer Protection Act (RCW 19.86). The Act parallels the federal statutes in several ways, but also protects individual consumers against effects of these unfair practices. The language is often amazingly terse. Here are the major prohibitions under the Act:

- UNFAIR METHODS OF COMPETITION and UNFAIR OR DECEPTIVE ACTS OR PRACTICES in the conduct of any trade or commerce are hereby declared unlawful. (RCW 19.86.020)
- Every contract, combination, in the form of trust or otherwise, or conspiracy in restraint of trade or commerce is hereby declared unlawful. (RCW 19.86.030).

- It shall be unlawful for any person to monopolize, or attempt to monopolize or combine or conspire with any other person or persons to monopolize any part of trade or commerce. (RCW 19.86.040)
- The statute outlaws agreements not to compete when such agreements lessen competition. (RCW 19.86.050)

ENFORCEMENT OF THE ACT is vested in the Attorney General, who may seek court injunction to restrain unlawful acts, recover costs, and cause the restoration of property.

PRIVATE CAUSE OF ACTION. The Act also provides individuals with a private right to sue.

> "Any person who is injured in his or her business or property by a violation ... or any person so injured because he or she refuses to accede to a proposal for an arrangement which, if consummated, would be in violation ... may bring a civil action in superior court to enjoin further violations, to recover the actual damages incurred by him or her, or both, together with the costs of the suit, including a reasonable attorney's fee." The Act also allows the court to award additional damages of up to 3 times the actual damages, subject to monetary maximums depending on which portion of the statute was violated. (If the actual damages are less than $75,000, a suit may be filed in district court as well.)

BEING ABLE TO ASSERT A CONSUMER PROTECTION ACT (CPA) CLAIM AGAINST A BUSINESS IS A POWERFUL CIVIL LITIGATION STRATEGY, BECAUSE THE BUSINESS IS FACED WITH POSSIBLE TREBLE DAMAGES AND ATTORNEYS' FEES.

False or misleading advertising, bait-and-switch marketing tactics, high pressure sales techniques, and the like are considered deceptive practices, for which consumers may sue if damaged.

AVOIDING AGREEMENTS THAT RESTRAIN TRADE. Pharmacists, pharmacies, and pharmacy associations must avoid agreements that restrain trade. Pharmacies cannot agree with one another to a fee schedule, a minimum fee, or to boycotts, to agree on a standard bid for government or private contracts, or to allocate markets or customers. In the past, local associations have been charged with these kinds of behavior when discussions about how to respond to certain market situations have led to apparent agreements to take collective action. For example, WSPA members concerned about rate cuts by Medicaid cannot agree to withdraw from the Medicaid program; each pharmacist or pharmacy must decide whether to participate on its own, without any collective understanding.

Meetings of state or local associations, political action committees, or other pharmacy groups often will begin with a reading of a policy on avoiding any discussions that might be seen as agreements to restrict trade.

MANUFACTURER PRICING POLICIES have come under scrutiny over the years. Community pharmacies have long believed that they are unfairly charged higher prices than many of their major competitors. Ultimately, the courts have upheld the ability of pharmaceutical manufacturers to sell drugs to hospitals and HMOs at rates significantly below the prices sold to retail pharmacies. In an important court decision, it was held that manufacturers could sell drugs at lower prices to hospitals under terms of the Non-Profit Institutions Act, which exempts from the Robinson-Patman Act "purchases of their supplies for their own use by ... hospitals, and charitable institutions not operated for profit." "Their own use" is what could reasonably be regarded as use by the hospital [as] ... a part of and promotes the hospital's intended ... operation in the care of persons who are its patients."[543]

Subsequently, the Ninth Circuit held that non-profit HMOs, such as Kaiser, could sell drugs to outpatient members, even though it purchased them at deeply discounted prices. The Court held that the HMO is designed to provide a full range of health care to its members.[544]

However, institutions purchasing drugs at these low rates may not sell them to others, because to do so is to create unfair pricing in other market segments. This is why hospitals – even in emergencies – are reluctant to sell drugs to community pharmacies. They may, however, "loan" drugs to a community pharmacy, provided that the community pharmacy "returns" product it purchased within its market segment.

Manufacturers are allowed to sell at different rates based on total volume, which is why buying groups are an important tool for independent pharmacies.

TARGETED CONSUMER PROTECTION LAWS in Washington have been enacted to enforce standards in certain industries and to give consumers specific rights in particular instances. Some of these laws include:

- Lemon law, which gives consumers certain rights to new vehicle owners who have substantial continuing problems with warranty repairs.
- Prohibited automobile sales practices
- Automobile repair – consumer's rights
- Credit reports (governed by the Federal Fair Credit Reporting Act). Businesses that extend credit, or access credit reports, are governed by these laws.

JUNK MAIL AND RELATED MARKETING

UNORDERED MERCHANDISE. Goods mailed to you without your authorization are gifts. Unless otherwise agreed, you have the right to accept delivery of unordered goods, and to keep them as gifts, and you are not obligated to pay for them or return them. Under Washington law, goods are not considered to have been requested if you fail to respond to an invitation to purchase and they are sent anyway.

TELEMARKETING, FAXES, TEXT MESSAGES

The FEDERAL TELEPHONE CONSUMER PROTECTION ACT OF 1991 restricts telemarketing, including automatic dialing systems, SMS text messages, and faxes. Pharmacies must be cautious in enrolling or participating in advertising activities that may violate this law. Unless the recipient has given prior express consent, the TCPA

- Prohibits calls to residences before 8 a.m. or after 9 p.m. local time
- Establishes the National Do Not Call Registry and maintain a "do-not-call" list of persons who have asked not to be called; these must be honored for 5 years
- Prohibits solicitations to residences using an artificial voice or a recording (doesn't apply to non-solicitations, such as political "robocalls")
- Prohibits automated calls, or artificial or pre-recorded voice messages to 9-1-1 lines, hospital emergency numbers, a physician's office, a hospital/health care facility/elderly room, cellular telephones, or any service for which the recipient is charged a fee
- Prohibits unsolicited advertising faxes

A subscriber may sue for up to $1,500 for each violation of the act, or to recover actual monetary loss, whichever is higher. Subscribers may also seek injunctions against future violations.

In recent years a number of cases have been filed against pharmacies or PBMs arising from various faxes or robocalls. If the calls are reminders to patients about a needed refill of their prescriptions, or suggesting certain monitoring needed for drug safety, the calls have been allowed by the courts, but in at least one case, the suit was permitted to go forward when the chain pharmacy continued calling a patient about refills after he asked them to stop.

UNSOLICITED FAXES - WA. Washington law prohibits unsolicited faxes unless there is a prior contractual or business relationship between the sender and the recipient. If you tell a fax sender to stop faxing you, they must stop, and you can sue in small claims court and receive damages of $500.

UNSOLICITED OR MISLEADING COMMERCIAL E-MAILS - WA. Washington law (RCW 19.190) prohibits the sender of a commercial e-mail message from a computer in Washington or to an e-mail address held by a Washington resident that

- Uses a 3rd party internet domain name without permission of the 3rd party, or otherwise misrepresents or obscures any information in identifying the point of origin or the transmission path of the message; or
- Contains false or misleading information in the subject line

Such actions are a violation of the Consumer Protection Act, and it is also a violation of the CPA to use e-mail to knowingly or intend to violate the CPA

Damages to the recipient are $500 or actual damages, whichever is higher; damages to an interactive computer service are $1,000 or actual damages, whichever is greater

Unrequested commercial text messages are prohibited when sent to a cell phone, absent the prior consent of the recipient, or messages that are sent at no cost and the recipient has not requested that such messages not be sent

WASHINGTON'S LAW AGAINST DISCRIMINATION (WLAD)

Washington's broad statutory prohibition against discrimination has its origins in a general law to prohibit discrimination in employment in the State of Washington because of "race, creed, color, or national origin" that was first enacted in 1949.[545] The statute has been amended over a dozen times since its inception, and now provides citizens of the state with statutory rights of freedom from discrimination in:

- Employment
- Public accommodation (including resorts, assemblage, amusement or accommodation)
- Real estate transactions, including discrimination against families with children
- Credit transactions
- Insurance transactions or transactions with health maintenance organizations
- Engagement in commerce without boycotts or blacklists
- Breastfeeding in any public resort, accommodation, assemblage, or amusement

Prohibited under the statute is discrimination as listed above based on any of the following individual characteristics:

- Race
- Creed
- Color
- National origin
- Sex
- Sexual orientation
- Honorably discharged veteran or military status

- Presence of any sensory, mental, or physical disability
  - Use of a trained dog guide or a service animal by a person with a disability is recognized as a civil right

PHARMACIES ARE PUBLIC ACCOMMODATIONS. The definition of "place of public resort, accommodation, assemblage, or amusement" includes places used for

- Entertainment
- Housing
- Lodging of transient guests
- Accommodation of those seeking health, recreation or rest
- Burial or other disposition of human remains
- Sale of goods, merchandise, services, or personal property
- Rendering of personal services
- Public conveyance or transportation including stations, terminals, and garages for vehicles
- Food or beverage consumption on the premises
- Public amusement, recreation, entertainment, sports, or recreation
- *MEDICAL SERVICE OR CARE*
- Public halls, elevators, washrooms
- Housing of two or more tenants
- Public libraries or educational institutions
- Schools of special instruction, day care, children's camps

Certain fraternal organizations not open to public use, and bona fide religious or sectarian institutions and their properties are not included.

Although the protections of WLAD overlap in many ways with federal antidiscrimination laws, the legislature in 2007 made it clear that "the law against discrimination affords to state residents protections that are wholly independent of those afforded by the federal Americans with disabilities act of 1990, and that the law against discrimination has provided such protections for many years prior to passage of the federal act." This means that employers and public accommodations in Washington may be held to standards and be subject to suit in situations where federal statutes do not apply.

As noted below, the procedures and necessary elements of employment discrimination claims are essentially the same for suits based on WLAD or federal employment antidiscrimination laws. In addition to WLAD, other statutes provide for protections in employment and for workers, including affirmative action in hiring, domestic violence leave, family leave, and military family leave (see below).

A major lawsuit invoking the WLAD outside of the employment discrimination setting was the *Stormans* case (see Chapter 3) because as part of their suit, plaintiffs sought an injunction against enforcement of WLAD against them. During the development of WAC 246-869-010, the Washington Human Rights Commission issued an opinion that refusing to dispense Plan B® would constitute discrimination based on gender in contravention of WLAD. However, when the 9th Circuit upheld the Pharmacy Commission's rules, it also held that plaintiffs' claims relating to WLAD were not ripe for adjudication because the HRC's opinion was not an actionable enforcement decision.[546]

In 2017, the Washington Supreme Court unanimously ruled against a business that refused to provide services to a same-sex couple on the basis that providing the service violated the owner's freedom of religion.[547]

In 2018, the Washington Supreme Court ruled that an employer operating a place of public accommodation, in this case a health system, is vicariously and directly liable to the plaintiff when one of its employees sexually harasses a member of the public, whether or not the employer was aware of or authorized the discrimination.[548]

EMPLOYER-EMPLOYEE ISSUES

In the US and Washington, employer-employee relationships are governed by a variety of statutes and common law principles.

THE NATURE OF THE EMPLOYMENT CONTRACT

AT WILL. Most employees are "at will," meaning that they may be terminated without notice, and they may quit without notice. If a pharmacist does not have a written contract, or a company employee's manual that specifies otherwise, he or she should presume that he or she is an at-will employee.

COMPANY MANUALS may constitute a contract. For example, if they specify certain procedures to be followed before an employee can be terminated for cause, the company must follow those procedures. In general, employers must follow their own policies.

TERMINATION. At will employees can be terminated "for cause", or can be terminated with no reason given. If a reason is given, the employee may be able to challenge the underlying facts

MEMBERS OF A UNION are governed by the terms of the union contract, and the union has a right to represent their members' interests.

Private-sector collective bargaining is federally regulated by the National Labor Relations Act of 1935 (the Wegner Act), as amended by the Labor-Management Relations Act of 1947 (the Taft-Hartley Act; 29 USC 141). The National Labor Relations Board enforces the law.

Once a union has been recognized, it is mandatory that employer and union negotiate on "wages, hours, and other terms and conditions of employment." Refusal to bargain is an "unfair labor practice."

EMPLOYEES OF GOVERNMENTS obtain property and liberty interests in continued employment, and have constitutional due process rights that can be asserted, in additional to provisions of state civil service laws, agency policies, and written contracts of employment. States may by statute specify the rules for collective bargaining by state employees. Washington has done so.

TERM CONTRACTS. Employees with contracts are said to be "term" employees, and have rights to continued employment during the term of the contract

- They may be terminated, furloughed, laid off, or reduced in hours under the terms of the contract, including a certain notice period;
- They may be restricted from quitting without a minimum notice, or lose certain benefits or be forced to pay damages;
- They may be terminated "for cause," such as
  - Non-performance
  - Inadequate performance
  - Violations of law or company policy
  - Actions against the interest of the company
  - Insubordination (failing to follow orders of superiors)

COVENANTS NOT TO COMPETE. Some employers may seek to have certain professional employers sign "non-competition" clauses, preventing them for working for a competitor or setting up a competing business in the same locale. This is unusual for pharmacists working in retail pharmacies or chains, but is often done for consultant pharmacists, who might take substantial business away from the employer upon their leaving.

If a lawsuit arises from such non-competition agreements, courts will look to the REASONABLENESS OF SUCH CLAUSES:

- They must be for a reasonable *TIME LIMIT*
- They must be reasonable in *SCOPE* (e.g., cannot prohibit all employment, only that which is truly competitive with the employer)
- They must be reasonable in *GEOGRAPHIC AREA*
- There should be *SPECIFIC CONSIDERATION* related to the non-competition portion of the employment contract, such as a specific payment to the employee if the employer exercises the options under the non-competition agreement. In Washington, specific consideration is considered to exist if the non-competition agreement is entered into at the time of employment. However, specific independent consideration must be proven if the non-competition agreement is developed after the start of employment.[549]

PERSONNEL FILES ARE REQUIRED. Every employer in Washington is REQUIRED TO MAINTAIN A RECORD OF EVERY EMPLOYEE, and to permit the Department of Labor and Industries to inspect the record.

- EMPLOYEES MAY INSPECT THEIR OWN PERSONNEL FILES AT LEAST ANNUALLY. (RCW 49.12.240)
- EMPLOYEES MAY PETITION EMPLOYER TO REVIEW their personnel files and correct or remove irrelevant or erroneous information. If the employee disagrees with the employer's determination, the employee may have his or her rebuttal or correction statement placed in the file. The right to rebut or correct the file shall continue for 2 years following termination of employment. (RCW 49.12.250)
- Inspection rights do not apply to the records of an employee related to investigation of a possible criminal offense, or to records compiled in preparation for an impending lawsuit which would not otherwise be discoverable. (RCW 49.12.260)

PROVIDING REFERENCES. Employers are often asked to provide references concerning, or information about the performance of former employees. Employers often limit themselves to reporting the bare facts of employment, such as dates of employment. They fear being sued for defamation if they make negative comments concerning an employee's performance. As a result, "problem employees" are often passed on from one firm to another. In the case of health care practitioners, this perpetuates danger to patients.

STATUTORY IMMUNITY WHEN PROVIDING EMPLOYMENT INFORMATION. The 2005 Washington Legislature established immunity for disclosure of employee information to a prospective employer in RCW 4.24.730. If an employer provides information to another prospective employer, or employment agency, at the specific request of that employer or agency, he or she is "presumed to be acting in good faith and is immune from civil and criminal liability for such disclosure or its consequences," provided that the disclosed information relates to:

- The employee's ability to perform his or her job
- The diligence, skill, or reliability with which the employee carried out the duties of his or her job; or
- Any illegal or wrongful act committed by the employee when related to the duties of his or her job.

The Act states that the employer making the report should KEEP A RECORD of the identity of the person or agency to whom the disclosure was made for a minimum of 2 years. The former employee has a right to inspect such a written record upon request, and such a written record becomes part of the employee's personnel file.

The *PRESUMPTION OF GOOD FAITH MAY BE REBUTTED* by the former employee by showing clear and convincing evidence that the information was

- Knowingly false;
- Deliberately misleading; or
- Made with reckless disregard for the truth.

IS THE EMPLOYER LIABLE FOR THE ACTS OR OMISSIONS OF HIS OR HER EMPLOYEES?

VICARIOUS LIABILITY: Common law makes employers "vicariously liable for the acts of their employees." This is sometimes called the doctrine of "*respondeat superior*" ("let the Master answer"). Any act or omission of an employee, which is committed within the scope of his or her employment, can make the employer liable for damages to a third party. As noted above, an employee's violation of WLAD's prohibitions against discrimination in places of public accommodation (such as pharmacies) triggers vicarious liability on the part of the employer.

EMPLOYER NEGLIGENCE IN HIRING, TRAINING, SUPERVISING, OR RETAINING EMPLOYEES. Employers can also be sued for damages arising from their negligence in selecting, training, or supervising their employees. For example, a pharmacy that hires a pharmacist without demanding to see a current license, and without checking to see if the pharmacist is currently disciplined or suspended, may be found negligent in selecting that employee if the employee injures a patient through his or her actions.

WASHINGTON RULES REQUIRE REVIEW OF QUALIFICATIONS. Note that WAC 246-869-060 requires pharmacy employers to obtain suitable evidence of the pharmacist's licensure and qualifications before allowing the pharmacist to practice in the pharmacy.

CRIMINAL BACKGROUND CHECKS are important to protect the pharmacy from potential harm and theft, and are essential when hiring staff who will have access to

- Controlled substances. The DEA prohibits registrants from employing individuals with felony convictions related to controlled substances.
- Vulnerable individuals. State laws prohibit persons with a conviction for a violent offense, or for sexual offenses, from caring for children or vulnerable adults.[550]
- Pharmacies receiving payments from programs that are federally funded (Medicaid, Medicare, TriCare, etc.), may not employ individuals who are excluded from participation in federal programs. Employers should check the Online Exclusions Database[551] of the DHHS OIG prior to hiring an individual, and should check the status of all employees at least annually.
- Many pharmacies and hospitals use services such as FACIS® (one of several Verisys® products)[552] to assist them in these checks.

See also the discussion below regarding discrimination in hiring; while questions may be asked about criminal convictions or arrests during the hiring process, there are limits to the use of this information.

WASHINGTON'S EMPLOYER LIABILITY LAW IS FAIRLY STRINGENT, and regards an employee's acts as being imputed to the employer as long as any portion of the act is done for the employer's benefit.

> For example, a technician agrees to deliver several prescriptions to a nursing home on his way home after his shift has ended. Believing that there is "no rush," the technician stops off at a tavern and

becomes intoxicated. On the way to the nursing home, the technician's car collides with a pedestrian, severely injuring him. Under Washington law, the pharmacy may be held liable for the injuries. This hypothetical example relating to pharmacy is loosely based on actual cases involving other businesses, including *Smith v. Leber*, 34 Wn.2d 612 (1949).

LAWS PROVIDING FOR NON-DISCRIMINATION IN EMPLOYMENT

A very significant percentage of lawsuits against pharmacies are based on employment discrimination. The consequences for the employer can be substantial. In a recent case, a verdict of $2 million, which included $1 million in punitive damages, was upheld by the Massachusetts Supreme Court against a pharmacy chain for failing to pay a woman pharmacist a salary equivalent to her male counterparts, and for retaliating against her when she complained.[553] The FEDERAL LAWS listed below typically have state counterparts; Washington's equivalent is WLAD.

TITLE VII OF THE CIVIL RIGHTS ACT of 1964 (42 USC 2000) is the principal federal anti-discrimination law, and it applies to all firms who employee 15 or more employees. It makes it an unlawful employment practice for an employer

To FAIL OR REFUSE TO HIRE OR TO DISCHARGE ANY INDIVIDUAL, or otherwise discriminate against any individual with respect to his

- Compensation
- Terms
- Conditions, or
- Privileges of employment

BECAUSE OF SUCH INDIVIDUAL'S

- *RACE*
- *COLOR*
- *RELIGION*
- *SEX, OR*
- *NATIONAL ORIGIN.*

OTHER FEDERAL LAWS PROHIBIT DISCRIMINATION based on

AGE (GREATER THAN 40) – THE AGE DISCRIMINATION IN EMPLOYMENT ACT (ADEA) OF 1967

- Applies to employers of 20 or more people
- Prohibits mandatory retirement for most employees
- Prohibits Title VII-type discrimination based on age greater than 40

PREGNANCY – THE PREGNANCY DISCRIMINATION ACT OF 1978

- Prohibits discrimination in hiring or employing individuals on the basis of their pregnancy
- Requires pregnant employees to be treated the same as other individuals with medical disabilities
- Prohibits "fetal protection policies" restricting pregnant women from "dangerous" jobs as long as the woman can perform the essential functions of the job (e.g., prohibiting a pregnant pharmacist from working with chemotherapy agents)
- Requires that employers who provide parental leave for new mothers must provide same leave for new fathers

Gender – Equal Pay Act of 1963

- Applies to employers of 2 or more employees engaged in interstate commerce or in the production or handling of goods in interstate commerce (eg, prescription drugs)
- Requires "equal pay for equal work" – may not pay one gender more than the other gender for the same work, or work requiring
  - The same skill,
  - The same effort,
  - The same responsibility, and which is
  - Performed under similar conditions

Disability – The Americans with Disabilities Act of 1990

- Applies to employers with 15 or more employees
- Prohibits discrimination against individuals with disabilities in
  - Employment
  - Public services
  - Public accommodations (a pharmacy open to the public generally is considered a public accommodation)

IN EMPLOYMENT, CANNOT DISCRIMINATE AGAINST "QUALIFIED" INDIVIDUALS based on their disability

A QUALIFIED INDIVIDUAL is one who

- can perform the "essential functions" of the job
- with or without accommodation

EMPLOYERS MUST MAKE "REASONABLE ACCOMMODATIONS" for employees with disabilities to help them perform a job function

- Not required to make an accommodation that would be an "undue financial hardship"
- Financial hardship is measured against the size and resources of the employer
- For employers with multiple divisions or units, the resources are measured at the corporate level
- Not required to make an accommodation that would pose a danger to the employee, the public, or co-workers

THE REHABILITATION ACT OF 1973 applies to employers with $2,500 or more worth of federal government contracts (including pharmacies accepting Medicaid or Medicare payments); also to states receiving federal assistants

- May not discriminate on the basis of mental illness or physical handicap
- Must make accommodations similar to those required under the ADA
- Qualified individuals determined as under the ADA

Other Protected Classes

Federal law also prohibits discrimination in employment based on receipt of black lung benefits, bankruptcy or bad debts, genetic information or citizenship status (except for unauthorized immigrants).

FEDERAL AFFIRMATIVE ACTION REQUIREMENTS - applies to "federal contractors." In addition to the antidiscrimination laws reviewed above, federal contractors are subject to the requirements of Executive Order 11246 (1965), which prohibits discrimination and requires written affirmative action plans. This order is enforced by the Office of Federal Contract Compliance Programs in the Department of Labor.[554] Recent policy announcements by the OFCCP suggest that health care providers such as pharmacies may be considered federal subcontractors subject to the same requirements as prime contractors.

Recipients of over $10,000 in federal business in 1 year are required to

- Avoid discrimination in employment decisions
- Take affirmative action to insure that equal opportunity is provided in all aspects of their employment

Contractors with 50 or more employers and $50,000 or more in government receipts in 1 year must

- Have a written affirmative action plan for each establishment
- Specify how it will deal with problems
- Specify expanded efforts it may undertake to deal with problems

Covered entities are subject to OFCCP compliance reviews and inspections.

WASHINGTON STATE DISCRIMINATION LAWS

ADDITIONAL PROTECTED CLASSES. Washington's laws related to discrimination typically parallel federal laws, but, in addition to the protections in federal law, ALSO PROHIBITS DISCRIMINATION based on

- Marital status
- Sexual orientation
- Disability (sensory, mental, or physical) including AIDS/HIV or Hepatitis C infection
- Membership in state militia
- Use of a service animal
- Gender identity
- Status as a domestic violence victim

Companies with 1 or more employees are subject to prohibitions against gender-based discrimination, and with 8 or more employees are subject to other provisions of employment antidiscrimination laws.

AVOIDING DISCRIMINATION IN HIRING

Several important considerations relate to hiring of individuals so as to avoid unlawful discrimination.

ESSENTIAL FUNCTIONS OF THE JOB

It is important to define the essential functions of any given position for which a hiring decision or recruitment effort is made. The functions should be reasonably related to accomplishing the job responsibilities, and should not include tests or abilities that are not needed. For example, a pharmacy technician may need to be able to lift boxes containing shipments of medications from the wholesaler, but would not typically be required to lift or move heavy objects.

When essential functions are defined properly, it is lawful to exclude individuals who cannot carry them out. However, if they are essential, then persons who cannot complete them should not be hired. If an essential function may be waived, it is not "essential."

The employer may also specify "desired" abilities, which may be used to distinguish among qualified individuals based on demonstrated differences in skills, experience, or training.

Several pharmacists have sued employers when they were required to provide immunizations and the employees sought accommodation under the ADA for physical disabilities (e.g., MS) or mental issues (e.g., needle phobia) that prevented them from safely immunizing patients. The majority of these cases are now being resolved in favor of the employer if the essential functions statement for the position of pharmacist has been revised to include immunizations.[555]

PRE-EMPLOYMENT INQUIRIES

Pre-employment interviews and questionnaires should seek only such information that is necessary to determine if the prospective employee is qualified to perform the essential functions of the job. Information related to protected classes (race, sex, national origin, age, religion, etc.) are generally irrelevant to a person's qualifications and abilities.

Explicit prohibitions under federal law include questions about disability. Also, a request for a photograph as part of an application is not allowed. Once a person is hired, photographs for identification and security are appropriate.

Because background checks are specifically recommended for hiring pharmacists and other staff who will have access to controlled substances or vulnerable individuals, pharmacy employers should become familiar with guidelines on these types of checks, available at www.eeoc.gov/laws/practices/index.cfm.

GENERAL PROCEDURE FOR PROVING A CASE OF DISCRIMINATION

Discrimination can take one of two forms

DISPARATE TREATMENT – an individual protected by the law is actually treated differently than similarly situated persons because of his membership in a protected class

> Example: a woman staff pharmacist in a hospital is paid less than the three male staff pharmacists

DISPARATE IMPACT OR ADVERSE IMPACT – members of a protected class are treated differently as a result of an ostensibly neutral company policy

> Example: "job sharing is allowed (a policy whereby two employees can share the same position, with each working less than full time – desirable to many working mothers), but no one in a job sharing situation can be the Head Pharmacist."

PROCESS FOR FILING A COMPLAINT

It is critical that an aggrieved employee carefully follow the steps outlined in federal and state laws to preserve a cause of action for discrimination in employment.

EEOC FILING. The employee files a complaint with the federal Equal Employment Opportunity Commission (or a state equal opportunity commission which has been delegated authority to investigate these claims – in Washington, employees contact the EEOC)

- The employee must establish a "prima facie" case of discrimination
- Must show that the employee is in a protected class
- Must show that the employee was treated differently than other members who are not in the class, either because of disparate impact or disparate treatment
- The evidence must create an "inference of discrimination"

If this burden is met, then the EEOC certifies the action and a suit may be filed in court.

EMPLOYER OPPORTUNITY TO REBUT INFERENCE OF DISCRIMINATION.

The employer now bears the burden of rebutting the inference of discrimination, by demonstrating a "legitimate nondiscriminatory reason for the action or policy that the employee alleges is discriminatory."

> Example: "We paid the woman pharmacist less, but she has a BS degree with no advanced training, whereas all three male employees have PharmD degrees and have completed residencies or MS degrees."

EMPLOYEE MUST PROVE "PRETEXT"

The burden then shifts to the employee to demonstrate that the "legitimate nondiscriminatory reason" is a pretext, that it is unworthy of belief.

> Example: "I only have a BS degree, but I have 20 years of experience, and all of us do exactly the same thing – compound IV admixtures, so their extra credentials aren't a bona fide qualification for the position."

MANAGERIAL RESPONSIBILITY. Managers or supervisors can make the firm liable for discrimination even if they are not the person doing the discriminating, as long as they have notice and have not taken immediate and appropriate corrective action.

This is especially an issue when sexual harassment is being alleged.

Harassment can be "quid pro quo," where employment or benefits of employment are conditioned upon exchange of sexual favors, or are threatened if sexual favors are not granted.

Harassment can also arise from a hostile or offensive environment, where the employer and managers tolerate unwelcome sexual advances, jokes, or ridicule, or other behaviors that are based on sex and interfere with the employee's work performance or create an intimidating, hostile or offensive working environment.

A PHARMACIST MAY BE A MANAGER OR SUPERVISOR TO WHOM A REPORT OF HARASSMENT CREATES A NEED FOR THE COMPANY TO TAKE ACTION. In a recent Washington case, an employee of a large retailer alleged harassment by a manager of a non-pharmacy department. The employee worked at part time in the pharmacy, and part-time in another department, but not the one managed by the harassing manager. At one point, the employee mentioned to the head pharmacist that she was being harassed by the other employee. She alleged that the head pharmacist did not notify anyone above him in the organization, and that the company failed to take action until after she reported additional incidents to another assistant manager some months later. The court held that the communication to the pharmacist created knowledge on the part of the firm of the harassment, thus making them liable for not taking immediate corrective action.[556]

SALARIES AND PAYMENT OF OVERTIME

The federal FAIR LABOR STANDARDS ACT (FLSA) affects salaries for employees engaged in interstate commerce or in the production of goods for interstate commerce.

- It sets a federal minimum wage -- $7.25 per hour is the rate as of 2019.
- It requires premium pay for more than 40 hours work in a given week
- Executive, administrative, and professional (EAP) employees are exempted from the overtime and minimum hourly wage requirements of the FLSA.
    - Employee must be paid a predetermined and fixed salary that is not subject to reduction because of variations in quality or quantity of work performed (the "salary basis test")
    - The salary must meet a minimum level ("salary level test")
        - Under revisions proposed on December 1, 2016, EAP employees must meet a minimum salary of $913 per week, set at the 40th percentile of weekly earnings of full-time salaried workers in the lowest wage Census region, i.e., the South.

        - EAP employees with only minimal EAP duties may also be exempt if they are highly compensated employees (HCE); the 2016 proposed standard is the 90th percentile of earnings of full-time salaried employees nationally, or $134,004 annually.
    - The employee's duties must primarily involve executive, administrative or professional duties ("duties test"); as noted above HCE employees must have at least minimal EAP duties.

The 2016 proposed revisions to the rules for overtime exempt employees may affect pharmacists who are enrolled in residency programs, and most residents will not meet the test for HCE employees.[557] (Medical residents, but not pharmacy residents, are specifically exempted under federal law.) Also, the majority of non-managerial practicing pharmacists in the US are hourly employees, not salaried, as a result of chain compensation practices and/or union contracts. Note: as of January 2019, the Department of Labor website indicates that the proposals from 2016 are ongoing rulemaking, and the Department is currently enforcing the rules in effect in November 2016.

In February 2014, President Obama signed an executive order establishing a minimum wage of $10.10 per hour for certain employees of federal contractors that provide services directly for the federal government, effective January 1, 2015, and indexed to inflation thereafter.[558] As of January 1, 2019, the wage is $10.60 per hour.

STATE MINIMUM WAGE LAWS – Washington's minimum wage was addressed in Initiative 1433, passed by the voters in November 2016. The minimum wage is $12 /hr in 2019, with a mandatory time-and-a-half for work beyond 40 hours in a week (14- and 15-year old workers may be paid 85% of the minimum wage, or $10.20 per hour). In 2019, Washington, California and Massachusetts tie for the highest state-level minimum wage in the U.S. Under Initiative 1433, the minimum hourly wage will increase to $13.50 in 2020; in 2021 the increases will be tied to inflation using the CPI-W.

Employers may not retain any tips and gratuities, but must pay them to their employees, and tips and gratuities may not be used to offset the minimum wage. As a result, consumers are beginning to see "service fees" added to restaurant bills, especially in the Seattle area. These are income to the employer (except at Sea-Tac – see below).

MUNICIPAL MINIMUM WAGE ORDINANCES – Some cities have adopted higher minimum wages than the state level, such as

- City of SeaTac, WA, which has established a minimum wage of $15 per hour for workers in hotels with more than 100 rooms and at least 30 nonmanagerial employees and parking lots with more than 100 spaces and at least 25 nonmanagerial employees. About 1600 workers were estimated to be affected by the new wages as of February 2014.[559] The minimum wage increases annually with inflation. The 2019 minimum wage for covered workers in SeaTac is $16.09/hr. SeaTac ordinances require any "service fees" to be passed on to employees.
- City of Seattle –
    - Employers with less than 500 employees, with a "guaranteed minimum compensation responsibility" of $15/hour ($15.75/hour in 2020) that includes wages, employer-paid health care contributions, and tips
        - $12.00 in 2019
        - $13.50 in 2020
        - $15.00 in 2021
        - $15.75 in 2022
        - $16.50 in 2023
        - $17.75 in 2024

- Employers with 500 or more employees.
  - 16.00, adjusted for inflation starting 2020

  Because Seattle's wages allow tips and medical benefits to be included in the compensation goals, the minimum wage levels are expected to be overtaken by state law over time.

- City of Tacoma – $12.35/hour in 2019, which will be annually adjusted for inflation starting in 2020. It is likely that by 2020 the state minimum wage will overtake the Tacoma minimum.

EMPLOYMENT OF TEEN WORKERS

State laws govern employment of minors; for Washington, the minimum age for most jobs is 14, and employers of minors under age 18 must have a Minor Work Permit endorsement issued by the Department of Labor and Industry, which is renewed annually. Each minor must have a Parent/School Authorization form. There are limits on how many hours can be worked by minors during a school week.

PROHIBITED WORK ACTIVITIES FOR MINORS INCLUDE:

- Regular driving of motor vehicles to make deliveries. 17 year old minors may drive only during daylight hours, if properly licensed for the type of driving involved, subject to other restrictions.[560] (RCW 49.12, WAC 296-125-030)
- Working at heights greater than 10 feet off the ground or floor level.
- Working past 8 p.m. without supervision by someone 18 years or older who is on the premises at all times
- Working in jobs with possible exposure to bodily fluids, or radioactive and hazardous substances.

UNEMPLOYMENT COMPENSATION. The Washington Employment Security Department provides unemployment compensation that is funded through mandatory employer contributions. It also provided job training and retraining programs, and employment assistance resources statewide. Its website is http://www.esd.wa.gov/

LAWS GOVERNING EMPLOYER-PROVIDED HEALTH CARE PLANS OR OTHER BENEFITS. (See also Chapters 6 and 8)

ERISA. Retirement and benefit plans are established under the federal Employee Retirement Income Security Act (ERISA) which preempts state laws to the contrary for qualifying plans. Companies' prerogatives to use Pharmaceutical Benefits Managers or limit employees to certain providers have generally not been assailable by state insurance laws because of ERISA protection.

COBRA AND HIPAA. The right to maintain insurance protection upon termination of employment is covered by certain provisions of COBRA-86 and HIPAA, which are discussed in Chapter 6.

AFFORDABLE CARE ACT. See discussion in chapter 8.

OCCUPATIONAL SAFETY

OSHA. Federal law governs provision of safety in the workplace under the Occupational Safety and Health Act, which is administered by the Occupational Safety and Health Administration (OSHA). Similar state requirements for on-the-job safety are established by the Washington Industrial Safety and Health Act (WISHA), administered by the Department of Labor and Industries.

WASHINGTON DEPARTMENT OF LABOR AND INDUSTRIES.
WORKPLACE SAFETY. The fundamental rules governing workplace safety require that employers provide a safe workplace, including (1) freedom from employees under the influence of alcohol or narcotics; (2) protection from exposure to hazardous substances and chemicals; and (3) protection from exposure to biological agents. See http://www.lni.wa.gov/safety/rules/

See Chapter 4's discussion of the handling of hazardous drugs in pharmacies and other health care settings, the rules for which have been established by L&I and are due to become effective in 2015.

WORKMEN'S COMPENSATION. Most employers in Washington are required to participate in a state-sponsored insurance program that compensates individuals who are injured on the job, a program administered by the Department of Labor and Industries. Prescriptions issued to beneficiaries are filled in Washington pharmacies who submit claims to the Department. (See also Chapter 8)

- Employers may set up a self-insurance program to provide equivalent coverage
- Sole proprietors may elect to participate in order to provide protection for themselves
- General information is available on the DLI website at http://www.lni.wa.gov/ClaimsIns/Insurance/Learn/default.asp

FAMILY MEDICAL LEAVE

THE FEDERAL FAMILY MEDICAL LEAVE ACT and the WASHINGTON STATE FAMILY LEAVE ACT require employers to allow employees leave from work for certain medical reasons, for birth or adoption of a child, and for care of certain family members with a serious health condition. The Washington law extends additional benefits to women who are pregnant and to registered domestic partners or spouses in same-sex marriages. Covered employers are those who employ 50 or more persons and are engaged in interstate commerce. Pharmacies, hospitals and other healthcare facilities are covered employers if they employ the requisite number of people.

UP TO 12 WEEKS PER YEAR OF UNPAID LEAVE ARE PROVIDED.
OTHER STATUTES OR REGULATIONS PROVIDE ADDITIONAL PROTECTED FAMILY LEAVE. A comparison of applicable state and federal laws is available at http://www.lni.wa.gov/WorkplaceRights/files/FamilyLeaveLawsTable.pdf

MANDATORY PAID SICK LEAVE. Several state and municipal jurisdictions passed legislation in 2011 and 2012 requiring all employers to provide paid sick leave or "paid safe time." Among these was Seattle, Washington.[561] A similar ordinance was passed in Tacoma, WA in January 2015.[562]

With passage of Initiative 1433, all employers in Washington were required to provide paid sick leave starting in 2018:

- Accrual – leave will accrue at a minimum of 1 hour of paid sick leave per 40 hours worked
  - Employees are entitled to use paid sick leave starting on the 90th calendar day after start of employment
  - Unused paid sick leave of 40 hours or less must be carried over to the following year
  - More generous sick leave and carry over benefits are allowed
- Usage – may be used to care for the employee or a family member
  - May be used when the employee's workplace or the employee's child's school or place of care has been closed by order of a public health official for any health-related reason
  - May be used for absences that qualify for leave under the Domestic Violence Leave Act

    - Employers may allow use of sick leave for additional purposes

WASHINGTON PAID FAMILY AND MEDICAL LEAVE AFTER 2019[563]

The 2017 Legislature enacted SSB 5975 – Paid Family and Medical Leave – which extends paid family medical and leave coverage to all Washington workers who work at least 820 hours during a qualifying period. The statute excludes federal workers, Native American tribes, or self-employed persons, but tribes and self-employed individuals may opt in. Employees covered by a collective bargaining agreement prior to October 2017 are not included until the CBA is reopened, renegotiated, or expires.

The program is an insurance program which is funded by premiums (0.4% of wages in 2019) shared by the employee (63%) and employer (37%). Premiums are being collected during 2019 for benefits to begin in 2020.

EMPLOYEE ELIGIBILITY, PREMIUMS, AND BENEFITS

- Employees qualify if they work 820 hours in the first 4 of the last 5 completed calendar quarters prior to making a claim for benefits.
- A claim is made when there is a qualifying event, which is either Family Leave or Medical Leave:
    - Family leave
        - Care and bond after a baby's birth or the placement of a child younger than 18
        - Care for a family member experiencing an illness or medical event
        - Certain military-connected events
    - Medical leave
        - Care for the employee in relation to an illness or medical event
- Premiums and benefits are based on gross wages.
    - Premiums are 0.4% of gross wages.
    - Benefits depend on wage, paid per week of leave:
        - <50% of state average weekly wage – 90% of employee's average weekly wage
        - >50% of state average weekly wage – 90% of the employee's average weekly wage that is below 50% of the state average, plus 50% of the remaining portion of the employee's average weekly wage
    - An example employee making $50,000 per year would pay $2.44 per week in premiums, the employer would pay $1.41 per week, and benefits of about $778 per week would be available for up to 12 weeks (18 weeks in certain exceptional circumstances).

MILITARY SERVICE LEAVE AND REINSTATEMENT. The Uniformed Services Employment and Reemployment Act of 1994 (USERRA)[564] provides certain rights to employees who are called to serve in the uniformed services. Reemployment rights end after five years cumulative total of military service.

EMPLOYERS MUST PROVIDE LEAVE to an employee who is

- Drafted or
- Enlists in a uniformed service; and is
- Called to active duty for combat, training, or inactive duty.

EMPLOYEE MUST GIVE ADVANCED NOTICE OF MILITARY DUTY, and notice of intent to return to work; notice should be in writing

EMPLOYER MUST

- Place employee in same position if leave < 91 days; or
- Place employee in position of like status, pay and opportunity if leave >90 days; and

- Reasonably accommodate any disability due to injury while on military duty

REINSTATEMENT NOT REQUIRED if employee would have been involved in a layoff during the leave

LEAVE FOR RESERVE OR NATIONAL GUARD TRAINING DUTY or response to local disasters is up to state law

- WASHINGTON mandates a military leave of absence for a period not to exceed 21 days during each year beginning October 1. (RCW 38.40.060)
- EMPLOYEES WITH A MILITARY SPOUSE are entitled under WA law to up to 15 days of unpaid leave while their military spouse is on leave from a deployment or before and up to deployment once the spouse receives official notification of an impending call to active duty.[565]

EMPLOYEES CARING FOR A FAMILY MEMBER INJURED IN MILITARY ACTION are entitled to up to 26 weeks of leave under the Family Medical Leave Act. (National Defense Authorization Act of 2008[566])

EMPLOYERS IN WASHINGTON MUST TREAT REGISTERED DOMESTIC PARTNERS OR SAME SEX SPOUSES OF EMPLOYEES THE SAME WAY THEY TREAT OPPOSITE SEX SPOUSES OF EMPLOYEES

All insurance, retirement, and other employee benefits that are extended to spouses of heterosexual employees must, after December 2009, be extended equally to registered domestic partners of employees. Any notices, e.g. regarding garnishments, change of benefits, etc., that would be sent to an employee's wife or husband, must be sent to an employee's registered domestic partner.[567] The Marriage Equality Act[568] requires all employers to treat spouses in same-sex marriages equally to other spouses. ERISA plans were formerly exempted from these requirements under the provisions of the federal Defense of Marriage Act (DOMA),[569] which was declared unconstitutional by the US Supreme Court in 2013.[570]

LAWS GOVERNING WHISTLE BLOWERS

Employees who report employer violations of laws or rules to an appropriate agency are protected in their jobs from discharge, demotion, or other retaliation because of their "whistle blowing" activity.

Washington recognizes a "PUBLIC POLICY EXCEPTION" to the at-will employment doctrine that protects employees in four situations:[571]

- Employees who are fired for refusing to perform an illegal act
- Employees are fired for performing a public obligation, such as jury duty
- Employees are fired for exercising a legal right or privilege, such as filing workers' compensation claims
- Employees are fired in retaliation for reporting employer misconduct to an appropriate body outside the company

Establishing a claim for wrongful discharge in violation of public policy is done in the same manner as for discrimination claims, generally.[572] These cases are not easy to establish however; a disagreement between an pharmacist and his employer over the meaning of a rule or regulation may be insufficient to establish a public policy violation. Also, the pharmacist who alleges a public policy violation claim must show that some other reason was not the basis for her termination. A pharmacist in Washington was terminated when she took prescription files home to "organize" on her own time, and she was fired for violating a company policy against removing company property from the store. She alleged in part that she was required to keep prescriptions organized and thus was carrying out public policy by taking the prescriptions home when she had insufficient time to organize them during work hours. The court ruled, however, that since federal and state law require all prescriptions to remain on the premises, her own actions violated public policy.[573]

EMPLOYEES OF THE STATE OF WASHINGTON are protected by the State Employee Whistleblower Act of 1982 (RCW 42.40).

HEALTHCARE WORKERS, AS WELL AS CONSUMERS AND OTHER CITIZENS IN WA are specifically protected against retaliation or other adverse employment actions, and immune from civil liability, for complaining in good faith to the DOH about improper quality of care. (RCW 43.70.075, WAC 246-15)

REFERENCES

[509] "I do not wish to contend" – also interpreted as "no contest; accused doesn't admit guilt, but doesn't contest or challenge the charges.
[510] *Wright v. Jeckle*, 158 Wn.2d 375; 144 P.3d 301 (Wn. Supr. Ct., 2006).
[511] *Stormans, Inc. et al. v. Wiesman et al.*, No. 12-35221, 9th Cir., July 23, 2015.
[512] *Stormans, Inc. et al. v. Wiesman et al.*, No. 15-862, *Cert. denied*, S.Ct., June 28, 2016
[513] *Client A & B, P.T. PhD v. Yoshinaka et al*. 128 Wash. App. 833, 844; 116 P.3d 1081, 1086 (Wash. App. Div. I, 2005)
[514] This approach, in place since 2010, was established to comply with a Washington Court of Appeals decision in *Seymour v. Dept. of Health et al.*, No. 61494-1I, 152 Wash. App. 156, 216 P.3d 1038 (Wash. App. Div. I, 2009)
[515] The panel may include 1 or more temporary commission members, appointed to serve as hearing panel members; this helps spread the workload; temporary members are often former commission appointees
[516] *Hardee v. Dep't of Soc. & Health Servs.*, 172 Wn.2d 1, 256 P.3d 339 (Wash. 2011)
[517] Article No. 987, Washington State Board of Pharmacy Newsletter 2009 Jan; 30(3):1.
[518] 2008 c 134 § 12.
[519] FTC. Offering Layaways. https://www.ftc.gov/tips-advice/business-center/guidance/offering-layaways
[520] Brushwood DB. Refusing a prescription and defaming the prescriber. Pharmacy today 2015; 21(12):58.
[521] *Washburn v Rite Aid Corp*, 695 A.2d 495 (Supr. Ct. R.I., 1997)
[522] *Murphy et al. v State of Washington*, 115 Wn. App. 297, 2003.
[523] See, e.g., *Mckown v. Simon Property Group, Inc., et al.*, No. 87722-0, S. Ct. Wash., March 5, 2015, at 6-9.
[524] *Helling v. Carey*, 519 P.2d 981 (Wash. 1974)
[525] https://ori.hhs.gov/sites/default/files/rcrintro.pdf
[526] *Schloendorff v. Society of New York Hospital*, 211 N.Y. 125, 129-30, 105 N.E. 92, 93 (1914)
[527] *Cruzan v. Director*, MDH. 497 US 261 (1990)
[528] *Washington v. Harper*, 491 US 210, 1990; 759 P.2d 358 (1988)
[529] *McKee v. American Home Products*, 782 P.2d 1045, 1054 (1989)
[530] *Silves v. King*, 93 Wn. App. 873 (1999)
[531] This author (Fassett) has been permitted to testify or opine in at least 2 cases in Washington that under the circumstances of the case, the pharmacist or pharmacists involved in the patient's care had a duty to obtain informed consent when they were initiating or modifying drug therapy in accordance with RCW 18.64. Both cases settled shortly thereafter.
[532] *DeYoung v. Providence Medical Ctr.*, 136 Wn.2d 136 (1998)
[533] 2006 c 8 §§ 301-302.
[534] *Schroeder v. Weighall*, No. 87207-4, Wash. S.Ct., January 16, 2014.
[535] http://www.templehealth.org/ICTOOLKIT/html/ictoolkitpage1.html
[536] *Young v. Key Pharmaceuticals Inc.*, 112 Wn.2d 116, 770 P.2d 182 (1989)
[537] *Colwell v. Holy Family Hosp.*, 104 Wn. App. 606, 15 P.3d 210 (2001)
[538] *Hall v. Sacred Heart Med.* Ctr., 100 Wn. App. 43, 995 P.2d 621 (2000)
[539] *Hill v. Sacred Heart Med. Ctr.*, 143 Wn. App. 438, 177 P.3d 1152 (2008)
[540] *Davies v. Holy Family Hosp.*, 144 Wn. App. 483, 183 P.3d 283 (2008)
[541] See, e.g., *Watts v. Medicis Pharmaceutical Corp.*, No. 1 CA-CV 13-0358, Ariz. App. Div. 1, 2015 Ariz. App. LEXIS 12, January 29, 2015.

[542] http://access.wa.gov/topics/consumerprotection
[543] *Abbott Laboratories et al. v. Portland Retail Druggists Ass'n, Inc.*, 425 U.S. 1, 96 S.Ct. 1305 (1976)
[544] *DeModena V. Kaiser Foundation Health Plan, Inc.,* 743 F.2d 1388 (9th Cir.1983)
[545] 1949 c 183
[546] *Stormans, Inc. v. Selecky*, 571 F.3d 960, 975 (9th Cir. 2009)
[547] *State of Washington v. Arlene's Flowers, Inc., et al.*, No. 91615-2, S.Ct. Wash., February 16, 2017
[548] Floeting v. Group Health Cooperative, No. 95205-1, S. Ct. Wash., January 31, 2019.
[549] *Labriola v Pollard Group, Inc.,* 152 Wn.2d 828, 2004.
[550] RCW 43.43.832
[551] http://exclusions.oig.hhs.gov/
[552] https://www.verisys.com/
[553] *Haddad v. Wal-Mart Stores, Inc.,* 455 Mass. 91, 914 N.E.2d 59 (2009)
[554] http://www.dol.gov/ofccp/
[555] See, e.g., *Stevens v. Rite Aid Corp.,* 851 F.3d 224 (2nd Cir., 2017), Cert. denied 138 S. Ct. 359 (2017)
[556] *Francom v Costco Wholesale Corp.,* 98 Wn. App. 845, 991 P.2d 1182 (2000)
[557] http://www.pharmacist.com/new-federal-overtime-rules-likely-have-implications-pharmacy-residents
[558] E.O. 13658; 78 Fed. Reg. 9849
[559] Martinez A. $15 wage floor slowly takes hold in SeaTac. Seattle Times 2014 Feb 13.
[560] http://www.lni.wa.gov/workplacerights/files/policies/esc43.pdf
[561] Paid Sick and Safe Time Ordinance, City of Seattle Ordinance No. 123698, passed 9/23/11; SMC 3.14.931; http://www.seattle.gov/civilrights/documents/PSSTPSAforemployersfinal81412.pdf, accessed 3/31/13.
[562] Martin K. Tacoma sick leave law passes. *The News Tribune*, 2015 Jan 27; http://www.thenewstribune.com/2015/01/27/3610629_tacoma-sick-leave-law-passes.html?rh=1
[563] https://paidleave.wa.gov/
[564] 38 U.S.C. § 4303 et seq.
[565] 2008 c 71.
[566] Pub. L. 110-181, § 585.
[567] 2009 c 21
[568] 2012 c 3
[569] Pub. L. 104-199.
[570] *Windsor v United States*, No. 12-63, 570 U.S. ____, S.Ct. 2013.
[571] *Dicomes v State*, 113 Wn.2d 612, 1989;
[572] *Gardner v Loomis Armored, Inc.*, 128 Wn.2d 931, 1996.
[573] *Kelleher v. Fred Meyer Stores, Inc.,* No. CV-13-3108-SMJ, E.D. Wash., 2015 U.S. Dist. LEXIS 10576, January 29, 2015.

8 - LEGAL ISSUES INVOLVING PAYMENT FOR PHARMACEUTICAL SERVICES AND THIRD PARTY PAYERS

OVERVIEW OF PRESCRIPTION DRUG BENEFITS

Primarily since the end of World War II, it has been a growing assumption that health care is a necessity of modern life, and that it is inappropriate in a society and economy such as that in the United States for individuals to suffer from lack of health care simply because they do not have the funds. Since the 1960s, the role of drug therapy has grown to occupy such an important place in health care that affordable drug therapy is considered a necessity as well. Currently, the many ways in which health care is paid for in the US include:

PRIVATE HEALTH CARE

Private health care coverage is generally individually purchased or employer-provided. Private payments for health care include:

CASH, OUT OF POCKET

PRIVATE HEALTH INSURANCE

- Individually-purchased
- Employer-provided

PREPAID HEALTH CARE COVERAGE (INDIVIDUALLY PURCHASED OR EMPLOYER PROVIDED)

- Health care cooperatives
- Health Maintenance Organizations

EMPLOYER-PROVIDED DIRECT CARE

- Industrial health programs
- Vaccinations and/or travel medicine
- Company owned clinics

COMPETENCY AREAS IN THIS CHAPTER

2016 MPJE COMPETENCY STATEMENTS – With the possible exception of area 3.1.1, the MPJE blueprint largely ignores issues related to 3rd party payers, insurers, or federally-funded health programs

2016 ACPE REQUIRED ELEMENTS – Pharmacy Law & Regulatory Affairs; Medication Dispensing, Distribution, and Administration; Healthcare Systems; Public Health

GOVERNMENT PROGRAMS

Government-provided health care programs include patient care services provided directly by government agencies and/or government-provided insurance or financial subsidies.

Federal Programs

- Public Health Service
- Merchant Marine, etc.
- Indian Health Service
- Federal prisons
- Military health care
- Military Hospitals and Clinics
- TRICARE program
- Veterans Affairs
- Public employees
- Medicare
- 340B drug program eligible clinics

State and Municipal Programs

- Public employees insurance
- Special programs for firefighters and police
- Public health programs and services (vaccinations, etc.)
- Basic health plans
- Mental health hospitals and programs
- TB sanitariums
- Jails
- State soldier's homes (prior to VA)
- Workman's compensation programs and care for on-the-job injuries

Federal/State Shared Funding

- Medicaid
- SCHPs

Federal and/or State Tax Preferences

- Flexible spending health care accounts
- Health care savings accounts

Each of these approaches or programs is associated with specific legal issues for pharmacists relating to receipt of payment for services rendered.

IMPORTANCE OF FEDERAL PROGRAMS TO PHARMACISTS

Federal expenditures for prescription drugs and pharmacy services arise from payments for federal employees, military personnel and defendants, and beneficiaries of Medicaid, Medicare, Children's Health Insurance Programs, and veterans. Recent figures put federal prescription drug expenditures at around 40% of all prescription drug purchases. Also, as noted in Chapter 7, certain convictions or discipline may place pharmacists or technicians on the list of individuals excluded from participation in federal programs; this virtually excludes these individuals from being employable in most pharmacy settings.

"CASH" PAYMENT MECHANISMS

FEE FOR SERVICE. The pharmacist determines a fee for the service he or she provides, which may include a portion covering professional services, and another portion covering the cost of drugs, packaging, etc., plus a margin for profit. This calculation results in a USUAL AND CUSTOMARY FEE (UCF). In general, pharmacies are expected to charge the same UCF to all patients who belong to the same class of trade, or in other words, not to discriminate unlawfully.

UNFAIR OR DECEPTIVE PRACTICES are prohibited by Washington's Consumer Protection Act (RCW 19.86). The CPA parallels federal antitrust and price fixing law as well as providing protection for consumers. As related to pharmacy, these may include:

ANY UNFAIR OR DECEPTIVE PRACTICE, such as charging for a brand name drug but substituting a generic, charging for services never delivered, knowingly dispensing fewer doses than charged for, or acting in a way so as to economically injure a patient or customer. Failure to pass on to the consumer 60% of the savings from generic substitution could be a basis for a CPA claim in WA.

PRICE FIXING AGREEMENTS. Pharmacies not under the same ownership may not agree, directly or indirectly, to charge a set price for any service or product. Local or state associations must be careful not to allow their organizations to act in any way that would be considered price fixing. It was common in the 1950s for local associations to publish pricing guides or tables from which pharmacies would calculate prescription fees. In the early 1960s, the Justice Department took action against a variety of trade associations including associations of physicians, dentists, attorneys, realtors, and pharmacists. Two key lawsuits were won by the government against pharmacy associations in California[574] and Utah.[575]

AGREEMENTS TO RESTRAIN TRADE. Pharmacies may not agree or conspire to restrain trade. The WSPA ended up in the early 1980s settling a lawsuit because of discussions among members of ways to vitiate a certain contract for nursing home services.

CONSUMER LAWSUITS. Any consumer who is "injured in his or her business or property" by a violation of the CPA can bring a civil lawsuit and recover damages, costs, attorney fees, and up to 3 times the damages as a punitive award. In a recent Washington Appeals Court case, a patient sued her surgeon for negligently performing surgery, and also filed a CPA lawsuit alleging that the surgery as recommended was unnecessary, and therefore its recommendation was a deceptive practice. The court held that even though she lost on her negligence claim, the plaintiff could proceed with a CPA claim against the surgeon as it related to the business aspects of his profession.[576]

ACCEPTED BUSINESS PRACTICES. It is generally accepted to allow discounts or other enticements as long as they are not deceptive, unfair, or based on unlawful discrimination (see below, however, regarding Medicaid and Medicare Part D). Some examples include:

- Senior Citizen Discounts
- Quantity Discounts
- Promotional Discounts, such as when a new pharmacy opens, or on certain days.
- Promotions may include points, stamps, coupons, etc.

Note: some Boards of Pharmacy may restrict promotional discounts, including promotions such as "double savings stamps," if they believe the promotion encourages overuse of drugs or creates situations (such as overly busy pharmacy) that are not conducive to patient safety.

- Lower fee for delayed service (e.g., calling in for refills in advance, or picking up prescriptions on "slow days")
- Free shipping or delivery
- Reduction in fee to meet specific competition

PRICE POSTING OR DISCLOSURE. Many states have at times required posting of drug prices to the public. Washington did this formerly, but now merely requires that pharmacies provide their price to any consumer on request. (WAC 246-881-040)

ADVERTISING OF DRUG PRICES. At one time, pharmacies were prohibited from advertising prescription drug prices, but rising consumerism led to a change in public policy. Pharmacies may, but are not required, to advertise prescription prices, subject to the following (WAC 246-881-020):

- Advertising must comply with federal laws and the Washington Consumer Protection Act
- The advertising is not intended to promote the use of prescription drugs, but is solely to advice the public of prices
- The following information must be provided concerning the drug product advertised:
    - The proprietary name, if any
    - The generic name,
    - The strength,
    - The dosage form, and
    - The price for a specified quantity.
- If the price advertised compares a generic to a brand name, the advertising may not imply in any way that the brand name is the product advertised.

DISCLOSURE OF PATIENT COSTS TO PRESCRIBERS (RCW 18.64.430). A Washington statute enacted in 2000 requires that "The registered or licensed pharmacist under this chapter shall establish and maintain a procedure for disclosing to physicians and other health care providers with prescriptive authority information detailed by prescriber, of the cost and dispensation of all prescriptive medications prescribed by him or her for his or her patients on request."

OUT OF POCKET EXPENSE REIMBURSEMENT TO PATIENT. In this situation, the patient pays the usual and customary fee, and receives an appropriate receipt from the pharmacy, which the patient submits to a third party for reimbursement. In many cases, the third party deducts a co-pay amount from the reimbursement. Insurance that reimburses an insured after the fact for actual costs is termed "indemnity" insurance. The cost-sharing involved with a co-payment is intended to encourage the insured to attempt to purchase at a reasonable cost.

THE PHARMACIST'S RECEIPT MUST BE TRUE AND ACCURATE. The pharmacist will be complicit in fraud if he or she knowingly provides the patient with a deceptive receipt. The receipt should accurately reflect the actual amount charged for the transaction.

It is appropriate to provide a receipt for charges when the patient has a credit account with the pharmacy, and the amount on the receipt is debited to the patient's account with good faith expectation of ultimate payment.

It may not be appropriate to issue an inflated receipt to "cover" the patient's co-pay, and later waive the co-pay as a credit to the patient's account. In some cases, the third party payer has policies that are communicated to the pharmacy to allow the pharmacy to waive the co-pay, but this is unusual in the case of indemnity insurance.

TrOOP is the acronym used in the Medicare Part D program to stand for "true out-of-pocket expense." The government considers it fraud when the pharmacy manipulates TrOOP to either push a beneficiary through the coverage gap so that the beneficiary may gain catastrophic coverage, or manipulates TrOOP to keep a beneficiary in the coverage gap.

CONTRACTED OR VOLUNTARILY ACCEPTED PAYMENT MECHANISMS

These mechanisms require that the participating pharmacy voluntarily accept them by contract or other means. Acceptance of them indicates acceptance of the terms offered by the third party.

REIMBURSEMENT TO THE PATIENT BASED ON A FEE SCHEDULE. This approach is used by indemnity insurers as well as other third party payers. The pharmacy must submit the claim electronically to the insurer, which informs the pharmacy of the allowable charge, which is then charged to the patient, who is later reimbursed for their out of pocket expense, with or without a co-pay. It may be possible for the pharmacy to "accept assignment" of the amount due to the patient, and the payment is made directly to the pharmacy. If co-pay is involved, the pharmacy must collect it from the patient.

FEE SET BY A THIRD PARTY, WITH NO REIMBURSEMENT TO PATIENT OR PHARMACY BY THE THIRD PARTY. This approach is taken by the various "discount cards" available to consumers. The patient pays cash for the prescription, but the price is determined by the issuer of the discount card.

The 2009 Legislature passed the Health Care Discount Plan Organization Act,[577] establishing standards for discount plan organizations, protecting consumers from unfair or deceptive marketing, sales, or enrollment practices, and to facilitate consumer understanding. It requires licensing of discount plans by the Insurance Commissioner, and plans must have written provider agreements that include the services and products that are discounted and the amount of the discounts. Plans may not restrict access to providers, must refund plan charges to a member who cancels within 30 days of enrolling, charge no more than a one-time $30 processing fee, and must provide written materials to the customer on request.

REIMBURSEMENT TO THE PHARMACY BASED UPON A CONTRACTED FEE SYSTEM, WITH OR WITHOUT A PATIENT CO-PAY. The pharmacy electronically exchanges information with the third party, and is reimbursed based on a calculation by the third party payer, typically within 15 to 45 days following the transaction. This is now the predominant form of reimbursement to pharmacies for dispensing of prescription drugs. Washington statutes prohibit an insurer who has previously approved a prescription claim prior to its dispensing from later rejecting that claim. (RCW 48.20.525; RCW 48.44.465)

PRIVATE CONTRACTS VS. GOVERNMENT CONTRACTS

PRIVATE CONTRACTS ARE ENFORCEABLE BY CIVIL LAWSUIT, OR BY ARBITRATION AS SPECIFIED IN THE CONTRACT

In general, a pharmacist who disputes a payment with a private third party must file a civil lawsuit to gain redress. If the contract specifies, the pharmacist may need to submit to binding arbitration. Only if the contract allows it can the pharmacist recover legal fees if he or she is successful. Likewise, the recourse that a private third party has is to sue the pharmacy. Either or both parties may terminate a contract in accordance with its provisions.

State laws protect consumers from unfair conditions in consumer contracts which they are typically unable to change and which they often are unable to fully read. However, contracts between pharmacies and third party payers are treated as commercial contracts and are treated by the courts as binding documents on both parties. Pharmacies that are offered contracts by PBMs are free to make modifications to contracts before they sign them, such as striking certain clauses. If the PBM accepts the modified contract, the pharmacy's changes are likely to be binding.

GOVERNMENT CONTRACTS ARE ENFORCEABLE BY CIVIL SUIT, BUT ALSO BY ADMINISTRATIVE ACTION, AND ARE SUBJECT FEDERAL OR STATE FRAUD STATUTES

Unlike private contracts, the terms of government contracts are set by law or regulation, and are typically not negotiable. However, government programs usually have other mechanisms for resolving problems, including appeals to the relevant agency, prior to filing a lawsuit. These mechanisms ("administrative remedies") must be fully utilized or "exhausted" before a suit can be filed. Violation of a government contract can expose the pharmacy to civil or criminal fraud charges and severe consequences and penalties. Finally, patients have legislatively been given certain rights under federal contracts that may not exist under private insurance contracts

RISK IS ASSOCIATED WITH 3RD PARTY CONTRACTS, AND VIGILANCE IS THE KEY TO RISK REDUCTION

As will be seen from the discussion below, pharmacies are at risk for numerous problems with 3rd party payments, and are not always in a good position to deal with inequities in the plans or their contracts. A pharmacist should not assume that 3rd party payers are guaranteed to deal fairly or even honestly with the pharmacy, and since they are debtors to the pharmacy, they should be taken on with care and vigilance. Third party payers and PBMs may include requirements in contracts that restrict actions pharmacists may take, including refusing to dispense a given prescription because the payment under the contract is inadequate. Pharmacists may also be prohibited by the contract from making comments to beneficiaries regarding the adequacy of reimbursement under the contract or other derogatory comments concerning the plan.[578] Once entering into a contract, it is critical to know the terms and requirements, for failure to abide by all of the terms can be very costly.

Many of the audit problems discussed below arise from careless day-to-day claims and prescription processing on the part of the pharmacists and technicians in the pharmacy. Management of the pharmacy must develop a compliance monitoring plan to assure its staff is properly trained, that they follow proper procedures, and that records are kept and secure.

EMPLOYEE RETIREMENT INCOME SECURITY ACT (ERISA) PREEMPTION OF STATE LAW

ERISA IS THE MAJOR FEDERAL STATUTE DEALING WITH EMPLOYEE BENEFIT PLANS. Its primary impact on legal issues related to 3rd party payments for pharmacy benefits is that its provisions preempt state law. In general, state law affecting the design of benefits, denial of benefits, or enforcement of beneficiaries' rights under the plan is preempted by ERISA. A variety of state lawsuits by individual patients against plans, related to denial of benefits (such as denying "experimental" cancer treatment) have been deemed preempted by ERISA. However, state rules regarding same-sex marriages apply to plans that provide coverage for spouses of employees.

PHARMACISTS' ATTEMPTS TO BE INCLUDED IN HEALTH PLANS

As the percentage of health care covered by 3rd party payers has grown, pharmacies – particularly independent community pharmacies – have worked hard to operate on a "level playing field," where their opportunities to provide services to patients in their communities are not foreclosed by the tendency of health plans to work only with big business. Two forms of legal protection have been sought in state legislatures: one requiring plans to pay any provider who is willing to abide by the plan's fee schedule, and requiring plans to pay pharmacists for providing for non-dispensing services, such as immunizations or medication therapy management, if the services are otherwise covered by the plan.

FEDERAL RECOGNITION OF PHARMACISTS AS PROVIDERS – THE PROVIDER STATUS INITIATIVE. One barrier to payment for pharmacists' non-dispensing patient care services has been that, unlike physicians, nurse practitioners, psychologists, nurse midwives, nurse anesthetists, clinical social workers, physician assistants and some others, pharmacists are not listed as providers in the Social Security Act (SSA), which determines who may be eligible for payment by federal health care programs such as Medicare Part B (see below). Many private insurers and state plans have cited the omission from Medicare Part B as a reason for not paying for pharmacists' services. In addition, not being listed as providers affects the ability of pharmacists to participate in accountable care organizations (ACOs).

The APhA, in concert with other organizations, has set achieving some level of provider status under the SSA as its primary legislative goal, and in 2018 was lobbying in support of H.R. 592/S. 109,[579] the Pharmacy and Medically Underserved Areas Enhancement Act, which would amend the SSA to allow payment for pharmacist-provided services under Medicare Part B if provided within state-authorized scopes of practice in a setting located in or serving any of the following designated areas or populations:

- Health professional shortage area (HPSA)
  An HPSA is designated by HRSA as having shortages of primary care, dental care, or mental health providers – may be geographic (county or service area), population-based (e.g., low income or Medicaid eligible, or may be a federally designated health center, state, or federal prison. Some examples:[580]
  - In King County, several health centers, including Sea Mar CHC, Seattle Indian Health, and Snoqualmie-North Bend Family Clinic are designated as HPSAs.
  - All of Benton County is an HPSA
  - In Grant County, Moses Lake CHC, 5 rural health clinics, seasonal migrant workers, and over a dozen census tracts are HPSA designated

  - In Spokane County, CHAS, the N.A.T.I.V.E. Project of Spokane, Deer Park/Colbert, Rockford, and numerous census tracts are designated
- Medically underserved area or population (MUA or MUP)
MUAs or MUPs are defined only based on primary care. Qualifications for these areas or populations are based on an index that includes infant mortality rate, poverty rate, percentage of elderly, and primary care physician-to-population ratio. MUAs and MUPs are found throughout the state:[581]
  - Washington counties containing MUAs include Asotin, Garfield, Columbia, Okanogan, Douglas, Grant, Franklin, Ferry, Pend Oreille, Yakima, Pierce, Lewis, and Pacific counties, and parts of Stevens, Lincoln, Spokane, Grays Harbor, Cowlitz, Clark, King, Snohomish, Island, San Juan and Clallam counties.
  - Washington counties containing MUPs include Klickitat and Kittitas counties, and parts of Whatcom, San Juan, Clallam, Thurston, Kitsap, King, and Spokane counties

If the bill is passed, this would mean that pharmacist providers could be used to augment the primary care of many citizens of every county.

As of February 2019, neither bill appears to have been reintroduced in the 116th Congress.

ANY WILLING PROVIDER LAWS

Pharmacies have worked for many years to achieve a goal of not being "locked out" of 3rd party contracts, whereby a 3rd party contracts with some, but not all willing pharmacies. For many years, the federal courts held that such state laws did not apply to ERISA plans. However, Kentucky passed a law that stated that a "health insurer shall not discriminate against any provider who is located within the geographic coverage area of the health benefit plan and who is willing to meet the terms and conditions for participation established by the health insurer, including the Kentucky state Medicaid program and Medicaid partnerships."[582] In 2003 the US Supreme Court reversed its previous decisions and held that ERISA did not preempt the Kentucky statute because of the provision in ERISA that "nothing in this title shall be construed to exempt or relieve any person from any law of any State which regulates insurance, banking or securities." In its opinion the Court indicated that "Today we make a clean break from the McCarran-Ferguson factors and hold that for a state law to be deemed a 'law ... which regulates insurance' under *§ 1144(b)(2)(A)*, it must satisfy two requirements. First, the state law must be specifically directed toward entities engaged in insurance. Second ... the state law must substantially affect the risk-pooling arrangement between the insurer and the insured."[583] The Washington State Pharmacy Association has attempted for several years since the Kentucky decision to persuade the Legislature to adopt a similar statute in Washington, but the attempts have so far been unsuccessful. This remains a legislative goal for the WSPA.

ANY CATEGORY OF PROVIDER LAWS

Another agenda for pharmacies has been to become eligible for payment for services, such as immunizations or medication therapy management, for which plans pay physicians but won't pay legally authorized pharmacists. Washington law (RCW 48.43.045) requires that

> Every health plan delivered, issued for delivery, or renewed by a health carrier on and after January 1, 1996, shall:
> (1) Permit every category of health care provider to provide health services or care for conditions included in the basic health plan services to the extent that:
> (a) The provision of such health services or care is within the health care providers' permitted scope of practice; and
> (b) The providers agree to abide by standards related to:
> (i) Provision, utilization review, and cost containment of health services;

(ii) Management and administrative procedures; and
(iii) Provision of cost-effective and clinically efficacious health services.

An informal letter opinion by the Washington Attorney General's Office in 2013 indicated that "Pharmacists are health care providers and must be compensated for services included in the basic health plan that are within the scope of the pharmacist's practice if the pharmacist agrees to abide by stated standards related to cost containment, management, and clinically efficacious health services."[584] Therefore, these requirements apply to private insurers who offer individual health plans in Washington; it does not require them to contract with any specific provider, but if they do, they must pay contracted providers for any covered services that are within the provider's scope of practice. These rules do not apply to other state programs, such as Medicaid. Pharmacies who have been denied participation in violation of this rule must file claims with the Insurance Commissioner.

WASHINGTON'S PHARMACIST PROVIDER LAW

In May, 2015, the Governor signed ESSB 5557 – Health Carriers—Services Provided by Pharmacists,[585] which is the first such state law in the nation to require health insurance carriers to include pharmacists as network providers within their scope of practice. It became effective on January 1, 2017 for health plans issued or renewed on or after that date (RCW 48.43.094):

- Benefits shall not be denied for any care service performed by a pharmacist licensed under chapter 18.64 RCW if:
    - The service performed was within the lawful scope of such person's license;
    - The plan would have provided benefits if the service had been performed by a physician, ARNP, or PA; and
    - The pharmacist is included in the plan's network of participating providers
- Plans must include an adequate number of pharmacists in its network of participating medical providers
- Participation by a pharmacy in the plan's network drug benefit does not satisfy the requirement for pharmacist medical providers within the network
- The provisions of this statute do not supersede RCW 48.43.045 (see above)
- These requirements apply only to private plans issued to large group, small group, individual, and family plans; they do not necessarily apply to federal plans or other state plans such as UMP or Apple Health, or to commercial self-insured plans.

The statute directed the Insurance Commissioner to designate a lead organization to develop a collaborative work group report during 2015 regarding implementation of the statute. OneHealthPort was so designated and their report was delivered on November 30, 2015. It presents FAQs, a set of Health Plan Policy Directives that plans will need to put in place, and a Pharmacists and Other Providers Expectations document that describes the expectations that will need to be met by pharmacists who wish to participate as providers.[586]

BASIC ELEMENTS NEEDED TO PARTICIPATE IN 3RD PARTY PLANS

Although in recent years a number of independent pharmacies have stopped accepting third-party plans,[587] it remains the reality that most pharmacies do accept at least Medicaid and Medicare, as well as local private plans.[588] Key elements needed to accept 3rd party reimbursement include the following:

- Application to the plan and agreement to the plan's contract.
- Ability to transmit and receive electronic claims data. This involves
    - Claims processing software integrated with the pharmacy's patient medication record and billing systems.

        - For most prescription claims, this software must adhere to the current protocols adopted by the National Council on Prescription Drug Programs (NCPDP)
        - NCPDP D.0 is the standard protocol for pharmacy claims.
        - Transaction standards for other transactions are handled by the X12 HIPAA version 5010.
    - Dial-up or internet access to a "switch" which routes claims to the 3rd party's claims server
- Administrative systems in place to monitor and reconcile claims, and retain the records and documentation required to withstand subsequent audits
- Staff who are trained in the software, plan rules, and resolving issues with claims.

CLAIMS FOR PAYMENT

DETERMINATION OF THE VALUE OF THE PRESCRIPTION CLAIM

Under almost all 3rd party plans, the value of a prescription claim is composed of two elements, a dispensing fee, and reimbursement for the cost of the drug dispensed.

DISPENSING FEE

The fee is determined by the contract. In most cases the pharmacy cannot negotiate the fee as an individual participant, but may be able to do so as part of a provider group.

For government programs, it is possible to lobby the legislature or agency for changes in the rules by which the fee is determined; this is not always a successful effort, but it is an important advocacy agenda for state associations.

State Medicaid agencies are required by federal rules to pay providers "a reasonable dispensing fee established by the agency."[589] Fees for Medicaid programs may vary for different pharmacies depending on location (e.g., rural versus urban) and volume.

In states that have moved to an AAC-based estimate of drug cost (see below), these changes may be accompanied by an increased fee, based on the Cost of Dispensing (COD). It was reported in 2012 that First Databank was participating with Ernst & Young in New York to develop an estimate of the COD which it will publish for New York pharmacies.[590]

REIMBURSEMENT FOR THE ESTIMATED COST OF THE DRUG

Depending upon the plan and contract, the estimated replacement cost of the drug dispensed may be defined according to nearly a dozen different approaches. The most widely used are listed below.

PHARMACY'S ACTUAL ACQUISITION COST (AAC). The *Actual* Acquisition Cost has been known as the cost that the pharmacy *actually* pays for the particular drug product that it dispenses to a patient at a particular time. It varies from day-to-day as manufacturers alter their prices (generally upwards for brand names, sometimes downwards for generics), or if the product is purchased from different sources. Thus, it is difficult for a pharmacy manager to determine how much it cost for a particular patient's medication on a particular day. It is therefore even more difficult for 3rd party payers to determine this cost. They generally are unwilling to take the pharmacy's word for it.

Medicaid programs in several states, as well as CMS, are involved in efforts to determine *Average* Actual Acquisition Costs (*also* known as "AAACs") for Medicaid program use (see below). Sometimes, these are also confusingly called AACs. In the context of Medicaid programs, AAC typically means that the state is estimating the average actual acquisition cost, not that it is relying on a specific pharmacy's cost.

The AVERAGE WHOLESALE PRICE (AWP), which does not ever reflect what a pharmacy actually pays for the drug (it is often said that AWP means "Ain't What's Paid"), but which is set forth in commercially-developed databases and is based on manufacturers' reports to those database vendors. Because most pharmacies, and virtually all pharmacy chains are able to buy drugs from wholesalers at prices significantly below the AWP, it is rare for plans to pay based on AWP without some form of discount.

FEDERAL AND STATE LAWSUITS AGAINST MANUFACTURERS, WHOLESALERS AND THE DATABASE PROVIDERS ALLEGING FRAUD IN THE SETTING OF AWPS. Some generic manufacturers have been charged with setting artificially high AWPs, then covertly dropping their actual prices to pharmacies to gain sales, a strategy called "marketing the spread."[591] Cases against wholesalers and the database vendors include a specific claim that in the period after 2000, the spread between what wholesalers actually charged pharmacies and the AWP price was arbitrarily increased by wholesaler and database provider conspiracy. A proposed settlement in one such lawsuit resulted in across-the-board reductions in AWPs published by First DataBank to by 4%.[592] The settlement was approved by the court, and changes took place on September 26, 2009. By the end of 2011, FirstDatabank independently discontinued publication of AWPs.

Micromedex and Redbook continue to publish AWPs as determined by theTruven Health Analytics division of IBM Watson Health. Medispan, a division of Wolters Kluwer, uses the same approach as Micromedex and Redbook.[593] The AWP listed by these sources is the one listed by the manufacturer, or a markup specified by the manufacturer, which is typically based on the WAC (see below) or DIRP (see below), or the manufacturer's SWP (see below). If the manufacturer does not specify an AWP or markup guide, Red Book uses sets the AWP at 120% of the WAC, or, if no WAC, the AWP is 120% of the DIRP.[594]

AWP MINUS A SPECIFIED PERCENTAGE. This is still a common approach for estimating the cost of brand-name drugs, with AWP – 15% to AWP – 18% being fairly typical pricing factors.

MAXIMUM ALLOWABLE COST (MAC). Because of the wide range of prices available for generic drugs, and a desire to encourage pharmacies to use generics, many programs set a MAC for covered generics. The pharmacy may use that price basis for generic drugs. If they can buy a generic below the MAC, they make a larger profit.

AVERAGE MANUFACTURER'S PRICE (AMP). One particular pricing basis is currently of importance for pharmacists providing services to federal programs. As a condition of OBRA 90 (see Chapter 6), manufacturers were required to provide rebates to Medicaid programs, which are set as a percentage of the cost of drugs paid for in a particular state. The AMP was established as the measure of the costs of these drugs, and is defined as the average price paid to manufacturers by wholesalers (less discounts) for a particular dosage form and strength of a prescription drug distributed solely to the retail pharmacy class of trade. Until recently, the AMP has not been published, nor has it been used for any purpose other than calculating rebates.

The Patient Protection and Affordable Care Act[595] modified the calculation of AMP, and its uses, in 2010. The statute replaced a former regulatory definition of AMP with a statutory formula:

> AMP means, with respect to a covered outpatient drug, the average price paid to the manufacturer for the drug in the US by
>
> - Wholesalers for drugs distributed to retail community pharmacies; and
> - Retail community pharmacies that purchase drugs directly to the manufacturer.

Exclusions from calculation of the AMP include

- Customary prompt pay discounts extended to wholesalers;
- Certain "bona fide service fees" paid to wholesalers or retail community pharmacies;
- Reimbursements for recalled, damaged, expired, or otherwise unsalable returns;
- Payments received from, and rebates or discounts provided to PBMs, MCOs, HMOs, insurers, hospitals, clinics, mail order pharmacies, long-term care providers, manufacturers, or any other entity that does not conduct business as a wholesaler or a retail community pharmacy, unless the drug is not normally dispensed through a retail community pharmacy.

Another important use of the AMP is for calculating Federal Upper Limits (FUL) for payment for a particular drug (see below).

WHOLESALE ACQUISITION COST (WAC), which is the "catalog price" a wholesaler pays to the manufacturer. It does not include rebates or promotional discounts. For many wholesalers, their net profit consists of rebates, promotional fees, and a discount for early payment. Many wholesalers depend on the fact that manufactures frequently increase prices, and make a profit by buying in quantity and selling at the increased WAC. Some wholesalers set their prices to pharmacies as WAC plus a %, typically up to 5% for smaller accounts, and WAC minus some % for large volume purchasers.

DIRECT PRICE (DIRP OR DP). This is the price published by a manufacturer for sale directly to non-wholesalers. It does not include rebates, reductions, prompt pay discounts.

SUGGESTED WHOLESALE PRICE (SWP). This is the manufacturer's published suggested price from the wholesaler to its customers. It does not represent actual prices charged by wholesalers, and is likely to be less accurate than even the AWP.

FEDERAL SUPPLY SCHEDULE PRICE (FSS) is the price that federal agencies purchase drugs from the manufacturer. It cannot be greater than the lowest price the manufacturer charges any non-federal purchaser. Clinics that are eligible for 340B pricing (see below) are able to purchase at approximately the FSS price.

AVERAGE SALES PRICE (ASP). The Office of the Inspector General entered into a Corporate Integrity Agreement with Tap Pharmaceuticals. As part of that agreement, the ASP was defined as the average of all final sales prices charged for a prescription drug in the United States to all purchasers (including mail order pharmacies) excluding those sales that are exempt from inclusion in the "best price" for Medicaid drug rebate purposes.

BASE LINE PRICE (BLP). This measure was formerly used by Washington's Department of Labor & Industries for generic drugs. It is calculated by taking the mean AWP of all generics in a particular group, determining the standard deviation, and then calculating the mean of those products within one standard deviation of the grand mean.

MEDICAID DRUG COST ESTIMATION APPROACHES

Medicaid is operated by states, but the federal government reimburses the states for a large percentage of their costs. Federal rules require the states to reimburse pharmacies based on the state Medicaid agency's "best estimate of the price generally and currently paid by providers for a drug marketed or sold by a particular manufacturer or labeler in the package size of drug most frequently purchased by providers."[596] However, many states, including Washington, have received approval for Medicaid State Plans that provide services to recipients through managed care options. Pricing to pharmacies under managed care plans is handled like other third party payment programs.

Where individuals are covered under traditional Medicaid – a small number of patients in Washington –, the following bases for reimbursing drug costs to pharmacies are currently being used by Medicaid programs:

MACs FOR GENERIC DRUGS

Washington determines two types of MACs: the State Maximum Allowable Cost (S-MAC), and an Automated Maximum Allowable Cost (A-MAC) (see below).

ESTIMATED ACQUISITION COSTS (EACs) for SINGLE SOURCE DRUGS, for which the states often use an "AWP minus" or "WAC plus" approach.

STATE-LEVEL AVERAGE ACTUAL ACQUISITION COST (AAC, OR AAAC). Alabama, Colorado, Idaho, Iowa, Louisiana, and Oregon now use AAC for Medicaid pricing. All six states contract with Myers & Stauffer, a national accounting firm, to regularly collect a sample of actual invoices from pharmacies and calculate statewide average AACs. AACs may be applied to both single-source and generic drugs.

Because of the "generally and currently" and "most frequently purchased" language in federal regulations, the states are not attempting to determine anything but average or weighted AACs. Therefore, even the best efforts at determining AACs will set them at levels where some pharmacies may pay less than the AAC and some may pay more.

Where AAC is being used, it may accompany an increase in dispensing fee; the announced intent is to base the revised fee on periodic surveys. Among the 6 states using AAACs, the dispensing fee in early 2019 ranges from $10.64 in Alabama to $15.11 in Idaho.[597]

A 2014 report by the Kaiser Family Foundation noted that in late 2013 12 states were still using AWPs, 16 states were using WACs, and 6 states were using AACs to determine costs of Medicaid drugs. 17 states were using a mixture of methods.[598]

NATIONAL AVERAGE DRUG ACQUISITION COST (NADAC)

The NADAC is determined by an accounting firm under contract with CMS, which surveys invoices from independent and chain retail pharmacies. CMS publishes weekly and monthly updates to the NADAC, and this information is available to state Medicaid agencies. States may submit a state plan amendment to CMS to use NADAC data to set reimbursement rates.

FEDERAL UPPER LIMIT (FUL)

No cost basis can exceed the FEDERAL UPPER LIMIT (FUL), which the federal government calculates when there are 3 or more versions of a generic available in a given geographical area. The FULs are calculated using a method required by the Affordable Care Act that uses the AMP; as of 2016 the FUL for most multiple source drugs is set at either

- 175% of the weighted monthly average AMPs where that amount is greater than or equal to the NADAC; or
- where 175% of the AMP average is less than the NADAC, the NADAC will become the FUL

STATE MEDICAID REIMBURSEMENT PROFILES

CMS publishes quarterly reports of information on reimbursement for Medicaid outpatient drugs.[599] As of the quarter ending in December 2018, WASHINGTON STATE uses the following bases for determining acquisition costs: Single source drugs, and multisource drugs with 4 or fewer sources, AWP – 16%; Multisource drugs with 5 or more sources and no MAC or FUL, AWP – 50%. S-MAC or A-MAC applies to multisource drugs that are on the MAC lists. OREGON uses AAC for all drugs and no state MAC. IDAHO uses AAC, or if no AAC established, WAC.

PROFESSIONAL SERVICE FEES may be billed for non-dispensing activities, usually in accordance with either a

- Set fee schedule established by the plan; or
- A resource-based relative value scale (RBRVS) which applies a particular fee range to the complexity of the service and the time involved.

PRICE CHARGED TO GOVERNMENT MAY NOT BE GREATER THAN THE PHARMACY'S UAC. Usually, and especially for government programs, the resulting claim value cannot exceed the pharmacy's UAC for the same quantity of drug. In certain government programs, the contract may also specify that the claim value cannot exceed that which would be charged to any other 3rd party. In late 2016 several lawsuits were filed against various national chains alleging that the chains had established a list of generic drugs that could be purchased by the public at set rates, e.g., $4 for a 30-day supply. To be eligible for those prices, the pharmacies often required joining a discount club or use of an affinity card, but in fact these plans were widely available to the public. The plaintiffs alleged that the chains failed to report these prices as their UCF and thus violated a state or federal False Claims Act, or a contract with a 3rd party payer. These suits are in the early stages in February 2017.[600]

DETERMINATION OF THE DRUG OR SERVICE PROVIDED

DRUGS are almost universally identified in claims by the National Drug Code (NDC), an 11-digit code that indicates the manufacturer, the drug product, and the package quantity. Drugs are normally billed using NCPDP claims processing standard D.0.

FRAUDULENT TO RECORD INCORRECT NDC. It is considered fraudulent to misrepresent the product actually used by entering a different NDC than the one actually on the package from which the drug was dispensed.

For example, 65427-*158-73 is the NDC for Lipitor 20 mg tablets purchased from Pfizer in bottles of 500, and 65427-*158-30 is the NDC for bottles of 30. A pharmacy could conceivably buy Lipitor at a significantly lower cost per tablet by buying in 500s than in 30s. If the computer is set, to record "65427-*158-30" whenever Lipitor is dispensed, then the cost basis for a Lipitor claim will be greater than if "65427-*158-73" is recorded. Certainly under Medicaid, and most private plans, this would be considered fraudulent, and if discovered on a subsequent audit, could result in denied claims, fines, and other penalties.

Similarly, "13411-*524-06" and "58016-*529-60" are NDCs for two different bottlers' propranolol 20 mg tablets, in bottles of 60. Dispensing one product but entering the NDC for the other is not only potentially fraudulent, but it also violates the state rule which requires recording the manufacturer of the drug actually dispensed in the patient medical record. It is very common to use a different product on refills of a generic drug, and if the technician or pharmacist does not be sure to change the NDC when the refill is dispensed, the pharmacy may be unwittingly committing a fraud. At least one national pharmacy chain is now under the terms of a Corporate Integrity Agreement (see below), in part because of lack of care of its personnel to properly record NDCs on generic drug prescriptions.

DEVICES in federal programs are identified by a "Healthcare Common Procedure Coding System (HCPCS – pronounced "Hick-Picks") code, which indicates the *type* of device used. HCPCS codes and associated reimbursement levels are established by Centers for Medicare and Medicaid Services (CMS). The codes for most devices distributed by pharmacies are alpha-numeric codes called HCPCS Level II codes. The pharmacy will be reimbursed the set amount for that device, regardless of their cost, and is not required to identify the particular manufacturer or source. Here are two examples for a similar device (in this case, a wheelchair):

K0836 -- POWER WHEELCHAIR, GROUP 2 STANDARD, SINGLE POWER OPTION, CAPTAINS CHAIR, PATIENT WEIGHT CAPACITY UP TO AND INCLUDING 300 POUNDS

K0838 -- POWER WHEELCHAIR, GROUP 2 STANDARD, SINGLE POWER OPTION, CAPTAINS CHAIR, PATIENT WEIGHT CAPACITY 301 TO 450 POUNDS

In 2016, the reimbursement in Washington was $477.77 per month for the K0836 chair, and $503.46 per month for the larger chair. Entering the incorrect code could cost the pharmacy revenue, or result in increased revenue, which would be considered fraudulent. Devices are normally billed using electronically-submitted CMS-1500 claim forms.

SERVICES. Professional services billed by physicians and other providers are encoded by the Current Procedural Terminology codes maintained by the American Medical Association. CMS uses these codes for payment in federal programs, where they are called HCPCS Level I codes. Pharmacists who are eligible under collaborative practice agreements to evaluate and prescribe drugs may be able to use existing codes for medication Evaluation and Management (E&M) codes that apply to other prescribers. However, after many years of effort, pharmacists have persuaded AMA to adopt a set of CPTs for use by pharmacists in face-to-face medication therapy management sessions; these can be used by all pharmacists. These codes allow for complexity and time involved, so they constitute a type of RBRVS codes. Pharmacist providers using these codes will be subject to audits and their records must justify the complexity and nature of service provided. Services are billed electronically using a standard known as ASC X12N-837 or X12-837, developed by the Accredited Standards Committee (ASC) X12, a group chartered by the American National Standards Institute (ANSI); the pharmacy-specific version of the standard is known as ASC X12N-837P.

PHARMACIST OPTIONS FOR BILLING FOR PROFESSIONAL SERVICES

INCIDENT-TO-PHYSICIAN SERVICES. The primary care provider (physician, ARNP, etc.) adds a charge for a pharmacist's time and service provided using a CPT code related to the visit. Payments by providers are made to the clinic or physician. Pharmacist provides a SOAP note in medical record to document service provided and justify level/complexity of service. This approach is most appropriate for pharmacists employed in clinics.

This approach is limited to in-clinic encounters. It does not provide for a service rendered in a separate pharmacist-run clinic, nor to services provided in nursing homes or hospitals.

PHARMACIST BECOMES CREDENTIALED PROVIDER TO 3RD PARTY PAYER and bills using CPT codes for medication therapy management services, or in certain cases for Medicaid or Medicare, a HCPCS code. The Pharmacist Services Technical Advisory Coalition is a key source for information on billing for pharmacist-provided health care services.[601] The following is only a partial list of billing codes that may be used by pharmacists; for the complete master code list, see the PSTAC website.[602]

POS CODES – PLACE OF SERVICE

- POS Code 01 – Pharmacy
- POS Code 11 – Office
- POS Code 99 – Other place of service

DIAGNOSIS CODES – All provider claims must include an appropriate diagnosis code. Pharmacists may obtain a diagnosis code from a referring practitioner, or the patient's record, in the form of ICD10 (International Statistical Classification of Diseases and Related Health Problems, version 10) codes. Diagnosis codes assigned by a physician or other practitioner authorized to make diagnoses are in the range from A00 to Y99. For other encounters, not associated with an injury or disease, such as immunizations, a pharmacist may select from the series Z00-Z99, which are "reasons for care codes." For example, a patient may have a primary diagnosis of paroxysmal atrial fibrillation that is the reason for anticoagulation management; this code – I48.0 – would have been assigned by the patient's physician. Or the encounter is for providing an immunization that is not otherwise billed under a dispensing claim; the code would be Z23. Diagnosis codes are freely available at ICD10Data.com.

PROCEDURE CODES are used to specify the particular billable service provided by the pharmacist, using Current Procedural Terminology (CPT) codes maintained by the American Medical Association. AMA charges a license fee to have access to the full code set. However, a pharmacist aware of a CPT code provided by sources other than the AMA may not be enjoined from using that code on the basis of a copyright violation.[603] Within the CPT are several code sets, of which medication therapy management, and evaluation and management codes are most relevant to pharmacy primary care services. Some medical codes, such as immunization codes, are also used by pharmacists. The examples below are far from all-inclusive. Medical coding is a specialized occupation, and certified medical coders may receive salaries in the $15 to $30/hour range. Pharmacists, fortunately, are able to restrict their activities in ways that do not require a full-time medical coder, or may rely on the medical diagnostic coding provided by other members of the health care team.

MTM CODES – MEDICATION THERAPY MANAGEMENT

- CPT code 99605 – medication therapy management service(s) provided by a pharmacist, individual, face-to-face with patient, initial 15 minutes, with assessment, and intervention if provided; or initial 15 minutes, new patient
- CPT code 99606 – initial 15 minutes, established patient
- CPT code 99607 – each additional 15 minutes; code 99607 is billed in addition to 99605 or 99606 to code for the primary service

E&M CODES – EVALUATION AND MANAGEMENT

- CPT 99201-99205 – office or outpatient visit for evaluation and management of a new patient, based on complexity
- CPT 99211-99215 – office or outpatient visit for evaluation and management of an established patient, based on complexity, for example:
    - 99213 – visit includes 2 of 3 key components: expanded problem-focused history, expanded problem-focused examination, or medical decision making of low complexity;
    - 99214 – visit includes 2 of 3 key components: detailed history, detailed examination, or medical decision making of moderate complexity
- CPT 99241-99245 – office and other outpatient consultations: requires a comprehensive history, a comprehensive examination, and medical decision making of varying levels of complexity, for example:
    - 99244 – might be used for office visits with extensive counseling about the drug for a patient newly placed on warfarin and the pharmacist will be monitoring INR and making dosing adjustments
- CPT 99371-99373 – telephone calls
- CPT 99381-99397, 99401-99404, 99411-99412, 99420, 99429 – preventative medicine services
- CPT 99499 – other E&M services

IMMUNIZATION CODES

- CPT 90471 – administration of medically necessary vaccines other than pneumococcal, hepatitis B, or influenza vaccines.
- HCPCS G0008, G0009, G0010 – administration of influenza, pneumococcal, and hepatitis B vaccines, respectively.

PHARMACIST ESTABLISHES RELATIVE VALUE UNITS (RVUS) – one approach was to examine RVUs within clinic for E&M codes and compare to services provided by pharmacists who will use MTM codes. One pharmacist-run clinic in Wyoming determined that most of their visits for MTM services would be coded 99606 (initial 15 minutes, established patient) or 99607 (additional minutes), and found that these were similar to E&M codes

99213 (for shorter visits) and 99214 (for extended visits). For their clinic the RVUs were, respectively, 0.92 and 1.42. Thus, they submitted RVUs of 0.92 for CPT 99606, and 1.42 for 99606 combined with 99607.[604]

A fee schedule is determined based on financial evaluation of the cost of the professional's time.

WASHINGTON HEALTH CARE AUTHORITY RBRVS FEE LIMITS

The Health Care Authority has established the following limits on payments for certain medication therapy management services or specialty pharmacy services in state-covered programs (effective July 1, 2018):

Code	Modifier	Comments	Maximum Allowable Rate
90471			$12.11
99605	FP		$13.50
99605	HE	Per week, per client	$10.00
99606	HE	Per week, per client	$10.00
G0008			$12.11
G0009			$12.11
S9430			$10.00
T1999	UE	Limit of 4 per client, per year	$6.00
T1999	SC	Limit of 4 per client, per year	$16.91
T1999	NU	Limit 4 fills per client, per month	$3.00
T1999	TS	Limit 4 fills per client, per month	$2.50

The codes beginning with S or T are HCPCS codes relating primarily to covered devices under the Apple Health FFS program.

CMS ENCOURAGES PHARMACIST PRESCRIBING IN MEDICAID PROGRAMS. On January 17, 2017, the Center for Medicaid and CHIP Services sent an announcement to state program directors that in the Center's view, states have "flexibilities" to "facilitate timely access to specific drugs by expanding the scope of practice and services that can be provided by pharmacists, including dispensing drugs based on their own independently-initiated prescriptions, collaborative practice agreements ... 'standing orders' issued by the state, or other predetermined protocols for Medicaid beneficiaries."

The announcement cited naloxone distribution, tobacco cessation therapy, immunizations, and emergency contraception as examples of options that states could choose to pay for when delivered by pharmacists to Medicaid beneficiaries.[605]

BILLING FOR MTM SERVICES UNDER MEDICARE PART D. A specific set of MTM services are established in Medicare Part D, and Part D plans must provide these services. However, they are not required to always use pharmacists to provide these services. Plans contracting with community pharmacies or individual pharmacists to provide MTM services vary in whether they require pharmacists to be credentialed, whether they require pharmacist to also be enrolled in providing drug benefit services, and which mechanisms they use for submitting claims.

Many complexities are involved in establishing billing for pharmacist services under Medicare, Medicaid, or other 3rd party plans. Several of these are discussed by Stump in the presentation cited above. Considerable additional resources are available at MTM Central on the American Pharmacists Association website: http://www.pharmacist.com/mtm

IDENTIFY OF THE PHARMACIST PROVIDER. HIPAA established a National Provider Identifier which is to be used on all electronic interchange of patient data. The NPI is available to pharmacists to be used to identify individuals as providers of care. (See Chapter 7)

COMMON AUDIT PROBLEMS FOR PHARMACIES

Third party payers, whether private or governmental, are entitled by contract or statute to conduct audits of pharmacies to assure that services and drugs supplied were actually delivered to the patient, were covered by the plan, and the charges were appropriate according to the plan requirements. Problems that arise from audits have significant consequences, including possible recapture of payments by the payer, fines and penalties, federal or state fraud prosecutions, and costs to the pharmacy for dealing with the discrepancies or retaining legal representation. Problems may be categorized as related to the claim submitted, the eligibility of the patient, documentation or authorization for the claim, improper or invalid claims, or failures of the point-of-sale system.

ORDER OR PRESCRIPTION OR CLAIM AS ENTERED.

Claims are frequently denied because the order or prescription is considered invalid for authorizing the drug, device, or service provided.

PRESCRIPTION MUST MEET ALL THE LEGAL REQUIREMENTS. SOME POSSIBLE EXAMPLES:

- Prescription not written, when program required written prescription.
- Prescription incomplete or not dated.
- Prescription not valid because it was "illegible" under Washington law (i.e., written in cursive)
- Prescription for Medicaid not valid because it is not written on tamper-resistant pad
- Patient's full name not specified on prescription.
- Prescription is a transfer and all required information is not present
- Prescription not valid on date of service
- Identity of person who called in prescription not recorded
- Drug is for an unapproved use, as indicated by directions
- Prescription exceeds guidelines (e.g., methadone once daily for pain)
- Faxed prescriptions fail to meet state requirements
- Directions for use incomplete (Washington doesn't allow "ud")

DRUG, DEVICE, OR SERVICE ORDERED AND PROVIDED MUST MATCH THE CLAIM.

- Wrong NDC entered.
- NDC entered for a non-covered drug.
- NDC is not for package size used (discovered by comparing claims to invoices from wholesalers)

PRESCRIBER IDENTITY AND AUTHORITY

- Invalid prescriber identifier (e.g., DEA number or NPI)
- Beyond scope of practice of prescriber
- Wrong prescriber identified on claim
- Prescriber not registered with the plan

Patient Eligibility Issues

- Patient was eligible under more than one program, and pharmacy did not properly bill all payers
- Patient was not eligible at the time of the claim.
- Patient hadn't properly met spend down requirements and this was known to pharmacy
- Patient was deceased at time of service. This happens when the date of service was entered incorrectly or sometimes because a relative or other person was using a medical card of a deceased patient.

Documentation, Justification, or Prior Authorization

- DAW documentation not available
- Documentation of step therapy not in place.
- Documentation of need for MTM service not in records.
- Certificate of Need for DME not on file.
- Inadequate record that refill was authorized by prescriber
- Original record of claim not available at audit time
- Prior authorization not documented when needed
- Failure to have a record that the patient actually received the drug, device, or service.

Improper or invalid claims

- Failure to correct claim or reverse claim for partial fills that aren't picked up or prescriptions never picked up.
- Evidence of waiving required co-pays (note; it is possible under certain circumstances to waive co-pays for Medicare Part D patients – see below).
- Early refills
- Unauthorized refills
- Using a dosage form not covered by FUL pricing instead of a covered form (e.g., ranitidine capsules dispensed instead of tablets)

Point-of-Sale (POS) System Failures. Most claims are adjudicated in real time using a POS system. Theoretically, this should avoid many of the eligibility, identification, excess quantity, early refill, and similar problems. Government rules are usually written in such a way as to put the burden on the vendor, not the government, even though the government has failed to implement its POS system properly. At best, the vendor should be able to avoid penalties, but may still have to repay the claim, even though the drug was dispensed in good faith. Private 3rd party payers are more likely to have to accept responsibility for failures of their adjudication system, but they may have contract language that insulates them in some way. Medicare Part D plans are likely to be backed by federal rules that place more of the burden on the pharmacy.

The ability of the government to place the burden on pharmacies even when the failure is the government's arises from the State's (or federal government's) *sovereign immunity* (see Chapter 1).

TYPICAL CONDUCT OF AUDITS

The following discussion is derived primarily from Medicaid audits, but private 3rd party payers use similar audit procedures and, in some cases, the same auditing firms. Medicare Part D plan providers (see below) are required to implement similar audits, following federal guidelines.

RECORD AUDIT AT 3RD PARTY OFFICE. A sample of claims and providers selected from claims submitted to payer are reviewed.

PROVIDERS MAY BE SELECTED AT RANDOM, based on a randomized schedule to audit all providers over a certain time frame, and/or "outlier" providers are selected based on total volume or unusual volume of claims per enrollee, etc. Some states will do an audit that looks at all providers.

CLAIMS ARE USUALLY SAMPLED FOR AUDIT. A set of claims, typically less than 1%, are selected at random. Some programs always review the most expensive group of claims, such as those comprising some set percentage of total payments to the vendors.

OFF-SITE AUDITS. In many cases, an on-site audit is not performed unless the initial sample reveals a certain level of non-compliance. In such a case, a request may be made for documentation of selected claims by the auditor, and the vendor must supply copies of relevant documents. Discrepancies detected during this phase may be reported to the vendor with a proposed level of settlement for presumed invalid claims. In some cases, agreement to the proposed settlement will forestall an onsite audit.

ON-SITE AUDITS. An onsite audit will examine a variety of elements of the vendor's operation, including a claim-by-claim review for all of the claims selected in the sampling process.

ELEMENTS OF INSPECTION. According to Prudent Rx, one of the nation's major Medicaid contract auditors, the following are elements of the on-site review in one state:

- Physical prescription
- Signature log/Delivery Receipt
- Inventory review (physical or purchasing records)
- Documentation of DAW requirements
- Tamper-proof prescription requirements
- Usual and Customary pricing

RECOVERY CALCULATION

EXTRAPOLATION FROM SAMPLE. Some states require extrapolation based on the random sample. In this process, the recovery value of each sample prescription is determined, and the total for all the sample prescriptions is then extrapolated to the total claims during the sampling period. If 1% of claims were sampled for a pharmacy, and the total recovery value of those claims were set at $800, then the amount of recovery sought from the pharmacy would be $\frac{\$800}{0.01}$ = $80,000. Washington Medicaid audits use extrapolation techniques.

Washington statute enacted in 2014 provides that private health insurers and PBMs may not use extrapolation techniques during pharmacy audits. (See below)

FULL RECOVERY FROM HIGH-COST CLAIMS. The high-cost claims that were specifically examined were excluded from the calculations involving sample claims, so the recovery value of those claims is added to the extrapolated amount.

AUDIT FINDINGS are provided to the vendor.

Proposed recovery amounts well exceeding $100,000 are not uncommon in Washington, and in at least one case an independent pharmacy in western Washington was issued an initial recovery claim of over $550,000, an amount that would have bankrupted the pharmacy.

APPEAL. The vendor has a set time limit to appeal the audit findings. If the appeal date is missed, the findings are final. Particularly where extrapolation is used, a detail appeal of each claim is usually necessary, which is very costly in staff time. Often, at the point of appeal, the vendor will find it necessary to hire an attorney and/or an audit consultant.

PHARMACEUTICAL BENEFITS MANAGERS (PBMS)

PBMs contract with insurers to manage all aspects of the insurers' pharmaceutical benefits; they serve as a "middle man" between the insurer and all the other players in the pharmaceutical marketplace: manufacturers, wholesalers, pharmacies, and (through mail order pharmacies operated by the PBMs) patients. In theory, PBMs save insurers money by obtaining lower prices for drugs from suppliers, by reducing dispensing costs through either mail order or contracting with community pharmacies, and by implementing benefit design changes that affect drug utilization. Critics challenge the efficacy of PBMs, and cite the lack of transparency among traditional PBMs as a factor which make it difficult for customers of PBMs to determine whether they are realizing savings.[606] Some critics of the traditional PBMs have proposed a "transparent PBM model" in which the transparent PBM is paid a per-member-per-month (PMPM) management fee as opposed to the per-claim fee/profit on which traditional PBMs tend to operate.[607]

The criticisms of traditional PBM structures and activities have led to calls for increased transparency as a means of insuring that PBMs contribute to better care at reduced costs to plan sponsors, government payers and individual patients who pay premiums. Federal and state legislation has been passed since 2007 to pursue this goal.

FEDERAL PBM TRANSPARENCY LEGISLATION

A provision of the Affordable Care Act[608] requires PBMs and health benefit plans that offer pharmacy benefit management services under Part D or through an insurance exchange to report to HHS (and to the insurance plan where relevant) the following data on a calendar year aggregate basis: (1) percentages of retail and mail order dispensing; (2) their generic dispensing rate; (3) the types and numbers of dispensing pharmacies; (4) the amounts of negotiated volume-related rebates, discounts, and other price concessions; (5) the amounts passed through to the plan sponsors; and (6) the number of prescriptions dispensed. The reported information will be kept confidential except where HHS deems disclosure necessary, or to enable the Comptroller General or Congressional Budget Office to conduct reviews, or to assist states in establishing health care exchanges.[609]

PBM MAC PRICING AND AUDIT REFORM IN WASHINGTON

On April 3, 2014, Governor Inslee signed ESSB 6137,[610] a PBM audit reform bill supported by WSPA for several years. The statute created a new chapter – RCW 19.340, and requires PBMs to annually register with the Department of Revenue. The statute parallels laws adopted in nearly 30 other states in recent years.[611] The statute was amended in 2016 by transferring enforcement and regulatory authority from the DOR to the Office of the Insurance Commissioner (OIC) and providing for some pharmacies the ability to seek a review of appeals from the Commissioner.[612] The statute does not apply to state medical assistance programs.

REGISTRATION OF PBMS. PBMs must register annually with the OIC, and pay an initial or renewal registration fee set by the Commissioner. (RCW 19.340.030) The OIC's fee regulation is found in WAC 284-180-210:

- The initial registration fee is $200
- The renewal fee will be assessed on PBMs based on the annual cost of renewal and oversight experienced by the Insurance Commissioner;
  - The minimum renewal fee is $500;

  - Each PBM's proportional share will be based on annual filings with the OIC by March 1 of the PBM's prior year gross income from activities in Washington;
  - By June 1 of each year, the OIC will calculate and set the renewal fees from the ensuing fiscal year of July 1st through June 30th.
  - Unexpended balances remaining at the close of each fiscal year will be carried forward to reduce renewal fees in the succeeding year.

PENALTIES. Failure by a PBM to register, or to timely pay renewal fees, or any other violation of the chapter, shall subject the violator to a civil penalty of $1,000 per violation, or, if the violation was knowing and willful, $5,000 per violation. (RCW 19.340.110)

MAXIMUM ALLOWABLE COST LIST REQUIREMENTS. The statute also creates requirements for multisource drugs listed by PBMs as being subject to a MAC price. The statute now refers to "predetermined reimbursement cost for multisource generic drugs, such as a maximum allowable cost or maximum allowable cost list, or any other benchmark prices.", but for convenience, we will continue to use "MAC." Each PBM must:

- Not subject a drug to MAC pricing unless at least 2 therapeutically equivalent multisource drugs, or at least one generic drug available from only one manufacturer, are generally available for purchase by network pharmacies from national or regional wholesalers.
- Ensure that all drugs on a MAC list are not obsolete.
- Provide each network pharmacy at the beginning of the contract, and upon renewal, the sources utilized to determine MAC pricing.
- Provide a list to a network pharmacy on request in a readily accessible to and usable by the pharmacy.
- Update each list every 7 days, and make updated lists available to network pharmacies.
- Ensure that dispensing fees are not included in the calculation of MAC pricing. (RCW 19.340.100(2))

MAC PRICING APPEALS. The PBM must establish a process by which network pharmacies may appeal reimbursements for drugs subject to MAC pricing. Pharmacies may appeal a MAC that is lower than the price actually paid by the pharmacy to its supplier, and the appeal must be completed within 30 days after the pharmacy submitted the appeal. If no decision is received within 30 days, the appeal is considered denied. If a pharmacy that is independent or part of a corporation with fewer than 15 retail outlets in Washington can demonstrate it is unable to purchase a drug from a suppler doing business in Washington, the appeal must be upheld.

- PBMs must provide the pharmacy with a phone number of a person who handles appeals.
- If the PBM denies the appeal, it must provide the pharmacy with a reason for the denial and the NDC of a drug that can be purchased by similarly situated pharmacies at a price that is equal to or less than the MAC.
- If an appeal is upheld, the PBM must make an adjustment within one day of the determination.
- A pharmacy with fewer than 15 outlets may provide information about its appeal to the Insurance Commissioner for the purpose of information collection and analysis.

Dispute resolution by Insurance Commissioner. A pharmacy whose appeal is denied, or if the pharmacy is unsatisfied with the outcome of the appeal, the pharmacy or pharmacist may dispute the decision and request a review by the commissioner

- The pharmacy must be a firm with fewer than 15 retail outlets in Washington to avail itself of this review
- The request must be filed within 30 days after receiving the decision from the PBM

- Within 30 days of the request, the Commissioner shall review all relevant material submitted to the office, and may enter an order directing the PBM to make an adjustment, may deny the pharmacy's appeal, or take other actions deemed fair and equitable.
- Upon resolution, the Commissioner shall provide a copy of the decision to both parties within 7 days.
- The Commissioner may authorize the Office of Administrative Hearings to conduct appeals under this section

PHARMACY AUDIT REQUIREMENTS. (RCW 19.340.040) With regards to the conduct of audits, the Washington statute generally mirrors other states, and requires the PBM to

- Establish a written procedure for appeals the findings of an audit, and provide the procedure to the pharmacy prior to an audit
- Restrict its audits to claims filed within 24 months prior to the audit
- Provide the pharmacy with at least 15 days' advance written notice of an on-site audit
- Avoid on-site audits on the first 5 days of any calendar month, without the pharmacy's consent
- Conduct the audit in consultation with a pharmacist licensed in Washington or another state if the audit involves clinical or professional judgment
- Review in on-site audits more than 250 unique prescriptions during a 1-year period, except in cases of alleged fraud
- Conduct no more than 1 on-site audit in any 12-month period
- Audit each pharmacy under the same standards and parameters used to audit other similarly situated pharmacies
- Pay outstanding claims of a pharmacy within 45 days after the earlier of the issuance of a final audit report or the conclusion of all appeals
- Exclude from the calculation of overpayments any dispensing fees or interest on a claim unless the overpaid claim was for a prescription that was not filled correctly
- Not recoup costs associated with clerical errors or other errors that do not result in financial harm to the entity or a consumer.
- Not charge a pharmacy for a denied or disputed claim until the audit and appeals are final.

PROHIBITION OF SAMPLING OR EXTRAPOLATION PROCEDURES. A finding that a claim was incorrectly presented or paid must be based on identified individual transactions. Probability sampling, extrapolation, or other means that "project an error using the number of patients served who have a similar diagnosis or the number of similar prescriptions or refills for similar drugs," is prohibited. (RCW 19.340.050)

AUDITOR COMPENSATION. An entity that contracts with a third-party auditor may not compensate the third-party auditor on the basis of a percentage of the amount of overpayment recovered. (RCW 19.340.060)

EVIDENCE OF VALID CLAIMS. PBMs or third party auditors must allow the following evidence to validate a claim under review:

- An electronic or physical copy of a valid prescription if, within 14 days of the dispensing date the prescription was (1) picked up by the patient or patient's agent; (2) delivered by the pharmacy to the patent; or (3) sent to the patient using the US Postal Service or other common carrier
- Point-of-sale electronic register data showing purchase of the claimed drug or item
- Electronic records, such a beneficiary signature logs, scanned and stored patient records, and other reasonably clear and accurate electronic documentation. (RCW 19.340.070)

TIME LIMITS. Preliminary audit reports must be provided to the pharmacy within 45 days of the audit, and final reports within 60 days of the preliminary report or the date that the pharmacy contested the audit under the appeals process. (RCW 19.340.080)

PBM "GAG CLAUSES"

Many PBMs have included "gag clauses" in their contracts with pharmacies that prohibit pharmacies from disclosing information to patients that they have options under their plan to obtain the drug at a lower cost by paying out of pocket rather than submitting the claim. Bills introduced into the Washington Legislature in 2018 passed the House but not the Senate.

However, the U.S. Congress enacted two statutes in 2018 prohibiting these clauses. The Patient Right to Know Drug Prices Act, S. 2554, prohibits gag clauses in plans offered by private health insurers, and became effective immediately.[613] The companion statute, the Know the Lowest Price Act, S. 2553, applies to plan sponsors of Medicare Part D plans, and becomes effective for plan years beginning on or after January 1, 2020.[614]

ANTI-KICKBACK AND ANTI-INDUCEMENT LAWS

Most states and the federal government prohibit provision of kickbacks, which are considered a form of bribery, to persons in a position to refer government-paid for services, and these extend to payments for prescription drugs. In addition, most states have specific laws making it illegal for providers of health care to offer or receive kickbacks as they relate to referral of patients for healthcare services. It is also illegal under federal and many state laws to provide inducements to patients to obtain business paid for by federal or state programs.

WHY HAVE ANTI-KICKBACK LAWS? Two major concerns have led to this kind of legislation: (1) the concern that kickbacks to referral sources, particularly physicians, will diminish the referral source as an independent decision maker, and will likely lead to unnecessary utilization of services or use of more expensive services than appropriate; (2) physician self-interest will lead to unethical choices regarding patient care.

WHAT ARE KICKBACKS? Kickbacks are payments or benefits given to a referral sources in return for directing business to the payer. They may be actual monetary payments, made either directly or indirectly, or they may be other items of value, such as free space or equipment.

WHAT ARE INDUCEMENTS? Under a federal statute known as the Civil Monetary Penalties (CMP) statute, prohibited inducements include "offering or transferring remuneration to a Medicare or Medicaid beneficiary when the provider of the inducement knows or should know that the remuneration is likely to influence the beneficiary to use a particular supplier, provider, or practitioner to obtain an item or service paid for – in whole or in part – by Medicare or Medicaid.

As they pertain to pharmacy practice, here are some examples of kickbacks or inducements:

FEE-SPLITTING IN ANY FORM. Any arrangement whereby the prescriber obtains a percentage or set amount for each prescription written, or each patient referred for services (e.g., MTM), is an obvious kickback, and is the source of the term "kickback:" the pharmacy "kicks back" a portion of its fee to the prescriber. The following indirect returns of items of value to a referring physician are also considered kickbacks.

ALLOWING PHYSICIANS TO BILL PATIENTS FOR PHARMACY SERVICES, AND THEN GIVING THE PHYSICIAN A "COLLECTION DISCOUNT." This has sometimes been done with injectable drugs, whereby the pharmacy sends a "prescription" for an individual patient to the physician for administration, and the physician collects the prescription price from the patient, but pays the pharmacy some amount, e.g., 80% of the price. The discount amount is almost always greater than the physician's actual billing and collection costs, so it is truly a kickback.

PERCENTAGE RENTS BASED ON PRESCRIPTION VOLUME. Pharmacies may be located in physician-owned clinics, and it is not unreasonable to pay rent for the space. However, if the rent is related to the volume of prescriptions generated by the clinic and referred to the pharmacy, such an arrangement amounts to paying the physician a percentage of the amount collected for each referred prescription, and is a kickback.

MORE THAN NOMINAL ENTERTAINMENT COSTS. Pharmaceutical sales representatives now are explicitly restricted in the amount they can spend on taking physicians to lunch or other expenditures related to continuing education programs, etc. (see below). Pharmacy owners who would fly local physicians to their condos in Hawaii or Cabo San Lucas, or who take physicians golfing at exclusive clubs and pick up the tab would be probably providing kickbacks under current rules. It's fun to assume that pharmacy owners have these kinds of resources, but even less extravagant expenses – dinners and lunches, may be out of bounds.

SALES OF GOODS AT A REDUCED PRICE. Pharmacies may sell supplies to physician's offices at less than retail prices, providing the prices are consistent with competition and fair business practices. (Remember that if these sales are > 5% of total business, the pharmacy must register as a wholesaler – see Chapter 1). However, providing physicians or their families who refer patients to the pharmacy with personal discounts below what would be charged to the general public may constitute a form of kickback.

PROVIDING FREE SERVICES FOR NURSING HOMES. A pharmacy may seek a consulting contract with a nursing home based on implementation of a particular, e.g., unit dose, system, which includes pharmacy-maintained patient medical records or other services. These may legitimately reduce nursing costs and be of benefit to the home when compared to other ways of delivering drug therapy. However, pharmacies have sometimes offered additional services, such as bookkeeping services, provision of free dispensing carts, etc. To the extent that these confer a benefit to the home beyond the services contracted for, they represent a kickback.

RECEIVING A FEE FROM A MANUFACTURER to contact patients to urge them to obtain their refills of the manufacturer's product, unless the amount of the fee simply covers the actual cost of making the contact.

RECEIVING A FEE FROM A DRUG COMPANY TO DISCUSS COMPANY'S DRUG WITH PATIENT could be a kickback if payment is based on success in improving compliance or switching the patient to the manufacturer's drug.

PROVIDING COUPONS to patients to encourage them to transfer prescriptions to the pharmacy. Under federal rules, nominal gifts of $15 or less per gift and $75 or less per person per year are excluded from enforcement. However, coupons cannot normally be provided to beneficiaries of federal programs; although certain loyalty programs are among "safe harbors" established by the HHS OIG (see below).

MEDICARE ANTI-KICKBACK STATUTE. This principal federal anti-kickback legislation has been described as "the mother of all anti-kickback/anti-rebate statutes."[615] Kickbacks are a form of bribery, and to be involved in a kickback is defined in the federal Medicare Anti-kickback statute as to "knowingly and willfully" solicit, receive, offer or pay any remuneration in return for (1) referring or arranging for services payable by any federal or state health care program, or (2) purchasing, leasing ordering or arranging for any goods, facilities or services which may be paid for in whole or in part by any federal or state health care program. Under the federal law, participating in a kickback scheme is a felony, punishable by up to 5 years in prison and a $25,000 fine (42 U.S.C. §§1320a-7b). Although this is labeled the "Medicare Anti-kickback Statute," it applies to any federal program.

The statute also includes prohibitions on inducements to Medicare or Medicaid beneficiaries to use any particular provider, practitioner, or supplier to obtain items or services paid for by Medicare or Medicaid.

Additional sanctions include exclusion from participation in Medicare and Medicaid, and additional civil monetary penalties of up to $50,000 per violation, and assessments of up to 3 times the amount of remuneration paid under the agreement.

Violations of the statute can also be considered violations of the Federal False Claims Act, bringing its civil penalties to bear.

Generally, violations of the Medicare Anti-Kickback Statute must be "knowing and willful," so the government must prove that the violator knew the action was a violation and committed it intentionally.

The Act is enforced by the Office of the Inspector General (OIG) of the Department of Health and Human Services. The OIG also establishes "safe harbors," which are guidelines for certain situations, which, if followed carefully, protect individuals from being charged with violations of the Act.

The statute does not apply to any payments "by an employer to an employee (who has a bona fide employment relationship with such employer) for employment in the provision of covered items or services." While this is important particularly for hospitals, it also suggests that a pharmacy could employ a physician or nurse practitioner – on a non-volume-related basis (such as hourly) – to see patients in the pharmacy and write prescriptions to be filled in the pharmacy, without violating the Act (other state provisions might apply, however.)

STARK ACT (THE "ETHICS IN PATIENT REFERRALS ACT").[616] One commentator has suggested that "If the Anti-kickback statute is the mother of all anti-rebate statutes, then the Stark Law is the Gordian Knot of such laws."[617] This law, passed in 1989 and expanded in 1993, is designed to prevent physicians from referring Medicare or Medicaid patients to entities in which they or family members have an economic interest. Originally, it applied to referrals of Medicare patients to clinical laboratories in which the physician had a financial interest, but was extended later to referrals of Medicare *and* ten additional "designated health services" (DHS): physical therapy; occupational therapy; radiology; radiation therapy; DME equipment or supplies; parenteral and enteral nutrition services; prosthetics and orthotics; home health services, outpatient prescription drugs; and inpatient and outpatient hospital services.

Enforcement of and regulations under the Stark Act are the province of the Centers for Medicare and Medicaid Services (CMS). The most recent regulations were promulgated in 2008.

The statute imposes strict liability for violations of its requirements: no intent is necessary, unlike the Medicare Anti-kickback statute. The Act's civil penalties are quite severe, and can trigger charges of violation of the Federal False Claims Act. Both the physician and the participating entity (e.g., pharmacy) can be penalized and/or excluded from participation in Medicare or Medicaid.

In November 2009, Omnicare, the nation's largest nursing home pharmacy, and IVAX paid $14 million to settle claims that Omnicare solicited, and IVAX paid Omnicare $8 million in return for Omnicare's purchase of $50 million worth of drugs from IVAX.[618]

The many implications and exclusions under the Stark regulations are beyond the scope of this text; pharmacies must consistently seek legal counsel when entering into relationships with physicians that might bring them under the ambit of the Stark Act.

SAFE HARBORS ESTABLISHED BY OIG.

A final rule issued by the OIG that became effective in January 2017 has provided amendments to certain safe harbors and exemptions from civil monetary penalties (CMPs) that relate to pharmacy services and operations. Some of the more important amendments are:[619]

- Waivers or reductions in co-pays or other cost-sharing amounts owed to pharmacies by financially-needy federal beneficiaries if
  - The waiver or reduction is not offered as part of an advertisement or solicitation;
  - The pharmacy does not routinely waive or reduce cost-sharing amounts;
  - The reduction or waiver is made only after a good faith determination that the individual is in financial need or after making reasonable failed efforts to collect the owed amount
- Offering of coupons, rebates, or other rewards from a retailer if
  - The rewards are offered on equal terms available to the general public, regardless of health insurance status; and
  - The rewards are not tied to the provision of other items or services reimbursed in whole or in part by federal funds.

    This would allow Medicare Part D patients, for example, to participate in loyalty programs by a grocery chain which provides points for purchases in the pharmacy; it would not allow giving of coupons or rebates to a Medicare Part D patient or Medicaid patient for transferring prescriptions to the pharmacy.
- Provision of certain services or products that promote access to care by encouraging compliance with prescribed drug therapy are allowable if they pose a low risk of harm. Included in this category might be timed dispensing containers or "Med-packs."

WASHINGTON ANTI-KICKBACK LAWS

STARK ACT AND MEDICARE ANTI-KICKBACK ACT ADOPTED IN WASHINGTON.

Washington has incorporated the Stark Act and Medicare Anti-kickback statutes into state law as they apply to the Medicaid program (RCW 74.09.240). Equivalent provisions also apply to the health care programs funded by the Department of Labor and Industries industrial insurance pool (RCW 51.48.280). Certain differences exist between the state and federal acts, including that the state adoption of the Anti-kickback Act did not specify that intent was necessary to violate the statute, so it may be easier to convict under the state law than the federal law.[620]

WASHINGTON ANTI-REBATE LAW (RCW 19.68).

First enacted in 1949, the Washington anti-rebate law was one of the earliest attempts to deal with physicians' business practices that were seen as disreputable.[621] Its construction is quite awkward; Black notes that this statute "consists of one of the longest and most poorly worded sentences in the entire Revised Code of Washington."[622] A footnote to the most recent Supreme Court opinion interpreting the law noted dryly that "More precisely, we are as asked to interpret a 156-word sentence. We are up to the task."[623] Here is the sentence in question (RCW 19.68.010(1)):

> It shall be unlawful for any person, firm, corporation or association, whether organized as a cooperative, or for profit or nonprofit, to pay, or offer to pay or allow, directly or indirectly, to any person licensed by the state of Washington to engage in the practice of medicine and surgery, drugless treatment in any form, dentistry, or pharmacy and it shall be unlawful for such person to request, receive or allow, directly or indirectly, a rebate, refund, commission, unearned discount or profit by means of a credit or other valuable consideration in connection with the referral of patients to any person, firm, corporation or association, or in connection with the furnishings of medical, surgical or dental care, diagnosis, treatment or service, on the sale, rental, furnishing or supplying of clinical laboratory supplies or services of any kind, drugs, medication, or medical supplies, or any other

goods, services or supplies prescribed for medical diagnosis, care or treatment.

In essence, the statute makes it unlawful to pay a physician, drugless healer (e.g., naturopath), dentist, or pharmacist a rebate for referral of patients for care or provision of health care supplies or services. A violation of the statute is a misdemeanor, and can lead to charges of unprofessional conduct. It is rarely enforced by state agencies,[624] but, as in the case discussed below, can be the basis for a law suit under other laws, such as the Consumer Protection Act.

IT IS NOT A VIOLATION OF RCW 19.68 TO MAKE A PROFIT ON SALES OF PRESCRIPTION DRUGS TO ONE'S OWN PATIENTS. A case (Wright v. Jeckle, 158 Wn.2d 375; 144 P.3d 301, 2006) regarding the statute was of particular interest to pharmacists, and the WSPA joined 26 other state or local health care associations as *amici curiae* (friends of the courts). The trial court had held that Dr. Milam Jeckle of Spokane Valley had violated the Anti-Rebate Statute when he sold his patients fen-phen tablets at a profit. It was permissible, the court held, to sell drugs to patients, but not at a profit. As a result, he could be found to have engaged in a deceptive practice under the Consumer Protection Act. (Such a finding would obviously have implications for pharmacists with prescriptive authority.) On appeal to the Supreme Court, Justice Chambers wrote in the opinion that "We are asked today to determine whether RCW 19.68.010 is an 'antikickback' statute or an antiprofit statute. We conclude the legislature intended to prohibit kickbacks, not profits. Accordingly, we reverse the trial court."[625]

Pharmacists who engage in prescribing drugs under CDTAs, such as envisioned by the minor ailments project,[626] or birth control distribution, are not prohibited from charging a fee for the service and a fee for the dispensed prescription. For example, provision of immunization may be paid based on reimbursement for the drug and payment for the administration of the drug. However, it is probably a good practice to give notice to patients that the prescription may be filled at any pharmacy of their choice, and any specific restrictions arising from a third party payment contract (private or governmental) must be observed.

HEALTH CARE FRAUD, WASTE AND ABUSE

HEALTH CARE FRAUD IS A SIGNIFICANT PROBLEM. According to legend, when asked by a reporter, "Why do you rob banks?" Willie Sutton replied, "Because that's where the money is."[627] In 2005, total public spending on health care was $847 billion, with $653 billion of that total due to Medicare and Medicaid. Not surprisingly, a government enterprise with that much money involved will be of real interest to persons who wish to commit fraud. Federal government recoveries from false claims pursued in 2010 exceeded $3.1 billion, with $2.7 billion coming from the top 10 cases, all of which involved healthcare.[628] One national organization of *qui tam* plaintiffs' attorneys, Taxpayers Against Fraud, maintains a website that chronicles a variety of judgments and settlements in the courts for fraud against the government (http://www.taf.org/).

FEDERAL FALSE CLAIMS ACT (FCA)

Originally enacted following the Civil War, to deal with fraud by federal defense contractors, the Federal False Claims Act (31 U.S.C. §§3729-3733), is the principal federal statute that provides a mechanism for recovering from federal contractors for claims that are made fraudulently. It applies to all claims against the government, except it does not apply to tax collections under the Internal Revenue Act. Congress amended the FCA in 2009 by enacting the Fraud Enforcement and Recovery Act (FERA).[629]

ACTIONS CREATING LIABILITY UNDER THE ACT include the following:

- Knowingly presenting a false or fraudulent claim for approval, or causing one to be presented, to an officer or employee of the US government or to an employee of the Armed Forces.
- Knowingly making or using a false statement or record, or causing a false statement or record to be made or used, to get a false or fraudulent claim approved by the Government.
- Conspiring to defraud the Government by getting a false or fraudulent claim approved.
- Intending to commit fraud by shorting the Government in money or goods in any transaction.
- Acting as an individual authorized to deliver a receipt to the Government, intentionally commits fraud by delivering the receipt without knowing that the information on the receipt is true.
- Knowingly buying government property from a government officer or employee, or member of the Armed Forces, who may not lawfully sell the property.
- Knowingly making or using a false statement or record, or causing a false statement or record to be made or used, to conceal, avoid, or decrease an obligation to pay or transmit money to the Government.
- Knowingly and improperly avoid[ing] or decreas[ing] and obligation to pay or transmit money or property to the government. Under FERA, it is not a requirement that the defendant submitted a claim directly to the government, so pharmacies may now be in violation of the FCA by knowing retention of government overpayments, even if the provider made no false or improper claim for the payments.

  Another federal statute, the Medicare Secondary Payer Act, requires that parties to personal injury claims (including defendants), protect Medicare's interests when settling cases. If a pharmacy is sued by a Medicare beneficiary, and the pharmacy or its insurer agrees to a settlement, Medicare must be notified of the settlement and any funds that would have been paid to the plaintiff for treatment costs must be paid to Medicare to reimburse it for its share of those costs. Failure to do so is now considered, under FERA, to be avoiding or decreasing an obligation, and subjects the pharmacy to FCA litigation. It is important for pharmacies (and pharmacists) involved in settlements with Medicare beneficiaries to assure through their attorney that the MSPA is complied with.

PENALTIES UNDER THE ACT INCLUDE:

- Civil penalties of not less than $10,781 nor more than $21,563 per false or fraudulent claim or action, plus 3 times the amount of damages sustained by the Government.
  - Under certain circumstances, the person committing the violation may notify the Government within 30 days of the violation and, if they cooperate fully with the Government will be subject to no more than 2 times the damages sustained.
  - All individuals violating the Act may be assessed the costs to the Government of bringing the action.

CLAIMS INCLUDE THOSE MADE TO ANY GOVERNMENT CONTRACTORS IF ANY FEDERAL DOLLARS ARE INVOLVED IN PAYING FOR THE GOODS OR SERVICES INVOLVED. Therefore, for example, pharmacy claims to Medicaid, even though submitted to the State of Washington, are subject to the Act.

"KNOWING" AND "KNOWINGLY" MEAN THAT A PERSON, WITH RESPECT TO INFORMATION:

- Has actual knowledge of the information;
- Acts in deliberate ignorance to the truth or falsity of the information; or
- Acts in reckless disregard of the truth or falsity of the information. In this last case, the Government will not need to prove intent to defraud.

INDIVIDUAL PRIVATE CITIZENS MAY BRING *QUI TAM* LAWSUITS ON BEHALF OF THE GOVERNMENT FOR VIOLATIONS OF THE ACT.

If an individual has knowledge of a false claim or other practice that violates the Act, that person may file a lawsuit for the person and for Government in the name of the Government. The person bringing the lawsuit is called a *"qui tam* relator." The term *qui tam* is an abbreviation of the Latin phrase *"qui tam pro domino rege quam pro se ipso in hoc parte sequitur"*, meaning *"he who sues for the king as well as for himself."* The complaint must be filed with the US Attorney General as well, and depending on the decision by the US Attorney, the government may take over the case and its prosecution, or the relator may pursue the case with his or her own attorney. If the case is won or settled, the relator may be awarded (with some exceptions):

- Not less than 15% nor more than 25% of the total recovery if the Government prosecuted the case; or
- Not less than 25% nor more than 30% of the total recovery if the relator pursued the case.
- Attorneys' fees. In either case, the relator may also be awarded costs and attorneys' fees needed to pursue the case, which shall be paid by the defendant. However, if the relator pursues the case after the government has declined to do so, and loses, the defendant may be awarded its costs and attorneys' fees, to be paid by the relator.

Relators are protected by whistleblower provisions in the Act. Several *qui tam* relators retain employment in the firms that they sued.

SOME EXAMPLES OF PRACTICES IN PHARMACY SETTINGS THAT HAVE LED TO QUI TAM SUITS[630]

Note that many of these would also be subject to rejection of claims in an audit (see above), but would only be sustained in a *qui tam* suit if intent or reckless disregard of the truth could be proven.

- Billing for goods or services that were never delivered (e.g., failing to reverse a claim for prescriptions that were never picked up, or for unclaimed partial fills that were returned to stock)
- Upcoding – billing for a higher class of service or goods than provided
- Billing for brand name drugs when generics were dispensed.
- Billing for a more expensive dosage form of the prescribed drug.
- Being overpaid on a prescription claim and not reporting that overpayment.
- Obtaining prescription business by kickbacks.
- Billing for unapproved drugs, or for approved drugs for indications not recognized by USP-DI or AHFS.
- Forging physician signatures when such signatures were needed to authorized billing to Medicare or Medicaid.

MOST QUI TAM SUITS ARE BROUGHT AGAINST MAJOR CORPORATIONS. The principal reason is that the case must have sufficient value to be worth the cost of investigating and prosecuting it, and the defendants must have sufficient resources to pay the civil fines. Smaller firms typically declare bankruptcy when faced with treble damages in these suits.

STATE FALSE CLAIMS ACTS

The Deficit Reduction Act of 2005 enacted an incentive for states to adopt false claims acts that mirror the federal act: they obtain a 10% increase in their share of false claims recoveries. Jurisdictions with false claims acts that are equivalent to the federal act include: California, Colorado, Connecticut, Delaware, Georgia, Hawaii, Illinois, Iowa, Massachusetts, Montana, New York, Rhode Island, Tennessee, Texas, and Washington.[631]

The Washington Legislature adopted a state Medicaid Fraud Act in 2012.[632] It largely parallels the federal statute, and provides that the Attorney General may bring false claim suits on behalf of the state, and allows for *qui tam* suits. An assessment by a law firm that represents health care entities identified some differences between the state act and the federal law that it considers to be additional risks for providers not covered by the federal statute:[633]

- The AG may impose civil administrative penalties for claims determined to violate the Act, requiring repayment of excess payments and up to treble damages. The director of the Health Care Authority has had this same authority, but a section of the law specifies a right to an adjudicative proceeding. This provision does not appear to apply to the AG's imposition of penalties. (RCW 74.09.210(2).
- It does not appear that the state law has a statute of limitations, whereas the federal law has a 6 to 10 year limit.
- Under both statutes, *qui tam* suits may not be based on "publicly disclosed" information, but the state limits this to information disclosed to state agencies, which may open entities to suits based on information disclosed to federal agencies, which would be barred under the federal law.
- Some business insurance policies exclude coverage for "intentional acts," and the state statute defines an "intentional act" to include any submission of a false claim, which may affect the business liability insurance of health care entities.

FEDERAL CRIMINAL STATUTES. The False Claims Act provides civil penalties for fraud against the government, but there are a large number of corresponding criminal statutes under which violators may be fined or imprisoned. These are not confined to one statute, but fraud against the Government may be criminally prosecuted under many laws. Without going into great detail, here's a partial list:

- SUBMITTING FALSE CLAIMS (18 USC § 287). This is the criminal statute companion to the False Claims Act, and was also first passed in 1863. Penalties include fines and/or imprisonment up to 5 years.
- MAKING FALSE STATEMENTS (18 USC § 1001). This was a companion to § 287, with similar penalties, adopted first in 1863.
- MAIL OR WIRE FRAUD (18 USC §§ 1341, 1343). The major statute used by the Department of Justice to prosecute fraud, including healthcare fraud, because almost every scheme to defraud at some point involves transmitting information, claims, contracts, etc., through the mails or by "wire."
- MEDICARE AND MEDICAID FRAUD (42 USC §§ 1320A-7B(A)(1)). This statute is found as part of the Medicare Anti-kickback statute (see above), with similar penalties, and it applies to all federal health programs, covering fraud other than kickbacks or self-referrals.
- HIPAA FRAUD STATUTES. HIPAA included three major sections devoted to health care fraud, and unlike the Medicare and Medicaid fraud laws, the HIPAA statutes apply to fraud against "health care benefit programs," which would include private insurers. The three sections are similar to equivalent sections of the Civil War statutes and the Medicare and Medicaid fraud and kickback statutes, with somewhat different sentencing rules.
- HEALTH CARE FRAUD (18 USC § 1637)
- THEFT OR EMBEZZLEMENT IN CONNECTION WITH HEALTH CARE (18 USC § 669)
- FALSE STATEMENTS RELATING TO HEALTH CARE MATTERS (18 USC § 1035).
- OTHER FEDERAL STATUTES that may be involved include the following (citations to the USC omitted):
  - MONEY LAUNDERING
  - RICO (RACKETEER INFLUENCED AND CORRUPT ORGANIZATIONS ACT)

- CONSPIRACY
- THEFT OF GOVERNMENT PROPERTY
- OBSTRUCTION OF JUSTICE
- DISPOSING OF ASSETS TO OBTAIN MEDICAID COVERAGE (18 USC § 1320-7B(A)). This statute applies to prospective Medicaid recipients who "knowingly and willfully dispose of assets (including by any transfer in trust) in order for the individual to become eligible for medical assistance under a State plan under title XIX, if disposing of the assets results in the imposition of a period of ineligibility for such assistance under section 1917(c)." One commentator has suggested that actually prosecuting a person under this section will be difficult, in part, because it is otherwise legal to do exactly what the statute prohibits, and it results in a delay of eligibility for Medicaid.[634] Fraudulent concealment of assets by a prospective Medicaid recipient could be dealt with by any number of other federal fraud statutes.

DEFICIT REDUCTION ACT OF 2005 FRAUD REDUCTION PROVISIONS

State Medicaid agencies must provide in the state plan that any entity that receives $5 million or more in Medicaid receipts must

- Establish written fraud control policies
- Include in those policies procedures for detecting fraud, waste, and abuse
- Include in the employee handbook a statement informing employees of their rights to be protected as whistleblowers.

The DRA expanded funding for federal anti-fraud resources:

- Increased CMS' Program Integrity Team from 8 individuals to 100 nationwide
- Increased CMS anti-fraud funding from $5 million/year in 2006 to $75 million per year in 2009 and thereafter.
- OIG received an additional $25 million/year for FY 2006 through FY 2010 for Medicaid integrity activities

HEALTH REFORM LAW FRAUD AND ABUSE REQUIREMENTS IN 2010 AND LATER

- The Patient Protection and Affordable Care Act (ACA) has 32 sections devoted to fighting fraud, waste, and abuse, and allocates $350 million over 10 years to increase enforcement activities.
- Increased screening of providers, including a national pre-enrollment screening program for Medicare or Medicare providers.
- Expanded federal audits
  - Medicare rule allows CMS to audit records of pharmacies
  - An Integrated Data Repository of claims will allow data mining to help identify targets for audits
  - The Office of Inspector General has greater subpoena power for any documents needed to validate claims
- Recovery Audit Contractors are auditing firms that contract to audit pharmacies and other providers. Under the law audits are extended to Medicare Part C and D
  - RACs are reimbursed in proportion to how much they collect
  - Will be able to audit Part D plans and pharmacy part D claims
  - States must hire RACs for Medicaid
- Medicare Part D plans must implement new fraud programs
- Use of National Provider Identifier will become mandatory for Medicare and Medicaid claims, and for applications to become a provider

- Knowingly keeping an overpayment constitutes a violation of the False Claims Act, even if no false claim was ever filed
    - Must return an overpayment within 60 days of discovery, and must "explain in writing the reason for the overpayment"
- Penalties for failing to repay are up to $10,000 fine for each overpayment plus 3 times actual damages
- The ACA amends the Anti-Kickback statute to make any claim for payment "resulting from" a kickback a violation of the False Claims Act

CORPORATE INTEGRITY AGREEMENTS

As a result of adverse audits, and/or settlements in civil false claims or fraud lawsuits, the OIG may impose a Corporate Integrity Agreement (CIA) as a condition of the settlement or continuation of eligibility for participation in federal programs. The OIG may also impose (or negotiate) Certification of Compliance Agreements (CCA), or may supervise Settlements with Integrity Provisions. Collectively, these are all considered Compliance Agreements. A related alternative for criminal settlements is a Deferred Prosecution Agreement (DPA), by which defendants charged with criminal offenses agree to adhere to the DPA, and after a period of time of compliance, the charges will be dismissed. The OIG website currently lists several hundred of these agreements.[635] Agreements are posted for at least: 12 pharmaceutical manufacturers, 3 national pharmacy chains, 1 national long-term care pharmacy chain, 6 independent pharmacies, 2 national PBMs, 4 medical device manufacturers, and 14 major university medical centers. The CIAs for the pharmaceutical manufacturers are all related to settlements which total at least $4.35 billion.[636]

TYPICAL ELEMENTS of a CIA include the following obligations:

- Hire a compliance officer and appoint a compliance committee
- Develop written standards and policies
- Implement comprehensive employee training programs
- Review claims submitted to federal health care programs (may include submitting samples to CMS and/or use of an Independent Review Organization (IRO) to do the review and submit reports.
- Establish a confidential disclosure program
- Restrict employment of ineligible persons
- Submit reports to OIG

TYPICAL LENGTH OF CIA. CIAs typically operate for 5 years, but terms can vary and have included as little as 3 years and upwards of 9 years.

EXCLUDED PERSONS

The OIG may exclude individuals or corporations from participation in federal programs. Excluded persons may not be hired by government contractors to do work related to any government program from which they are excluded. Entities may not bill federal programs for any claim that involves work or participation by an excluded individual. This applies whether or not the employer has a CIA. So, an excluded pharmacist cannot really work for any pharmacy that serves Medicare or Medicaid patients. This is a professional "death sentence," and is another reason for seeking the advice of an attorney when faced with possible disciplinary action by the Pharmacy Commission.

REASONS FOR EXCLUSION INCLUDE:

- Misdemeanor conviction related to health care fraud

- License revocation or suspension
- Default on federal student loans
- Felony conviction related to controlled substances.

LISTS OF EXCLUDED PERSONS ARE AVAILABLE ON FEDERAL AND SOME STATE WEBSITES.

OIG – http://exclusions.oig.hhs.gov/

GSA – http://www.epls.gov/

STATE AGENCIES may also exclude individuals, and may do so for different reasons than the federal government.

IF EXCLUDED, MUST REAPPLY; REINSTATEMENT IS NOT AUTOMATIC. For example, a pharmacist's license is suspended for 6 months, leading to exclusion. Upon reinstatement of the license, the pharmacist must apply for reinstatement of eligibility to participate in federal programs, and reinstatement is neither automatic nor immediate.

HEALTH CARE OPTIONS IN WASHINGTON

Washington has elected to develop a statewide system of health care coverage for all citizens, and has taken full advantage of the opportunities under the Affordable Care Act (ACA), including establishing a state-run insurance exchange. As summarized by Northwest Health Law Advocates,[637] the range of coverage options include:

WASHINGTON APPLE HEALTH

This program includes federally-assisted and state programs for individuals and families with low incomes: Medicaid; CHIP (Child Health Insurance Program), also called the Apple Health for Kids program; and other state assistance programs for special populations. The former Basic Health Plan, which provided state subsidized premiums to purchase private insurance coverage from qualifying plans has been incorporated into Apple Health and/or options from the insurance exchange. These programs are operated by the Health Care Authority in partnership with the Department of Social and Health Services, and are coordinated with the Washington Health Benefit Exchange, also known as Washington Healthplanfinder, so that individuals who are not eligible for Washington Apple Health can find potentially subsidized plans from the Exchange.

MEDICAID TRANSFORMATION. In 2017, the state embarked on a 5-year demonstration project to significantly reform Medicaid. The principal initiatives of the project include (1) creation of Accountable Communities of Health; (2) offer new services – including services and supports for family caregivers – for long-term Medicaid beneficiaries; and (3) provide for supportive services that help beneficiaries get and keep housing and/or services to support employment.

In 2019, Apple Health began a statewide transition to "whole-person care," in which both medical and mental health services are combined in a single program "so that people will receive the help they need for boday and mind, including mental health and substance abuse treatment. On January 1, the move was instituted in 4 regions (Greater Columbia, King, Pierce, and Spokane). The remaining regions will move to integrated care in July 2019 (North Sound) and January 2020 (remaining regions).

ACCOUNTABLE COMMUNITIES OF HEALTH are established in each state region – one ACH per region – and will pursue transformation projects agreed to between the ACH and the state in building health systems capacity, redesign of how care is delivered, and disease prevention and health promotion. Certification of ACHs is scheduled to be completed by mid-2017.[638]

PUBLIC EMPLOYEES

The state provides employer-covered health care for its employees. Employees pay a portion of the premiums for this coverage and, depending on their location, may choose the Uniform Medical Plan (statewide), a managed-care option, or a consumer-directed health plan integrated with a Health Savings Account (HSA). Retired employees are able to continue coverage at higher premiums in coordination with Medicare coverage.

MEDICARE

Medicare is a fully-federally-funded program for persons 65 and over and for persons who are disabled or fit other categories such as end-stage renal disease. Medicare enrollment is handled by the Social Security Administration, and the program is managed by the Centers for Medicare and Medicaid Services (CMS). Some individuals eligible for Medicare may be able to have assistance in purchasing Part B Supplement Insurance (see below) from the Washington State Insurance Pool.

QUALIFIED HEALTH PLANS

QHPs are private insurance plans that meet requirements established under the ACA that allow for federal subsidies for certain individuals whose income is too great to qualify for Washington Apple Health. These insurers are regulated by the Washington State Insurance Commissioner, and by the Health Benefit Exchange, and are found using the Washington Healthplanfinder.

COMMERCIAL INSURANCE PLANS

These are plans offered by private health insurance companies and are available to individuals or employers. They are purchased through agents or brokers, and are regulated by the Insurance Commissioner.

WASHINGTON HEALTH INSURANCE POOL

A former program available primarily for individuals needing Medicare Supplement insurance who cannot afford it. After January 1, 2014, the program was largely closed to new enrollees, except for the Medicare supplement program.

DETERMINING INCOME LEVELS FOR FEDERALLY-ASSISTED PROGRAMS: MAGI

The MODIFIED ADJUSTED GROSS INCOME (MAGI) is used to measure individual or household income for a variety of federal purposes, including calculating limits on an individual's tax-free contributions to an Individual Retirement Account (IRA), premiums for Medicare Part B, C, and D, and qualification for Medicaid or premium supplements available through state or federal insurance exchanges. The MAGI for most individuals is determined by the IRS from the individual's federal income tax return. The MAGI adds back income from certain deductions that are used to calculate the ADJUSTED GROSS INCOME (AGI) for other income tax purposes.

- The AGI is calculated by taking all of your income and *deducting* certain amounts, which typically include: IRA and self-employed retirement plan contributions; alimony payments; self-employed health insurance payments; one-half of self-employment taxes paid; health savings account (HAS) deductions; penalties on the early withdrawal of savings; educator expenses; student loan interest; moving expenses; qualifying tuition and fees; and certain other uncommon deductions.

- The MAGI starts with the AGI and *adds back:* student loan interest; one-half of the self-employment tax; qualified tuition expenses; any deducted tuitions and fees; IRA contributions and taxable social security payments; exclusions for income from US savings bonds; certain excluded adoption expenses; rental losses; and losses from publicly-traded partnerships. For many, if not most, individuals, particularly those with lower incomes who cannot itemize deductions, the MAGI will differ little from the AGI.

MEDICARE – OVERVIEW

SERVICE OR PRODUCT	PART A	PART B	MEDIGAP	PART C	PART D
Hospitalization	✓		Copays, coinsurance, deductibles	✓	
Nursing homes	✓		"	✓	
Home care			"	✓	
Hospice	✓ palliative care drugs		"		✓ drugs for treatment
Devices		✓	"	✓	✓ drug-device combos
Drugs	✓ inpatient	✓ administered	"	✓ optional	✓ outpatient
Mental health	*	✓	"		
Office visits		✓	"		
Surgeries		✓	"		
Care outside US			✓		
Dental care	X	X	X	X	X
Glasses	X	X	X	X	X
Acupuncture	X	X	X	X	X
Hearing aids	X	X	X	X	X
Foot care	X	X	X	X	X

*Mental health inpatient care or partial hospitalization are covered under Part B, not Part A.

Medicare is a federal system of health care for the elderly, and certain other permanently disabled persons. The Medicare legislation is part of the Social Security Act, and the program is administered by CMS. The SSA was first enacted in 1935, and did not cover medical care. Title XVIII of the SSA, "Health Insurance for the Aged," was enacted in 1965, to provide health care coverage to complement existing Social Security provisions for retirement and survivors. Benefits were added in 1973 for disability insurance beneficiaries. Medicare is now a four-part program.

IRMAAS – Individuals who are eligible for Medicare but who have MAGIs of more than $85,000 (or $170,000 for a couple filing jointly) are assessed additional premiums known as IRMAAs, or income-related monthly adjustment amounts for Part B, C, and D plans. The adjustments are based on MAGIs from 2 years prior, so 2017 incomes are used to determine IRMAAS for 2019.

PART A – HOSPITALIZATION. Pays for care provided to SSA beneficiaries in hospitals, skilled nursing facilities (SNFs), hospices, and home health care programs. Eligibility is automatic for citizens of the US if they or their spouse worked for 10 years in Medicare-covered employment and they are 65 years of age or older. As of November 2018, 60.1 million persons were enrolled in Medicare.

No premium is charged for persons 65 or older if they are receiving or eligible to receive Old-Age, Survivors and Disability Insurance (OASDI) or Railroad Retirement (RR) benefits, or had Medicare-covered government employment.

- A premium may be paid to purchase Part A coverage for persons 65 or older who do not meet these requirements ("uninsured aged") which is reduced for individuals who have accrued 30 quarters of qualifying covered employment. For 2017, the monthly premium maximum is $413.
- Persons under age 65 who have received OASDI or RR benefits for 24 months are eligible for Part A without a premium; persons with amyotrophic lateral sclerosis (ALS) may waive the 24-month waiting period.
- Persons with end-stage renal disease (ESRD) who require kidney dialysis or renal transplant may enroll in Part A without a premium.
- Part A benefits are limited to a "benefit period," which begins when the beneficiary first enters a hospital, and ends with a break of at least 60 consecutive days since inpatient hospital or SNF care was provided. There is no limit on the number of benefit periods that will be covered for a particular beneficiary during his or her life, but there is a limit on the number of days of care that are paid for during a single benefit period.
  - Inpatient hospitalization – 90 days of care per benefit period, with an up-front deductible, and with co-pays required from days 61 through 90. A lifetime reserve of 60 days can be drawn upon, again with co-pays. In 2019, the up-front deductible is $1,364, and co-pays are $322 per day or $644 per day if reserve days are used.
  - Mental health inpatient stay – lifetime limit of 190 days. Co-insurance payments are the same as for inpatient hospitalization.
  - SNF care – 100 days of care per benefit period. Generally, care must start within 30 days of a hospitalization of 3 days or more. No deductible is charged, and 20 days of SNF care are fully covered per each benefit period, with co-pays for days 21-100 per benefit period. In 2019, the co-pay is $161 per day.
  - Home health care – there is no deductible or coinsurance payment for home health care services covered under Part A; Part A pays for DME during this period of home care with a 20% deductible.
  - Hospice care – No cost for hospice care, with a copayment of up to $5 per prescription for outpatient prescription drugs for pain and symptom management, if not otherwise covered under Part D. There is 5% copay for inpatient respite care, which may range from $5 to $12 per day.

PART B – MEDICAL INSURANCE. Part B pays for physicians' services, outpatient hospital care, and other services not covered under Part A. It also covers home health care services not associated with a prior hospitalization or SNF care. Enrollment is voluntary, and requires a monthly premium. Persons eligible to purchase Part A may also purchase Part B, even if they do not participate in Part A, Almost all persons entitled to Part A choose Part B as well.

Among its other coverages, Part B pays for approved DME for home use, such as respiratory care, oxygen, prostheses, mobility aids, surgical dressings, and braces. It also pays for injectable drugs that are not normally self-administered (e.g., vaccines, immunosuppressive drugs) and certain self-administered oncology drugs. It pays for drugs that are administered by approved devices (e.g., bronchodilators administered by nebulizer, but not MDI). It also pays for certain services and supplies to patients with diabetes.

To be covered, services must be one of several enumerated preventive benefits, or must be medically necessary. Documentation of the medical need must be retained by the provider of the service.

Certain services are subject to special payment rules, including deductibles (for blood), maximum approved amounts (for non-hospital based PT, OT, or speech therapy), or higher cost-sharing levels (e.g., outpatient treatment of mental illness).

COST-SHARING UNDER PART B INCLUDES:

- One annual deductible ($185 in 2019)
- 20% co-insurance for most services (based on remaining allowed charges)
- A deductible for blood
- Patient pays in full for non-covered services.
- 20% co-pay for outpatient mental health services.

PREMIUMS FOR 2019 PER PERSON ARE AS FOLLOWS

ANNUAL INCOME – INDIVIDUAL*	ANNUAL INCOME – JOINT FILERS	PREMIUM WITH IRMAA	2019 IRMAA
< $85,000	< $170,000	$135.50 per month	$0.00
$85,001 - $107,000	$170,001 - $214,000	$189.60 per month	$54.10
$107,001 - $133,500	$214,001 - $267,000	$270.90 per month	$135.40
$133,5001 – $160,000	$267,001 - $320,000	$352.20 per month	$216.70
$160,001 - $500,000	$320,001 - $750,000	$433.40 per month	$297.90
> $500,000	> $750,000	$428.60 per month	$325.00

*Modified Adjusted Gross Income (MAGI) from 2 years prior. Incomes used are from 2017.

** Higher rates reflect IRMAAs

PART C – MEDICARE ADVANTAGE

The original approach to Medicare is called the "fee-for-service" (FFS) program or "original Medicare," in which individual providers are paid a fee for allowable services provided to Medicare patients. Part C allows participants in both Part A and Part B to receive their care from organizations that will provide Part A and B services as a package of benefits. Enrollees may pay their Part B premium plus an additional MA premium. Some plans charge no premiums for Part D or for the MA plan. Most MA plans include Medicare Part D benefits within their programs. Four major types of Part C providers currently are available:

- HEALTH MAINTENANCE ORGANIZATION (HMO) plans
- PREFERRED PROVIDER ORGANIZATION (PPO) plans
- SPECIAL NEEDS PLANS (SNP), which are tailored to patients with specific conditions or circumstances. They include Chronic Condition SNPs (C-SNPs) for severe or disabling chronic conditions such as cancer, dementia, diabetes, HIV/AIDS, or neurologic disorders, Institutional Special Needs Plans (I-SNPs) for institutionalized patients, or Dual Eligible Special Needs Plans (D-SNPs) for patients who are eligible for both Medicaid and Medicare.
- PRIVATE, UNRESTRICTED FFS (PFFS) PLANS, which allow beneficiaries to select certain participating private providers. These plans have an advantage for participating providers in that, as long as they accept the plan's payment terms and conditions, they are not at risk, nor do their payment rates vary based on utilization.

Medicare Advantage Plans available in Spokane in 2019 have premiums (in addition to the Medicare Part B premium) from $0 to $238 per person per month.

PART D – OUTPATIENT PRESCRIPTION DRUGS

Drugs ordered or administered in inpatient settings or physicians' offices have long been covered under Part A and/or Part B. Starting in 2006, Medicare Part D provided subsidized access to outpatient prescription drug insurance for individuals entitled to Part A or enrolled in Part B. Two types of offerings are available: stand-alone prescription drug plan (PDP) or a Medicare Advantage Plan that offers prescription coverage (Advantage-D plan). Additional detail on Medicare Part D is found in the next section. Approximately 42 million people enrolled in Part D in 2016. While enrollment is voluntary, delayed enrollment (i.e., after a person becomes first eligible for Medicare) is associated with a late enrollment penalty that increases the minimum premium by 1% of the national base premium per month of delay. For example, a person who enrolls in Part D 2 years after eligibility, and did not have equivalent coverage from another source during the delay, would be subject to monthly minimum additional premium of 24% of the 2019 national premium base of $33.19, or

$$24 \times 0.01 \times \$33.19 = \$7.97 \text{ per month}$$

Higher income beneficiaries will pay an IRMAA of from $70.90 to $77.40 per month in addition to the plan premium.

MEDIGAP INSURANCE POLICIES.[639] The payment limits and service restrictions under Part A, and co-pays under Part B have led to the development of private insurance offerings (also called Medicare Supplement Insurance) that fill in "gaps" in Medicare Part A and B (but not Medicare Advantage) plans. In most states, insurance companies can only issue a "standardized" Medigap policy, with variable benefits according type of plan. The plan types are labeled A through N. Plan type F has a "high-deductible" option. Some types available prior to 2012 (E, H, I, and J) are not available for new enrollees. Within a type of plan, the only major variable across insurance providers is the plan premium. State and federal laws restrict Medigap policies, among other rules:

- The policy must clearly identify it as "Medicare Supplement Insurance."
- It can only cover one person, so a husband and wife must each purchase their own policy.
- All plans cover Part A coinsurance and other uncovered items related to hospitalization, and all plans cover preventive care coinsurance. All plans cover all or at least half of Part B coinsurance or

copayments. Plan F covers virtually all coinsurance, deductibles, or co-pays. Plans C, D, F, G, J, M, and N pay 80% of charges for medically necessary care outside the US.

- Medigap insurance has guaranteed renewability, and patients have a guarantee of being able to purchase Medigap insurance if:
  - It is during a Medigap open enrollment period (6 months from a person's 65th birthday), or
  - The patient has "guaranteed issue rights," primarily because of the type of plan he or she is already enrolled in.

Typical monthly premiums for Medigap type F policies available in Washington range from $204 to $278, depending on the sponsoring insurance company.

MEDICARE MEDICAL SAVINGS ACCOUNT. Medicare MSA plans are a form of Medicare Advantage Plans that are consumer-directed, and are combined with a Medical Savings Account that is similar to Health Savings Accounts (HSAs) offered outside of Medicare. They provide health coverage similar to other Medicare Advantage Plans, except they do not cover Part D drugs. There is no premium for the MSAs, but beneficiaries do have to continue Part B premiums. MSA participants are not eligible to purchase Medigap policies. Persons covered by other insurance or Medicare plan are not eligible for MSAs.

Two important elements vary by plan and are key to making a decision to enroll:

- High deductibles. The plans feature a high deductible before Medicare-covered services are provided.
- Contribution to MSA. Medicare deposits a specified amount into the MSA at the beginning of the plan year; this amount also varies by plan.

Any health care costs that would be payable from a HSA or a Health Care Flexible Spending account may be paid from an MSA. However, only Medicare-eligible expenses count towards fulfilling the deductible.

Participants may not contribute funds to their MSA.

Funds remaining at the end of a plan year carry forward.

MSA participants may generally not spend more than 160 days per year living outside the MSA's coverage area.

RETIREES WITH CONTINUING EMPLOYER-PROVIDED COVERAGE are not required to enroll in Medicare Part D if their continuing coverage provides at least equivalent coverage to Medicare. Retiree insurance plans typically deal with Part A and Part B covered services as if Medicare is the primary payer, and the retiree insurance pays the remaining amount. A Medigap plan is typically not needed with retiree insurance.

SERVICES NOT COVERED BY MEDICARE. No part of Medicare provides coverage for certain services, including long-term nursing care, custodial care, dentures and dental care, eyeglasses, hearing aids, or routine foot care. Some of these services may be provided by a Medicare Advantage plan, but most, such as dental coverage, will require a separate monthly premium (the premium for one dental insurance plan available in Spokane for a person > 65, with coverage similar to that provided for state employees, ranges from $50 to $60 per month per person.)

PAYMENTS TO PROVIDERS. In general, the original Medicare plan is a fee-for-service plan where individual providers submit claims to Medicare for services rendered. Some of the Medicare Advantage plans reimburse providers on a FFS basis as well.

PART A. Payments to hospitals are based on a prospective payment system (PPS). Acute inpatient admissions are categorized by diagnosis-related group (DRG), and each DRG has a predetermined payment amount, which is the basis for payment. Certain adjustments may be made to the DRG's predetermine rate, but in the long run, the hospital is expected to make a profit on some admissions for a given DRG and lose on others. If the hospital is able to reduce its costs per DRG, then it will theoretically profit in the long run. Separately developed PPSs are used for SNFs, home health care, inpatient rehabilitation care, long-term care hospitals, and hospice. The pharmacy department's contribution to reducing length of stay and complications of care for a given DRG are essential to a hospital's financial success under a PPS.

PART B. Physicians and other primary care providers are reimbursed on the basis of allowable charges, which are the lesser of the submitted charges, or the amount determined by a fee schedule based on a relative value scale (RVS). Coverage for Durable Medical Equipment, Prosthetics, Orthotics, and Supplies (DMEPOS) is in Part B. Payments for DME and laboratory services are based on a fee schedule. Hospital outpatient services are reimbursed on a PPS, as is home health care. The HCPCS coding system described above is used to describe the services provided.

ACCEPTING ASSIGNMENT. If the provider agrees to accept the Medicare-approved rate as payment in full, this is called "taking assignment." The provider may not take any additional payments (aside from annual deductible and coinsurance) from the beneficiary or insurer. If the provider does not take assignment, then the beneficiary (or the Medigap insurer) will be charged for the excess, up to limits imposed by law. Physicians are "participating physicians" if they agree at the beginning of the year to take assignment for all Medicare services they provide during the year.

DME PROVIDERS MUST BE ACCREDITED. Suppliers of durable medical equipment, prosthetics, orthotics and supplies (DMEPOS) generally must meet accreditation requirements to be eligible for reimbursement from Medicare or Medicaid. Pharmacies are exempted from these requirements if they meet all of the following requirements:

- Total billings of DMEPOS to CMS are less than 5% of total pharmacy sales;
- The pharmacy has been enrolled as a DMEPOS prior to 2010 and has been issued a provider number for at least 5 years;
- No final adverse action has been taken by CMS against the pharmacy for the past 5 years;
- The pharmacy submits an attestation to CMS that it meets the first 3 criteria; and
- The pharmacy agrees to submit requested materials during the course of audits conducted in a random sample of pharmacies each year.[640]

PART C. Medicaid Advantage plans are paid on a capitation basis (a certain amount per beneficiary per month), but may pay contracting providers according to a FFS basis using their own rates.

PART D. PDPs and the prescription drug portions of the Advantage-D plans are reimbursed on a per enrollee per month basis based on a complex set of rules and the plan's "risk-adjusted" bid to CMS. Individual providers, such as pharmacies, who contract with a given PDP are reimbursed according to the contract rates agreed to between the pharmacy and the plan.

MEDICARE PART D IN GREATER DETAIL

CHOICE OF PROVIDERS. As noted above, Part D enrollees may purchase Part D coverage from PDPs or Medicare Advantage plans that are available in their area.

BASIC BENEFIT DESIGN. The Medicare Part D legislation established basic benefits, but individual plans may offer an alternated benefit design that provides the same actuarial benefit as the standard design. The basic design covers most FDA-approved drugs and biological, except for drugs covered under Parts A or B. Note in particular that the drugs must be FDA-approved in order to be covered. The deductible, co-pay, and limits are recalculated by CMS annually. For 2019, the following benefits are available under the basic design:

- $0 to $415 initial deductible
- For each covered prescription, beneficiary pays a plan-specified co-payment or percentage of the remaining cost, based on a price calculated by the plan. For a given plan, the price will be the same at all participating pharmacies.
- There is an initial coverage limit of $3,820 in total costs, which includes plan payments and co-payments.
- The patient then pays 25% of costs for brand name drugs and 37% of costs for generics until his or her total out-of-pocket expenses reach $5,100. This gap in coverage has been called the "donut hole." Calculation of the patient's actual out-of-pocket expenses is established by Medicare Part D rules, and the resulting measure is called the beneficiary's True Out of Pocket Expenses, or TrOOP. An amount equal to 95% of the cost of brand name drugs (25% paid by patients and 70% paid by manufacturers) will be allocated towards TrOOP. Note that the pharmacy's dispensing fee does not count towards TrOOP.
- The generic cost proportion will decline annually until the patient generic copay is 25%
- Some plans provide additional coverage during the coverage gap, which can be applied toward the patient's TrOOP.
- Once the TrOOP limit is reached, for the rest of the remaining year the catastrophic coverage provisions come into play, and the patient pays the greatest of 5% coinsurance or a defined copayment set at $8.50 for non-preferred drugs or $3.40 for generic/preferred drug.

DRUGS NOT COVERED IN STANDARD PLAN. The following drugs or indications are *not* covered by standard plans, but may be covered by plans using alternate designs:

- Anorexia, weight loss, or weight gain
- Fertility promotion
- Hair growth
- Symptomatic relief of cough and colds
- Prescription vitamins and minerals (except prenatal vitamins and fluoride)
- Nonprescription drugs
- Outpatient drugs for which the manufacturer seeks to require that associated tests or monitoring services be purchased exclusively from the manufacturer or its designee as a condition of sale
- Any drug covered by Part A or Part B
- Drugs or indications not approved by the FDA, however, non-approved indications (other than those listed above) for approved drugs will be covered if the indication is supported by one or more citations in at least one of the following compendia:
    - AHFS Drug Information
    - USP-DI
    - DRUGDEX Information System

All plans, including those with alternate designs, must ensure that drugs are used for medically acceptable indications.

ALTERNATE DESIGNS. The majority of patients have enrolled in Part D plans with low or no deductibles, flat payments for covered drugs, and/or partial coverage in the donut hole. Choosing among available plans is one of the challenges facing the elderly, and the opportunity to change plans occurs annually.

LOW INCOME MEDICARE BENEFICIARIES are eligible for reduced cost-sharing, and if otherwise qualified for Medicaid, may have Medicaid coverage, but Medicaid will not pay for covered drugs; rather, individuals receive a low-income subsidy (LIS) for their Part D premium. (See dual-eligible patients, below.)

MEDICATION THERAPY MANAGEMENT (MTM). All Part D plans are required to provide for MTM services as an effort to reduce total Medicare costs for patients with multiple chronic diseases (MCDs), multiple Part D drugs (MPD), and the likelihood of incurring high annual costs. These services may be performed in a variety of ways, and plans may reimburse pharmacists for performing them. (See above.)

PHARMACIST REFERENCE GUIDES. CMS provides a variety of Medicare resources specifically for pharmacists, in the CMS Pharmacy Center (https://www.cms.gov/Center/Provider-Type/Pharmacist-Center.html).

ASSISTING PATIENTS IN SELECTING A PLAN.

THE OFFICIAL CMS MEDICARE WEBSITE FOR PATIENTS IS WWW.MEDICARE.GOV. CMS provides a plan finder tool on their website.[641] Pharmacists may assist patients in using any unbiased plan finder tool, but may not steer the patient toward a plan that may be economically preferable to the pharmacy.

PHARMACIES MUST INFORM BENEFICIARIES ABOUT GENERICS. Plans must ensure that pharmacy staff members inform beneficiaries of any price differential between a covered Part D drug and the lowest priced generic version of that drug that is available under the plan at the pharmacy. Pharmacy staff must provide this information at the time the beneficiary purchases the drug, or in the case of drugs purchased from mail service pharmacies, at the time of delivery.

PHARMACISTS MAY WAIVE PATIENT CO-PAYS UNDER CERTAIN CIRCUMSTANCES. The Medicare Part D legislation modified the Anti-kickback statute to allow pharmacies to waive or reduce cost-sharing amounts provided they do so in an unadvertised, non-routine manner after determining that the beneficiary in question is financially needy or after failing to collect the cost-sharing amount despite reasonable efforts. Pharmacies may also waive or reduce a LIS beneficiary's co-pay or cost sharing amount without determining the patient is financially needy or attempting to collect the cost-sharing amount. However, they cannot in any way advertise the provision of the waiver or cost-sharing reduction. As long as pharmacies follow these procedures, the waived amounts can still count toward the beneficiary's TrOOP.

REQUIRED NOTICE TO PATIENTS ABOUT THEIR RIGHTS. Plans must distribute the following or equivalent notice to participating pharmacies, to make available to enrollees. A pharmacy is required to provide the notice when the patient's plan denies a prescribed drug at the point of sale. The pharmacy is expected to provide the patient with the information necessary to submit the coverage determination request. The notice is not required for a list of specific scenarios that may be found in Chapter 18 of the Part D Manual,[642] where the appropriate NCPDP rejection code is not communicated at the point of sale:

- Claims rejected only because they lacks all the necessary data elements;
- Claims for an OTC drug not covered by the plan sponsor;

- Claim is for a prescription written by a sanctioned provider who has been excluded from participation in federal health care programs;
- Claims for drugs not listed on the participating CMS Manufacturer Labeler Code List;
- Claims for drugs not listed in FDA electronic drug file;
- Claims rejected for "refill too soon/early refill" edit;
- Claims for drugs not covered by Part D benefit, but covered by a co-administered benefit managed by a single processor.

Medicare Prescription Drug Coverage and Your Rights

YOUR MEDICARE RIGHTS

You **have the right to request a coverage determination** from your Medicare drug plan if you disagree with information provided by the pharmacy. You also **have the right to request a special type of coverage determination called an "exception"** if you believe:

- you need a drug that is not on your drug plan's list of covered drugs. The list of covered drugs is called a "formulary;"
- a coverage rule (such as prior authorization or a quantity limit) should not apply to you for medical reasons; or
- you need to take a non-preferred drug and you want the plan to cover the drug at a preferred drug price.

WHAT YOU NEED TO DO

You or your prescriber can contact your Medicare drug plan to ask for a coverage determination by calling the plan's toll-free phone number on the back of your plan membership card, or by going to your plan's website. You or your prescriber can request an expedited (24 hour) decision if your health could be seriously harmed by waiting up to 72 hours for a decision. Be ready to tell your Medicare drug plan:

1. The name of the prescription drug that was not filled. Include the dose and strength, if known.
2. The name of the pharmacy that attempted to fill your prescription.
3. The date you attempted to fill your prescription.
4. If you ask for an exception, your prescriber will need to provide your drug plan with a statement explaining why you need the off-formulary or non-preferred drug or why a coverage rule should not apply to you.

Your Medicare drug plan will provide you with a written decision. If coverage is not approved, the plan's notice will explain why coverage was denied and how to request an appeal if you disagree with the plan's decision.

MEDICAID -- OVERVIEW

The 1965 Social Security Amendments established a second federally-funded health care program in Title XIX, called "Grants to the States for Medical Assistance Programs." It is more commonly known as Medicaid. Under the plan, states would continue to provide medical assistance for low income persons, but the federal government would share in the costs. One commentator has suggested that Medicaid may have been considered a "stopgap" piece of legislation, because it was widely expected that if Lyndon Johnson or Hubert Humphrey were elected to the Presidency in 1968, then a national health care system would shortly follow.[643] By 2016, Medicaid and CHIP provided some form of coverage or assistance to 73 million Americans, or about 1 in 5 individuals. On January 1, 2014, the Affordable Care Act allowed states to expand their coverage to individuals and families earning 138% of the federal poverty level, and if every state did so, another 10 million individuals would have been covered. As of January 2017, 32 states have adopted the expansion.[644]

FEDERAL MATCHING FUNDS FOR OPERATION OF MEDICAID PROGRAMS. The federal government provides grants to the states that fund the majority of Medicaid costs, with the states required to provide a percentage of the funding. The funding for the pre-expansion Medicaid program is according to a Federal Medical Assistance Percentage (FMAP) that varies by state. For Children's Health Insurance Programs (CHIPs), a slightly different matching percentage, known as the "enhanced" FMAP, or eFMAP, is used.

For 2019, the FMAP for Washington is 50% and the eFMAP is 88%.

The net impact on the state budget in terms of federal reimbursement is relative to the percentage of state citizens enrolled in traditional Medicaid versus CHIP. In 2016, total federal and state spending in Washington for Medicaid and CHIP was $10.9 billion; 38.3% was paid by the state and 61.7% by federal funds. Thus the state received about $1.60 from the federal government for every $1 dollar it spends on traditional Medicaid.

The care for citizens covered by Medicaid expansion in Washington will be funded 88% by the federal government in 2019.

WASHINGTON MEDICAID

The majority of existing Medicaid programs, including the Children's Health Insurance Program (CHIP), are now merged into a program called the APPLE HEALTH Plan, which is Washington's brand name for Medicaid and CHIP. Most beneficiaries are covered by the Apple Health Managed Care program, which, from a pharmacy perspective, operates like other PBM-managed programs. Certain beneficiaries, particularly Medicare-Medicaid dual-eligible beneficiaries, including aged, blind, or disabled individuals, children in foster care, and individuals receiving supplemental security income (SSI) (administered by DSHS), are covered by the Apple Health Fee-For-Service (FFS), or "classic Medicaid" system, with pharmacies submitting claims directly to the HCA via the "Provider One" POS system.

Certain services, such as treatment of chronic HCV infection, are also excluded from managed care and are handled through the FFS system.

A single portal, the Washington Health Plan Finder (www.wahealthplanfinder.org) is available for all citizens to determine if they are eligible for Apple Health or assistance with an insurance plan from the Washington State Health Benefit Exchange.

FEDERAL RULES GOVERNING STATE OPTIONS.
States administer Medicaid programs under broad federal regulation. In Washington, Medicaid is administered by the Washington State Health Care Authority in coordination with the Department of Social and Health Services. Washington's Medicaid program is part of Washington Apple Health. In order to be eligible for federal Medicaid matching funds, each state must have in place a CMS-approved State Plan or an approved State Plan Amendment allowing changes since the first plan was approved.

MANDATORY BENEFITS
Every state *must* provide at least the following benefits:

- Inpatient and outpatient hospital services
- Services by physicians and clinical laboratories
- Nursing home care
- Home health care

OPTIONAL BENEFITS. States have fairly broad authority to administer the program and determine its scope. Some of the more common options adopted by states are:

PRESCRIPTION DRUGS – all states provide for categorically needy; more than half cover prescription drug for all recipients. If a state provides prescription drug coverage to any group of enrollees, it must cover:

- All FDA-approved prescription drugs marketed by drug manufacturers who have entered into a rebate agreement with the Secretary of Health & Human Services;
- All additional FDA-approved drugs that are on the state-developed Medicaid formulary;
- Any non-formulary FDA-approved prescription drug that is specifically requested and approved through a prior authorization process.

Notwithstanding the above, states *may* exclude the 9 categories of drugs that are also excluded from the standard prescription drug plan under Medicare Part D (see above). Note, however, that Washington does cover several of the optional 9 categories (e.g., cough and cold, smoking cessation).

DENTAL COVERAGE
States may seek federal waivers to allow them to provide benefits and cover groups that would otherwise be excluded under Medicaid.

FEE-FOR-SERVICE OR MANAGED CARE. Medicaid recipients may be covered under traditional FFS programs, or may be required or encouraged to participate in a managed care organization. In the latter case, the MCO is paid a fixed monthly payment; federal law allows deviations from the normal formulary requirements, but most states enforce the basic coverage requirements in their contracts with MCOs.

APPLE HEALTH managed care plans offer the following choices in 2019, based in part on the individual's county of residence:

- *AMERIGROUP (AMG).* Amerigroup is a national plan which is owned by WellPoint. Pharmacy services are provided by network pharmacies contracted with Caremark. The plan encourages members to utilize the same pharmacy every time.
- *COMMUNITY HEALTH PLAN OF WASHINGTON (CHPW).* CHPW is a non-profit health plan founded by the federally-qualified community health centers in Washington. The pharmacy network is operated by Express Scripts, Inc. CHPW has specific provisions for payments to qualified pharmacy providers of medication therapy management services, when the provider is "working with the member's primary

care team to coordinate therapeutic goals, medication recommendations, and provide ongoing monitoring of implementation and results. Collaboration with the member's primary care team ... is a requirement for reimbursement." CHPW pays for covered MTM services according to the RBRVS schedule established by the Health Care Authority (see above).

- *COORDINATED CARE CORPORATION (CCC).* Based in Tacoma, CCC uses network pharmacies that have contracted with US Script, a PBM that is a subdivision of Centene with headquarters in Fresno, CA.
- *MOLINA HEALTH CARE OF WASHINGTON, INC. (MHC).* Part of a national plan, MHC uses CVS/Caremark as its PBM.
- *UNITEDHEALTHCARE COMMUNITY PLAN (UHC).* The plan's PBM is Optum Rx, headquartered in San Diego.

APPLE HEALTH FFS clients are in a fee-for-service plan and pharmacies bill HCA directly through the "ProviderOne" system.

PROVIDER REQUIREMENTS FOR PARTICIPATION

- Properly licensed
- Have a signed core provider agreement (CPA)
- Follow guidelines in billing instructions and applicable WACs
- Retain documentation that all other possible payers have been billed appropriately
- Participating pharmacies may be required to
- Obtain authorization on a drug or product
- Ascertain and document that certain diagnosis requirements are met
- Meet other requirements for client safety and program management.

BILLING FOR PHARMACY SERVICES. Patients covered under Apple Health will have a ProviderOne Services Card, or may be identified by using the ProviderOne system. Pharmacies must be contracted with the network serving the managed care system in which the patient is enrolled, unless the patient is in the classic (FFS) system.

PATIENTS IN MANAGED CARE PLANS. The pharmacy bills prescriptions to the patient's managed care plan. If the prescription or service is not covered by the plan, but is otherwise eligible for coverage by Apple Health, then the FFS system may be billed.

PATIENTS IN FFS PROGRAM. The pharmacy follows the rules in the Health Care Authority's Guide to the Prescription Drug program, which, along with other important information is found on the HCA's Pharmacy Information page: http://www.hca.wa.gov/medicaid/pharmacy/pages/index.aspx

WASHINGTON HEALTH BENEFIT EXCHANGE

Washington has opted to operate its own insurance exchange under the ACA, which is found at www.healtplanfinder.org. Qualified health plans (QHPs) may enter the exchange and provide benefits for individuals, families, or small businesses, who may receive tax credits or other financial help to pay for premiums or copays, depending upon income or business size. Individuals or families with existing employer-provided plans are not eligible for the exchange.

INDIVIDUALS AND FAMILIES who do not qualify for Apple Health may receive tax credits to help them pay for a QHP. Note that these are tax credits which are recovered at the time that the individual or family files its annual form 1040 with the IRS. Families with annual incomes between 138% and 250% of the FPL may also qualify for cost sharing subsidies if they buy a Silver plan. In 2019, a family of 4 in Washington is at 250% of the FPL if its income is $64,375 or less.

Actual premiums depend on which of 3 plan levels (Bronze, Silver, or Gold) is selected. The premium is linked to income, as are the tax credits.

SMALL BUSINESSES are eligible for tax credits if they have fewer than 25 FTE employees, pay an average wage of less than $50,000 per year, and pay at least half of employee health insurance premiums.

The maximum credit is 50% of premiums paid for small business employers and 35% of premiums paid for small tax-exempt employers. The credit will be available to an individual employer for a total of any 2 taxable years.

LABOR AND INDUSTRIES

The Department of Labor and Industries administers a program to compensate injured workers in covered industries, and will pay for medical care for job-related injuries. Because these are state funds, all of the normal state laws concerning accountability and fraud are in operation, as they are for Medicaid. Participating pharmacies may fill prescriptions written by physicians or other prescribers only if the prescriber is also a participating L&I provider.

ELIGIBLE PATIENTS are those who are covered by an approved and open Labor and Industries State Fund (SF) claim. Upon initial injury, a worker completes a Report of Accident (ROA) and obtains an examination, diagnosis, and initial treatment from a participating physician. The ROA contains a Claim ID number and a Claim ID card. Upon review by L&I of the ROA and physician's report, the claim is approved or denied.

CRIME VICTIMS. L&I also administers a medical care program for Crime Victims. Participating pharmacies may provide covered services to these patients as well, under the same rules.

PATIENT RESPONSIBLE FOR ULTIMATE PAYMENT

Pharmacies may bill L&I according to its rules if they have a claim number, but if the claim is later denied, they must seek to recover from the patient.

FIRST FILLS. However, L&I guarantees to pay for the first fill of prescriptions issued during the initial visit for any new claim.

- Pharmacists must verify the claim ID using the L&I POS system, or actually see a copy of the ROA or Claim ID card. (It's advisable to make a copy for the pharmacy records.)
- L&I will not pay for any refills or additional prescriptions until claim is approved.
- L&I will not pay if it is a federal claim or a self-insured claim, but pharmacies can submit the bill to the proper insurer. Self-insured claim numbers begin with S, T, or W.

COVERED DRUGS. Drugs must be on the L&I Formulary, or approved by prior authorization.

The provisions of the Preferred Drug List apply to L&I prescriptions.

Specific control policies exist for certain drugs that are frequently misused in the workman's compensation arena. In particular, L&I will not pay for prescriptions for carisoprodol or oral fentanyl products. Other specific control policies[645] are listed on the L&I website.

BILLING FOR SERVICES. Claims may be submitted in 3 ways:

- POS system
- Paper form
- Using 3rd party billers. A specific agreement with L&I is necessary.

L&I FEE SCHEDULE FOR PHARMACIES:

GENERICS	AWP – 50%, plus $4.50 fee
SINGLE SOURCE BRAND	AWP – 10%, plus $4.50 fee
BRAND NAME DRUG INSTEAD OF GENERIC EQUIVALENT (DISPENSE AS WRITTEN)	AWP – 10%, plus $4.00 fee
COMPOUNDED DRUGS	AWP – 10%, plus $4.00/15 minutes compounding fee, plus $4.50 fee. Prior authorization required.
COVERED OTC DRUGS WRITTEN ON RX – THESE ARE NOT SUBJECT TO SALES TAX.	40% margin (i.e., $\boldsymbol{AWP \div 0.6}$)

340B PRICING OF PHARMACEUTICALS

The federal government purchases drugs for the military and the VA at significant discounts. Under 1992 amendments to the Public Health Service Act, which became Section 340B of that act, manufacturers who participate in Medicaid must also participate in a program that sells drugs to qualified entities at the federal price. Drugs purchased under this program are called "340B drugs." The pricing schedule for these drugs may also be called "PHS pricing" or "602 pricing." The program is administrated by the Health Resources and Services Administration (HRSA). HRSA maintains a 340B website for pharmacists at http://www.hrsa.gov/opa.

THE 340B PRICE is a ceiling price, or the highest price that may be charged to a qualified entity. CMS determines and updates the 340B pricing schedule quarterly, using a formula designed to set the price at least as low as what Medicaid would pay after manufacturer rebates. 340B prices are typically 50% lower than AWP.

A NATIONAL PRIME VENDOR is the single "preferred" wholesaler that serves 340B covered entities, provides value added services, and attempts to negotiate sub-340B prices with manufacturers based on volume. The current prime vendor manager is Apexus, and the three major national wholesalers (AmerisourceBergen, Cardinal Health, and McKesson Pharmaceuticals) serve as distributors, along with numerous regional or specialty distributors.

340B-QUALIFIED ENTITIES include the following:

- FEDERALLY-QUALIFIED HEALTH CENTERS (FHQCS) are community-based health care providers that provide health care for underserved areas, and which may take the form of
  - Community health centers
  - Migrant health centers
  - Health care for the homeless
  - Health centers for residents of public housing
- FHQC LOOK-ALIKES provide care to underserved areas and meet the requirements of the HRSA Health Center Program, but do not receive HCP funding. These may include
  - Consolidated Health Centers
  - Health Schools/Health Communities
  - A family planning project receiving certain federal grants
- NATIVE HAWAIIAN HEALTH CENTERS
- OFFICE OF TRIBAL PROGRAMS OR URBAN INDIAN organizations
- RYAN WHITE ACT for Early HIV Intervention Services grantees
- A state-operated AIDS DRUG ASSISTANCE PROGRAM
- A BLACK LUNG CLINIC receiving certain federal funds
- A comprehensive HEMOPHILIA DIAGNOSTIC CENTER receiving certain federal grants
- Certain entities certified by the Secretary receiving funds for treatment of STDS OR TUBERCULOSIS
- A "DISPROPORTIONATE SHARE" HOSPITAL
- Certain CHILDREN'S HOSPITALS
- FREE-STANDING CANCER hospitals
- CRITICAL ACCESS hospitals
- RURAL REFERRAL centers
- SOLE COMMUNITY hospitals

QUALIFIED PATIENTS are any patient of a 340B entity if the entity maintains control of the patient's medical records and has primary responsibility for the patient's care.

PHARMACY SERVICES CONTRACT. 340B entities may contract with a local pharmacy to provide services and dispense 340B drugs to their patients. This allows the entity to avoid the startup and ongoing costs associated with maintaining its own in-house pharmacy.

- The entity must have an agreement with the pharmacy that meets the elements outlined in the Contract Pharmacy Services Model Agreement.[646]
- The covered entity will order the drugs from the distributor, arrange to be billed directly for the drugs, and arrange to have the drugs shipped to the pharmacy.
- The covered entity will use the pharmacy's business records to verify that a tracking system exists to assure that 340B drugs are not diverted to individuals who are not patients of the covered entity.
- The entity will have opportunity to inspect the tracking system prior to start of services.

- The contract pharmacy will dispense covered drugs only upon presentation of a prescription from the entity indicating that the patient is eligible for 340B drugs
- The covered entity must certify to the PHS Office of Pharmacy Affairs that they have signed an agreement with the pharmacy.

REFERENCES

[574] *Northern California Pharmaceutical Association v. United States*, 306 F.2d 379 (9th Cir. 1962)
[575] *United States v Utah Pharmaceutical Association*, 201 F.Supp. 29 (D. Utah 1962)
[576] *Ambach et vir. v French, et ux. et al.*, Case No. 24784-8-III, Wn. App. Div. III, November 27, 2007.
[577] 2009 c 175; RCW 48.155; WAC 284-38-005
[578] Akers J. Should I sign this contract? Contract law and case examples. New Drugs, New Laws 2015, Washington State Pharmacy Association, Seattle, WA, 2015 Mar 1.
[579] http://www.pharmacistsprovidecare.com/article/provider-status-legislation-reintroduced-us-house-representatives
[580] WSDOH, Rural Health, Health Professional Shortage Areas; http://www.doh.wa.gov/ForPublicHealthandHealthcareProviders/RuralHealth/DataandOtherResources/HealthProfessionalShortageAreas
[581] WSDOH, Rural Health, Medically Underserved Area Designations; http://www.doh.wa.gov/ForPublicHealthandHealthcareProviders/RuralHealth/DataandOtherResources/MedicallyUnderservedAreaDesignations
[582] KRSA § 304.17A-270
[583] Kentucky Association of Health Plans v Miller, 123 S Ct 1471, 155 L Ed 2d 468 (2003)
[584] Steele JS, Assistant Attorney General of Washington, Letter to Hon. Linda Evans Parlette et al., January 22, 2013.
[585] 2015 c 237; RCW 48.43.094
[586] https://www.insurance.wa.gov/about-oic/reports/commissioner-reports/documents/onehealthport-report-on-essb5557-november2015.pdf
[587] http://www.drugtopics.com/drugtopics/article/articleDetail.jsp?id=110964
[588] Some commentators see major chains well-positioned to deal with increased 3rd party following expansion of insurance coverage following the Affordable Care Act ("Pharmacy Stocks, Post ACA: Walgreen more undervalued than CVS, safer than Rite Aid, Seeking Alpha 2012 Jul 19; http://seekingalpha.com/article/733411-pharmacy-stocks-post-aca-walgreen-more-undervalued-than-cvs-safer-than-rite-aid, accessed 03/30/13). Others believe that unintended consequences of the ACA will lead to openings for innovative practices in health care that will reform health care practices, not just insurance approaches (Cochrane JH. After the ACA: freeing the market for health care, http://faculty.chicagobooth.edu/john.cochrane/research/papers/after_aca.pdf, accessed 03/30/13)
[589] 42 CFR § 447.331
[590] First Databank to participate in an effort to identify New York state pharmacy drug acquisition costs. First Databank Company News, 2012 Jan 24
[591] Ven-a-Care of the Florida Keys, et al. v Mylan Laboratories et al. C.A. No. 98-3032G, Fla. 2d Jud. Cir., Leon County, 2005.
[592] *New England Carpenters Health Benefits Fund et al. v. First DataBank and McKesson Corp*. US Dist. Ct. (D.Mass.), Case No. 1:05-CV-11148-PBS.
[593] https://www.wolterskluwercdi.com/sites/default/files/documents/WKH_AWP_Policy.pdf
[594] http://truvenhealth.com/Portals/1/Assets/AWP%20Policy_Oct%202014.pdf (Revised 6/9/18)
[595] Pub. L. 111-148 (2010).
[596] 42 CFR § 447.502
[597] https://www.medicaid.gov/medicaid-chip-program-information/by-topics/prescription-drugs/downloads/xxxreimbursement-chart-current-qtr.pdf, accessed 2/14/19
[598] Bruen B, Young K. Paying for prescribed drugs in Medicaid: current policy and upcoming changes. Issue Brief, Kaiser Family Foundation, 2014 May.
[599] https://www.medicaid.gov/medicaid/prescription-drugs/state-prescription-drug-resources/drug-reimbursement-information/index.html

[600] See, e.g., U.S. et al. ex rel. Proctor v. Safeway, Inc., No. 11-3406, C.D. Ill., November 30, 2016; Sheet Metal Workers Local No. 20 Welfare and Benefit Fund et al. v. CVS Health Corp., C.A. No. 16-046 S, D. R.I., November 1, 2016.
[601] http:/www.pstac.org
[602] http://www.pstac.org/services/master-code.html
[603] Practice Management Corporation v. AMA. 121 F.3d 516 (9th Cir. 1997)
[604] Stump AL. Creating a fee schedule for the pharmacist CPT codes based on Revenue Value Units (RVUs); http://www.ashp.org/doclibrary/membercenter/webinars/fee_schedule_revenue_value_units.aspx, accessed 3/19/15.
[605] USDHHS, CMS, CMCS. State flexibility to facilitate timely access to drug therapy by expanding the scope of pharmacy practice using collaborative practice agreements, standing orders, or other predetermined protocols. CMCS Informational Bulletin 2017 Jan 17.
[606] Eban K. Painful prescription. Fortune 2013 Oct 10.
[607] Beste P, Eberle B. The transparent PBM pass-through model: managing drug spending through aligned incentives. Employee Benefit Plan Rev. 2008 (Jan); 62(7)
[608] 42 U.S.C. 1320b-23
[609] Social Security Administration, Compilation of the Social Security Laws: Pharmacy Benefit Managers Transparency Requirements;
[610] 2014 c 13
[611] Fassett WE. Washington is latest state to enact PBM statute, requires PBM registration and MAC list clarity. Rx Ipsa Loquitur 2014 (Mar/Apr); 41(2): 2-3.
[612] 2016 c 10
[613] Pub. L. 115-263, 10/10/2018
[614] Pub. L. 115-262, 10/10/2018
[615] Black DW. Hospital/physician compensation under state and federal anti-kickback laws. Seattle: Ogden Murphy Wallace PLLC, 2001, p. 3.
[616] 42 U.S.C. §1395nn.
[617] Black DW, *op. cit.,* p. 10.
[618] USDOJ. News Release No. 09-1186, Civil Div., 2009 Nov 3; http://www.justice.gov/opa/pr/2009/November/09-civ-1186.html
[619] DHHS, OIG. 42 CFR Parts 1001 and 1003. Medicare and State Health Care Programs ... Revisions to Safe Harbors ..., 81 Fed. Reg. 88368, December 7, 2016.
[620] Black DW. *Op. cit.*, p. 27.
[621] For example, in the American Optical case (*US v American Optical Co.,* 97 F.Supp. 66, (4th Cir. 1951)), the Justice Department sued over 2000 physicians for allegedly referring patients to American Optical to have their eyeglass prescriptions filled, at inflated prices, for which the physicians received a kickback.
[622] Black DW, *Op. cit..,* p. 28.
[623] Opinion of the Court, *Wright v Jeckle,* 158 Wn.2d 375, 375 (Fn. 1), 2006.
[624] Black, DW, *Op. cit.,* p. 28.
[625] *Ibid.*, at 375.
[626] Garza L. Clinical community pharmacists. Northwest Pharmacy Convention, Coeur d'Alene, ID, June 3, 2016; http://c.ymcdn.com/sites/www.wsparx.org/resource/resmgr/Northwest_Pharmacy_Convention_Presentations/2016/Lisa_Garza-_Community_Forum.pdf
[627] Willie Sutton denied he ever made that statement: "Why did I rob banks? Because I enjoyed it. I loved it. I was more alive when I was inside a bank, robbing it, than at any other time in my life." See http://en.wikipedia.org/wiki/Willie_Sutton.
[628] http://www.taf.org/total2010.htm
[629] Pub. L. 111-21
[630] http://www.taf.org/whyfca.htm, accessed 1/5/08.
[631] http://www.taf.org/states-false-claims-acts, accessed 3/17/15
[632] 2012 c 241; ESSB 5978.
[633] Robbins DB, Howard RM. Washington Medicaid Fraud False Claims Act awaits Governor's signature. Perkins Coie News/Blogs 2012 Mar 3; http://www.perkinscoie.com/news/pubs_Detail.aspx?publication=89485f0f-a3a1-4d89-a8dd-d2ed077cbea1, accessed 3/19/15.
[634] Bucy P. Health Care Fraud: Criminal, Civil and Administrative Law. New York: Law Journal Seminars Press, 1997, p. 3-52.
[635] http://www.oig.hhs.gov/fraud/cia/cia_list.asp
[636] http://www.taf.org/top100fca.htm, accessed 1/6/08.

[637] Northwest Health Law Advocates. Coverage Options in Washington State; http://nohla.org/infoAnalysis/coverOps.php, accessed 4/25/2014.
[638] http://www.hca.wa.gov/about-hca/healthier-washington/medicaid-transformation#what-is-medicaid-transformation
[639] CMS, 2015 Choosing a Medigap Policy: A Guide to Health Insurance for People with Medicare. (https://www.medicare.gov/Pubs/pdf/02110.pdf, accessed 3/19/15.)
[640] CMS. DMEPOS Accreditation. http://www.cms.gov/Medicare/Provider-Enrollment-and-Certification/MedicareProviderSupEnroll/DMEPOSAccreditation.html, accessed 3/19/2015.
[641] https://www.medicare.gov/find-a-plan/questions/home.aspx
[642] https://www.cms.gov/Medicare/Appeals-and-Grievances/MedPrescriptDrugApplGriev/Downloads/Chapter18.zip
[643] Wolfgang A. Medicare and Medicaid, Chapter 17 in McCarthy R and Schafermeyer K, Eds., Introduction to Healthcare Delivery, 4th Ed., Sudbury, MA: Jones & Bartlett, 2007, p. 467.
[644] http://kff.org/health-reform/state-indicator/state-activity-around-expanding-medicaid-under-the-affordable-care-act/?currentTimeframe=0
[645] http://www.lni.wa.gov/ClaimsIns/Providers/TreatingPatients/Presc/Billing/default.asp
[646] 61 FR 43549, August 23, 1996.

INDEX

SUPPLEMENT: MPJE COMPETENCY STATEMENT MAP

PURPOSE AND SCOPE

This supplement is prepared for the candidate taking the Multistate Pharmacy Jurisprudence Examination for the State of Washington, using this textbook as a source for preparation. Use of this guide will help the candidate review each competency statement to assess his or her knowledge in the area. We recommend doing this after first studying the textbook. As can be seen, most of the MPJE competency statements are covered in Chapters 2 through 7 of the text.

Each competency statement in this guide is accompanied by a list of chapters in the textbook, and specific pages in which information related to the competency statement may be found. NOTE: the listing attached is not necessarily a complete listing of every page on which material related to a given competency statement may be found and generally lists the first page of a possible range of pages on that topic. See the listing below of competency statements by chapter to assist you as well.

CITATIONS

In addition, specific references to relevant state or federal statutes or regulations are listed where applicable. The following citation formats are used:

WAC – Washington regulations contained in the Washington Administrative Code;

RCW – Washington statutes contained in the Revised Code of Washington;

CFR – federal rules from the Code of Federal Regulations;

USC – federal statutes contained in the United States Code

Pub. L. – major laws cited by their Public Law (Pub. L.) number;

USP – relevant chapters of the United States Pharmacopeia (USP) are cited with the chapter in brackets, e.g., USP <795>.

In general, a specific WAC, RCW, CFR, or USC citation may be pasted into a search engine, such as Google, as listed herein. Among the choices for Washington citations, the best site is apps.leg.wa.gov.

CONTROLLED SUBSTANCE REGULATIONS

Earlier editions of this textbook recommended review of the Pharmacist's Manual, published by the DEA, in addition to the material in Chapter 5. This may be helpful, but the DEA manual was last revised in 2010. More up-to-date information is available on the DEA Diversion Resources webpage for the following areas that have been changed by statute or regulation since 2010:

- Current controlled substances schedules
- DATA waived physicians
- Drug Disposal
- E-commerce Initiatives, including electronic prescribing

RECOMMENDED PLAN FOR PREPARING FOR THE WASHINGTON MPJE

We strongly recommend that new pharmacy graduates without a great deal of practice experience do not attempt to prepare for any state's MPJE by simply reviewing a power point or a list of questions and answers for that state. If you have purchased this book, then your best use of it is to carefully read the book and reflect on the ways in Washington's rules and statutes differ from the state(s) in which you gained your practical experience.

As noted above, most of the MPJE competency statements are dealt with in Chapters 2 through 7 of the book. Chapter 1 is, nevertheless, a good introduction to how the State of Washington is established and organized. Chapter 8, on third party programs, will be a useful reference for you – particularly if you enter community practice, but it is not essential to prepare for the MPJE.

As you read the chapters in the textbook, if you find material you don't understand well, or if it raises questions you can't answer, feel free to e-mail Dr. Fassett – his email address is in the front of the book. He is happy to respond to your questions.

After reading the book, then you should use the MPJE Competency Statements from the MPJE Candidate's Guide as a guide to systematic review of what you know. Note that approximately 83% of the MPJE will come from Area 1, 15% from Area 2, and only about 2% from Area 3.

The NABP has published an analysis of competency areas in which candidates performed very well, acceptably, or poorly in April, 2016. Candidates did above expectation on competency statements 1.1 and 1.5. They were "on target" for statements 1.2, 1.3, 1.4, and 2.1. Candidates performed below expectation on statements 1.6, 1.7, 2.2, 2.3, and 3.1.[1] First-time passing rates are typically lower for the MPJE than for the NAPLEX, possibly because the candidates feel the NAPLEX requires a more serious and focused approach than the MPJE.

We recommend that for each competency statement you write out what you believe is important to know in that area regarding Washington law. Use this guide then to help you confirm that what you know is correct and complete.

AN EXAMPLE

For example, consider statement 1.7: "Procedures for keeping records of information related to pharmacy practice, pharmaceutical products, and patients, including requirements for protecting patient confidentiality."

We would see this statement has having 4 parts: How to keep records related to (1) pharmacy practice; (2) pharmaceutical products; (3) patients; and (4) how to protect patient confidentiality. Implied in the statement is knowing what records are required. So, here are some example starting questions that we would want to know the answers to:

(A) What records are required to be kept for a pharmacy practice setting? Do not limit your review to

[1] Catizone CA. MPJE Content-Area Performance Patterns: 2016. Chicago, IL: National Association of Boards of Pharmacy; 2017 (Mar). https://nabp.pharmacy/wp-content/uploads/2016/07/MPJE-White-Paper_FINAL.pdf.

community pharmacy, but think of long-term care, institutional, and home IV pharmacies. Our list might include: copies of any state or federal registrations; copies of inspection reports; records of who is the pharmacist in charge; license numbers and registrations of all employees; required policies and procedures manuals and their updates; copies of any collaborative drug therapy agreements; copies of any prior authorizations for therapeutic substitution. You should be able to add others.

(B) Ask the same or similar question to (A) for drug records and for patient records.

(C) Who must keep them, where and how must they be stored (off-site, on-site?), and how long must they be retained?

(D) In addition to requirements for protecting patient confidentiality (note that WA law differs in some ways from HIPAA), what are the procedures that must be used? For example, how do you comply with requests for patient information, or patient requests for changes to their records, or what procedures must be followed if a release of patient information is discovered? How long do you have in WA to respond to requests?

This is just an example drawn from one of the statements. It may seem a daunting task to do this for every statement, but if you want to help assure that you'll pass the MPJE on your first attempt – isn't it worth the effort?

MPJE COMPETENCY STATEMENT	Chapter(s)	Page(s)	Regulation or Rule
1.1 Legal responsibilities of the pharmacist and other pharmacy personnel	2	33, 41, 61	WAC 246-863-095, WAC 246-901-070, WAC 246-901-035, WAC 246-901-020
1.1.1 Unique legal responsibilities of the pharmacist-in-charge (or equivalent), pharmacists, interns, and pharmacy owners **• Responsibilities for inventory, loss and/or theft of prescription drugs, the destruction/disposal of prescription drugs and the precedence of Local, State, or Federal requirements**	**2, 5**	35, 230, 242	WAC 246-858-040, RCW 18.64.020, RCW 18.64.43, RCW 18.64.245, RCW 18.64.250, WAC 246-869-160, WAC 246-869-020, RCW 18.130.180, 21 CFR §1304.04
1.1.2 Qualifications, scope of duties, and conditions for practice relating to pharmacy technicians and all other nonpharmacist personnel **• Personnel ratios, duties, tasks, roles, and functions of non-pharmacist personnel**	2	39-45	RCW 18.64A.020, WAC 246-901, RCW 18.64A.040, RCW 18.64.580, RCW 18.64A.060, WAC 246-874,

YOUR NOTES:

MPJE COMPETENCY STATEMENT	Chapter(s)	Page(s)	Regulation or Rule
1.2 Requirements for the acquisition and distribution of pharmaceutical products, including samples	2, 3, 4, 5	61, 70, 85, 105, 107, 212, 242	RCW 18.64.245, RCW 18.64.046, RCW 18.64.044, RCW 69.45.050, RCW 69.70, WAC 246-879-010, 21 CFR §1304.04, 21 CFR §1306.24, RCW 69.70.050, 21 CFR 203.39, RCW 69.45.050
1.2.1 Requirements and record keeping in relation to the ordering, acquiring, and maintenance of all pharmaceutical products and bulk drug substances/excipients **• Legitimate suppliers, pedigrees and the maintenance of acquisition records**		215	
1.2.2 Requirements for distributing pharmaceutical products and preparations, including the content and maintenance of distribution records **• Legal possession of pharmaceutical products (including drug samples), labeling, packaging, repackaging, compounding, and sales to practitioners**		203, 291	

YOUR NOTES:

MPJE COMPETENCY STATEMENT	Chapter(s)	Page(s)	Regulation or Rule
1.3 Legal requirements that must be observed in the issuance of a prescription/drug order	4, 5	145, 155, 156, 238	RCW 18.79.250; WAC 246-840-410 et seq.; RCW 69.50.100(w)(3), RCW 18.79.240r, RCW18.32, RCW 18.57, RCW 18.22, RCW 18.59.160, RCW 18.74.160, RCW 18.92; WAC 246-933-340(5)b, RCW 18.06, WAC 246-803, RCW 18.79, RCW 18.71, WAC 246-834-250, RCW 18.36A, WAC 246-836-210, RCW 18.53; WAC 246-851-580, 590 , RCW 18.57A; 18.71A; WAC 246-854-030; WAC 246-918030, 035, RCW 18.64; WAC 246-863-100, RCW 69.50.402,
1.3.1 Prescription/order requirements for pharmaceutical products and the limitations on their respective therapeutic uses **• Products, preparations, their uses and limitations applicable to all prescribed orders for both human and veterinary uses**		121, 128, 233, 250	
1.3.2 Scope of authority, scope of practice, and valid registration of all practitioners who are authorized under law to prescribe, dispense, or administer pharmaceutical products, including controlled substances **• Federal and State registrations, methadone programs, office-based opioid treatment programs, regulations related to retired or deceased prescribers, internet prescribing, limits on jurisdictional prescribing**		145, 151, 184, 187, 231, 236, 238, 273	

YOUR NOTES:

MPJE COMPETENCY STATEMENT	Chapter(s)	Page(s)	Regulation or Rule
1.3.3 Conditions under which the pharmacist participates in the administration of pharmaceutical products, or in the management of patients' drug therapy **• Prescriptive authority, collaborative practice, consulting, counseling, medication administration (including immunization, vaccines), ordering labs, medication therapy management, and disease state management**	2, 4	27, 28, 146	RCW 18.64.011, WAC 246-863-110, RCW 69.41.030
1.3.4 Requirements for issuing a prescription/order **• Content and format for written, telephonic voice transmission, electronic facsimile, computer and internet, during emergency conditions, and tamper-resistant prescription forms.**	4, 5	157, 158, 160, 175, 178, 231, 233, 244	RCW 69.41.040, RCW 69.41.120, RCW 69.41.101, RCW18.64.500, WAC 246-869-100, WAC 246-871-050, RCW 69.50.308, WAC 246-875-020, RCW 18.64.246

YOUR NOTES:

MPJE COMPETENCY STATEMENT	Chapter(s)	Page(s)	Regulation or Rule
1.3.5 Requirements for the issuance of controlled substance prescriptions/orders **• Content and format for written, telephonic voice transmission, electronic facsimile, computerized and internet, during emergency conditions, conditions for changing a prescription, time limits for dispensing initial prescriptions/drug orders, and requirements for multiple Schedule II orders**	5	244, 248, 249, 250, 252	RCW 69.41.050, RCW 69.41.120, RCW 69.50.308, 21 CFR §1306.21, WAC 246-870-050, 21 CFR §1306.25, RCW 69.04.560, WAC 246-887-020, RCW 18.64.245, 21 CFR §1306.12, 21 CFR §1306.14; see also 1.3.4, since legend drug requirements also apply to scheduled drugs
1.3.6 Limits of a practitioner's authority to authorize refills of a pharmaceutical product, including controlled substances	4, 5	159, 73, 247, 250	WAC 246-869-100, WAC 246-871-050, RCW 69.50.308

YOUR NOTES:

MPJE COMPETENCY STATEMENT	Chapter(s)	Page(s)	Regulation or Rule
1.4 Procedures necessary to properly dispense a pharmaceutical product, including controlled substances, pursuant to a prescription/drug order	4, 5	235, 261, 262	RCW 69.50.308, 21 CFR §1306.04
1.4.1 Responsibilities for determining whether prescriptions/orders were issued for a legitimate medical purpose and within all applicable legal restrictions **• Corresponding responsibility, maximum quantities, restricted distribution systems, red flags/ automated alerts, controlled substances, valid patient / prescriber relationship, and due diligence to ensure validity of the order**		155, 231, 278	
1.4.2 Requirements for the transfer of existing prescription/order information from one pharmacist to another	4, 5	158, 162, 178, 254	WAC 246-869-090, 21 CFR §1306.25, WAC 246-870-030
1.4.3 Conditions under which a prescription/order may be filled or refilled **• Emergency fills or refills, partial dispensing of a controlled substance, disaster or emergency protocol, patient identification, requirement for death with dignity, medical marijuana, and conscience /moral circumstances**	3, 4, 5	75, 174, 175, 176, 232, 249, 250, 275, 281	42 U.S.C. §300, WAC 246-978, WAC 246-887-020, RCW 18.64.245, WAC 246-70, WAC 246-72

YOUR NOTES:

MPJE COMPETENCY STATEMENT	Chapter(s)	Page(s)	Regulation or Rule
1.4.4 Conditions under which prospective drug use review is conducted prior to dispensing **• Patient-specific therapy and requirements for patient-specific documentation**	3, 6	66, 78, 87, 95, 96, 101, 300	WAC 246-875-040
1.4.5 Conditions under which product selection is permitted or mandated **• Consent of the patient and/or prescriber, passing-on of cost savings, and appropriate documentation**	4	166, 168	RCW 69.41.100-190, WAC 26-866-030(3)
1.4.6 Requirements for the labeling of pharmaceutical products and preparations dispensed pursuant to a prescription/order **• Generic and therapeutic equivalency, formulary use, auxiliary labels, patient package inserts, FDA medication guides, and written drug information**	4	137, 140, 142, 306, 307	RCW 18.64.246, WAC 246-875-020(1)(h), WAC 246-869-255, WAC 246-869-210(2), WAC 246-869-210(1)), WAC 246-869-210(3), WAC 246-869-210(4), WAC 246-869-220, 21 CFR Parts 201, 208, 209, WAC 246-873-080(5)c, WAC246-873-080(5)a, WAC246-871-050, WAC 246-865-060(4)a 21 CFR 208.26(b)), USP <17>

YOUR NOTES:

MPJE COMPETENCY STATEMENT	Chapter(s)	Page(s)	Regulation or Rule
1.4.7 Packaging requirements of pharmaceutical products, preparations, and devices to be dispensed pursuant to a prescription/order **• Child-resistant and customized patient medication packaging**	2, 4	181	WAC 246-869-230, WAC 246-875-020, WAC 246-869-235, WAC 246-869-255
1.4.8 Conditions under which a pharmaceutical product, preparation, or device may not be dispensed **• Adulteration, misbranding, and dating**	4	129, 144	21 USC §351, 21 USC §352, WAC 246-869-210
1.4.9 Requirements for compounding pharmaceutical products **• Environmental controls, release checks and testing, beyond use date (BUD), initial and ongoing training**	4	207, 210	USP <795>, <797>, RCW 18.64.270, WAC 246-878-020
1.4.10 Requirements for emergency kits **• Supplying, maintenance, access, security, and inventory**	3	85, 89, 90	WAC 246-865-030, WAC 246-865-040, RCW 69.70.050
1.4.11 Conditions regarding the return and/or reuse of pharmaceutical products, preparations, bulk drug substances/excipients, and devices **• Charitable programs, cancer or other repository programs, previously dispensed, and from "will call" areas of pharmacies**	3, 4	70, 189, 213	RCW 69.70, WAC 246-869-130

YOUR NOTES:

MPJE COMPETENCY STATEMENT	Chapter(s)	Page(s)	Regulation or Rule
1.4.12 Procedures and requirements for systems or processes whereby a non-pharmacist may obtain pharmaceutical products, preparations, bulk drug substances/excipients, and devices • Pyxis (vending), after hour's access, telepharmacies, and secure automated patient drug retrieval centers	3	73, 78, 79, 93	WAC 246-873-050, WAC 246-874
1.4.13 Procedures and requirements for establishing and operating central processing and central fill pharmacies • Remote order verification	3	93	WAC 246-874, WAC 246-873-080, WAC 246-875-020
1.4.14 Requirements for reporting to PMP, accessing information in a PMP and the maintenance of security and confidentiality of information accessed in PMPs	5	266	RCW 70.225.020, WAC 246-470
1.4.15 Requirements when informed consent must be obtained from the patient and/or a duty to warn must be executed • Collaborative practice and investigational drug therapy	4,7	148, 349, 352	WAC 246-919-855, 21 CFR §50.24

YOUR NOTES:

MPJE COMPETENCY STATEMENT	Chapter(s)	Page(s)	Regulation or Rule
1.5 Conditions for making an offer to counsel or counseling appropriate patients, including the requirements for documentation	6	302	WAC 246-869-220
1.5.1 Requirements to counsel or to make an offer to counsel			
1.5.2 Required documentation necessary for counseling	6	305	42 USC §1396r-8
1.6 Requirements for the distribution and/or dispensing of non-prescription pharmaceutical products, including controlled substances	4	123, 129	RCW 69.41, RCW 69.50, WAC 246-869-150
1.6.1 Requirements for the labeling of non-prescription pharmaceutical products and devices		130, 132	
1.6.2 Requirements for the packaging and repackaging of non-prescription pharmaceutical products and devices	4	130, 131	16 CFR § 1700.14, RCW 18.64.246, WAC 246-869-230
1.6.3 Requirements for the distribution and/or dispensing of poisons, restricted, non-prescription pharmaceutical products, and other restricted materials or devices **• Pseudoephedrine, dextromethorphan, emergency contraception, and behind the counter products as appropriate**	4	119, 120, 122, 123, 126	RCW 96.36, RCW 69.38, RCW 69.40, RCW 69.75 (restricts sales of dextromethorphan to persons 18 or older)

YOUR NOTES:

MPJE COMPETENCY STATEMENT	Chapter(s)	Page(s)	Regulation or Rule
1.7 Procedures for keeping records of information related to pharmacy practice, pharmaceutical products and patients, including requirements for protecting patient confidentiality	4, 5	242, 261, 269	RCW 69.43, RCW 69.75.020
1.7.1 Requirements pertaining to controlled substance inventories	5	243	21 CFR §1304.11
1.7.2 Content, maintenance, storage, and reporting requirements for records required in the operation of a pharmacy **• Prescription filing systems, computer systems and backups, and prescription monitoring programs**	5	253, 292	WAC 246-887-020, RCW 225.020
1.7.3 Requirements for protecting patient confidentiality and confidential health records **• HIPAA requirements and conditions for access and use of information**	6	307, 309	RCW 71.05.390, RCW 70.24, 45 CFR §164.501, 45 CFR §164.502, RCW 70.02.230

YOUR NOTES:

MPJE COMPETENCY STATEMENT	Chapter(s)	Page(s)	Regulation or Rule
1.8 Requirements for handling hazardous materials such as described in USP	4	198, 200	USP <800>, <795>, <797>, WAC 296-800; 296-62-500
1.8.1 Requirements for appropriate disposal of hazardous materials		191, 195	
1.8.2 Requirements for training regarding hazardous materials **• Reverse distributors, quarantine procedures, comprehensive safety programs, Material Safety Data Sheets**			
1.8.3 Environmental controls addressing the proper storage, handling, and disposal of hazardous materials **• Ventilation controls, personal protective equipment, work practices, and reporting**		201	
1.8.4 Methods for the compounding, dispensing and administration of hazardous materials **• All hazardous materials including sterile and non-sterile compounding**			

YOUR NOTES:

2.1 Qualifications, application procedure, necessary examinations, and internship for licensure, registration, or certification of individuals engaged in the storage, distribution, and/or dispensing of pharmaceutical products (prescription and non-prescription)	2	29-50	RCW 18.64.020, WAC 246-12-030, WAC 246-861-090, RCW 43.70.270, RCW 18.340, WAC 246-12, WAC 246-863-080, RCW 18.64.080, WAC 246-858-040, WAC 246-858-060, WAC 246-901-060, WAC 246-907-0301, WAC 246-873-040,
2.1.1 Requirements for special or restricted licenses, registration, authorization, or certificates **• Pharmacists, pharmacist preceptors, pharmacy interns, pharmacy technicians, controlled substance registrants, and under specialty pharmacist licenses (Nuclear, Consultant etc.)**			
2.1.2 Standards of practice related to the practice of pharmacy **• Quality assurance programs (including peer review), changing dosage forms, therapeutic substitution, error reporting, public health reporting requirements (such as notification of potential terrorist event, physical abuse, and treatment for tuberculosis), and issues of conscience and maintaining competency**	2, 4, 7	50–52, 52, 163, 171, 320	RCW 74.34.035, RCW 26.33.030, WAC 246-101-101, RCW 9.02.150, 42 USC §300, RCW 69.41.100-108, WAC 246-899-030, RCW 69.41.190, WAC 182-50-200, RCW 70.41.200, WAC 43.70.510

YOUR NOTES:

MPJE COMPETENCY STATEMENT	Chapter(s)	Page(s)	Regulation or Rule
2.1.3 Requirements for classifications and processes of disciplinary actions that may be taken against a registered, licensed, certified, or permitted individual	7	325, 331	RCW 18.130, RCW 34.50, WAC 246-16-800,
2.1.4 Requirements for reporting to, and participating in, programs addressing the inability of an individual licensed, registered, or certified by the Board to engage in the practice of pharmacy with reasonable skill and safety **• Impairment caused by the use of alcohol, drugs, chemicals, or other materials, or mental, physical, or psychological conditions**	2, 7	55, 326	RCW 18.130.170, WAC 246-16-200, WAC 246-16-270,
2.2 Requirements and application procedure for the registration, licensure, certification, or permitting of a practice setting or business entity **2.2.1 Requirements for registration, license, certification, or permitting of a practice setting** **• In-state pharmacies, out-of-state pharmacies, specialty pharmacies, controlled substance registrants, wholesalers, distributors, manufacturers/repackagers, computer services providers, and internet pharmacies**	3	60, 61, 63, 68, 73, 84, 91, 93, 98, 102, 105	21 CFR §1301, WAC 246-869, RCW 18.64. 020, WAC 246-869-070, WAC 246-873, RCW 18.64.043, WAC 246-873A, RCW 18.64.011, WAC 246-865, RCW 18.64.510, WAC 246-874, WAC 246-871, WAC 246-903, RCW 18.64.046, RCW 18.64.044

YOUR NOTES:

MPJE COMPETENCY STATEMENT	Chapter(s)	Page(s)	Regulation or Rule
2.2.2 Requirements for an inspection of a licensed, registered, certified, or permitted practice setting	3	68, 69	WAC 246-869-190, 21 USC § 374
2.2.3 Requirements for the renewal or reinstatement of a license, registration, certificate, or permit of a practice setting	3	61, 68	RCW 18.64.043
2.2.4 Classifications and processes of disciplinary actions that may be taken against a registered, licensed, certified, or permitted practice setting	3, 7		RCW 18.130.040, RCW 18.130.070, RCW 18.130.080, RCW 18.130.090, WAC 246-16-800,
2.3 Operational requirements for a registered, licensed, certified, or permitted practice setting	3	61, 63, 73	WAC 246-869, WAC 246-873
2.3.1 Requirements for the operation of a pharmacy or practice setting that is not directly related to the dispensing of pharmaceutical products **• Issues related to space, equipment, advertising and signage, security (including temporary absences of the pharmacist), policies and procedures, libraries and references (including veterinary), and the display of licenses**			

YOUR NOTES:

MPJE COMPETENCY STATEMENT	Chapter(s)	Page(s)	Regulation or Rule
2.3.2 Requirements for the possession, storage, and handling of pharmaceutical products, preparations, bulk drug substances/excipients, and devices, including controlled substances **• Investigational new drugs, repackaged or resold drugs, sample pharmaceuticals, recalls, and outdated pharmaceutical products**	3, 4	64, 77, 78, 89, 189, 212	WAC 246-879, WAC 246-865, WAC 246-873-080, WAC 246-869-150, WAC 246-873-100
2.3.3 Requirements for delivery of pharmaceutical products, preparations, bulk drug substances/excipients, and devices, including controlled substances **• Issues related to identification of the person accepting delivery of a drug, use of the mail, contract delivery, use of couriers, use of pharmacy employees, use of kiosks, secure mail boxes, script centers, use of vacuum tubes, and use of drive-up windows**	4, 5	101,246, 267 260, 266	21 USC § 802, WAC 246-869-020, RCW 18.64.011, WAC 246-470

YOUR NOTES:

MPJE COMPETENCY STATEMENT	Chapter(s)	Page(s)	Regulation or Rule
3.1 Application of regulations **3.1.1 Laws and rules that regulate or affect the manufacture, storage, distribution, and dispensing of pharmaceutical products, preparations, bulk drug substances/excipients, and devices, (prescription and non-prescription), including controlled substances** **• Food, Drug, and Cosmetic Act(s) and Regulations, the Controlled Substances Act(s) and Regulations, OBRA 90's Title IV Requirements, Practice Acts and Rules, other statutes and regulations, including but not limited to, dispensing of methadone, child-resistant packaging, tamper resistant packaging, drug paraphernalia, drug samples, pharmacist responsibilities in Medicare-certified skilled-nursing facilities, NDC numbers, and schedules of controlled substances**	1, 3, 4, 5, 6	20, 59, 111,129, 160, 181, 216, 218, 230, 247, 273, 275, 282, 305, 306, 390	RCW 18.64, 21 USC Chapter 9, RCW 69.50, 21 USC, RCW 69.36, RCW 69.40, ORBR-90, RCW 18.64.246, Narcotic Addiction Treatment Act, CARA (Pub. L. 114-198), DQSA (Pub. L. 113-54), 42 CFR 483.25, 42 CFR 483.60

YOUR NOTES:

ABOUT THE AUTHORS

William E. Fassett is professor emeritus of pharmacy law and ethics at Washington State University (WSU) in Spokane, WA. He earned his BS in Pharmacy from the University of Washington, an MBA from the University of Puget Sound, and his PhD (in leadership and policy studies) from the University of Washington. He is a licensed pharmacist in Washington, having been so continuously since 1969, and he has maintained a litigation support and management consulting practice since 1983. He joined WSU in 1999 as dean of the College of Pharmacy, and in 2005 returned to full time teaching. Prior to coming to WSU, he taught pharmacy law and other topics in the field of social and administrative sciences at Drake University (Des Moines, IA) and at the University of Washington. He has also taught at Pacific University of Oregon and in the online MS Pharmacy program at the University of Florida. The 2019 edition of *Fassett's* Washington Pharmacy Law is the 14th iteration of the text, which began as a compilation of his lecture notes for the pharmacy law class at WSU. He retired from WSU in 2014 and lives with his wife, Sharon, in the Five Mile Prairie neighborhood in north Spokane.

Shannon G. Panther practices as a clinical pharmacist at Kaiser Permanente in Spokane, WA. Her PharmD is from Washington State University and she is a Board Certified Ambulatory Care Pharmacist (BCACP). She was previously clinical assistant professor of pharmacotherapy at Washington State University in Spokane, where she taught, among other classes, Pharmacy Law & Regulatory Affairs. Dr. Panther has also served as an upper level manager of a mail order operation for a national pharmacy retailer and has been previously licensed in 13 states. She is a director of the American Society for Pharmacy Law.

Made in the USA
Middletown, DE
17 February 2019